SOCIAL SYSTEMS: THE STUDY OF SOCIOLOGY

SOCIAL SYSTEMS: THE STUDY OF SOCIOLOGY

by

Charles P. Loomis
University of Houston &
University of Texas School of Public Health

and

Everett D. Dyer
University of Houston

In Co-authorship With

M. Francis Abraham
Grambling State University

Anthony Gary Dworkin
University of Houston

Robert F. Eshleman
Franklin and Marshall College

Zona K. Loomis
Houston Public Library

Proshanta K. Nandi
Sangamon State University

Schenkman Publishing Company, Inc.

Cambridge, Massachusetts
02138

CONTENTS

*To locate pages for specific concepts see the Index at the end of the volume.

*To locate pages for specific concepts see the Index at the end of the book.

PREFACE

Schemas are helpful in making analyses and comparisons among organizations. In many term papers, graduate dissertations, and published articles, the concepts of the Processually Articulated Structural Model, worked out mainly by the senior author, have been instrumental in enabling users to go beyond mere journalistic description to scientific analysis. The first part of the title of this book, *Social Systems,* derives from the senior author's work and writings (as does the PASM).

All projects have a history; the present Preface examines the genesis of *this* work and the subsequent contributions made to it. Certain chapters were prepared at an earlier date by Zona Loomis before she and the senior author took assignments in India, a circumstance which delayed the work's final preparation and publication. Ms. Loomis' contributions are important to all parts of the book, but particularly to the illustrative cases, which remain virtually unchanged. She contributed significantly to the chapter on "Social Systems Delimited by Rank: Class, Caste, and Ethnic Groups."

The original chapters were updated by Everett D. Dyer, who added distinctive materials of his own. Professor Dyer made revisions in three chapters and updated materials, particularly on the subjects of the family, stratification and ethnic relations, and government — all representing areas of his own specialization. He also edited the whole final manuscript with the assistance of his wife, Jacqueline.

Francis Abraham contributes to two chapters: "Religious Social Systems," which he authored, and "Small Informal Social Systems," which he co-authored. His life in India and in other parts of the world, and his whole background, have provided him with a cross-cultural perspective attained by few. Being thoroughly familiar with the conceptual scheme of this book, he has used it in professional articles, some of them co-authored with the senior author.

Robert F. Eshleman gives us the chapter "Production Systems: The Division of Labor, The Community, and Society." He does this by updating and revising a chapter in the senior author's earlier *Social Systems: Essays on Their Change and Persistence,* and the end result is a very important contribution to the present volume. He has, incidentally, used the earlier *Social Systems* as a classroom text ever since its publication in 1960.

Anthony Gary Dworkin joined the senior author in preparing the chapter on "The Mexican American Community." He not only contributed data from his outstanding studies of the stereotyping of Mexicans and Americans by and about themselves and each other; he also updated the chapter as it was originally written by introducing recent data and providing background and perspective.

Proshanta K. Nandi has contributed most significantly to the chapter on "Educational Social Systems." He collaborated with the senior author under Ford Foundation support in the planning for educational, health, and other systems in his native country, India. Dr. Nandi has specialized in social psychology and complex organizations. He has published previously with the senior author.

Finally, the senior author is indebted to Benjamin S. Bradshaw of the University of Texas School of Public Health for encouraging and facilitating him in his contribution to the chapter on the Mexican American community. These materials were used in the joint seminar held at UTSPH on Social and Health Problems of the Border Region. All the authors are indebted to Jean Blalack of UTSPH and Arlene Thomas of U. of H. for excellent typing done as they worked on the manuscript through its various stages.

It is hoped that this volume will provide both the specialist and the beginning student of sociology with a clearly written and well documented text exploring social systems, their structures, and their patterns of change.

Charles P. Loomis

Chapter **1**

Social Systems: Their Elements, Processes, and Patterns*

THE FRAME OF REFERENCE OF SOCIOLOGY

An effective understanding of human society and group life would be difficult, if not impossible, without consideration of relevant social systems, the elements comprising them, and the important processes involved. This chapter is devoted to an attempt to isolate and explain those elements and processes believed to be essential to the understanding of social entities.

The purpose of the present chapter is to acquaint the reader with the terms of our conceptual scheme. Two procedures will be employed. First, pertinent excerpts and definitions from the senior author's book *Social Systems* will be presented.[1] Second, a summary description of a particular social system — that of the *Old Order Amish* community in Lancaster County, Pennsylvania — organized in terms of the pertinent concepts will be given to introduce the concepts and illustrate their use in analytical application. The scheme which provides that organizational device is called the Processually Articulated Structural Model, hereafter referred to as the PAS Model.

As the first step in familiarizing the reader with that model the following excerpts from *Social Systems* are presented.[2]

Activity may be defined as any event involving the use of energy. It is thus a generic term. The social sciences in large measure limit their frame of reference to human activity and approach its analysis by use of the "action" frame of reference which, although similar to some usages of the behavioral frame of reference in that it concerns what people do, avoids some of the limiting connotations of stimulus-response "behaviorism." Social action is the activity of social units.[3]

*By Charles P. Loomis

(1)

Interaction, the core datum of sociology, has been defined as any event by which one party tangibly influences the overt actions or the state of mind of the other.[4] It is a reciprocal and interdependent activity, designated as having the quality of complementarity or double contingency.[5] Reciprocal activity or interaction that is repeated and persists comprises *social relations*.

Interaction tends to develop certain uniformities over time, some of which tend to persist. As they are *orderly* and *systematic*, they can be recognized as *social systems*. Because the *social system* is composed of identifiable and interdependent parts it is said to possess *social structure*. Sociology, like other sciences, is concerned with the *orderliness* or *uniformities* involved in its particular class of phenomena, and it finds this order in the *social system*. It is very much concerned with two very different kinds of order found in interaction. On the one hand it is concerned with order resulting from factors in the situation over which the members of a given social system have no control or order imposed from what may be called the conditions of action. An example of this type of order is that imposed by man's limited physical mobility as related to the factor, geographical space, which makes it impossible for an actor to be at two geographical points at the same time. On the other hand sociology is concerned with norms which determine what is evaluated as just or unjust, true or false, beautiful or ugly, and what are considered appropriate responses to these evaluations.

The *social system* is composed of the patterned interaction of a plurality of individual actors whose relations to each other are mutually oriented through the definition and mediation of a pattern of structured and shared symbols and expectations.

A means of delineating a social system is furnished by the more intense and frequent occurrence of *specific types of interaction* among members than among non-members, within a situation having both physical and symbolic aspects. However, this simplified means of delineating social systems requires accurate use. It has been observed, for instance, that actors of a given family whose members are scattered about in an industrial society may retain solidarity as a family but interact less frequently with family members than with non-members on the job and in other places. Because there is a difference in the type of interaction and resulting bonds among the family and non-family members, the phrase "specific types of interaction" in the definition is important. Among the dimensions that may determine the type of interaction are extensity, intensity, duration, direction (i.e. whether solidary or antagonistic), and nature and extent of integration.[6]

THE ELEMENTS

An element is simply one of the constituent parts of some larger whole. Thus in chemistry an element is one of a limited number of distinct varieties of matter which, singly or in combination, compose every material substance. An element, then, is the unit of analysis employed in explaining interaction from the point of view of a given discipline. An explanation of social interaction calls for the examination of the elements of the social system. It is not implied here that there is in sociology the same universal agreement as to what the elements are as in chemistry, but it is maintained that in the accumulative work of sociologists certain analytic aspects of interaction have been consistently used. From among these aspects those that are considered elements are 1) belief (knowledge); 2) sentiment; 3) end, goal, or objective; 4) norm; 5) status-role (position); 6) rank; 7) power; 8) sanction; and 9) facility. At any given moment in time the structure of a given social system may be described and analyzed in terms of these elements.

THE PROCESSES

The elements that stand in a given relation to each other at a given moment do not remain in that relation (except by abstraction) for any length of time. The processes mesh, stabilize, and alter the relations between the elements through time; they are the tools through which the social system may be understood as a dynamic functioning continuity — a "going concern." The concept "process" is commonly employed in various of the sciences. A mere listing of such processes as osmosis, metamorphosis, succession, or evolution indicates the diversity of the specialities to which the term is applicable. Regardless of the diversity, each process is characterized by a consistent quality of regular and uniform sequences and is distinguishable by virtue of its orderliness. This same orderliness is the essence of any social process through which transition from one social condition to another is accomplished. For the present purposes the social processes may be classified under two headings: the specialized elemental processes by which the separate elements are articulated and the comprehensive or master processes by which several or all of the elements are articulated or involved. Those of the first category, along with the elements that they respectively articulate are:

1) cognitive mapping and validation by which the element belief (knowledge) is articulated

2) tension management and communication of sentiment by which the element sentiment is articulated
3) goal attaining and concomitant "latent" activity as process by which the element end, goal, or objective is articulated
4) evaluation by which the element norm is articulated
5) status-role performance by which the element status-role (position) is articulated
6) evaluation of actors and allocation of status-roles by which the element rank is articulated
7) decision making and its initiation into action by which the element power is articulated
8) application of sanctions by which the element sanction is articulated
9) utilization of facilities by which the element facility is articulated.

The social action categories shown in Figure 1 are handy names by which any structural element and its particular functional process (both being ingredients of the social action category) may be designated as a closely connected bundle of phenomena. In the sections of this chapter which follow, and in subsequent chapters the elements and the specialized processes by which the elements are articulated will be treated together. The comprehensive or master processes by which many or all of the elements are activated will follow.

WHAT DOES THE FUTURE HOLD? WILL WE MOVE TOWARD GEMEINSCHAFT OR GESELLSCHAFT?

When thousands agree that we are a nation and world of strangers leading meaningless lives, when knowledgeable people talk about the danger of nuclear exchanges which may destroy most of mankind, when we hear daily about the possibility of our environment becoming so poluted that life will be undesirable or impossible and when it is evident that the main sources of energy on which we now rely are petering out, our question, "What does the future hold?" plagues us all. Sociologists try to describe what is and will be but they are also concerned about what should be and what people want it to be. Sociologists with the background and training of the senior author of the present volume frequently use the German terms developed by Ferdinand Toennies[7], *Gemeinschaft* and Gesellschaft in addressing such questions. The terms appear many times in the chapters to follow. Although there are no exact English equivalents for these terms they are sometimes translated as community and society. In

FIGURE 1

**Elements, Processes And Conditions Of Action Of Social Systems
The Processually Articulated Structural Model (PAS Model)**

Processes (Elemental)	Social Action Categories	Elements
1) Cognitive mapping and validation	Knowing	Belief (knowledge)
2) a) Tension management and b) Communication of sentiment	Feeling	Sentiment
3) a) Goal attaining activity and b) Concomitant "latent" activity as process	Achieving	End, goal, or objective
4) Evaluation	Norming, Standardizing, Patterning	Norm
5) Status-role performance	Dividing the functions	Status-role (position)
6) a) Evaluation of actors and b) Allocation of status-roles	Ranking	Rank
7) a) Decision making and b) Initiation of action	Controlling	Power
8) Application of sanctions	Sanctioning	Sanction
9) Utilization of facilities	Facilitating	Facility
Comprehensive or Master Process 1) Communication 2) Boundary maintenance	3) Systemic linkage 4) Institutionalization	5) Socialization 6) Social control
Conditions of Social Action 1) Territoriality	2) Size	3) Time

Chapter 6, in which we relate the other terms discussed in this chapter to Gemeinschaft and Gesellschaft, we argue that as traditional or developing societies modernize the relationships of their members become more Gesellschaft-like and less Gemeinschaft-like. We also know that as this happens suicide rates increase, people become alienated, use of various harmful drugs often increases and many condemn and some withdraw from conventional urbanized, commercialized and mechanized societies to form John Birch and similar groupings, countercultures and communes. A few others such as the Amish discussed below throw up boundaries in the attempt to retain Gemeinschaft qualities.

Since Chapter 6 details the nature of these changes and Gemeinschaft-like and Gesellschaft-like groupings we shall here only briefly and perhaps in over-simplified terms discuss them. Pluralities which are Gemeinschaft-like are those in which the inter-personal relationships are *ends in and of themselves*. Toennies designates the mother-child relationship as the prototype of Gemeinschaft-like relations but he also specified that other relationships such as those among kin, friends, members of crafts and guilds of earlier times and many cliques, buddy and work groups of present times as Gemeinschaft-like.

Again speaking in simplistic terms members of Gesellschaft-like pluralities place primacy on those characteristics of social relationships which are *means to other ends*; that is, they are thought of as instrumental, usually not expressive and they may involve ulterior motives. Toennies specified trading relationships between and among merchants as the prototype of Gesellschaft-like relations. Whether the Gesellschaft-like plurality be an army, a factory or a university and whether the ends be those of winning battles, making profits or developing and disseminating knowledge relationships are not *ends in and of themselves* but rather means to the ends of the organization or unit. In modern societies those bureaucracies of a comparable type which achieve the most with the least investment of energy and/or money (in business organizations those which achieve the highest profit combination) are considered the most efficient and are usually the most Gesellschaft-like.

How to provide organizations with efficiency and also furnish arenas in which creative, satisfying and meaningful relationships among workers prevail is perhaps the most important problem of the age. Toennies and others have described buying and selling cooperatives as syntheses of Gemeinschaft and Gesellschaft.[9] Many other approaches to the problem are made in both totalitarian and free enterprise societies. Sociology must contribute to the solution of these major problems of our age.

Of course, an ultimate objective in the development of such concepts as those discussed in the preceding paragraphs is that of facilitating scientific explanation and prediction. To this end propositions involving such variables as goal attaining potential and goal attaining efficacy for instrumental organizations and social solidarity (or cohesiveness as the variable is called by some) for all pluralities have been developed for various ongoing investigations not reported in the present volume. These propositions have assisted in the development of hypotheses of the "x varies as y" variety involving these variables and/or those represented by the concepts of the PAS Model. The use of these concepts in the present volume is, however, confined in large part to codification and comparison.

THE OLD ORDER AMISH AS A SOCIAL SYSTEM

The purpose of this presentation is to give the reader in as succinct a form as possible a working knowledge of the concepts of the PAS Model; the means employed is to demonstrate their use by actual application to an empirical community viewed as a social system.

The effort to acquaint the reader with the terms of the PAS Model is a consequence of the authors' conviction that understanding and appraisal of various social system analyses must be based upon common denominators which will insure categorical treatment of comparable phenomena. The paragraphs immediately to follow should serve the purpose of further initiating the reader into an organizational framework with which he will be very familiar by the time he finishes this book.

Attention is now turned to a community study of the Old Order Amish of Lancaster County, Pennsylvania.[10] The study of such a group offers many advantages. It is traditionally difficult to be objective about one's own concerns, one's own memberships in social systems; the Old Order Amish system is sufficiently different from the larger society that it is possible to view it fairly objectively. Still it is a part of the larger society, and being an offshoot of our own Western culture and the Christian religion, it is sufficiently similar to familiar systems in the larger society to be understood. Finally, it is sufficiently slow-paced that the observer can have a better look at it than he can at a feverishly changing social unit. The study of the Old Order Amish helps provide the reader with a pattern by which he can look systematically at a more complex or more rapidly changing system.

ELEMENTS AND ELEMENTAL PROCESSES APPLIED TO THE OLD ORDER AMISH

KNOWING

Belief as an element. A belief is any proposition about the universe which is thought to be true. The Old Order Amish share common religious beliefs with all Christians, but they also subscribe to specific beliefs that differentiate them from other Christians and from other members of the larger society. The Amish are monotheistic; they have internalized God as a Father and Christ as the Son of

God. Unlike Catholics, the Amish do not believe in salvation through the sacraments mediated by formally trained and ordained priests. They believe, as do other Protestants, in the supremacy of the Bible and the necessity for living and worshipping as prescribed by their interpretation of the Bible. Strict adherence to the Bible leads the Amish to the following tenets:

1) baptism only upon confession of faith;
2) complete separation of church and state;
3) absolute religious toleration for others;
4) absolute nonresistance;
5) opposition to the use of the oath;
6) individual determination of each person's salvation;
7) that church buildings and other facilities are unnecessary and inappropriate for the worship of God;
8) that each individual is responsible for his own salvation and that the Amish are a chosen people.

The Old Order Amish share with the larger society the belief in the scientific conduct of agriculture, but to a lesser extent than does the larger society. Scientifically demonstrated improvements in seed, in breed, and in crop and animal husbandry are accepted. Their belief system encompasses other aspects of science too, but the belief that they are God's people and a separate people drastically restricts their application of scientific beliefs to any pursuit except agriculture. Even in agriculture many technological devices are restricted in their use.

Cognitive mapping and validation as a process may be defined as the activity by which knowledge, or what is considered true and what false, is developed. The cognitive mapping done by the Old Order Amish takes its unique slant from two points of view. One comes from the bloody tales of martyrdom contained in *The Bloody Theatre*, or *Martyr's Mirror*; its tales of retribution and punishment which occurred centuries ago are so completely internalized that they are relived in the present. In the Amishman's perception of reality the persecution of his forebears keeps him keenly aware of a past tragedy which could be repeated if he does not behave as behooves a member of God's chosen people. The second distinctive phase of apprehending reality is at once a cognitive mapping and a validation process; it is the utter reliance placed upon the Bible as interpreted by the group through the centuries, and especially upon particular Biblical verses. Among the most important bits of validation for the Amish cognitive mapping of the universe are Biblical injunctions which emphasize that they are separate from the world. One such injunction concerns "the unequal yoke" which validates the belief that an Amishman should not participate in any formal organizations and activities of the larger society. "Be ye not unequally yoked together with unbelievers: for what fellowship hath righteousness with unrighteousness? and what fellowship hath light with darkness?" From the Amishman's point of view he has the perfect validation for his most important beliefs; he has Biblical justification for nonresistance, adult baptism, humility, and separation of church and state. The belief virtually contains its own validation.

The Amishman validates his belief in part of scientific agriculture by reproducing the conditions of the experimental process and getting the expected result through improved crops, herds, farm buildings, and so on. The Old Order Amishman is seriously hampered in full-fledged scientific validation, however, because of restrictions placed on "worldly" technical equipment. These restrictions are validated by the Bible. He shows much ingenuity in substituting efficient horse drawn equipment for tractor drawn machinery and in making other substitutions which approximate "scientific agriculture" without violating his taboos on equipment. His resourcefulness in bridging a scientific belief and a religious belief that are incompatible demonstrates the religious center of his cognitive mapping. It also shows the successful attempt to build a rationale which takes the existence and application of science into account. In short his is a religious belief system based upon the fundamental premise that he "be not conformed to this world" and that he "be separate from the world."[11] All cognitive aspects of reality including scientific agriculture are shaped and molded according to this basic belief. For example, many farmers believe that the use of tractors which is forbidden by the norms would decrease profits. These beliefs are rather surprising and contrary to fact, a state of affairs which indicates that the process of cognitive mapping is capable of neglecting some pieces of evidence and over-emphasizing others in validation. The influence of the basic belief extends beyond the area of knowing; it affects feeling, achieving, and all of life.

FEELING

Sentiment as an element. Whereas beliefs embody thoughts, sentiments embody feelings about the world. The predominating patterns of emotion and sentiments of the Old Order Amish can easily be discerned. Awe and reverence are evoked by contemplation of the sacred, and this contemplation pervades nearly all activities. The Amish have sanctified the chores and tasks of every day life. They feel reverence, awe, and holiness in farm work, in contact with the market, and in accumulation of material goods as well as in religious services. The whole way of life is God-directed and therefore sanctified, and an Amishman feels the sanctification.

Although reverence is the dominant sentiment of the Amishman, it by no means precludes happiness and even occasional gaiety. He is sustained by a real enjoyment of his religion which provides him with a satisfaction and feeling of security with the universe. This religious-pastoral way of life nourishes the specific sentiments of self-discipline, love without over-indulgence for family members, affection and sympathy for a large number of relatives, intimate friendliness with other members of the church district, merriment on festive occasions, humility on all occasions, disgrace and embarrassment upon defection of any family member from the Amish way of life, and suspicion and uneasiness about those more secular aspects of life characteristic of the larger society.

Tension management and communication of sentiment as processes. Tension management may be defined as the process by which the elements of the social system are articulated in such manner as to 1) prevent sentiments from obstructing goal-directed activity and 2) avail the system of their motivating force in achieving goals. Communication of sentiment is the process by which members of a social system may be motivated to achieve goals, to conform to norms, and to carry out systemic action through transfer of feeling by symbols. The most important Amish activities for tension management are their religious rites of passage and rites of intensification. Birth, death, baptism, and marriage temporarily upset the equilibrium of interpersonal relations in the home, in friendship groups, and in the community. Rites of passage are the institutionalized religious means of giving emotional support until a new equilibrium is established. Particular attention will be paid here to those rites of passage involving Amish youth — baptisms and weddings, for example — and to other tension management devices which seem particularly equipped to support the affected individuals through stressful periods.

The baptismal ceremony inducts into the fellowship of the church the young people from ages 16 to 18 and up to the age of 20. Amish permit baptism only to those who give evidence of "true conversion." Parents encourage children to be baptized sometime after they finish school at fourteen and before they are twenty. The service is not as elaborate as one might think, in view of the great opposition and persecution met by the sect when it rejected infant baptism during the 16th century and afterwards. After baptism young people regularly attend the singings, which in themselves must be regarded as tension management devices, providing as they do an institutionalized means of courting, having fun, and interacting with other Amish youth. The other concessions to near-adult status perform the same function. Trips of families to Amish settlements in other parts of the country also lead to marriage. Secrecy, which may be a design to insure some privacy and thus be a tension management device, shrouds most of the preliminary preparations for the wedding, including the courting. During the courting period, for instance, the young man calls on the girl after she (apparently) and the family (actually) have retired. The young man drives up to the house and with the aid of a flashlight or buggy light makes his presence known. If the girl is interested, she quietly descends the stairs to meet the caller.[12]

Sometimes before the wedding a Schteckleimann, a deacon or minister, acts as a go-between to learn the attitude of the girl's parents concerning the possibility of the boy's marrying her. In the past this go-between carried a proposal to the girl; in more modern times the action of the Schteckleimann has been more a formality because the young people have usually decided to marry before his mission is made. The mission of the Schteckleimann must be performed in strict secrecy. Several weeks prior to the wedding date, the announcement is made at a church service. Custom decrees that the bride-to-be is not present at this service.

Weddings are important rites of passage, constituting the most important social events among the Amish and an occasion when the whole community communicates sentiment. In weddings as in singings the community intergroup relations are clearly evident. From 100 to 300 friends and relatives attend in response to verbal invitations. Weddings usually occur during November, after the crops have been harvested and when there is time for elaborate preparations. The couples are usually in their twenties. Civil law requires that the young couple present themselves at the County Court House to apply for a marriage license. Sometimes as many as six to twelve Amish couples appear at the court house for the same reason and at the same time. State law requires that the couples must wait three days after application for the granting of the license. From then on the church handles proceedings. In fact, the church has a hand during the whole courtship and honeymoon period.

Tuesdays and Thursdays are favored wedding days which are occasions for great merriment. The noontime and evening feasts which are prepared would stagger even other rural people who are accustomed to large meals. After the wedding the couple makes special visits to all close relatives and friends many of whom participated in the wedding. On these visits they receive wedding gifts. This round of visiting may require several weeks and the young couple frequently spends a night or several nights at the houses of the numerous hosts. This is the Amish honeymoon.

Events other than the changed status of meaningful individuals can also disturb the equilibrium of a society. The threat or the fact of war is particularly disturbing to the Amish because of their non-resistance convictions. For such upsets in life's routine, rites of intensification help to restore the balance. Special prayers for divine guidance under such stressful conditions provide the Amish, like other members of religious systems the world over, "an opportunity to 'act out' some of the psychological products of strain . . . (and) give people a sense of 'doing something about it.' "[13] Silent mealtime prayers are observed by all Amishmen; they are rites of intensification too, in that they mark the end of one set of activities and the beginning of another communal activity calling for a different rate of interaction among the family members.

Communication of sentiment follows a typically Gemeinschaft-like pattern, being interspersed throughout activities that are not primarily social in nature. Work bees get certain work done, but they are also festive social occasions with good food, good fellowship, gaiety, and merry-making. Since many ordinary pleasures are prohibited — music, movies, radio, most reading, television, dining out, and dancing — the Amish turn to each other for fun, relaxation, and pleasure. Visiting takes on an importance almost impossible for the outsider to comprehend. Before church services, after church services, on Sunday afternoons, and on many holidays, families visit with each other. They go to each others' homes incessantly and nevertheless complain about getting behind in their visiting obligations. In the midst of severe restrictions on expressive activity and on such expressive items as furniture or dress, which if used would indicate lack of humility, they use colorful items which combine utility with beauty. The flower gardens, bright but solid colors, embroidery designs, brightly colored dishes, and large picture calendars testify to the fact that these "plain" people also enjoy the expression of other than sober sentiments. Indeed the proper expression of sentiment does not deny enjoyment; it denies pride. A certain deliberateness and simplicity must accompany the display of sentiment, in order to be properly reverent before God to whom the most important of all expressions of sentiment are made. The Amish expression of sentiment is characterized by humility and by the rule that "love, not compulsion . . . must rule both the church and the world."[14]

ACHIEVING

End, goal, or objective as an element.   The end, goal, or objective is the change (or in some cases the retention of the *status quo*) that members of a social system expect to accomplish through appropriate interaction. Eternal life is the ultimate goal of the Amish. In the past the founders of the movement condoned certain methods of achieving this end, and some of these methods of achieving salvation have now become ends in themselves. "Full fellowship" with other Amishmen has become one such objective. Thrift, industry, good stewardship of resources, and even accumulation of goods also have become objectives in themselves.

Goal attaining and concomitant "latent" activity as process.   Whether the Amishman attains the goal of eternal life can never be proven or disproven. However, when all Amishmen are motivated toward this goal their unified and varied activity is discernible. These activities are called "latent" because the results are neither recognized nor intended. If thrift, industry, and careful stewardship lead to ultimate salvation, a certain measure of worldly success becomes equated with pursuance of the ultimate goal. Industry has become an end in and of itself, as well as serving a goal attaining function. Thus, when Christopher, the father and husband of the family overslept one morning, arising at 5:00 instead of the regular 4:00, he and the family talked about this as an important happening which required endless justification.[15] When Amish people talk about the "gay" people in the area, in contrast to themselves and similar sects who are "plain," they refer to laziness and spendthriftiness. There is continuous discussion and delaying of needed purchases in an effort to avoid spending money. There is more talk about the money wasted on cars, tabooed modern conveniences, going to movies, and other practices of "gay" people than there is about the inherent immorality in these items and practices.

By almost all standards the Amish are successful farmers. The pressure to increase yields and improve products and income is tremendous. Although goal attaining activity requires a heavy expenditure for modern efficient facilities, it stops short of becoming involved in the use of "worldly" machinery, conveniences, or devices. The rationale for "worldly" is not clear to the outsider who wonders, for example, why the tractor for the use of belt power is accepted but its use for draft power in the field is taboo. Why is the gasoline engine on the washing machine or battery charger all right and the rubber-tired tractor for draft power or the family automobile "wicked"? Why can a farmer who needs the telephone in his business use a pay-station or even have one installed in his out-house, but not in his home? The utilization of such facilities is based directly on the goal as it is viewed and the activity related to realizing that goal. It is hypothesized that in the pursuit of the goal those practices are in-stitutionalized which will not plunge the sect into deep contact with the outside world; that those practices are prohibited which would encourage a rapid interaction with the outside world, even though their use might sizeably increase profits.

"Full fellowship with other Amishmen" is a goal-attaining activity in that Biblical directives are compatible with it. And it too has become an end in itself. Those Amishmen deprived of full fellowship suffer extreme frustration, whereas for those in "full fellowship" the "Amish system provides 'social security' . . . from the womb to the tomb, and a certain guarantee of security even beyond the tomb."[16]

NORMING, STANDARDIZING, AND PATTERNING

Norm as an element. The rules which prescribe what is acceptable or unacceptable are the norms of the social system. The most visible norms among the Amish are those that govern personal grooming, dress, house furnishings and farm operation. Amishmen wear long, bobbed hair, parted in the middle and banged across the forehead. Married men wear beards but not mustaches; unmarried and unbaptized men are usually clean-shaven. All males wear broad, full trousers which are held up by plain suspenders. Their dress coats have no lapels and no outside pockets; hooks and eyes are used rather than buttons. Broadrimmed, flat straw hats are worn in summer and broadrimmed, flat, black hats are worn in the winter.

The women's dress is similarly standardized. Dresses are always of a solid color. Unmarried girls wear white aprons and married women wear aprons which may match the color of their dresses. Women's hair must not be cut or curled. Identical home-made bonnets and devotional head coverings are worn by both girls and women. Style changes over the generations are at a minimum and are made only after group deliberation and approval, and when scarcity or other factors make change necessary. Jewelry, pictures, and photographs are prohibited.

Hand flashlights with batteries are permitted, but electric current cannot be used as power in any form. Although many houses have running water from wells powered by ingeniously designed water wheels linked by cables, none may have indoor toilets. Fancy decorations in the houses are taboo. In the technological field autos, telephones, radios and tractors for draft power are prohibited.

Perhaps the most important of the norms of the Amish deal with vocations. Only agriculture and a few related occupations such as rural carpentry and masonry are open to them. Only farming is thought to be harmonious with God's way; the city is considered the epitome of that which is "worldly." The importance of the taboo on non-agricultural occupations for a people with a relatively high replacement rate is obvious. The Amish farms have been reduced in size, the community boundaries have been moving outward, and new colonies have been established to meet this pressure on the land.

Most of the norms reinforce Amish belief in separation from the world and non-conformity to it. The cultivation of humility is reinforced by these norms. Pride is regarded as a cardinal sin. The norms barring membership in non-church organizations and affiliation with non-Amish people mean that the Amish avoid the organizations so common to the middle classes of the Western world. The doctrine of the "unequal yoke" supports this non-joining. "They do not join cooperatives, insurance companies, political groups, parent-teacher organizations, civic or social clubs, and they take no part in government-sponsored plans designed to aid them and other farmers."[17]

Interesting as the norms are in themselves, the constellation of different dress, non-joining, distinctive grooming, non-resistance, and agriculture-limited vocations represents the core of boundary maintenance.

Evaluation as a process. Evaluation is the process through which positive and negative priorities or values are assigned to concepts, objects, actors, or collectivities, or to events and activities, either past, present, or future. Despite the ready-made decisions in the form of norms which confronts each Amishman, his life is nevertheless beset with problems which require choices; in short he must evaluate. Amish family life is replete with cases of exceedingly difficult evaluative choices. One family became interested in dairy-cattle breeding. Time, money, and study went into the creation of a pure-bred herd which became so fine that in the eyes of the Amish community it represented sinful pride. The family had to make a choice: to dispense with the dairy herd which meant disposing of the work of years which had, by this time, become a compelling interest and achievement or to risk ex-communication. Other families face similar decisions. The congregation as a whole makes a group evaluation each time that it deliberates on the reported moral short-coming of a member. It must weigh the transgression and mete out the punishment. Figure 2 gives some perspective to the evaluative process as carried out by the Amish relating concepts used by Merton to some used in the PAS Model.

It presents different methods of adaptation to life's situations, or as its author termed it, a "typology of modes of adaptation."[18] What is here called ends and objectives Merton calls "culture goals" as shown on the chart. What Merton in this article calls "institutionalized means" includes norms, utilization of facilities, and goal attaining activities. The member "evaluates" when he calculates the results of his action in terms of his ends, and norms. For the Amishman to remain an Amishman he must accept the complex of items included in culture goals and must also use only the institutionalized means for the goal's attainment. He clearly falls within Type I from the point of view of his own communal social system. If he does not, sanctions are brought upon him and he must conform or leave. Both his ends and norms are at variance with those of many other important social systems in the larger society, but within his own social system he is a strict conformist as compared with members of most other social systems.

FIGURE 2*

A Typology of Modes of Individual Adaptation

Modes of Adaptation	Culture Goals Ends	Institutionalized Means Norms
I. Conformity	Acceptance	Acceptance
II. Innovation	Acceptance	Rejection
III. Ritualism	Rejection	Acceptance
IV. Retreatism	Rejection	Rejection
V. Rebellion	Rejection of prevailing ends and substitution of new ones.	Rejection of prevailing norms and substitution of new ones.

*Robert K. Merton, *Social Theory and Social Structure* (New York: University of Columbia Press, 1949), p. 133.

Utilization of Merton's typology as extended by Robert Dubin provides some insights into the adaptation of the Amish.[19] Since Dubin uses the concept "cultural goal" to describe what we call societal goals and "institutional norms" to describe the norms of a sub-system, the general society and the Amish as systems may be considered at one time. He divides Merton's concept "institutionalized means" into institutional norms and means, the latter being "actual behaviors of people." Thus, the Amishman who developed the fine herd of dairy cows accepted the cultural goal and institutional norms but rejected and substituted means. In the Amish community's eyes, the family has substituted "pride" for the appropriate sentiment, "humility"; they had substituted an ostentatious herd for a utilitarian one. They were, therefore, cast out. A form of Type IV, retreatism, is always latent for the Amish. Should the greater society exert pressures which would make the larger societal goals and norms mandatory, the Amish might reject both goal and norm and retreat by moving to some other location. The evaluative process has led to this result for a great many Amish groups in the past. The present location of Mennonite groups, of which the Amish are an off-shoot, in Manitoba, Canada, and in Latin America is the result of adaptation to "outside" goals and norms by retreat.[20]

DIVIDING THE FUNCTIONS AND ACTIVITIES

Status-role incorporating both element and process. The two-term entity "status-role" contains the concept of status, a structural element implying position and the concept of role, a functional process. Both are important determinants of what is to be expected from an incumbent and how it is performed by him as he occupies any social position. Simplicity marks the status-role pattern of the Amish where almost every family is a farm family, where conformity within the group is paramount, and where few sub-systems with differentiated status-roles exist. The division of labor is prescribed by sex roles in the family and community. The males carry on the heavy farm work and entrepreneural functions of the farm enterprise; the females do the housework, care for the fowls, and do lighter field work. Age differentiation is indicated in part by grooming. The braided hair of the little girl gives way to the smoothly drawn tresses and bun at the nape of the neck as she matures. The smooth-shaven face of the youth becomes the bearded face of the married man who assumes a new status-role of head of a household. His open buggy used during courting days is replaced by the closed family-style buggy. Similarly, baptism brings the status-role of church member to the Amish youth, and he participates in church decisions, thus functioning in a status-role formerly closed to him. The youth as a suitor, as a worker, as a church member, and as a son holds a number of status-roles, the expectancies of which are seldom uncertain. Though he may become restive and try to find out about the outside world, question the existing order, and cause his parents much anxiety before he marries and settles down, he is never uncertain about what he should expect of himself and what others expect of him. Other family status-roles in existence because of age and family position are those of

> . . . the Grossdawdy and the Grossmutter who retire to their part of the house and find as much work outside as they care to do. Grossmutter

sews during the day for children and grandchildren. This work keeps
both of them healthily occupied as long as they are active. If they need
attention younger members of the family are near. It is doubtful that old
people anywhere are more contented than the occupants of the
Grossdawdy house who can associate daily with their children and
grandchildren and yet be separate.[21]

The most important church-community status-roles in this social system, devoid of formally trained leaders, are those of minister,
deacon, and bishop. Ordinarily each of the 33 districts in Lancaster
County, Pennsylvania has several ministers, one deacon, about
80-100 baptized members and that many or more younger people.
Every two districts has one bishop.

After the status-role of family members, church members, and
officials the most important role is that of teacher. Since only the
vocation of farming and closely related occupations are open to the
Old Order Amish, the teachers are usually from more liberal "plain
people" sects. The Amish attempt to have such teachers for their
small district schools because they understand and sympathize with
the strict norms of the Amish better than those of "gay" origin. Her
grooming and dress may resemble but not be the same as those of the
children.

Though the choice of status-roles seems extremely limited to the
outsider accustomed to the highly specialized division of labor of the
larger society, those of the Amish community feel that the status-
roles available in their system give much scope to individual differences in interests and ability. When informants were asked about
varied ambitions on the part of their children, they replied that
farming offers adequate opportunity to give expression to these differences. Even in a specialized form of farming, variations are possible in approach and execution. The opportunity to exercise special
talents in farming was also stressed. Soil, stock, crop, and marketing
problems are cited in abundance to demonstrate this point. "Why, a
good farmer does not even treat two cows, two horses, or even two pigs
alike."[22]

RANKING

Rank as an element.   Rank or standing represents the value an
actor has for the system in which the rank is accorded. Among the
Amish rank differences are not extreme. The Amish community
eliminates some rank differentiation available to non-Amishmen. In
the Amish social entity everyone has the same amount of schooling;
everyone is in farming or allied trades; everyone wears the same kind

of clothes; everyone drives the same kind of buggy. Nonetheless ranks can be distinguished. The individual who has been successful as both a church leader and a farmer is ranked higher than the church leader who in turn outranks the successful farmer. The farm owner has a higher rank then the farm renter who outranks the farm laborer. The old person, other things being equal, commands higher rank than the young. Young men and women often line up by age to march into the church services and the position in the line often indicates ranking. Of the approximate 16 bishops in Lancaster County, it is the five oldest whose counsel is regarded as most important.

Evaluation as a process in ranking and allocation of status-roles. Rank differentiation foretells the bases of the evaluative process. The community gives a high evaluation to the successful Amish farmer who demonstrates church leadership. This means that he must familiarize himself with the scriptures and show that he is in sympathy with church regulations and practices. An exemplary life is highly esteemed. So are those whose farming enterprises have been so successful that their houses are large enough to hold 200 or more persons in church meetings. They are generally evaluated more highly than those with smaller houses. Also the more valuable the livestock, the better it is cared for, the more productive and fertile the farm, and the better it is kept the higher the social rank of the owner.

Age and wisdom are assumed to be related. In general, the older the person the higher the rank. When old age impairs faculties, especially the mental ones, however, rank likewise suffers. The importance of achievement and capacity to achieve is always important in rank among the Amish. Despite such mundane evaluations, it is important to remember that the basic ends, beliefs, and sentiments of the Amish emphasize Godliness, humility, and "full fellowship." Honor and high standing are accorded to those whose lives exemplify these qualities. Once an Amishman ceases to incorporate these qualities in his life he ceases to be an Amishman. Hence the basic evaluative process tends to accord undifferentiated standing to individuals; the rank differences are hardly more than subtle over-lays in an evaluative process which, more than any other known to the author, results in near equality of rank.

The nearly equal accordance of rank is of course related to the lack of specialization of status-roles within the system. Only one important status-role among the Amish is allocated in an unusual and dramatic fashion; its allocation depends to a degree on the evaluation of the actor before the assignment, and after its allocation the

rank of the incumbent is almost bound to increase. A minister is
chosen from among the members of the congregation as Matthias was
selected to become one of the Apostles.

All baptized members of the congregation participate and any
man who receives as many as three votes is entered for the selection
ceremony which is solemn and formal. Bibles of similar outward
appearance are placed on a table, one for each candidate. A slip of
paper is hidden from view in one Bible. On this slip is usually a
Biblical verse which designates that the chooser must give his life to
his new post. Candidates file past the table and each picks a Bible.
The one who chooses the Bible with the slip of paper is said to be
chosen by God to serve and is ordained immediately. The status-role
of bishop, considered higher than that of preacher, is filled from the
preacher's ranks. In spite of the great honor that assignment to the
status-role of minister carries with it, the family of the chosen minister is usually sad and he is usually filled with trepidation. He has
placed upon him a tremendous responsibility. Large segments of the
Bible must be memorized in High German, and sermons of one hour
and a half or longer must be memorized since the use of notes is
prohibited. Hundreds of hours of reading and studying are in prospect
although the new minister may not necessarily be studious by inclination. A large part of the heavy farm work load that had been his
must be taken over by other members of the farm family. Families
whose husband-father is chosen as minister are often said to go
through a period of weeping and mourning not unlike those experienced at the death of a member.

CONTROLLING

Power as an element.   Power is the capacity to control others. It
has many components which may be classified as authoritative and
non-authoritative control. Authority is the right as determined by
the members of the social system and built into the status-role to
control others, whereas unlegitimized coercion and voluntary
influence are nonauthoritative. Influence may rest on personal
characteristics, social capital, and many other bases. The control of
the parents over the child is the most prominent example of Amish
power relations. There is no question but that the husband and father
holds the authority of the family. His power is cushioned by the
Christian doctrine that stresses mercy and understanding and by his
anxiety that his children might go "gay" or break with the church.
The wife and mother holds authority too. The Amish family, like most
American families, has an authority pattern that is discernible but

much less rigid than that which operates within a work team in a factory or other bureaucratic setting. Both father and mother influence the controls of each other, and there is a reciprocal influence exerted between the children and their parents, although the children have less power than do the parents. The fact that the parents hold the purse strings and make the necessary contributions to substantial dowries and toward the later economic independence of the children is a controlling factor of great importance.

The ministers, deacons, and bishops exert more control over community affairs related to the church than do ordinary members of the congregation. The authority of the deacon is illustrated by his right and duty to initiate the disciplining of members who have violated regulations. He also manages the poor fund. In crises that involve the whole community the influence of the ministers, deacons, and bishops becomes more obvious and it is usually those of highest rank who exercise the greatest power. This is not always true, however, for in a given situation special experience or abilities may carry more influence than does rank.

Decision making and its initiation into action as process. Decision making is the process by which the alternatives available to the members are reduced and a choice made. The locus and balance of power in the family as well as in the church and community can best be observed when decisions are made. The husband and father initiates important family decisions and usually directs their execution. He is the primary initiator of action in external activities. Nevertheless, the rarity of arbitrary decisions is impressive. The tempering effect of the children's and wife's influence on paternal authority is illustrated in the following instances of decision making. Conversations such as these at meal-time often led to decisions. "David, you might mend the fence in the south pasture today. The cows are going to get into the corn." "The fence in the ridge pasture is in much worse shape, Father; there are at least three places there where the stock can get out if they try hard enough." "Well, then, why don't you fix the fences in both pastures. Do the ridge pasture first if you think it's so much worse, but I want the south pasture fence fixed before tomorrow, or we're going to lose our corn." There were decisions to make concerning the mother's sphere of work too. "I made a deal with the poultry farm yesterday. They are holding four dozen chickens for us. Maybe you could take time this afternoon to go over with me and help me bring them home." "I don't know where I'm going to put four dozen chickens. We'll need another coop first. Do we have to get them today?" "No, I guess the poultry farm could hold them for another day or two. I'll get the chicken wire and lumber and make the coop this afternoon or tomorrow. We'll get the chickens tomorrow afternoon instead."

A recurring cause for decision making revolves around the disciplinary problems handled by all the baptized of the congregation. The person charged with the breach of the rules and all unbaptized persons leave the meeting. The deacon repeats the charges and reviews the circumstances. Unanimity of decision concerning the offender is the ideal, but frequently this cannot be attained. Actually, majority vote carries less weight than a decision by the ministers and deacons who are, it is believed, chosen by divine influence. On very important congregational matters or on community matters which involve a number of congregations the bishop may be summoned. The bishop is usually slow to arrive at a decision, but once he nods his head in approval the opinions of the congregation are likely to coalesce in agreement. Thus, "the bishop's nod" has come to be practically synonymous with ultimate decision.

SANCTIONING

Sanction as an element. Sanction may be defined as the rewards and penalties used to attain conformity to ends and norms. The most interesting and powerful sanction among the Amish is negative — the *Meidung* or shunning. The *Meidung* shuts off the violator from communication with any member of the congregation — his family, his friends, his neighbors. Its very existence as a possible consequence of indiscreet behavior is a powerful force toward conformity. Other negative sanctions include public "confession of fault" accompanied by promises not to repeat the offense and public apologies. Positive sanctions include the support the conforming member feels from the knowledge that aid and comfort in time of need would immediately be forthcoming.

> The program of brotherly love and mutual aid, founded on definite scriptural injunctions, is still maintained . . . . The Amish take care of their own poor, and none of them is now on relief. Members in distress still receive aid from fellow members, particularly if reverses result from "acts of God."[23]

Application of sanctions as process. The cases of offenders are brought before the entire baptized congregation. A serious offense such as cursing or operating an automobile may result in being refused participation in the Lord's Supper and full fellowship until amends are made. If the violator refuses to make amends he may be shunned by all the church members including his own family and may eventually be excommunicated. The example of David Sussfuss and his milk truck illustrates the process of Meidung or shunning.

David Sussfuss had a milk route in Lancaster which he and his family had built up over a period of seven years. Customers began to cancel their standing orders and usually they gave the same reason — the milkman failed to deliver regularly. This was not the first time that the Sussfuss family had failed to get a responsible and dependable non-Amishman with a truck to act as their delivery man. Customers had fallen off gradually and now with such alarming rapidity that the livelihood of the family was at stake. The whole family had spent long hours in prayer over the matter, and they finally decided to buy a truck by which to make their own deliveries. Immediately in executive session after the biweekly sermon the deacon consulted the congregation. David was told to get rid of the truck and ask forgiveness. In the following weeks while David made deliveries with the truck, not one person of the community spoke to him or to any member of his family or in any way acknowledged their existence. Close friends and neighbors of many years walked past them with unseeing eyes; playmates simply did not see or hear the Sussfuss children; they disregarded them completely. Close relatives of David's wife — her sisters and parents — were deaf and blind to her presence. It was as if they did not exist. The Sussfusses cried and prayed day and night but could see no way to remain dairy farmers without having a truck. Finally they looked into joining the Church Amish or New Order Amish which permits the use of cars and trucks. When last heard of, they were gradually becoming acquainted with the Church Amish, many of whom had gone through similar experiences. Few forgot the horrible experience of being shunned by their closest friends and kin. It is reported that some Old Order Amish who have been shunned and returned to the fold tell of suffering for days from such ailments as amnesia. Suicide under these conditions is not unknown.

Those who follow the norms, however, can count on aid and assistance when they need it. The financial aid given one father is an example of a positive sanction. Sickness in the family had caused a financial crisis. The father found that he could borrow money from the bank at six percent interest but that he would have to get someone with property to sign for security. He described trying to get a cosignatory:

The first Amish fellow I went to said he guessed he better not. He hated to turn me down but his father said "never go anybody's note." The

second fellow didn't know what to do. He went to ask his mother and I
saw him come out of the door with a check book and a note pad. I didn't
know what would happen. He said "I can't sign for you but I can give you
the money if you'll pay me four per cent. You don't have to pay this
year." I was so glad I could cry. I was in a tight place . . . .

FACILITATING

Facility as an element.   A facility is a means used within the
system to attain the members' ends. The Amish emphasis upon
humility and their avoidance of sinful pride makes them peculiarly
unliable to the collection of material things. The facilities of worship
and of everyday living are consequently not nearly so plentiful as
they are for more ritualistic and more materialistic social systems.

On the other hand the self-conscious avoidance of religious
paraphernalia and of personal, occupational, and household luxuries
carries with it a preoccupation about "things." In this sense every
item prescribed by custom and church rule is essential in that it
cannot be substituted by another item; it becomes a facility. The
house or barn serving as a church, since special church buildings are
sinful, is obviously a facility as is all the agricultural equipment of
the farmyard and the household. Those items particularly distinctive
of Amish culture — the open buggies of the young men and the closed
ones of the family, their clothes, the particular style of household
architecture which allows great areas to be opened into each other for
church meetings, must all be regarded as facilities. Facilities necessary for the religious services may, at the outset, seem simple as
compared with religious services rich in symbolism and ritual. But in
lieu of church buildings, pews, altars, flowers, organ music, choirs,
and other common Christian religious facilities, other facilities have
come to prevail for the Amish.

Utilization of facilities as process.   The fortnightly Sunday
church meetings among these people involve longer and more intimate interaction than do the church services of any other group
known to the author. First of all the family which is to hold the
meeting must put house, barn, and yards in order. Kitchen ranges
and heating stoves are polished and even the walls may be freshly
painted or washed. Since the service may be held in the barn, particularly in the summer, the lower story barn walls may be whitewashed
and the cement floor swept. Meeting-benches must be hauled to the
place, bread and food must be bought or baked. Bread, butter, apple
butter, pickled beets, other pickles, apple or schnitz pies and coffee
are prescribed for the Sunday meal by church regulations. On Sunday
morning everybody shakes hands and preachers greet each other

with the holy kiss as commanded in the Bible. The religious services usually last from 9:00 a.m. until noon or frequently until 1:00 p.m. but many worshippers arrive by 8:00. There is considerable singing from the old hymn book, the *Ausbund* written in High German. More visiting takes place after the church services. If there are disciplinary problems these are considered after the last hymn by those of the congregation who are members. Visiting goes on for hours after the noon meal and close friends and relatives of the host may stay for supper. The thirty-three church districts each contain some 70 to 100 members but since membership is withheld until people are in the late teens, at which time they can be baptized, these church meetings are usually attended by twice as many people as there are members.

The very avoidance of facilities in the pursuit of agriculture makes them extremely important. In fact the rejected facilities both in the church service and in farming reveal as much about the evaluative judgments of the members of the social system and about their objectives as do the approved facilities. The forbidden facility is often not disapproved of because of any intrinsic characteristic of the facility, but because interaction patterns in the group itself might be disrupted if the facility were adopted.

COMPREHENSIVE OR MASTER PROCESSES

Communication. Communication is the process by which information, decisions, and directives pass through the system and by which knowledge is transmitted and sentiment is formed or modified. The intense interaction of the Amish serves an important function in passing information, decisions, and directives throughout the system. This interaction for a people denied much of the mass media of the larger society becomes the chief method of communication. Newspapers may supply the information and knowledge, but it is face-to-face interaction that reinforces opinions and attitudes. The spectacle of similar sects that have allowed the abolition of a few taboos only to be rapidly acculturated into the prevailing "worldly" society is another form of communication uniquely important to the Old Order Amish. The bi-lingual and sometimes tri-lingual ability of the Amish must also be regarded as an important communication method by which they can interact with the greater society in business and other pursuits on the one hand, but on the other, maintain through language itself a sustained integration. In a way not common to the larger society, normatively prescribed appearance constitutes a communication medium. The young Amishman communicates, in effect, by his high visibility, were he to attempt to enter a cinema or tavern. Likewise, he communicates his status-role by his grooming and his dress. Despite the limitations placed upon the mass media, the Amishman is informed of outside affairs through his newspaper and has a most efficient system of communication for the parochial happenings of his immediate world.

Boundary Maintenance.   Boundary maintenance preserves the solidarity, identity, and interaction pattern within the system. No process is more important in the life of the Amish than boundary maintenance; without hard and fast boundaries of conduct as well as spatial boundaries, their ways would change and their system disintegrate. This process is therefore related to every single element and process that makes up Amish life and puts it in motion. What appears here is a selection from all the elements and processes which forms the core of the boundary maintenance process.

The Amish have specialized in a way of life founded on the belief that they are "God's peculiar people" who "are not conformed to the world" and who should not be "unequally yoked together with unbelievers." Every act of life becomes one designed to keep the group intact and untouched by meaningful contacts with individuals outside its own boundaries.

The sanctified nature of farming permits the maintenance of certain boundaries. No Amishman needs further education; no Amishman needs to seek a job in a non-Amish community; and no Amishman engages in an occupation that does not involve the whole family. The sentiment of humility provides a rationale for "plain" and standardized grooming and dress, boundary maintenance devices in themselves. "Full fellowship" with other Amishmen demands strict conformity to the system's norms. Grooming, dress, house furnishings and farm operation methods and facilities tend effectively to set the Amish off from members of the larger society.

The simplicity of the status-role pattern and the limited number of status-roles available to the individual insures against little pyramids of special occupational interests. Commonly shared status-roles means commonly shared life styles; it maximizes integration and minimizes the splintering of interests. A uniform and clearly understood power and rank system which leaves the most important allocation of power up to God minimizes the competition for power and rank and fosters integration. The awful fate of him who is either shunned or excommunicated can scarcely be imagined by those who have a number of important reference groups and whose ideas of a personal heaven and hell may be hazy. The Amishman has only one membership group and very few reference groups and his idea of heaven and hell is explicit. Each sanction has been described as "a living death."

The excommunication of members was an awful and solemn procedure. The members to be expelled had been notified in advance and were absent. An air of tenseness filled the house. Sad-faced women wept quietly; stern men sat with faces drawn. The bishop arose; with trembling voice and with tears on his cheek he announced that the guilty parties had confessed their sin, that they were cast off from the fellowship of the church and committed to the devil and all his angels.[24]

Every article used by the Amish that marks them as "different" from the members of the larger society is a boundary maintaining device. If they should forget for one moment that forbidden facilities maintain boundaries they have but to look at what has resulted for other Old Order Amish groups when they have compromised on facilities.

They see this in the difficulties other nonconformity groups are having after modifying their conduct with reference to certain "worldly" practices or conveniences. For instance, after some branches of the Mennonite and Amish churches made concessions regarding the automobile, the tractor for field work, and the English language for religious services, it was difficult to maintain certain other long-established practices. Men cut their hair shorter and shorter and eventually some adopted the prevailing hair cut; beards became shorter and in time were discarded by some; suits became less extreme in appearance, and some men even bought "store suits." Women departed from old standards in that printed goods were used in dresses, devotional head coverings became smaller, and some of the women curled their hair. In services, part-singing was introduced by stages. One change has led to another, until most of the outstanding nonconformity practices have become things of the past.[25]

Under a system which makes the old a sacred trust and the new something to be wary of, the Amish have succeeded in erecting a boundary against the surrounding society which tends to be scornful of the past and uncritical of the new.

Institutionalization. Through institutionalization human behavior is made predictable and patterned, social systems are given the elements of structure and the processes of function. The most essential features of the institutionalization of the elements of the Amish social system began to be formed 400 years ago as their antecedents, the Swiss Brethren, denied the efficacy of organized religion. As a result of their revolt against the Catholic, Lutheran, and Reformed churches "thousands of harmless, pious souls, with no other desire than to worship God in their own way, were put to death with the concurrence of both state and church, often under great

torture . . . wherever . . . they were found."[26] Their beliefs and need
for support under such conditions led to the postulate of "a separate
people," "a people apart," unyoked to the worldly groups about them.
Practices consistent with the postulate emerged and gradually were
institutionalized in the norms elaborated above. Resulting status-
roles about which the division of labor is organized are perhaps the
simplest of any collectivity of comparable size in the modern world
and because they are so highly institutionalized are among the most
predictable.

If the reader were to focus his attention completely on the Amish
community, and not for the moment see it surrounded by other
"worldly" communities, it would be easy to conclude that here was a
life pattern, institutionalized in a completely harmonious way
around the three chief interlocking social sub-systems — the family,
the church, and the occupation. Expectancy patterns would be so
completely fulfilled at each point of interaction that solidarity, security, and freedom from stress would seem inherent in the system.
The Amish created a new way of life for themselves. To protect that
system all the most ordinary pursuits were prescribed — where to
live, what to wear, when to quit school, when to marry, how to rear
children.

Systemic linkage.   This is the process whereby the elements of
at least two social systems come to be articulated so that in some ways
and on some occasions they may be viewed as a single system.
Whereas the processes previously discussed deal chiefly with interaction within a system, systemic linkage relates members of at least
two systems. But let the reader broaden his focus to include the larger
social groups among which the Amish as individuals move, and
points of strain immediately become apparent. Despite the communal aspect of worship, mutual aid, and blood interrelatedness,
Amish enterprise is private. Property is owned and taxes paid by
families interacting within the total society. Families buy and sell in
the non-Amish market and are dependent upon the general economy.
They compete economically with non-Amish families in the production and distribution of goods. Their methods of farming and hauling
are subject to many prohibitions, designed to preserve the Amish
community, not to help the farmer compete. When there is pressure to
change — a dairy farmer may, for example, feel it necessary to have a
newly invented item of equipment — tremendous stress may develop,
in part at least, because none of the existing norms of the Amish apply
to the new situation. Can the unmarried men have a car? Under what
circumstances if at all can mixed couples go riding? Linkage with
another and different social system requires reestablishment of

norms and new institutionalization of behavior, and weakens boundary maintenance.

Some of the institutionalized patterns of behavior designed to preserve the Amish society are incompatible with the basic laws and norms of the general society. Compulsory attendance at a school which meets minimum standards is a case in point. Since the Amish do not believe in education beyond the primary grades, they cannot recruit from their own group teachers who meet state standards. The teacher, who holds an influential position, is consequently recruited from another community. She may represent a highly valued role-model to which the Amish youngster can not aspire and still maintain his faith. This bit of linkage with another social system provides a situation which can be beset by conflict and strain.

To the Amish parents the stress is no less great. They see their children, whom they fervently hope will remain in the faith, influenced by a person who commands the children's admiration and respect and who is in a prestigeful position which is denied them. Petitions from the Amish for control of their own schools have usually been met with rebuffs from those in control in the larger society to whom it seems wicked and un-American to deny children a broad education under well-trained teachers.

A similar strain threatens the Amish youth when they solicit services from outside professionals — doctors, lawyers, and the like. The prestige of these roles is no less apparent to the Amish than to the non-Amish, and desire of Amish youth to emulate these professionals and gain the same kind of prestige can be a deterrent to the full use of professional services. Thus, the attempt is made to regard the hiring of all such services as a purely business proposition and to avoid any affective or diffuse relations.

When a young Amishman leaves his church to become a member of a more liberal one the typical expression is: "He got his hair cut." Should he leave both Amish and Mennonite fellowship, "He went English."[27] Parents continually worry lest children be "lost" in this manner. The Amish community is in constant fear that the general society will pass laws or enforce existing laws that will force the Amish to violate their norms. Compulsory high school attendance, consolidated schools, and enforced military service are continual threats. In the last war Amish youths served in various capacities in conscientious objector camps which, it is claimed, led many to lose their faith. Under similar threats many groups have moved to countries promising freedom from obligations that violate their basic norms. The Amish must maintain a readiness for leaving farms and homes which are the work of many years and in some cases generations. Material things "of this world" must be devaluated and group integration fostered to maintain this readiness.

Although voting has been discouraged in the past, Amishmen and even their wives have recently voted in school elections to prevent the consolidation of schools. This voting indicates the nature of the dilemma confronting the members of a social system that is integrated around beliefs, ends, and norms that are at variance with those of the dominant larger society. Voting may violate the norms and taboos designed to avoid the "unequal yoke," but non-voting would permit the non-Amishmen to force school consolidation thus establishing "the unequal yoke" in another form and subjecting the Amish children to forces which would call into question their values and beliefs. The Amishman is "bedamned if he does" and "bedamned if he doesn't" vote. As yet no institutionalized mechanism has been developed to remove the stress from either voting or non-voting, but one must emerge if effective linkage between the Amish system and the general society is to be maintained.

By definition systemic linkage is the process whereby the elements of at least two systems come to be articulated so that in some ways they function as a unit. For the most part, the Amish community illustrates resistance to linkage at all costs. Nevertheless, a small but increasing linkage with the outside world is actually taking place. Only in recent years have the Amish participated in cow-testing associations sponsored by the county agent. A good many have joined a Cooperative Egg and Poultry Association and some have joined the Inter-State Milk Producers' Cooperative. The Lancaster County Swiss Cheese Company, although controlled by the Amish, has some non-Amish members and represents at least a slight tolerance of the "unequal yoke."

Various government programs developed through the agencies of the United States Department of Agriculture also force participation. Not to participate and not receive various available payments would result in penalizing family and community. Thus systemic linkage with the outside cannot be said to be absent, but it is relatively less important here than in most social groups. Specific examples of technological change resulting from social cultural linkage are the following: Electricity, though it may not be used for power or light, has been used for wire fences and in hen houses, to increase production. The various facilities of non-Amish neighbors such as telephones are frequently used. Gasoline engines are used to power washing machines and other equipment in the place of tabooed electricity. Increasing use is made of various professions and vocations related to medicine, law and finance which are tabooed as status-roles for Amishmen.

Socialization. Socialization is the process whereby the social and cultural heritage is transmitted. The chief job facing parents in transmitting the social and cultural heritage of the Amish is to see that the child accepts his "difference" from members of other groups, that he accepts his occupation of farmer or associated work, and that he accepts the Amish idea of God and religion.

> Children must be told why they cannot have clothes, bicycles, and many toys like those of other children; why the family cannot have electric lights, a car, a radio. The total impression of the children must be one of separateness, difference and one of strong disapproval of the world and all its doings. That the children may understand the religious services and read available religious books, including the Bible, they must be taught to speak and read German.[28]

The same writer commends the success with which the parents cultivate in their children a sense of values which centers their interests and plans on farming. The chief adult model is of course a farmer. Definite farm tasks are assigned each boy and girl at an early age, and it is always taken for granted that the children will some day farm. Boys and girls of eight and nine regularly help in the house and do chores and field work; nearly all of them milk cows at this age and the boys have usually begun doing field work with horses and implements by this time. Failure to farm or engage in a closely related activity is regarded as total failure and is a disgrace to the family and to the community. Children's play impressively brings out the limited scope of life for which the Amish child is being socialized. Children play that they are mothers and fathers and, of course, children; but not that they are policemen or any of dozens of status-roles enacted by children in the "gay" society of the outside world. Since there is no place in the belief system for war and strife, boys do not carry on mock gun battles; actual fighting among siblings and peers is at a minimum. The author marveled at the relative absence of conflict in the family with whom he lived. He concluded that the pattern of struggle was not internalized because the children were kept from the outside world and the virtues of love and kindness were extolled. These virtues and other elements of the Amish culture are nurtured within the family, church, and community. Boundary maintenance devices reduce to a minimum the outside influences, for children who in school or elsewhere internalize to any considerable extent incompatible ends, norms, beliefs, and sentiments from the outside may "go gay" and leave the community.

CONDITIONS OF SOCIAL ACTION

Territoriality. The Lancaster County Old Order Amish community is composed of approximately 150 square miles with 33 church districts and several schools. A larger proportion of people are known to each other than in any community of similar geographical size and population known to the author. Most families are linked to the various areas of the community by close family ties.

The social processes and elements in the system lead to a most interesting ecological phenomena. The high value placed on separation from the non-Amish people places a high premium upon living near the center of the community. Almost all community members prefer to live in the center so that all children attend a given school and most contacts are with other Amishmen. The fact that the horse and buggy, not the automobile, must be used places relatively greater centripetal pressure on the land than is so in other rural areas in the United States. Also a factor of selectivity operates. Families who develop liberal tendencies or "go gay" and who own land in the center of the community often sell their land for very high prices to the more conservative who desire that location. This tends to increase the conservatism of the center. In time the value of farms is determined by the distance from the center of the community rather than by their relative productivity or money-making potential. Wealthy Amishmen who live in the center may buy land from non-Amishmen on the fringes and by hiring or renting to Amishmen of lower rank build up the usually rundown land left by non-plain people.

Time. Time as a facility is reflected in the sequence of events in church ritual and other ways. Time as a condition and uncontrollable by man is reflected in the conceptions of eternity and the concern that each accomplish as much good as possible before he dies.

Size. The size of the various subsystems of the Amish, with the exception of the family, is to a considerable extent controlled. Obviously the limited land available and the consequent migrations from the Lancaster site have made the community less powerful than if all could have been retained.

AN AMISH CHURCH ADOPTS THE AUTOMOBILE[29]

A CASE OF SUCCESSFUL SYSTEMIC LINKAGE

As in every instance of evaluation and decision making, the adoption of the automobile by the Old Order Amish, which we shall call The Hoog Church, has a particular history. The Hoog group was one of four House Amish religious communities in Pennsylvania

County. The House Amish groups were more conservative than the four Church Amish groups in the County. The Hoog group was the most progressive of the House Amish, resembling the most conservative of the Church Amish as much as they did the next most progressive group of House Amish. The Hoog group originated fifty years ago as an offshoot of the then most progressive of the House Amish. While the group shares the same general culture as other Amish in the territory the details differ considerably. Shirts, suspenders, and in some instances broadfall trousers are purchased when available at the nearby store. Buttons are permitted on work jackets. The men's hair extends over part of the ear, which is considerably shorter than the hair length for men in the next most progressive group. Tractors, including those with rubber tires, are used for farming operations. The brims of men's hats are smaller than those of all other Amish. Until the acceptance of automobiles carriage tops were black. The ban on the use of electricity was lifted 10 years ago; since that time farms have been modernized considerably. Farming is completely modern and tractor-oriented but religion centers in house worship. *Norms and boundary maintenance devices had already been relaxed. Partial systemic linkage with the larger society in agricultural practices had already been achieved.*

For a number of years members of the Hoog Group used tractors in the field and for farm work. With the appearance of pneumatic tires, they were also used on the road, to pull wagons to town and to run errands to nearby farms. Several members installed high speed transmissions especially for road work. During deer hunting season tractors could be seen on the mountain where they were parked while their operators were hunting. The tractors were equipped with huge platforms on the rear for hauling milk. Boxes were also attached in which Amish youngsters were transported. One church official of the group commented to the writer: "This seemed inconsistent to me and I was afraid to be seen on the road anymore with the tractor." *The objective of occupational efficiency was added and was sometimes in conflict with the old objective of remaining "God's peculiar people." New norms were institutionalized, new facilities added to accomplish the old objective of making money, an objective given a higher priority by the evaluative process.*

Some of the younger members commented on the inconsistency of driving rubber-tired farm tractors on the road, but using horses for transportation to church. One informant predicted, "It won't be long until some change will have to be made. When the youngsters grow up they will not understand why horses must be used on Sunday, when rubber-tired tractors can be used during the week."

Members often traveled long distances, to and from other Amish settlements in the state or even beyond in order to maintain contact with relatives who had migrated. They often hired taxi-cabs or the service of a neighboring Church Amish member for whom automobiles were not taboo. *Communication and interaction patterns could not be maintained under the old norms. Strain resulted.* One of the bishops of the Church Amish informed a minister of the group: "You cannot expect to keep up this practice."

Some of the parents bought or financed autos for the young men who had become members of the Church Amish. There were no dominant negative sanctions for such generous acts on the part of the House Amish father to his Church Amish son as there was in stricter Amish groups. In this way the entire family had transportation. *Note that members of the same family held memberships in two different church groups, a type of systemic linkage.*

The desire for automobiles became dominant in informal conversation among some of the members. One farm hand in particular constantly kept ribbing his employer, a minister of the group, about inconsistency, and the difficulty of hitching up horses. Horses were too much trouble, too slow a form of transportation, and besides it was dangerous to drive a carriage on the open highway. This informal conversation and "egging" undoubtedly played a significant part in preparing the minister for a favorable decision later when the time came for a nod in the church. *Communication about new norms to a person holding a status-role vested with power was important.*

No amount of informal conversation concerning the desire for an automobile could make the subject legitimate for discussion in church. Only if some person violated the restriction could it be discussed. Early one spring a young man of a well-thought-of family became the first offender. Without the consent of his family and church he purchased a used automobile under considerable pressure from a used car dealer. The youngster had secured a learner's permit; he drove the automobile to the home of his parents. The father objected to having the car on his property, and after a good deal of persuasion on the part of his parents, the sixteen-year-old boy returned the car to the dealer with the promise from his parents that he could have it back if the church should come to a favorable decision whenever the subject came up for discussion. *The objective of full fellowship was important to the family as was the Godliness represented by the Church.*

In the following week, a young married man who was employed in the nearby village purchased a new automobile. He kept it at the place of his employment, continuing to use his tractor to commute to and from work. With the aid of another friend he had taken a driver's test and satisfactorily passed it.

In the latter instance the offender was immediately excommunicated for purchasing a car, and in order to be received again into full fellowship he was advised to put it away until the church could come to a unanimous decision on the ownership of automobiles. He sold his new auto to a friend for one dollar, and after the church had approved, he took it back. Meanwhile, a brother of the young married man was offended that his brother was excommunicated; in retaliation he also purchased an automobile. Like his brother, he too was promptly excommunicated. *Rank is evidenced here; evidently the two excommunicated brothers had lower rank than the first offender who was granted an immunity from the negative sanctions.* By this time the officials of the church had enough justification to bring up the question for discussion and taking the "Rot" or vote of the membership. *The status-role of the officials is here articulated. They use their power to initiate the evaluation and decision-making processes.*

Following the excommunications, informal discussions continued. Meetings were held informally in the homes. The second offender, in desperation for help, on a Sunday afternoon went to see the bishop of one of the Mennonite (Church Amish) congregations. He informed the bishop of his predicament and stated his desire to become a member of the Mennonite Church. The bishop advised him not to be in a hurry about joining another church. The next day the third offender came to the same bishop stating his desire to join the Mennonite Church. The bishop suggested to him that he call a meeting with other persons who, like himself, wanted to have an automobile. About 30 persons, both men and women, came to the meeting which was held in a private home. *Members intimately acquainted and sharing the same need, continue to reinforce sentiments and opinions and evaluate action through informal communication.* The bishop, accompanied by one of his assistant ministers, stated his position and read the Bible and led prayer. He explained that for people to join a church because they want an auto "usually doesn't help the church they jump into." He advised them to take the matter to their own ministers and see whether they couldn't come to some solution. The bishop's position was that in the previous years he had received many of the Amish members for no other reason than that they wanted automobiles. He was not interested in having more members of that kind, or just for that reason. *The bishop realized that his church as a social system was a complex of belief, sentiments, objectives and norms. Agreement on one norm, perhaps this one concerning automobiles in particular, is not enough to insure dedication to the whole system.*

The six ordained men of the Hoog group in the meantime had counselled with each other informally. None of them opposed the on-coming automobile question, but one wife did. "Where will this lead to, if our young people are given the privilege of going wherever they want?" was the chief objection she raised. *Sentiments and opinions were formed and modified by the communication process.*

The decision finally came before the assembled church. The process of decision making has been defined as the reduction of the alternate courses of action available so that some course of action can take place. Since the Amish church provides that each district maintain its own regulations and discipline it was up to the Hoog group to decide.

The "Rot" is usually taken at the members' meeting following the worship se vice. The two deacons polled the church, one taking the vote among the men and the other among the women. The bishop as a rule states the opinion of the ministry on any issue up for consideration, after which the membership affirms the minister's decisions, disapproves of them, or remains neutral on the question. *The process of decision making had become institutionalized.* The terms used to describe the outcome of the vote may be three: unanimous, practically unanimous, or not unanimous. In this case the report was practically unanimous in favor. Only four persons did not give assent, and they chose to join a stricter conservative Amish Church in the community. *Those in conflict with the new norms sought a group whose objectives, norms and sentiments would be like theirs.*

On the following Sunday at worship services eight automobiles were present. Several weeks later most of the members came in automobiles, and today from 40-50 automobiles are parked in a single barnyard with perhaps one or two carriages present. Only four of a total of 70 household heads have not purchased autos, and all of these are old people. Members were advised to secure only black automobiles or to have them painted black, and they were not to drive trucks.

The bishop had his own view of what had happened. The general practice of using tractors for road work and business trips to town helped to bring on the automobile. The bishop felt it was not so much the fault of the young people as it was the fault of the parents — those who purchased automobiles for their boys who were either not yet members or were members of Church Amish groups. The frequent practice of young drivers dropping their parents off at preaching and then returning for them after the service was a primary reason for the innovation, according to the bishop.

The legitimation of the automobile by the Amish Church is a case of successful linkage of the Amish social system with that of the outside world. The change agent in this case was the group of Amish "young Turks" who advocated and successfully introduced the automobile into the Amish community. The target system, as the recipient of the "egging" and the direct attempt at innovation, was the Amish community represented by the ministers whose objectives, at first, were the maintenance of the status quo.

The results of the systemic linkage which brought the automobile to the Hoog group will take some time to manifest themselves. After all the boundary maintenance devices failed to prevent the invasion of sacred norms, and in a matter of weeks forces were released which in the larger society required half a century to partially regularize and to control through continuous institutionalization. Except for infrequent and expensive "taxi" rides, the community had been the chief arena of interaction; now the interaction arena has been increased in size to cover the eastern part of the nation. Young people who formerly courted in prescribed ways now have the automobile, a facility viewed with mixed feelings by almost every parent with children of courting age even in the larger society. Such are the problems which the automobile has brought to the Hoog group.

NOTES

1. Charles P. Loomis, *Social Systems: Essays on Their Persistence and Change* (Princeton, N.J.: D. Van Nostrand, Inc., 1960).

2. Ibid., Essay 1.

3. Social action for Florian Znaniecki stressed conscious performances, i.e., those in the course of which the agent, the X who acts (whoever he may be), experiences the data included in his performance, and is aware of the changes which he is producing. *Cultural Sciences* (Urbana: University of Illinois Press, 1952), p. 187.

4. Pitirim A. Sorokin, *Society, Culture and Personality: Their Structure and Dynamics — A System of General Sociology* (New York: Harper and Brothers, 1947), p. 40.

5. Talcott Parsons, "The Social System: A General Theory of Action," in *Toward a Unified Theory of Human Behavior*, edited by Roy R. Grinker, (New York: Basic Books, 1956), pp. 55-56. Here Parsons gives Robert R. Sears credit for the term, "double contingency."

6. Pitirim A. Sorokin, *Social and Cultural Dynamics* (Boston: Porter Sargent Publisher, 1957), p. 444.

7. Ferdinand Toennies, *Community and Society — Gemeinschaft und Gesellschaft* (East Lansing, Michigan: Michigan State University Press, 1957). Also (New York, London: Harper & Row, 1963). Translated to English by Charles Loomis.

8. Charles P. Loomis, "Wanted — A Model for Understanding and Predicting Change in Natural and Theraputic Groups and Systems which are Gemeinschaft-like," *Group Psychotherapy*, 21, (June-September 1968).

9. R. Weber, "Das Konsumgenossenschaftswesen als Syntheses von Gemeinschaft und Gesellschaft," Koelner Vierteljahrsheft fuer Sociologie, 5, (1925). See also Charles P. Loomis and Zona K. Loomis, "Social and Interpersonal Trust — Its Loss by Disjunction," *Humanitas*, 9, (November 1973).

10. The principal source of information about the Amish is Walter M. Killmorgen, *Culture of a Contemporary Rural Community — The Old Order Amish of Lancaster County, Pennsylvania* (Rural Life Studies) (Washington, D.C.: Department of Agriculture, September 1942). For additional references see John A. Hostetler, *Annotated Bibliography of the Amish: An Annotated Bibliography of Source Materials Pertaining to the Old Order Amish Mennonites* (Scottsdale, Pa.: Mennonite Publishing House, 1951).

11. Stanley A. Freed, "Suggested Type Societies in Acculturation Studies," *American Anthropologist*, 59, (Feb. 1957), p. 591.

12. Walter M. Kollmorgen, op. cit., p. 62.

13. Talcott Parsons, *Religious Perspective of College Teaching in Sociology and Social Psychology* (New Haven, Conn: The Edward W. Hazen Foundation, 1952), p. 12.

14. C. Henry Smith, *The Mennonite Immigration to Pennsylvania in the Eighteenth Century* (Morristown, Pa.: The Pennsylvania German Society, 1929), pp. 12 and 13.

15. Charles P. Loomis, "Farm Hand's Diary, Amish Family," (Typewritten Manuscript, Earnst Correll Collection, Archives of the Mennonite Church, Goshen, Indiana). See John A. Hostetler, *Annotated Bibliography*.

16. John A. Hostetler, *Amish Life* (Scottsdale, Pa.: Herald Press, 1952), p. 10.

17. Charles S. Rice and John B. Shank, *Meet the Amish, A Pictorial Study of the Amish People* (New Brunswick: Rutgers University Press, 1947), p. 9.

18. Robert K. Merton, *Social Theory and Social Structure* (New York: University of Columbia Press, 1949), p. 133.

19. Robert Dubin, "Deviant Behavior and Social Structure: Continuities in Social Theory," *American Sociological Review*, 24, (April 1959), p. 147.

20. "Withdrawal, flight, emigration — this was by now their institutionalized reaction to any major threat to the dogmas of their faith, particularly to principles which distinguished them from other Christian persuasions." E.K. Francis, *In Search of Utopia — The Mennonites in Manitoba* (Glencoe, Ill: The Free Press, 1955), p. 35.

21. Walter M. Kollmorgen, op. cit., p. 63.

22. Ibid., p. 59.

23. Ibid., p. 22.

24. John Umble, "The Amish Mennonites of Union County, Pennsylvania," *Mennonite Quarterly Review*, 7, (1933), p. 92.

25. Walter M. Kollmorgen, op. cit., p. 103.

26. C. Henry Smith, op. cit., p. 17.

27. John A. Hostetler, op. cit., p. 27.

28. Walter M. Kollmorgen, op. cit., pp. 58-59.

29. This case resulted from field research carried on by John A. Hostetler who wrote the original case. Hostetler, a former Amishman who became a Mennonite and is now a social scientist at Temple University is an authority on the "plain people." The adaptation of the original case written by Hostetler was made by the senior author.

Chapter 2

Family and Kinship Social Systems*

INTRODUCTION: FAMILY TYPES AND VARIATIONS

Throughout the world and throughout the ages the family or kinship group has been an important social system in all known societies. The forms of the family are myriad and have been classified by scholars according to many principles. For example whether the father or mother in families is the authority, is the figure around which descent is reckoned, and is the family member who plays the dominant status-role may determine whether the kinship system is a patriarchy or matriarchy. The number of mates allotted a given spouse is basic to another classification: polygamy (more than one wife for each husband), polyandry (more than one husband for each wife), and monogamy (one husband for each wife). Irrespective of its varying patterns the so-called nuclear family composed of parents and their immediate sons and daughters is always apparent.[1] This is the type that is most common among the middle classes of the industrialized and urbanized west. The nuclear family will be one point of reference in the analysis to follow.

The second type of family which will be used as a point of reference is the "extended family." Essentially it includes other relatives besides the married pair and their children. The norms of the society determine what other relatives are to be counted as "family." Some societies specify that the recognized family relatives will be the mother's, others the father's, and still others prescribe combinations of these two. Whatever its composition, the extended family includes persons other than the wedded pair and their children. The societal norms usually specify what relatives shall be included in "family" as well as those to be excluded, and very often stipulate that a wedded

*By Everett D. Dyer and Charles P. Loomis

pair reside with or near a given set of relatives. A child born in an extended family may feel fully as related and close to a host of other relatives as he does to his mother and father. In fact, a boy child in pre-Communist China was much more closely bound in some ways to his father and grandfather than toward his mother, brothers or sisters. All family or kinship systems provide for their members personal relations of the kind which are bound up with sentiments, which are directed toward the whole person rather than a small segment of the person, and which are adapted in part at least to the individual's emotional needs. In terms of the Gemeinschaft-Gesellschaft continuum, they fall near the Gemeinschaft pole.

In the pages to follow a distinction will occasionally be made between *the family of procreation* and *the family of orientation*, terms which may apply to any of the above mentioned forms of family organization. Upon marriage the wedded pair creates a family of procreation. From their point of view they and the children subsequently born to them constitute a family of procreation. From the point of view of the children born to them, theirs is a family of orientation; when the children marry their new families will be for them families of procreation.

The social relations within the family and between it and other social systems constitute the focus of analysis of this chapter.

THE FAMILY AS A BASIC AND UNIQUE SOCIAL SYSTEM

As seen in Chapter I, there are many different kinds of social systems in a given society. Some are short-lived and of relatively little importance to the community or larger society. (e.g., The Society for the Preservation of Barber Shop Quartet Singing, or the Blond Watcher's Society of Lower Almeda Street). Others are more durable, and a few have been so durable and nearly universal throughout time and space that they are considered to be among the very few basic and functionally necessary units of human society. Such a social system is the family.

The family is one of the universal social entities, and in certain ways is unique. The family not only performs more very important societal functions than most other social systems, it also is the main foundation of the larger society. William Goode points out that "the role behavior that is learned in the family becomes the model or prototype for role behavior required in other segments of the society. The content of the socialization process is the cultural traditions of the society; by passing them on to the next generation the family acts as a conduit or transmission belt by which the culture is kept alive."[2]

Another striking feature of the family is that while its major functions are analytically separable one from another, in fact they are not found to be separated in any known enduring family system. The family contributes such services or functions to the society as reproduction of the young, physical maintenance of the family members, social placement of the child, socialization, and social control. Separations of these activities could be made, of course, and some attempts have been made here and there, such as in the Russian child training centers and the Israeli Kibbutzim experiments in relieving parents of child care. Goode contends that when one or more family tasks are assigned to another institution the change can be made only with the support of much ideological fervor, and that when the fervor declines there is a gradual return to the more traditional family patterns.[3]

ELEMENTS AND PROCESSES OF THE FAMILY AS A SOCIAL SYSTEM

How does the family as a social system pursue its goals and perform its functions? How are the social actions and relations of its members structured and directed? One way to seek answers to these questions is to examine the family as a social system in terms of the elements and processes of social systems outlined in Chapter 1.

ACHIEVING

Ends or objectives.   As suggested above, the ends or objectives of the family may be many and varied and may relate to societal, community, or individual needs. Individuals may have various objectives for their marriages, (e.g., personal happiness, status improvement, parenthood, etc.). When the married couple become parents and start rearing children we may say the family is at the same time satisfying certain individual goals and contributing to the societal goals of replenishing the population and socializing the new-comers to fit into their community and society.

From the point of view of a given family, the family itself may be its own reason for being. For the individual the circumstance and satisfaction of having a family and being in a family may itself be an objective, and other goals such as providing for family members, educating them and nurturing them in diverse ways are sub-goals premised on the basic objective of being a family. From the point of view of society, the objectives of the family systems may be many: they may organize the defense of the country, mobilize the economy, constitute the educational system, and many other societal objectives.

According to Parsons "the basic and irreducible functions of the family are two: first, the primary socialization of children so that they can truly become members of the society into which they have been born; second, the stabilization of adult personalities of the population of the society."[4]

Goal attaining and concomitant "latent" activity as process. In most societies outside the orbit of the industrialized west the adult individual's achievement is measured largely by the size of his family and the relative success of it as a cooperative unit. In pre-Communist China to a very great degree and in present-day Mexico to a lesser degree a sense of complete achievement and attainment can be enjoyed only if one marries and has children.

In industrialized societies where great emphasis is placed on occupational success, as in the United States, it is possible for people not to marry and consequently not to have families of procreation or children, but nonetheless to achieve a satisfying and serviceable mode of life. There is no simple measure of success either in achieving a family or in accomplishing the family objectives.

High birth rates are usually correlated with low standards of living. American families which have achieved very well by the single measurement of production of children are not viewed too favorably if it is thought that they cannot provide well for the children, or do not instill accepted norms. Childless families of procreation, on the other hand, which may enjoy acceptable material and normative standards are sometimes thought of as being less successful than those with children.

Some trends and changes in ends or objectives. In keeping with the trends in sentiment and beliefs, (to be discussed below) the trend in contemporary marriage and family systems is toward an emphasis on individual needs and goals such as love, affection, and companionship rather than on the more traditional goals of having and rearing many children. One of the results has been a reduction in family size in the U.S.A. A small-size family of two children or less has become a planned goal for increasing numbers of married couples. Family planning involving birth control methods is the means being followed to attain this goal. It should be mentioned that the increasing concern with over-population coupled with the belief that a family should only have as many children as it can amply provide for have been motivating factors in the emergence of the small-sized family goal. Middle class families have been in the fore in this trend.

There have been many other changes or reordering of priorities in family ends. For example, in recent decades factors such as upward social mobility striving and the emphasis on equalitarian values have led to the increased employment of wives and mothers outside the home.

KNOWING

Belief (knowledge) as an element. Most significant beliefs held by large segments of a given population are likely to be in part engendered by members of the family social system and transmitted by the family from one generation to another. This situation comes about because of the family's contribution in the socialization process of its members, and because of the strong systemic linkages which exist between the family and the other important social systems within a society, such as the school, the occupational system, and the governmental system. Quite aside from beliefs and knowledge subscribed to by families and reciprocally extended to other social systems, there are beliefs and knowledge about the family itself and the relationships between its members which vary tremendously from society to society. Basic in family life are the beliefs about sex and the knowledge which may be applied to its regulation. A belief dramatically at variance with that commonly held in most parts of the world is that of the Melanesians. They believe in a spirit world inhabited by the rejuvenated spirits of the dead who are reincarnated through new-born children. This belief in a spiritual and transmigratory source of life denies any relationship between sexual intercourse and reproduction. The Malanesians believe that vaginal penetration by some means is essential to pregnancy but do not believe that the male makes any contribution to fertilization.

Beliefs and knowledge of maternal and child care vary as much as do beliefs about sex. The Melanesians possess beliefs which require sexual abstinence from the fifth month of pregnancy until the child can walk, and which require the observation of a great many food taboos during pregnancy. In the United States knowledge of venereal disease and antagonistic blood types lead to pre-marital physical examination of prospective bride and groom. Babies tightly swaddled and babies wearing no clothes at all may be living examples of different normative beliefs entertained by the families and societies into which they are born. Nursing patterns and maternal care show similar variations exemplifying norms usually grounded in beliefs peculiar to the family systems of the various societies. Some investigators from societies given to observation, comparison and generalizations, subscribe to beliefs that methods of dress, nursing, weaning, toilet training, and other child rearing practices are responsible for discernible differences in adult personalities. Such beliefs, of course, result from cognitive mapping and validation.

Cognitive mapping and validation as process.   An anthropological investigator suggested to the Melanesians that there was a biological connection between the male's contribution to intercourse and
subsequent female pregnancy. His suggestion was received deri-
sively as being too silly to listen to. An ugly and unprepossessing
woman who had borne a child was cited as proof that children were
born irrespective of sexual intercourse because no Melanesian man,
it was claimed, would think of having sexual relations with this
woman. The biological father, the anthropologist notes, obviously did
not acknowledge his relations with this woman scorned by his peers.
Although pre-marital free sex relations are a common and prescribed
mode of courtship among the Melanesians very few pregnancies occur
before marriage, a further proof to the Melanesians that copulation
and pregnancy are unrelated.[5] The Melanesians' cognitive mapping
and belief validation of this aspect of the family is clearly rooted in
and harmonious with the basic religious belief of a spirit world and
reincarnation. Other social systems including parts of western, industrialized and rationalized societies validate beliefs about conception, pregnancies and birth by non-scientific means. The widespread
belief in pre-natal influences is validated by its subscribers by a
method of *post-hoc* reasoning. The pregnant woman, for example,
may experience a fire raging out of control. When her child is born
with a firey red birth mark on its leg she remembers that in her
excitement over the fire she slapped her thigh with her hand and
screamed for help. It is reported that some pregnant women in the
industrialized west consciously expose themselves to fine art, music,
and literature in an effort to predispose the unborn child to an artistic
sensitivity, a cognitive mapping related to the belief in prenatal
influence. Validation of the beliefs stemming from scientific and
rational approaches to sex is based in the effectiveness of controls
emerging from belief application: fewer mothers and babies die who
practice the beliefs of scientific maternal and child care, unwanted
pregnancies occur less frequently by the application of scientific birth
control, and so on. The validation of the beliefs are, however, no less
rooted in the general pervasive belief in scientific procedure and in
the controllability of the universe than the Melanesian belief is
rooted in their prevailing religious belief system. Moreover, many a
childless couple who has prayed earnestly for a child would, upon
becoming parents, find validation of their religious beliefs no less
than for scientific beliefs.

FEELING

Sentiment as an element.   Probably no sentiment can be mentioned which is foreign to family life: love, hate, jealousy, pride,

greed, sorrow, and a host of others. Sociologically, the element of sentiment is important in the family system in that it provides to family members the one universal and sustained experience of primary and internally patterned relationships involving love. Perhaps even more important is the training provided in how to manage emotional tensions and how, according to the norms of the society, to communicate emotion, both processes by which sentiment is activated.

Tension management as a process. The potential for tension among members of a family is great, and under no circumstances can be eliminated completely. There are societal mechanisms, however, which greatly reduce the incidence of the unthinkable disorder which could arise with the absence of these mechanisms. By far the most prevalent is the incest taboo which decrees who cannot marry. "In no known society is it conventional or even permissible for father and daughter, mother and son, or brother and sister to have sexual intercourse or to marry."[6] If such sexual relations were not tabooed it scarcely need be elaborated how disruptive could be the rivalry between mother and daughter and between father and son. A mother's control over her daughter could scarcely be exercised were the daughter to be also a wife to her mother's husband. Parental authority, control, and responsibility would be disrupted as would property and inheritance rights based on family relationships. What legacy would belong to the incestuous child of a father-daughter union whose mother would be his own sister? Incest is variously defined as unlawful sexual relations among members of the immediate nuclear family as in most states in the United States, to cousins to the sixth degree as in parts of India. Thus, who shall not marry whom is an important mechanism which mankind has constructed to keep the family system intact and protect it from unendurable tensions.

Also important for many societies is the stipulation of who *shall* marry whom. A society which prescribes that marriage take place only between the holders of certain status-roles is said to have a system of preferential mating. Sons and daughters of sisters must marry in some societies; sons and daughters of brothers in others. Such matings are between parallel cousins. A brother's and sister's children of opposite sex must marry in some societies, in which case the matings are between cross-cousins. The details of who must marry whom are not important to remember, but rather the hypothesis that in those societies where preferential mating exists, the mechanism has been set up because without it society would be disrupted. In each society authority patterns and the rates of interaction dictate that the greatest potential for smooth cooperation or for bitter strife takes place between specified status-roles. The status-roles which must be linked by marriage are those which are mutually cogenial, complementary, cooperative and peaceful; those which must be avoided are by their nature mutually distant, formal, competitive and controversial. Tensions between certain status-roles are so great in some societies that avoidance patterns develop. Thus the Navajo husband is not supposed to see his mother-in-law; he must avert his eyes if he knows that she is in his vicinity. The same stressful status-role relationship exists in a less intense fashion in the United States and in Mexico where there are more barbed jokes about mothers-in-law than about any other status-role.

Communication of sentiment. Family sentiments, as family beliefs and knowledge, are transmitted among family members by the process of communication. (The topic of communication will be treated more fully later under Comprehensive or Master Processes.)

Language is the principal means of communicating family sentiments, but also various gestures and acts, such as embraces, kisses, and sexual intercourse itself convey sentiments and intimate feelings among family members.[7] Sentiments of family loyalty, and loyalty to each other, faithfulness of spouse to spouse, love and affection between spouses and between parents and children are communicated via terms of endearment, promises, exchanges of gifts, etc., in various family situations. Bossard and Boll found that various family rituals and traditional activities serve to communicate feelings and to refresh, renew, and keep alive family sentiments, e.g., wedding and birthday anniversaries, family oriented holidays such as Christmas and Thanksgiving, family reunions, and everyday table-talk, etc.[8]

Some trends and changes in belief, knowledge, and sentiment. As contemporary society becomes more Gesellschaft-like, many families are changing their beliefs and sentiments in keeping with the secular and rational trends. There has been a long-term decline in familistic sentiments and beliefs. Sentiments of loyalty to and beliefs in one's obligations to one's family or orientation (parents and kinfolk) have diminished in the 20th Century, and are being replaced by sentiments and beliefs stressing the reciprocal conjugal obligations between husband and wife. Sentiments of love, happiness, and companionship in marriage are being stressed, supported by beliefs that marriage and family life should bring the satisfaction of individual needs and yield personality growth. The 20th Century has seen a change from the belief that marriage is primarily a social obligation toward the view that marriage is a means of pursuing individual happiness and that divorce is approved if the marriage does not bring happiness and personal fulfillment.

In recent years, especially during the 1960's, there has been emerging a set of beliefs and sentiments called the "New Morality" or

"Situational Ethics." This means that "one judges all acts in terms of the degree to which they promote love between human beings, love being the summum bonum and all other aspects of life being means — more or less — to this end."[9] Such situational ethics support the newer pre-marital sex codes such as "permissiveness with affection," and the youth's belief in tolerance and interest in alternative ways of doing things, and in "doing your own thing" in your own way. Related to the new situational ethics is the wide dissemination of birth control knowledge and the availability of more reliable and simpler techniques such as "the pill." Also, in the late 1960's abortion was legalized, and information and advice on abortions for unmarried as well as married women became available. Information on birth control and abortions, etc., available in family planning agencies, clinics, and increasingly in colleges, is giving young people greater freedom and control over sex and reproduction than ever before.

The 1960's has seen some increase in "living together" among young people of this persuasion. Studies by Johnson (1969) and Machlin (1972) of unmarried college couples living together indicate that this may be an alternative form of courtship rather than a sign of the breakdown of the marriage system.[10] The couples were highly committed to each other, and the likelihood of marriage in the future was quite high for most of the couples.

What effect is the New Morality having on pre-marital and extra-marital sexual relations? Regarding pre-marital sex, there is evidence that the proportion of non-virginal unmarried females has been about 50 percent since the 1920's in the U.S.[11] Reiss sees a possible rise to 65 or 70 percent of non-virginal unmarried females at marriage before the end of the century. The present generation of young people are asserting the belief that one has the right to choose his own sex codes. With respect to extra-marital sex, new types such as mate-swapping (swinging), and mate-sharing are being discussed and written about, mostly by novelists and journalists so far. Reiss feels that old-fashioned adultery is still more prevalent, and will continue to increase somewhat.[12] Kinsey reported that by age 40 half of the husbands and a quarter of the wives had committed adultery.[13]

There is very little research evidence on mate-swapping. Estimates run from 1 percent to 10 percent of all marriages.[14] We may expect some of this kind of equalitarian adultery in a society becoming more equalitarian and open in its beliefs and practices.

With respect to mate-sharing types of communes, any firm conclusions must await careful and more adequate research. Reiss suggests that couples with "segmental role-relations" are more suited to this (or to mate-swapping) than those whose beliefs and sentiments embrace the ideal, total self-sharing type of marriage.[15]

Mate-sharing is not likely to involve a very large segment of the population in the future. Such multiple-matings are apt to be so complex as to be highly unstable, and only a few of those practicing them could stay in such a setting very long.

Reiss feels that "In sum, if the increased openness on sex and on autonomy has any impact on adultery, I believe it will show itself very largely on increased adultery rates for those who are in process of getting a divorce and for those who are unsatisfied with their marriages and those with narrow self-involvement in their marriages. I do not believe there will be a noticeable impact on happy marriages with diffuse self-involvement."[16]

NORMING, STANDARDIZING, PATTERNING

Norms.   The norms which prescribe the relation of the sexes to society and to each other are basic to the family patterning which occurs in every society. Each society has developed accepted ways of behaving in the universal pursuits of obtaining a mate, practicing sexual intercourse, producing children and caring for them, and interacting with relatives. Connected with these pursuits which are generally performed in ways prescribed by each society is a mass of supporting customs concerning shelter, cooking, eating, care of the sick, clothing and many other intimate aspects of life. The member of one society who is suddenly confronted with the norms of another society, especially with respect to these extremely personal parts of life, is likely to see the bizarre and to conclude that what he is beholding is exotic and unexplainable. The observer from most western societies might be shocked at the sight of the Arunta woman who must sit over a hole in the ground during her entire menstrual period. Some might scorn the Pukapukans for whom sexual intercourse is a pleasant form of play for adolescents and for whom the woman who has borne a child out of wedlock is especially desirable as a wife because she has proven her fertility.

A host of norms mark family life as it is lived from day to day. Holiday celebrations, family rituals, what is considered funny, what naughty, the treatment of friends and guests, the food the family eats, the kind of house lived in, are all normatively determined by the society and class of the family. The process by which this vast panorama of norms is articulated by particular families in particular societies is called *evaluation*.

Evaluation as a process.   Members of family social systems select from the various ways of conducting family affairs; they put some considerations before others. The basis of their selection is evaluative. Most couples do not consciously select and act upon the advantages and disadvantages of early or late marriages, of small or large families, of family involvement or independence, or analyze their choice of intergeneration relationships. Yet, from generation to generation and from decade to decade, in an industrialized society, great ebbs and flows of marriage rates, birth rates, divorce rates, household compositions, and age structures testify to aggregate activating of varying sets of norms for the conduct of family life. And in traditional societies family organization tends to reflect the evaluative choices of the past which are either reinforced or changed by the realities of the present. The vital statistics of a society reflects the results of the evaluation process of the many families within the society. Among the basic demographic indices are 1) the birth rate; 2) the infant mortality rate; 3) household composition.

The birth rate. Throughout most of man's history the size of a given society was determined by births, deaths and migration. The number of children borne by the average woman has generally remained at a fairly constant high level. Despite the traditionally high reproductive level it is important to remember that

> ... The wish for offspring is not an innate component of human nature; it is not a basic drive. On the contrary it is an acquired motive which is continuously being reinforced by social rewards and punishments. Promises of security, approval, and prestige support the desire for children; threats of insecurity, punishment, and ridicule block incipient wishes to escape the pains and cares of childbirth and parenthood ... In existing societies conditions are such that the majority of their adult members are motivated more strongly to have children than they are motivated to avoid the annoyances of childbearing and parenthood. Nevertheless, it is important to remember that tendencies are continuously generated which threaten to undermine the desire to bear children. If people are to reproduce, social life must offer enough rewards for bearing children to more than outweigh the punishments involved in reproduction.[17]

Crude means for prevention of conception, for abortion after conception, or for killing the newly born are known and available to most societies. That the latter birth reduction methods are frowned upon and the former used to limit rather than to prevent childbirth is one evidence of the positive evaluation placed upon children. The continuation of societies is of course, proof of mankind's choice of life over death. Individual families demonstrate their evaluation of prospective or newly born family members by a host of practices all of which have negative alternatives not usually practiced by the parent adults. Among the common evaluative practices are those which follow. As soon as a woman knows she is pregnant, in most societies she takes all the precautions dictated by the norms of her society to carry the fetus to term successfully. This effort often involves help from her husband, as when coitus is tabooed during some stages of pregnancy, and help from other family and community members, as when the pregnant woman is spared tasks believed to be potentially harmful. A barren couple make great effort to determine the reason for barrenness and to correct it. The mother is assisted during childbirth, and both infant and mother are given special care during the period regarded as critical after birth.

Families in societies which have placed a high evaluation upon children often employ patterns of family organization and rules of conduct which in fact if not in purpose, tend to limit the number of children born, or tend to make less than maximal the number of pregnancies of each woman. Prohibitions of sexual intercourse for long periods after birth, requirements of long periods of lactation, some forms of polygamous family organization, marriage partners of strikingly disparate age, and other practices followed under some conditions in some societies, tend to cut down the total number of children born to one union. They may also reflect societal evaluations against too numerous pregnancies which are considered to be detrimental to health and against too high a birth rate which is judged to jeopardize the physical and human resources of the society. The individual family member follows the normative custom of his society which function to limit the birth rate with no thought in mind of helping to limit the population. He generally marries with the expectation of having children; the evaluations by which he initiates and carries out his family life usually are functionally adapted within an institutional framework, to adjust family size to the needs of the society.

The infant mortality rate. Different ways of life accompanied by different standards of living create tremendous differences in the infant mortality rate; a high rate is one of the most dependable indices of a low standard of living. The evaluations concomitant to differential infant mortality rates are but an extension of those associated with the birth rate. A high birth rate usually means a high death rate, much of which is accounted for by the death of infants. When the death rate is lowered by the adoption of rational Gesellschaft-like practices it is characteristic that the birth rate after remaining at a constantly high level for a while, follows the downward dip indicative of a lowering rate. Whether the physical resources become too scant for a constant population (as in famine or

extreme economic depression) or whether a bulging population becomes too great a tax upon a constant quantity of physical resources
(as when the death rate decreases faster than the birth rate) the
eventual result seems to be a lowering of the birth rate. During the
precarious first year of life, a period in which in some parts of the
world some 20 to 50 percent die, there are great differences in the
time, energy and care expended on the infants.[18]

Household composition.   It was seen above under *tension management* that the definition of family — that is, what relatives are
considered family — varies greatly from society to society. So too, will
the family members who reside in one household reflect great societal
differences. Inter-sibling and inter-generation relationships are
among the basic considerations which determine household composition; evaluations leading to different household compositions include
the respective judgments made on age, sex, mobility, and occupation.
The extended family is usually portrayed as being highly ubiquitous
and interdependent with household compositions which more often
than not include relatives other than the wedded pair and their
children. The nuclear family is often referred to as *isolated* and
neo-local, terms which describe the family as living in a place where
no other family members live and conducting their affairs in a manner which is virtually independent of considerations of family which
extend beyond the nuclear family group. The evaluations leading to
the first or extended type of household composition are prompted by
respect and need for the grandparent generation from whom the
young mother learns vital child-rearing and home-making practices.
The older generation may be the authority figures and the property
holders, status-roles which may further enhance their importance to
the young couple. The young couple may revere their elders even
though the latter be dependents or semi-dependents with the full
expectation that the same evaluation be extended to them by their
children when they are old.

Trends and changes in family norms.   As changes in family
beliefs, sentiments, and goals come about, there will be corresponding changes in family norms and evaluative choices relating to these
things. To illustrate, the beliefs that a couple should only have as
many children as they can well provide for and that there is great
danger to the world in over-population, led to a change in the family
size ideal (and goal) from a large family to a small family. Consequently, there has been emerging a set of family norms prescribing
family size limitations via various birth control methods. Such norms
have not been uniform in all social classes, however. The middle and

upper classes have been the strongest subscribers so far. A brief review of the historical context of these normative changes and the evaluative processes by which they are applied follows.

About 150 years ago in the Western world, family norms with respect to birth rates began to change dramatically after an unprecedented fall in the death rate. The death rate fell sometime before the decline in the birth rate with the result that for a period after 1750 there was a very rapid increase in the population. When the birth rate responded to the new social condition and the tendency toward a smaller number of children became entrenched the surplus of births over deaths diminished so that some countries, e.g., Austria and France, actually experienced population decreases. What had happened to mankind's evaluation upon new life, upon babies? Was Western man indeed so engrossed in occupational efficiency that the reproduction of life held no value for him? Were the well-off and the educated who were the first extensively to adopt the birth control techniques eventually to be eliminated by the lower-classed and poorer educated who maintained a proportionately high birth rate? The "baby boom" after World War II provided a tentative answer to some of these questions. It showed that

> planned families need not be small families . . . The groups in our population whose birth rates were low in the depression years are usually those whose birth rates rose more after the war, namely, the better educated, the white-collar workers, the urban population, and the higher-income groups. These are also the groups known to use family limitation methods most extensively. Apparently, the groups who effectively planned to have fewer births in the depression also planned to have more births in the favorable postwar years . . . Also . . . couples have been marrying younger . . . [and] have been starting their families within 2 years after marrying.[19]

Freedman's investigation of family planning in the United States demonstrates that family limitation is almost universally approved and is widely practiced, education being the most important factor associated positively with differences in family planning. Further it establishes that the American population is rapidly approaching a point at which a common set of values about family size is evident. "The traditionally high fertility of the farm population and of urban couples with low socio-economic status is no longer supported — if it ever was — by a desire for large families. Lack of knowledge about effective means of preventing conception may always have been the most important reason for the extra children."[20] The investigators further relate the rapid fluctuations in birth rates to a highly developed "system of communication and interdependence that even on such a basic matter of how many children a couple should have" functions effectively to establish "new values . . . developed, diffused, and put into action on a massive scale very quickly." Other values such as those of a religious or economic nature effect the value attached to family size.

DIVIDING THE FUNCTIONS

Status-role. The irreducible number of status-roles in the family social system are husband and wife. The incubents to each are determined by the sex of the individual and thus are ascribed. Together they produce children who assume the status-roles of daughters and sons in respect to their parents, and of siblings in respect to each other. The nature of the respective status-roles of father and mother are universally affected by the biological fact of the mother's bearing and caring for the young child. The description of status-roles in the family as in other social systems answers the question "Who does what?" In the family social system sex and age are the obvious determinants for the assignment of duties, although there is little consistency from one society to another in what is men's work and what is women's.

By far the most common of such internalizations is that of boy-child, girl-child, and man and woman, father and mother. The family everywhere is the arena for this internalization, but the circumstances attending status-role internalization in the slow-paced traditional Gemeinschaft-like society are very different than those of the rapidly paced, changing Gesellschaft-like society.

In the former the internalization of status-roles by the children of a family fits them for an adult status-role which, with minor variations, will be theirs forever. The boy in the traditional society who, in his moments of play *is* his father for that moment, imaginatively plowing the field, raking the hay and hunting the deer, is practicing for the status-role which he'll enact in reality later. Real too will become his expectations that his children will obey him, his wife be respectful of his male prerogatives (if such are the norms of his society) and that he as the task-leader will be recognized as leader. There will be little that this child will have to unlearn or find meaningless from his man-father status-role internalization of his early youth. His daily contact with his father is so steady that there is little that his father does which he does not observe, come to understand, and gradually to assist in.

Contrast the self-sufficient and traditional family with the ordinary nuclear family of the western industrialized world. Fathers leave home each morning to do something which earns a pay-check. What he does can only be described to and may be little understood by the rest of the family. Mother may work also, in which case her work away from home is little comprehended by the others. Or she may conduct the household affairs which increasingly means handling the arrangements with the vendors of goods and services, and with the organizational personnel important in the children's lives. The children are, like their father, away from home at school and in youth activities. Although the father, mother and each child in the traditional family had a multitude of duties to perform in the execution of his status-role, each always *remained in status-role* as father, mother or child. Father did not become the blacksmith, he still was father, when he shod the horses. Mother did not become the baker, she was still mother, when she made bread. In the urbanized family father, mother and the children assume many different status-roles during the day, and each is quite irrelevant to his status-role of father, mother and child of a particular family. Father is a salesman, and nobody's father particularly to the customer. Mother is a shopper, and nobody's mother in particular in the market. The child is a student in school and a girl-scout after school. Whose child she is makes little or no difference in the roles she is playing. There is no point at which these family members in their dealing with people in other social systems are seen or treated as whole individuals. This small nuclear group, therefore — father, mother and the children bear the whole traffic of each other's encounters with social systems relatively unknown to any except the individual family member who has the primary contact. Each family member feels the necessity of making his experiences known in terms of himself as a whole individual. It is as though the industrialized family has been able to "farm out" all of its duties except the emotional one. Compared to the common extended family, the nuclear family is so small that its saturation point is low and always near the point of what the traffic can bear.

Worse, just when the status-roles for handling emotional needs are most in demand, they fade because their duties are not clearly defined. Mother, the traditional comforter and emotional pivot, is also the discipline-wielder in father's absence, many times a complementary breadwinner, the family bursar, and a decision-maker far beyond what she was in the pre-industrial family. Many of these necessary roles prevent her from slipping effectively into the role of the all-loving comforter. Father, who regards himself and is so regarded by the family as the member who ought to articulate authority is not sure how it happens that his wife is making decisions, paying the bills, and disciplining his son. The norms supporting family status-roles are in arrears of current economic and social life, although nostalgia for the traditional family is imbedded in the beliefs and sentiments of the society. The difficulties of the child in internalizing the status-roles as exhibited by his father and mother are clear, and of course have their impact not only upon the presently segmented family but upon the families of the future whose adult status-roles will be negatively affected by the present normative inadequacies of internalization.

In recognition of the importance to the child of the socializing process of internalization, a single parent, usually the mother in cases of the death or absence of the father, is often urged to supply to her child through a male neighbor or friend enough familiarity with the male status-role that it can be successfully internalized. The junior author has observed in a number of underdeveloped countries such as Mexico, Costa Rica, Salvador and Peru that literally thousands of children, particularly those of domestic servants, were born out of wedlock and has speculated that this condition may be self-perpetuating since neither the boys nor the girls born from such uninstitutionalized unions ever have the opportunity to internalize the behavior of a male in a real father status-role or the behavior of a wife and children to a male in that status-role. Evidently the family structure in communities with a slave heritage tends likewise to be mother-centered and exhibits other evidences of the historical absence of a well entrenched father status-role.[21]

Trends and changes in status-roles. With the long-term development of the urban-industrial Gesellschaft has come a number of important changes in marital and family status-roles. The conjugal emphasis has replaced the old consanguine emphasis, resulting in a relatively independent nuclear family where the husband-wife status-roles come first. Sentiments and norms of individualism, equalitarianism, and feminism — important elements of the Gesellschaft development and trend — have brought about redefinitions of the status-roles of not only husband and wife, but also parent and child.

An important factor in the changing definitions of husband and wife status-roles in the 20th Century has been the big increases in the employment of married women outside the home. In 1970 the U.S. Census found 41 percent of American married women in the labor force.[22] Fifty-eight percent of these women had children under age 18, and 30 percent had children under age 6. In 1920 only 9 percent of American married women were so employed. The biggest increases have come since World War II.[23] From 1947 to 1962, three-fifths of the increase in the entire labor force was made up of women, with married women living with their husbands contributing most to the trend, comprising more than half of the total female labor force.[24] Since 1940 there has been a rapid increase in the number of women over 35 in the labor force, indicating that women who have completed their child-rearing role are entering the labor force more. College-educated women are at the forefront of this trend. In 1964, 74 percent of women who had completed 5 years or more of college were in the labor force. Of married college-educated women living with their husbands, 63.4 percent were employed.[25]

Some re-division of family functions was inevitable with this massive entry of wives and mothers into the labor force. This involves changes in the status-role definitions of the husband and father as well as the wife and mother. Originally one aspect of the traditional male family status-role definition was that the male carried the full responsibility for the economic support of the family. As the wife entered the labor force, this could now be relaxed with the wife's earnings taking on increasing significance. The male's traditional definition of "housework" as essentially women's work must change as women compete in the labor force. In a study of working-couple families in Wisconsin in 1953, the senior author found that the employment of the wife led to increased participation by the husband in routine household tasks.[26] In family role-expectations, husbands as well as wives were becoming increasingly emancipated from traditional conceptions of "man's place" and "woman's place" in the family. Many recent studies have corroborated these trends.[27] These changes are now seen in farm families as well as in city families.[28]

Since children are influenced by the sex role-models their parents present, it is logical to expect more overlapping in domestic sex role definitions and performances as the present generation of children grows up. In a study of sex-role conceptions, Hartley found that boys showed more awareness of male participation in domestic work than did girls, mentioning more often men's performance of household tasks, and indicating that they thought men as well as women took care of children.[29] Other studies have also shown that where mothers work, sons as well as fathers share in traditional household tasks.[30]

The trend toward equalitarianism and "women's liberation" is very apparent. Women's right to work and to equal treatment at work are being advanced and protected by such laws as the Equal Pay Act of 1963, and Title IV of the Civil Rights Act of 1964 prohibiting discrimination in employment on the basis of race, color, religion, sex, or national origin.[31] However, it is doubtful that complete equalitarianism in sex roles will occur soon. Even in families where the wife is employed full time, there is seldom an equal sharing by the husband in the housework.[32] In their study of married couples, Blood and Hamblin (1958) found the median husband's share of the housework where the wife was not employed was 15 percent, and this increased only to 25 percent where the wife was employed.[33] In his study of the Israeli Kibbutzim, Spiro noted that males were prone to avoid the laundry, kitchen and day care activities.[34] Reiss feels that American fathers probably will not change very drastically in their sharing of the various mother and wife roles, and that greater equality will come to American wives and mothers with the increase in collective upbringing facilities, i.e., in day care centers where mothers can bring their pre-school children and leave them under proper care from 9 to 5 while the mothers work.[35] Also, it seems most likely that these day care centers will be run by women. The children would still be under the care of women rather than men, and many women would merely be changing scenes, not roles.

What have such changes meant for marital adjustment or marital satisfaction? The literature reveals that there is a growing acceptance of job-holding wives on the part of men, and that probably the wife's employment is less a source of strain on the marriage than it was earlier.[36] In his study of 129 Wisconsin working couples the junior author found a high degree of marital happiness in the whole sample. Also, marital happiness was greater where the husband and wife had become "partnership-equalitarian" in their family role patterns. That is, they had become partners in other areas of family life as well as in providing for the family. It was also found that marital happiness was greater where there was a close agreement between the expectations of the husband and the wife as to the way the family roles should be performed.[37] The attitude of the husband toward his wife's employment appears to be a crucial factor in the marital adjustment of working couples.[38]

CONTROLLING

Power. The law and custom of all societies prescribe the authority and rights of members of the families. In all societies too, individual families vary in their interpretations of authority within the family. Whether the authority figure be the father or the mother or the mother's brother, certain significant behavior within the family revolves around the locus of authority. Parsons and Bales develop the theory that all effective social systems designate one status-role as responsible for getting the job done, or the so-called instrumental or task leader, and another status-role as the manager or assuager of tensions which result from that action, or the popular leader. Viewed thus, the instrumental leader holds the authority and the popular leader the influence. An example of this in a traditional family system might be the father as instrumental leader who gives commands, makes decisions, expects obedience and has the authority to discipline; the mother as popular or expressive leader may soften the command, intercede for the disciplined, explain to children the reason for the command and for the discipline, and emphasize that parental love is always available even in times of interpersonal stress. It is very likely that the authority figure in the family as in other social systems receives less affection than does the expressive figure.

It has been claimed that the child internalizes the authority figure of his family in such a manner that he establishes for himself a generalized pattern of response to authority. The response he builds to the authority figure of his childhood thus becomes his response to all life situations in which authority is a component. His reactions to his teacher or to his boss, in later life, are not to these individuals as such, but to them as though they were his father, or the authority figure of his childhood. According to this theory, the people who in adult life "can't handle authority" — that is, cannot accommodate themselves to the person in authority, or are contemptuous of it — have failed earlier to come to terms with the parental authority status-role.

Decision making and its initiation into action, as process.   Biblical accounts record the decision-making of family power figures. The patriarch Abraham and his successors decided again and again to uproot the large extended family until they finally settled in the land of Canaan. He chose wives for his sons and decided which fields would be theirs for grazing purposes. Even in the much changed and democratized nuclear family of the western world today it would be rare indeed for the father not to have a good deal to say about the decision of where to settle, what occupation to follow, and the relative opportunities to be proffered the children. Decision-making in the family can be seen to be the action aspect of the power that each person holds according to his accepted status-role. The process is likely to be precise and unequivocal when power is clearly located in certain status-roles, as in most pre-industrial societies. It is imprecise and amenable to many interpretations when the status-roles and the power vested in them are not clear-cut, as in most western industrialized societies. Even for the rural family where it is assumed that a high integration between household and farm operation exists, the lack of a generalized decision-making pattern is evident.[40]

Trends and changes in power.   Changes in power distribution within the American families, especially middle class families, have accompanied changes in status-roles discussed above. With the change from a Gemeinschaft sacred type society toward a Gesellschaft secular type society, there has been a corresponding change from a traditional-patriarchal family power or authority pattern toward a democratic-equalitarian pattern. As American women have been gaining in rank in the family — with the reorganization of family status-roles — they have also been gaining in power. The junior author learned in his Wisconsin study of working couples that they had become highly equalitarian in their authority patterns. In 84 percent of these families policies were determined and family decisions made jointly by the husband and wife. Also, a striking feature was that for both husbands and wives there was a similarity between their highly equalitarian performances and their authority-expectations.[41]

Recent literature shows a continuation of this trend toward a more equalitarian distribution of power in American families.[42] These equalitarian trends mean that family life in America no longer exhibits clear-cut distinctions between the traditional instrumental power role of the father and the expressive role of the mother. Although the middle class father remains the chief power figure actually and symbolically, the actual power of the father is considerably less than that held by family authority figures in preindustrial societies. Much of the western father's power in industrialized communities has been transferred to the mother. In middle class families both the mother and father frequently act as though the mother's power were not an intrinsic part of her status-role, but something delegated to her rather reluctantly, because the father's absence from the family demands such delegation. This pretense of delegation, when often it is a true assumption of power, allows the mother to shift more easily into the expressive leader status-role, the demands of which are often incompatible with the status-role of authority. Thus the mother may say, "For the present do as I tell you, and we'll ask father when he comes home what we ought to do about it in the future." The authority is wielded by the mother in a way that escapes the appearance of exercising ultimate authority in case she should soon have to be the loving and sympathetic mediator. Lasswell gives some idea of the social results of this situation.

> ... One consequence of life in America has been the partial dissolution of the family pattern in which the father rules the home. The democratiza-

tion of family life, with the resulting increase in the authority of the mother, has tended to obscure the sharp differentiation of masculine and feminine types . . . Although masculine and feminine functions are somewhat obscured in the democratized family, the heterosexual code of adulthood adheres to explicit distinctions. Since the emotional experiences of the child prepare him less adequately than in earlier times to conform to the code, a great burden of repression and adaptation is put on the child; hence we are justified in expecting a relatively large incidence of neurosis, psychosis, psychopathic personality formation, together with such crude efforts at adjustment as excessive alcoholism and sexual promiscuity . . .[43]

The democratization process has spread to the children too, allowing them to share to some extent the power formerly held exclusively by their parents. When the child becomes closely linked to an outside social system which is important to the parent, some power is shifted to the child. Thus when the children in immigrant families spoke English better than their parents and understood norms of the new society when their parents did not, the father's and mother's power was correspondingly lesser and the child's correspondently greater. Thus the activities of family members prescribed by the society helps to determine their authority. Any society in which the man is expected to wield the authority and does not may be predicted to place him in a stressful position, as well as the children who are learning authority patterns.

RANKING

Rank.   Social rank and ranking apply to the family in two ways.

1. Social rank of members of a social system is based on evaluations and consensus as to what is to be rated high and what low as these things are relevant to the family system. Family status-roles tend to be ranked partly according to the amount of prestige and power built into the status and partly according to the esteem derived from role performance as noted for status-roles in general in Chapter 1.[44] Factors such as age and sex are, of course, important in the ranking of family status-roles, e.g., husband and wife, son and daughter.

2. Social rank of families in the community or larger social system.

The second aspect of social ranking pertaining to the family concerns the ranking of the family as a whole in the community or larger society. As noted earlier, one of the very important functions of the family is that of "status-conferral," or placement of family members in the larger society. The individual's placement in the community is based largely on his family of orientation's rank and placement in the stratification system of the larger society. (See Chapter 3 for detailed discussion of social stratification.) His or her family will be grouped with other families of similar rank, and they may be said to constitute a social strata in the stratification system. (e.g., a social class in America or a caste in India). Various differences between the classes have been observed in family organization and life-styles. We'll look at some of these differences briefly as they exist in the United States.

Upper class established families pay more attention to one's relatives than to achievement. Marriage determines membership in the group so the question of the fiance's background is very important. The upper class family of long standing is basically an extended kin group. Maintenance of rank is accomplished by a combination of wealth, education, leadership, and control of marriages generation after generation. The new upper class family has had to have decisive and phenomenal economic success during a short interval. They have all the purchaseable symbols of wealth but systematic linkage to the established upper class families cannot be purchased, so the new upper class finds itself generally excluded from the most prestigeful upper class group.

The upper middle class family is characterized by self-discipline, by great geographic mobility, by serious responsibility for the demands of the job, by a high value placed on cleanliness and orderliness, by belief in education and a high value placed on achievement. The lower middle class family usually exhibits ability, hard work, a desire for a good education but a willingness to compromise for some education, vocational or otherwise, which might be less than the ideal but enough to enable the family to be upward mobile. A sizeable number of individuals from this group are educated beyond the family level, a somewhat divisive factor which makes for a degree of conflict both for the individual and the family.

The working class family is completely dependent on the swings of the business cycle, the wife very often is a supplementary wage earner, a high sense of responsibility toward relatives in need is felt, and about twice as many families are broken by desertion or divorce or death of the father or mother before the children are reared than is true in the middle class. The lower class family is the most unstable family in the United States. Lower class people do the most menial, the poorest paid and the dirtiest jobs which also tend to be seasonal and of short duration. Orderliness and cleanliness is sporadic. Companionate or common-law marriages are common, changes in marital partner are made comparatively frequently, relationships within any one given family may be complicated. From one-half to two-thirds of wives are employed, often as the sole support of the family.

Of all the systems which lend support to the class structure by behavior consonant with the class, the family is by far the strongest in that support. Each family with its own class heritage tends to inculcate in its children the behavior and attitudes designed to fit them for a life in the same class. This can be said to be generally true, even though there are classes as noted above which strive to have their children rank higher than the parents. Nonetheless, all of the early rearing practices and other socializing forces of early childhood are perforce carried out by the parent in the manner he knows, which is a manner determined by his class.

Evaluation as a process in ranking and allocation of status-roles. The process of evaluation is continuous and characteristics ranked high at one time in one society may be ranked low at another time in the same or another society. Rare skills which earn a high rank for their possessors may be rendered valueless by technological or social changes with a resultant drop in the rank of the skilled individuals. Despised activities such as money-lending once was can in another era become respectable. Thus individuals and families and aggregates of both are unconsciously and continuously judging others and being judged as to the degree of indispensability and worth of certain characteristics. The families described above as constituting certain classes within the United States hold their rank because they possess certain characteristics which have been differentially judged as being useful, less useful, desirable, less desirable, and so on.

As sociologists attempted to understand the criteria by which ranking is achieved they discovered a unity and complementarity of all of the parts of a family's life commonly called a "life-style". For example, a family in an industrial society in which the father's job concern is security is likely to rear children whose fears center in such security items as fear of being hungry, the fear of having no home, or of having the furniture repossessed. This concern with the material things of life is again reflected in the father's work where his job is likely to limit him to handling *things* in a physical sense. In his home he "handles" his children too, in a physical sense by physical punishment; they learn physical aggressiveness as a substitute for achievement. They are likely to view the authority of the law or the authority of the occupation not as an ally but as an enemy. Thus behavior becomes "all-of-a-piece" and isolated characteristics which in themselves may be praiseworthy such as honesty and willingness to work hard become less significant criteria than the comprehensive life-style. A family in which the father's job concern is skillful human relations is likely to rear children whose fears center in not being loved, or not living up to parental or teacher expectations. This concern for relational success is again reflected in the father's job where it is likely that his success is gauged by his skill with interpersonal relations and ideas. He and his wife tend to punish their children by withdrawal of love and by appeal to the child to put himself in the place of the one he has wronged. Achievement by skill and knowledge is valued over skill of physical aggressiveness. The family tends to regard the authority of the law and the authority of the occupation as protectors. Thus behavior for this family too, becomes consistent; isolated characteristics which in themselves may be considered undesirable such as shallowness or smugness become less significant criteria than the comprehensive life-style. It seems to be this complementarity of characteristics which is evaluated. The product of the evaluation is attached to the group which exhibits the characteristics.

Trends and changes in social rank and social mobility. As noted earlier, families in a community or society are ranked differently, depending upon the extent or degree to which they possess or exhibit certain valued qualities or activities. Similarly ranked families are seen as constituting a social class, and the families in a given class pursue somewhat different life-styles. When a family changes its rank, moving either to a higher or a lower social class, we call this process social mobility. In a Gesellschaft-like society stressing universalism, achievement, and a readiness to change, it is inevitable that there would be a lot of social mobility, that many families would be in process of moving either up or down on the social class ladder.

The American Dream embodies the sentiments and goals of success through ambition, hard work, and "right living," as basic parts of the American heritage.[45] Horatio Alger heroes are still being extolled in America. Although the opportunities for upward social mobility have scarcely been equal in the U.S.A., and the extent of upward movement for any individual or family in one generation is more likely to be one rung rather than from bottom to top of the ladder in "rags to riches" fashion, still upward social mobility rates have been high in our expanding industrialized society.[46] There has also been downward mobility, as individuals or families are unable to maintain their social rank, or otherwise fail in their efforts. In either upward or downward mobility, the family experiences a change in social rank and normally must change its style of life and otherwise adjust to its new class position.

In a Gesellschaft type society emphasizing achievement, one of the principal means to upward mobility for the family is success in an occupation by one or more members of the family. This responsibility has traditionally been borne by the husband-father, but as earlier noted the wife-mother is now joining her husband more frequently in this role. Their combined occupational efforts may enable the family to "move up" faster and further than the husband's alone. The crucialness of occupational careers for the social ranking of families points out a very important systemic linkage between the family system and the economic productive system.[47] The family's rank in the community, including its prestige and privileges, as well as economic fortune, appears to be tied directly to the performance of one or more family members in a non-family role in another social system.

We are all familiar with the numerous benefits of upward social mobility for the individual and the family — they have long been proclaimed by Commencement Day speakers and Fourth of July orators. Only fairly recently however has much attention been given to the possible negative effects of upward social mobility for the individual or the family.[48] In a study undertaken in Uppsala, Sweden in 1964, the junior author investigated possible dysfunctional consequences of upward social mobility for nuclear family integration and for extended family cohesion.

In a sample of upwardly mobile families, nuclear family integration (measured in terms of marital adjustment, parent-child closeness, and shared leisure time interests and activities) was found to be negatively affected where the husband and wife had different mobility orientations (i.e., one or the other was more ambitious to move up), and where the husband and wife had differential ambitions for their children. Also, nuclear family integration was weaker where (1) the husband and wife had different friends and role-models from different social classes, (2) the couple had moved up from the lower to the middle class, and (3) where the husband and wife had moved up farthest from their social class origins.[49]

Extended family cohesion (measured by various ties, activities and contacts of nuclear family members with parents and relatives) was also examined in these upwardly mobile families. Differential upward mobility between the couple and their adult siblings was found to be detrimental for extended family cohesion. Also, the higher the husband's present occupation in relation to his father's last occupation, the less likely the couple were to retain close ties with his parental family. Social mobility was found to be definitely detrimental to extended family cohesion where the nuclear family is geographically removed from their parents and kin. They not only see each other less, but other kinds of ties and contacts are diminished, including correspondence. However, the findings of this study were far from conclusive as to the effect of upward social mobility on extended family cohesion.[50] As Turner has suggested, tendencies toward both "class consciousness" (identity with and loyalty to one's social class combined with out-group attitudes toward other classes), and "prestige identification" (enhancement of one's prestige by identification with a person of higher prestige, e.g., parents identifying with a very successful son or daughter) co-exist in varying degrees in today's mobile families.[51] Further study is needed to seek those conditions (1) under which prestige identification may prevail in family systems where some members are upwardly mobile and others are not, and (2) under which family ties are weakened or severed due to the intensification of class consciousness.

SANCTIONING

Sanctions. Sanctions were defined in Chapter I as "those potential satisfaction-giving or depriving mechanisms at the disposal of the system which induce compliance with ends and norms." Sanctions may be either positive or negative, i.e., rewards or punishments.

Sanctions and their application occur on different levels within the family social system and are closely associated with evaluation. Choice of mate, the bearing of children, the support and care of dependents and many other family-connected activities are kept within the normative bounds of any given society by a system of rewards and punishments. For example, the unmarried mother and her child are sanctioned severely by public disapproval in one society while in another pre-marital conception and birth are rewarded by a choice marriage. In order that a sanction system work well, the proper conduct must be at no time in question, and the results of conduct, either deviant or conforming, must be consistent and conclusive. This principal is generally recognized although not always adhered to in the rearing of children.

Two basic sanctioning methods of inducing desired child behavior are the giving or withholding of desired material objects, and the giving or withholding of parental approval and love. There are some areas of conduct which are not clear-cut. In achievement oriented middle class of the achievement conscious larger industrial society, the child measures his own achievements in a wide range of activities at a very early age. It is probably true that a child's peer group, his parent's friends, and his parents themselves show by their degrees of approval how important it is that he excel in his studies, excel in sports, excel in social relations, make the school team, be well adjusted, and a host of other accomplishments. Under such competitive circumstances it is difficult for the parent to reward a child sufficiently and honestly for a mediocre performance which may be the child's best. It is such pressures that are meant when some social scientists maintain that middle class Europeans and North Americans exert more severe pressure on the young child than any other people in the world.[52]

Trends and changes in sanctions.   When changes are occuring in family sentiments, beliefs, norms, and status-roles, questions may arise as to what sanctions are appropriate or acceptable within the family system. As society becomes less traditional and the norms frequently in doubt, the modern parent can say less often than his own forbears, exactly what constitutes desirable and undesirable behavior. As a result the parent uses punishment inconsistently, and children become adept in helping the parent to feel guilty over punishment that neither is sure is justified. The untraditional society, too, offers many ways of behaving in a seemingly simple situation. The question arises as to what clothes to wear, how late to stay out, what activities are appropriate for certain ages. Children moving in school groups not identical with their parents' friendship groups, apply sanctions based on their parents' desire for reasonable conformity coupled with ignorance of other families' norms. If all subsystems were known to the parents and an agreed upon ranking were available, as would be the case in a traditional society, this particular power of sanction of the child over the parents, based as it is on societal segmentation, would not exist.

In a study of social life in ten high schools, Coleman was impressed with the power and affluence of teen-age society.[53] While these students did not necessarily ignore nor reject the values of their parents, Coleman observed that the parents found themselves in constant competition with the teen-age society, and they were never sure when their wishes would prevail with their children.

In his studies of parents in modern America, LeMasters finds that many American parents are having a difficult time with their teenagers, and that many of these parents feel that the mass media contribute to their parental problems, along with the pervasive youth society and its subcultures.[54]

FACILITATING

Facility.   Facilities are the means by which a social system achieves its ends. Applied to the family social systems as they flourish in the industrialized world this principle reveals the development of facilities as being among other categories, space saving, time and labor saving, mobile and portable. The nuclear family's household and surrounding property cannot be bigger than the family can easily take care of; facilities are thus often multi-purpose and compact. Time and labor saving devices permit the performance of household activities in fewer man-hours, a necessary arrangement for the small labor force represented in the nuclear family. Facilities which increase spatial mobility allow the family members to go their separate ways and to reunite. They also permit the whole family to make numerous moves to new locations, a circumstance which has fostered the development of portable household facilities. Communication facilities provide connecting links between family members while they are separated.

Trends and changes in facilities. Families in our highly industrialized and secularized world are both ready — indeed often eager — to adopt new time or labor-saving or space-saving facilities, and are also presented with a plethora of such devices and techniques by our ever-expanding technology. Changes in housekeeping methods and materials, in transportation and communication, etc., not only affect family life styles and role performances of family members, but also may have consequences for family integration. Facilities which have freed family members from onerous duties have had a dual effect on family integration. They have reduced the need for family team-work in the production of goods and the rendering of services and thus have allowed families further to splinter their activities. On the other hand they have provided time which otherwise would not be free for families to be together in leisure. One sociologist maintains that it is the need, ability, and opportunity to achieve together which provides the conditions in which members develop sentimental bonds.[55] If the need and opportunity to work together is diminished by technology or facilities, it is unlikely according to this theory that the time saved by the use of the facilities can be used successfully in enjoying leisure together. Actually, in industrialized society, family members tend more to enjoy recreation organized in relation to their own age and interest groups and less to enjoy family recreation than was true in the traditional family.

COMPREHENSIVE OR MASTER PROCESSES OF FAMILY AND KINSHIP SYSTEMS

As indicated in Chapter I, the elements of social systems are manifested or articulated via social processes both elemental and comprehensive. We turn now to a discussion of the latter.

Communication. The process of communication pervades all the elemental and processual aspects of family life. Intimacies among family members are portrayed in some societies by the language

used. Many societies reserve a familiar, intimate form of address for
family members and other intimates. Whether or not the language by
its form communicates the degree of intimacy in the interaction, the
emotional meaning of words used in the family transcends their
ordinary significance. Despite the intimacy which exists among family members no family member can say with impunity anything he
wishes. The norms will determine what one ought not to say, what
jokes are told before everyone and before only those of the same sex,
what subjects are prohibited or permissible, and the communication
should be in accordance with the sensitivities of other family members. Thus the family which provides a wide communication latitude
because of the intimacy of its members at the same time imposes some
of the severest restrictions for the same reason.

Trends and changes in communication.   As pointed out earlier,
communication pervades all the elemental and processual aspects of
family life. The Gesellschaft-like or secular trend has meant that
family members have become more "mentally accessible" to new
ideas and are more amenable to changes based on rational persuasion. These trends were generally felt earliest in the more educated
middle-class families, but are now affecting working class families
too. Radio, T.V., and movies, as well as the printed word now pommel
family members of all ages and classes with information, opinions,
and cosmopolitan views. Higher education for girls as well as boys,
and increasingly for working class youth, means the introduction of
advanced secular knowledge and ideas into family circles where
parents and other older relatives may still be clinging to more traditional orientations and narrower views (e.g., the T.V. show "All in the
Family"). While such generation gaps have likely always existed,
they seem especially acute in mid-20th Century. The family planning
movement is an area of family life that well illustrates the process of
intimate family communication for the purpose of achieving a rationally determined goal, the restriction of family size. Rational
planning of family size probably is based on a composite of information and attitude, both of which are influenced by the efficiency of the
communication process. At least it is known that

> the small-family pattern probably was adopted first by the better edu-
> cated, those in higher-status white-collar occupations, those with
> higher incomes, some of the Protestant and Jewish groups, and people in
> large urban centers.[56]

Not only do large urban centers afford superior access to centers of
information and communication; the better educated are known to be

greater users of multiple communication media and to be involved in a wider network of inter-personal communication than are the less well educated. The specific knowledge of contraceptive methods is diffused widely among such groups as is training in positive attitudes concerning man's control over the universe including the size of his own family. At any rate

> availability of information about contraception is not sufficient to bring about its widespread use. In addition, there must be attitudes which are favorable to family planning and social or economic conditions which make it advantageous.[57]

Some sub-groups within the larger society are more aware than others of the social and economic climate in which they live. Those with superior communication facilities are likely, other things being equal, to be more aware than the more isolated. However,

> there is evidence that all major sectors of our population are being drawn toward a single urbanized society in which information and standards of behavior are quickly communicated throughout the social system. The eventual result of such developments may be that all major groups will adopt effective means for limiting family size, which will bring a large reduction of the fertility differentials that have been common in the Western world for more than a century. In the United States as in some European cities traditional fertility differences may be reversed, with higher-income groups having more children than lower-income groups because they can afford more children without sacrificing the other amenities . . .[58]

In the area of parent-child communication the much discussed generation-gap is especially pertinent. As Kingsley Davis points out in his article "the Sociology of Parent-Youth Conflict", there is a basic birth cycle differential between parents and their children. Each generation is born into a different period of social history.[59] This situation becomes a problem for parent-child relations and communication especially in times of rapid social change, and the last 3 or 4 decades have brought some of the fastest and most far-reaching social changes in human history. Young people coming of age in the 1970's have to cope with social problems relating to the Atomic Age, space travel, population explosion, and our involvement in many foreign wars, whereas their parents had to cope with problems arising from the introduction of the automobile, the airplane and the Depression.

Also, the role of parents seems to be less clear in our increasingly complex modern life, and traditional parental authority is often undermined by the secular emphasis on freedom, individualism and change. As Kirkpatrick points out, a breakdown in parental control is often characterized by a breakdown in communication between parents and their sons and daughters.[60] Whereas parents seem to view many teenage problems in terms of impulse control for which they believe parental guidance and control are necessary, adolescents tend to interpret their problems in terms of autonomy, self control, and judgement based on exploratory experience and a re-ordering of goals and priorities.[61]

Socialization.   The process of achieving the primary socialization of children is accomplished in families by the spontaneous events of family life as well as by channeled efforts to prepare the children to live in their native society. Despite the many studies devoted to the formation of personality and the process of socialization there is no precise understanding of what happens. Psychological, biological and sociological factors involved are difficult to separate and almost as difficult to synthesize. Certain observations and concepts from sociological literature have through the years proven useful in understanding the process; other empirical studies have in many cases substantiated the intuitive observations of early sociologists. Among the most useful are the following: (1) Internalization; (2) The "looking-glass self"; (3) Attitude molding.

1. When a person has *internalized* the actions of others he is able, as George Herbert Mead noted, to put himself in the other's place, and, therefore to understand and predict what another will do in various situations. A child learns early in life a bundle of actions, attitudes, emotions, responses, gestures, and meanings typical of situations in which his mother, father and other family members are actors. He has internalized these when spontaneously they become his mode of operating in a similar situation, or when he spontaneously expects that others will react in a way which he has internalized as appropriate for the situation. A young child's play often involves pretending he is someone else; he is internalizing or practicing other status-roles as will be shown later.

2. An early sociologist named Cooley conveyed by the figure of speech "the looking-glass self" that the individual develops an impression from his intimates (early in life usually from his family) as to what kind of person he himself is. He displays this image of himself to his family and to others and elicits a response appropriate to the self that he has projected. Thus if parents have frequently told others that he is a shy child, and have protected him from social encounters on the basis of his shyness, he is likely to display to them and to others the picture of himself as a shy child. Subsequent reactions on the part

of others to him will be those ordinarily given a shy child which will serve to reinforce his shyness and cause him to project this same image again and again. The individual according to this concept, repeatedly sees in the responses from others the image of himself that he has given to them.

3. Although attitudes are formulated, shifted, and changed throughout life there is evidence that basic attitudes are molded by the family as by no other social system. Piaget discovered by experimental work that a child does not wonder whether or not something is true.[62] He believes as soon as the thought occurs to him; *what* he believes is because of what his elders say and do. Although the meaning of the belief usually eludes the child, he believes because "father told me." Thus beliefs are viewed first as rules — rather infallible rules — that cannot or should not be questioned or broken. As Bossard points out, the emotional intimacy and the all-importance of the parents, coupled with the mere fact of constant exposure combine to create the indelible impression.[63] How indelible the impression is has not been definitely established but it is certain that beliefs of older children resemble those of parents more than they resemble those of other status-roles, such as those of teachers, friends, and others. It has also been demonstrated that the family provides a very definite climate of political belief. Its members of voting age have a strong inclination to vote in the same way.[64]

Psychologically oriented child-training texts frequently emphasize the process of the emotional socializing tendered children by the adults of the family. They tend to reiterate that the emotional climate is more important in the answering of questions than is the content of the answers. The emotional overtones in family talk about the neighbors, business dealings, church affairs, explanations of sex, or whatever the subject will be remembered when the subject of the conversation is forgotten.

Systemic linkage. Systemic linkage not only is achieved by the marriage of two persons as was described earlier as preferential and assortative mating was discussed. The life-cycle of families changes the composition of the family from time to time, and the linkages of families to other social systems fluctuate accordingly. Although the consanguine or extended type of family has a much longer existence than the conjugal or nuclear family because replacement of members in the latter does not provide for the perpetuation of a single social system, all family systems pass through life cycles. The life cycle of the nuclear family begins at marriage, and systemic linkage is achieved at that point between the families of orientation of the bride and groom. The family grows in size as children are born; it remains constant in size from the last child's birth to the time when one of the children leaves home. It decreases in size as each child subsequently leaves home, and passes out of existence when the last parent dies. In the Gemeinschaft-like society adults know each other rather intimately before they have children and continue to do so when the children marry and settle nearby. The stage of the traditional family's life cycle therefore, does not involve so many different sets of systemic linkages (except the all-important one of marriage) as is true for the families in the Gesellschaft-like society. In the latter, family linkages with other families are not ordinarily very extensive before children are born; what linkages exist occur largely because of occupational connections. The situation is changed, however, when children of different ages comprise the family. The greater spontaneity of children's friendships relate the children's families in the same neighborhood and in the same school district in meaningful interaction. It has been suggested that one reason for the intense attention devoted to child training by middle class families in the United States is the realization on the part of parents that they are being judged by their peers on the basis of their children.

Trends and changes in systemic linkage. Family life was more restricted and outside contacts more limited for rural traditional families in Gemeinschaft-like societies than for urban modern families in present Gesellschaft-like societies. Traditional rural family life tended to be all inclusive, with most of the needs and interests of family members being met within the family system itself. The Gesellschaft-like secular trend has emphasized functional specificity, instrumental roles, and contractual relationships. As we have seen, linkages between the family system and the economic productive system are increasing with increased employment of female family members. Women and children as well as men in the family are increasing their contacts and memberships in a variety of educational, recreational, cultural, civic, health, and military groups and institutions.

As the family moves through its life-cycle, the nature of its linkages will change from stage to stage. The social systems responsible for the organized activities for children are similarly linked to the family social systems in a pattern dictated by the family life-cycle. Even linkages which are not children-based as those between families and churches are frequently strengthened and broadened during the period of the life-cycle when the children are growing up. The importance of the life cycle to explain variabilities in systemic linkages is shown by investigators who report that family linkages with various marketing social systems are much more sensitive to life cycle stage than to age of the married couple.[65] The importance of the life-cycle of families is being increasingly recognized as, for example, when welfare agencies differentiate between their aged clients and their clients with large numbers of dependent children. The familiar annual income tax levy with its special provisions for minor children and for aged adults is one of the best known examples of systemic linkages between family and government. Although the linkage exists irrespective of life cycle stage, the latter exerts a great influence upon the terms of the linkage.

Boundary maintenance. Although it is inevitable that families are systematically linked to other social systems, it is imperative for the continued identity and solidarity of the family that such linkage be limited. Some boundary maintenance devices against such disruptive circumstances as "dispersal of kin, contacts with strangers, and prevalence of market values" are imbedded in most societies; others arise or are altered in order to cope with these and other disruptive forces at times of fundamental societal change.[66] Some of the most general will be noted here.

Systems of land tenure, property holding and rules for inheritance in a given society tend to be supportive to the family social systems within that society. (There are some notable exceptions, such as property rights in the U.S.S.R.) The immediate effect of many violent changes by revolution is redistribution of land and other property in a manner believed to be more consonant with family solidarity, although in this instance too, some revolutions affected by totalitarian states provide exceptions. Inheritance rights may distribute patrimony very unequally, as in primogeniture, or in a very complicated way, as in inheritance from grandparent to grandchild on a differential sex-legitimacy basis. There are often the disinherited who simply must go elsewhere to try to eke out a living. Basically, however, the laws and customs of property ownership and use in primitive, peasant, and most other societies, support the family form, and at the expense of the disinherited, permit a fairly constant number of families to exist.

Trends and changes in boundary maintenance. As suggested in our earlier discussion of this topic, family systems often experience problems of boundary maintenance in the face of disruptive forces and conditions related to social change. The trend from a rural Gemeinschaft-like society toward an urban-industrial Gesellschaft-like society has been conducive to some long-range changes in family systems bearing directly on family boundary maintenance. The familistic solidarity and member dependence of the earlier rural traditional family type has given way to the emergence of the small,

independent, equalitarian, mobile, urban-oriented family type.[67]
Urban nuclear families are less apt than traditional rural families to
have sentimental attachment to land or even to their homes — if
indeed they have such ownership at all. And very few urban families
have a family business to help hold members together. Under these
conditions, the family property inheritance system is weakened as a
family boundary maintenance device.

In contemporary Gesellschaft-like societies, the emphasis upon
universalism and achievement has been accompanied by a trend
away from familistic particularism and nepotism as a boundary-
maintaining device. In Gemeinschaft-type societies family power
arrangements were generally patriarchal and quite rigid. Family
disintegration in varying degrees is often observed to follow the
breakup of traditional power alignments. In the contemporary
equalitarian family the redistribution and diffusion of power makes
it more difficult for the husband-father — or any family member — to
use authority as a means of holding family members together. Consequences are felt in parent-child relations as well as in husband-wife
relations. It was noted earlier that characteristics of the emerging
nuclear equalitarian family were emphasis on personal needs and
goals and the definition of marriage as a freely entered upon, interpersonal relationship which must be mutually satisfying to both
marriage partners. Accordingly, freedom to choose one's mate has
become a very strong norm in Gesellschaft-type societies. Americans,
for illustration, have taken this "right" of free choice for granted for
many decades. Not that American parents don't exert various kinds
of influence upon their children in the courtship process, but the idea
that American parents should have the power to actually choose the
mate for their son or daughter would probably strike most Americans
as very un-American.

Japan is a case in point of a rapidly secularizing society where
such changes are being observed today. Well into the 20th Century
the predominant family type in Japan was the traditional-
patriarchal family. Marriages of sons and daughters were arranged
by the parents, often via a marriage broker or go-between, with the
son or daughter having little or no voice in the choice of his mate.[68]
Alliance with a suitable family, and prevention of an alliance with an
unsuitable person or family were foremost in the minds of the parents. Their power over the choice of mates for their children
functioned as an effective family boundary maintaining device. In
urban industrial Japan, especially since World War II, these patterns
are being undermined as emancipated young people insist on having

a voice in choosing their mates. In his Toyko study, Blood found that about 65 percent of his sample of 444 couples were "love matches" decided upon by the marriage partners, as compared to only about 30 percent Miai marriages arranged by the parents of the couple.[69]

As discussed earlier, increases in both spatial and social mobility may be disruptive to family stability and continuity.[70] However, there is evidence that the mobile, urban, nuclear family is not quite so isolated from its kin, physically nor socially, as thought earlier.[71]

There is some concern today that current rejection of middle class beliefs, sentiments, and norms by many of today's youth may pose a threat to established marriage and family systems in American society. Rejection of traditionally established marriage and family roles and responsibilities has increased the number of broken marriages, marriage and family dropouts and desertions, and has been instrumental in increases in couples living together without marriage, and in the rise of commune type quasi-families. The possible lasting effects of such deviations and variations on marriage and family institutions awaits further study.

CONDITIONS OF SOCIAL ACTION

As noted in Chapter I there are a number of attributes of social action and change that are not generally under the control of the actors but which affect their actions. These have been called "conditions of social action." Among the important conditions are those involving time and space. Space or territoriality will be discussed briefly.

Territoriality. In at least two respects spatial considerations are important conditioning determinants of family organization in many societies of the world. Some societies prescribe that marriage partners be sought from *outside* the group, a pattern known as exogamy. Other societies prescribe that marriage partners be selected from *within* the group. The pattern is known as endogamy. Although both exogamy and endogamy exist within narrow spatial confines, the former pattern is more likely than the latter to involve the families in systemic linkages over a wide range of territory.

A second family spatial condition observed in many societies of the world describes the place of residence of the newly married pair. When societal norms require that the marriage partners live in the village of the husband's family, the wife's family, or in a new location the residence patterns are referred to respectively as patri-local, matri-local, or neo-local. The lines of descent, property ownership and inheritance, the reckoning of kin and the authority pattern are among the social factors intimately bound up with the spatial condition of residence.

Where the newly married pair resides is less structured in most Western societies. The pattern is often neo-local, the new family establishing itself in a place which is the residence of neither the bride's nor groom's family. Families must usually be ready to move. The importance of the occupational systems and the huge territorial expanse of many of the large economic enterprises together with the average middle class man's drive toward occupational achievement mean territorial changes sometime in the life cycle of many middle class United States families.

Trends and changes in space or territoriality. The Gesellschaft secular trend has brought about greater freedom of choice of mates, more equality, emphasis on individual needs, and greater social and mental accessibility. A consequence of such changes has been a diminishing of many traditional endogamous marriage prescriptions. Young people are courting and marrying across social class, religions, ethnic and even racial lines more. This exogamous trend means a widening of the territory over which family linkages are made by marriage.

Different types of family residence according to the place of residence of the newly married couple were mentioned in our earlier discussion of territoriality. In older Gemeinschaft-like societies the types have generally been either patrilocal or matrilocal.[72] These types fit with the patrilineal or matrilineal descent and inheritance systems, and the strong authority patterns generally found in traditional family systems. On the other hand, as societies become more Gesellschaft-like, the typical residence pattern becomes neo-local. This fits the independent, socially and spatially mobile, nuclear family, jealous of its independence from relatives, and with its eye on economic and social improvement. Such a family must be willing and able to move over a wide range of territory, its destinations generally determined by the occupational opportunities beckoning the husband-father and/or the wife-mother. Business and professional careers may now take American families anywhere in the U.S.A., or in fact in the world. The world is now becoming the territory of such families.

Ecologically, recent developments in population-space interrelations have brought about far-reaching changes in the residential patterns of family systems. Urban industrial trends of the 19th and 20th Centuries brought mass migrations of families from rural areas to American cities. In 1790 about 95 percent of the people lived in rural areas, with the remaining 5 percent city dwellers. By 1970, the figures were 26.5 percent rural and 73.5 percent urban dwellers.[73] As families moved to cities, their residential space was generally small and more crowded compared to farm and other rural residential space, especially for lower and working class families. Urban residential neighborhoods became separated and often segregated according to the social class, ethnic or racial identity of its families. Life-chances as well as family life-styles were strongly affected by these urban family residential ecological conditions. Middle and upper class families were affected too, but generally could provide better conditions of life for their children and themselves. In recent decades the movement of urban families out to suburban and commuter residential zones has been the predominant trend. This has tended to perpetuate social class, ethnic and racial residential separation, since the more affluent white middle and upper class families move out to seek more living space for their families, while the poor and the ethnic and racial minority families tend to remain behind and live in the older more crowded parts of the cities.

FIGURE 1

FAMILY VARIATION AND FAMILY CHANGE

A. Gemeinschaft-Gesellschaft (Sacred-Secular) typologies as conceptual frame-works for analysis of variation and change. Types of action and relationships articulated in the elements, processes, and conditions of social action.*

Gemeinschaft (Sacred) Type	*Gesellschaft (Secular) Type*
Social System:	*Social System:*
Particularism	Universalism
Affectivity	Affective Neutrality
Functional Diffuseness	Functional Specificity
Expressive Consummatory	Instrumental
Ascription (Quality)	Achievement (Performance)
Traditional	Rational
Familistic	Contractual
Sacred	*Secular*
1. Greatest reluctance to change	1. Greatest readiness to change
2. Social and mental inaccessibility	2. Social and mental accessibility

B. Family types identified with Gemeinschaft and Gesellschaft types of social systems.**

Gemeinschaft Social System: Traditional-Patriarchal Family Type	Gesellschaft Social System: Modern-Equalitarian Family Type
Extended family organization (consanguine ties emphasized)	Nuclear family organization (conjugal ties emphasized)
Familism	Individualism
Multi-functional	Limited functions
Traditional role and authority patterns (patriarchy)	Flexible roles and equalitarian authority
Strict sex division of labor	Flexible and experimental sex division of labor
Male dominance and masculine privileges	Equal rights and privileges for sexes
Patrilineal descent	Bilateral descent
Primogeniture	Equal inheritance
Patrilocal residence	Neolocal residence
Large size; fertility emphasized	Small size; family planning emphasized
Subordinate status or rank of women and children	Equal status or rank of sexes and ages
Marriages arranged by parents	Freedom of choice of mate
Age prestige	Youth prestige
Marriage a sacred obligation	Marriage an interpersonal relationship of compatibility and satisfaction of personal needs
Marriage relatively indissoluble	Divorce approved if marriage regarded as a failure

*See Charles P. Loomis, *Social Systems* (Princeton New Jersey: D. Van Norstrand, 1960), Figure 2, p. 61.
**Developed by Everett D. Dyer

NOTES

1. G.P. Murdock, *Social Structure* (New York: The Macmillan Co., 1949), p. 11.
2. William J. Goode, *The Family* (Englewood Cliffs, New Jersey: Prentice-Hall, 1964), pp. 4-5.
3. Ibid., p. 5.
4. Talcott Parsons and Robert F. Bales, *Family: Socialization and Interaction Process* (Glencoe, Ill.: Free Press, 1955), pp. 16-7.
5. Bronislaw Malinowski, *The Sexual Life of Savages in Northwestern Melanesia* (New York: Liveright, 1929).

6. G.P. Murdock, op. cit., p. 12. See also his treatment of rare exceptions, p. 13.

7. Harvey J. Locke, *Predicting Adjustment in Marriage: A Comparison of a Divorced and a Happily Married Group* (New York: Henry Holt and Co., 1951).

8. James Bossard and Eleanor Boll, *Ritual in Family Living* (Philadelphia: University of Pennsylvania Press, 1950).

9. Ira L. Reiss, *The Family System in America* (New York: Holt, Rinehart, and Winston, 1970), p. 394.

10. See Michael P. Johnson, "Courtship and Commitment: A Study of Cohabitation on a University Campus," Master's Thesis, unpublished. (Iowa City: University of Iowa, 1969); and Eleanor D. Macklin, "Heterosexual Cohabitation Among Unmarried College Students," *The Family Coordinator*, 21, (October, 1972), pp. 463-471.

11. Ira L. Reiss, op. cit., p. 407.

12. Ibid., p. 408.

13. Alfred C. Kinsey, et al., *Sexual Behavior in the Human Male* (Philadelphia: W. B. Saunders Co., 1948), p. 587; and Alfred C. Kinsey, et al., *Sexual Behavior in the Human Female* (Philadelphia: W. B. Saunders Co., 1953), p. 442.

14. Richard W. Lewis, "The Swingers," *Playboy*, 16, (April, 1969), p. 149. Gilbert Bartell, "Group Sex Among the Mid-Americans," *The Journal of Sex Research*, 6, (May, 1970), pp. 113-130.

15. Ira L. Reiss, op cit., p. 409.

16. Ibid.

17. Clellan Stearns Ford, *A Comparative Study of Human Reproduction* (New Haven: Yale University Press, 1945), p. 88.

18. Ibid.

19. Ronald Freedman, Pascal K. Whelpton, and Arthur A. Campbell, *Family Planning, Sterility, and Population Growth* (New York: McGraw-Hill Book Co., 1959), p. 7-8.

20. Ibid., p. 403.

21. Yehudi A. Cohen, "Structure and Function: Family Organization and Socialization in a Jamaican Community," *American Anthropologist*, (August 1956), p. 664 ff. Some argue that the presence of many families without males functioning as husbands and fathers disproves G.P. Murcock's claim for the universality of the nuclear family. *Social Structure*, op. cit.

22. *World Almanac*, 1972: Table 332, p. 203.

23. Current Population Reports — Labor Force, no. 662: (1955), p. 50.

24. Esther Patterson, "Working Women," *Daedalus*, 92, (Spring, 1964).

25. Ruth E. Hartley, "American Core Culture: Changes and Continuities," in Georgene H. Seward and Robert C. Williamson, eds., *Sex Roles in Changing Society* (New York: Random House, 1970), p. 128.

26. Everett D. Dyer, "Some Trends in Two-Income Middle-Class Urban Families," *Southwest Social Science Quarterly*, 39, (September 1958), p. 127.

27. Ruth E. Hartley, op. cit., p. 129.

28. Eugene Wilkening and Lakohnu Bharadwaj, "Dimension of Aspirations, Work Roles and Decision-making of Farm Husbands and Wives in Wisconsin," *Journal of Marriage and Family*, 29, (November 1967), pp. 703-711.

29. Ruth E. Hartley, "Children's Concepts of Male and Female Roles," *Merrill-Palmer Quarterly of Behavior and Development*, 6, (1959-60), pp. 83-91.

30. Robert O. Blood, "Long Range Causes and Consequences of the Employment of Married Women," *Journal of Marriage and Family*, 28, (February), 1965.

31. Ira L. Reiss, op. cit., p. 403.

32. Everett D. Dyer, op. cit.

33. Robert D. Blood and Robert Hamblin, "The Effects of the Wife's Employment on the Family Power Structure," *Social Forces*, 36, (May 1958).

34. Melford E. Spiro, *Kibbutz: Venture in Utopia* (Cambridge, Mass.: Harvard University Press), 1956.

35. Ira L. Reiss, *op. cit.*, p. 404.

36. Robert O. Blood, "The Effect of the Wife's Employment on the Husband-Wife Relationship," in Jerold Heiss, ed., *Family Roles and Interaction: An Anthology* (Chicago, Rand McNally and Co., 1968), pp. 255-269.

37. Everett D. Dyer, "Marital Happiness and the Two-Income Family," *The Southwestern Social Science Quarterly*, 40, (Supplement, 1959), p. 102.

38. Harvey J. Locke, and Muriel Mackeprang, "Marital Adjustment and the Employed Wife," *American Journal of Sociology*, 54, (May 1949), pp. 536-538.

39. George C. Homans and David M. Schneider, *Marriage, Authority, and Final Causes: A Study of Unilateral Cross-Cousin Marriage* (Glencoe, Ill.: The Free Press, c1955), p. 58. The conclusion that "jural ties tend to be segregated from affectionate ones" is reinforced by Dorrian Apple, "The Social Structure of Grandparenthood," *American Anthropologist*, (August 1956), who reports that authority centered in the status-roles of grandparents made for formal relations with grandchildren, dissociation of grandparents from family authority made for indulgent, close, and warm relationships with grandchildren.

40. Eugene A. Wilkening, "Joint Decision-Making in Farm Families as a Function of Status and Role," *American Sociological Review*, 23, (April 1958), p. 187 ff.

41. Everett D. Dyer, 1958, op. cit.

42. Robert O. Blood and Donald M. Wolfe, *Husbands and Wives: The Dynamics of Married Living* (Glencoe, Illinois: The Free Press, 1960). Robert O. Blood, *Marriage* (New York: The Free Press, 1969). Bert N. Adams, *The American Family* (Chicago: Markham Publishing Co., 1971).

43. Harold D. Lasswell, *World Politics and Personal Insecurity*, p. 230; bound with *Political Power*, by Charles E. Merriam, and *Power and Conscience Beyond Conscience*, by T.V. Smith, separately paged and carrying the overall title *A Study of Power* (Glencoe, Ill.: The Free Press, 1950).

44. Kingsley Davis, *Human Society* (New York: The MacMillan Co., 1949), pp. 93-94.

45. R. Richard Wohl, "The 'Rags to Riches Story': An Episode of Secular Idealism," in Reinhard Bendix and Seymour M. Lipset, eds., *Class, Status and Power* (New York: The Free Press, 1953), pp. 388-395.

46. Seymour M. Lipset and Reinhard Bendix, *Social Mobility in Industrial Society* (Berkeley, Calif.: University of California Press, 1959).

47. Talcott Parsons, "The Social Structure of the Family," in Ruth Aushen, ed., *The Family: Its Function and Destiny* (New York: Harper and Brothers, 1959), pp. 241-74.

48. Morris Janowitz, "Some Consequences of Social Mobility in the United States," *Transactions of the Third World Congress of Sociology*, 3, (1956), pp. 191-196.

49. Everett D. Dyer, "Upward Social Mobility and Nuclear Family Integration as Perceived by the Wife in Swedish Urban Families," *Journal of Marriage and the Family*, 32, (August, 1970), pp. 344-348.

50. Everett D. Dyer, "Upward Social Mobility and Extended Family Cohesion as Perceived by the Wife in Swedish Urban Families," *Journal of Marriage and the Family*, 34, (November, 1972), pp. 717-22.

51. Ralph H. Turner, *Family Interactions* (New York: John Wiley & Sons, 1970).

52. W. Allison Davis and Robert I. Havinghurst, *Father of the Man* (New York: Houghton Mifflin Co., The Riverside Press, 1947), p. 10.

53. James S. Coleman, *The Adolescent Society* (New York: The Free Press, 1961), Chapter 1.

54. E. E. LeMasters,*Parents in Modern America: A Sociological Analysis* (Homewood, Ill.: The Dorsey Press, 1970).

55. George C. Homans,*The Human Group* (New York: Harcourt, Brace and Co., 1950).

56. Ronald Freedman, P.K. Whelpton, and A.A. Campbell, op. cit., p. 100.

57. Ibid., p. 101.

58. Ibid., p. 102.

59. Kingsley Davis, "The Sociology of Parent-Youth Conflict," *American Sociological Review*, 5, (August, 1940), pp. 523-535.

60. Clifford Kirkpatrick, *The Family as Process and Institution* (New York: Donald Press, 1963), p. 266.

61. David A. Schulz, *The Changing Family, its Functions and Future* (Englewood Cliffs, New Jersey: Prentice-Hall, 1972), Chapter one.

62. Jean Piaget, *The Moral Judgment of the Child* (Glencoe, Illinois: The Free Press, 1932).

63. James H. S. Bossard, *The Sociology of Child Development* (New York: Harper and Brothers, 1948), p. 95. Citation constitutes the summary of Chapter 4.

64. Paul F. Lazarsfeld, Bernard Berelson, and Hazel Gaudet, *The People's Choice* (New York: Columbia University Press, 1948).

65. J. B. Lansing and Leslie Kish, "Family Life Cycle as an Independent Variable," *American Sociological Review*, 22, (October, 1957), p. 512 ff.

66. Jean L. Comhaire, "Economic Change and the Extended Family," *Annals of the American Academy of Political and Social Science*, (May, 1956), p. 45.

67. Ernest W. Burges and Harvey Locke, *The Family* (New York: The American Book Co., 1945).

68. Robert R. Blood,*Love Match and Arranged Marriage: A Tokyo-Detroit Comparison* (New York: The Free Press, 1967), Chapter 27.

69. Ibid.

70. Everett D. Dyer, 1972, op. cit.

71. Eugene Litwak, "Geographical Mobility and Extended Family Cohesion," *American Sociological Review*, 25, (February, 1960).

72. George Peter Murdock, "Family Stability in Non-European Cultures," *Annals Academy of Political and Social Science*, (November, 1950), p. 197.

73. *American Almanac*, 1972: Table 15, p. 16.

Chapter 3

Social Systems Delimited by Rank: Class, Caste, and Ethnic Groups*

INTRODUCTION

There are distinguishable social systems in which the memberships are defined and limited by commonly shared life styles or by commonly shared ethnic or racial characteristics, and wherein the members are imputed the rank accorded the group. A previous chapter has shown that rank is closely related to the manner in which family life is expressed; the following list enumerates the main points about stratification which were covered in that chapter.

1. When aggregates of individuals and groups are given a similar ranking by the major ranking systems they may be said to constitute a caste, an estate or a class.

2. Families can be distinguished by attributes discernibly different from strata to strata.

3. Strata differences are seen to extend into every area of life and encompass much more than is shown by the common indicators of wealth, education and occupation.

4. Since each social system in all of its elements and processes displays differences by strata which are in the main consistent and complementary, stratification can be seen to pervade everything about a given individual or a given family or a given group and hence is expressive of a "life-style."

5. The ranking system, therefore, besides providing the basis for society's distribution of its rewards creates classes or strata — groups of people who, although they may not constitute closed systems or organizations, nevertheless have the nucleus of structure in the common "life-style."

*By Zona K. Loomis, Everett D. Dyer and Charles P. Loomis

If the group thus distinguished by stratification is very rigidly ranked so that none within the stratum, including offspring, can ever be a member of another stratum, a caste is said to exist. Marriage solely within the stratum (endogamy), restricted occupations, segregated residence as well as segregation in all public places, and special food and dress are common characteristics of a caste. A less rigid ranking which allows a person born into one stratum to pass into another under prescribed circumstances and with recognized ritual is called an estate. Least rigid of all is the so-called open-class system where nothing but a person's achievement determines his standing. India will come to mind as a nation which has long been known for its caste system, although there are many evidences that the castes are not nearly so rigidly demarcated as they have been thought to be.[1] Northern United States will come to mind as an area in which something approaching the open-class system operates, although never has society there or elsewhere been completely open in the sense that there is a one to one relation between rank and competence.

Although stratification is universal the patterns it assumes are numerous, varying in rigidity (as shown by the caste — open-class continuum), in relative durability, and in relative size of the various stratified segments of society. A well known stratification pattern is the pyramid as shown in Figure 1 in which there is a tiny segment at the apex representing the aggregate of individuals with a very high rank supported by a broad base composed of common people. Variations of the pyramid pattern show middle layers between those ranked highest and those lowest. Other profiles are not pyramids at all, but rather resemble a diamond figure; the top peak represents those of very high rank, the opposite peak upon which the figure is resting those of very low rank, and the great center mass representing those who do not belong at either extreme.

A pattern of class in the United States would at the present time tend to resemble that portrayed in Figure 3, although until fairly recently the basic contour would have resembled Figure 2. Involved in these varying contours is more than a segmented picture of society by class. The factor of vertical mobility is revealed by them. America's stratification has always been marked by rapid change in the direction of upward mobility.

Certain sub-systems are infinitely more important than others in ranking the individual. In the United States the occupational system overshadows all others. The educational system, although of tremendous importance, usually bestows an enabling rank which entitles a person to compete for an occupational rank; this latter

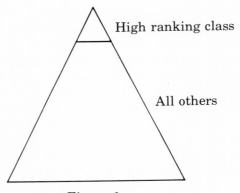

Figure 1.

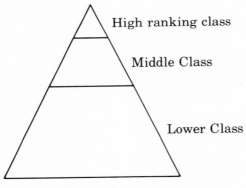

Figure 2.

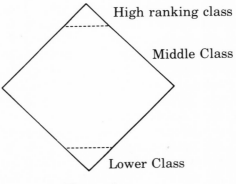

Figure 3.

constitutes the appraisal by which the individual is most widely known. Subsequent chapters will treat both the occupational system and the educational system and their ranking and stratification function will be duly noted. The family system in the United States is still an important ranking system also; its ranking and stratification function was noted in a chapter dealing with the The Family and Kinship Systems. The remaining important ranking system in the United States is the ethno-racial system.[2]

> Ethnic belongingness is another possible basis in diffuse solidarity for differentiation of status. It is probably, along with certain aspects of religion, the most important basis which is independent of occupation and kinship in the narrower senses, except perhaps for the rural-urban and the regional aspects of community. The case of the Negro, even in the North, is the most conspicuous one . . , ethnicity to some degree tends to preserve relatively independent 'pyramids' in the more general system.[3]

This chapter, then, will devote major attention to these "relatively independent 'pyramids' "; since they are inevitably intertwined with the class and caste structure of the United States, the analysis of the ethnic groups will perforce be concerned largely with stratification.

Identification of the ethno-racial groups and factors contributing to differential ratings. Most helpful in the identification of the ethno-racial groups is Table I[4] which also suggests what factors are most important in differential ratings among the various groups. Its data show that in the United States some people (the proto-type being the Anglo-white Protestant) are so completely accepted by the society that nothing but their own individual limitations restricts their achievements, and that others (the prototype being the non-white, non-English speaking, non-Christian) are so excluded that no amount of individual achievement entitles them to a higher ranking. All others fall between these extremes with the factors of religion, ethnic and national background and skin color determining to a large extent not only the degree of assimilation, but the levels of stratification. Most ethnic groups in the United States have lost their distinct identity. Assimilation has worked for most of the 32 million immigrants who have come to the shores of the United States. This chapter will deal chiefly with those "relatively independent 'pyramids,' " as Parsons designated them, whose members find that ethnic or racial extraction is, along with the sex of the individual, *the* most important condition of life. Such racial and ethnic sub-systems are negative products in the sense that they exist because their members *are not* what the members of the dominant society are. The elements and processes characteristic of social systems will be applied to those unabsorbed, unassimilated racial and ethnic systems of the United States, and where necessary, will be contrasted to the social system of the larger society.

The social scientist must be wary of unwarranted generalizations. Worthy of noting here is an ethnic group which is clearly an exception to the assimilation as compiled by Warner and Srole in Table I.

> Chicago's share of Southern 'hillbillies' . . . is, in a sense, the prototype of what the 'superior' American should be, white Protestants of early American Anglo-Saxon stock; but on the streets of Chicago they seem to be the American dream gone berserk . . . Clannish, proud, disorderly, untamed to urban ways, these country cousins confound all notions of racial, religious, and cultural purity.[5]

Whenever a sub-group, whatever its composition, is limited in interaction with members of other sub-groups, the members of the isolated group will of course intensify their reactions with members of their own group; the social changes occurring within the sub-group will not necessarily parallel those occurring in the greater society. Many times the factors which limit interaction or facilitate boundary maintenance are taboos and prohibitions. The factor in the case of the "hillbillies" was geography. Their news story serves the purpose of emphasizing that no generalization about stratification is universally true of each member within any one class or caste or racial or ethnic system nor universally applicable to all such systems. If the student remembers that there can be individual exceptions or exceptions involving "pockets" of individuals such as the "hillbillies" he can read the following analysis and find it by and large applicable to the ethnic and racial systems treated here.

ELEMENTS AND ELEMENTAL PROCESSES

KNOWING

Belief (knowledge) as an element. The dominant beliefs about ethnic and racial groups, held by the larger society and shared in a sometimes ambivalent way by racial and ethnic sub-groups, are contradictory in nature. Consider the following paradoxes:

1. Equality of man vs. class society with a recognizably superior elite.

2. Achievement vs. ascription.
3. Efficiency vs. the worth of the individual.

Both sets of beliefs serve a function in the larger society, and in some respects these opposites support and sustain the conditions necessary for America's chief accomplishment — integration and solidarity constructed out of diverse peoples. Although America has been among the great innovators in science and technology, among the distinguished nations in the creation of capital wealth, and among the respectable in the development of the expressive arts, unique distinction cannot be accorded in any of these fields. An accomplishment duplicated nowhere else in the world on such a broad scale, however, is America's integration into a solidary whole the millions of people with hundreds of very different cultural pasts. This has been called "the American dream" and it is both a belief and a sentiment.

> Above us all hangs the ancestral command which we call the American Dream. It has come here in the hold of every westward-bound ship since the Mayflower and before. The image in dream may have been a city of gold or a city of God, but always it was perfect and always it was here. It had to be found or it had to be founded. It has made us rich, beneficient, idealistic, and democratic, and also blind, bigoted, and cruel.[6]

As Thompson implies, the beliefs, perhaps especially the paradoxical ones, were basic to the achievement of the American dream and held up until about two decades ago.

Consider the conditions under which "the American Dream" began to operate. A motley array of people at different levels of development and with different standards of living quickly gave rise to the conviction "some people clearly are superior to others," a tacit class and elite system. This non-equalitarian belief was tempered by the basic equalitarian conviction: "Everyone has a chance; even if you are low on the ladder, if you try hard, you'll make it; you'll get there." And those who did not speak English, learned English. The timid learned to push. Those with "different" grooming and clothing watched and copied. The unhappy knowledge that people *weren't* equal unless in certain measures they conformed led to the mighty struggle to conform in manners and to excel in output. Chances for success were enhanced by the business orientation that the United States social system was increasingly taking on. Whereas the new-comer could fail dismally in polite society, occupationally he was needed, economically he was rewarded, even though at times exploited, and in the market places of his new land, his dollar was good, his trade was desired. If America's dedication to business had

TABLE I. THE ORDERING OF ETHNIC AND RACIAL GROUPS*

Racial Type I-Light Caucasoids			Racial Type II-Dark Caucasoids		
Cultural Type	Degree of Subordination	Time for Assimilation	Cultural Type	Degree of Subordination	Time for Assimilation
I. English-speaking Protestants (e.g., English, Scots, Canadians)	very slight	one generation or less	I.		
II. Protestants not speaking English (e.g., Danes, Dutch, French)	slight	1-6 generations	II. (e.g., Protestant Armenians and other dark-skinned Protestants)	slight to moderate	6 generations or more
III. English-speaking non-Protestants (e.g., South Irish)	slight	1-6 generations or more	III.		
IV. Non-Protestants not speaking English (e.g., French, Belgians)	slight	1-6 generations or more	IV. (e.g., dark skins of Racial Type I, also Sicilians, Portuguese)	moderate	6 generations or more
V. English-speaking non-Christians (e.g., English Jews)	moderate	1-6 generations or more	V.		
VI. Non-Christians not speaking English (e.g., fair-skinned European Jews and Mohammedans)	moderate	1-6 generations or more	VI. (e.g., dark-skinned Jews and Mohammedans)	moderate to great	very long

TABLE I. THE ORDERING OF ETHNIC AND RACIAL GROUPS* cont.

Racial Type III-Caucasoid Mixtures			Racial Type IV-Mongoloids and Racial Type V-Negroids (combined)		
Cultural Type	Degree of Subordination	Time for Assimilation	Cultural Type	Degree of Subordination	Time for Assimilation
I.			I. (e.g., most American-born Chinese, Japanese, Negroes)	great to very great	very long to indefinitely long
II. (e.g., small groups of Spanish Americans in the Southwest)	great	very long	II.		
III.			III. (e.g., some American Negroes)	very great	indefinitely long
IV. (e.g., most of the mixed bloods of Latin America)	great	very long	IV. (e.g., Filipinos and Negroid Puerto Ricans)	great to very great	indefinitely long
V.			V.		
VI.			VI. (e.g., Orientals and Africans)	great to very great	indefinitely long

*Originally developed by W. Lloyd Warner and Leo Srole. Presented here as adapted by Leonard Broom and Philip Selznick, *Sociology* (Evanstown, Ill.: Row, Peterson and Co., 1955), pp. 460.

been second-fiddle to family, if America's business had been conducted on the personal basis of the master-apprentice relationship, or
in the tradition of the family-friendship group, it is unlikely that the
hordes of immigrants could have been assimilated. If achievement
was not the criterion, if children were ascribed to the same position in
life that their parents held, if men were not encouraged to pull
themselves up by their own boot-straps, integration could not have
been achieved. The great success of the job of integration makes all
the more conspicuous those points of imperfect integration. Particularly conspicuous is the failure to allow the black to progress by
achievement to the same extent that most others have. Few believe
that those sub-systems which have not become integrated either
because of biological or cultural differences, will not in time become
an organic part of American society. In the meantime "there is a
great struggle in white people's minds — the struggle between the
democratic ideals of equality in the American Creed and the obvious
lack of equality in the treatment of the American black. This struggle
we have called 'an American dilemma.' "[7]

The range of beliefs about the unassimilated ethnic groups and
the non-white racial groups extends from convictions of biological
and racial superiority and inferiority to the scientific findings which
indisputably disproves the claim for native superiority of any race. At
least one study[8] establishes that in situations in which beliefs about
minority groups are prejudiced and stereotyped notions about *who
constitutes* minority groups are at best hazy, nebulous and indistinct.
Jews or Negroes, for example, were thought to have certain characteristics; when non-Jews displayed these "Jewish" characteristics
they were thought to be Jews by the respondents. Similarly, when
Jews displayed "non-Jewish" characteristics they were not believed
to be Jews. In other words, the belief concerning racial or ethnic
characteristics remained unchanged in light of evidence which dis-
proved the stereotype; the belief concerning who constituted the
group changed to allow the basic belief about the racial or ethnic
group to remain unchanged. The conclusion is inescapable that
ethnic and racial systems are viewed with the prejudices as often as
they are viewed with objectivity. The civil rights movement of the
1950's and 1960's was accompanied by a resurgence of the equalitarian beliefs of the American Creed. These beliefs were appealed to
for support of the Supreme Court decision in the Brown case in 1954
which legally desegregated public schools in America. Emerging
black civil rights movement leaders such as Martin Luther King
made appeals to the American conscience in terms of traditional
American beliefs in justice, fair play, and equal opportunity for all

Americans in education, employment, use of public facilities, etc. Scientists continued to accumulate evidence in support of the position that races and nationalities are essentially equal in biologically inherited achievement potential. Such trends in racial beliefs and knowledge were in keeping with the Gesellschaft-like direction of social change. It should be noted that there is still a wide range of beliefs and attitudes in America concerning race and ethnic groups, as will be made apparent in the following discussion.

Cognitive mapping and belief validation as process. As indicated above, beliefs in America about ethnic and racial groups, and to some extent about social classes, are mixed and may be contradictory. The beliefs range from convictions of social and ethnic superiority and inferiority to full acceptance of scientific position that no racial or ethnic groups are innately superior or inferior.

Those holding the former types of beliefs tend to have their cognitions or perceptions directed along certain *a priori* routes where stereotypes serve as their guides. Walter Lippman said, "We do not first see and then define, rather we define first and then see."[9] Dominant or majority groups frequently hold highly ethnocentric stereotyped definitions of ethnic and racial (and social class) minority groups. If the stereotype of race X says its members are basically lazy, shiftless, dirty, undependable, and unable to learn much, then people holding the stereotype will tend to "see" such characteristics in members of the group, at the same time ignoring other characteristics which are not included in the stereotype, especially if such characteristics contradict the stereotype.

It has been observed that prejudiced and stereotyped beliefs about racial and other minority groups tend to create a vicious cycle which has a self-fulfilling function.[10] Once a dominant group accepts such beliefs it then treats the minority group members as inferior, denying them admittance to the best schools, the better paying occupations, the better dwelling areas, etc. Such treatment produces people who are in fact "inferior" in that they do not have as good an education, nor as much money, nor as good clothes or homes, etc., as members of the dominant group. This in turn reinforces the original prejudiced belief in their inferiority and increases the likelihood that they will continue to be treated as inferiors — and the vicious cycle continues. In other words, the "end product" tends to validate the original beliefs regarding the inferiority of the ethnic or racial minority group.

On the other hand, those espousing the equalitarian beliefs of the American Creed would be expected to be able to perceive things in a less prejudiced or ethnocentric way, looking beyond the narrow and distorted perspective of the stereotype. Validation of equalitarian beliefs would be seen in the expanding achievements and contributions in business, professions, and government by minority group members.

FEELING

Sentiment. Man who fancies himself to be a creature of reason tends to bolster his sentiments with whatever beliefs seem appropriate. Three and a half centuries ago Pascal tells of an acquaintance of his who declared to him: "Reasons come to me afterwards, but at first a thing pleases or shocks me without my knowing the reason, and yet it shocks me for that reason which I only discover afterwards." And Pascal, contemplating this puzzling sequence reported by his friend concludes: "But I believe, not that it shocked him for the reasons which were found afterwards, but that these reasons were only found because it shocks him." Pascal's conclusions are certainly reinforced in the matrix of sentiment-belief which is the core of racial and ethnic social systems. A white woman was shocked and resentful that a black saleslady waited on her in a clothing store. She exclaimed, "This is going too far. I know that the Negro girl must have a job, but it shouldn't be one which requires her to handle the clothes that *I* wear." When it was pointed out that her black laundress handled her most intimate clothes in the laundress' own home and that this had never seemed like "going too far" the white woman was resentful not only of the black saleslady but of her interrogator as well. There is no doubt that her sentiment preceded her "reason" and exerted a great influence on it. In communities where there had been no integration of the races the shock of sitting in the same school room with a child of another color, or the resentment and fear on the part of whites when black men were added to the assembly line invariably ended in the impassioned question of possible and seemingly imminent inter-marriage. The fact that many co-workers are unsuited to each other as marriage prospects but nevertheless are not regarded as a threat seems not to weaken the convictions of those who have "reasoned" out this inter-marriage rationale for continued segregation.

No less prejudiced are those whites who are predisposed to see nothing but good and admirable traits in every member of a minority ethnic or racial system. Who could deny that sentiments are lurking very near the surface of Dorothy Parker's nameless character:

"I liked him," she said. "I haven't any feeling at all because he's a colored man. I felt just as natural as I would with anybody. Talked to him just as naturally and everything. But honestly, I could hardly keep a straight face. I kept thinking of Burton. Oh, wait till I tell Burton I called him 'Mister.' "[11]

Or that Wouck's upper class Willie was emotionally reacting to an ethnic group rather than to an individual:

Willie's reaction to the discovery that May Wynn had an Italian name was complicated, and quite important: a mixture of relief, pleasure, and disappointment. It struck away most of the girl's mystery. A night-club singer who could carol a Mozart aria with understanding was a wonder, for in Willie's world familiarity with opera was a mark of high breeding — unless you were an Italian. Then it became a mere racial quirk of a lower social group, and lost its cachet. Marie Minotti was someone Willie could cope with . . . He knew perfectly well that he would never marry an Italian. They were mostly poor, untidy, vulgar, and Catholic. This did not at all imply that the fun was at an end. On the contrary, he could now more safely enjoy being with the girl, since nothing was going to come of it.[12]

Whether the sentiments are violent like those of the six Ku Klux Klansmen in Alabama who castrated a black they chose at random "to scare the hell out of,"[13] or superior and paternal like those of the stereotyped southern white who "loves our nigras so long as they're in their place," or guilt-laden and grovelling like the distressed liberal who, after the Detroit race-riot "felt like bowing down to every Negro he met and beg his pardon", there is no question that attempts at systemic linkages between racial and ethnic systems are fraught with emotion. It is the sociologist's job to analyze this body of sentiment and find whence it springs and what, if any, function it performs.

Undoubtedly the intensity of sentiment expressed as classes, castes and ethnic groups change social rank and standing is in large part due to two forces: 1) the strains which accompany change with the inability to predict the behavior of others and to know what to do one's self; and 2) the possibility and actual occurrence of actions on the part of others in the anomalous and unstructured situations which disparage the self-image of the individual. Thus, if the self-esteem of X in ethnic system No. 1 is in any way dependent upon assuming higher rank than Y in ethnic system No. 2, the change in No. 2 for the better may affect the self-esteem of X. Frequently, the resulting sentiments manifest by X and through No. 1 will be violent and their cause unknown to X. Conditions of *anomie*, of normlessness, of unpredictable human behavior set in as soon as conditions for one or both racial or ethnic groups change. And the conditions are changing constantly. In the vast ebb and flow of whites and blacks from the country to the cities, from the South to the North and back again to the South, almost everyone whose orbit passes through that of the other racial system is puzzled about how he should behave.

In the history of man's relation to man none are more bitter or filled with hate and rancor than those expressed when subordinate strata are rising or threaten to rise. This aspect of sentiments revolving about class and caste distinctions has been summarized by Robert E. Park:

> All our sentiments, love, loyalty, patriotism, homesickness, contempt, arrogance, hate, are based upon and supported by prejudices. Furthermore, mankind is incurably sentimental . . . Prejudice . . . has its source and origins in the very nature of men and their relation to one another . . . Race prejudice, so conceived is merely an involuntary expression of conservatism . . . The Negro is rising in America and the measure of the antagonism he encounters is, in some very real sense, the measure of his progress.[14]

This should give a clue to the possible function of sentiments which suffuse racial and ethnic social systems. This clue will be traced out in greater detail as the process of boundary maintenance is discussed. Suffice it to note in passing that the kind of conservatism which makes of everyone who is not of the "in-group" a foreigner is the conservatism which preserves social systems. The student might try to imagine the consequences upon his family, his friendship group, his university, his fraternity, his football team of completely uninhibited "joining" by anyone who might have the notion to do so.

Whitehead develops the idea that these same sentiments, the bulwark of any social system, are "triggered" by symbols, even when the symbol-sentiment combination is no longer appropriate to the situation. Under the heading *Communication* later in the chapter the symbol-sentiment matrix in relation to ethnic groups will be discussed.

Sentiments, being emotional in nature, are generally more difficult to change than beliefs which are cognitive in nature. With increases in education, sophistication, and scientific knowledge come increases in intellectual enlightenment for more people. But one may not always easily accept on the level of feelings or emotions what one's mind has learned. Therefore, changes in sentiment tend to lag behind changes in knowledge and belief. However, increasing white contacts with blacks and other minority group members in schools and at work, etc., are not only expediting changes in beliefs regarding the essential humanness, goodness, and equal potential of these minority peoples, but also seem to be gradually changing older sentiments of prejudice and fear to sentiments of acceptance, respect, and often warmth. This is especially true for many youth, who are not only mingling more in schools and on college campuses and in church groups, but who are also more socially accessible to new contacts and mentally accessible to new ideas and sentiments, in modern secularizing America.

Tension management as process.   As indicated above, intense sentiments tend to suffuse racial and ethnic social systems. Thus the potential for tension is great in the area of social and ethnic relations, especially in times of stress and change as today when we are experiencing the rising expectations and demands of minority peoples.

Societies have used various mechanisms in their attempts to reduce or manage tensions and potential conflict. Appeals to commonly held beliefs or values which would justify or rationalize the status quo have been made by dominant groups in many societies. The Brahmans in India have historically based their ascendancy on their superior spiritual development, a belief all good Hindus are expected to accept. Not unlike this were early Christian beliefs which were used to justify slavery. Based on such beliefs, those in positions of power may impose norms backed by strong sanctions to maintain the status quo and keep minority groups in their place. American racial segregation laws and mores from the Reconstruction period to mid-20th century would be an example. Such efforts may be only partially successful in managing tensions, and may break down under the challenge of changing beliefs and sentiments. The 20th century has witnessed many such breakdowns often accompanied by violent conflict in race relations.

During times of changing beliefs and sentiments, efforts to reduce tensions and conflict may be made by educational, religious, and political leaders who understand and support the changes. For example, scientists and educators may expose the old myths of racial inferiority; religious and political leaders may appeal to the commonly held beliefs and sentiments of equality, justice, and fair play. Also, legislation outlawing discrimination in schools, employment, housing, etc., will generally function to reduce tensions in the long run — while often increasing them in the short run — by breaking into the vicious circle discussed above. This will (a) undermine some of the basis for continued prejudice on the part of majority-group members, and (b) help reduce tensions and hostility in the minority groups by providing wider opportunities, etc.

Communication of sentiment as process.   Communication will be discussed at some length later under Comprehensive or Master Processes. Here we need only to point out that communication of sentiments within and between class, racial, and ethnic systems takes place through the use of symbols and emotion-laden terms in daily social interaction. Words such as Dago, Polack, Nigger, or Gringo communicate strong negative sentiments. Terms such as "the upper crust," "the fat cats," "the hoi-polloi," "the scum of the earth," etc. communicate sentiments of invidious social class distinction.

ACHIEVING, NORMING, STANDARDIZING, PATTERNING

Ends and norms as values.   The current state of affairs for both the minority and majority ethnic and racial groups is one of flux; there is neither the clear-cut caste and class system of slavery and early immigration days nor is there any dependable degree of integration which enables anyone to say with certainty: "As regards matters between the races and the partially assimilated ethnic groups, this is the way it is." Since no generalization will suffice, a clear picture of ends and norms would emerge only from a look at all the major sub-groups within the main ethnic and racial social systems — a look at the North and the South, at the educated and uneducated, at the Latino or Chicano and Anglo of the Southwest, at the liberal and the conservative, and at many, many more sub-groups. A few of the most important sub-groups and their ends and norms are given here.

There is a heartening convergence and consistency between the items that the blacks want of the larger society and the items that the majority of whites are most willing to give. Table II presents evidence that the ends of the two groups are closer than is often assumed, and that the high-priority black ends will be realized in an institutionalized manner earlier than the low-priority ends.[15] As a matter of fact Fair Employment Practices legislation is already having some effect on the realization of the first black objective, and at least two important sub-systems are involved, the governmental system and the occupational system.

Reference has already been made a number of times to the beliefs, sentiments, and ends of the Southern whites. It would certainly be a mistake to impute to northerners completely liberal and integrative norms and to southerners completely prejudiced and seg-

TABLE II.*

Blacks want those items in decreasing order	Whites will yield those items in decreasing order
1. Opportunity to secure land, credit, jobs and other means of earning a living; non-discrimination in public relief and other social welfare activities.	1. Fair employment practices and equitable public relief and welfare.
2. Non-discrimination by law courts, by police, and by other public servants.	2. Equal treatment by law courts, by police, etc.
3. Political enfranchisement.	3. Political enfranchisement.
4. Non-discriminative use of public facilities such as schools, churches, and means of conveyance.	4. Non-discriminative use of public facilities.
5. Non-discrimination in such things as attendance at dances, bathing beaches, restaurants, etc.; cessation of rules which deny equality such as mode of hand-shaking, hat lifting, use of titles, and the like.	5. Non-discrimination in the public kind of personal relations involved in the list to the left.
6. Legal intermarriage.	6. Legal intermarriage and sex relations of white women with blacks.

*Adapted from Arnold Rose, op. cit., p. 24.

regative norms. A brief look at the history of some of the inter-racial practices will show that discriminatory practices flourished in the north as well as in the south even preceding the War between the States. The North for example had laws against intermarriage which remained on the law books after the war was over and in many northern states they still exist. Separate schools for blacks and whites existed in the North before and after the Civil War. The North had always segregated its military units and this practice was strengthened by the Civil War. Some token integration in the military occurred in World War I, and more took place in World War II.

To point out such practices of northern discrimination is not to say that the North and South were entirely alike, however, or even very much alike. There flourished in the South practices which were not supported by law but were deeply ingrained by custom; these folkways were more powerful than laws in demeaning the black. Shortly after the Civil War the southern states enacted into law what up to that time had existed only as social custom. Folkways which, uncodified, were free to shift as attitudes shifted, became solidified and less subject to change by becoming law.

The present-day structure of these norms as well as their historical development tell the sociologist much of significance when their location is plotted on the Gemeinschaft—Gesellschaft scale.

> We may generalize . . . for each community there would seem to be less
> discrimination and segregation where the service is less personal.
> Barber shops and beauty parlors are, both in the North and in the South,
> the most completely segregated while clothing stores allow Negroes to
> buy but discriminate more than do hardware stores.[16]

Social systems of the South have been markedly more Gemeinschaft-
like than those of the North. The white southern house-holder, for
example, may not pay his Negro employee very high wages, but his
concern for his welfare is likely to extend beyond the strictly
employer-employee relationship. The northern white householder is
more likely to pay good wages and limit his relationship to that
required by the job at hand. Similarly, the kind of discriminatory
practice of the south is more likely to invade the Gemeinschaft-like
items of every day life — the manner of address, the door used to enter
the home, the common courtesies of social intercourse between
equals. Said the northern housewife of her maid:

> Rose is a good worker, but I don't know how to cope with some of her
> expectations. In order to help her with some ailment, I got from my
> doctor and passed on to her the names of doctors who live near her
> residence and are competent to treat her. All she said was, "Folks sure
> are different from what they are in Alabama. If I told my missus that I
> was ailing she would call her doctor and tell him to come right over. She
> would say, 'Come right along now, and mind you take care of Rose,
> because she's my girl.' " The fact that I pay Rose more than three times
> as much as did her 'missus' in Alabama, apparently does not decrease
> her expectation that I should be interested in all of the problems of her
> and her family.

The more universalistic, affectually neutral and functionally specific
North may very well be less discriminatory precisely because of its
more Gesellschaft-like orientation than the more particularistic, affectual and diffuse South with its Gemeinschaft-like orientation.

The Gesellschaft-like rationale for the 1954 Supreme Court decision which outlawed school segregation was rationally aimed at
creating a favorable picture of the United States in the minds of the
black people of the world who outnumber the white and who, in many
instances, are at a juncture of casting their lot with Russia or with the
United States. It was a matter of importance that Russia whatever
her "faults may be — has no color prejudice. Again and again she has
demonstrated that she does not regard colored people as inferior . . .
Laws against discrimination or the manifestation of prejudice are
strictly enforced."[17] Many Americans whose private disposition and
tradition favor discrimination see rationally that their country's wel-

fare demands an end to discrimination. A clear statement of the rational approach has been given by Blumer: "It is not essential in efforts to change human conduct to alter, on the part of individuals, the feelings and attitudes behind the conduct, or, on the part of the group, the collective values, claims, and expectations which sustain the conduct."[18] Americans may, by a desire to "save their skins," whether the skins be white or black, find a more compelling objective in integrating the races than in nurturing the prejudices.

Race relations in time of crisis do not, of course, necessarily follow the rational (as opposed to the traditional) approach. Majority Americans were notably apathetic about American citizens being denied Constitutional rights as Japanese-Americans were whisked off to Relocation Centers during World War II, thereby tacitly agreeing with Westbrook Pegler who declared "the Japanese in California should be under armed guard to the last man and woman right now and to hell with habeas corpus until the danger is over."[19]

How the original Spanish and Mexican settler of the Southwest who originally held their ranches and other possessions lost most of them at the hands of the more aggressive and business-minded Anglos of the North after those areas were taken from Mexico has been recounted elsewhere.[20] Throughout the Southwest this ethnic group which is economically subordinated to the Anglo but in many places in control politically retains relationships toward the Anglo which have been named by the senior author "polite separatism." Through closed family, friendship, and other groupings distinct systems are retained. Despite separate gangs in schools focused in *pachucos* or Spanish-speaking students and *stompers* or Anglos which carried on vicious fights, the norm of "polite separatism" reduces interaction between the pertinent systems and requires that relationships be on formal terms and for the most part negotiated by those in special status-roles developed for this purpose.

The 1960's brought changes in the "polite separatism" pattern in Mexican American-Anglo relationships. The Chicano movement developed with a more militant activism for the pursuit of the goals of this minority group. Patterned in part after the Black militant movements, Mexican-Americans began to organize and marshal "Chicano Power" to pursue goals in education, politics, and employment. A recent example would be the Raza Unida Party of Texas.

The general trend in the U.S.A. — as in many other lands today — is toward a diminishing of discriminatory norms and an increasing of equalitarian norms and goals. This is in keeping with the Gesellschaft-secular direction of change, and supports the efforts of the minority groups to achieve equal opportunity for their members to pursue the valued American goals of a good education for their children, good jobs, good homes, and to otherwise share in the good things of life to be found in American society.

Goal attaining and concomitant latent activity as process.   Goal attaining activities of racial and ethnic minorities may range from peaceful efforts to improve their lot within the system such as through better education, job training, voter registration drives, etc., to boycotts, strikes, sit-ins, and more militant activities aimed at achieving "freedom now" and full equality goals immediately. The Black Power movement of the 1960's and the more recent Chicano Power efforts illustrate such goal-attaining drives.

An example of the goal attaining activity in the Negro's struggle for racial equality would be the classic speech of Martin Luther King, titled "I Have a Dream," delivered at Washington, D.C., August, 1963. Here are some excerpts:

I say to you today, my friends, that in spite of the difficulties and frustrations of the moment I still have a dream. It is a dream deeply rooted in the American dream. I have a dream that one day this nation will rise up and live out the true meaning of its creed: 'We hold these truths to be self-evident; that all men are created equal.' I have a dream that one day on the red hills of Georgia the sons of former slaves and the sons of former slaveowners will be able to sit down together at the table of brotherhood . . . I have a dream that my four little children will one day live in a nation where they will not be judged by the color of their skin but by the content of their character. This is our hope . . .[21]

Organizations such as C.O.R.E., the Southern Christian Leadership Conference, and the Black Panthers arose to pursue the various goals of black minorities. Activities ranged from passive resistance to mass marches to destruction of property. These activities saw the emergence of a variety of leaders, to be discussed below under status-roles.

Evaluation.   Sociologists recognize that a very great number of items in the total environment are pre-judged, among which would be ethnic or racial groups. Some animals and reptiles, for example, may be needlessly feared in some societies. Children born into such societies take on by the process of internalization the pre-judgment of their elders about the supposedly fearsome and threatening animals. Likewise, foods are pre-judged as edible and inedible, and what is a tasty tidbit of worms, or snakes, or snails to one society is vermin to another. The tendency to evaluate and classify everything in the environment and transmit these stereotypes from generation to generation is indeed universal. Applied to humans it is this tendency which forms the basis of the ranking system shown in Table I. "No one is neutral on this subject."[22] In spite of the irrationality of the pre-judged (or pre-judicial, the more common word) evaluation as regards racial and ethnic groups, of great importance are changes which over time do occur in both the evaluator and the group being evaluated. The change does not necessarily herald a more rational evaluative process but it does demonstrate that prejudicial evaluations are not eternal.

Mr. and Mrs. Rosselini left Italy in 1910 and settled in New York state just in time to give their eldest child the privilege of being born in the United States. They were glad that it worked out this way, but their joy soon was dimmed by the increasing difficulty Mr. Rosselini had in getting any carpentry work to do. A friend advised him "Change your name; no American with money enough to hire work done is going to hire an Italian called Rosselini." So Mr. Rosselini became Mr. Rose, and enough carpentry work poured in to take care of the family which in time numbered four children. The son Norman, was particularly gifted. His academic accomplishments propelled him onward so that almost before they knew it, he had a PhD after his name, and he was ready to be a professional engineer. There were so many jobs for which he seemed to have just the right requirements, but somehow he never got the job. A friend advised him "Change your name; no engineering outfit is going to hire a Mediterranean-type guy with a name like Norman Rose. They think you're a Jew." Norman Rose became Norman Rosselini. He got the job he interviewed for, and Grandma and Grandpa Rose are very proud of their little Rosselini grand-children.

There are many investigations which attempt to answer the complicated questions about the evaluative process in relation to ethnic and racial groups. Moral convictions, rational observations, propinquity, self interest and situations both local and global no doubt have been effective in changing the evaluative process of an increasing number of individuals. More and more white Anglo-Americans realize that their one-language Anglo-tongued representatives are at a tremendous language disadvantage in the conduct of foreign affairs and that a favorable evaluation of the brown-skinned people of the United States may prevent millions of the brown-skinned peoples of the world from rendering an evaluation on America which would be devastating and lethal.

By what evaluative process are individuals relegated into the various classes irrespective of ethnic or racial identity? In the United States strict conformity to middle class norms is an important evaluative measure. Writers and critics like George Bernard Shaw poke

fun at "middle-class morality," and intellectuals eulogize individualism and decry the "vast mediocrity," which has become conforming middle-class America. The high degree of conformity in the
United States which some think stifles creativity has been the price
paid by the society for integration and near-integration of vast millions of diverse peoples. As the cultural differences which have served
as evaluative factors have been swallowed up in the integrative
process, occupational appraisal has become the most important
evaluative factor in the class structure. In some societies it would be
necessary in "placing" a person to ascertain what family tree and
what particular branch he comes from. In the United States an
evaluator has not "placed" the other person until he knows what the
head of the family does as he works. If evaluations based on other cues
are used — speech, dress, manner — and these turn out to be disparate to the occupational cue, it is the latter that will take precedence.
The college graduate who becomes a truck driver, in other words, will
be evaluated as a truck-driver; the successful businessman who only
finished seventh grade will be evaluated as a successful businessman.

The Gesellschaft-secular trend means a continued emphasis on
achievement (e.g., on education and occupation), and less on ascription (e.g., on family lineage, ethnicity, and race), in the evaluative
process. With increasing spatial and social mobility young people are
able to move away from and up from their families of orientation and
their original social class, ethnic, and in some ways racial origins,
and move into new communities where they are evaluated on the
basis of their occupational achievements and their life-style patterns.

If evaluations were solely by the achievement criteria of occupation or income each ethnic or racial system would be distributed up
and down the range of occupations and salaries in much the same
proportion to their total number that obtains for the general population if it is accepted that ability to achieve is not afforded by ethnic
identity. Tables III and IV show that this is not the case. Whereas
both tables show a remarkable integration of most ethnic groups,
they also establish that Parsons was right when he saw certain
unassimilated ethnic groups as constituting relatively independent
pyramids in the total population.

Freedman and his associates, in the work which originally cited
Tables III and IV, observe that in general "the northern and western
European ethnic groups reveal the largest concentrations of persons
in the high-status business and professional occupations. These, it
should be noted are the groups which have generally been in this
country for the longest period of time."[23] The Tables, of course, lend
further authenticity to the Warner-Srole Table of Assimilation (Ta-

ble I) and render it in effect an evaluative device. It will be noted that the persons coming originally from the U.S.S.R. form an exception to the general pattern of the Tables III and IV. Many of these persons are Jews; they enjoy a relatively high occupational status in view of their relatively disadvantaged place on the Warner-Srole scale.

Tables III and IV sum up the evaluative process regarding the ethno-racial systems by demonstrating that in the United States the society evaluates highly income, education, and occupation, but imputes a separate minority ethnic evaluation to members of unassimilated groups.

DIVIDING THE FUNCTIONS; RANKING

Status-role and rank as elements and processes. The student will remember that each ethnic system, as the term is here used, is distinguishable from the larger society either by virtue of cultural or biological differences between the members of the ethnic system and the members of the larger society. (See Note No. 2.) Status-roles peculiar to the particular ethnic system characterize each sub-group and generally serve to integrate the ethnic group and to mitigate strains between it and the larger society. It would be necessary to

TABLE III. PERCENTAGE DISTRIBUTION OF NATIVE-BORN (OF FOREIGN PARENTAGE) URBAN MALES 14 YRS. OF AGE AND OLDER IN NON-FARM OCCUPATIONS, BY ETHNIC AND RACIAL CATEGORIES, U.S., 1950.*

Ethnic-Racial Categories	Professional and Business	Clerical and Sales	Craftsmen and Foremen	Operatives	Service Workers & Laborers	Total
English and Welsh	29	20	23	18	10	100
Swedish	29	19	27	16	9	100
Norwegian	27	18	26	17	12	100
German	25	17	27	19	12	100
Irish	23	23	20	17	17	100
U.S.S.R	45	27	10	13	5	100
Italian	18	16	22	29	15	100
Polish	17	15	24	32	12	100
Czechoslovakian	16	15	27	29	13	100
French-Canadian	13	13	25	35	14	100
Mexican	6	10	18	31	35	100
Negro	6	6	10	29	49	100
A. U.S. Males	22	15	20	25	18	100

*Source: Data adapted from *U.S. Census of Population: 1950*, Vol. IV, *Special Reports,* Part 3, Chapter A, Nativity and Parentage, Table 20 and Vol. II. Characteristics of the Population, Part I, Table 128. Figures for ethnic groups are based on native whites of foreign or mixed parentage. The Negro group includes all Negro males residing in Urban areas. After Ronald Freedman, et. al.,*Principles of Sociology: A Text with Readings* (New York, Henry Holt, c1956), p. 543.

Social Systems

TABLE IV. INCOME AND EDUCATION MEDIANS OF SECOND-GENERATION ETHNICS (NATIVE-BORN OF FOREIGN PARENTAGE) RESIDING IN URBAN AREAS, AGE 25-44, BY ETHNIC AND RACIAL CATEGORIES, U.S., 1950.**

Ethno-Racial Categories	Median Year of Education	Median Income
English and Welsh	12.5	$2,967
Swedish	12.3	3,047
Norwegian	12.3	2,925
German	11.8	3,005
Irish	12.2	2,861
U.S.S.R	12.7	3,213
Italian	10.5	2,573
Polish	10.7	2,740
Czechoslovakian	11.1	2,788
French-Canadian	9.5	2,338
Mexican	7.9	1,784
Negro	8.3	1,330

**Source: Data adapted from *U.S. Census of Population: 1950*, Vol. IV, *Special Reports*, Part 3, Chapter A, Nativity and Parentage, Table 20 and Vol. II, Characteristics of the Population, Part I, Table 163, and Table 115. Figures for ethnic groups are based on native whites of foreign or mixed parentage. From Ronald Freedman, et. al., *Principles of Sociology: A Text with Readings* (New York, Henry Holt and Company, c1956), pp. 543-4.

examine each ethnic group in order to locate and specify the particular status-roles which exist in each. Some of the more common are the rabbi, the cantor, and the professional mourner among the Jews; the priest, the father-confessor, the alter-boy among the Catholics; the Dons and Donnas and the *patrones* among the Latinos. Among the blacks is a type which some Southern whites call the "good Negro," faithful, meek, humble, and unaggressive.[24] He and his counter-parts among other ethnic groups no longer find favor with most members of the minority groups. Other status-roles commonly found are those of "the agitator," "the defender," "the spokesman," "the pioneer." The latter may be typified by Jackie Robinson, the baseball player who when he began to play with the Dodgers could not object to an umpire's decision, had to grin and bear it when he was insulted by other players, who wore the "armor of humility" so well that for a long time fans did not realize that this was not the real Jackie. As he finally allowed himself to emerge as the fiery competitor he always had been he had earned "the right of every white player — the right to squawk."[25]

Starting in the 1950's and continuing through the 1960's there arose an increasing number and variety of "protester," "agitator," and "militant" leader status-roles within American minority groups (e.g. Martin Luther King, Malcolm X, Stokely Carmichael, Cesar Chavez, etc.). Most shared the general goals of improving the lot of their people. Strategies and tactics ranged from passive resistance to revolutionary and destructive acts aimed at fundamentally changing the existing social institutions. Great courage and dedication to the equalitarian cause was shown by many such leaders, some of whom achieved remarkable success in the face of bitter opposition by those in power in "the establishment." A few leaders gained great esteem not only in the eyes of their followers, but in the nation and the world at large. Such a charismatic leader was Martin Luther King, whose efforts gained him world-wide respect, a Nobel Peace Prize, and a martyr's death.

Less obvious is another aspect of status-role peculiar to ethnic systems. Membership in a minority ethnic group constitutes a status-role in and of itself in the eyes of the dominant society, and this ethnic status-role transcends, affects and controls the selection and execution of most other status-roles for the minority ethnic group member. The dominant society sees not only "the porter," "the doctor," "the father," "the neighbor." It sees "the Negro porter," "the Jewish doctor," "the Mexican father," "the Italian neighbor." It is the purpose of this discussion to reveal that status-role for a member of a minority ethnic group is largely controlled by the ascribed factor of ethnic identity; further, that since minority ethnic identity carries with it a group rank, the selection and execution of most status-roles become in part, functions of group rank for the member of the minority ethnic system. The discussion will be limited to status-roles held by minority ethnic group members in a few of the key sub-systems of the general society: 1) the occupation pluralities, 2) the family, 3) the governmental.

1. Occupationally, the blacks and others low on the Warner-Srole scale (Table I) are under-represented in the so-called "clean" jobs, and over-represented in various service jobs and in the least wanted jobs in manual labor. Rose examines the Negro's position in respect to agriculture where he was typically the share-cropper. In the circles of unskilled labor he is typically filling the status-roles least wanted by the whites.[26] Among the "white collar jobs" where he is generally under-represented he is practically non-existent in finance, and although represented in business and the professions he is marginal in those spots inasmuch as his trade or practice is usually almost exclusively dependent upon the Negro market, a marginal and unstable part of the total economy at best. Lastly Rose examines the black in relation to what he terms "the shady occupations." Racketeering, gambling, dope pushers, and organized vice, often done for white employers catering to white customers, can more

easily be executed within the Negro community because of its greater disorganization, inadequate police protection and graft-seeking political bosses. "The last hired and the first fired" makes of him the marginal man occupationally, and this is the true status-role which he has learned to play. He and his marginal counterparts among other ethnic groups are prompted for the sake of survival to use labor tactics or business tactics considered to be unethical by the dominant society. Thus, when the black, in order to get a job at all, is willing to "scab" or when a small businessman of a minority ethnic group engages in sharp business practices he intensifies and perpetuates the unfavorable image that the dominant group already holds. Although there is considerable evidence[27] that there is now less discriminatory occupational treatment — i.e., a wider selection of status-roles for those of the minority ethnic groups, not even the most sanguine of the equalitarians would deny that when black youth examines many attractive status-roles in which they could make a contribution they find a "not for you" tag attached to it.

2. Family-wise, the member of a discriminated against ethnic or racial group finds that even those status-roles played within the intimate circle of the family are affected. The failure of families in unassimilated ethnic groups to provide adult models whose behavior can be copied and whose beliefs and sentiments can be internalized will be treated later under the heading *Socialization*. Here will be mentioned some of the mental "hells" of the second generation ethnic group member. To the incumbent of this status-role falls a number of dilemmas: the struggle between filial love and the desire not to be "different;" the extremes of a ruthless casting off of all nationality moorings and an equally intense embracing of ethnic heritage; the decision to keep a "foreign" name or the trauma of changing it; the conflict within the individual who denies his nationality one moment and donates super-abundantly to "the cause" the next.

3. Election prognostications take into account "the Negro vote," or "the Spanish vote" or "the Polish vote." Once in office, the official with a name which shows him to be of an ethnic group not totally assimilated is often expected to execute his status-role with special considerations for the ethnic group from which he sprang. Even on the higher levels of government at which impartiality is paramount, it is often necessary for the official to make self-conscious efforts to eradicate ethnic thinking from the performance of the status-role.

One who belongs to the most vilified and persecuted minority in history is not likely to be insensible to the freedoms guaranteed by our Constitution . . . But as judges we are neither Jew nor Gentile, neither Catholic nor agnostic . . . As a member of this Court I am not justified in writing my private notions of policy into the Constitution, no matter how deeply I may cherish them or how mischievous I may deem their disregard.[28]

It is scarcely necessary to point out that it is the dominant society's insistence that the minority individual remember his minority status-role which renders any status-role for that individual a dual affair.

The status-role of the minority ethnic is further complicated by uneven desegregation practices which force individuals into status-roles in at least two ethnic or racial social systems at once. Thus it becomes "increasingly common for both blacks and whites to play pluralistic roles inside and outside the uneven color line."[29] How for instance does the young Negro male who works elbow to elbow with the young white female behave when he meets the same girl in the bowling alley or in the cafeteria? Until the desegregation is complete the strains of marginality will be frustrating to all concerned. Thus the white worker "may fight for his Negro co-worker in the plant, but at home with his wife and his neighbors and their wives he will fight the same Negro co-worker with fire and dynamite when the Negro tries to move into his neighborhood."[30] It is at such times that the "pioneers" like Jackie Robinson and the "statesmen" such as Walter White and Charles Johnson help the marginal man to reinforce the sense of his personal worth, to foster hope that the stigma of inferiority will some day be lifted, and to believe anew in the "equality of opportunity," an ideal which remains a basic belief-sentiment constellation for both whites and blacks.

Status-roles and the rank imputed to the group are related too when the class system (irrespective of race or ethnic membership) is considered. Children of lower class families, for example, less frequently elect to persist in the status-role of "student" than do children of the middle and upper classes. Certain occupational status-roles which require long and expensive training like that of doctor tend obviously to be filled by incumbents from those classes which can afford to pay for the long educational process. There is evidence that lower-class people often become school dropouts and play fewer status-roles.

In every type of group without exception — church, fraternal, service, recreational, patriotic, political, cultural — membership on the part of the lower income class was markedly lower . . .[31]

The important distinction between the status-role – class-system relationship and the status-role – ethnic system relationship is the relative rigidity of the latter by which the individual, regardless of his own achievements tends to be imputed the rank of his ethnic group. In contrast, there is a relative flexibility of the class system which allows a relatively unobstructed flow of individuals from class, both upward and downward.

> One . . . of the most notable features of the American system of stratification is its relative looseness, the absence of a clear-cut hierarchy of prestige except in a very broad sense, the absence of an unequivocal top elite or ruling class; the fluidity of the shadings as well as mobility between groups and, in spite of the prestige-implications of the generalized goal of success, the relative tolerance for many different paths to success. It is by no means a 'classless society,' but among class societies, it is a distinctive type.[32]

Sociological literature on rank, class, caste and stratification is voluminous,[33] expanding and dynamic; its concepts are being used to probe new fields and to gain new insights in old fields. The following generalizations are basic in the relationship between the element "rank" and the class and ethnic subsystems of the United States.

1. Although strata are discernible at any one moment in the total society, the individuals composing that class are not always the same individuals. From time to time individuals leave the class to which they have belonged. They either rise in rank in which case upward mobility is said to have taken place, or descend in rank in which case downward mobility is said to have occurred. Many people remain relatively stationary in rank. Certain classes are characterized by having a particularly strong upward mobile drive. They tend to be composed of individuals who already have succeeded in some measure of vertical mobility. The lower middle class and the new upper class show a strong upward mobile impulse, for example. (See the treatment of *Social Rank* in the chapter on *Family and Kinship Systems.*)

2. Marginality of position is characteristic of those who have "just arrived" in a class. For the most part they have cast off old friendships, old customs, the old "life style;" the new "life style," whether coveted as in upward mobility or deplored as in downward mobility, is not yet established as habitual. They are firmly established neither in the old class nor the new. The new-comer too, whether he has gone up or down shows some evidence[34] of being more sensitive than individuals whose rank is more stable or stationary to threats from ethno-racial groups. The upward mobile or downward mobile seem to impute to the Jew and the Negro, for example, more of the stereotyped ideas about them than do people whose rank has remained stationary. People of any class tend to impute more negative attributes and form more hostility toward those immediately

above or below them in the class scale than they do to individuals several notches removed from them.

3. No class is without its own intra-class ranking system. The versifier meant this when he designed his lines: "The Lowells talk only to Cabots and the Cabots talk only to God." Scrutiny would show that the lower-class "Martins and McCoys, those feudin' mountain boys" would also hold a rank in their class system higher than some and lower than others.

4. Some maintain that the black and white are not divided by caste restrictions. Although it is not literally true that no black can rank high the prohibitions preventing his rise are so numerous and so stringent, generally in the land, that to disclaim a caste system anywhere in the United States is to attach an overly literal connotation to the caste concept. Figure 4 describes Warner's schematic portrayal of the class and caste system in the South.[35] It will be noted that a diagonal bar separates the black and white castes. The arrangement of this bar expresses the restrictions that separate the two castes. The more the restrictions are removed the more the bar AB will move on the axis C until it approximates the vertical line DE. That is, it is necessary for the occupational and other groups of Negroes to resemble comparable white groups in the prestige and other measures of standing accorded them in society at large. On the other hand, if the restrictions were increased, if the black's rights and privileges were decreased, and if he were again to be relegated to slave rank so that no black group, not even those who had the highest rank in the community, were higher than the lowest white group, then the bar would become horizontal, with only blacks below and only whites above.

From these generalized statements concerning rank attention will now be turned to the element of the social system which is positively correlated with status-role and high rank, namely, power.

CONTROLLING

Power as an element.   Some aspects of power in relation to class and ethnic sub-systems will be considered subsequently under occupational systems and production systems. Here is the place to note, however, that much of the power held by the principal class-caste and racial-ethnic subsystems is not the power to initiate wanted action, but rather the power to *stop* unwanted action, or what Riesman has called "veto power."

The lobby in the old days actually ministered to the clear leadership, privilege, and imperative of the business ruling class. Today we have substituted for that leadership a series of groups, each of which has

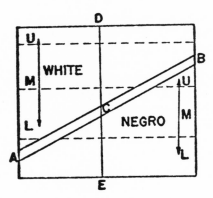

Figure 4. Warner's Schematic Diagram of Class and Caste in America. The diagonal lines (AB) separate the Negro from the white caste. The dashed lines within each caste distinguish Upper (U), Middle (M), and Lower (L) classes. The line (DE) indicates a hypothetical position to which the diagonal (AB) may move. Source: W. Lloyd Warner, "American Class and Caste." *American Journal of Sociology*, Vol. XLII, No. 2, September 1936, pp. 234-237.)

struggled for and finally attained a power to stop things conceivably inimical to its interests and, within far narrower limits, to start things. The movie-censoring groups, the farm groups and the labor and professional groups, the major ethnic groups and major regional groups, have in many instances succeeded in maneuvering themselves into a position in which they are able to neutralize those who might attack them. The very increase in the number of these groups, and in the kinds of interests (practical and fictional) marks therefore, a decisive change from the lobbies of an earlier day. There is a change in method, too, in the way the groups are organized, the way they handle each other, and the way they handle the public, that is, the unorganized.

These veto groups are neither leader-groups nor led-groups. The only leaders of national scope yet in the United States today are those who can placate the veto groups.[36]

Pertinent groups which attained a degree of power "to stop things conceivably inimical to its interests" number among them the National Association for the Advancement of Colored People, various organized labor groups, the B'Nai B'rith, the Urban League, and the Civil Liberties Union. Memberships in any of these groups are not limited to those of a particular class or race, but tend to be dominated by the groups which are being protected plus a number from outside the group who espouse the protective cause by reason of their being liberal, or humanistic or conscious of civil rights.

Rose[37] describes as a uniquely unrewarding position the power position which comes to a few within the black community. Any real power cannot come to a black without its coming from a white group. The white group usually is willing to part with some power and bequeath it to a black because they think that this particular one can influence other blacks. Since the white group is not willing to allow anywhere near as much privilege to go to the Negro as the latter would desire, in a short time the Negro power-figure is regarded as a failure by other blacks since he has not achieved what they wanted. His power wanes as his influence with the blacks vanishes and he is replaced by another power-figure who goes through the same cycle; or a number of would-be power figures, none with unassailable influence, compete as the leader-figure in the black community. "Uncle Tom" is a derisive term applied by blacks to those black power-figures who according to the judgment of the black community, are more willing to cater to what the white man wants than to work for what the black needs.

As seen above, in the 1960's a new type of leader emerged in the black and Chicano minority groups. These leaders depended neither upon white or majority support, nor did they exercise mainly a veto-power role. Rather, they drew their support and power resources from their own groups, and exercised their power in direct action efforts in confrontations with the majority group establishment power figures. Martin Luther King and his Southern Leadership Conference made use of a bus strike by blacks in Birmingham, Alabama, to successfully force the bus company and the local government to desegregate the seating on buses. "Sit-ins" were instigated by black groups to force desegregation of restaurants and lunch counters. Marches and demonstrations were held to force white officials to register black voters. While such efforts brought significant improvements for blacks in the South, little was being done to improve the lot of the masses of black people in the urban ghettos of the North and the West. Living in poverty, with closed opportunities, and de facto school segregation, these people were ripe for more militant leadership. It came in the form of activist leaders such as Stokely Carmichael and Rap Brown who rejected King's "non-violent" means and "working within the system" approach, advocating instead "freedom now" for blacks by separating themselves from the white community, building their own independent positions of power in order to achieve such goals as economic and political independence, and black pride and unity. Militant strategies were called for, including armed resistance against "whitey," and extracting "an eye for an eye" in confrontation with white police. In the mid-1960's white America was shocked at the outbreak of wide-spread destructive "riots" in the black ghettos of many major cities. Short periods of near-anarchy saw the burning and looting of stores and other business establishments and proper-ties. Some loss of life occurred. Post-riot analysis indicated that these disturbances of the 1960's differed significantly from most "race riots" of earlier times. Instead of being primarily clashes between particular groups of blacks and whites, the recent violent activities seemed to be aimed at the most visible symbols of white dominance: property, local merchants, public officials, and the police.[38]

For the Chicanos, the new La Raza Unida Party represents an effort by the Mexican-American minority in the Southwest to marshal its latent political power, and thus to improve the lot of its people via more participation in the political processes. They feel a significant start was made in the 1972 elections when their candidate for Governor of Texas, Ramsey Muñiz, drew 6.7 percent of the total vote.

Decision-making. The organization of neither the class systems nor the ethno-racial systems has become so institutionalized that any one vehicle or body speak authoritatively for a whole class, a whole ethnic group or a whole racial group. Even these organizations which represent one or another such system in the popular mind generally are neither all-inclusive of that system nor exclusive of members from other systems. Thus, the various labor organizations might be thought to be synonymous with the "working man" or "labor." To some this might mean that it is an organization of lower-middle class and lower class memberships. Yet large numbers of white-collar workers as well as smaller numbers of teachers, physicians, librarians, and other middle class persons belong to the ranks of organized labor. The National Association for the Advancement of Colored People which to some means an organization of blacks not only does not include all blacks, but it does include many whites. Pressure groups frequently are designated by some term by which strata is suggested such as "the working class" or "property owners" or "taxpayers," although no such group is discrete by class. Insofar as class-caste or racial-ethnic systems are represented by local organizations, decisions are made which represent the welfare of the systems. A local of a labor union must decide whether to accept the terms of an employment contract or to strike. A local branch of NAACP reports cases of discrimination to the national office which must decide whether to sit tight or to make a public protest. Many actions that appear to be those of an individual protesting the right to work or the right to attend school may actually represent the test case of a much larger group which has decided to take this method of determining the boundaries and of establishing new ones. Decisions about what action will be taken and when is likely to lie with the elite at the top of the organization.

The massive black liberation movements of the 1960's and the somewhat similar Chicano movement of the late 1960's and early

1970's have brought the emergence of more formal organizations and new leaders in these ethno-racial systems, and the identity of higher percentages of minority group members in such organizations. Organizations such as the Southern Christian Leadership Conference, the Congress on Racial Equality, the Black Muslims and the Black Panthers have attracted black members from a wide range of ideological views, but all concerned with black liberation. Chicano groups such as La Raza Unida are appealing to increasing numbers of Mexican-Americans. While such organizations do not encompass nearly all the blacks or Spanish-speaking people in the U.S.A., their membership is now substantial, and the decisions made and actions taken by such organizations often have consequences for the larger racial and ethnic groups themselves.

SANCTIONING

Sanction as an element and application of sanctions as process. In the above treatment of *Sentiments,* the intensity of the sentiment was seen to be related to the degree that the situation was unstructured and unpredictable, and to the degree that improvement of status of one group was destructive of the self-image of another group. The same two factors contribute toward the sanctions, both positive and negative, that are likely to be exercised. The Southern black who migrates to the North will find favor at one job for using the full repoirtoire of black "acts" that are put on for the benefit of the white man; this same stereotyped behavior will lose him his job at another place. In either South or North it is much easier to find negative sanctions which are applied to the black for his deviations, both real and imagined, than it is to enumerate similar positive sanctions offered to induce desired behavior. The acme of the negative sanctions has become the lynching. The most common justification for lynching is "protection of white womanhood." However, the fact that there was a correlation from year to year between low cotton prices and a high number of lynchings and that among the total number of lynchings only 23 percent were allegedly for rape or attempted rape bely this rationalization. Walter White has stated that " . . . Lynching is much more an expression of Southern fear of black progress than of Negro crime."[39] Rose indicates that "All the forms of violence against Negroes — striking, beating, robbing, destroying property, exiling, threatening — still occur often in the South."[40]

Negative sanctions against other ethnic groups sound mild in comparison but are effective in reminding the individual ethnic group member that he has not been accepted in full fellowship into American society. Jewish high school graduates debate over a decision like a name change when a particularly well suited job opening comes to their attention after a number of failures in gaining employment. Young Jewish college students who have been told by several colleagues how hard it is for a Jew to get hired in any of the chemical or engineering industries decide to try the longer and more expensive route to scientific achievement in medicine. Although the medical schools are reported among the Jews to have quotas, at least those who make it, they argue, can practice with fewer job difficulties.

Sanctions as they apply to class sub-groups are documented by an increasingly large body of studies. The public school teacher embodying middle-class standards of behavior, for example, very often makes it difficult for the lower-class child to feel at ease in school or to continue schooling.[41] Both high school and college attendance is seen to be affected by the father's occupation fully as much as by the native intelligence of the child. The law enforcement agencies and the court systems have been shown to deal differentially with people from different classes. Even in the most Gesellschaft-like situation in the market place where according to principle "one man's dollar is as good as another" negative sanctions of a snobbish or condescending nature are used to discourage the trade of those whose appearance and manner reveal a class which is lower than the ordinary clientele.

Sanctions as they apply to class and caste reveal well that an established pattern of expectation which is invariably fulfilled under certain prescribed conditions is very much less stressful and painful than the condition which exists under generally kinder but unpredictable conditions. The author's experience in the high sierras of the Andean country of South America included a visit with a missionary group which had the following story to tell.

> The Indians hereabouts have done all the labor on the haciendas for years; they have been the peons, the laborers, the share croppers, for the non-Indian owners who in most cases have never seen the farm they own. A hired manager usually runs the place and through the years a custom of management by extreme cruelty has evolved.

> Our mission was to change all this. In the name of Christ, we set out to settle a large area of land and have it put into agricultural production not as an hacienda but as family-sized farms worked by the Indian families who previously had worked under one of the managers. We visualized each family working harder since their labors would be for themselves; we knew that each individual would gain in self-respect and grow in the image of God just as he would gain in material wealth. But instead of bringing him increased stature, we almost ruined him. They never had had to make one little decision before; they always had had to do only what they were told. If they deviated at all, they were reminded right away by a whipping with a leather-tonged whip.

Not long after our noble experiment had begun a delegation from nearby haciendas called on us. We found that "our Indians" had been stealing, philandering, and pillaging throughout the area. Drunken orgies, "raids" into other haciendas, and generally uncontrolled behavior had made of them the scourge of the countryside and they threatened to burn us out if we did not get the Indians under control. We had to hire a manager who knew the traditional way to handle the Indians, and we look back now with shudderings at that dismal period when the church had to sanction whippings. Then starting from where they had been and with procedures that everybody understood we were able to move slowly step by step to the point where we are now where each Indian family is an independent agent. But we did have to go back to the old system and pull out of it.

This story, inapplicable as it is in extremity of deprivation, punishment and degree of dependence is entirely applicable to any group of any class, caste or ethno-racial system in demonstrating the debilitating force of unfulfilled expectations, or of *anomie*, and that no sanction can be understood without knowing the expectancy pattern.

In the U.S.A. in the 1950's and 1960's, negative sanctions, often severe, were imposed by white authorities and citizens upon minority group members actively engaged in the Civil Rights and Black Power movements, e.g., the police use of fire hoses and turning of police dogs on blacks marching in Birmingham and Selma, Alabama, the bombing or burning of homes of black leaders by the Ku Klux Klan. These violent sanctions brought about a big wave of adverse public reaction. The American public seemed to be saying loud and clear that no Americans in positions of power should be allowed to deny other Americans their rights of full citizenship. Strong Civil Rights laws were enacted by Congress in the late 1960's, backed by legal sanctions enforceable in Federal Courts.

As already discussed above under *Power*, the past two decades have seen the use of a variety of sanctions by racial and ethnic minority peoples in the pursuit of their goals, ranging from the peaceful "passive resistance" techniques of marches and "sit-ins" to the destructiveness of a "Watts-type riot."

FACILITATING

Facility as an element and utilization of facilities as process. The facilities which underlie the class-caste, and racial-ethnic subsystems in the United States range all the way from those essentials of life — food, shelter, and clothing — without which man could not exist, to the class symbols — those facilities which are enjoyed or used not exclusively for themselves but as advertisements to the world that its possessor belongs to a certain class. Both the essential and the symbolic facility are most available, of course, to the people in the upper left hand corner of the Warner-Srole Scale (Table I) and decreasingly available to those in the various steps of the scale until the individuals in the bottom right hand corner are reached; those individuals have the least facilities of all.

Nowhere among the facilities essential to life are differences expressed more conspicuously than in housing. Here segregation in all parts of the United States as exercised against all minority groups has been crucial in preventing amelioration. The Federal Government and other agencies in initiating huge slum clearance schemes have often worsened rather than bettered living conditions for the very low income groups. Slum clearance has often further overcrowded the remaining slum areas, the only areas remaining where the poor can live, the rent of the new units being too high or various forms of exclusion preventing low ranking ethnic groups from using them.

Dress and grooming are among the most common facilities which are used as class symbols but none is more characteristic of the United States, perhaps, than the automobile. Indeed, the student can perhaps quite easily think of the makes of cars the ownership of which to some extremely upward mobile people is synonymous with "arriving." Such cars allow the possessor to think at least some of the time and make others believe most of the time, that now he is like the upper middle class. Bona fide members of the upper middle class who owe their position to education and culture often of course, would not allow themselves to be persuaded to own what to them would seem such a flamboyant symbol. It would seem to them pretentious and in bad taste. They perhaps would employ class symbols which are not so easily bought on the market place, but are fully as symbolic and fully as conspicuous, but usually attended with subtleties. The well-controlled, modulated voice, the choice vocabulary, a familiarity with certain abstract or cultural subjects would be a more acceptable symbol of class to this kind of middle-class person.

There are many articles which a lower-class person usually thinks of as "classy" and aspires to own and display which a person of a higher class immediately labels "lower class." Cheap perfume, prominent and large gold fillings, cheap fur treated to look like more expensive fur, and garish or sentimental pictures are among the many possessions which are lower-class symbols.

Education must certainly be regarded as a facility in the class-structure. As important as the actual availability of a good school system is the nurturing of attitudes about school, a phenomena which varies greatly by class, which will be explored further under the heading *Socialization*.

People themselves have been regarded as a facility. In feudal times serfs and land were considered as constituting in an inseparable manner one of the factors of production; he who owned the land also owned a certain portion of the labor of the serfs. Under slavery human beings are regarded as capital. In the southern part of the United States where that pattern was most dominant it is not surprising to find that the descendants of the people who were thought of as capital are still relatively disadvantaged.

With the long periods of sustained economic prosperity and growth following World War II, and the Civil Rights and other related movements toward more equal opportunities in education, employment, etc., more racial and ethnic minority peoples, as well as working and lower class peoples, have been able to improve their facilities. With upward social mobility, individuals and families normally experience improvements in economic facilities as well as increases in prestige and power. Today more ethnic, racial, and lower class people are achieving incomes sufficient to enable them to dress better, eat better, drive better cars, and live in better houses or apartments. As noted earlier, educational opportunities are improving for minority peoples, both in public schools, and in higher education. Also, sentiments and norms supporting the value of higher education are extending downward into the working and lower classes. Thus, lower and working class families are making greater efforts to keep their children in school and to help them to go on to college.

COMPREHENSIVE OR MASTER PROCESSES OF CLASS, ETHNIC, AND RACIAL SOCIAL SYSTEMS

Socialization. It will be recalled from a preceding chapter that each child acquires by the process of internalization a self-belief or self-knowledge basic to his personality system. Besides the family and the intimate friendship systems which furnish to members of all ethnic systems the models which are internalized, another all important reference group furnishes self-images to the minority ethnic group member. The minority group member sees himself (and believes himself to be) not only what his most primary associations reveals him to be, but what the majority system thinks him to be. The black, for example, may believe himself to be lazy or unpunctual or happy-go-lucky, if this is what he perceives to be the belief of the dominant whites. Even if he does not believe that he is any of these things, he is almost certain to be aware that "they" think he is. He might respond by measuring up to "their" expectations or by proving that "they" are wrong. In either case his conduct springs from a degree of internalization of beliefs about himself through white man's eyes. This in part, is what is meant by Rose: "We have pointed out that what is important in the black problem is what is in the minds of white people, and that changes for good or evil in the black problem depend primarily on changes in people's beliefs and values."[42]

A preceding chapter has also pointed out that the stabilizing of the adult personality is one of the functions of the family. For the newly arrived immigrant the degree of acceptance and the rank which the larger society tenders his ethnic group is an important factor in his self-image and his stabilization. Even under very difficult conditions, however, the *first* generation, newly arrived from "the old country" can often make itself somewhat impervious to the different normative demands of a new country by keeping alive the beliefs, goals and norms of "the old country" and by associating with others whose lives are guided by the same principles. The *second* fits in a social milieu which demands a kind of behavior of which the parents are incapable. Consequently, the sons and daughters are deprived of an adequate adult model upon which to fashion their own casting of the status-role of "mother", "father" and other adult roles. The common phenomena of peer-group gangs, strongly ethnic or racial in membership make-up as the *pachucos* mentioned above is thought to be related to the absence of an effective adult model of behavior.[43] The gangs of course, further intrench racial or ethnic segregation.

The lower class child, too, lacks an adult model whose behavior he can imitate advantagiously in the many life situations dominated by people from the middle class. The lower class child is not being "bad" when he is visually aggressive, anti-gentlemanly, physically combative and precocious in the acceptance of adult roles including occupational roles and sex roles. He is merely behaving in a manner consistent with his training, just as the middle class teacher is behaving in a manner consistent with her training when she repudiates lower class behavior in the classroom.

Recent studies of lower class black family life have emphasized this problem for black youth, especially boys. In many of these families the absence or weak presence of a father means the boys grow up without a real father figure and adult male role-model. This hampers the development of a strong masculine ego for the boy and inhibits his identification with male family status-roles such as husband and father.[44] Thus, the lower class black male youth lacks socialization in the beliefs, sentiments and norms conducive to the development of conventional marriage and family status-roles and responsibilities, including the family provider status-role. According to Moynihan, this pattern tends to perpetuate the female and mother-dominated urban poor black family.

Communication.   How does the process of communication make of the caste-class and ethno-racial systems a going concern? The most obvious answer is in the language spoken. As was shown on the Warner-Srole scale (Table I), the inability to speak English is one of the major factors leading to non-assimilation. People in a country like the United States, which by and large has a common language, sometimes are unaware of the tremendous integrative force this is. Communication difficulties resulting from the dozens of languages in Mexico and the multi-language problems of Guatemala, China, India, Ecuador, Peru, as well as the various dialects of advanced countries such as Germany, Spain, and France are less prevalent in the United States. The major exception is the Spanish-speaking group which has flourished in the Southwest for a longer time than the United States has embraced that territory; more recently the Spanish-speaking population has been augmented by new arrivals from Puerto Rico who have settled for the most part in New York. Many such settlers have black blood and very soon become aware of the low rank given blacks on the United States mainland. Some feel that they are protected from this onerous classification if their language is Spanish and they claim "Latino" background. Thus, the learning of English is often inhibited even though inability to talk English well cuts down their earning power.

While it is without doubt true that a common language is of inestimable value in diminishing ethnic differentiations, there is considerable evidence that figuratively, all English-speaking people "don't speak the same language." Schatsman and Strauss[45] found that differences in thinking and in perceiving and differences in relationships to other persons showed up in the communication patterns of lower class individuals as contrasted with those of middle class persons. The inability of the lower class person to respond and interact in the manner in which the middle class person is accustomed may certainly have a good deal to do with the maintanance of the class-system in its present form. In inter-class communication it is possible for the true meaning of the communication symbol to slip right past its intended recipient. It is not surprising that law or justice or business practices seem to work to the relative disadvantage of the lower class person whose responses seldom meet the requirements or expectations of the middle class judge or business man who, from their point of view must probe and ferret out answers necessary for the transaction.

The word itself can and does carry very different meanings to different classes. Consider such words as "policeman" or "truant officer" or "hungry." Then there are a host of emotion-laden words which sound like battle cries to the lower class and like slander and calumny to the upper middle class. Demagogues like Hitler, Huey Long, and Father Caughlin all knew how to manipulate such symbolic words as "war lords," "imperialists," "robber barons," "fat-jowled capitalists," "the salt of the earth," "the scum of the earth," to set class against class. Symbol manipulation reaches its height, probably when it is used to set race against race and ethnic group against group. The brief Nazi triumph in Germany with its attendant persecution of the Jews, and the public frenzy in the United States which permitted the Japanese Re-Location centers are but two wide-scaled results of communication techniques as applied to the ethnic-racial systems.

So culture-bound are individuals to words, sights, scents, and sounds that it is even difficult sometimes for the beginning social science student to distinguish between "fact" and "symbol." The Japanese bride clothed in red and the mourner in white would seem "wrong" to many Americans, accustomed as they are to color symbols with different meanings. These same Americans automatically "go" on the green light and automatically "stop" on the red light, bringing into play another set of situational color symbols. The sentiments, actions, and meanings associated with particular symbols often outlive their appropriateness. As Whitehead[46] points out, when a symbol evokes responses which are no longer appropriate either the social system accommodates to the situation by withdrawing or changing the meaning of the symbol, or by itself passing out of existence. The ancient Romans failed to accommodate their social system to the sign of the cross which remained a derogatory symbol long after Christians were non-threatening to the stability of the Roman Empire. The Roman Empire passed out of existence to be replaced by another social system. Years later in England feudalism had run its course; a new social situation demanded cities and citizens rather than fiefs, lords, and vassals. Much of feudal symbolism lost its old meaning, England accommodated to out-moded symbols and to newer ones, more appropriate to the new social situation, and by so doing survived as a nation. In the United States the major ethnic and racial systems respond discriminatingly to the symbol of a dark skin. Such reactions, appropriate to a social system supported by slavery, and well enough suited to a situation in which there was unequal achievement in an achievement-oriented society, are inappropriate now because of new elements in the situation. Slavery is dead, dark-skinned people have demonstrated their ability to achieve, and furthermore, the total social system is in jeopardy in a world which places a high premium on non-discrimination by skin color. History would teach that the social system will die to be replaced by another, or it will accommodate to the new situation by rendering the symbolism of the dark skin meaningless.

One aspect of the black liberation movement of the 1960's in the U.S.A. focused on this very thing. The expression "Black is beautiful" was coined and used extensively by black leaders to help counter the older notion of "black is inferior." The achievements of present day black Americans, and belatedly, the recognition of the contributions by blacks in America's past, were publicized not only in black groups but throughout the land via the mass media and in schools and colleges. "Black Studies" programs hit college and university campuses, aimed, among other things, at changing the image of blacks and engendering pride in blackness by emphasizing their contributions to America as well as the richness of their African heritage. Among the various symbolic expressions of this black pride movement were the adoption by black youth of special traits such as Afro hair styles, distinctive clothing, "soul food," the raised arm and clinched fist sign, and the use of expressions such as "soul brother" and "soul sister." Communication among blacks in terms of these symbolic expressions and traits has brought about a dramatic change in the meaning of being black in America today.

Symbols which stand for class differences, on the other hand, are fraught with meanings which are appropriate but little understood. Interaction between individuals who have different ends, sentiments, beliefs and norms can be stressful. Symbols of class differences are cues to the individuals which enable them to act in a manner likely to limit or formalize interaction so that stress is reduced. One of the most confused areas of symbolic meanings by the middle class white is the reaction to the lower class ethnic or racial minority member. The sentiments and reactions triggered off by the encounter are largely in response to the *class* symbols of grooming, cleanliness, dress, speech and general air of self-confidence. The reactions are often thought to be in response to the symbol of the cultural or biological difference, i.e., to the "foreign-sounding English," to the dark-skin, to the exotic appearance. Limited communication on the part of middle class Anglo whites with middle or upper class Negroes perpetuates the mistaken identity of symbols.

Boundary maintenance. It has already been demonstrated that boundaries *are* maintained — boundaries that prevent unlimited intermingling of class with class, of race with race, of main-stream population with unassimilated ethnic groups. To suppose that under any set of circumstances — complete integration, for example —

boundary maintenance would cease is contrary to any sociological knowledge that has ever been accumulated. Even in a society like Russia which is solely dedicated to the formation of a classless society, individuals are ranked and the various aggregates of similarly ranked people are demarked from other aggregates by boundary maintenance mechanisms. The equalitarian beliefs of the United States society makes it necessary to give particular attention to the function performed by boundary maintenance, for sometimes boundaries are mistakenly thought to be inconsistent with the belief that "men are born equal." As Blumer observes, "segregation is a primary means by which a human society develops an inner organization — an allocation of diverse elements into an articulated arrangement."[47] The student should note carefully that Blumer does not say "racial segregation," but simply "segregation" by which he means boundary maintenance of society's sub-systems. Thus for all the social systems discussed in the text, boundary maintenance brings into play

> a continuous process of preserving group domains and of excluding outsiders from ingress into such domains . . . If groups could not draw lines and exercise control over accessibility to their ranks and their privileges, their existence would be intrinsically doomed and group life would be chaotic.[48]

It would be helpful for the student to think of some of the functions performed by boundary maintenance. Basic to such an attempt is the knowledge that different life styles attend the broad class divisions characteristic of the society.

By respecting the aggregates of individuals who have been accorded a similar rank (and who by that token tend to share a common pattern of life) it is easier, for example, to communicate within the group. It is also easier for an outsider (for example, a "boss" who is responsible for giving instructions on a new process) to communicate with the group. The group will be much more free of emotional tension if everyone in the group shares roughly the same expectations than if there are those in the group whose expectations are different. Common expectations and common communication symbols make the performance of a group task very much easier than if outsiders were present. Those generally stated functions applied to a particular system like the family or the occupational system will soon demonstrate the kind of strain which would be present were one middle class family to attempt to rear children in a lower class neighborhood, or if an upper class person were to take a job on the line where lower middle class men were working. The student will be able to expand his list of reasons for boundary maintenance.

In relation to the systems with which this chapter is concerned, it is very soon apparent that some kinds of boundary maintenance can perform *dysfunctions* to the whole society. Blumer, as well as noting the functional aspect of "segregation" as he calls it which was noted above calls attention to the condition under which certain boundary maintenance mechanisms must be repudiated; namely, when segregation devices violate norms of the "larger inclusive group, such as an embracing political society with legal rights of citizenship or a transcending moral community with a set of ethical expectations."[49] Clearly, such a situation exists when large sections of the black population cannot vote and otherwise are tossed a "second-class citizenship;" when large numbers of Jews must choose their occupation not by their natural talents but by what they will be allowed to do; when large sectors of the population of the Southwest are limited in their choice of where to live, what to do and whom to marry by virtue of a Spanish surname; when subtle social pressures are applied to the grade-school student of a lower class family so that regardless of his natural ability, he is likely to drop from school at the earliest opportunity. The dysfunctions performed by certain kinds of boundary maintenance devices can be summed up very briefly. In an achievement-oriented society such as that of the United States, boundary maintenance devices based upon ascription perform a disservice to society as well as to the individuals concerned. Among others, the following disservices or dysfunctions have been identified: (1) Persons ascribed to a lower class status or to a racial or ethnic group evaluated as inferior may develop self-images that are less favorable than those in the more fortunate middle and upper classes or majority groups. Favorable self-images are important to the development of one's potentials, while unfavorable self-images may result in lack of self-confidence and feelings of apathy or even shame. (2) Such differential self-images in a community may result in unequal motivation among people to participate in the life of a community. (3) This would be followed by an unequal sense of significant social membership within the community. (4) A consequence of these developments could be unequal feelings of loyalty among members toward the community or society.[50] Truly incalculable are the losses to society caused by the unequal chance; losses in terms of crime, slum, welfare load, production of material goods, creativity and fulfillment of personal growth. These are a few of the prices society pays for the privilege of using an ascriptive boundary maintenance device.

Systemic Linkage. When any group becomes wholly assimilated so that the nationality, language, religion or race of its forefathers is of little or no consequence in the conducting of every-day affairs systemic linkage has been completely accomplished and the group merges into the main-stream of the society, no longer perceptible as a separate sub-system. At the other extreme is the group that is so little assimilated that few facets of life of any consequence exist outside the group. Student life in a few all-Negro colleges is sometimes cited as approaching the acme of non-systemic linkage. For most of the ethno-racial groups which are still discernible, however, and for the lower classes, a marginal position exists which demands that the members at some times belong to the greater society and to so conduct themselves, and at other times belong to the ethnic, racial or class system and to so conduct themselves. In general it is the transitional generations which are subjected to the greatest strain in systemic linkage through acculturation to the larger society. Groups such as French-Canadians and Spanish-Americans which as indicated on Table I assimilate more slowly than Protestants, English-speaking, or northern Europeans, but assimilation is inevitable. Thus a study in Woonsocket, Rhode Island indicated the following percent of intermarriage with non-French Canadians: 8.8 per cent of second generation, 35.0 per cent third generation.[51] Studies made during the period of highest immigration to the United States showed higher rates of criminality and suicide among the off-spring of immigrants than among the immigrants themselves; this of course reflected the strain due to the marginal position of the second generation.

A social phenomena characteristic of system linkage is worthy of special note. The marginal person who gains a toe-hold in the main-stream system holds a precarious position there for a while. The black who has succeeded in leaving behind him a lower class status, who is successfully competing in a white man's occupational world, and who is living in a middle class neighborhood; the Pole who no longer teaches Polish to his children, who perhaps has changed his name and has moved away from the Polish neighborhood; the Irish-Catholic who has clipped the brogue from his tongue, swept the pig from his parlor, and no longer wears his religion on his sleeve; all these and their counterparts so completely accept the ends, norms, sentiments and beliefs of the larger society that they tend to look upon the newcomers and the unassimilated as "foreigners." Systemic linkage of few other systems require such a denial of the members' roots. Only time and success in the new system can give the newly linked person the security necessary for him to function as a wholly effective link to the old system. Although the immigrant child serves as a link by translating for the old-world parents and the immigrant adolescent serves as a link by introducing the old-world parent to different customs, generally a great deal of security and sophistication in the new system is necessary before the assimilated adult can go to the old family and neighborhood and dedicate his assimilative experience to group integration. For this reason, some of the newly assimilated persons are systemic linkages only in the weakest sense in that they attempt to sever the link with the old system rather than strengthen it.

Since World War II there has been a trend toward more systemic linkage between ethnic and racial minority groups and the majority group in America, as well as between the social classes. As the Gesellschaft-secular trend continues with its emphasis on universalism, achievement, and social accessibility, both the quantity and quality of the interaction between these groups is increasing. The rate of cultural and social assimilation of many ethnic and racial groups into the mainstream of American society has speeded up rather dramatically. This would be true of Italian-Americans, Polish-Americans, and other "New Immigration" peoples of southern and central European origin, and of blacks and Mexican-Americans in certain respects in the 1960's and early 1970's. Urbanization, mobility, increased education, internationalism, and increased knowledge of cultural differences, etc., are yielding greater tolerance of ethnic and racial differences, with more appreciation of the values of human and cultural variety which make for a richer and fuller society. It is not certain, of course, how far such "cultural pluralism" will go in America. True cultural pluralism should stimulate more linkages between the various racial and ethnic groups, while still enabling them to maintain their separate identities.

Among black and Chicano minorities, the past decade or so has seen the emergence of a number of separatists movements and organizations, such as the Black Muslims. Such could be construed as movements to reduce integration and systemic linkage. The question always arises as to how representative such groups are of the whole racial or ethnic group. It is likely that the great majority of blacks probably agree with Representative John Conyers of Michigan, who said, "All we (blacks) want is for America to be what it says it is."[52] The goal is to share equally with whites the good things America advertises that it has — freedom, equality of opportunity, respect for the individual, and impartial justice.

In his article, "Toward Pluralism",[53] James Farmer presented this view: "Blacks are coming to terms with their collective self and celebrating ethnic being. Despite rhetorical excesses, the current black self-pride can be as creative and positive as the past self-hate was destructive. It becomes creative when it is seen not as 'separatism' . . . , but as a necessary phase through which black Americans must go to achieve full equality in a pluralistic culture." Perhaps more and more Americans, black as well as white, will come to define black power as a recognition of the need for pluralism as well as for integration. This would enable blacks to see themselves, and to be seen by others, "as a sub-society that is a part of a unified, yet diverse America — with freedom to remain within their group for primary relationships and to cross its borders equally freely if they wish to do so."[54]

Institutionalization. Members of ethnic, class and racial systems by and large know how to predict the behavior of their associates. The fact that relationships fall into patterns which meet expectations is proof that institutionalization exists. Nonetheless, the preceding pages of this chapter have demonstrated that many norms governing interracial interaction are unstandardized, that ethnic assimilation is uneven, and that the class structure is marked by a constant ebb and flow. To the extent that responses to situations are uncertain, unpredictable and unstandardized, norms governing interaction can be said to be uninstitutionalized.

It is unnecessary here to repeat all the phenomena which show the presence or absence of institutionalization of interaction within and between the ethnic, racial and class systems. Here the student's attention will be directed to the *nature of the change* taking place among institutions of the relevant systems in the South particularly but also in the North. The whole assortment of norms characteristic of the *Gemeinschaft* are those which have governed inter-system relationships generally. Those characteristics of the *Gesellschaft* are being substituted. The profiles in Figure 5 illustrate comparative regional institutionalization patterns. Before complete institutionalization could be said to exist the profiles would have to be identical in shape and similarly located on the Gemeinschaft-Gesellschaft continuum. The gradual institutionalization of rational legalistic norms has the effect of making violations of the American creed of equalitarianism very conspicuous. Many societal changes like industrialization, urbanization, and mobility are converging to bring about an increasingly Gesellschaft-like society in which it is easier at least in some aspects of life for even the most traditional southerner to conform to the Gesellschaft-like norms.

Thus the black spouse married to the white spouse is expected to interact in both North and South in accordance with Gemeinschaft-like norms. The black domestic servant interacts with her white

Figure 5

Stylized Profiles Describing Differences in the Institutionalization
Of Norms for Status-Roles for Negro Incumbents in
Interacting With White Incumbents In The
North and South of the United States

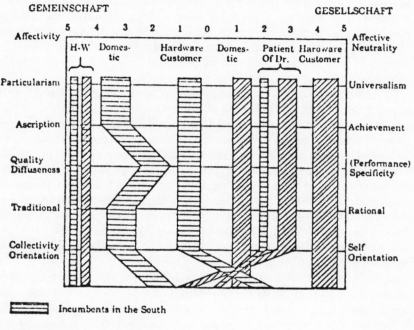

Incumbents in the South

Incumbents in the North

As the American creed of equality and norms which reward in terms of achievement become institutionalized, incumbents of status-roles develop expectancy patterns which are more characteristic of the North than the South of the United States. To illustrate this process of institutionalization the above hypothetical profiles are drawn. The zero point represents a neutral position between the polar types, Gemeinschaft and Gesellschaft and their sub-types, the extremes in both directions being at point 5.

mistress in the South in a more Gemeinschaft-like manner than would be the case in the North. The black customer in a hardware store is expected to interact in terms of Gesellschaft-like norms in the North. In the South this interaction is governed more by Gemeinschaft norms. Professionalized services differ less than nonprofessionalized services in these respects in North and South and the more personal the service offered through non-professionalized status-roles, the greater the difference in North and South. Even the physician in the South may find it more difficult to follow Gesellschaft-like norms in dealing with blacks as patients than a colleague in the North.

As discussed above under Systemic Linkage, the Gesellschaft-secular trend brings increases in contacts, communication, and interaction between minority and majority group members and between members of the different social classes. These contacts generally lead to more mutual understandings and reductions in ethnocentrism. This in turn helps undermine the older stereotypes and sentiments of race and class prejudice, and challenges the related norms of discrimination. Thus the "vicious circle" is broken; empirical evidence accumulates supporting a view of the essentially equal potential of peoples regardless of race, ethnicity, or class. All of which contributes to the institutionalization of the equalitarian beliefs, sentiments, and norms of the American Creed.

Territorality: A condition of social action. As a general rule, whenever social systems composed of color castes exist in the same geographic area, space comes to have symbolic and sacred significance. For some situations one caste may be excluded from a given area. If two castes are allowed to be in a given area at the same time elaborate ritual may be required as, for example, separate doors, separate seating arrangements, correct and differential address and the like. In the United States the most elaborate ritual handling interaction between castes existed earlier in the "deep" or "plantation" South which is an area of significance territorially because it was the core area of slave-master relations between black and white. Even within this core area places comparatively short distances apart have different subtleties of propriety concerning white-Negro relations. Outside of the deep South different norms have attended the relationship between the two races. Despite the wide-spread variations which were territorially marked, there have been widely used devices to handle the territorial aspects of class, caste, ethnic and racial social systems. Among the most common:

1. Gerrymandering of school districts, more common in the North than in the South, is sometimes a device for drawing school

district lines so that black children and lower class white children live outside of preferred white districts. This is more difficult in the South because of the more scattered pattern of black habitation.

2. Zoning and plotting of residential districts is used to prevent Negroes, Jews, Orientals, and other minority ethnic or racial groups from living any place where they can afford to live. The same codes, by setting minimum prices on structures in various sub-divisions, effectively segregate by class.

3. Nationality neighborhoods were important sanctuaries for the immigrants or migrants arriving in great numbers. Since the residents of "little Africa," "Mexican town," "China town," and others often had cultural and language differences, they were thought of as un-American and subjected to discrimination. If the tight little neighborhoods persisted, defense mechanisms often were created which further delayed acculturation.

4. The opposite situation in which a kind of forced interaction between different ethnic or racial group is fostered, usually follows a progression of events: people who are thrown together must interact; increased interaction produces increased understanding; increased understanding often produces decreased hostility. Examples of these situations lie in the desegregated army units and in inter-racial housing projects. Stouffer reports that although two-thirds of the men in the platoons were opposed to having black soldiers intermixed with the white units, after desegregated platoons had been tried only 7 percent said that they disliked having mixed companies.[55] Integrated interracial housing projects in comparison with segregated bi-racial projects were characterized by an increase in friendly, neighborly contacts, a more closely knit project community, more favorable attitudes toward blacks in general on the part of the whites in the project, and heightened acceptance of interracial residence.[56] Although there are certain to be exceptions it appears that when members of different ethnic and racial groups are of the same class, the territorial situation of being brought together tends to decrease adverse attitudes and prejudices. Particularly is this true if the two groups share similar life styles including basic beliefs, sentiments, norms and ends.

The 1970's find most American cities and towns still roughly divided along racial and ethnic lines as well as along class lines. But with the equalitarian trends and increases in upward social mobility — and especially following the desegregation legislation of the 1960's — territorial boundaries between the various racial, ethnic and class groups are becoming less apparent. There are

numerous cases of previously all-white working, middle or upper
class residential areas being gradually invaded and often succeeded by blacks or other minority peoples in cities such as Chicago, Washington, or Houston. At times most or all the whites
may move elsewhere, leaving the area to the "invaders." However, more mixed neighborhoods are to be found now also. As
noted above, the trend toward attitudes of acceptance of blacks
and other minorities, plus the greater understanding engendered
by more contacts between the groups, has meant less unwillingness on the part of more whites to live in the same residential
area with minority group people.

SHOPPING TRIP

It all started with the unintentional mistake the cashier in
the shoe store made. The shoes cost $7.00 and we gave the clerk
our only money, a twenty dollar bill. When only $3.00 change
came back the clerk said she did not have anything to do with
that; we'd have to see the cashier. The cashier said we would have
to wait till the end of the day when the receipts would be checked
against the sales slips. She thought we would go away, but we
needed that money for our groceries so we had to sit there and
wait. When she wasn't going to get rid of us very easily she
finally did some figuring from the little pack of sales slips she had
and counted the money and found that she had short-changed us
by ten dollars. She had also wasted three hours of our afternoon
and the children were home alone doing goodness knows what.
We found that it had been raining hard and as we sidled along
the car bumpers toward our car a woman who must have hated
"colored" drove full speed right through a big mud-hole. We were
dressed in our good clothes and now we were plastered in mud.
Myrtle wanted to get the mud mopped off her good suit before it
caked on, and I knew I had better tend to mine too. The nearest
store at the shopping center had a public rest-room, but the floor
manager stopped us and told us to go to the community rest-
rooms in the middle of the center. We were so discouraged by the
time we finished washing up that Myrtle said we ought to go
home but we *had* to buy a few groceries. I raced up just as the
super-market was closing. The young fellow said "Sorry it's quit-
ting time." I don't know what happened to me, because it wasn't
his fault, but I hauled back and pasted him one. I don't know
exactly how Myrtle got home. I landed in jail and most of our
money went to pay a fine. Sometimes I try to pretend it's not true,
but right now I know it as a fact: They hate us. They just plain
hate us. And by God, I'm going to hate them back.

CAMPAIGN WIFE

I haven't seen you, have I, since Blake was appointed to Congress? But of course you have read about it what with all the fanfare made over his being the first Negro from this district ever to be a Congressman. Well, now the unexpired term which the governor filled by appointing Blake is just about over and he's running for re-election. I thought that I was in-the-know politically but I'm finding how wrong I was. His legal training, his knowledge of this district, his extensive experience on important boards, seem to have so very little to do with his chances of getting elected.

It seems much more important to find a Polish candidate whose name can be linked with Blake's so that their campaigns can be conducted together. Yes, I didn't know it either, but in this district it seems that the Negroes and the Poles are the low men on the totem pole. They are competitors for places to live, for jobs and for the scraps of political patronage which might come their way. If Blake's name were not associated with a good Polish name every Pole in the district would vote against him as a Negro. From the Pole's point of view, if their candidate were not linked with a Negro, every Negro in the district would vote against the Pole. In this district they practically have to pair a Negro and a Pole together so that both groups won't cut their collective throats. And it's all figured out where his support has to come from. He has to get up at 4:00 every morning to be on the spot to shake hands with the garbage collectors, the foundry workers, the street repair gangs and the construction "stiffs." There'll be a number of liberals who will vote for him because he is a Negro and a group of the prejudiced who will vote against him for the same reason. No one that I know of will cast their vote one way or the other because of whether he has what it takes to be a good congressman.

Blake and Joe — that's his running mate — can't possibly make all the meetings they're supposed to appear at so Joe's wife, Mary Jowikowski, and I attend a good many luncheons and other meetings as sort of proxies. I've had a bigger social whirl among "my people" — so called — than any Negro woman in this district and it really has been from rags to riches, from imitation rabbit to mink. I drew the line at Little Father Celestial Goodness, and told Blake that even if he lost the election I absolutely could not go out and socialize in that colony of crack-pots.

Our biggest strain came from Blake's family itself. Have I ever told you about Madame Marvel's Mud-Pack Skin Bleach? Well, it *is* sort of a family skeleton. But in the old days when Blake's father, in spite of his excellent experience and education, failed to get promotions in the branch of Civil Service work he was in, he occasionally turned to the home manufacture and packaging of this bleach. Sev-

eral times Madame Marvel's mud-pack has recouped the family fortunes. But he always is low on funds when he turns to it and usually
has to start out on borrowed capital. So right after the campaign was
off to a good start he blew in for a two week stay with the idea of
borrowing money from families he knew (and who knew Blake of
course) to start the Mud-Pack business again. Blake was so busy with
campaigning that he scarcely knew his father was in town. He would
just fall into bed for a few hours sleep and be off and away again before
any of us were up. There was once a period of ten days when Delores
did not even see her daddy and became quite concerned about
whether he lived here any more. But I *knew* as I saw the old man
operate that Blake's campaign would be a failure and even his future
practice as a lawyer would be hurt if any of the big-city newspapers
got hold of a banner head-line "Congressman's Father Solicits Local
Funds" followed by a story about Madame Marvel's Mud-Pack Skin
Bleach putting him through law school. Blake finally had to call his
brother Ned and have him come from Philadelphia to talk to the old
man. He told him that Blake's appointment was a great honor to the
family as well as to the race, and that the father's activities during
the campaign were about to bring ruin to everyone.

His father could not see that his manufacture of Madame Marvel
was any different than that of any of the great cosmetics houses which
advertise "hormone creams" "skin food" and so on, and of course it
isn't in principle. But I think that an educated man with a mind like a
steel trap who has become bitter and disillusioned is pretty hard to
handle. At least he has withdrawn for the duration of the campaign,
and I hope that he never makes the stuff again, or if he does, that he
raises the money elsewhere. The trouble is, Blake is so conspicuous
now that whatever his family does is bound to be reported in the
Negro Press, and the big-city presses will pick things up too.

I so want to move. Both Blake and I had experiences from our
earliest years in associating with mixed groups — both white and
colored, I mean. Delores' school has no white children in it, and she is
in for a terrific shock one of these days when she discovers that she is
not nearly as big a cock of the walk as she thinks she is. Right now is
the time when she should be learning the give and take that she can
only get in a mixed school situation. But Blake is afraid that if he is
successful in the election and then moves a rumor will get going
among the Negroes that his success went to his head and that he
didn't want to live among all colored any more. That would be political suicide for him, he says. The present situation in a northern city
like this will be social suicide for our little girl. It's a funny thing that
beyond a certain point, each successful advance that Blake has made

has not reduced the racial pressures but really has doubled them. We now have to think of behavior — really conspicuous behavior — in both groups, both white and colored, and it isn't very often easy.

NOTES

1. John Useem and Ruth Hill Useem, *The Western-Educated Man in India* (New York: The Dryden Press, 1955), pp. 88-89.

2. "Ethno-racial systems" are characterized by a distinctive cultural tradition or by biological distinctness or by both. The Amish, for example, would qualify as an ethnic group according to the following definition: "An ethnic group is normally endogamous and recruitment is by birth, though of course, assimilation by intermarriage or even other mechanisms is in a certain proportion of cases possible. The biological distinctness of an ethnic group will presumably only be significant to the social structure if the group is characterized by a distinctive social status in the larger social system, a status which is very often at least marked and symbolized by a distinctive cultural tradition." Talcott Parsons, *The Social System* (Glencoe, Illinois: The Free Press, c1951) p. 172. Parsons further elaborates that the Jew is distinguished by a distinctive cultural tradition, whereas the color of the Negro renders him visibly different in the total society and in a sense takes the place of a distinctive culture.

3. Talcott Parsons, "A Revised Analytical Approach to the Theory of Social Stratification", in Reinhard Bendix and Seymour M. Lipset, eds. *Class, Status and Power* (Glencoe, Ill.: The Free Press, 1953), p. 118.

4. Originally developed by Lloyd Warner and Leo Srole, *The Social Systems of American Ethnic Groups: TheYankee City Series*, Vol. 3 (New Haven, Connecticut: Yale University Press, 1945), Chap. 10. The form of the Table as given here is taken from the adaptation made by Leonard Broom and Philip Selznick, *Sociology* (Evanston, Ill.: Row, Peterson and Company, 1955), pp. 460 ff.

5. Albert N. Vota. "The Hillbillies Invade Chicago", in *Harper's Magazine*, 216, (Feb. 1958), p. 64.

6. Lovell Thompson, "Spirit of Our Times", *Harper's Magazine*, (Sept. 1957), p. 64.

7. Arnold Rose, *The Negro in America: The Classic Condensation of Gunnar Myrdal's The American Dilemma* (Boston: Beacon Press, 1948), p. 312.

8. W.B. Brookover and J.B. Holland, "Minority Group Attitude Expressions", *American Sociological Review*, 17, (April, 1952), p. 196.

9. Walter Lippman, *Public Opinion* (The Macmillan Co., New York, 1932).

10. Robert Merton, "Discrimination and the American Creed", in R.M. MacIver, ed. *Discrimination and National Welfare* (New York: Harper and Row, Inc., 1949), pp. 99-126.

11. Dorothy Parker, "Arrangement in Black and White", *Short Stories from the New Yorker* (New York: Simon and Schuster, 1940), pp. 99-103.

12. Herman Wouk, *The Caine Mutiny* (Garden City, N.Y.: Doubleday & Co., 1951), p. 15.

13. *Civil Liberties* — Monthly Publication of the American Civil Liberties Union, No. 155, October 1957.

14. Robert E. Park, "The Bases of Race Prejudice", *Annals of the American Academy of Political and Social Science*, 140, (Nov. 1928), pp. 12 and 13.

15. Adapted from Arnold Rose, op. cit., p. 24.

16. Arnold Rose, op. cit., p. 216.

17. Ibid, p. 320.

18. Herbert Blumer, "Social Science and the Desegregation Process", *The Annals of the American Academy of Political and Social Science*, 304, (Mar. 1956), p. 320.

19. Dorothy Swaine Thomas and Richard S. Nichimoto, *The Spoilage* (Berkeley: University of California Press, 1946), p. 19. After Arnold Green, *Sociology* (New York: McGraw-Hill, 1952), p. 329.

20. Charles P. Loomis, "El Cerrito, New Mexico — A Village Undergoing Accelerated Change at Mid-Century", *New Mexico Quarterly Review*, 33, (Jan. 1958), and Charles P. Loomis and J. Allan Beegle, *Rural Social Systems*, (New York: Prentice-Hall, 1950), p. 313.

21. M. L. DeFleur, et al, *Sociology: Man in Society* (Glenview, Ill.: Scott Foresman and Co., 1971), p. 325.

22. Arnold Green, op. cit., p. 316.

23. Ronald Freedman, et al. *Principles of Sociology: A Text with Readings* (New York: Henry Holt, 1956), p. 543.

24. Such status-roles find their support in various Biblical quotations. "The last shall be first, and the first shall be last" and "the meek shall inherit the earth", were often used by black ministers. Hortense Powdermaker, "The Channeling of Negro Aggression by the Cultural Process", in Clyde Kluchohn and Henry A. Murray, eds., *Personality in Nature, Society, and Culture* (New York: Alfred A. Knopf, 1949), p. 479.

25. Paraphrased from Leonard Broom and Philip Selznick, op. cit., p. 501.

26. Arnold Rose, op. cit., pp. 82-113.

27. Lloyd H. Bailer, "Organized Labor and Racial Minorities", in *Annals of the American Academy of Political and Social Science*, 273, (Mar. 1951), p. 101.

28. Felix Frankfurter, "Faith in a Free Society" as cited by Charles P. Curtis and Ferris Greenslet, eds., *The Practical Cogitator* (Boston: Houghton Mifflin Co., 1945), p. 301.

29. Hylan Lewis and Mozell Hill, "Desegregation, Integration, and the Negro Community", in *Annals of the American Academy of Political and Social Science*, 304, (March 1956), p. 122.

30. Jessie Bernard, *Social Problems at Mid-Century* (New York: Dryden Press, 1957), p. 555.

31. Genevieve Knupfer, "Portrait of the Underdog", in Reinhard Bendix and Seymour M. Lipset, op. cit., p. 257.

32. Talcott Parsons, "A Revised Analytical Approach to the Theory of Social Stratification", op. cit., p. 122.

33. Among the many good books on the subject the reader's attention is directed to Reinhard Bendix and Seymour M. Lipset, op. cit. for some five dozen selected articles on the topic. Older studies famous in this field are Talcott Parsons, "An Analytical Approach to the Theory of Social Stratification", *American Journal of Sociology*, 45, (May 1940); Pitirim Sorokin, *Social Mobility* (New York: Harper & Brothers, 1927); W. Lloyd Warner, "American Caste and Class", *American Journal of Sociology*, 42, (Sept. 1936).

34. Joseph Greenblum and Leonard Pearlin, "Vertical Mobility and Prejudice; A Socio-Psychological Analysis", in Reinhard Bendix and Seymour M. Lipset, op. cit., p. 480.

35. W. Lloyd Warner, "American Caste and Class", *American Journal of Sociology*, 42, (Sept. 1936), pp. 234-237.

36. David Riesman, "Who Has The Power?", in Reinhard Bendix and Seymour M. Lipset, op. cit., pp. 153-4.

37. Arnold Rose, op. cit., pp. 231-255.

38. DeFleur, et al., op. cit., 1971: p. 324.

39. Walter White, *Rope and Faggot* (New York: Alfred A. Knopf, 1929), p. 11; as cited in Arnold Rose, op. cit., p. 186.

40. Arnold Rose, op. cit., p. 187.

41. W. Lloyd Warner, Robert J. Havinghurst, and Martin B. Loeb, *Who Shall Be Educated* (New York: Harper and Brothers, 1944).

42. Arnold Rose, op. cit., p. 312.

43. Leonard Broom and Eshref Shevky. "Mexicans in the United States, A Problem in Social Differentiation", *Sociology and Social Research*, 36, (Jan.-Feb. 1952), pp. 150-8.

44. Moynihan, Daniel P., "The Negro Family: The Case For National Action." U.S. Department of Labor. Washington D.C.: Government Printing Office, (March, 1965).

45. Leonard Schatzman and Anselm Strauss, "Social Class and Modes of Communication", in *The American Journal of Sociology*, 60, (Jan. 1955), pp. 329-338. Genevieve Knupfer's article "Portrait of the Underdog", op. cit., further tends to confirm that lower class respondents attach meanings, particularly meanings of validity, to "messages" different from those perceived by middle class respondents.

46. A. N. Whitehead, op. cit.

47. Herbert Blumer, op. cit., p. 137.

48. Ibid, p. 138.

49. Ibid.

50. Tumin, Melvin, *Social Stratification* (Englewood Cliffs, N.J.: Prentice-Hall, Inc., 1967), Ch. 12.

51. Nathan L. Whetten and Arnold W. Green, *Ethnic Group Relations in A Rural Area* (Storrs, Connecticut, Ag. Exp. Sta. Bull. No. 244, (1943), p. 27.

52. M.H. Biesanz, and J. Biesanz, *Introduction to Sociology* (Englewood Cliffs, N.J.: Prentice-Hall, Inc., 1973), p. 307.

53. Farmer, James, "Toward Pluralism," *The Humanist*, (Nov.-Dec., 1971), p. 21.

54. M.H. Biesanz, and J. Biesanz, op. cit., p. 312. Also see Paul Bohannan, "Our Two-Story Culture", *Saturday Review of Literature*, (September 2, 1972), p. 56.

55. Samuel A. Stouffer, "A Study of Attitudes", *The Scientific American*, 180, (1949), pp. 11-15.

56. Morton Deutsch and Mary Evans Collins, "Interracial Housing", in William Petersen, ed., *American Social Patterns* (Garden City, New York: Doubleday Anchor Books, 1950), pp. 51-52.

Chapter 4

Governmental and Political Social Systems*

INTRODUCTION

Mankind has long dreamed of a world in which no man would be controlled by another, but those who yearn for completely uncontrolled individual liberty must find the historical record disappointing. "All evidence indicates that as long as man has been man, he has known authority in some form."[1] Governmental social systems exhibit many forms. Despite its variety the purpose of government is basically the same: to establish authority in such a way that man can best reap the benefits of association and be protected from its dangers.[2] Governmental forms have been classified in many different ways.[3] The best known, perhaps, is the classification which uses as criteria the number of people in whom power resides. Under this system of classification, monarchy, oligarchy, and democracy are the classical types, representing respectively government by one, government by a few, and government by many. In the analysis to follow, distinctions will most often be made on the basis of this classification, specifically between a democracy and an oligarchy. Other classificatory forms which will be mentioned are those which provide the forms of integration of political activity. The United States as a two-party state might be contrasted with the Soviet Union as a one-party state, or with France as a multi-party state under this classification. Other classifications, as by degree of centralization, or by theory of elite rule, are relatively less important for the forthcoming discussion.

It is true that were this to be a thorough-going discussion of governmental systems the governments of those people, for the

---

*By Charles P. Loomis and Everett D. Dyer

most part primitive, which have vested authority in the heads of families would have to be considered. Beals and Hoijer have depicted such peoples and have shown the anthropological speculations which surround the sequences by which a government moves from a family or tribal stage to that of a conquest state.[4] More recently, Lenski has traced the evolution of institutionalized power and governmental systems in whole societies.[5] Small hunting and gathering societies were generally extremely primitive politically. There was very limited development of specialized political or governmental roles, with minimal power vested in such roles. Often a single head man provided limited leadership for the group, and he was able to hold his position often only so long as the people were satisfied with him.[6] In simple horticultural societies the power of political leaders was quite restricted also. Local villages were largely autonomous, and the village head man or tribal chieftan depended more on persuasion than on coercion to get things done, and to stay in power. In agrarian societies, the shift from horticvlture to general agriculture brought increases in technological and economic development, which led to population growth, social stratification, and the rise of definite ruling classes who often turned from a preoccupation with "the conquest of nature to the conquest of man."[7] The exercise of power and the manipulation of people became absorbing interests of the governing classes desirous of increasing wealth and power. (Examples would be ancient Egypt and Mesopotamia.) Government was autocratic, with power residing in a central ruler supported by a privileged elite. (Further discussion of power and its forms appears below under Controlling.)

Democratic nations have arisen largely from agrarian societies that were originally monarchical. The type of democracy existing in most industrial societies today was unknown prior to the Industrial Revolution. In fact, industrialization has generally been accompanied by the rise of democratic politics and government.[8] Democratic political and governmental systems have not been universal in industrial societies, however. Dictatorships, Communistic or Fascistic, have arisen in some of these societies in the twentieth century, and still exist in modified form in Eastern Europe, Spain, and Argentina. Some other industrial nations such as Britain, Japan, and the Scandinavian countries still retain certain monarchical trappings, but real political power lies in the hands of democratically elected officials. While the level of democratic participation may still be low in countries like Poland and Czechoslovakia, it is important to note the trend toward democratic institutions. It should be understood that democracy, or rule by all the people, is always a matter of degree. No large society has ever achieved pure democracy, and even the most democratic of nations achieves no more than a representative democracy. Once this point is recognized, it is easier to distinguish the varying degrees of democracy existing in different nations, and at different historical periods for a given nation.[9]

Although it is true that a large portion of humanity has lived without the benefit of large-scale political operations, it is equally true now and for the forseeable future, that most of mankind must live under the control of governments which are increasingly complex and functionally interrelated. The ever accelerated rate of the development of technology and the increasing size of most social systems including governmental bureaucracies are important and related events in modern existence. Indeed, as has been pointed out, each new invention may change the form and size of political bodies. States suitable for bow and arrow weapons and messenger communications may not be compatible with intercontinental missiles and television.[10]

Despite the comprehensiveness of a government as a social system, it is not synonymous with society. Even in a totalitarian state like Russia, the state has not been able, try as it might, to usurp the functions and all the power of the other social systems. In fact the family, cliques and friendship groups worry the politicians and administrators in all walks of life. "The state then is an essential part, but never the whole, of the social structure."[11] In the following analysis of governmental social systems the government of the United States of America will constitute the core of the system to be examined, with emphasis on the present and immediate past of that governmental social system. Contrasts will be provided by examples from other governmental social systems and by the case which will appear at the end of the chapter. And as becomes a textbook in sociology, the political and governmental events or conditions, though important, are basically background material against which to view the elements and the processes of the governmental social system — one of the most pervasive of the social systems which mark man's interaction with man.

ELEMENTS AND PROCESSES OF GOVERNMENTAL AND POLITICAL SOCIAL SYSTEMS

KNOWING

Beliefs.   Membership in governmental social systems is exhaustively inclusive and therefore much more likely to be varied. Beliefs to be held as true in a great modern state must of necessity be broad and general. They must be subscribed to quite generally throughout the land; if they are not, the government must change or perish.

> The Great Community ... the community which embraces all other communities, is the political community. Holding it together are systems of beliefs, flexible bands weaving through and around each member of the community. The basic denominator of citizens is these belief-systems which express their ideas concerning their relationship to one another and to their rulers. Without them, without this fundament of commonness, no political community can be said to exist.[12]

The United States possesses "this fundament of commonness." Nonetheless there are paradoxical beliefs concerning government which spring in part from the nature of government itself and in part from the diversity of regions, peoples, backgrounds and social classes. Almost all social systems, for example, may be said to be concerned with the dilemma of maintaining rights for the individual and at the same time governing wisely for the common good. Since government is so uniquely a matter of allocating rights and powers the dilemma is of large proportions here.

So many of our American beliefs and values are relevant to our political and governmental systems that it would be very difficult to enumerate them all. Americans believe in freedom, justice, morality, and happiness, and tend to see progress in America in such terms. Lenski notes that the further a society advances technologically the greater the number of people who care about such things, and the more pressure the people put on their political and governmental systems to protect and foster these beliefs.[13]

Lipset says that Americans believe strongly in equalitarianism, individual achievement, and universalism, in contrast to elitism, ascription, and particularism traditionally found in Great Britain.[14] Such beliefs affect the political processes and operations of government. For example, while civil liberties may be stronger in some ways in elitist democracies such as England, equalitarian democracies such as the U.S.A. may be more "democratic" in that the whole electorate has more access to or power over those who actually run the government.[15]

We may attempt to identify some of the main traditional beliefs directly related to our American political and governmental systems. Both inclusions and exclusions may be open to question, of course. But the reader will probably detect that the list includes what a great many Americans believe, or think they believe, or say they believe, presently as well as in the past.[16]

1. The equality of man. The Constitution, the Declaration of Independence, and the Supreme Court reiterate this belief. Conflict

between this and the opposing belief that only *some* men are equal constitutes what Myrdal has called the great American dilemma.

2. The perfectibility of man. Actually, the belief stops short of thinking that mankind can be perfect. But there is an insistent belief that most social problems could be improved by a more broadly educated populace, that each generation tries to set its goals of life a little higher than its predecessor, that it is the duty of mankind to keep on trying to make the world in which we live a better place to be.

3. The controlability of the universe. Americans appoint committees and pass laws because they tend to think that a rational system of cause and effect underlies flood, disease, exhaustion of resources, and so forth, and that they can do something about it.

4. The rightness of free enterprise for individuals and groups of individuals smaller than the state. Conversely, Americans also believe in the cause of general welfare as propounded in the Constitution.

5. The institution of private property. The Constitution is as concerned with private property rights as it is with the protection of life itself.

6. The axiom "That government is best which governs least." This belief is obviously related to the belief in the individualism of free enterprise cited in numeral 4 above. Conversely, Americans also believe that in time of crises "the government should do something," or "there ought to be a law." This latter belief is related to the controlability of the universe cited in numeral three above.

7. Control by influence and persuasion rather than by coercive force and physical power.

These, then are among the chief traditional American beliefs. Since most of the readers of this text are likely to be American it may very well occur to many that there is surely nothing remarkable about this belief system. What other way is there to believe? The following enumeration of Russian beliefs should dispel the notion that there is anything inevitable or "natural" about the beliefs which happen to predominate in the United States.[17]

1. Class struggle is inevitable, and will characterize every stage of technological development until the proletariat, by force of their greater numbers and the rightness of their position will be victoriously in control of the means of production.

2. That the proletariat are already in control in Russia which thus has a classless society; that upon the achievement of a classless society there is no more need for the state which in class societies must arbitrate power between classes, and that the end of the state comes about by a withering away process.

3. The achievement of a classless society for every nation of the world by the establishment of Communism will be accompanied by the withering away of governments and the coming into being of a true internationalism.

4. That the worth and the importance of the individual is small compared to the worth and importance of the victory of Communism. To achieve this it is quite proper that power be concentrated in the hands of those few who have demonstrated the greatest loyalty and proficiency in serving the Communist cause.

Besides these beliefs central to Communism, Soviet Russia shares with a democracy like the United States at least three fundamental beliefs: a mechanistically conceived universe, the controlability of the universe, and man's perfectibility. It would seem that beliefs concerning the importance and worth of the individual, embraced by the United States and de-emphasized by the Russians, are central in their differences in governmental structure.[18]

Some of the above-mentioned traditional American beliefs probably never were fully believed in by certain segments of American society; and some of these beliefs are coming under increasing criticism and pressures for modification and change in recent years. Beliefs such as the equality of men, the perfectability of man, and the controlability of the universe by man, might better be viewed as ideal-beliefs that man sets up to strive toward.

Others, such as beliefs in free enterprise, private property, and business enterprise, have been held less by working and lower-class people than by middle and upper-class Americans; further, these beliefs have come under increasing criticism in recent times up and down the American class structure and across political party lines. The 1960's saw a pronounced modification of these beliefs to the effect that now the businessman should not be free to deplete our natural resources or pollute the environment at will, and that he has definite responsibilities to protect the public interest as well as to garner profits for the company stockholders.

This trend was accelerated faster in the early 1970's. Sharply increased awareness of the dangers from pollution and waste brought further modifications in beliefs regarding property rights. Realization that pure air and water are not private property, but rather public property, and that they, along with other such natural resources, are finite and becoming scarce, coalesced beliefs that such precious resources must now be placed under governmental control and planning. To still further crystalize such socialistic beliefs, the sudden recognition of the energy crisis in 1973 created an almost universal support in the U.S.A. for more governmental planning and

regulation of virtually every sector of the American economy in order
to conserve our scarce energy resources and to try to allocate fuel on a
rational and hopefully fair basis. Also, beliefs in the rightness of the
welfare state have grown stronger in recent years with the viewpoint
now that the government should be more active in helping the poor,
the racial and ethnic minorities, and the consumer, as well as continuing its protection and subsidies for business, financial, commercial, and agricultural groups.

Cognitive mapping and belief validation.   Political beliefs are
nurtured, articulated, and validated in many groups and social situations. Traditional political beliefs may be expounded, criticized, and
debated in the home, in schools, and colleges, and in church, as well as
in more specialized political and governmental groups such as court
rooms, legislative bodies, political party conventions, and during
political campaigns. Political beliefs may be validated by general
appeals to patriotism or by appeal to specific authors or articulators of
our political beliefs such as the Founding Fathers, and to the classical
statements of our political beliefs such as the Declaration of Independence, the Bill of Rights, etc. In intellectual circles political beliefs
are frequently validated in terms of Western Democratic ideologies
and Natural Rights doctrines.

In democratic nations as well as in totalitarian countries, people
are indoctrinated with the dominant political beliefs of their society
and with the view that their political beliefs and institutions are the
best anywhere.

FEELING

Sentiments.   Sentiment, always evasively difficult to isolate
and measure, is nevertheless fairly palpable on the political and
governmental scene. A news story carried the tale of a violent death
in California. The victim, a Californian, had made some remark
construed to be disrespectful of Texas, whereupon a native son of that
great state drew out his six-shooter and gave the slanderer his just
due. Many a wise man has refrained from arguing about politics or
religion, recognizing them as particularly incendiary subjects. Politicians who kiss babies, on the other hand, have learned that pleasant
and kindly sentiments may have as much effect as a sound program
in winning votes. No doubt the whole gamut of sentiments from holy
reverence to a murderous heart could be found in the political scene
For sociologists it is not the sentiments themselves, but the function
of the sentiments and what they mean that is important. Insofar as
various sentiments have function or meaning in shaping the governmental social system, or are so widespread as to create a social
phenomenon, they will be treated here.

Americans are considered to have a positive emotional response to what has been called "the old-fashioned virtues." The
sincere, the honest, especially when it appears in home-spun form
appeals; the witty, the clever, the smart technique repels. Although no one will dispute the virtue inherent in the admired
traits, the forthright expression of sentiment they evoke at the
polls does pose a danger. Every campaign in democracies is focused not only upon issues but also upon the personal image of
the leader. The danger in the sentimental reaction to the honest
virtues lies in the doctored-up parodies which are presented to the
public by public relations experts as being a true picture of the
candidate. It opens the possibilities for the villain to be portrayed
as a hero.

Though both instances immediately to be given may be "portrait images" rather than "public relations images" there can be
no doubt that Harry Truman was swept into office despite Gallup
polls and other predictions to the contrary through creating the
image of the "little but determined man" fighting the "big interests" with the "give 'm hell" challenge. The carefully cultivated
image of Eisenhower evoked the sentiments of the solid citizens
who wanted honesty and sincerity in government. If such a tendency were to become pronounced, so that the candidate's personality completely obliterated the issues, a kind of government
would prevail which would be similar to certain Latin American
governments. There the rallying point of sentiment is almost
completely the leader's personality. Just as a candidate is elected
on personal attributes, so does he conduct the government by a
consideration of personal sentiments: his family, his friends, his
supporters. Such a government of relatively unrestrained sentiment revolving around a popular leader, called a "caudillo" government in Latin America, is a very different thing than the form
to which the United States is accustomed.

There is the constellation of sentiments about honesty, red-
tape and efficiency. Americans are willing to forego some of the
comforts of the Gemeinschaft in their government for efficiency.
But the government bureau which exhibits neither Gemeinschaft
nor efficiency truly provokes the scorn of the citizenry.

Should the North American reader question what other sentiments would be appropriate or possible in relation to a governmental system, the sentiment system prevalent in Soviet Russia is suggested in the following paragraphs.

A study of the Russian Soviet system reports that even
though the people expect the government to be stern and demanding, in general they fear and do not love their leaders.[19] The Rus-

sian people are depicted as sentimentally in need of warmth and love by their superiors. Instead of providing this warmth the ruling elite has developed into an affectively neutral bureaucracy. A "new Soviet man," "puritanical" and dedicated to his status-role stands out in this description against the "warm-hearted Russian masses." In answer to the question as to whether it is better to be loved or feared Machiavelli reveals much of the nature of the status-role of the dictators, most of whom follow his advice in this respect. "It is much safer to be feared than loved, if one of the two has to be wanting."[20] But the problem faced by Russia in this respect is the problem faced by large-scale government everywhere. On the one hand bureaucratic and Gesellschaft-like efficiency is demanded by the people and required for survival and this requires dedication to specialities of government and affective neutrality. On the other hand people want officials to be responsive.

The growth of the Gesellschaft in American government is highly related to the following common expression of sentiment in government:

> There is sometimes bad blood between the 'politicians' and the 'bureaucrats.' The politicans dislike the aloof, technically competent, and sometimes condescending bureaucrats. The latter resent the hurly-burly methods and attitudes of the politicians and the pressure sometimes put on themselves to do favors for politicians' friends ... The bureaucrat criticizes the politician for his constant ear-to-the-ground attitude and his personal rather than impersonal approach to problems ... He represents the human and personal side of government ... The bureaucrat has no constituents. He is checked by rules and regulations, not by vote-getting considerations. We need both types.[21]

Lastly is the sentiment of loneliness felt increasingly as the nation becomes more bureaucratized and Gesellschaft-like: ". . . men stand today in this twilight zone of a 'society,' uneasy, distressed, feeling joined to their fellows only in war or crisis; and behind the inner doors of their mind they welcome war or crisis for the feeling of community it gives them."[22]

Tension management and communication of sentiment. Political parties seek to communicate and dramatize political sentiments among the people of a given society. Party rallies and conventions, fund-raising dinners, and political campaigns all serve as vehicles for communicating political sentiments of sincerity, honesty, dedication, and other old-fashioned virtues, which only their candidates can bring to governmental offices. Public relations experts become highly sophisticated in the art of appealing to sentiments in their efforts to sell the people on a given candidate for high office.[23]

Political leaders, especially those of "statesman" stature, often play important roles in tension management and in directing the energies created by strong political feelings into constructive channels and toward desired goal-pursuing activities. Such political leaders — "politicians" in the true sense of the word — are past masters in the arts of soothing feelings, reducing conflicts, and bringing about compromise among individuals and factions in the party or in a governmental body such as Congress. As a Senate majority leader, Lyndon B. Johnson performed legendary feats along these lines.

ACHIEVING

Ends. Many great political writers have noted that legitimized power is the single essential characteristic of all states. The function of such legitimation is *the establishment and maintenance of order* which thus can be recognized as one of the most universal of governmental ends. Once the government is established, whether by written compact as in the case of the United States, by unwritten tradition as in the case of Great Britain, or by fiat as in the case of Nazi Germany, policies emanate from the locus of power; another end of government is *to carry out these policies.*

More specific objectives emerge when a particular government is viewed. The objectives of the government of the United States of America constitute the well known preamble to the Constitution of the United States.

We The People of the United States, in Order to form a more perfect Union, establish Justice, insure domestic Tranquility, provide for the common defence, promote the general Welfare, and secure the Blessings of Liberty to ourselves and our Posterity, do ordain and establish this Constitution for the United States of America.

That an understanding of the ends of a social system are absolutely basic to an understanding of that system will continually be demonstrated throughout the chapter. Although the United States and Russia may actually share some beliefs (such as the belief in the controlability of the universe), and some sentiments (such as patriotism), the antithetic nature of the two countries is revealed nowhere better than in the statement of objectives. Compare the preamble of the Constitution of the United States with the Soviet objectives (here called morality).

... whatever furthers the cause of communism is moral ... The only scientific criterion of morality is the defense of the interests of the victory of communism ... Another writer puts the point more bluntly: "In our time only what furthers the destruction of capitalism and the victory of communism is moral."[24]

Current Soviet works in 'ethical theory' are chiefly exhortations aimed at making the Soviet citizen meet his 'moral obligations,' so defined — subordinating his individual interests to collective, socio-political interests in all cases of conflict between the two. This general obligation entails such specific obligations as 'respect for social property'; Soviet patriotism . . .; socialist internationalism . . . All of these 'principles' are variations on the central theme of the individual's absolute subordination, loyalty, and devotion to the 'collective.'[25]

Goal attaining activities. The apparatus of government is supposed to function in pursuing and achieving the general and specific political goals and ends of the given society. In complex industrialized Gesellschaft-like societies with rational legal governmental structures are found legislative bodies to enact laws, executive branches to administer the laws, and judicial bodies to adjudicate the laws. Through their operations and efforts the general political goals of the society are pursued, such as the establishment and maintenance of order, the protection of the rights and freedom of individual citizens and the establishment of justice.

Other social systems also function to assist the governmental systems in achieving political ends and goals. Familial, educational, and religious systems all help in the socialization and direction of the individual to make him into a generally responsible citizen who is willing to abide by the laws and support the

CONTROLLING AND SANCTIONING

Power, facilities, sanctions. The maintenance of law and order, that is, the routinization of power relations, is one of the ends of all governmental systems. Governmental power is obviously crucial to the attainment of these ends. "The sense of the social order as controlling the behavior of human beings . . . requires the establishment of social sanctions to secure it against the strains and pulls of contrary impulses."[26] These social sanctions institutionalized by custom and formalized by law, constitute the authoritarian aspects of power. Authority, the student will remember, may be defined as the right as determined by the system, to control the actions of others. The authoritative aspect of governmental power, then, consists of rights meted out by law to a select number of governmental sub-systems and vested in various status-roles of those sub-systems. Influence, or a non-authoritative control over others, also exists in the governmental system as a part of the power component as it does in other social systems. When these terms are used in connection with a governmental system there may be connotations which obstruct the true meaning. Lest power mean domination, authority officiousness, and influence control of a clandestine sort, let it be remembered that both authority and influence are as often used to defend the citizen's rights as they are to apply negative sanctions on the deviant citizen, and that power, besides signifying the mailed fist also signifies rapid postal service, good highways, pure food and drugs, reasonably safe banking and other such "peaceful" services.

Let us look briefly at views on the nature of power in human societies. There are two quite varying views prevalent, and each view relates to a different view of the nature of man and of society. The two views have frequently been identified as first, a conservative view, and second, a radical view of society and the state.[27] Those holding the first view have generally been distrustful of man's nature, seeing man as naturally weak and inclined toward evil, and thus in need of social controls and restraints, including government and laws. Those holding the radical view tend to see man's nature as essentially good, thus in need of much less social and legal restraint. Men of this persuasion tend to view society and its institutions as being overly restraining, corrupting, and the sources of evil.[28] Conservatives have generally viewed society as a social system with needs which must be met for the survival of society and its members. On the other hand, radicals see society as the setting within which various struggles and conflicts take place. Its institutions influence the outcome of the struggles between various contending groups. Radicals see coercion as the chief factor undergirding social institutions (such as private property), and in the rise of economic and social inequalities. Conservatives disagree, saying that consensus is far more important than coercion in the functioning of social institutions and the related development of inequalities.[29]

Radicals and Conservatives are also in major disagreement regarding the nature of law and the state. The former argue that the state with its laws and agencies of government are instruments of oppression used by the ruling classes for their benefit and ascendency; Conservatives see the state and its legal and governmental institutions as essentially organs of the whole society, functioning basically to promote the common good.[30]

Those holding the radical view are attracted by the "Zero-Sum" concept of power. Power is here defined as the capacity of one unit in the system to gain its ends over the opposition of other units.[31] The Zero-Sum concept is that a finite amount of power exists in a society or social system. Therefore, "a gain in power by unit A . . . is the cause of a corresponding loss of power by units B, C, D."[32] Non-radicals, such as Parsons, argue against this Zero-Sum idea, contending that there may be net additions or subtractions to the total amount of power in a system at various times. Parsons defines power as "the generalized capacity of a social system to get things done in the interest of collective goals."[33] Thus power is a generalized category of means in a society, applied toward the achievement of collective goals, in order that these goals can be achieved in a balanced and integrated manner in the best interests of society. Power in a society must be allocated to the different sub-systems proportionate to the differentiated needs of the products of the sub-systems. The network of collectivities called government is the primary, but not the only, instrumentality responsible for the allocating of power.[34]

In order to examine power, this section will turn its attention to the United States government. Since no more than a suggestion can be given here of what the power consists and where that power lies, power will be treated from the point of view of the chief executive, the President of the United States. This one point of reference does not at all limit the discussion to the powers of the President, however. If, for example, there is a power restraint on the Presidency it follows that some other body has power to restrain that office. The line dividing authority and influence becomes very fine indeed in the governmental sphere. The President, for example, has the power to veto, obviously a power of authority since it goes with his office. The veto, as will later be shown, can be used, however, not only to represent the presidential disfavor of a particular measure, but also as a sanction which punishes Congress for not complying with the presidential wish on another matter, or as a goal to follow proposed presidential policy in the future. The veto, so used, has the impact of coercive power even though it is based on an act of authority.

1. The President as an executive. The President in his executive's role, deals with a bureaucracy which in many respects is not unlike the bureaucracies of other governments and of giant businesses. He articulates his authority as head of the bureau-

cratic structure, but must use influence not specifically built into his status-role because, although he is the head, there are concentrations of particular powers, little and big, which stud the vast network of departments, bureaus, agencies, and commissions. Consider the following aspects of his position.

The President is vested with the ultimate responsibility for the working of the bureaucracy. He has much more to do than one man could possibly do; so the President is authorized to employ people to do some of the work for him. Ideally (from the point of view of the President's retaining his power) each person hired should be in complete accord with the President and, in effect, become another pair of hands and another brain working merely to accomplish what the President himself would do if he had time to devote himself to that particular task. Anyone would know, of course, that such an ideal is impossible for the some two million workers who do some job in the executive branch of the bureaucracy. It is perfectly obvious that the people who clean the offices, run the linotypes, order the paper-clips can and do think different thoughts than the President as they go about their work and this need not result in cracks appearing in the ship of state.

The problem, then, in determining where the power lies in the executive branch, must be pursued through the echelons of those officials who are responsible for policy. Where policy is molded wholly in conformity with the President's, his power is unassailed. Where policy is molded in orbits outside the presidential orbit the presidential authority is restrained. There are a number of such echelons to examine.

A. The Cabinet. The President has the authority to make appointments to the cabinet posts. He can also ask for resignations, withhold facilities, and fail to pay attention to the recommendations of a cabinet member. And he can pursue the opposite course, all of which are sanctions which normally are regarded as devices by which an administrator can surround himself with people who hold views harmonious with his own. Yet there is evidence that

> . . . rarely in our history have the visible political executives in the federal bureaucracy been solely and continuously 'the President's men.' Even when they have started out as 'his' men, personal fealty has often been weakened or destroyed by lateral pressures from Congress, by subterranean pressures from clientele groups or from within the bureaucracy itself; by the corrosive acid of personal ambition; or by honest differences over what was best for the country or the party. And many of our political executives have not even started out as 'the President's men.'[36]

This quotation identifies some of the means by which presidential power restraints, or counter-power groups become entrenched in the bureaucracy. Immediately upon examining them, the reader is thrust into a consideration of the division of power provided for by the Constitution. For Congress, thought of chiefly as a legislative body, is given strong directives by the Constitution to keep its eye on the executive branch. Officials hired ostensibly to administer a program, for example, report spending up to half their time telling a Congressional committee about the program they are supposed to be administering.

It is clear at once that the executive in one of the bureaus must at least be as sensitive to the shifts of opinion in Congress as he is to national policy as enunciated by the President. When the President, in his turn, asks the assistance of a particular department by way of information or opinion concerning a national matter, it is hard to tell whether the advice he receives is from his own henchman or from the henchman of the Congressional Committee who has as powerful a sanction upon the official as the President himself.

Despite the tremendous powers vested in the Presidency, "power is where you find it." Political reporters of the current scene observe that roughly fifty percent of people at cabinet meetings are not heads of federal departments, that top policy determiners and coordinators are not at the departmental level, that various professionals within the career services become little clusters of power and that Congress has a constitutional and compulsive mandate to compete with the President in the field of executive management. He who is called a "strong President" has exactly the same authority potential as the "weak President." The difference lies in the influence potential, or what has been called "the art of accomodation." To the extent that the President can align for his own support those whose sanctions are attractive to the executive officials, to this extent can the President be said to have real power beyond that of an ordinary office holder.[36]

B. Another echelon to examine is the President's executive staff which has increased tremendously in size since World War II. This staff, composed of many hundreds of people, exists for no other reason than to serve the President — to provide information, to spot possible troubles, to see that he does what he must do at the appointed time and be prepared for emergencies likely to arise. Many of the tasks formerly done personally by the President are institutionalized as part of the work load of the executive staff in a way that would have seemed fantastic to an earlier era of Presidents. For example, it is the duty of some of the executive staff to be up-to-date continually on legislative proposals, and as such proposals move toward final enactment, a number of veto messages may be completely prepared, so that should the President wish to veto the bill he can make a choice of veto message depending upon the emphasis he wishes to give. The people composing the executive staff, including the hundreds in the Bureau of the Budget, constitute a layer of influence and/or authority between the President and his cabinet which many political writers believe is having the effect of greatly decreasing the effectiveness and prestige of the cabinet and its departments. The extensive powers, control of facilities and application of sanctions by the heads of President Nixon's staff, Messrs. Halderman and Erlichman, were much discussed in 1973.

The executive office, many of the bureaus and departments, and the skilled bureaucrats who man them compose some of the primary facilities of the President. "The legal resources of the office, the practices, precedent, and protocol . . . the physical plant, and finance; the place of the office in society and in the culture as a medium for confronting and responding to challenges and problems; the facilities of the office, would be comparatively useless without the staff and the bureaucratic skills shaped, in large measure, after the presidential policy."[37]

2. The President as a Legislator. Study of the play of forces between the legislature and other branches of government is one of the most fruitful in exploring and evaluating the locus of power. Consider the following conditions and their relation to power.

The President is one of the chief initiators of legislation; his annual "State of the Union" message has come to be regarded as a policy-enunciating speech which calls upon the Congress to respond in the months ahead with appropriate legislation.

In spite of vast powers, the office of the Presidency can become a mere masquerade of power if Congress chooses to make it so. It is not only that many of the powers of the President are derived from acts of Congress, and what Congress gives it may also take away. Even those Presidential powers derived directly from the Constitution depend in large measure for their effectiveness upon congressional co-operation. Without congressional approval of men and money, the President may be Commander-in-Chief, but of a phantom force. Even the President's foreign policy requires congressional support if it is to succeed . . . Thus it is literally true that, while the President proposes, Congress ultimately disposes. Hence the importance of good relations between the President and the legislature if an administration is to succeed.[38]

Most important roll calls of Congress reveal voting done by a coalition of common interests — regional, economic, attitudinal — rather than by party lines. Each Congressman is responding by his vote to quite a different set of pressures from his constituency and from fellow Congressmen than to those to which the President is reacting. Even when Congress is made up predominantly of the same party which the President heads, the President in order to win enough support for his proposals must use many devices which sometimes shade into a twilight zone between authority and influence. Among the common devices are distribution or withholding of patronage, the sanctioning use of the veto, the discretionary power to convene Congress in special sessions, and the wooing of crucial supporters from Congress. Congress is not without recourse as the quotation above from Odegard shows.

However, trends in recent years show that the President has been gaining in power, often at the expense of Congress. This is especially apparent in the areas of foreign relations and national defense. In 1973 Congress engaged in a power struggle with President Nixon. It reclaimed its constitutional power as the only branch of the government having authority to declare war.[39]

The following excerpts have been chosen to show some of the seesawing which goes on between the legislature, their constituents, and the President, as each one attempts to make the most of the power at his command; and they illustrate the utilization of facilities and the application of sanctions by the President.

The Veto.

A bill involving the Federal Trade Commission's duties which would have legalized certain price-fixing practices came to President Truman for his signature. After having the Democratic National Chairman poll the constituencies of the Truman administrative strength he vetoed the bill.

Had Truman signed the bill he would have risked alienating the very base of his political power — labor, farmers, and small business. He would thereby have repudiated his own supporters and given aid and comfort to his bitter enemies, the Dixiecrats.[40]

The Power to Convene Congress.

Lincoln set July 4, eleven weeks after the fall of Fort Sumter, as the date of the special session. Meanwhile Lincoln had a free hand and exercised half a dozen powers that the Constitution vests in Congress. Lincoln's ... delay in convening Congress underscored the extraordinary power inherent in the President's exclusive discretion as to whether or not to call special sessions ...[41] President Wilson warned his first Congress, which was planning to postpone action on the Federal Reserve banking bill to a later session, that if they adjourned without action on the bill he would promptly convene Congress in special session — a threat which produced the desired effect.[42]

Patronage.

During the 'Hundred Days' of emergency relief legislation President Franklin Roosevelt would now and then whisper to an importunate Congressman, "We haven't got to patronage yet." The result of this coyness led Pendleton Herring to the conclusion ". . . the session indicated that the consummation of a national program of legislation is greatly aided by transmitting through patronage the localism of our politics into support of the Chief Executive." Patronage is a means by which a President may, when it is available, persuade Congressmen to risk the displeasure of important constituent interests by strengthening their position among influential and 'deserving' party leaders at home.[43]

3. The President and the Judiciary. The President's great advantage in relation to the Supreme Court and to certain federal courts is the authority of appointment. The corresponding negative sanction of dismissal is denied him, however. More than any agency of government the courts are regarded as being nonpolitical, although it is not true that blind-folded Justice is so unable to see that she does not recognize the political scenery. Among the powers that the supreme court exercises which tend to modify the presidential powers are: the testing of presidential prerogative (power stemming from the constitution itself); the final enunciations of presidential and congressional power; and the subtle temperings of decisions in relation to the political climate. A noteworthy aspect of Supreme Court legal philosophy was enunciated during the Truman administration when a decision acknowledged for the first time the relativity (in contrast to the former absoluteness) of the President's power. Under the "relativity" philosophy, the power of the President depended not only upon the specific legal provisions but also upon both the seriousness of the emergency and the consent of Congress.

4. Other Presidential powers. There are a few forms or loci of power which have not been mentioned above. The President's power to use a special personal agent augments his power in emergencies. The power in the form of influence held by many groups throughout the country have been hinted at: they may greatly augment or limit the President's power. How power relates to the political parties is scarcely mentioned above, but of course, it is a force. A very real power that the President has to a greater extent than any other official is the power to get his message publicized. This may be as great as any mentioned here but its implications will be explored under the process of communication, later in the chapter, e.g., free T.V. time is a great "facility."

Scarcely a greater contrast could be found than power in the

United States and power in the Soviet Union. The detailed functioning of Soviet power cannot be given here, but the locus of power can be found without such detail. Power lies not in the governmental structure but in the Communist Party. The core of the Communist Party is the Central Committee. Under Stalin the Secretariat of the Central Committee, a post filled by Stalin, was the primary instrument of rule in the party, and thence in the government. Stalin's death posed the question of his successor. No greater evidence of his thorough-going dictatorship exists than the fact that none of the remaining members of the powerful Central Committee could marshall forces quickly enough to take over the rule of the party.

Decision-making and initiation of action. The section above devoted to power has shown sufficiently that in the United States decision-making does not reside in any one locus of power. The process has been greatly diffused even in such clear-cut presidential policy enunciations as the Budget Message and the Economic Report. There are literally thousands of decisions made in the governmental bureaucracy of the United States governmental system, as there are in other bureaucracies, which never come to the attention of top-level executives.

> Yet . . . the President's high rank does not necessarily mean that he makes more 'decisions' than other political executives below. Indeed it is arguable that in our government the higher one's rank the fewer decisions one makes . . . As you go up the ladder of authority each official is beset with more committees, more horizontal clearances, more veto groups and political personalities whose views must be reconciled or discounted before the 'final decision' is reached.[44]

Once decisions are made it is necessary to implement them, that is, to initiate action along appropriate lines. In the early 1970's the Federal Government enacted laws aimed at protecting the environment and meeting the energy crisis. These decisions were implemented in part through the establishment of agencies such as the Federal Environmental Protection Agency and the Federal Energy Administration. An example of action initiated by the F.E.P.A. would be administration of the program set up by the Clean Air Act of 1970. Under this act, the F.E.P.A. specifies the maximum emissions of impurities into the air to be allowed motor vehicles, industrial plants, etc., and imposes penalties and sanctions for violations of these standards.

On the energy front, when the Arab oil embargos brought the energy crisis to a head in late 1973, President Nixon reorganized the Federal Energy Administration under Energy Czar William Simon. Americans were asked to voluntarily use less gasoline for their cars and less fuel and electricity for their homes and businesses. Simon set up a priority plan for allocation of fuels to public, business, and private consumers. A stand-by gasoline rationing plan was announced which could be put into effect on short notice if the petroleum shortage should warrant it. And in January 1974 President Nixon signed legislation that would deny federal highway funds to states which do not lower highway speed limits to 55 miles per hour.

It has been observed that the structure of political decision-making and action in the U.S.A. demonstrates the traditional concern in American society for democratic freedom and the diffusion of power. Local government seems to be becoming more rather than less pluralistic, reflecting the growing interdependence of economic and political systems. The structure of the federal government is based on the diffusion of power, as is true of American government generally. However, a complete separation of executive, legislative, and judicial powers has never been possible in practice. As the DeFleurs and D'Antonio point out "Studies of the national power structure, like those of community power structures, disclose a pattern of multiple influences, despite some plausible attempts to show a power elite."[45]

NORMING, STANDARIZING, PATTERNING

Norms. The most tangible norms of the governmental social system are those, of course, which are incorporated into law. As MacIver has observed, the norms of the state differ from all other norms in two ways.[46] They receive the sanction of socialized and unconditional compulsion (there can be no uncertainty about whether or not one "should" conform to them) and they apply without exception to everyone within a geographic area. Some laws are expressive of norms much more basic to the conduct of life than others. Of the laws governing the United States among the most basic are these found in the Bill of Rights.

As everyone knows from his first introduction to American history, the first ten amendments to the Constitution of the United States spell out in the basic law of the land, the rights of individuals against their government. They are of tremendous importance to the United States, but are not unimportant elsewhere in the world since they specify in legal form the norms of a people for whom citizens, not the state, are in control. This circumstance makes all the more amazing the results of a study in the 1950's which reports that "less than 2 percent of a sample of school teachers in Wisconsin and of students in two great universities agreed to the provisions of the United States Bill of Rights."[47] The questions were worded in modern conversational language but revolved around the essential liberties guaranteed by the Bill of Rights. Those of liberal persuasion were more supportive of the Bill of Rights than the conservatives. The attitudes thus revealed were in response to a questionnaire, not to a crisis. But there is ample evidence to substantiate the thesis that when questions deal with an actual situation people are often willing, unknowingly, to answer "No", thereby forfeiting liberty and freedom. Voting behavior in Germany, for example, answered "No" to the same kind of question as the electorate swept into office the Nazi regime.[48] Conservative support during the McCarthy hearings in 1953 embraced the same attitudes as the Wisconsin school teachers who cast their "straw vote" against the liberties guaranteed in the Bill of Rights. Since the core of democratic government is the substance of this discussion it is worth while, in our consideration of governmental norms, to trace a course of public thinking which can lead to the trap which annihilates personal freedom.

First, war or depression or some other untoward circumstance leads to general frustration and dissatisfaction. Second, the radicals, including Communists, intent upon disruption through violence and shrewd about timing it for peak effectiveness, stir up a row and while being protected by the norms of democracy, prepare for the liquidation of those norms. Third, conservatives who correctly preceive the rabble-rousing radicals for what they are, attempt to rid society of them. The radical is safe in his legal armour of democratic liberties (the Fifth Amendment, for example) and harm cannot be done him without irreparable harm befalling the legal armour. But the radical and his shocking behavior are so much more tangible than a civil liberty that the most important thing of all seems to be his riddance and the establishment of a situation where no other scoundrel can behave similarly. So the legal armour is ripped and riddled and the scoundrel is destroyed, or at least routed. But there is no more legal armour left for the scoundrel, or for the peaceable man unjustly accused, or for the newsman who wants to print the truth as he sees it. And the conservatives who rent the armour and cut down the villain take over and establish a new government. Thus was born Nazi Germany. Since the norms having to do with individual liberty are the true cornerstone of democracy people's indifference to their preservation is a key weakness of democracy. The further entrenchment and institutionalization of these basic norms of liberty by quite deliberate design would seem to be indicated.

To treat all the normative aspects of governmental behavior is as impossible as it would be undesirable. It is hoped that the following will expose the very pith of important and recognizable norms in the governmental system.

1. In order to get anything done, compromise measures must be made. When many men must give and take to produce a result, that result is often more easily defended on grounds of its workability than

it is on grounds of consistency, or truth, or virtue. However, what is judged by those in power to be expedient must also be made to sound as though it were right too. It must be legitimized.

2. The mere fact of standing for "special interests" does not negate the interest as a public interest; only those who represent "special interests" come what may, and despite any and all other circumstances to be considered in the governmental system, are regarded as retarding the broader "public interest."

3. Cleavages are natural in public thinking about a great many governmental issues. Cleavages integrate whole groups of people around a few issues, and their integrative force is as important as their divisive force, which arrays one group against the other. Many leaderships are based upon certain alignments composed of cleavage groups. Disturbances of this alignment, i.e., conditions which would entice some of the old supporters to switch to another camp, or re-arrangements within the class structure of a society, or a crisis which posed a more compelling issue and therefore a cleavage on a subject over which the leader had no control, is alarming to leaders whose power lies in the old alignment.

4. Refusal to consider the opponent's interests and position, to deal, to compromise, is justifiable only when the most sacred morals prevent it. It is a sign of strength to "give and take," not of weakness.

Other normative areas, especially those which are less well institutionalized with the consequence that the expectancy pattern on the part of the public and on the part of the official and/or politician are poorly defined, will be treated more fully under institutionalization later in the chapter.

Norms in Soviet Russia. Perusal of the growing literature on Soviet Russia is outside the scope of this chapter. It seems fair to say, however, that the general difficulty of the western world in understanding the Russians lies in norms that are basically different. What the rules of the game are in Soviet Russia has kept everyone in the western world guessing for several decades. That they still support autocracy there seems to be little doubt, but that they also support a way of looking at things that is quite different than what the western mind is accustomed to seems to be certain too. Thus, what the western world would call autocratic appears to be somewhat democratic through a different normative point of view. This is demonstrated in the belief concerning the rightness of a one-party system. To the western world the denial of the right to disagree would mean autocracy. To the Russian world, the need to disagree and subsequent need to compromise shows class struggle and decadence. Without probing what the difference in norms is — indeed, without the wherewithal to

discover exactly what makes the difference, it is perfectly obvious
that very different norms obtain in a governmental system whose
leader was able to declare:

> We have no contending parties any more than we have a capitalist class
> contending against a working class which is exploited by capitalists.
> Our society consists exclusively of free toilers of town and country —
> workers, peasants, intellectuals. Each of these strata may have its
> special interests and express them by means of the numerous public
> organizations that exist. But since there are no classes, since the divid-
> ing lines between classes have been obliterated, since only a slight but
> not a fundamental difference between various strata in socialist society
> has remained, there can be no soil for the creation of contending parties.
> Where there are not several classes there cannot be several parties, for a
> party is part of a class.[49]

It would also seem safe to venture that Soviet operating norms
very often stray out of line with the norms as imbedded in basic law
and historical documents and proclamations. Grave inconsistencies
between stated policy and actual policy seem not to be tolerated, so
that the norm demanding rationalization is rampant. Almost any
report of a party congress will contain an elaborate apologetic for the
way that actual events have deviated from the idealized state of
affairs. This is probably consistent with the rational scientific orientation of the Russians, and perhaps not unlike the norm which in the
United States requires that the expedient be made to appear "right."

Evaluation.   Certainly in the area of evaluating and planning
the democracies differ greatly from the dictatorships. In democracies
a basic belief frequently is held that most of the long-term objectives
will automatically be provided in the self-adjusting mechanisms of
free enterprise, supply and demand, and natural adjustment. In more
recent times depressions, war and the development of totalitarian
dictatorships with elaborate planning systems have forced all major
governments to evaluate possible long and short-range goals and to
plan for the future. Therefore, in most of the important government
bureaus of the major democracies planning is carried on. Thus, for
example, in the United States Department of Agriculture research
and production resulting from the new practices are planned many
years into the future relating production to population change, consumer preferences, and many other factors.

The energy-environmental crises of the 1960's and early 1970's
produced an unprecedented state of governmental planning activities to deal with these complex problems. The Federal Environ-

mental Protection Agency was created to set goals, design and administer programs to protect and conserve the nation's air, water,
and land resources. In 1973 President Nixon set forth the goal of
energy self-sufficiency for America by 1980, and asked Congress to
appropriate billions of dollars to increase our gas and petroleum
production and develop additional sources of energy such as solar
energy, nuclear energy, and the conversion of coal to oil, etc. As
discussed above, a strong Federal Energy Administration Agency
was established to plan the best uses of existing energy resources and
plan the development of new resources at home.

On the international level the Administration planned additional moves to help solve the energy crisis. Secretary of State Henry
Kissinger told a news conference (January 3, 1974) that President
Nixon was planning personal initiatives to promote solution to the
world energy crisis. Kissinger said that "Nixon's diplomatic offensive
would seek to build cooperation between oil-producing and oil-
consuming nations . . . There is no way that one nation can solve it
(the crisis) by itself, not even a nation as powerful as the United
States."[50]

The totalitarian nations have made planning a central feature of
government. In Russia lip service is paid to the Marxian theory of the
processes of history but "in practice . . . the leadership acts as if events
could be controlled by a rational calculus and by resolute effort."[51]
Rationality is the central key to the various decision-making and
planning bureaus. The so-called law-making bodies function more or
less as a rubber stamp for the Central Committee of the Party and
Politiburo (or the Presidium as it is now called) which are the most
important planning and decision-making bodies.

DIVISION OF FUNCTIONS AND ACTIVITIES

Status-role.   So varied are the status-roles played by the official
and political actors in the governmental social system that few
generalizations can be made. It may be true as some have claimed,
that the bureaucrat very often hired on the merit system and
qualifying for his job because of technical or professional competence,
is more oriented toward the Gesellschaft. The prototype is pictured as
an individual of little imagination, coming to the same office year
after year, arriving at an accustomed hour, doing habitual tasks,
"closing shop" promptly when the clock says the day's work is done,
doing tasks that may be meaningless, and that even with meaning
are certainly without warmth and heart. The blustery and affable
politician who stops to shake hands of neighbors, friends, nodding
acquaintances, and strangers, who flatters the women and kisses the

babies, who blows hot and cold as the political climate around him dictates, who finds a job in the system for his friend and makes his promises in terms of "influence," is the epitome of the Gemeinschaft for whom there are no universalistic principles, but only specific and individual ones. It is unlikely that either picture comes close to being correct. Certainly there are many devoted, inspired, inventive, and admirable bureaucrats whose warmth can infuse their whole agency with spirit and drive. And, while it is true that the hall-mark of the successful politician is his successful human relations, they are certainly not all offensively breezy and overly affable.

It may be true, however, that in politics more than in any other social system the specifications of the job and the behavior of the incumbent in the job tends to vary with the individual who holds the office. This is another way of saying that the governmental status-role is not as functionally specific, universalistic, and affectively neutral as are many others. Probably more than a different attitude on policy matters determined the differences in the articulation of office between Hoover and Roosevelt, for example. Insofar as the status-role of the President of the United States is concerned, certain observations can be made. He functions as

> the nation's chief executive ... the commander-in-chief of the armed forces and the director of our foreign affairs. He is further a pre-eminent participant in the legislative process, charged with recommending measures to Congress and with reviewing bills enacted by it for his approval or veto. As chief of staff the President performs a variety of ceremonies and social duties. No less importantly, he is the accepted leader of his political party. And finally, transcending all of these functions, the President is an indispensable source of national leadership.[52]

Status-role performance. It has often been said that each occupant of a given status-role interprets it in his own way and therefore performs the role somewhat differently from other occupants of that status-role. Perhaps no better example of this phenomena could be found than that of the 37 different occupants of the status-role of the Presidency of the United States. As described above, the status-role of the Presidency includes many different functions and responsibilities, including those of leader of the American people and leader of his political party. In these areas the differences in interpretation and role performance may be quite striking, revealing individual differences among occupants in acuity of political appraisal, in persuasiveness in coalescing conflicting strands of the body politic, etc.

As Sidney Hyman notes, such executive positions, or status-roles are part institution and part man.[53] Historically, terms coined out of various President's names have come to stand for particular interpretations and qualities imparted by certain Presidents to the status-role.

Buchananism stands for a Presidency marked by legalistic interpretation of duty. James Buchanan was the "starkest exponent" of this kind of incumbency in contrast to Abraham Lincoln whose attempts to bring to the country "new political readjustments, a rekindling of social hopes, and a will to resolve what is in dispute" has stamped this kind of presidential behavior with the term Lincolnism. Clevelandism represents the middle ground between the two extremes.

There can be little doubt that crises of one sort or another emphasize the President's personal expression of his status-role. During a crisis period the institutional restraints of office are eased; there is consequently less of the institution and more of the man in evidence. Foreign affairs have provided yet another situation in which this same easing of the institutional restraints is accomplished. As Louis Koenig points out, "the twentieth-century Presidents have operated in an era of personal diplomacy, witness Eisenhower at Geneva, Truman at Potsdam, F.D.R. at Yalta, Wilson at Versailles."[54] And more recently Nixon at Peking and Moscow.

Lest there seem to be overemphasis on those fairly broad areas in which "the man" seems to dominate "the office", let it be said that political literature is replete with conclusions that many a man has been made, or at least greatly improved by the office. Polk and Lincoln, to take two notable examples, grew strikingly in stature after brief exposure to the trials and tribulations of office.[55]

Presumably, they along with many others were able to rise to the levels equal to or surpassing their eminent predecessors whose precedents and practices became as great foot-prints which become easier to follow the more the path is trod.

RANKING

Social rank and stratification. In the "classless society" of Russia, the elite are the members of the Communist party, and among this group, are the special elites which compose the Central Committee and the Politburo, now known as the Presidium. In the United States, too, some political activities mark greater social rank than others. The President, of course, ranks the highest. This ranking has entered the folk-lore by depicting every mother of a new-born son dreaming of his future as the President of the country. The Supreme

Court judge is held in very high esteem; the senator tends to be rated higher than the representative. A nationwide cross-section sample of Americans ranked the following occupations in the order listed. At the top of 94 occupations:[56] U.S. Supreme Court Justice, physician, nuclear physicist, scientist, government scientist, state governor, cabinet member in the federal government, college professor, United States Representative in Congress, chemist, lawyer, and diplomat in the U.S. foreign service.

Rankings of governmental systems themselves do occur, and change through the years. As a matter of fact various studies of the adjustment of foreign students in the United States reveal that the extent of adjustment and favorable attitudes toward the United States is closely related to the ranking these students believe Americans give their country and its culture.[57] Few would claim that Great Britain, for example, would be accorded the same rank now as might have been true fifty years ago. Ranking of governmental social systems by comparatively low ranking sovereignties are of extreme importance to the United States and to Soviet Russia. The latter, of course, succeeds in the ultimate objective of spreading communism throughout the world each time a lesser nation embraces communism and, tacitly at least, acknowledges Russia and/or China top rank. Each country added to a power alignment means more potential force should the contest for rank and power come to a point where it is to be decided by force. To the United States, being accorded top rank is important because of the obvious desire not to be left in the position of standing alone in a world of all-communist nations. Many subtleties establish this kind of national ranking among which are demonstrated attitudes of the members of the governmental social systems towards color of skin, toward cherished beliefs, degree and quality of what are regarded as colonial practices, the degree to which the dominant country shows respect for the lesser country and develops mechanisms by which the lesser country can maintain its dignity, and the personal example of nationals from the greater country abroad in the lesser country. Not at all subtle is the more important factor of power — power to vanquish as well as power to help provide means to the lesser country to get where it wants to go in its own development.

Evaluation of actors and allocation of status-roles. As was pointed out under status-role, governmental and especially political activity, gives so much latitude to the individual as he performs in his status-role that individuals who hold identical status-roles from which they derive comparable prestige can very possibly be ranked quite differently because of variations in role performance and the resulting esteem accorded. Then, too, some of the sub-systems within the governmental social system have criteria other than achievement for the awarding of signally important status-roles. Thus, in Congress the chairmen of the various committees are the chairmen because of seniority in the legislative chamber. Prestige derived from such status-roles cannot be very stable with esteem fluctuating extremely in accordance with the measure of the man in the status-role. A built-in ranking of sorts exists in the U.S. governmental system as succession to the Presidency is spelled out through the office of the Vice-President, down through various cabinet posts. It would not necessarily follow, of course, that outside of the actual situation of Presidential succession, a Vice-President would always, or indeed very often, out-rank the Secretary of State, and so on.

The rank of governmental officials is a key element to watch as a society becomes stratified. The other great hierarchies of the modern world each have their own kind of power. Great industries and the communities of which they are the sub-systems, for example, might be cited as important hierarchies in the United States. If examination of each of the power-laden hierarchies, including the national governmental social system, reveals that each has high ranking *men who are the same men* as those found to be high ranking in the other hierarchies, then a ruling class can be said to exist. This is no doubt one of the reasons that the Soviet amalgamation of industry, party, government and society makes it very difficult for the West to believe that theirs is truly a classless society. The fact that the very top status-roles in each of these four great hierarchies are allocated to *the same men* makes most Westerners conclude that Soviet Russia has a ruling class. It is interesting to note that in Soviet Russia in which the communists under the Marxist ideology set out to eliminate all classes except the proletariat, there have emerged new "classes somewhat similar to western society."[58] The very highest ranks in Russia converge in governmental and party posts. By contrast in the United States the prestige and esteem which is associated with high rank is often greater in business than in government, particularly local government. However, public office may provide additional rank and attract people from the highest and most powerful classes during war time or when the society is thought to be threatened. When tensions exist in society as in the case of the traditional rural South with regard to the race issue even local offices may be filled from the top.

Some contend that there is a power-elite in America. C. Wright Mills argues that there is a self-conscious elite drawn from the upper-classes in America which dominates the top positions in business, the military, and the executive branch of the federal government.[59] These high-ranking persons mingle socially and may move from the top military to top business to top governmental posts. Critics of this view point out that Mills has not been able to offer proof that such a power elite has been able to get its way on most of the important national issues. Arnold Rose is such a critic. He presents a multi-influence thesis, as follows: "Segments of the economic elite have violated democratic and legal processes, with differing degrees of effort and success, but in no recent period could they correctly be said to have controlled the elected and appointed political authorities in large measure. The relationship between the economic elite and the political authorities has been a constantly varying one of strong influence, cooperation, division of labor, and conflict, with each influencing the other in changing proportion to some extent and each operating independently of the other to a large extent."[60]

CONDITIONS OF SOCIAL ACTION

Of the several conditions of social action and interaction (time, size, and territoriality), probably territoriality is the most significant for political and governmental systems.

Territoriality. To no kind of social system is the condition of territoriality more important than to the governmental social system. The great conflicts of history generally were territorial in nature; some of the more minor and contained struggles of the modern world are territorial as well. The desirability of annexing a territory and having access to its resources, both natural and human, is probably the most obvious expression of territoriality. Other less obvious territorial conditions deserve mention also.

Centralization and decentralization rest upon conditions of territoriality no less than they do upon the ideal of a responsive and informed electorate. In the United States regionalism, an aspect of territoriality, is both a phenomena whose various alignments contributes to political power, and a conditioning factor which affects the kind of representation to the legislature, the make-up of important committees, the kinds of services required, the location of the men who are likely to get the nod for presidential candidacy, and so forth. Even vast uninhabited territory can become very important to a governmental system as it is sought out and used for the testing of dangerous nuclear devices.

The old political dodge known as gerrymandering (arbitrarily arranging the political divisions of a state, county, etc. to give one political party an unfair advantage in elections), and the tenacity of established methods of apportionment of representation are further evidences of the importance of territoriality. A hapless householder who built his house right on the Michigan-Ohio state line found out the effects of territoriality when he sought to have various services installed. The telephone companies, the gas company, the various community water works, and electric departments all declined to run services to the new house for fear it lay in someone else's jurisdiction. The boundaries of various governmental and political social systems are important whether marked by an "iron curtain", "bamboo curtain," Mason-Dixon line, or other device; unless their existence is recognized, governmental social action can neither be understood or implemented.

COMPREHENSIVE OR MASTER PROCESSES OF GOVERNMENTAL AND POLITICAL SOCIAL SYSTEMS

Communication. In his book *The Web of Government*, McIver said that "of all . . . monopolies the most immediately fatal to democracy is the monopoly of the media of opinion, or any approximation of it."[61] Totalitarian governments make widespread use of their monopolization of the media to propagandize and indoctrinate the masses.

To cite the lack of freedom of communication media in totalitarian dictatorships is not to say, however, that the same media function in complete harmony with public interest in a democracy. In the United States the Communications Act of 1934 which created the Federal Communications Commission, and libel laws, are controls which set forth and could establish the rights of the citizens. Professionals engaged in the use of each media have codes of ethics which if obeyed would protect the public. Both the editors' code of ethics and the Broadcasters' Creed are admirable statements of the high purpose to which it is proposed the respective informational instruments be dedicated. Nevertheless, the charges that mass media harm people and society are not without foundation. Among the detriments of mass media are the following: they tend toward economic conservatism, an overemphasis on violence, an expansion of the trivial and an over-looking of the fundamental, an emphasis on happenings of the moment to the detriment of the importance of what happened yesterday. The mass media in the United States tend to reinforce the commonly held values and the ideas existing in American society, and may disparage efforts to improve life.

In the Soviet Union the completely one-sided propagandist use of all normal communication media has created interesting counter-agents. There is every evidence to believe that an important system of informal, unofficial oral communication has grown up. Such a system of course has difficulties in a country where it is possible to receive a severe sentence in a forced labor camp for telling a joke which has the wrong political implications.[62] The investigators who sought to determine the importance of this informal communication system concluded that it is, in the main, dysfunctional to the ruling regime, even though the regime knowing of its existence occasionally encourages its action, both to allow steam to be blown off and as feedback. For the individual citizen it may have the function of providing him with information not available anywhere else.

The brashness of American newspapermen is legendary. Because it will serve to remind the American reader that during the periodic news conferences of the President of the United States, it is the newsmen, not the President, who pose the questions and "call the shots," the following is given: One such occasion was the press conference on November 11, 1953, when the reporters took President Eisenhower to task . . . From abroad, Harold Callender of the New York Times cabled an account of the astonished European reaction to this Presidential interrogation:

> Few would believe that the reporters would dare address the President with the challenging questions asked or that their editors published the questions and answers. No European Premier or even a foreign minister would dream of according to the press the privileges accorded by President Eisenhower. Few European Members of Parliament and fewer reporters would venture to treat even a minor minister as American reporters treated the President.[63]

Though no doubt a discomforting experience and one of which the pressmen present were a little ashamed themselves, the incumbent of the Presidency of the United States is willing to put up with a bad time or two with the newsmen for the tremendous advantages their services give to him. The President

> more than any other person in the nation, perhaps in the world, has access to the eyes and ears of the people. The press, radio, television, are if not at his beck and call, ever alert to report what he says or does or proposes to do. Nowhere is his skill as a political leader more clearly revealed than in the use he makes of these facilities to mold and mobilize public opinion.[64]

By the same token, the media of communication have a great deal of power too. They determine what is newsworthy, where it goes in the paper and how it is commented upon by newscasters, as well as what questions are asked at the press conference and what issues the President talks about. It is reported that the President often prepares ready answers about matters which he considers grave and important which he feels surely must come up, only to have them neglected in favor of questions the newsmen consider important.

It also happens that when the President's position is opposed by Congress the President by virtue of his singular position tends to get better coverage than does plural, many-voiced Congress. It is said that Franklin Roosevelt had only to glance at the microphone in the presence of a delegation of protesting Congressmen to have them drop the matter. They dreaded the flood of letters from constituents that every Fireside Chat had been bringing.[65]

The means of communication is indeed great. That the democratic controls are at work in this medium as in any other may be demonstrated, however, if the student tries to imagine an American President by virtue of his access to newspapers, television, and radio, accomplishing the personal aggrandizement job that was accomplished in the Soviet Union for Stalin. It is impossible to imagine pictures of the President adorning every home, building, street, and tree; to hear his opinions extolled as exalted, to breathe his name as a deity. Unlimited access to and use of the communication media does not exist in the United States.

Boundary maintenance and systemic linkage.   Two levels of the application of boundary maintenance can be seen among governmental social systems. One concerns the literal maintenance of geographic boundaries by those within the system against the encroachments of those outside the system. Military and productive forces constitute the core of this kind of boundary maintenance, and is abetted by alignments through diplomatic maneuvers (a systemic linkage of a sort) whereby areas of influence are established beyond the actual boundaries of the governmental system in question. Such governmental phenomena as customs inspection, border patrol and immigration services protect the country from illegal entrance of people and goods.

The second kind of boundary maintenance perceptible among governmental social systems is that maintained by the governmental sub-systems. The norms which articulate the anti-trust laws are actually supportive of boundary maintenance measures to insure that no sub-system can monopolize power to the disadvantage of society. The much criticized loyalty oaths, government investigations of personnel, State Department investigation for passports, etc., are in actuality an attempt at boundary maintenance too. In most areas of life in a democracy, however, there is a fluidity of membership and consequently, of boundaries. An individual can be a member of the Democratic Party for example, and leave it to become eventually a leader of the Republican Party. Nonetheless, it is also true that the significant sub-groups come to stand for a certain position, and that any individual's memberships probably tend to be in sub-groups whose causes are harmonious, one with the other. Thus, although it is possible, it is not likely that a member prominent in the Civil Liberties Union would also be prominent in the American Legion; that a member prominent in a labor union would also be prominent in the Chamber of Commerce. The kind of labels by which sub-groups tend to become identified are evidences of boundary maintenance practices by most of the members despite the actual freedom of the individual to join what he chooses.

In Soviet Russia, to provide for constant checks on loyalty as well as execution of decisions, the rules call for continuous cleansing of party ranks. The party arranges for periodic review of the record of each member. Matters may be brought out from the distant past, and excellent work is required to redeem one who has deviated sharply from the party program at some early date. The thought of this periodic cleansing is sufficient to keep the average member alert to his responsibilities.

Membership is not gained easily. Rules have always required that applicants be supported by recommendations of party members, who are held responsible for the good quality of their recommendations . . .

A candidacy of one year is required after admission, during which the candidate studies the party's history, its policy, and its techniques of operation and takes part in assigned tasks. Those who pass the strict tests are admitted to full membership by decision of a general meeting of the primary party organization, following ratification by the district (or city) committee.[66]

The totalitarian systems have been exceedingly successful in systematic linkage through what the German Nazis called fifth column activity or peaceful infiltration previous to military attack and what the communists call penetration or the establishment of cells. Through these devices a good many countries lost their independence. The United States' attempts at systemic linkage have usually taken the form of grants-in-aid for economic recovery and loans of men and material designed to start areas with undeveloped human and natural resources on the road to technological proficiency. Such programs, incorrectly estimated by many to be good-hearted philanthropic gifts, are as necessary to the country's defense by way of establishing systemic linkage with prospective allies as is defense measured by men and artillery. Note the case at the end of this chapter on unsuccessful systemic linkage in Mexico.

Institutionalization. In the very nature of politics and the governmental system, those practices which are successful and properly timed to the needs of the hour tend to be institutionalized fast. "So extensive . . . are the institutional changes in the Presidency that we properly speak of the 'modern Presidency' as dating from the era of Theodore Roosevelt."[67] Theodore Roosevelt established a trend of Presidential leadership in legislation which was institutionalized by Woodrow Wilson who recognized the Constitutional provision for the Presidential message to Congress as a splendid vehicle for dynamic legislative leadership. Today the State of the Union message has great significance because it has been institutionalized to signify a Presidential statement of policy and an exhortation to Congress to act accordingly. The importance of institutionalization in the governmental social system is found in "The authority which adheres to precedent and practice and has worked to convert the achievement and advance of "strong" Presidents into an enduring legacy for their gifted successors."[68]

Presidents of the U.S.A. have become increasingly strong since World War II. Some of the precedents and practices initiated by President Franklin D. Roosevelt and institutionalized in the office of the President have been discussed above under *Power*. Critics argue that Americans have given too much power to their Presidents in recent years. It is even contended by some that the American public today surrounds the Oval office in the White House with a mystique that approaches a national quasi-religious cultism.[69] Watergate may be seen as a latent function of these developments.

The Watergate exposures demonstrated the lengths to which President Nixon's advisors and certain officers of his Administration went to assure his re-election in 1972. Campaign contributions were illicitly obtained and used, Democratic Party headquarters were broken into, "enemies" lists were drawn up, and efforts made to use agencies of the Federal Government such as the Federal Bureau of Investigation and the Internal Revenue Service to "screw" these enemies.

The Watergate scandals brought strong reaction against such practices. New stricter norms regarding obtaining and using money in elections and in the conduct of politics and government appear to be emerging. (Some of the specific new norms being urged will be discussed below shortly.) An interesting case in point is seen in former Vice President Agnew's statement during his resignation speech in October 1973 that some things he did while Vice President and Governor of Maryland may appear now to be wrong in terms of the "new post-Watergate" standards.

Under a totalitarian system there would exist, logically, opportunities for the institutionalized practices of one dictator to break down or be discarded under a successor's regime. This sequence could represent only a limited institutionalization which would permit the exercise of caprice rather than that of tradition. An excellent chance to observe whether or not this was true was given the world at the death of Stalin. The principle of concentration of power had apparently become well institutionalized; the regime in fear of being deposed concentrated power still further than had been true under Stalin. Twenty-five ministries replaced fifty-one, for example. Other immediate measures were similar. An inner cabinet of five men replaced the old one of ten. To ward off wide-spread unrest more emphasis for a while was given to the production of consumer goods; the severity of the criminal code was somewhat relaxed. Thus, for more than a year control was maintained by reducing the number of people in command on the one hand, and creating through certain popular measures a favorable impression among the rank and file on the other.

Future institutionalization in the United States governmental system is likely to come at those points where the norms are not solidly legitimized at present. The whole matter of how much a prospective office holder should spend to achieve the authority of office which he seeks, how much his campaign should cost, how much any one individual should be allowed to contribute, what his obligations are to those who most heavily support him are normative questions. Certain laws passed to safeguard the public interest have not been too successful. Once an acceptable norm which works is contrived it is reasonable to assume that it will be quickly institutionalized. As technology creates Gesellschaft-like bureaucracies requiring that more emphasis be placed upon achievement, functional specificity and universality, norms which reduce the graft, bribery and nepotism of the old system tend to become institutionalized. Such has been the history in countries such as some in South America which traditionally have had sanction systems which reward by ascription, and in which norms are particularistic, functionally diffuse, and affective.

Recent national elections, especially the Presidential election of 1972, have pointed up — in fact the Watergate scandals and the Vice President Agnew resignation have dramatized — the need for changes and reforms in political norms governing campaign and election procedures and practices in America. Some of the areas needing change and some suggested reforms follow:

1. Campaign financing. The tremendous amounts of money seemingly used to finance Presidential or Congressional campaigns has led to proposals that such campaigns be publicly financed, and/or that limits be set on the amount any individual may contribute to a given candidate, and that the names of each contributor be made public along with the amount of his contribution.

2. Campaign ethics and anti-corruption. Proposals were made to curb unethical and unfair campaign practices. The need for stronger norms and sanctions here was pointed up by the "Dirty tricks" practices of the Committee to Re-Elect the President in the 1972 campaign, uncovered in the Watergate hearings. The Agnew case has pointed up the need for clearer norms and stronger sanctions aimed at reducing corruption connected with political campaigns, and with actions of office holders in their relations with their political supporters.

3. Presidential power. The need for better checks and balances in the federal government. At the time of this writing, (Oct., 1973), the power struggle between President Nixon vs. the courts and Congress had reached historic proportions and had become a serious constitutional crisis. The Watergate tapes confrontation and the firing of Special Prosecutor Cox brought to a climax the power struggle between the three branches of the federal government. Among the proposals to restore a better balance of powers and provide checks on Presidential power are: (1) Creating a congressional counsel to serve as a "watch-dog" over the Executive branch of government; (2) Requiring congressional confirmation for members of the President's Executive staff; (3) Imposing limitations on the Executive Privilege power of the President; (4) Requiring that the Attorney-General be an officer of the Judicial Branch of government, and thus be independent of White House pressures and control; (5) Enacting a freedom of Information Act, in order to strip away some of the governmental secrecy in which the Watergate activities flourished.

UNSUCCESSFUL SYSTEMIC LINKAGE IN MEXICO

UNITED STATES TECHNICAL COLLABORATION: AN ATTEMPT THAT FAILED.

Throughout the world the industrialized societies are promoting alignments with other nations both large and small, developed and underdeveloped. Leaders in the effort to develop friendly alignments or at least to neutralize hostile ones are such opposing powers as Russia and the United States. Both are expending millions in various types of technological assistance to under-developed areas. One of the favored approaches of the United States is that of fostering more or less direct relations between American institutions of higher learning, and comparable institutions in under-developed areas. An attempt to foster collaborative relationships between an American and a Mexican college in the field of agriculture will be briefly described. The account concerns actions of students in a Mexican college and actions of officials of the governmental social system. In order that both sets of actors be seen in proper perspective the recounting of the case will be preceded by (1) background data concerning the Mexican governmental social system, (2) background data concerning the particular Mexican college involved. The names of places and persons are fictitious in this account prepared by the senior author from reports available in the Area Research Center at Michigan State University and in Mexico.

(1) BACKGROUND DATA OF THE MEXICAN GOVERNMENTAL SYSTEM:

As various studies in the United States-Mexican Border region demonstrate, there are marked variations in the classes among the various ethnic groupings.[70] However, most of the interaction in the present study involved what is commonly called the middle class on both sides of the border. Our analysis will therefore, deal chiefly with this class as it is articulated in the case under discussion. In many instances the differences between the two ethnic groups do not appear directly in the following case but furnish background for hostility which has accumulated through the years.

Beliefs. The general Mexican ideology is more humanistic than the Anglo-American which is more puritanical; the Mexican intellectual interest centers more on logic and dialectics, the North American more on pragmatism. Mexican intellectual interests and background may include some elements such as Marxism, Spanish individualism, and a greater Catholic influence than do the comparable North American interests. In terms of broad systemic differences the following should be noted. The family is of much greater importance as a reference group for the Mexican than for the North American, and what is called *la raza*, which is really a glorification of Latin Culture as opposed to Anglo-Saxon culture, is also of great influence.[71] The beliefs that the universe is controllable is more often doubted or discredited by Mexicans than by North Americans.

Sentiments. South State has a long history of conflict with Mexico and although much effort in recent years has been devoted to the development of more friendly relations the hostile sentiments common to such borders as those between Germany and France are the rule. Cultural differences give the hostility a moral tone. The relative de-emphasis on family and close friends on the part of the North American and his devotion to occupational pursuits are interpreted by the Mexican in unfavorable terms. North Americans, on the other hand, judge Mexican morality harshly from the relatively greater prevalence of the *morbida* (the bribe), graft in government, and prostitution, which along the border exists as a major enterprise chiefly for a North American clientele.

Also the rising nationalism of the Mexican middle classes leads political leaders, teachers, students, and professionals to pride themselves upon past Mexican accomplishments and "makes them loath to accept outside help in solving the country's problems unless it is quite clearly under Mexican auspices and contrcl."[72] The combination of a rising sentiment of nationalism and a "longstanding fear of 'the colossus of the North' leads to resistance to American projects because as they say 'there is always danger in living in the same room with an elephant."[73]

Ends.   In the various technical and professional meetings of the Organization of American States and in other settings the desire of Mexicans to assume leadership in Latin America has been noted. In matters related to technical collaboration with the United States, success for Mexican officials and bureaus can be achieved only if the official demonstrates to his countrymen that he is not pro-North American or that he is anti-North American, and at the same time is able to get the facility which may be used to advance the country's position, which of course is a normative way of achieving an end.

Norms, status-roles, power, and rank.   The Mexican government is much more highly centralized with power located in the national capitol and particularly in the President who controls in large measure the election of other officials and the officials' actions after the election. "Inefficiency, corruption, cruelty — if personal — are all acceptable. What is not acceptable is the cold, impersonal, efficient government."[74] The President makes sure that his friends and only his friends control the Senate and decides who is the "rightfully" elected governor. "Like a good father, the President cannot say no, and if he does, the no is not final. Surely the father's heart can be mellowed, his kindness reawakened, his true virtues as the father of his children brought to bear upon the issues in hand."[75] The President like the kings of old rules. "He rules rather than governs, and must do so if he is to survive . . ."[76] These same norms are followed by the governors. Power must be guarded and the means for doing this are personal means with power remaining highly centralized. Various ministers on the federal level may become aspirants for the Presidency and the President and other ministers continually check the relative ranking of various potential candidates. Federal officials feel insecure if local authorities and institutions gain in power. Most tax monies are controlled by the states and federal governments and localities wanting schools and other facilities must make representation to the power centers at state and federal levels.

(2) BACKGROUND DATA FOR THE MEXICAN COLLEGE:

There had been indecision about closing a dormitory which was costing the college too much to maintain. The Governor of the state had recommended that student fees be higher, particularly in light of the considerable student population which came from out of state (from Mexican states other than Estado Norte where the college was located); he recommended further that if student fees could not be made high enough to carry the cost of the dormitory then the dormitory should close. The Director of the College Henrique Normano protested that if the dormitory were closed the students would strike. Nevertheless, the Governor ordered the dormitory closed, and a short time later the students used the strike as a protest, just as the Director of the College had predicted.

Sequence of events. The United States agency in charge of technical collaborative arrangements is the Economic Cooperation Administration of the Department of State. Since their program had been making little progress in advancing technical cooperation in Mexico, Dr. Ray Morley, Country Director of ECA in Mexico was encouraged when a former governor of Estado Norte, and then currently Minister of Navy, approached him in Mexico City concerning the possibility of technical collaboration for the Henrique Normano College, an agricultural school with some 300 students and some three dozen professors, located in Dulcity, a city of some 75,000 and the capitol of Estado Norte. Negotiations for the project took almost a year and Mexico's representation at the negotiations included the Minister of Agriculture, the Minister of Foreign Relations, the President and various collaborating agencies. Finally a contract was drawn up which specified that South State Agricultural and Mechanical College would furnish eight agricultural experts for the staff of Henrique Normano College, the United States government to pay half of the support, or one-half million dollars, and Estado Norte providing the other half. In due time the experts from South State A. & M. College arrived at Henrique Normano College and began their work. About six months later the student body of

College Henrique Normano went on strike. Since their organization, the Sociedad Estudiantil was an affiliate of the National Federation of Technical Students the local organization asked the national organization to join them in striking. The students listed many complaints, but the one carried most commonly in newspapers was the unexplained presence of the North Americans on the campus of Henrique Normano College; there were accompanying speculations that the North Americans were "taking over" the college. During the strike and very shortly afterward, two events reinforced the cause of the striking students. The Governor of Estado Norte requested the Director of Henrique Normano College to have the technicians from South State A. & M. College leave the campus. The President of Mexico made the same request of the United States Embassy and stipulated that he wanted the project terminated.

The striking students never did state formally that the presence of the North American technicians was the reason for the strike. Rather, they drew up a petition from the local Federation of Technical Students which listed a number of items which in their opinion would bear investigation. Item two in the petition was a "study of possible advantages or disadvantages that the Point Four Program would bring." The then current strike was attributed to "an internal struggle between members of the staff contributing to the neglect of fundamental school duties", and observed that a program comparable to the collaborative one between the two schools might be satisfactory provided "the personality of the professors and the host institution be respected." All the other items in the petition concerned local school conditions, such as the reopening of the dormitory, changes in entrance requirements, the fulfillment of past agreements with the students, and a change in policy concerning the qualifications and functions of the administrative positions in the school.

During the progress of the strike the Governor of the state sent three alumni of Henrique Normano from the neighboring city of Caballo which was also the home of the governor, to council with the students and arrange a meeting between representatives of the students and the governor. Subsequently twenty-five students represented the Sociedad Estudiantil "Henrique Normano" in negotiations with the Governor in a meeting which lasted almost through the entire night. In this meeting the Governor implied that there were Communist leaders among the student body, and by adroit references to a not-too-long-past trip to Moscow by the student president robbed him of his influence. Charges and counter-charges of this nature consumed the first three hours of the negotiations by which time the students had split their united front. Finally in the wee small hours of the conference the Governor took up the students' demands. The dormitory, the crux of the matter as far as the students were concerned, would be reopened immediately. He refused to discuss the South State A. & M.-Henrique Normano technical collaborative program, but did not fail, according to the student reports of the meeting, to discuss at great length his anti-North American senti-ments. He poured out a volume of anti-North American vituperation and bitter profane condemnation of the program and of Americans. Over and over he denied that he was a "malinchista" (disparaging term from the name of the Indian mistress of Cortes, conqueror of Mexico, symbolizing the attitude that foreign things are superior). During this outpouring of vindictiveness he reminded the students that it was he who during the Rio Grande flood declined the help of the "gringoes who came with their helicopters and all available equip-ment." He also recounted to the students some historical facts about the Mexican land taken away from Mexico by the North Americans.

In the meantime, of course, his directive had gone out to the college director telling him to get the North American technicians off the campus and shortly afterwards the national President's request to the United States Embassy to terminate the project spelled the end of this short-lived affair. Why did a project which on the surface represented the willing collaboration of neighboring nations and colleges, fail almost before it had begun?

Reasons for project's failure. The following brief statement represents the senior author's judgment of the reasons for failure based upon experience in and knowledge of the governmental system and upon first hand accounts given the author. The items are listed in an order which show a range of influence from the most local and parochial level to the international.

1. Mexican faculty members who became part of the project, including the director, were given increased salaries, other faculty members at Henrique Normano were not. This created jealousy and friction. In this connection it should be noted that about one fourth of the original staff at Henrique Normano were trained in United States institutions, some in South State A. & M. College.

2. The project created competitive strains among the colleges and among the ministries in the national government. The Minister of Education under whose jurisdiction Henrique Normano fell was opposed to the project. The Minister of Agriculture who originally favored it was accused of being interested in political advancement. The National College of Agriculture claimed to be threatened by the facilities and effort being channeled into a state college, Henrique Normano.

3. Ultra-nationalists felt that the United States Professors on the Mexican campus were a threat and it was reported that their "taking over classes was the straw that broke the camel's back."

4. Probably most important, the Governor of Estado Norte was glad to find an excuse to discontinue the project and the student strike, which was really focused upon another matter primarily, was an excellent pretext. The chief threat which the project created for the governor was its cost to his state of half a million dollars to match the American funds. Just as "influence", "accommodation", and "compromise" are necessary within the American governmental system for much action to take place, in Mexico funds are necessary both at the state and federal level which can be used when necessary to buy the help of influential people. The Governor's influence would be lessened tremendously by the cost of the collaborative project, because his wherewithal to buy influence would be markedly diminished. Moreover, both the Governor and the Minister of Agriculture were being accused of being pro-American, which if they were to have any political future, was an epithet which must be demonstrated to be false.

5. Communists in Mexico City were able to use the traditional sentiments mentioned above to stir up opposition to this and similar programs in Mexico. The case suggests that United States collaboration, to be successful, must be done in terms understandable to and compatible with the norms and ends of the host country, even though it means temporizing universalistic principles and forfeiting traditional norms concerning acceptable governmental behavior. An evaluation of ends and means is implied.

NOTES

1. Alfred De Grazia, *The Elements of Political Science* (New York: Alfred A. Knopf, 1952), p. 32.

2. Fritz M. Marx, ed., *Foreign Governments* (New York: Prentice-Hall, 1949) p. 3. The chief function being that of institutionalizing power is a conclusion common to many political writers. The statement used here is a re-wording of one used by Marx.

3. De Grazia, op. cit., p. 43-45.

4. Ralph L. Beals and Harry Hoijer, *An Introduction to Anthropology* (New York: Macmillan Co., 1953), p. 445.

5. Gerhard Lenski, *Human Societies* (New York: McGraw-Hill, 1970).

6. op. cit., p. 176.

7. op. cit., p. 249.

8. op. cit., p. 354.

9. op. cit., pp. 354-55.

10. F. Cotrell, *Energy and Society* (New York: McGraw-Hill, 1955).

11. R. M. MacIver, *Society: a Textbook of Sociology* (New York: Farrar and Rinehart, 1941), p. 284. How Marxian and Hegelian thought differentiates these aspects of societies see Ralph Milband, "Marx and the State," in Tom Bottomore, ed. *Karl Marx* (Englewood Cliffs, N.J.: Prentice-Hall, Inc., 1973).

12. Sebastian De Grazia, *The Political Community: a Study of Anomie* (Chicago: The University of Chicago Press, 1948), p. ix.

13. Lenski, op. cit., p. 470.

14. Seymour Lipset, *The First New Nation* (New York: Basic Books, 1963), Ch. 7.

15. op. cit., p. 270.

16. The beliefs enumerated here are found in one form or another liberally sprinkled through all kinds of literature which discusses America and Americans. To cite each instance in which similar ideas were found would be impossible. Nonetheless the author acknowledges his indebtedness to the following: F.S.C. Northrop, *The Meeting of East and West* (New York: The Macmillan Co., 1948); *The Annals of the American Academy of Political and Social Science*, 280, (March 1952) and 307, (September 1956); Carl L. Becker *New Liberties from Old* (New Haven: Yale University Press); Cora DuBois, "The Dominant Value Profile of American Culture," *American Anthropologist*, 57, (December 1955), pp. 123. f.f.

17. The beliefs enumerated here are widely distributed throughout the literature about the Soviet Union. The chief source to which the authors are indebted are Raymond A. Bauer, Alex Inkeles and Clyde Kluckhohn, *How the Soviet System Works* (Cambridge, Mass.: Harvard University Press, 1956).

18. The theme has been developed that in societies dominated by religious beliefs which exalt the importance of the individual (e.g. the Roman Catholic and Protestant traditions) democracies may be expected to flourish, whereas in societies dominated by religious beliefs which do not exalt the individual (including the Greek Orthodox Catholic tradition) dictatorships and feudal monarchies may be more compatible. See Paul Honigsheim, "Max Weber as Rural Sociologist," *Rural Sociology*, 11, (September 1947), pp. 207-218.

19. Bauer, Inkeles, and Kluckhohn, op. cit., p. 215.

20. Niccolo Machiavelli, *The Prince* (New York: A Mentor Book, New American Library, 1952), p. 98.

21. Jessie Bernard, *American Community Behavior* (New York: Dryden Press, 1949), p. 240.

22. Sebastian De Grazia, op. cit., pp. x-xi.

23. Theodore White's book on *The Making of a President, 1964*, spells out how this is done.

24. G. L. Kline, "Recent Soviet Philosophy," *Annals of the American Academy of Political and Social Science*, 280, (March 1952), p. 68.

25. Ibid., p. 134.

26. R. M. MacIver, *The Web of Government* (New York: The Macmillan Co., 1947), p. 42.

27. Gerhard Lenski, *Power and Privilege* (New York: McGraw-Hill, 1966), p. 23.

28. op. cit., pp. 22-23.

29. Kingsley Davis and Wilbert Moore, "Some Principles of Social Stratification," *American Sociological Review*, 10, (April, 1945), pp. 242-249.

30. Lenski, op. cit., p. 23.

31. See Talcott Parsons, "On the Concept of Political Power" in R. Bendix and S. Lipset, *Class, Status, and Power* (New York: The Free Press, 1966), pp. 255-56.

32. Ibid.

33. Charles P. Loomis, *Modern Social Theories* (Huntington, N.Y.: Krieger, 1975), p. 399.

34. op. cit., pp. 399-400.

35. Stephen K. Bailey, "The President and His Political Executives," *Annals of the American Academy of Political and Social Science*, 307, (September 1956), p. 25.

36. This discussion is based on the papers appearing in *Annals of the American Academy of Political and Social Science*, 307, (September 1956).

37. Louis W. Koenig, "The Man and the Institution," *Annals of the American Academy of Political and Social Science*, 307, (September 1956), p. 11.

38. Peter H. Odegard, "Presidential Leadership and Party Responsibility," *Annals of the American Academy of Political and Social Science*, 307, (September 1956), p. 66.

39. See Senator William Fulbright, *The Crippled Giant* (New York: Vintage Books, 1973).

40. Wilfred E. Binkley, "The President as Chief Legislator," *Annals of the American Academy of Political and Social Science*, 307, (September 1956), p. 104.

41. Wilfred E. Binkley, op. cit., pp. 99-100.

42. Ibid., p. 100.

43. Wilfred E. Binkley, op. cit., p. 104.

44. Harlan Cleveland, op. cit., p. 43.

45. Melvin L. DeFleur, William D'Antonio, and Lois DeFleur, *Sociology: Man in Society* (Glenview, Ill.: Scott, Foresman, and Co., 1971), p. 471.

46. R. M. MacIver, *Society,* op. cit., p. 285.

47. *Abstracts of Papers Delivered at the Fifty-Second Annual Meeting of the American Sociological Society* (Washington, D.C.: American Sociological Society, 1957), p. 43.

48. Charles P. Loomis, *Studies in Applied and Theoretical Social Science* (East Lansing, Mich.: Michigan State College Press, 1950), p. 4.

49. Statement of Stalin in interview to Mr. Roy Howard as cited by John N. Hazard, "The Socialist State: The Soviet Union and Its Orbit," in Fritz M. Marx, ed., op. cit., p. 147.

50. *Houston Post*, (January 4, 1974), pp. 1 and 13.

51. Bauer, Inkeles, and Kluckhohn, op. cit., p. 50.

52. Robert E. Merriam, "The Bureau of the Budget as Part of the President's Staff," *Annals of the American Academy of Political and Social Science,* 307, (September 1956), p. 16.

53. Sidney Hyman, "The Art of the Presidency," *Annals of the American Academy of Political and Social Science,* 307, (September 1956), p. 1.

54. Louis W. Koenig, op. cit., p. 12.

55. Ibid., p. 13.

56. Robert W. Hodge, Paul M. Siegel and Peter Rossi, "Occupational Prestige in the United States, 1935-1963," *American Journal of Sociology,* 7, (November 1964), pp. 286-302.

57. Richard T. Morris, "National Status and Attitudes of Foreign Students," *Journal of Social Issues,* 2. See also articles by M. Brewster Smith in this issue which point to the same conclusions.

58. Bauer, Inkeles, and Kluckhohn, op. cit., p. 26; Lenski, op. cit., pp. 327-332; Merle Fainsrod, *How Russia is Ruled* (Cambridge, Mass.: Harvard University Press, 1963).

59. C. Wright Mills, *The Power Elite* (New York: Oxford University Press, 1966).

60. Arnold M. Rose, *The Power Structure: Political Process in American Society* (New York: Oxford University Press, 1967), p. 2.

61. R. M. McIver, *The Web of Government* (New York: The Macmillan Co., 1947), p. 221.

62. Raymond A. Bauer and David B. Gleicher, "Word-of-Mouth Communication in the Soviet Union," *The Public Opinion Quarterly*, 17, (Fall 1953), p. 297.

63. Douglass Cater, "The President and the Press," *Annals of the American Academy of Political and Social Sciences,* 307, (September 1956), p. 59.

64. Peter Odegard, op. cit., p. 75.

65. Wilfred E. Binkley, op. cit., p. 104-5.

66. John N. Hazard, op. cit., p. 428-29.

67. Louis W. Koenig, op. cit., p. 13.

68. Ibid.

69. Professor Harvey Cox of Harvard University, as quoted in *TIME*, (January 7, 1974), p. 20.

70. Julio Rivera, Michigan State University, Ph.D. Dissertation, (1957). Roy A. Clifford, *The Rio Grande Flood: A Comparative Study of Border Communities in Disaster* (Washington, D.C.: National Research Council, National Academy of Sciences, 1956). Ozzie G. Simmons, "Anglo Americans and Mexican Americans in South Texas," Ph.D. Dissertation, Department of Social Relations, Harvard University, (1952). For a historical study by a sociologist which gives the background for conflict in one of the border states see S. H. Lowrie, *Culture Conflict in Texas 1821-1835* (New York: Columbia University Press, 1932).

71. Ralph L. Beals and Norman D. Humphrey, *No Frontier to Learning — The Mexican Student in the United States* (Minneapolis: University of Minnesota Press, 1957), p. 19.

72. James G. Maddox, "United Nations Technical Assistance to Mexico," American Universities Field Staff, A Report, December 17, 1956.

73. Ibid., p. 2.

74. Frank Tannenbaum, "The United States and Mexico," *Foreign Affairs*, 27, (October 1948), pp. 44-57.

75. Ibid.

76. Ibid.

Chapter **5**

Religious
Social Systems*

INTRODUCTION

There is nothing in the world which has at once been the object of such deep reverence and the center of such severe criticism as religion; it has been equated with salvation and characterized as the opiate of the people. On the one hand, it is viewed as the "group-supported road to salvation," the path of eternal bliss, or the light of mankind. On the other hand, it is said to be a survival of the primitive, or simply a vestige of an illusion or a collective phantasmagoria. Philosophers and scientists seldom agree on the nature and function of religion. And what Gibbon wrote of the religion of the Roman Empire could very well be said about contemporary forms of worship in the 20th century: "The various modes of worship, which prevailed in the Roman world, were all considered by the people as equally true; by the philosopher, as equally false; and the magistrate, as equally useful."[1]

The sociologist, of course, is not concerned with the truth or falsity of any given religion; he only takes an objective look at religion — its functions, social foundations and social consequences. He does not study religion per se, but the effect of religious beliefs and practices on the social and cultural system, socialization process and personality development. More specifically, the sociologist is concerned with the myriad ways in which society and religion interact, with profound consequences for the individual.

Although the viewpoints and perspectives on religion vary greatly, there seems to be a universal human impulse toward sacredness which manifests itself in the institution of religion, a

*By M. Francis Abraham. See the Preface for citation to a companion essay by Charles Loomis on religion.

(181)

codified system of beliefs, symbolic expressions and rituals. Of all creatures, men alone recognize their own mortality and ponder over death. This awareness induces in them a sense of awe and reverence for what is construed as the supernatural and gives rise to an elaborate system of rituals and ceremonies intended to propitiate the divine force that presides over human destiny. Thus, according to Freud, religion develops from the need to exorcise the horrors of nature, particularly the cruelty of death and also to compensate for the deprivations which culture imposes on the individual.

In his book, *Elementary Forms of Religious Life*, the great French sociologist Emile Durkheim gives a general definition of religion: "Religion is a unified system of beliefs and practices relative to sacred things, uniting into a single moral community all those who adhere to those beliefs and practices."[2] Paul Tillich says that religion is that which concerns man ultimately. Religion entails a form of worship, obedience to divine commandments and a concern with transcendental realms that are beyond the rational and the empirical. While it is difficult to formulate a universally acceptable definition of religion, the phenomenon displays at least three basic elements that are easily identifiable: (1) an irresistible obsession with the sacred, variously defined as God, *Totems*, supernatural, eternal or the ultimate, which manifests itself in ritualistic practices, ceremonies and symbolic expressions; (2) a social form with networks of institutional arrangements and status-roles; and (3) a moral philosophy which unites the mundane and the supernatural in a mystical blend.

There are eleven world religions today. Christianity has the largest group of followers with 986 million believers and Islam is the second largest religion with a following of 472 million. Whereas Christianity is the dominant religion of the West, Hinduism, Sikhism and Jainism are practiced primarily in India. Taoism and Confucianism are traditional Chinese religions and Shintoism is the ancient Japanese religion. Buddhism is concentrated in East Asia and Islam in West Asia.

ELEMENTS AND ELEMENTAL PROCESSES

KNOWING

Knowledge (belief). Any proposition about an aspect of the universe that is accepted as true may be called a belief. Religion is founded on many such beliefs, although they are not usually universal or easily demonstratable. A systematic belief, doctrine or theology is not necessarily a universal component of religion; not even belief in God — personal or transcendental — is essential to the existence of a religion. As a matter of fact, several major religions of the world like Buddhism, Confucianism, Shintoism and Taoism do not involve a god-figure; they constitute certain ethical and philosophical systems that emphasize correct behavior and a moral way of life.

Based on beliefs of members, religions are divided into two types, monotheistic and polytheistic. The former believe in only one God, the omnipresent, omnipotent, supernatural God, the center of Judaic-Christian theology and ethic. Polytheistic religions like the natural religions of ancient Greeks and Romans and many primitive religions of today worship several gods who preside over numerous forces of nature. Even Hinduism as a form of worship — as opposed to a philosophical system — is a loose association of numerous local religious cults which seek to propitiate different deities that preside over particular villages, castes or clans. Whether it is the one transcendental God of the Christians, a beautiful female deity of the Eskimos, the whole God of the Cherokee Indians, the totem of the Australian aboriginals or the Greek Gods of Mount Olympus, religion throughout the centuries was always emphasized and expressed in terms of a given belief or a system of beliefs. No wonder followers of any religion are called believers or "the faithful" and non-members of religious groups are characterized as those who have "lost" their faith.

Myths, legends and sacred texts provide a framework of knowledge within which the supernatural and the phenomenon outside the ordinary experience become meaningful to the believers. Similarly, the profuse use of symbols by believers is part of an attempt to explain the ultimate and unknown in terms of the mundane and the ordinary, while transcending the objects to the heights of veneration and sanctity. Thus, knowledge of a superhuman figure and his "demands" is transformed into a pattern of rituals and ceremonies. With this knowledge, doctrines and beliefs like retributive justice, last judgment, forgiveness, absolution, salvation, etc. become meaningful. As Malinowski observes:

> To us the most essential point about magic and religious ritual is that it steps in only where knowledge fails. Supernaturally founded ceremonial grows out of life, but it never stultifies the practical efforts of man. In his ritual of magic or religion, man attempts to enact miracles, not because he ignores the limitations of his mental powers, but, on the contrary, because he is fully cognizant of them. To go one step further, the recognition of this seems to me indispensable if we want once and for

ever to establish the truth that religion has its own subject-matter, its
own legitimate field of development; that this must never encroach on
the domain where science, reason, and experience ought to remain
supreme.[3]

Max Weber has provided an insightful synthesis of the world's
major religious beliefs. He identified two particularly consistent
belief systems: (1) The Hindu belief in the transmigration of souls
which grew directly out of the universally diffused representations of
the fate of spirits after death and in the principle of retributive justice
by which the sins of a previous life are expiated in the present life. (2)
The Calvinistic belief in predestination. Just as a Hindu believes that
the caste into which he is born is predetermined by his conduct in a
prior life, a Calvinist believes that all human souls are predestined to
either salvation or damnation. Weber also stressed the key role
played by intellectualism in the development of theodicy and ethical
prophesy. In this context he dwelt on the systematic elaboration of
the Talmudic law among Jews, intellectualism of early Christians,
ascetic Protestantism and the classical Brahminical intellectualism.
Referring to the latter he wrote: "Right thought and right knowledge
were held to be like sources of magical power. Here as elsewhere, such
knowledge did not retain the character of ordinary common sense.
The supreme good could be achieved only through a higher knowledge: a gnosis."[4]

One of the earthly consequences of religious beliefs particularly
relevant to modern sociology is prejudice. Anti-Semitism or prejudice
against Jews has always been prevalent in the Christian world in
varying degrees. The conflict between Catholics and Protestants in
the West, between Hindus and Moslems in India and between
Christians and Buddhists in Viet Nam are only manifest expressions
of certain religious beliefs. Historians have often argued that the
Christian church was largely responsible for the development of
anti-Semitism in medieval times. Most recently Glock and Stark[5]
argued that several Orthodox theological beliefs of Christians induce
in them a religious hostility toward the historic Jew who is held
responsible for the crucifixion of Christ. Several empirical studies of
the relationship between religiosity and anti-Semitism show that
more religious Christians tend to be more prejudiced against the
Jews. Simpson[6] and Vanecko[7] found a positive association between
Church attendance and anti-Semitism. However, findings have not
always been consistent. For instance, Middleton[8] and O'Reilly[9] found
no significant relationship between Christian belief and anti-
Semitism.

Cognitive mapping and validation as process. The Hindu doctrine of transmigration of souls, the Calvinist doctrine of predestination, the Catholic faith in the infallibility of Pope, the concept of last judgment and certainly the faith in God are all believed in by followers. Weber's critique on the religion of India is significant here: "For 'faith' in the typically religious sense does not necessarily intend facts and teachings to be true — such belief in dogmas can only be fruit and symptom of the actual religious sense. A religion of faith implies the religious devotion, the unconditional trust and obedience and the orientations of one's entire life to a god or redeemer".[10] Magical asceticism, mysticism, redemption religiosity, faith in the charismatic 'gurus' or magical redeemers, sorteriological entrenched power of religious traditions, and belief in ordeal, oracle and signs interfered with the process of rationalization. And Buddhism discouraged knowledge as a form of 'thirst' or desire and inquiry into the nature of *Nirvana* was treated as heresy because the "great cosmic mystery" remained unsolvable for human wisdom.

Similarly many Protestant sects believed in a God who was wholly transcendental, and therefore, incomprehensible to the finite minds of men. The best way to know him is to study his works, the world around us. This religious conception encouraged development of scientific research for the comprehension of natural order. Many schools of higher learning, among which are some of the earliest and the most prestigious in the United States, owe their foundation to the motivation of knowing God better through systematic study of the world's natural phenomena as well as theology. This shift away from the mystical and the otherworldly orientation and toward a more positive and pragmatic approach led to the development of modern rational, empirical science. According to Loomis:

> The Protestant, in search for an understanding of God, was cut off from such supports as church and priest, as found in the Catholic confessional, by virtue of the extreme anti-ritualism of Protestant belief. He was further thrust upon his own resources by the tenet that God must come before family members and friends. Furthermore, any of the friends or relatives upon whom one might otherwise rely, might be damned in accordance with the predestination principle of Calvinism. All of this led to an "inner isolation of the individual." The inner isolation in combination with the push toward a quest in nature for the essence of God, led to a rationalization of conduct.[11]

The dawn of the 19th century witnessed a scathing attack on religion in general and historic Christianity in particular. Religion has become increasingly imageless, having lost its moral authority among the working classes in industrial societies and its symbolic value among the intellectuals. The Darwinian theory of evolution, the Marxian theory of socialism, the purely intellectual interpretations of religion by Fraser, Comte, Nietzsche and others and the development of rational science have shaken the foundations of religion.

The new attempts at rationalization had two inevitable consequences: (1) The accelerating process of secularization; and (2) The reverberating process of resacralization as a counter-offensive to secularization.

Secularization. In his book, *The Secular City*, which so effectively captured the theological mood of the 1960's, Harvey Cox refers to secularization as the process that "simply bypasses and undercuts religion and goes on to other things."[12] He adds: "The gods of traditional religions live on as private fetishes or the patrons of congenial groups, but they play no significant role in the public life of the secular metropolis."[13] And in McKee's words, "As a cultural process, secularization is a desacralization of the world, in which there is no overarching religious symbolism for the integration of society, and in which man's understanding of himself and of his society are no longer primarily in religious terms."[14] Thus the world has become more rational and secular; economic, political and educational institutions have become separated from religious perspectives. Neither the laws of nature nor the laws of man are any longer interpreted in terms of traditional religious beliefs; rather religion itself is being radically transformed to meet the changing conditions of the modern world. The sources of secularization are many and varied. The intellectual interpretation of religion since the Renaissance, emergence of the Protestant ethic, the development of modern science and resultant technological revolution, movements to update the Catholic church since Pope John XXIII, the death-of-God theology and the many radical perspectives on religion, and the various contemporary movements aimed at making religion relevant — they all have contributed to the accelerating process of secularization. As Peter Berger and Robert Bellah suggest, today's religion has moved away from the institutionalized framework of dogma and devotion; it has become more subjective, personal, and a privatized form of inner faith which retains its influence primarily within the family.

Resacralization. Just as the Reformation was followed by counter-reformation the contemporary trends in secularization are countered by several new religious revival movements which *Time* magazine portrayed as "Searching Again for the Sacred." *Time* quotes California's Episcopal Bishop C. Kilmer Myers as saying: "We have become imageless. We have no symbols like Moses' passage through the Red Sea. We are empty people. The elements of mystery in the church have been almost systematically removed. But hunger for the mysterious is widespread in all people. We cannot be human unless we have the experience of transcendence."[15] This statement explains the growing momentum of various religious sects — evangelist, fundamentalist, transcendental and mystical. Membership in doctrinally conservative Protestant churches is booming and the ranks of Roman Catholic traditionalists are growing. Young Americans are returning to an appreciation of mysticism, particularly of the great Eastern religions. Robert Ellwood, Jr. estimates that there are at least 500,000 members of various Eastern religious groups in the United States, not counting the practitioners of transcendental meditation and fellow-travelers like students of Yoga and readers of books on mysticism who number several millions. The totalitarian disciplines of the Children of God, Jesus Movement communes, Krishna Consciousness movement, Zen Buddhism, Integral Yoga retreats, transcendental meditation of Maharish Mahesh Yogi, Pentacostal groups and the growing ranks of various fundamentalist groups within the established churches attest to a growing undercurrent of disillusionment about man's ability to transform either himself or his world, and the resultant quest for new religious roots.

The trend is clear: religion of today lays less emphasis on glorifying the given and the God-ordained or validating the inherent inconsistencies of faith but dwells upon the social and psychological functions of religion and takes advantage of the inability of modern science to provide a meaningful insight into the inner experience of man and to transcend it.

FEELING

Sentiment. Emotionalism plays a vital role in the cultural practices of world religions. It is hard to find a uniform pattern of sentimentalism; the feeling structure is determined by the intensity of one's faith, the doctrinaire orthodoxy of a religion, form of rituals and the formative influence of different sects. A comparative study of the types of religious communion would lay bare the motives for their foundation as well as the stages of their evolution. A sense of awe and reverence toward the over-powering forces of nature, a fear of the unknown, anticipation of death and contemplation of the supernatural built the sentiment structure which is the very foundation of religious symbolism.[16]

Durkheim believes that gods are simply transfigurations of social forces. According to him men have never worshipped any other reality — in the form of totem or God — than the collective social reality transfigured by faith. Societies are inclined to create gods or religions when they are in a state of exaltation, an exaltation which occurs when social life itself is intensified. Such moments of collective activity, masses of men dancing and shouting, partaking in feasts and religious services, and the trance of sacred enthusiasm carries each individual outside of himself and enables him to experience something extraordinary, immanent and transcendental. Here is the relevant passage from Durkheim:

> It is not difficult to imagine that, having reached this state of exaltation, man no longer knows himself, and feels himself dominated, carried away by a kind of outside power which makes him think and act differently than he ordinarily does. He naturally has the sensation of no longer being himself. He seems to have become a different creature. The decorations in which he is rigged out, the kinds of masks with which his face is covered represent this interior transformation materially even more than they help to bring it about. And since at the same time all his companions are transfigured in similar manner and express their feelings by their cries, their gestures, their attitudes, all proceed as if they really were transported into a special world, completely different from the one in which he ordinarily lives, into a milieu swarming with exceptionally intense forces which invade and transform him. How could experiences like these, especially when they recur daily for weeks, fail to convince him that there indeed exist two worlds which are hetereogeneous and not to be compared with one another? One is the world in which he languidly drags out his daily life; whereas he cannot penetrate the other without also entering into communion with extraordinary powers which stimulate him to the point of frenzy. The first is the profane world, the second is the world of sacred things.[17]

Tenets of faith as well as rituals perpetuated by different religious groups reinforce the feeling structure. For example, according to Calvinists and others of similar persuasion man stood alone before his Creator and there was no place for him to turn to for support. God's elect could understand the work of God in their own hearts only, and, since the church included among its members the doomed as well as the saved, support from church membership could not be relied upon. The sentiments of uneasiness, fear and worry evoked by these beliefs led to the orientation toward rational organization.

Sociologically speaking, the influence of religion may include a positive or cohesive integrating influence. The sharing of a common religion and the pervasive influence of symbolism have served to integrate the social and cultural fabric, particularly in primitive and traditional societies. However, the history of religion is also ridden with brutal and bloody contests, violent internal strife and destructive power struggle. Whether the overriding influence of religious sentiments has been integrative or disintegrative is hard to say.

Communication of sentiment as process. Symbolic communication of sentiment has always been a vital process inherent in all religions. It has three aspects. One is the manifest expression of solidarity, identity and awe-feeling among believers of the same faith. Another is latent or manifest hostility toward members of a different faith. Prejudice, discrimination, 'Holy' wars, crusades, communal riots, persecution, excommunication, burning at the stake, witch trials, festivals, ceremonies, prayers and worship are manifest expressions of religious sentiments. The third is universal as opposed to particularistic orientation which regards religion as a matter of personal faith and promotes tolerance of all faiths.

Communication of religious sentiments has involved the use or manipulation of the following:

1. Symbols — any sacred object like a cross, fire, totem, bone, tree, etc.
2. Movements — nativistic, messianic or proselytizing — which have played a major role in the spread of religious beliefs and ideology.
3. Holy texts — believed to be based on revelation and containing the tenets of faith and rules of conduct.
4. System of rituals including festivals, ceremonies, prayers, religious services, feasts, sacrifices, offerings, etc.
5. Expressive culture, particularly literature and the visual arts. From the earliest known artistic attempts of pre-historic man, through the Renaissance, to the present century, paintings and sculptures have served as vehicles for the communication of religious sentiments. Many of the master-pieces of world art testify to the association between religion and expressive culture throughout much of human history.

An objective look at the proliferating religious groups and communes of today will clearly bring out the importance of commitment and communication of sentiments in any fellowship of faith. Yinger writes:

If many of us today live in "the lonely crowd," we would expect to find "cults of re-assurance." It is not surprising that the title of a prominent

Protestant family magazine is *Together*, or that the "new religions" in Japan have spread most widely among recent migrants to the city who have been cut off from regular contacts with their families and villages. In the last several years, to be sure, the somewhat self-centered emphasis on the pains of loneliness has been modified by greater activism among some groups. This may only change the way in which isolation is dealt with, however, and not indicate its abatement. One can observe, without in any way criticizing programs of social action by religious groups, that joint efforts in "good works" can produce a powerful effect of communion, of attachment to others.[18]

Tension management as process.   Religion is probably the most enduring and imaginative tension-management device ever created by man. Man transformed his fears of the forces of nature into a cult of the unknown and invented a system of rituals in order to propitiate the supernatural, or the deity that presided over the overpowering forces of nature. The main undercurrent of all religions, from the primitive to the most modern, is a fusion of reverence and devotion to the ultimate which will enable man to overcome his fears by linking mundane existence with eternal bliss. Even the psychological interpretation of Freud rested on the assumption that man created religions in an attempt to thwart the anxieties he felt in a world that was beyond his control. According to him, the feelings men developed in their nearly helpless stages of infancy and childhood toward their parents were in adulthood transferred to the supernatural.

Most ethical systems proclaim absolute mastery over passions and desires to be an essential prerequisite to salvation. Orthodox Hinduism, Buddhism, and Jainism alike stress the importance of self-control in the process of holy-seeking. "Forbearance, patience, freedom from envy, purity, tranquility, correct life, freedom from desire, and freedom from covetousness are the eight good qualities of the soul in Gautama's law book."[19] The general principles and commandments of Hinduism include "abstinence from intoxicants and from the enjoyment of meat and honey, absolute avoidance of any sort of unchastity and strict loyalty in marriage, avoidance of status pride, of anger, and all passions."[20] Absolute indifference to world affairs including complete freedom from attachment to family is required of the seeker of eternal bliss.

The spirit of revival prevalent in the contemporary American religions is a response to the quality of life in the modern mass society where individuals feel lost in a "lonely crowd," unloved, unvalued and cut off from moral roots. Disenchanted with the moral barrenness of technocratic revolution and dissatisfied with the death-of-God theology, men wanted to escape the social dustheap of modern metropolises. As Yinger points out, "Most of the vigorous religious movements in American cities reflect the efforts of various groups to come to terms with urban life, to feel at home in a sea of strangers, to find some stability in a setting where so much is changing."[21] The communitarian communes, new utopias, and the numerous religious countercultures betray the sentiment of the mass man — the feeling of alienation, anomie, meaninglessness and self-estrangement attributable to technocratic revolution, gigantic industrial bureaucracies, the breakdown of primary relationships, the atomization of group life and the weakening of traditional authority-structures.[22]

Thus, when everything else seems to be crumbling, more and more young people are turning to the conscious manipulation of Eastern religions, the commitment-oriented communitarian communes or to secular religions that stress love and devotion more than hell-fire and brimstone. In short, religion accomplishes tension management in several ways.

1. It helps individuals reconcile to the hardships and inequities of society by interpreting failure and frustration symbolically and by advising believers not to take vicissitudes of mundane existence seriously.
2. It promises salvation or eternal bliss to those who have tread the prescribed path.
3. It provides a kind of psychic insurance policy by uniting believers into a fellowship of shared experience.
4. It offers support when other social institutions are rapidly changing, throwing the individual out of gear. This is particularly true of periods of crisis such as war, depression and the like.
5. It gives the individual a sense of personal identity, meaning and inner experience and may bring transcendence of the same.

ACHIEVING

End, goal or objective.   Spiritual values of a religion center on the ultimate goal, the direction of movement set for its followers. The advent of redemption religiosity and the birth of salvation religions have considerably influenced the concept of ultimate goal. Buddhism preached *nirvana* or salvation from existence as the supreme goal. The monks considered "freedom from life thirst" to be an essential prerequisite to the "sudden leap into the psychic state of illumination, a leap which can only be prepared for through methodical contemplation."[23] Similarly, Jainism also stressed *Nirvana* which, according to it, was "salvation from the body", the source of all sin, vice and lust. Likewise, in the monasteries of early Christendom,

> the end of . . . asceticism was to be able to lead an alert, intelligent life; the most urgent task (being to contribute to) the destruction of spontaneous impulsive enjoyment . . . (and to) bring order into conduct. In ascetic Protestantism 'every Christian had to be a monk all his life.'[24]

Now let us look on the instrumentality of religion from the functional perspective. Radcliffe-Brown and Malinowski have provided the most thorough-going functional interpretation of religion. According to these authors, every society must, in order to survive, meet a number of functional prerequisites, one of the most important being solidarity of its members or simply social integration. Religion is regarded as the integrative and legitimating institution which unite people in a cohesive and binding moral order. Also, religion is an agent of social control which threatened punishment in this world as well as beyond it. According to Marx, religion was a tool of the bourgeoisie who used it to secure the unquestioned services of the working class. Today religious belief is commonly recommended for its utilitarian value — for the "power of positive thinking," mental health, better family life, patriotism and richer and more meaningful life.

Contemporary religions mark a shift from the doctrine of predestination to a general extension of the Social Gospel which has come to view Christ as a social revolutionary and church as an instrument of social revolution. In the late 1950s and early 1960s there arose in the United States a series of church-centered activities directly related to civil rights, poverty, ecological balance, world peace and the like. In the new theology, the Calvinist interpretations of success in business and professions were overshadowed by the genuine concern for the sick, the poor, the maimed, the outcast and the down-trodden.

Goal attaining and concomitant latent activity as process. As the ends which individuals pursue are many and varied, so are the means which they adopt. For example, Jewish and Islamic traditions emphasize correct observance of the religious law. Right behavior is given primary attention in Hinduism and Buddhism. Partaking of sacraments was stressed in early Roman Catholicism and strict moral conduct was the corner-stone of Puritan ethic.[25] The Brahmin stressed gnosis, contemplation and asceticism as sacred means. Referring to Mahayana doctrine Weber writes: "Mahayanism, first through formalistic prayers, finally, through the techniques of prayer mills and prayer ships hung in the wind or spat-upon idols, attained the high point of cult mechanism and joined it to the transformation of the entire world into an immense magical garden."[26] And, Elaide points out that the use of opium and other drugs has been widespread among some Oriental religious movements, Muslim mystical orders and various Siberian and Indian tribes.

Yinger has outlined several types of religious behavior that serve as means to professed ends:

1. Addressing the supernatural (prayer, exorcism).
2. Music (dancing, singing, chanting, playing instruments).
3. Physiological exercise (physical manipulation of psychological states through drugs, deprivation, and mortification).
4. Exhortation (addressing others as representative of divinity).
5. Reciting the code (use of the sacred written and oral literature, which contains statements regarding the pantheon, cosmology, myths, and moral injunctions).
6. Simulation (imitating things for purposes of control).
7. Mana (touching things possessed of sacred power; laying on of hands).
8. Taboo (avoiding things to prevent the activation of unwanted power or undesired events).
9. Feasts (sacred meals).
10. Sacrifices (immolation, offerings, fees).
11. Congregation (processions, meetings, convocations).
12. Inspiration (pursuit of revelation, conversion, possession, mystical ecstasy).
13. Symbolism (manufacture and use of symbolic objects).

Perhaps the above categories of religious behavior treat religion too much as a static and isolated system, and therefore we might extend them in two directions:

14. Extending and modifying the code (in connection with category 5).
15. Applying religious values in nonreligious contexts (what later, following Charles Glock, we will call the consequential dimension).[27]

In *Feast of Fools*, Harvey Cox has put forth a strong case for the renewal of 'festival and fantasy' in modern life. The moral bankruptcy of modern life, the existential dread and alienation so pervasive in mass society and the rapidity with which contemporary social organizations are changing, have created a "declassification" of life which, in the opinion of Cox, can be set right by reviving religiously-oriented folk songs, drama, music, feasting and a variety of rituals. The introduction of guitars and drums into church choir, toe-tapping tunes, folk songs and new dance-forms adopted by different religious groups represent various attempts at regaining an aspect of lightness.

One significant latent activity stands apart from all the rest and has received the greatest attention in theoretical sociology. This is Weber's theory of the Protestant ethic and the spirit of capitalism. According to Weber,

> The religious valuation of restless, continuous, systematic work in a worldly calling, as the highest means to asceticism, and at the same time the success and most evident proof of rebirth and genuine faith, must have been the most powerful conceivable lever for the expansion of that attitude toward life which we have here called the spirit of capitalism.[28]

Weber believed that Protestant asceticism, particularly Calvinism, was highly influential in the appearance of the capitalist spirit. He was intrigued by the fact that full-fledged capitalism was developed in predominantly Protestant countries of Western Europe and North America, whereas many of the Catholic countries like Spain and Portugal in spite of their earlier glory failed to attain the economic arrangement of capitalism based on rational bureaucracy. Weber showed many areas in which the spirit of capitalism and the Protestant ethic are in harmony. The values embedded in Protestantism that facilitated the emergence of capitalism were:

1. A shift from mysticism and other worldly orientations to down-to-earth pragmatism and scientific inquiry into the natural order.
2. The belief that work is necessary and good and can contribute to the glory of God, as opposed to the Catholic conception of work as a punitive necessity.
3. The concept of predestination and the divine command to build the kingdom of God on earth.
4. Permission to collect interest on loans which was tabooed in the Catholic theology.
5. Emphasis on literacy based on the exhortation that everyone should read his own Bible.
6. Strictures on alcohol use.
7. Rejection of holy days, rituals, ceremonies, festivals, etc.

8. Protestant asceticism based on the teaching that earthly things and flesh belong to the order of sin and death and that salvation can come to man only through divine grace.

Thus, the relationship between the Protestant ethic and the spirit of capitalism is this: accept a calling, work hard, be successful in business or profession but abstain from the pleasures of the world. In effect, to accumulate, save, reinvest in productive process, was the essence of the new religious ethic — a condition par excellence for capitalism. Weber has convincingly argued that outside Western civilization we cannot find a religious interpretation comparable to the Protestant ethic. In China and India, there were many conditions favorable to the rise of capitalism but their combination in Calvinism is original and unique.

NORMING

Norm. Religious norms are twofold: prescriptive norms and proscriptive norms.

1. Prescriptive norms. These are norms that prescribe a form of conduct, and every religion commands its believers to fulfill certain basic obligations. The concept of *Dharma* or correct ritual behavior for the Hindus, the holy day of obligation for Catholics, the observance of Sabbath in the Judaic-Christian tradition and several of the commandments in the old testaments are prescriptive norms. "Honor thy father and thy mother, that thy days may be long upon the land which the Lord thy God giveth thee" is a typical example.
2. Proscriptive norms. These are norms that forbid or proscribe certain types of behavior. "Thou shalt not kill or thou shalt not commit adultery" are examples.

In his monumental work on *The Religion of India* Max Weber has carefully delineated the normative structure of Hinduism, Buddhism and Jainism. He has outlined the steps that constitute the eight-fold path contained in the famous sermon of Buddha in Banares: (1) Correct insight which involves rational understanding and insight permeating one's entire being; (2) Right will, the compassionate wise renunciation of all pleasures of life; (3) Right speech — the avoidance of untruths and loveless speech through mastery of one's own passionate nature; (4) Proper life conduct which involves the elimination from conduct of all impurities and particularly all interest in the results of one's own correct action; (5) *Sammo ajivo* — a spiritual

power of the holy will attained through tremendous exertion of all
one's powers in the service of the holy goal; (6) The right power of will,
that is, inner attitude of holy knowledge; (7) Perfection in which only
holy thoughts and feelings prevail; (8) the right concentration or the
last and highest step — *Nirvana.*

The Code of Manu, the great Hindu law-giver, lists the following
virtues:

> contentment, patience, self-control, non-stealing, purity, control of
> desire, piety, knowledge, truthfulness, and freedom from anger. These
> were also condensed into five commandments for all castes: to injure no
> living being, to tell the truth, not to steal, to live purely, to control the
> passions. Quite similar commandments appear as the first step of
> yoga.[29]

And Parsons concludes, "It is probably no accident that it is on a
Brahman-Hindu-Buddhist background that the radical doctrine of
Ahimsa — the prohibition of killing of any living thing, except plants
of course — has arisen, and that vegetarianism is very much a virtue
among high caste Hindus."[30]

The most recurrent theme in the normative system of Judaic-
Christian tradition is brotherly love enjoined by the Bible. The ascetic Protestants interpreted it "as a fulfillment of the daily tasks given
by the natural law." Max Weber contrasted the highly developed
rational legal procedures of the West with the scanty development in
the East. The West typically possessed a temporal law completely
distinguished from its sacred law whereas in the East secular law was
inextricably intertwined with sacred tradition.

Evaluation as a process. Religion as an inner state can have no
effect on reality until it has objectified itself into a concrete mood or
form through a communion of religious experience which can substantiate the emergent norms as well as transcend the collective
experience.[31] Sacred tradition and ethical systems to a great extent
reflect the attitude of each religion to the world. Some religions
present a cheerful evaluation of the world whereas the attitude of
other religions is decidedly negative, portraying the world in the
darkest colors. However, the Judao-Christian tradition presents a
combination of negative metaphysical and ethical interpretations of
the world which includes the possibility of sanctification in full or in
part.

Thus a comparison of classical Greek, Buddhist, and Hindu religious
evaluations of nature reveals characteristically different reactions.

Such differences in the interpretation of nature are well illustrated by an examination of the attitude toward nature held by Eastern and Roman Catholicism and by several types of Protestantism. Nature is variously accepted naively, is vigorously rejected, or is considered capable of sanctification.[32]

These differences have significantly influenced the variety and complexity of norms issued by different religions. Exhortation of asceticism, total abstinence, celibacy, meditation, renunciation, magical mysticism, alcoholic intoxication, sexual orgiasticism, drug addiction and the rejection of the mundane in favor of the other-worldly, or the commandment to build the kingdom of God on earth, were all different manifestations of varying attitudes to the world. Even the acceptance or rejection of the arts, music, painting, sculpture, drama and dancing — by the different religious groups — reflects their general orientation to the world. In this context it is worth remembering Hegel celebrated "characterization of the Chinese religion as one of measure, of the Syrian as religion of pain, of the Jewish as religion of sublimity, of the Greek as religion of beauty, and of the Roman as religion of utility."[33]

DIVIDING THE FUNCTIONS

Status-role as element and process. Analysis of status-roles in religion could be subsumed under three categories:

1. Professed role of the faithful. Redemption religions like Catholic Christianity and Buddhism glorified the status-role of saints and stressed meditations, penance, pilgrimage, poverty, celibacy, renunciation, monastic life, and even self-torture. But Calvinists and others of similar persuasion accepted "legitimate calling," hard work and success in business as means that fulfill their obligation to God as well as outward expression of brotherly love. Weber observes:

> The religious life of the saints, as distinguished from the natural life, was — the most important point — no longer lived outside the world in monastic communities, but within the world and its institutions. This rationalization of conduct within the world but for the sake of the world beyond was the consequence of the concept of "calling" of ascetic Protestantism.[34]

2. Projected role of prophets. Max Weber distinguished between ethical prophets and exemplary prophets. Ethical prophets of the Old Testament feel themselves to be the instruments of divine will and claim to speak the voice of a transcendental personal God. Exemplary prophets like ancient Buddha, on the other hand, set examples by which mankind could live in harmony with the world. Seers, charis-

matic leaders, prophets and saints were all men of wisdom, torch-bearers, who showed the "right" path. But in ascetic Protestantism turning to sages and prophets did not make sense, for the God's elect could understand Him in their hearts only. The difference in orientation explains the profound impact of saints and exemplary prophets in both messianic and secular movements in the East and almost complete absence of such status-roles in predominantly Protestant countries.

3. Communal role of contemporary clergymen. Blizzard identified three fundamental roles of Protestant clergymen involving three levels of analysis: (a) practitioner roles based on means; (b) integrative roles based on goals; and (c) master roles based on individual clergymen's conception of the ministry as distinctive from other occupations. The practitioner roles are those of administrator, organizer, pastor, preacher, priest and teacher.[35] The fourteen integrative roles including that of a "community problem solver" or "crusader with a social welfare orientation" concerned "the end toward which he (the minister) is working in his professional relationship with parishioners, church associations, community groups, and the general public.[36] The master role involves the perception of the minister as a servant of Christ, a social evangelist or an exemplary model for parishioners.

Fichter lists nine functional roles normally expected of the parish priest. Hargrove has succinctly summarized them as follows:

> The communal role, in which he is expected to relate to his parishioners as individuals and as a community; the administrative role, as coordinator of the many groups and activities; the businessman role of being responsible for soliciting contributions and making financial reports; the civic role as an influential person in the community and the official representative of his parish; the recreational role of working with boys' clubs and athletic leagues and the like; the ameloriative role of supervising and performing acts of mercy; the educational role of supervising the parochial school as well as teaching from the pulpit and in counseling situations; the sociospiritual role of supervising organizations of a spiritual or liturgical nature; and the liturgical role of presiding at services.[37]

RANKING

Rank as an element. An analysis of social rank in the context of religion may be undertaken at three different levels:

1. Rank order within the religious hierarchy. Wach identifies two fundamental principles that determine the nature and type of religious organization: authoritarian and conciliaristic. The Catholic Church represents a vast hierarchical organization of clergymen

based on the authoritarian principle. It has a pyramid of religious officials — Pope, Cardinals and Archbishops and so on, right down to the neighborhood curate whose rank and status-role are determined by the bureaucracy of church government. Congregationalism, on the other hand, is based on the "conciliaristic" principle and has rejected centralized or collective authority in favor of "the principle of regional crystallization." However, in recent years, there is a strong tendency toward bureaucratization in every religious organization. Modern churches represent a formal and hierarchical structure, with an army of officials, a chain of command from top to bottom, and a well defined rank-order characteristic of large organizations.

2. Social rank and religious affiliation of members. The relationship between religions and social stratification is a celebrated theme in the sociology of religion. Wach lists three occupations or professions which, through the ages, have preferably or exclusively united people who belong to the same occupations, or economic status, and speaks of "the religion of the warrior, of the merchant, and of the peasant."

A survey of recent sociological literature dealing with the relationship between religious membership and social class points up the following conclusions: (1) The Christian churches in most societies of the Western world are predominantly middle class, for whom participation in church activities is part of the expected behavior which stresses respectability, morality and security, (2) The members of higher social classes attend church services more regularly than those in lower classes. (3) Members of the lower class, particularly of the industrial working class and urban manual labor, are increasingly being alienated by the organized church. (4) In the devotional aspects of religious practice, however, lower classes exhibit deeper religiosity than higher classes, for they actively seek and value genuine religious experience in the absence of other sources of support like wealth and prestige which are the monopoly of the higher circles. (5) Conservative church bodies have higher proportions of lower class members than do liberal ones. (6) A separate Negro church has come into its own, which, in recent years, has attracted much of the potential leadership among the blacks and served as a powerful mechanism for integrating the culturally disadvantaged. (7) Religious affiliation is closely linked to income level and vertical social mobility in the United States. Jews and Episcopalians have larger shares of higher income, and Protestants in general have greater career success than Catholics.

3. Ranking and rating of religions themselves. The status of various religious denominations is a theme often overlooked in the sociological analysis. However, a closer look at the rank-order of

different religious denominations in the United States indicate that they are not all of equal esteem. Unitarian and Episcopal churches enjoy greater prestige than most other denominations. Congregationists and Presbyterians rank a little higher than Methodists and Baptists. In England, the Catholic church ranked highest until the formation of the Church of England. Generally speaking, it is the religion of the ruling classes and the elites that have the highest rank.

Evaluation of actors.   Both formal and informal methods may be used, and all religions have used a variety of criteria in evaluating the effectiveness of their leaders:

1. The idea of a mission which involves at least two basic elements — a prophet and a divine call! Even the greatest of the religious leaders did not attain their enlightenment and charisma entirely by themselves. They claimed to be the messengers of God, representing His divine will. Jesus was conscious of being sent by the Father; Mohammed was the messenger of Allah, and Zoroaster of Mazda.[38]

2. Development of a charisma. Charisma or the gift of grace is based on extra-ordinary personal or magical qualities of a person, actual, alleged or presumed. Many of the prophets, seers and saints have inspired horror, veneration and awe in the faithful.

3. Recognition of the moral authority and spiritual leadership of the clergy.

According to Wach:

> Not only in the hierarchically graded ecclesiastical bodies but also in religious groups of a more or less egalitarian constitution the pastor or minister, the regular or monastic spiritual leader, and even the sectarian elder, overseer, or 'bishop' may become the implicitly trusted, rightly revered, and indispensable guides of their followers. The religious guidance of souls involves the care of the physical, moral, social, and economic well-being of the 'flock.' Even in modern Western civilization, where a high degree of specialization had narrowed the activities of the priestly profession, a rapprochement has taken place between physicians, social workers, and priests in recent times which has tended to restore the unity of the priestly work never lost in the Orient.[39]

4. Distinct life styles and special privileges.

> The tremendous authority the priest enjoyed throughout almost all the history of human civilization is reflected in the manifold rights, honors, and privileges granted to priestly individuals and groups. High position and rank, special emblems, distinctions and dress, exemption from

public duties such as taxes, military service, etc., are indications of the high estimate and social prestige in which priesthood is held.[40]

5. Ascription.

The priestly office may be hereditary, as in Israel, Greece, Rome, and Japan and to a certain extent in the Russian church. Priests are at times organized as exclusive groups or castes, but elsewhere admission to this office is achieved.[41]

6. The prevalent system of stratification in a given society. New converts and members of various sects usually rank lower than followers of the dominant, established church. For example, Jews of the Middle Ages could not be integrated into the main stream of social and cultural life; and the Irish and Polish Catholics of modern United States would not be accepted among the Proper Bostonians.

Allocation of Status-roles. Religion as an institutionalized social structure has introduced a functional division of labor into society. As a result, all societies recognize the religious roles of priests and ministers, elders and laymen, missionaries and preachers, monks and seers, bishops and evangelists, prophets and saints. These roles are particularly specific and significant in ecclesiastical bodies with an elaborate hierarchy which has developed "a complicated order of duties, functions, and honors and corresponding differentiations of rank, privileges, and distinctions."[42] Wach has systematically traced the development of priestly roles in the world of religion.

Priestly functions are exercised among identical groups by their heads or leaders; such as the father in the family, the chieftain in the clan or tribe, the king in the nation or people. With the growing development and differentiation of social organizations and stratification, certain cultic functions of the leader are associated with special individuals or professional groups, and, as a result, professional magicians, diviners, and even prophets emerge in the more highly differentiated 'primitive' societies. Since it seems advisable to limit the term 'priest' to the holder of a special office, the above-mentioned functions of the paterfamilias, chieftain, or king might be called 'semipriestly.' This semipriestly activity is found among groups in which the religious and political bodies are identical. With the increasing complexity of cultural and sociological conditions, professional differentiation takes place, and a professional priesthood appears.[43]

Wach's celebrated list of types of religious authority includes founder, reformer, prophet, seer, magician, diviner, saint, priest, and "religious" or a layman leading a highly religious life. And, Sklare describes eight functions of contemporary church leaders: priest (conductor of public worship), preacher, cleric (a function of the state, empowered to perform certain ceremonies), rector (administrator of an organization), pastor (counsellor), father (head of a congregation in a psychological sense), parson (representative of the church to the community), and rabbi (teacher and interpreter of religious doctrines).[44]

Finally, the following passage from Hargrove's *Reformation of the Holy* is particularly relevant:

> The situation of the modern minister involves a series of important role conflicts. Blizzard lists a number of the most frequent. He says a minister is expected to be above all a man of belief, yet if he wants to keep his church strong and well supported, then he will express those beliefs only at certain times and under certain circumstances. As head of a large organization which according to American cultural standard needs to be doing things, he is expected to be a man of action, and yet as a man devoted to declaring the Word of God, he must be a scholar. He plays a very private role as pastor and counselor, yet in his public role as preacher he may be expected to speak to the problems that were confided to him in private. He is expected to serve as a teacher for his people, yet have time and talent for managing organizations. He is expected to be a generalist, able to apply religious insights to all of life, yet he is treated as a specialist who concentrates on religion. His training and status are those of a professional man, yet he seldom has the leisure or the opportunity to arrange his schedule as is expected of such persons. The simple service of God and fellow man which our culture deems the appropriate motivation for choosing the ministry as a vocation has developed into a complex executive position with many internal conflicts. The minister of a large church who has several colleagues with whom he shares his work may be able to divide some of the conflicts with them; however, if he is senior minister, he may have the added burden of coordination and supervision of the work of his staff.[45]

CONTROLLING

Power. Power, which is the ability to control, is free-floating in human society, and may become associated with any one of many distinguishing attributes — with physical strength (Eskimo), age (Andamanese) with being the first-born son of the first-born son (Polynesia), with knowledge (Zunis), psychic gifts or valor in war, with being born with a caul.[46]

In the case of religious groups the element of power may be treated under the following: (1) The traditional moral authority of religion, (2) the clerical hierarchy, and (3) intermingling of religion and politics.

1. Religion in the past exerted considerable moral influence on its followers, particularly in the primitive societies. The ethical system of all religions established an inevitable link between moral values and spiritual values which became inextricably intertwined with the philosophy of religion. "Right behavior" — ritualistic or moralistic — became an indispensable part of the means of salvation. And religion exercised its moral authority through sanctions in this world as well as beyond it. The Middle Ages represented the pinnacle of religious influence on general social organization.

However, like many other social institutions, religion has experienced a marked decline in its sphere of influence in recent years. Religion is no longer the primary integrative force in society; church can no longer sit in judgment over everyday human behavior. Economic, educational and political institutions have been separated from the Church — one of the major consequences of secularization we discussed earlier in the chapter. As Berger suggests, the primary influence of religion today is on a personal level and manifests itself within the family and kinship unit.

2. The power exercised by different churches varies with their organizational structure. There are three major forms of power-structure in Christian churches:

a. Episcopal. The episcopal organization represents a hierarchic pyramid, with final and almost absolute power vested in the person who holds the office at the top of the hierarchy. The Roman Catholic church, the Anglican Church and the Episcopal church illustrate this type of organization in which the priest or bishop is answerable and responsible only to his superior officials and the laity have no voice in their appointment or transfer.

b. The Presbyterian structure. Here the governing power is vested in a presbytery or council of elders, made up primarily of ministers. In the absence of bishops or superior officers, the decision-making power is vested in the council whereas the local congregation enjoys a limited amount of autonomy including the right to request the appointment of a minister and to select one from a list of available candidates.

c. The Congregational. Here, the power is concentrated in the local congregation which makes decisions and can hire and fire ministers without any interference from outside.

3. The intermingling of religion and politics. The relationship between religion and political institutions is one of the oldest in human history. The traditional authority of the tribal chief in the primitive societies was sanctified by religion. The Brahmins, the priestly caste of the Hindus, although possessing no organization

comparable to a church, retained their supremacy during most of the period in India's long history. In the West, the history of the Holy Roman Empire and the supremacy of church during most of medieval period testify to the enormous power wielded by church. However, the dawn of the age of enlightenment and the philosophers of Rennaissance initiated a new era which set in motion waves of reforms that radically altered the relationship between religion and society. With the accelerating process of secularization, the priest and the ministry have lost many of their traditional functions. The decline of their social and political prestige is particularly evident in contemporary nation-states characterized by professional specialization and structural differentiation.[47]

Yet in almost all contemporary societies, especially in the democratic countries, religions serve as important pressure groups trying to sway the balance of power one way or the other. Almost every religious group in the United States maintains lobbying groups in Washington D.C. charged with contacting legislators, and have a number of departments in charge of press, social action, education, youth, welfare, etc. The POAU (Protestants and Other Americans United for the Separation of Church and State), Quakers' Committee on National Legislation, and the National Catholic Welfare Conference are only some of the specific examples.

Decision-making and initiation of action. The various religious groups range from the most power-centered, authoritarian, hierarchic structure illustrated by the Roman Catholic Church, to the most power-diffuse situations, represented by the Quaker meetings in which decision-making is governed by the principle of consensus. Weber compares the activities of the Brahmans and of the Christian clergy: "The leading guru in a territory is similar to a bishop of a Western church . . . He had power to excommunicate individuals in case of grosser sins . . , bestowed absolution for penitence and . . . placed a tax on believers. He was father-advisor and father-confessor authority.[48]

Weber's celebrated classification of authority has immediate relevance for decision-making and initiation of action. He identified three types of authority.

1. Traditional, where authority is based on custom and tradition. Here the onus of decision-making and initiation of action rests exclusively in the hands of the traditional leader — tribal chief in a primitive society, or father, in a patriarchal system.

2. Rational-legal, where authority exists in formal organizations and is based on rules and regulations. Contemporary religious groups resemble well-established formal organizations with govern-

ing boards, directors, secretaries and committees where the process of decision-making is institutionalized and legitimized by formal rules.

3. Charismatic, where authority is based on extraordinary personal qualities of a leader, his magical aura, prophetic zeal, and dynamic personality. Christ, Mohammed and Buddha as well as a number of saints and prophets exerted tremendous influence on the strength of their charismatic qualities.

A review of the structure and functioning of contemporary religious groups in the United States points up three recent trends relevant to the process of decision-making. They are:

1. Increasing tendency toward bureaucratization of religious organization. Boskoff writes:

> The minister (or rabbi) — and often his wife — is a religious executive, supplemented by assistant or associate ministers, secretaries, governing boards, directors of religious education and music, laymen's committees, and a variety of intra-denominational organizations (local, state, regional, and national). Consequently, urban religion in its institutionalized forms is to many urban residents a poor substitute for traditional forms of religion. One typical reaction is passive participation; another is a gradual assumption of a secular attitude that blurs any previously meaningful distinction between the routine and the extraordinary. Still another reaction is the segregation of dissidents into factions jockeying for power. Most important, however, is a tendency toward stratification, which is understandable on historical and theological grounds as well.[49]

2. Trends toward greater participation by the laity in the decision-making process. The opening to experimentation in life style of religious orders, change in clothing styles and cloistered living patterns, greater participation on both ritual and internal government and the inclusion of women in the ministerial orders represent favorable response to various movements organized by change-minded men of the laity as well as the clergy.

3. The development of the philosophy of social gospel. One of the most important consequences of the mobilization of the laity was an attempt at making church more relevant. The philosophy of social gospel or "the prophetic minority of the church" and an active involvement on the part of the church in social action programs represent a growing concern for making the world a better place to live. As Hargrove observes:

> Ministers have often taken the lead in causes of community betterment, whether these have involved the prohibition of saloons and bawdy

houses; clean-up, paint-up, fix-up campaigns; social gatherings aimed at fostering good will; or the rights and needs of the poor or downtrodden. It is from this tradition that the Social Gospel developed, and that more recent activities in the area of civil rights and peace arose. It is this tradition that developed the idea of churches as political pressure groups.[50]

SANCTIONING

Sanction as element and application of sanctions as process. The term sanction refers to rewards and penalties meted out by the members of a social system in order to induce conformity to its norms and ends. Hell, heaven, excommunication and damnation are the most frequently mentioned sanctions in the religious literature. Max Weber explains the rationale behind such sanctions thus:

> The rationalization of taboos leads ultimately to a system of norms according to which certain actions are permanently construed as religious abominations subject to sanctions, and occasionally even entailing the death of the malefactor in order to prevent evil sorcery from overtaking the entire group because of the transgression of the guilty individual. In this manner there arises an ethical system, the ultimate warrant of which is taboo. This system comprises dietary restrictions, the proscription of work on taboo or "unlucky" days (the Sabbath was originally a taboo day of this type), and certain prohibitions against marriage to specified individuals, especially within the circle of one's blood relations. The usual process here is that something which has become customary, whether on rational grounds or otherwise, e.g., experiences relative to illness and other effects of evil sorcery, comes to be regarded as sacred.[55]

The Roman Catholic Church during Middle Ages exercised extreme negative sanctions against those who fell short of correct behavior. Torture, persecution and burning at stakes were part of the normative system of that era. The ascetic Protestants of the 16th century also imposed extreme negative sanctions upon deviants. Hinduism, Judaism and Catholic Christianity have made effective use of excommunication, one of the most powerful sanctions known to man.

Organized religion is an agent of social control which poses a threat of punishment to those who deviate from social norms. The unique advantage of religious sanctions is their supernatural character. On the one hand, the sin need not necessarily be detected and reported by another social actor; the supernatural power watches over everything. On the other hand, the effectiveness of religious sanction extends far beyond this world — into the life hereafter. Moreover, religion also provides a way for the deviant individual to atone for his deviance by repentance, release, penance, confession, fasting or a ritual of purification. This system, incidentally, reduces the strain on the individual who has been publicly branded as a deviant and facilitates his acceptance by the system.

FACILITATING

Facility as element and utilization of facilities as process. Any means used to attain given ends within a system are construed as facilities. Hence the numerous means of salvation recommended by different religions may be classified as facilities. Symbols, rituals, ceremonies, offerings, holy scriptures, hymns, the totems, prayer wheels, centers of pilgrimage, places of worship like temples, mosques, churches or synagogues, sacraments, sacred relics like a bone, or hair and idols are facilities within the context of religion.

Commenting on Max Weber's work on religion, Charles Loomis and Zona Loomis write:

> For the early Puritan to waste his time was a deadly sin because the span of life is so short and precious that he must use every minute to serve the Lord in the building of the Kingdom of Heaven on earth and also in providing his own election to salvation. The economical use of money in the construction of any place of worship was important and one of the features of the churches of the Puritans was their simplicity. Since a true Christian must not let man nor facility stand between him and his God, some Baptist sects avoided the construction of special church buildings, using instead their barns and their homes. The austerity of the church interior was unrelieved by musical instruments, by any adornments, and for the most part, was divested of creature comforts.

> The Hindu temple, by any standard, is ornate. Idols and other visual representations abound. Symbolism is rampant. What is considered to be suitable to the worship of gods and goddesses in India would be ranked idolatry, forbidden by God, for the ascetic Protestants. Weber observed, as he discussed religious art forms, that the Russians in the 17th century protested that the German depiction of saints was too fat for beauty. Indian art was the opposite. A mahapurusha must be fat because a visibly good nutritional state was considered a sign of richness and distinction.[52]

Urbanization as well as competition between faiths and denominations in the metropolitan religion have completely altered the pattern in which "the traditional" parish has utilized religious facilities. There are a number of experiments through which different religious groups act out their concept of Christian service. Some set up store-front churches and the so-called religious stones in the heart of the inner city slums in an attempt to bring religion to the doorsteps of the poor and the down-trodden. Some have cut out a segment of the city as the intensive service area of the church with a variety of programs and services like home visits, health care, fix-ups. Some Church groups specialize in working with minority groups such as blacks, the poor, homosexuals, the hippies and the mentally retarded.[53]

The following passage from Joseph Washington Jr.'s *Black Religion* illustrates how Negro congregations and folk religion utilize church facilities for purposes of amusement and recreation:

> The people want to be entertained. The church, depending upon its size and location, is an activities center complete with 'Rally day,' 'Men's Day,' 'Children's Day,' and special Sunday afternoon and evening programs. Musicals, dramas, pageants, movies, concerts, suppers, and 'gospel singers' are offered as free entertainment through the week and are enjoyed by the churched and the unchurched without discrimination. The value and quality of the entertainment varies from locale to locale.[54]

COMPREHENSIVE OR MASTER PROCESSES

Communication. Medieval Christianity emphasized the role of priests and bishops as channels of communication who mediated between God and the faithful. The Church controlled the process by which information, decisions and directions were transmitted to the laity and the ways in which knowledge, opinions, and attitudes were formed or modified by interaction. Another significant integrative force in society was the expressive culture, particularly literature and the visual arts which were always fostered and patronized by religion. With the coming of reformation, learning was more highly evaluated, because, according to the Protestant ethic, each man was supposed to read his own Bible rather than depend on priestly interpretations from the pulpit. This led to the development of schools of higher learning in New England. On the other hand, early Indian literature was developed by men who wished to excel in oratorical skills, for the Brahmin priests for a long time upheld the principle that sacred teachings could be transmitted only by word of mouth. As pointed out by Loomis,

Whereas the Chinese and also the ascetic Puritans combined graceful brevity with sober expression, Indian writing, according to Weber, appeared overburdened with an accumulation of embellishing adjectives, comparisons and expressive symbols. Hand and body gestures were of great importance to Indians for the communication of sacred epics and religious knowledge. Their use by the ascetic Protestants, who were famous for their blunt to-the-point communication, was limited.[55]

The work of Joseph Washington Jr. on *Black Religion* traces the role and development of Negro spirituals in the communication of their religious sentiments since the beginning of the 17th century. According to him:

> In addition to the African rhythms as a mode of expression, there are four fundamental elements without which Negro spirituals are not fully appreciated. These four elements are the cataloging of historical events, the various forms of protest, the individual and personal reflections, and the worshipful expressions. These elements are significant for the understanding of why many Negroes who found their life in religious communions independent of the mainstream of Protestantism were unable to hammer out an independent body of beliefs from the teachings codified in the Negro spirituals.[56]

Boundary maintenance. Through this process the identity of the social system is preserved and the characteristic interaction pattern maintained. Every religion or church has its own organizational style, form of services, membership requirements and fundamental tenets which distinguish between faiths or denominations and legitimize barriers between them. There are at least three factors that sustain boundaries in the context of religion:

1. The cultural values placed on family tradition and solidarity.

2. Opposition to intermarriage from family and church. Protestants, Jews and Catholics alike insist strongly in intra-faith marriage; and endogamy was always enforced in the past sometimes by threat of excommunication.

3. Prejudice and discrimination. Several scholars including Kennedy, Herberg, and Lenski have emphasized the strong tendency for Protestants, Catholics and Jews to remain separate in American Society despite the reduction of ethnic, class and regional differences within these groups. They tend to live in separate neighborhoods, to belong to separate associations and to frequent exclusive social clubs. While Lenski portrays the situations by referring to "our current drift toward a 'compartmentalized society,' "[57] Kennedy sees the

development, not of a single, but a triple melting pot. The emergence of the black religion and exclusive Negro churches represents another contemporary illustration of boundary maintenance.

Systemic Linkage.   In spite of the fissiparous tendencies inherent in religious groups, a persistent movement toward a stronger interreligious linkage has been growing in recent years. Since the calling of Vatican II by Pope John XXIII the ecumenical movement has been gaining momentum, stressing the open tradition of collegiality, denominational unity and interreligious cooperation. Robert Lee has identified a number of Social Sources of Church Unity, such as merger of denominations, federation of churches and attempts at building the so-called 'super-church', national and international organizations of churches, the use of common literature and lobbies, and the development of a "common-core Protestantism."[58] The Consultation in Church Union, which grew out of dialogue between Episcopalians, Presbyterians, and Methodists, the National Council of Churches of Christ in America and its larger counterpart the World Council of Churches provide the machinery of cooperation between denominations. And many of the activities particularly in the field of social services are carried on cooperatively with Catholic and Jewish agencies.

Recent studies by sociologists of religion suggest that the social sources of denominationalism are steadily weakening, although separation still remains. In the most effective terms, James Coleman describes the forces that criss-cross and mix-up in the prevalent society.

The economic, ethnic, and other groups which have paralleled religious groupings in the past are coming to cross-cut them now: Catholics have diffused upwards in the economic structure, and outward geographically to the suburbs; Jews similarly are less concentrated in particular economic roles and geographic locations than before; Protestants who grew up in one sect in a community are dispersed and recongregated in communities where sects must combine to survive. In sum, economic and geographic mobility is imposing new conditions of association and group identification on persons of different religious groups. These conditions will not break down religious cleavages; to the contrary, they may sometimes thrust together in a single community a combination of religious groups which makes for conflict; yet this dispersion has its effect in many ways; certainly by increasing the possibilities of cross-pressure; perhaps by bringing religious conflict more often to the community level, less often to the national or state level; perhaps by reducing intergroup suspicion and hostility which feed on disassociation; perhaps by initial disputes followed by gradual reduction of tensions. Little is known about such effects; much could be learned by research on communities faced with influx from a different religious group.[59]

Institutionalization. The Church is the institutionalized form of religion par excellence. The organizational style of contemporary churches has moved away from the emotionality of the folk religion and come closer to a bureaucratic structure with special interest groups, committees, women's and children's groups, educational, cultural, political and recreational interests; their services have become formal and dignified; and they have routinized the administration by formal means of membership and fund-raising.

According to Winter, Roman Catholic churches tend to be more client-oriented while Protestant churches are more member-oriented.[60] Member-oriented organizations are more strongly affected by mobility than client-oriented ones. Of course, not all members of a church are equally involved in its organizational activity. Studies of Protestant churches reported by Winter indicate that approximately two-thirds of their members are involved some way or other. However, Fichter found that less than four per cent of the members of Catholic churches over the age of fourteen are active in the organizational whirl.

Within the context of the institutionalization of religion there are a few concepts that must be clearly understood. They are: the ecclesia, the sect, denomination, and cult. The *ecclesia* is a religious bureaucracy with a formal and hierarchical organization, specialized division of labor and an established rank-order. The typical ecclesia is a universal world church inclusive in its scope, and earthly and power-centered in its orientation. The Roman Catholic Church and the Anglican Church are examples of ecclesia. A *sect* is a religious movement which represents an open and sometimes an articulate avowal of a value system inspired by an idealism that rejects the worldly society, seeks to fight the "establishment," and involves a fervent commitment to a belief. The Salvation Army in its initial stages in England and the Old Order Amish in Pennsylvania represented sects. The *denomination* is in between ecclesia and sect, a stable church with a relatively formal organization but less bureaucratized than the ecclesia. Finally, the *cult* is a small, nebulous religious organization in which membership is voluntary and no rigid adherence to any value-system is enforced. Cults appear most frequently in the urban centers, among uprooted migrants, store-front churches and in slums. The cults that emerge among middle class groups appear more fundamentalist and spiritualist. The Black Muslims and the 'I Am' movement began as cults.

Socialization. Family and church have long been recognized as the primary agents of socialization. As Yinger observes:

> In most of the world religions, there has traditionally been direct and powerful involvement of churches and of priests in education. Schools were attached to mosques in Islam; the rabbi has been central to Jewish thought and education; among the Hindus, the Brahman priestly caste was dominant in education and learning; and within Christendom, monasteries have been centers of learning, universities have been founded and supported by churches, and parochial schools have been of continuing importance. Societies within which Buddhism is important have varied more widely. In China, for example, priests have generally played only a small role in education; religion has been a minor subject of study. In lands of the Theravada tradition, however, (such as Burma, Ceylon, and Thailand), Buddhism has been of greater significance in education.[61]

In the United States, Harvard University and other similar institutions were founded primarily to socialize Puritans in their relation to God, His universe, and man. The continuing tradition may be followed to Utah where the same ethic as carried by the Mormons makes the state by far the most highly educated in the nation, considering the tax base supporting the institutions. The Old Order Amish and the Quakers illustrate the influence of religion in the socialization process through which values, beliefs and traditions are transmitted. Although the relationship between school and religion has always been a matter of controversy, most religious groups generally agree that schools must foster a commitment to values of morality, ethics and good citizenship.

Social control

> Whether it be the fear of hell and brimstone, which persisted for so long in Christianity, or the injunction to do good work, religions can clearly influence the daily behavior of its believers. The recognized, established religion can thus control human behavior and keep people 'in line' making it a useful instrument for ruling classes, and throughout history these classes have appreciated religion's utility, its instrumental value, regardless of the evaluation of religion in any other terms. Louis Schneider quotes F.E. Manuel that even skeptics and atheists in the eighteenth century recognized that 'religion was a mechanism which inspired terror, but terror useful for the preservation of society . . .' In short, religion was regarded as a useful discipline of the masses and an effective control of the working classes.[62]

The history of mankind is a story of religious subjugation. Through the ages men have not only failed to thwart religious social control but actually demanded more rigorous control of most aspects of life. For example, the Calvinists felt that there "was not too much supervision of life on the part of the Church, but too little." Excommunication, religious persecution, self-torture, crusades, burning at stakes and the like represented strong manifestations of religious control during the Middle Ages. In India, Sutee or the practice of women throwing themselves on the funeral pyre of their husbands, ban on widow remarriage and similar customs of the past had the backing of religion behind them. Asceticism, meditation, penance, renunciation, fasting and other aspects of religious preparation also testify to the influence of religion as an agent of social control. Even today religion is construed as the primary source of virtues and the basis of spiritual values which regulate as well as legitimize the standards of behavior in a society.

CONDITIONS OF SOCIAL ACTION

Territoriality. Here we consider the setting of the social system in space. Every religion emerged in a given social context and grew in a given geographic territory. Even today certain religious groups are concentrated in particular regions — Hinduism in India, Shintoism in Japan, Taoism and Confucianism in China and Islam in West Asia. And even within the United States, there are definite areas of concentration of particular religious groups:

1. Mormons in Utah and some counties of neighboring states, where a clear majority is held by members of this group;
2. Lutherans in two-thirds of North Dakota's counties, as well as Nebraska and South Dakota. In Minnesota and Wisconsin every county is predominantly Lutheran or Catholic;
3. Baptists in the South. Even when black Baptists are not counted, this denomination prevails in most Southern states;
4. Catholics in Louisiana, the lower Rio Grande valley of Texas, most of New Mexico, Arizona, California, and most New England states.[63]

In recent years, the suburban movement — or the continuous "escaping" of the middle class from central cities to the suburbs — has considerably affected the territorial segregation of churches and denominations. Suburbanization has led to the development of new, community-oriented, local churches catering to the needs of a well-educated middle class population. The process has also left behind the old churches to the care of the poor, the minorities and the old — a process which has perpetuated or even accelerated segregation of churches, black and white, middle class and lower class.

Time. Time as a condition of action is important in understanding the philosophy of religions. The ascetic Protestants stressed the shortness of human life and the necessity of using every second possible to build the Kingdom of God on earth and to prove the state of one's grace. Benjamin Franklin's assertions like "Time is money," "Early to bed, early to rise, makes a man healthy, wealthy and wise" are based on the religious philosophy prevalent in his days. Christians generally agree that mundane life is only a brief sojourn — to be followed by one of only two possible eternities — hell and damnation or heaven.

However, Hinduism and Buddhism believe in "timelessness" and the cycle of rebirths. According to Weber:

> Transitoriness adheres to everything, whether available to sense perception or to man's imagination as earthly, heavenly, or hellish forms and things. It is a quality of the world of forms as a whole. The world is an eternal, meaningless 'wheel' of recurrent births and deaths steadily rolling on through all eternity. Only two non-temporal realities are discoverable in it: the eternal order itself, and those beings who, through escape of ongoing rebirths, must be conceived as their subjects. They are the souls.[64]

The importance of time in Hinduism is also exemplified in the number and frequency of life-cycle ceremonies performed by a Hindu. Childbirth, attainment of puberty, marriage, death and anniversaries of death are all occasions for elaborate ritualistic ceremonies. And every ceremony must be performed during auspicious hours. The Catholics observe Lent and Mohammedans have a period of fasting. A devoted Muslim is required to pray five times a day and a Jain must say his prayers before dark. Thus, time is central not only to the philosophical system of religions but to the daily observance of rituals and ceremonies as well.

Size. Religions are of varying sizes and styles. Christianity is at present the world's largest religion and Islam the second largest. Sikhism, Jainism, Judaism, and Zoroastrism are among the smallest religions. In the United States, Catholics number over 48 million and the next largest single group is the United Methodist Church, with 11 million members.

> In the quarter of a century between 1926 and 1959, the population of continental United States increased 28.6 per cent; membership of religious bodies increased 59.8 per cent: in other words, church member-

ship grew more than twice as fast as population. Protestants increased 63.7 per cent, Catholics 53.9 per cent, Jews 22.5 per cent. Among Protestants, however, the increase varied considerably as between denominations: Baptist increase was well over 100 per cent, some 'holiness' sects grew even more rapidly, while the figure for the Episcopal Church was only 36.7 per cent, for the Methodist Church 32.2 per cent, for the Northern Presbyterians 22.4 per cent, and for the Congregationalists 21.1 per cent. In general, it may be said that practically all major types of American religion have staged what is popularly called a 'comeback.'[65]

In 1968, there was a total membership of 126 million persons in 241 religious groups in the United States. And the American Institute of Public Opinion reported that 97 per cent of Americans identify themselves with one of the major religious groups.

Scholars do not agree on the meaning of this religious "revival." There is no proof of a mass return to supernatural beliefs; nor is our everyday life more spiritualistic than before. However, there has been a definite increase in the search for a new meaning or a new spiritual discipline as evidenced in the growth of various fundamentalist as well as radical religious movements like the Zen Buddhism, Hare Krishna, Jesus movement, Transcendental Meditation and so on. Different types of renewal like "church-within-a-church," intensive small group activity provided by retreats, conferences and sensitivity training groups, store-front churches, and "religious store" seek to foster personal involvement in religious activities by maintaining a sense of commitment through small-group interaction.

NOTES

1. Edward Gibbon, *The Decline and Fall of the Roman Empire* (New York: Peter Fenelon Collier, 1914), Vol. 1, p. 49.

2. Emile Durkheim, *The Elementary Forms of Religious Life* (New York: The MacMillan Company, 1926), p. 47.

3. Bronislaw Malinowski, *The Foundations of Faith and Morals* (New York: Folcroft, 1936), p. 34.

4. Max Weber, *The Religion of India* (Glencoe: The Free Press, 1958), p. 164.

5. Charles Y. Glock and Rodney Stark, *Christian Beliefs and Anti-Semitism* (New York: Harper and Row, 1966).

6. Richard L. Simpson, "Negro-Jewish Prejudice: Authoritarianism and Some Social Variables As Correlates," *Social Problems*, 7, (Fall, 1959) pp. 138-46.

7. James J. Vanecko, "Religious Behavior and Prejudice: Some Dimensions and Specifications of the Relationship", *Review of Religious Research*, 8, (Fall, 1966), pp. 27-37.

8. Russell Middleton, "Do Christian Beliefs Cause Anti-Semitism?", *American Sociological Review*, 38, (February, 1973) pp. 33-53.

9. Charles T. O'Reilly and Edward J. O'Reilly. "Religious Beliefs of Catholic College Students and Their Attitudes Toward Minorities," *Journal of Abnormal and Social Psychology*, 49, (July, 1954), pp. 378-380.

10. Max Weber, op. cit., p. 187.

11. Charles P. and Zona K. Loomis, *Socio-Economic Change and the Religious Factor in India* (New Delhi: Affiliated East-West Press Pvt. Ltd., 1969).

12. Harvey Cox, *The Secular City* (New York: The Macmillan Company, 1966), p. 2.

13. Ibid., p. 15.

14. James B. McKee, *Introduction to Sociology* (New York: Holt, 1969), p. 541.

15. *Time*, April 9, 1973, p. 90.

16. Barbara W. Hargrove, *Reformation of the Holy* (Philadelphia: F.A. Davis, 1971), pp. 12-13.

17. Emile Durkheim, op. cit., as quoted by Raymond Aron, *Main Currents in Sociological Thought II* (New York: Doubleday, 1970), p. 59.

18. J. Milton Yinger, *The Scientific Study of Religion* (London: Macmillan, 1970), p. 157.

19. Max Weber, op. cit., p. 172.

20. Ibid., p. 201.

21. J. Milton Yinger, *Sociology Looks at Religion* (London: Macmillan, 1961), p. 23.

22. Leo Lowenthal and Norbert Guterman, *Prophets of Deceit: A Study in the Techniques of the American Agitator* (New York: Harper and Row, 1949), p. 15.

23. Max Weber, op. cit., p. 220.

24. Loomis and Loomis, op. cit., p. 45.

25. J. Milton Yinger, op. cit., p. 142.

26. Max Weber, op. cit., p. 255.

27. J. Milton Yinger, op. cit., pp. 16-17.

28. Max Weber, *The Protestant Ethic and the Spirit of Capitalism* (New York: Charles Scribner's Sons, 1930), p. 172.

29. Max Weber, op. cit., p. 172.

30. Talcott Parsons, "Introduction" to *The Sociology of Religion*, by Max Weber, (Boston: Beacon Press, 1956), p. lvi.

31. Joachim Wach, *Sociology of Religion* (Chicago: University of Chicago Press, 1962), p. 45.

32. Ibid., p. 48.

33. Annotated by Joachim Wach, op. cit., p. 45.

34. Max Weber, *The Protestant Ethic and the Spirit of Capitalism*, op. cit., pp. 153-54.

35. Samuel W. Blizzard, "Role Conflicts of the Urban Protestant Parish Ministers", *The City Church*, 7, (September, 1956), pp. 13-15.

36. Samuel W. Blizzard, "The Protestant Parishminister's Integrating Roles." *Religious Education*, 53, (July-August, 1958), pp. 25-32.

37. Barbara W. Hargrove, op. cit., p. 213.

38. Joachim Wach, op. cit., p. 343.

39. Ibid., p. 367.

40. Ibid.

41. Ibid.

42. Ibid., p. 338.

43. Quoted by J. Milton Yinger, *The Scientific Study of Religion*, p. 364.

44. Yinger, op. cit., p. 517.

45. Ibid., pp. 213-214.

46. Quoted by Joachim Wach, op. cit., p. 210.

47. Joachim Wach, op. cit., p. 368.

48. Max Weber. *The Religion of India*, p. 319.

49. Alvin Boskoff, *The Sociology of Urban Regions*, (Appleton: New York, 1970) p. 272.

50. Barbara W. Hargrove, op. cit., p. 187.

51. Max Weber, *The Sociology of Religion*, pp. 38-39.

52. Loomis and Loomis, op. cit., pp. 108-109.

53. Barbara W. Hargrove, op. cit., p. 243.

54. Joseph R. Washington, Jr., *Black Religion* (Boston: Beacon Press, 1968), p. 43.

55. Loomis and Loomis, op. cit., pp. 113-114.

56. Joseph Washington, Jr., op. cit., p. 208.

57. Gerhard Lenski, op. cit., pp. 326-30.

58. Robert Lee, *The Social Sources of Church Unity* (New York: Abington Press, 1960).

59. James S. Coleman, "Social Cleavage and Religious Conflict," *Journal of Social Issues*, 12, (1956): pp. 47-48.

60. Gibson Winter, *The Suburban Captivity of the Churches*, (New York: Doubleday, 1961).

61. J. Milton Yinger. *The Scientific Study of Religion*, p. 65.

62. James B. McKee, *Introduction to Sociology* (New York: Holt, 1969), p. 520.

63. Franklin H. Littel, *The Church and the Body Politic* (New York: Seabury Press, 1969), pp. 27-28.

64. Max Weber, *The Religion of India*, p. 167.

65. Will Herberg, "Religious Revival in the United States," in Amitai and Eva Etzioni, *Social Change* (New York: Basic Books, 1964), pp. 227-35.

Chapter **6**

Production Systems: the Division of Labor, the Community, and Society*

INTRODUCTION

The present study of work teams, communities[1], and societies[2] as social systems in the process of development, change, and adaptation to new environments views human productive behavior within the context of human ecology[3] and urbanization[4] on a world-wide basis. Differences in levels of development and population density are classified in Figure 1 where major territorial areas and regions of the world are identified as "less developed" and "more developed." As societies become increasingly urbanized, shifting patterns of emphasis among systemic elements and processes are discernible. These shifts are observable in the tribal and developing societies.[5] Some two-thirds of the people of the world live in developing areas and must contend with "a self-perpetuating vicious circle of poverty, disease, hunger, ignorance, and lack of technological skills and capital to improve their lot."[6] Shifting patterns are, likewise, observable in the more developed and over-developed societies facing ecological and socio-environmental change. Table 1 indicates for the societies in the "more developed" and the "less developed" regions significant differences which can be attributed to variations in normative elements regarding fertility control, to population composition, variations in the division of labor, and to technological development within the communities and societies.

The persistence of social systems in resistance to change, and the causes and consequences of change have significant implications for human well-being and health,[7] human productivity and freedom, and human welfare generally in the world community.

*By Robert F. Eshleman and Charles P. Loomis.

FIGURE 1

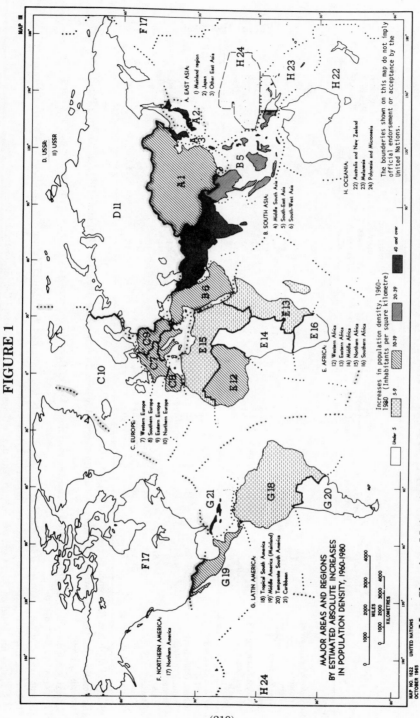

Map Showing Major Areas and Regions by Levels of Development and Population Density

MAP III

A. EAST ASIA:
 1) Mainland region
 2) Japan
 3) Other East Asia

D. USSR:
 11) USSR

B. SOUTH ASIA:
 4) Middle South Asia
 5) South-East Asia
 6) South-West Asia

H. OCEANIA:
 22) Australia and New Zealand
 23) Melanesia
 24) Polynesia and Micronesia

The boundaries shown on this map do not imply official endorsement or acceptance by the United Nations.

C. EUROPE:
 7) Western Europe
 8) Southern Europe
 9) Eastern Europe
 10) Northern Europe

E. AFRICA:
 12) Western Africa
 13) Eastern Africa
 14) Middle Africa
 15) Northern Africa
 16) Southern Africa

Increases in population density, 1960–1980 (inhabitants per square kilometre)

Under 5
5-9
10-19
20-39
40 and over

F. NORTHERN AMERICA:
 17) Northern America

G. LATIN AMERICA:
 18) Tropical South America
 19) Middle America (Mainland)
 20) Temperate South America
 21) Caribbean

MAJOR AREAS AND REGIONS
BY ESTIMATED ABSOLUTE INCREASES
IN POPULATION DENSITY, 1960-1980

MILES
1000 2000 3000 4000

KILOMETRES
0 1000 2000 3000 4000

MAP NO. 1822   UNITED NATIONS
OCTOBER 1983

TABLE I. 1970 WORLD POPULATION AND DATA FOR SELECTED COUNTRIES*

Region or Country	Population Estimates Mid-1970 (Millions)[a]	Births per 1,000 Population[b]	Deaths per 1,000 Population[b]	Infant Mortality Rate (Deaths under One Year per 1,000 Live Births)[b]	Population under 15 Years (Percent)[c]	Population Projections to 1985 (Millions)[a]	Per Capita Gross National Product (U.S.A.)[d]
World	3,632[1]	34	14		37	4,933	
More developed regions							
France	51.1	16.8	11.0	20.4	25	57.6	1,950
Japan	103.5	19	7	15	25	121.3	1,000
New Zealand	2.9	22.6	8.9	18.7	33	3.8	1,890
Sweden	8.0	14.3	10.4	12.9	21	8.8	2,500
United Kingdom	56.0	17.1	11.9	18.8	23	61.8	1,700
United States[3]	205.2	17.6	9.6	21.2	30	241.7	3,670
USSR	242.6	17.9	7.7	26.5	28	286.9	970
*Less developed regions***							
Brazil	93.0	39	11	170	43	142.6	250
China (Mainland)	759.6	34	15		47	964.6	90
Dominican Republic	4.3	48	15	73	44	7.3	260
Guinea	3.9	49	26	216	41	5.7	90
India	554.6	42	17	139	41	807.6	90
Mexico	50.7	44	10	64	46	84.4	490
Nigeria	55.1	50	25		43	84.7	80
United Arab Republic	33.9	43	15	117	43	52.3	160

*Source: Population Reference Bureau, Washington, D.C., April 1970.

[a]Estimates from United Nations. World Population Prospects, 1965-85, As Assessed in 1968, UN Population Division Working Paper #30, December, 1969.

[b]Latest available year. Except for North American rates computed by PRB, world and regional estimates are derived from World Population Prospects (see footnote a).

[c]Latest available year. Derived from World Population Prospects. (see footnote a and United Nations Demographic Yearbook 1967).

[d]1967 data: International Bank for Reconstruction and Development.

[3]U.S. figures are based on data from the U.S. Bureau of the Census and the National Center for Health Statistics.

**Note: In general, for many of the developing countries, the demographic data including total population, age reporting and vital rates are subject to deficiencies of varying degrees. In some cases, the data are estimates of the United National Secretariat.

FIGURE 2

PAS Model Profiles[1] Describing Major Types and Sub-types of Action of Primitive and Peasant Society (Gemeinschaft); and Action as Related to Norms in Work Teams of Bureaucracies in Urbanized Society (Gesellschaft)

Action of Primitive and Peasant Society		Action as Related to Norms in Work Teams of Bureaucracies in Urbanized Society
GEMEINSCHAFT*		GESELLSCHAFT*
Polar Evaluation Norms	——————— 0 PAS Model	Polar Evaluation Norms
Traditional # Familistic ## Sacred ###	Proverbial Prescriptive Principal Pronormless	Rational # Contractual ## Secular ###
Particularism** Affectivity** Functional Diffuseness** Expressive-Consummatory Ascription** (Quality)		Universalism** Affective Neutrality** Functional Specificity** Instrumental Achievement (Performance)**

[1]Processually Articulated Structural Model Profiles. Adapted from Loomis, Charles P., *Social Systems: Essays on Their Persistence and Change* (Princeton, N.J.: D. Van Nostrand Co., Inc., 1960), Figure 2, pp. 59-62. The continua presented in Figure 2 are based on observations of relations of students to their fathers; GI's to commanding officers in army camps during World War II; relations in a government bureau; relations in a Spanish/American cooperative; and relations in an Amish family.

*Ferdinand Toennies, op. cit. p. 224. Gemeinschaft: The "social order based upon consensus of wills — rests on harmony and is developed and enobled by folkways, mores and religions." Gesellschaft: The "social order which being based upon a union of rational wills — rests on convention and agreement, is safeguarded by political legislation and finds its ideological justification in public opinion." Ibid. p. 223.

#Action and norm types used by Max Weber, Howard Becker and others.

##Blanket types developed by Pitirim A. Sorokin. See *Social and Cultural Dynamics,* Vol. 3, (New York: American Book Company, 1937), p. 47ff.

###Howard Becker's Constructed Types. See "Current Sacred-Secular Theory and Its Development," Howard Becker and Alvin Boskoff, eds., *Modern Sociological Theory,* (New York: Dryden Press, 1957).

**Pattern Variables as Used by Talcott Parsons, et al., *Working Papers in the Theory of Action* (Glencoe, Ill: The Free Press, 1953), p. 57ff, and pp. 207-208, which he used as dichotomies at four different levels of action. These variables can also be conceived of as systemic attributes and treated as continua. We may therefore conceive of work teams and communities as going concerns whose behavior conforms and deviates in varying degrees from the polar ends of the continua.

IDEAL TYPOLOGIES:
GEMEINSCHAFT — GESELLSCHAFT

The differentiated patterning of social relations in peasant, nonindustrialized, and less developed societies, is in sharp contrast to relations in highly technological societies. This theme as Sorokin[8] has noted, has been a major preoccupation of philosophers and scholars through the ages, and was observed and explored by Toennies[9] in *Community and Society — Gemeinschaft and Gesellschaft* in the nineteenth and early twentieth centuries. In the work teams, families, communities, societies and other collectivities which are Gemeinschaft-like, human relations are ends in themselves: intimacy and sentiment are expected among the actors; norms are traditional and characterized by the features listed at the left of Figure 2. In the Gesellschaft-like associations, relations and actors are used instrumentally, interaction is impersonal and affectively neutral; actors are not known in their entirety to each other; and norms are rational rather than traditional.[10] The cluster of characteristics around each polar position of the Gemeinschaft and Gesellschaft respectively, as shown in Figure 2, reveals by their contrast the major differences in interaction as it takes place in the two differentiated ideal types of social systems.

No special system could persist if relations were completely Gemeinschaft or completely Gesellschaft. This fact does not prevent the human mind from conceiving of such "ideal types" and using them for comparative and ordering purposes. In fact this is their chief value.[11]

An ideal type, of which the Gemeinschaft—Gesellschaft dichotomy is one of the examples in Figure 2, is a "purposive, planned selection, abstraction, combination, and accentuation of a set of criteria that have empirical referents and that serve as a basis for comparison of empirical cases."[12]

Ideal typologies generally explain social changes as a transformation of society from one polar position toward the opposite pole — i.e. from Gemeinschaft toward Gesellschaft. The elements of the PAS Model as presented in Chapter 1 serve as a means of observing and conceptualizing human behavior, and the social relations of actors whose relations to each other are mutually oriented in terms of a pattern of structured and shared symbols and expectations in a dynamic process of interaction. Change in any element of the social system has implications for social change in the total system whether Gemeinschaft or Gesellschaft. The PAS Model enables the sociologist as an observer of society and social change to utilize theories of a "middle range" in the observation and microanalysis of elemental and cumulative phenomena in the social system,[13] rather than, for example, attempting to explain society and sub-systems in a macrosocietal sense of Marxian class conflict, and dialectical processes or unilinear evolutionary progress.[14]

THE DIVISION OF LABOR AND LARGE SCALE ORGANIZATION

The adaptation of a society to its physical and sociocultural environment in the development and utilization of available resources — land, human energy, capital, and in the production of goods and services requires economy in the organization of work. A high level of living has never been attained by a society without some division of labor and the introduction of such formal organizations as bureaucracies which concentrate the 'center activities,' and are involved in processing, distributing, and coordinating the field activities. The field activities result in the production of foods, fibers, ores, and raw materials and are usually carried on by small units scattered over the countryside.[15] In the less developed subsistence food-producing societies, social relations tend to be Gemeinschaft-like, based primarily upon family and kinship ties in the organization of work teams. As development takes place, large scale organizations emerge. Bureaucracies eventually replace the small family work unit.

As functions and processes are divided among the actors of the community in the ever proliferating division of labor, actors are provided with more opportunities for choice and are likewise subjected to conflicts from the demands of contradicting systems, norms, and status-roles. The more status-roles available in a society, the more varied is the impact of activities upon a given actor and the more functionally specific the demands are likely to be. Although there are exceptions, Gemeinschaft-like communities tend to be small and have relatively few sub-systems, the principal one usually being the family. In the extreme, the Gesellschaft-like commmunity has an infinite number of actors with an infinite number of sub-systems and status-roles which may serve as references for the actor.[16]

One of the distinguishing features of the "more" developed societies, in contrast to the "less" developed societies is the introduction and emergence of large scale organizations. By *formal* organization is meant "a *consciously*" designed set of activities which are distributed among the units of a system. Such a system has an interlocking of activities between the units which provide for communication and materials flow, and "feedback" or control activities which monitor the ongoing activities and set into motion correcting activity if actual performances do not fall within planned tolerance limits. We view such a system as a consciously contrived structure adapting to internal and external conditions, with control activities designed to monitor and regulate the correspondence between actual and planned activities.[17]

Modern bureaucracies do not emerge as fully developed entities at the initial steps of industrialization.[18] Intermediate stages between the simplest work group and the bureaucracy include differentiated work teams, variation in occupational specialties, and size and number of work teams determined by the maximally efficient use of labor and other resources. Wilbert E. Moore suggests the term rational work organizations to designate all such differentiated work teams which pursue their work goals in a rational rather than traditional division of labor and to this latter may be added the function of size as well as a related dimension, intensity of interaction, which latter constitutes in essence what the Wilsons designate as scale.[19] These are related devices pointing to the intermediate stages between the simplest work team and a full-blown bureaucracy.

The norms and work relations in a bureaucracy may be characterized as having the following five features: 1) a hierarchy of status-roles, 2) remuneration of members by fixed salaries related to competence or achievement in terms of the ends and norms of the system, 3) a status-role in the organization which is the primary one of the incumbent, 4) members who are subject to coercive discipline articulated to the hierarchy of status-roles, and 5) socialization (indoctrination and training) processes resulting in a high degree of internalization of ends, norms, beliefs and sentiments of the system on the part of actors.[20]

The PAS Model is designed to assist in the conceptualization and analysis of the impact of bureaucracies upon societies in the process of urbanization and social change. The nature and consequences of these kinds of phenomena are presented in this chapter. It is these reoccurring similarities (not necessarily identities) of patterns as well as the unique patterns which can be charted with precision by the application of the Processually Articulated Structural Model to a variety of on-going social systems. The varieties and similarities of the patterns thus described can be classified with some accuracy through the arrangement of their attributes on the Gemeinschaft—Gesellschaft scale, Figure 2. Certain constellations — division of labor, urbanization, and mobility, for example — occur with a high degree of regularity as societies of the same or different tradition change to a more Gesellschaft form,[21] with norms of social relations represented on the right side of Figure 2.

In presenting the Elements and Processes of workteams, communities, and societies, comparisons of work groups, divisions of labor, and work organizations will be made, using the Gemeinschaft-Gesellschaft typologies.

ELEMENTS AND PROCESSES OF WORK, COMMUNITY, AND SOCIETAL SOCIAL SYSTEMS

KNOWING

Belief (knowledge) as an element.   In the traditional, familistic, and sacred society and its sub-systems knowledge or beliefs about the universe tend to be varied from system to system, to be undifferentiated within any one system, and to be relatively static and persistant for all systems. Knowledge of the total production process is held by a large number of members of the social system and the knowledge held by each member closely resembles the knowledge held by all other members. In the simplest societies only the primary tool is known and little knowledge exists concerning forms of energy other than human energy.[22] The work team centers in family and kinship often composed of members of the same age or sex. Belief and knowledge are handed down from generation to generation by shared experience and tradition in the Gemeinschaft-like community, a process which tends to be resistant to new innovation and change. Members of the community are dependent upon the group and the immediate environment for survival which in many societies in the "less" developed areas of the world is barely a subsistence living.

According to Boulding development is "closely related to the process by which knowledge increases, and it is hardly an exaggeration to describe economic development simply as a particular aspect of the overall process of learning. Even the process of accumulation of physical capital, . . . must be interpreted primarily in terms of the imposition of a certain knowledge structure of the physical world. We do not get economic development by simply piling up stocks of old things. We do not get it, for instance, by simply accumulating big piles of wheat in warehouses. Rather it consists in the development of new machines, tools, habits of behavior, and social organizations, all of which derive essentially from changes in knowledge. A machine is merely human knowledge imposed on the physical world."[23] The

German sociologist, Max Weber[24] ascribed to religion and what people believed — the ideological — as a basis for the interpretation of social change, in contrast to Karl Marx[25] who belittled the influence of beliefs and norms as prime movers and who emphasized that economic factors were responsible for a dialectical struggle of class conflict and revolutionary change.

Development involves a change in belief, in cognitive mapping, in self-perception, and in social relations in the community. A significant element influencing change is *new* knowledge. Readiness to accept new knowledge, information or propositions about the universe is a common characteristic of rational, contractual, and secular oriented societies. The rational beliefs and knowledge of the Gesellschaft-like society and its sub-systems tend to be standardized from system to system, to be highly differentiated within any one system, and to be dynamic, in a state of readiness to change, for all systems.[26] Knowledge concerning piloting a jet plane is similar in London or in Houston, but knowledge of the total control system is held by no one member of the social system. Knowledge of tools and technology is extensive for the total system, but highly differentiated among members within the system.

As the social system exercises greater control over the immediate environment its members become increasingly dependent upon the knowledge and good faith of other members of the social system with whom they have limited contact.

Cognitive mapping and validation as a process. The Gemeinschaft-like society validates knowledge by tradition through personal interaction.[27] The validation process reinforces meanings and relationships of tradition in the face of social disorganization and systemic disintegration.

The members of a rational, contractual, and secular society validate knowledge in individual choices and personal obligations; and the empirical testing of propositions according to the methods of science validates new knowledge.[28]

In Gemeinschaft-like societies symbols of land, family, and religious significance are used in cognitive mapping: "The Good Earth," "God the Father," "The Way of Knowledge," or "Mecca." The ICONS of the Gesellschaft-like society capture the landscape of technology and leisure: "IBM," "747," "The Astrodome," "Three Rivers," and "Candlestick." The neon "GESELLSCHAFT" sign on Zurich's Bahnhofstrasse; the skyscrapers of New York's "Wall Street;" and Chicago's "O'Hare International," represent an expanding horizon where the "Big John," the "Big Stan," and now the world's tallest building, "The Big Buck," symbolize the bureaucratic society of larger scale organization. A minature ship hanging from the ceiling above the worshipers in the rear of the Grundvig's church in Copenhagen symbolizes both the integrative aspect of prayer and devotion of families in the Gemeinschaft-like community, and the separation and absence of fathers and husbands in the Gesellschaft-world risking their lives in vocation as fishermen at sea.

The respective cognitive maps are validated for consistency of meaning and sets of social relations by the members of the respective societies and subsystems. The Gesellschaft-like society is designed to absorb and transmit new knowledge within the internal pattern of social relations, which is sentiment-laden and expressive.

In Gesellschaft-like societies there emerges a community that is literate, heterogeneous, and rational with a system of beliefs that is rapidly evolving and changing and is shot through with sub-belief systems not necessarily harmonious with a central societal belief system. Institutional means are devised to act as shock-absorbers during the period of change resulting from knowledge absorption, but institutionalization does not keep pace with the introduction of validated items of new knowledge.[29]

FEELING

Sentiment as an element.   Durkheim treated "the community of beliefs and sentiments," common values, as "the fundamental fact of all social life."[30] Sentiment is highly articulated in the internal pattern of a social system, is primarily expressive, and represents attitudes about knowledge and belief held in high esteem by members of the interactive system.

In Yucatan, sentiment toward the physical and social environment is expressed in the way the Maya farmer teaches his son how to use the ax and machete, and that he should treat the maize plant with reverence.[31]

The relationship between high priorities and sentiment in the social system is especially noticeable in the traditional, familistic, and sacred societies. The norms are important in determining both what sentiment is expressed and how it is expressed.[32]

The polar evaluation norms which mark the scalar gradients of Becker's continuum (Figure 2) manifest the element of sentiment in varying degrees. The pole representing the extracted sacred is heavily saturated with evaluations charged with sentiment. Piety and awe, for example, accompany high evaluations of the holy; loyalty, allegiance, and patriotism accompany high evaluations of clan, nation, or other identifying membership group; and intimacy, friendship, and good faith prevail when bonds of intimacy are cherished. Strong emotional responses are attached to the familiar domestic environment and to the place of birth. Distress, fear, and strain accompany change or the suggestion of change to which there is emotional resistance. For Becker both poles of the constructed type exhibit greatest manifestations of sentiment; the intermediate gradient points on the scale (Figure 2) exhibit lesser or no sentiment. On the PAS Model, sentiment clusters primarily on the *Gemeinschaft* pole, affective neutrality being characteristic of the *Gesellschaft*.[33]

Gouldner as an interaction analyst of bureaucratic systems, however, indicates the importance of informal organization (and sentiment) as an equivalent counter to bureaucratic rules in the example of the mine head in the gypsum plant who steps out of his office and yells: "One of you, clean out the rock crusher!" How was a specific individual chosen for this "dirty job?" . . . "It's simple . . . we all just turn around and look at the newest guy in the group and he goes and does it."[34] Gouldner's development of the norm of reciprocity is clearly at work, an expression of sentiment. Thus men react adversely to the new rule which forbids their punching in early and accumulating a little overtime which they might later use in cases of emergency. "One mill worker said acidly, 'Well, if that's the way he wants it, that's the way he wants it. But I'll be damned if I put in any overtime when things get rough and they'd like us to.' Said another worker: 'O.K. I'll punch in just so, and I'll punch out on the nose. But you know you can lead a horse to water and you can lead him away, but it's awful hard to tell just how much water he drinks while he's at it.' "[35]

Gouldner suggests "that the occasional phenomenon of bureaucratic rule being replaced by charismatic rule may stem from the deadend eventually reached when the behavior of many actors is being directed by rules to which no one is committed . . . a charismatic leader [who] recharges the normative commitments of workers in a way which is completely inaccessible to the bureaucrat who typically entertains an abiding distrust of people and their intentions."[36] The persistence of norms and sentiments in informal social systems operates as sub-systems within large scale organizations so that "inevitably, a factory, like any other social organization, reflects a compromise between formal and informal organization, between rational and non-rational (sentimental) norms."[37]

Tension management as process and communication of sentiment as process. The incest taboo in the family, or the affective neutrality of the labor-management contract between organized labor and the corporation in modern bureaucracies, in each instance, is designed to process the management of social relations and tensions within the social system and between sub-systems.

According to Williams, "It is not a trivial matter of 'mere convention' or 'manners' that in the typical middle class, urban community, if either spouse is invited to a mixed 'social' gathering, the other spouse must be likewise invited." Any aggregate of persons becomes a real social group only by being identified as a unit, by sharing a common set of experiences, and hence by sharing a common universe of meanings and symbols.[38]

Affective neutrality, as a pattern variable (Figure 2), is a prime mechanism for the processing of tension management in societies on the bureaucratic, rational, contractual, and secular end of the continuum. The large scale organization as a

controlling mechanism consists of *administrative* or *organizational* coordination, enforced by a definite and identifiable social organization. Whether it be a factory, a corporation, a trade association, a labor union, a government bureau, or any other organized grouping . . . although the corporation as a whole is subject to the final test of profit and loss in the market, the allocation of resources within the organization itself is not necessarily dictated by 'free market' principles. Control of behavior, and thus of economic decisions, within the large industrial enterprise or grouping of enterprises is *social* in nature; it is established through established patterns of authority in an elaborate quasi-bureaucratic hierarchy, not through the impersonal pressures of the market.[39]

Social relations within the system are defined by contractual duties and obligations on the part of labor and management as collectivities. For teachers in public schools in Pennsylvania, Act 195, for example,

established rights in public employees to organize and bargain collectively through selected representatives; . . . collective bargaining is the performance of the mutual obligation of the public employer (The Board of Education) and the representative of the public employees (The Education Association) to meet at reasonable times and confer in good faith with respect to wages, hours, and other terms and conditions of employment, or the negotiation of an agreement on any question arising thereunder and the execution of a written contract incorporating any agreement reached, but such obligation does not compel either party to agree to a proposal or require the making of a concession.[40]

Such a contract incorporating any agreement reached is designed to effectively articulate the goal-directed activity of the system, as well as serve as a mechanism for effective tension management by minimizing interaction through routinized and formalized relations.

Communication of sentiment. In the internal pattern of a social system a primary purpose for interacting is "to communicate liking, friendship, and love among those who stand in supporting relations to one another and corresponding negative sentiments to those who stand in antagonistic relations."[41] Sentiment is communicated daily in the Gemeinschaft-like society, as for example, when members of the Amish family 1) assemble at mealtime, and 2) pause for a silent prayer of thanksgiving at the beginning and end of each meal. This periodic rite of intensification helps to maintain symbolically the importance of religious faith and commitment, as well as the status-role of each member of the family unit who occupies a particular age and sex position in the family circle. A wedding ceremony illustrates a non-periodic rite of passage which communicates to the respective families and to the community the new status-role relationship of members to each other and to the social system.[42] The importance of tension management and the communication of sentiment for integration, for cooperation and solidarity, and for commitment to group ends and willingness to sacrifice for them can scarcely be over-estimated.[43]

Large scale organizations share constraints on interaction. As Merton writes, "The substitution of personal for impersonal treatment within the structure [of a bureaucracy] is met with widespread disapproval and is characterized by such epithets as graft, favoritism, nepotism, apple-polishing, etc. These epithets are clearly manifestations of injured sentiments."[44] The bureaucratic structure "approaches the complete elimination of personalized relationships and nonrational considerations (hostility, anxiety, affectual involvements, etc.)"[45]

Williams notes that the affective neutrality so widely attributed to industrial bureaucracies as a means of channeling sentiment is not unlike that which prevails in schools where the norms of impartiality, formal equality and a degree of social distance have tension reducing significance.[46] By the minimization of personal attractions and antipathies, conditions disruptive to learning are controlled and the vulnerability of the teacher on matters outside his realm of authority is reduced.[47] The effective communication of sentiment affects the achievement of goals at all levels of the social system.

In the transition on the continuum from a Gemeinschaft-like to a Gesellschaft-like society, with the dissolution of older patterns of group interaction and its impoverishment of stable, recurring interaction patterns, tensions arise for members attempting to adapt to the new environment.[48] Williams notes that "Group membership in a Rotary Club may seem radically different from membership in the

American rural neighborhood of a half-century ago, but the loss of the latter has been a tangible factor in the growth of the former . . ."[49] Williams also notes a well-defined pattern of "withdrawal, aliena-tion, entrance, and assimilation" as individuals are confronted with vertical occupational mobility, or with transitions of residential mobility.[50] In *The Reduction of Intergroup Tensions*, Williams observes an inverse relation between amount of hostility and the number and adequacy of "harmless outlets" for aggression which do not violate the major norms of the social system. In the United States such outlets as competitive sports, swearing, joking, some uses of alcohol, drama and pageantry are indicated as falling in this class.[51] Jezernik points out that in Yugoslavia,

> In 1962, for workers of peasant origin, the most important problem was how to accommodate to their new, industrial environment, to their new social surrounding ; . . because of modernization and increased standard of living money became the main motivational factor, and where the society changed from a revolutionary to a consumer one, problems of integration of works into new social environments also became more and more severe. This happened particularly because the distribution of power remained *de facto*, unchanged, and because the latent conflict between management and labor did become institutionalized — the more dissatisfied workers were with their supervisors, the higher the rank given to the factor 'wages.'[52]

In the Gemeinschaft-like society, sentiment may be communi-cated in family, work, and religious settings of the community; in the Gesellschaft-like work setting the cost of affective neutrality in the contractual relationship of management and worker can be ex-pressed in money wages.

ACHIEVING

End, goal, or objective as element. In internally patterned interaction, relations are ends in themselves. Work is life and life is work. The child is socialized into a "way of life" which knows no sharp demarcation between social relations in work, rest, play, worship, quiet sociability, and festivity.

Externally patterned interaction as is commonly found in Gesellschaft-like societies is directed toward achieving instrumental goals and adapting to an environment where the work goal may be separated from other goals. Ends are situationally specified.[53] In an urbanization study in two villages in Turkey in 1962, Kiray observes attitudinal goal changes taking place in a society with a feudal traditional base: "Taking initiative for a better future, and offering rational reasons for success and improvement of conditions of life instead of fatalism, resignation and submission to authority . . . Both villages are positively future-oriented; . . . opinions concerning the ways to reach such goals are also nonfatalistic. Both of the villages indicate hard work and ability as the main road to success. Simple luck, fatalism, and/or good personal connections are far less frequent responses than diligence."[54]

Goals, ends, and objectives are elements in the "less" developed societies in process of change and, as Kingsley Davis observes, "ultimate ends are not inherited. They are not found in external nature. They must, therefore, arise as a cultural emergent. They must spring from the dynamics of communicative interaction,. . . they have a subjective and a transcendent quality — an existence only in the indoctrinated mind."[55] Goal attaining and the acceptance of new knowledge are important elements in the transition from "the old" to "the new" in the urbanization and development process.

Goal attaining activity and concomitant "latent" activity as process. The goal of the Gemeinschaft work team can be observed in the traditional complex of family and/or tribe activity in the tasks of daily living. The activity is manifest because its relation to the goal is both recognized and intended by the actor. Work activity is normatively integrative in that the relationships of members to each other and to work tasks embody the norms and beliefs of the group. Religious dedication of activities at seedtime and harvest are entwined with respect for the soil as well as devotion of the husbandman in his sharing the fruits of his labor with those less fortunate. This type of normative integration operates as a "latent"[56] activity in that it has a function for the system which is "unintended" and may be unrecognized by the actors.

When ends are functionally specific and sharply differentiated from other elements in the PAS Model, particularly norms and facilities, and when the norms of efficiency have priority, the action and the pertinent ends may be called instrumental and Gesellschaft.[57] "Production becomes increasingly precise, increasingly efficient by such goal-directed techniques as the efficiency expert, the assembly line, the automated plant, the job quotas, the time and motion studies, and the progress reports."[58] Sub-system activities, including "the coffee break," "the annual stockholders luncheon," "the inter-departmental bowling contest," and "the sales convention," which appear to be morally expressive, are nonetheless instrumental in goal attaining activity; and may be both manifest and latent in character. It is during such expressive activity that the

Gesellschaft work team can be said to have an internal interaction pattern.

Gouldner says the bureaucratic organization of large numbers of persons generally utilizes one of two approaches in the processing of goal attaining activity.

> In the rational model, the organization is conceived as an 'instrument' — that is, as a rationally conceived means to the realization of expressly announced group goals . . . The rational model assumes that decisions are made on the basis of a rational survey of the situation, utilizing certified knowledge, with a deliberate orientation to an expressly codified legal apparatus. . . . The natural-system model regards the organization as a 'natural whole' (which) strives to survive and maintain its equilibrium, and this striving may persist even after its explicitly held goals have been successfully attained. This strain toward survival may even on occasion lead to the neglect or distortion of the organization's goals.[59]

In the natural-system model, which stresses the interdependence of the component parts, planned changes are expected to have consequences for the whole organizational system.

Roethlisberger and Dickson[60] distinguished between the logic of cost and efficiency (the rational Gesellschaft-like model), on the one hand, and the logic of sentiment (the natural-system Gemeinschaft-like model), on the other. Planned change programs, designed by planners and professionals in the rational, Gesellschaft society, may fail when introduced into a developing Gemeinschaft society where "the logic of sentiment is important in the social system."

Alienation of the worker in his separation from the production process according to Marx[61], and the alienation of workers in all bureaucratically organized work situations according to Weber[62], are major consequences of large scale organization in the Western World. More recent work on alienation by Seeman illustrates five different aspects of relationships between goals and goal attaining activity as perceived by the individual in today's society; namely, powerlessness, meaninglessness, normlessness, isolation, and self-estrangement. *Powerlessness* is defined by Seeman as "the expectancy or probability held by the individual that his own behavior cannot determine the occurrence of the outcomes, or reinforcements he seeks. *Meaninglessness*, the individual is unclear as to what he ought to believe — when the individual's minimal standards for clarity in decision-making are not met. . . . a low expectancy that satisfactory predictions about future outcomes of behavior can be made . . . *Normlessness*, a high expectancy that socially unapproved behaviors are required to achieve given goals. *Isolation* . . . assigning low reward values to goals or beliefs that are typically highly valued in a given society. . . *Estrangement*, the degree of dependence of the given behavior upon anticipated future rewards."[63]

The French sociologist Durkheim observed that when normative integration is lacking in society, a state of "anomie," a condition of social disorganization or "disregulation" results.[64] In Durkheim's work on *Suicide*, he attempted to show differences in the rate of suicide by variations in anomie in society. Merton analyzes "the consequences for the behavior of people variously situated in the social structure in which the emphasis on dominant success-goals has become increasingly separated from an equivalent emphasis on institutionalized procedures for seeking these goals."[65] The process of goal attaining activity and concomitant latent activity has functional as well as dysfunctional consequences for adaptation of the society to the environment; and the modern bureaucracy as part of the socio-cultural environment itself demands human adaptation.

NORMING, STANDARDIZING, OR PATTERNING

Norm as an element. Norms of morality and conformity are characteristic in the Gemeinschaft-like work team.[66] Technical norms of efficiency and maximum profit are characteristic of the external pattern and the Gesellschaft-like corporation.

Williams observes that "values are closely related, conceptually and empirically, to social norms; but norms are more specific, concrete, situation-bound specifications; values are the criteria by which norms themselves may be and are judged . . . Values concern the goals or ends of action and are, as well, components in the selection of adequate means."[67]

The patterning of values has been observed by the senior author of this chapter in research in Southeastern Pennsylvania as stated in the following Propositions: *Proposition 1. "A unified cultural system (as well as a distinctive sub-system within the culture) has a consistent pattern of values."*[68] The cultural value profile consistency for the "high-conformity" members of the cultural system is significant as a normative system. *Proposition 2. "Processes which tend to disintegrate the culture will be reflected in the value system of its members."*[69] The cultural value profile for "low-conformity" members of the cultural system, identified by limited participation in religious activities and adherence to group practices, was also significantly consistent as a normative system.

The normative structures of the two sub-systems, however, are significantly differentiated, which not only supports the behavioral differences, but gives some indication of the direction in which the normative structure is moving. Traditionally high priority values of religion, family, and social service tended to show a decline in importance in the normative structure of the "low-conformity" sub-system; low priority values of excitement, wealth, and influence tended to increase in meaning and importance.

These propositions support the hypothesis that "as the normative structure of a social system changes, value profiles shift from one profile — 'familistic-traditional,' to an 'individualistic-achievement' profile in the urbanization process." The shift in value profiles is not random for a given society. The changing normative structure is relative to "new meaning" and "reference group" linkages of the society.

Usages of the reference group concept include the designation of that group which serves as the point of reference in making comparisons or contrasts, especially in forming judgments about one's self. In the original use of the concept Hyman spoke of reference groups as points of comparison in evaluating one's own status, and he found that the estimates varied according to the group with which the respondent compared himself.[70] Logically, then, any group with which an actor is familiar may become a reference group. A second referent of the concept is that group in which the actor aspires to gain or maintain acceptance. In the third usage, the concept signifies that group whose perspective constitutes the frame of reference of the actor. Thus, Sherif[71] speaks of reference groups as groups whose norms are used as anchoring points in structuring the perceptual field, and Merton and Kitt[72] speak of a "social frame of reference" for interpretations.[73]

Evaluation as a process.   Norms are established in a hierarchy and become the chief means of evaluating behavior and interaction in relation to the elements in the social system. Evaluation as a process involves both cognition and feeling (belief and sentiment) carried on in accordance with the norms of the system involved.

In an earlier work the senior author stated that "a value refers to the meaning a pattern of behavior has for the human organism and is defined as 'a qualitative phenomenon which is always relative to the self-realization of a given personality in a given situation.' The value of a pattern of behavior is its power to command preference over other known patterns of behavior in the human organism's drive to self-realization. In the process of evaluating a number of internalized behavior patterns the human organism makes choices according to its own definition of the situation and these choices or preferences are called its 'value pattern.' "[74]

Proposition 3. " 'The human organism when functioning in an interactive system(s) evaluates not only the significant behavior patterns representing its part in interaction but actually incorporates the evaluated behavior pattern of the other(s).' Interpersonal and intrapersonal action involves role and value-taking for others and for the self."[75]

The evaluation of norms and values as a process involves interaction of the self with members, as well as non-members of the society. Traditional norms may be reinforced or threatened as alternative choices must be made by members of the society in adapting to the physical and social world in which they live.

The rapid industrialization of Japan and the remarkable adjustment of the Japanese to industrialized and urbanized societies have been accounted for by the ease with which systemic linkage of the Japanese family to the larger system was accomplished. This linkage is reported to be particularly simple because of the convergence of certain ends and norms,[76] a factor presumably resulting from the evaluative process placing emphasis on similar items.[77]

The interdependent relationships between cultural, social, and personal value systems will be presented later in the review of socialization as a comprehensive or master process in the PAS Model.

DIVIDING THE FUNCTIONS

Status-role incorporating both element and process. The status-role differentiation in the external pattern of social systems varies with the stage of development of the society. A child born into a family in one of the "less" developed societies of the world can look forward to filling very few status-roles outside the family. Typically, he will follow an agricultural pursuit on a family-sized farm. His team-mates will be the other members of his family. On the family-sized farm he does a part of everything that there is to be done. He does these things at the same time that he performs his family status-roles of son and brother. His status-roles are *diffuse*. Neither the nature of his tasks nor the time allotted to do them is specified. Furthermore, his status-roles are *traditional*.[78]

In highly industrialized societies, the proliferation of status-roles in the technological, economic and political spheres is highly differentiated. The conceptual model of "The Occupation—Profession Continuum"[79] (Figure 3) as a heuristic device, suggests the existence of definite patterns in the life history of work groups along the lines of the continuum as social systems become increasingly contractual and bureaucratic in large scale organization. According to Povalko,

FIGURE 3
The Occupation-Profession Continuum*

Dimensions	Occupation	Profession
1. Theory, intellectual technique	Absent	Present
2. Relevance to social values	Not relevant	Relevant
3. Framing period	A. Short	Long
	B. Non-specialized	Specialized
	C. Involves things	Involves symbols
	D. Subculture unimportant	Subculture important
4. Motivation	Self-interest	Service
5. Autonomy	Absent	Present
6. Commitment	Short term	Long term
7. Sense of Community	Low	High
8. Code of Ethics	Undeveloped	Highly Developed

*Source: Povalko, Ronald M., *Sociology of Occupations and Professions.* (F.E. Peacock Publishing Co., Inc. 1971), pp. 17-27.

"Professional marginality represents the circumstance of work groups which, for a variety of reasons, develop to the point where inconsistencies and contradictions exist in the degree of development they display on various dimensions of work."[80]

Occupations as status-roles. In the status-role structure of the modern work team, "a perfect worker in the capitalistic enterprise is one who does exactly anything he is told to do, and does it for no other reason than because he is paid to do it."[81] Znaniecki observes that in communities undergoing development "where unexpected changes disturb established occupational patterns we find a demand for advisers whom people actively performing occupational roles can consult when in doubt. Because it is not the skill of the practical people, but their knowledge, which is in question, knowledge and skill is sought in an adviser. It is preferable — nay, often essential — that he should not be active in a practical role of the same kind as that of those who consult him; he must be beyond competition, so that men of action may be sure his advice is disinterested. In case of disagreement they will then defer to his judgment and subject their opinions to his arbitration."[82]

According to Povalko, professionals in bureaucracies experience the phenomenon of conflict, based upon two diametrically opposed characteristics. "Professions place a premium on autonomy while bureaucracies demand adherence to organizational rules, regulations, and procedures. From the professional perspective, the impetus for work behavior is internal to the individual. From the bureaucratic perspective it is located in the organization's goals and rules."[83]

The assignment of status-roles over which the individual has no control as in sex, birth order, ethnicity, and frequently occupational opportunity, is common in the traditional society. One of the unique characteristics of development is the emphasis placed upon personal achievement, in contrast to ascription.

RANKING

Rank as an element. Rank, as stated above, refers to the importance a specific status-role has for the system in which it is accorded. It has been observed that in any social system where it is possible to have a plurality of persons with similar standing, the step to class, caste, or estate forms of stratification is easily taken.[84] Sorokin writes, "Unstratified society, with a real equality of its members, is a myth which has never been realized in the history of mankind."[85] In the Gemeinschaft society, rank may be based upon age, sex, and kinship where everyone is known to everyone else. In the Gesellschaft societies status-roles are not only highly differentiated in the ranking of occupational and professional work and productivity, but there is demonstrated a display of conspicuous consumption as well. As Veblen observed, conspicuous consumption, leisure, and many activities may symbolize rank which entitles the actor to an "increment of good repute."[86]

Evaluation as process in ranking and allocation of status-roles. The standing or rank of an actor in a given social system is determined by the evaluation placed upon the actor and his acts in accordance with the norms and standards of the system.[87] Jones has shown how, when religious behavior is of paramount importance, it determines rank. Thus in Tregaron, a large Welsh village regarded locally as a town, religion largely determines status positions in work. Figure 4 derived from the Jones study[88] shows where "a non-religious person, however high his class position in terms of occupation, cannot achieve the highest status (or ranking) in the community. Comparable structural situations exist within most British rural communities, although the number of behavioral configurations which exist in a locality, their components, and the dominant institution may differ. They form the basis on which people are able to assess each other, and do."[89]

Allocation of status-role as stated previously, refers to the process or processes whereby incumbents come to occupy particular status-roles.[90] In a study of all high school seniors in Wisconsin public, private, and parochial schools in 1957, Sewell, Haller, and Ohlendorf found that "educational status attainment and the status level of one's first job are the most immediate variables influencing

FIGURE 4

A Diagramatic Representation of Status
Within a Community Evaluation*

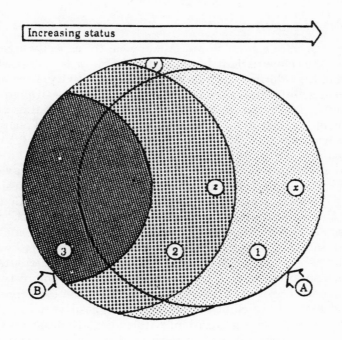

Key.   A   religious adherents
      B   non-religious element
      1   administrative, professional, managerial and proprietor category
      2   craftsmen and specialised worker category
      3   unskilled workers and labourers category

Individual x is of higher status than y, although both are in category 1, because x is in A and y in B. Individual z is of higher status than y although z is in category 2, because z is in A and y in B.

---

*Source: Jones, Gwyn C., *Rural Life Patterns and Processes*. (New York: Longman, 1973), p. 31.

later occupational status attainment."[91] As the individual experiences alternative status-role opportunities in the "less" as well as the "more" developed societies, he is, in fact, experiencing a transition in self-perception. Social mobility may be defined within the context of status-role evaluation by the actor, incorporating elements and process, as the internalization of new status-roles and values relative to social structure — a process of socialization.

CONTROLLING

Power as an element. Power is defined as the capacity to control others. In the Gemeinschaft-like community power is almost wholly confined to the informal controls within the collectivity. In contrast, the Gesellschaft-like societies are systemically linked and functionally integrated. Each such linkage is a potential or actual control over the operations of each bureaucracy, so linked reciprocal controls are exercised by (1) the corporate community, (2) other organized interest groups, and (3) government.[92]

Etzioni identifies three types of control on the behavior of members of the organization, and the involvement or type of response suggested in each instance.[93] The types of control are: (A) Coercive control: the application or threat of physical sanctions, such as the restriction of food or movement. (B) Remunerative control: manipulation of salaries, wages, fringe benefits. (C) Normative control: allocation of prestige symbols and influence over the distribution of prestige. The corresponding involvement of actors in the respective types of control are: (A) alienative: hostility to the organization's rules and goals; (B) calculative: neither strong positive nor negative attitudes toward the organization, with major attention upon the rewards for appropriate participation; and (C) moral: positive attachment to the organization's goals held to be desirable and valued.[94]

Organized labor and trade associations represent major social organizations linked with the corporation and government exercising spheres of control on the worker in the "more" developed societies.

Decision-making and its initiation into action. The patterns by which power is articulated vary greatly.[95] Two dimensions may be mentioned: 1) the extent to which it is concentrated or dispersed among the status-roles and actors and 2) the manner of acquiring, maintaining, and buttressing the possession of power.[96]

Max Weber identified three kinds of authority: charismatic, traditional, and legal-rational.[97] Each kind of authority is based upon different sources of power, and the relationships between leaders and followers in each case differs. Charismatic authority is vested in the personal attributes of the leader endowed with charisma — the gift of grace — and so recognized by his followers. In traditional societies, persons who occupy age and kinship status-roles may be granted the authority of charismatic leadership.

Traditional authority is a combination of the "right" to a position of authority, and the legitimacy of the person who occupies the status-role. Such persons hold traditional wisdom as it has been handed down from generation to generation, from father to son.

Legal-rational authority is vested in the status-role of the office, irrespective of who the occupant may be. The initiation of action is generally impersonal, applies to all occupants of equal status-roles, and subordinates are obligated to comply with the decision of the authority holder. As in all typologies, there are no "pure" types of authority in a given organization. The leader of a large scale organization may, in addition to the legal-rational authority vested in his office, hold personal attributes in addition; age, sex, ethnic identity or personal ability and charm which will attract a following of members who would not otherwise comply with his directives. Decision-making in Gesellschaft-like social systems is predominantly universalistic, affectively neutral, functionally specific, achievement oriented, contractual and rational; in the Gemeinschaft-like system it tends to have the opposite attributes[98] (Figure 2).

SANCTIONING

Sanction as an element and application of sanctions as process. Sanctions can be either positive or negative, and are manifest in the potential satisfaction-giving or depriving mechanism at the disposal of the members.[99] The application of sanction is illustrated in the following letters recorded in *The Polish Peasant*.[100]

Gazeta Swiqteczna, 1898.

I asked one of the farmers (of the village Kowalowka) why nobody there is afraid of theft and he said: "Formerly there used to be awful thefts, particularly they were stealing horses, but we decided at a communal meeting that whoever committed a theft would be forever excluded from the commune, and if he did not want to leave voluntarily his property would be sold at auction, the money would be given him and he would be driven away. Since that time there has been no stealing in our commune."

Gazeta Swiqteczna, 1903.

In Makoszyn . . . Andrej Lekarczyk with the help of his son Antoni, beat with flails his father-in-law, a white-haired old man, Josef Majda. The wronged Majda brought a complaint against his son-in-law and his grandson and the court condemned Andrzej Lekarczyk to 3 months and Antoni to 3 weeks imprisonment. But Majda begged the court to commute this punishment to a church-penance. And so it was done. In conformity with the demand of Majda, the Lekarczyks stood with the flails with which they had beaten the old man, in such a place that everybody could see them. It was a great shame for them. Now people laugh at them, point at them with their fingers and will remind them for a long time about their disrespect for gray hair. You should see the Lekarczyks running home from the church with their flails hidden under their coats. They ran without looking around; only dust rose behind them.

The informal and symbolic application of sanctions in the Polish peasant community imposed both coercive and normative control (Figure 5) on non-conforming members of the social system. In a more recent context and within American society, the Watts community in 1964 demonstrated an alienative involvement of its members toward the impersonal bureaucratic "City Hall" and in the application of negative sanctions toward store owners for their high prices and hostile manners; at the same time, "passing by" the business of a "Blood Brother." Bayard Rustin observes:

At a street-corner meeting in Watts when the riots were over, an unemployed youth of about twenty said to me, 'We won.' I asked him: 'How have you won? Homes have been destroyed, Negroes are lying dead in the streets, the stores from which you buy food and clothes are destroyed, and people are bringing you relief.' His reply was significant: 'We won because we made the whole world pay attention to us. The police chief never came here before; the mayor always stayed uptown. We made them come.' Clearly it was no accident that the riots proceeded along an almost direct path to City Hall.

Nor was the violence along the way random and 'insensate.' Wherever a store-owner identified himself as a 'poor working Negro trying to make a business' or as a 'Blood Brother,' the mob passed the store by. It even spared a few white businesses that allowed credit or time purchases, and it made a point of looting and destroying stores that were notorious for their high prices and hostile manners. The McCone Report itself observes that "the rioters concentrated on food markets, liquor stores, clothing stores, department stores, and pawn shops." The authors 'note with interest that no residences were deliberately burned, that damage to schools, libraries, public buildings was minimal.'[101]

The application of negative sanctions was designed to bring to public attention norms and ends which were unrealized in community living.

FIGURE 5
Control and Involvement Relations*

Type of Involvement	Type of Control		
	Coercive	Remunerative	Normative
Alienative	Prisons Custodial Hospitals		
Calculative		Industrial and Commercial firms Peacetime military units	
Moral			Churches, Schools and Universities Research Units Voluntary Organizations

*Source: Adapted from Amitai Etzioni, *A Comparative Analysis of Complex Organizations*, (New York: Free Press of Glencoe, 1961), pp. 12 and 66-67.

Bureaucratic organizations impose strong sanctions, positive and negative, as rewards or punishment for loyalty or disloyalty of workers in the attainment of organizational goals. Sanctioning behavior may involve public recognition or preferential treatment in group activity; it may involve a threat of dismissal or the administration of the "silent treatment" by associates or officers. The primary type of sanction as indicated by Etzioni (Figure 5) is "remunerative"; the involvement of the worker is "calculative." The "calculative" behavior of workers in the case of organized labor is expressed in the contractual agreement ensuing from collective bargaining, where "wages, hours, and other terms and conditions of employment[102] are negotiated. The greater need for functional and normative integration in the Gesellschaft-like system "requires a societal" machinery for the application of sanctions, both of punishment and reward, not found in the Gemeinschaft-like society. The whole legal system, both legislative and judiciary, are parts of that machinery. The hierarchical activities of the external pattern involving rating sheets, pay plans, rules of tenure, and standards of achievement are mechanisms by which rewards can be distributed according to universal standards which are functionally specific and in accordance with achievement.[103]

The Hawthorne studies found that the application of positive and negative sanctions were applied by the members of the work team to those who violated the group norm.[104] Those who produced beyond the group norm were "rate busters;" those who worked below standard were labeled "chiselers."

FACILITATING

Facility as an element.   Physical facilities, including mass communication, transportation, mass production assembly lines in factories, and technology in agriculture and industry directly influence the structuring and development of society. Likewise, the availability and control of the facility, as determined by the normative structure of the social system, is influenced by the internal pattern which is sentiment-laden, and the external pattern which is goal directed. Williams emphasizes the social nature of facilities. "Property consists first not of *things*, but of *rights*; it is not a concrete object of reference, but a socially recognized claim. The essence of property is *an institutionalized right* of persons as *other social units* to scarce values."[105]

Utilization of facilities as process.   The uses to which the resources of society are put are subject to the directive influence of common cultural goals.[106] Horowitz indicates that "the psychological characteristics of developing man directly affect the economic take-off point. It is widely presupposed that, however diverse the motives for development may be, dissatisfaction with the existential conditions and some sort of program for an optional approach are both necessary . . . Even if we ignore the dilemmas arising out of a direct correlation of actions and interests, there is a policy issue involved: the degree of social unrest necessary to stimulate a person to think along developmental lines without creating complete revolutionary upheaval."[107]

In Mosher's "Concept of Agricultural Development," the whole society is not the target.[108] The highest priorities are given to the infrastructure, which includes agricultural extension education and credit, research and technology and supplies and equipment. Underlying Mosher's discussion is what may be called central place theory and integrated community development. The first four items listed among his eight priorities or "elements" all take place territorially, that is within a region.

Mosher's first four priorities in Agricultural Development are: (1) agricultural expansion by bringing additional high potential land into production; (2) agri-support activities of transport and communication networks relating the rural structure to the total economy; (3) agricultural research to improve farm technology; and (4) measures to produce and distribute the material findings of research. The four additional priorities include (5) upgrading the quality of the land, i.e., irrigation, drainage, leveling or terracing; (6) providing production incentives for farmers; (7) education of agriculturally related techniques; and (8) a public administrative framework for executing the public activities (such as policing standards of weight, measurement, and quality; establishing public market information services; and enforcing fair trade practices), large-scale land development programs, the maintenance of roads and highways.

Societies that are, in fact, existing in a "less than subsistance" level of development, dislocated, and poverty-stricken may be motivated to some kinds of change by the desire to survive. This motivation can encourage the utilization of new facilities and programs of development linked to systems outside the infrastructure. Horowitz indicates that:

> a myth has been propogated that external stimulants are necessary to place the masses of Third World nations (the less developed societies) into a 'take-off' position. While there are certainly great differences between levels of achievement and aspirations, the poor do not require much motivation for change beyond their own existential situation. If we take the 'case histories' of two slum people — Carolina Maria de-Jesus in the Sao Paula *favelas* and Jesus Sanchez in the Casa Grande of Mexico City — what emerges is a picture of dislocated, no less than developing, people in changing circumstances.[109] We might outline the common characteristics among the poor who are part of the development process. (1) Ability to move from a rural society to an urban society, and also from a society based on barter and property to one based upon money and contract; (2) discontent with low-grade economic status, which is expressed in a variety of ways — shifts from house to house and from job to job, concern with the education of children, willingness to postpone immediate gratification; (3) politicalization, as expressed in voting, concern with candidates and party issues, and even membership in organized political groupings; (4) secularization of personal values, as expressed in a 'free' love pattern, a lessening of the bonds of religious fervor, or even sometimes conversions to other religious faiths, and a general acculturation to the impersonal, anomic life of the large industrial city; and above all (5) an unwillingness to return to the agricultural communities from which they have immigrated.[110]

The utilization of planned change is significantly expedited when supported by "rising expectations."

Planned change programs are facilitated by unrest within the "less" developed community, and, by reference group identity in the external pattern. As observed by Mbithi of The University of Nairobi:

> Kenya's development problems, which have dictated development policy in the 1960's and 1970's are, as in many African countries, determined by four major factors: first, the structural, institutional and racial class barriers to access to opportunities for the majority estab-

lished during 60 years of colonial rule; second, the emergent post-independence system of inequalities, unrealistic aspiration among the majority of its population, especially school-leavers, leading to inequalities in incomes, access to employment, education, land and an increasing flood of rural to urban migration; third, an open economy extremely sensitive to international trade, political, foreign exchange and aid policies, and finally, the structure of natural resource endowment which preempt certain development strategies . . . Kenya has an estimated population (1973) of about 12 million people, 90 percent rural.[111]

In the 'more' developed societies, the utilization of facilities is marked by 'overdevelopment' which Horowitz operationally defines as follows:

First, overdevelopment occurs when maximum levels of production are not achieved even though the plant capacity for full production is available. Second, overdevelopment results when the disparity between wealth and poverty grows, despite a constant increase in the gross national product and in the over-all accumulation of wealth. Third, overdevelopment occurs when conventional human skills available are outdistanced by technological advancements. Fourth, overdevelopment is therefore an excess ratio of industrial capacity to social utility, while underdevelopment refers to an excess number of social demands in relation to the available production and consumer outlets.[112]

COMPREHENSIVE MASTER PROCESSES

Communication. It is communication through preservable symbols and the development of culture which sharply distinguishes human beings from other animals . . . Communication is a primary process basic to the articulation of each of the elements of a social system and to the unity of the whole.[113] In the Gemeinschaft-like society, levels of literacy may limit effective communication to members of the family and the immediate community. Communication with outside social systems is limited. In contrast, the Gesellschaft-like society is able to interact readily within the society and with audiences linked systemically in contrasting settings across language and territorial barriers.

The diffusion of the urbanization process in developing areas is attributed by Frey to what he calls a "communication hypothesis."

Look at a series of overlays reflecting urbanization, industrialization, literacy, roads, railroads, death rates, assorted measures of productivity, cinemas, newspapers, income, education, and so on. Granted that there are variations in the hatchings and shadings, nevertheless in most developing societies there is usually an impressive similarity of pattern across all these maps . . . Initially, it strikes one that development seems to be some sort of suffusion of epidemiologic process. In grossest terms, it seems to move from coastal areas to the interior, along rivers and trade routes. It seems to be held up by natural barriers which increase isolation. Moreover, its movement seems to depend not just upon topography or climate but also upon proximity to external modernizing forces and upon the technology of transport and communication. In short, such a geographic gestalt strongly suggests a communications theory of development, namely, that modernization suffuses primarily according to ease of communication with more modern sources.[114]

Frey's "communication hypothesis" projects patterns of development along lines of human interaction. This hypothesis is comparable to Mead's hypothesis regarding mind (as regarding the self in social interaction) in that "the mental emerges out of the organic life of man through communication. The mind is present only . . . when significant symbols are being used by the individual. This view dispenses with the substantive notion of mind as existing as a box-like container in the head, or as some kind of fixed, ever-present entity. Mind is seen as a *process* (of communication) which manifests itself whenever the individual is interacting (with himself) by using significant symbols."[115] Society, self, and mind are emergent phenomena which, according to the action frame of reference, are products of the process of communication and socialization; a process of human development in the social system.

In the "more" developed societies, the networks of large-scale organizations are "instrumental in carrying the communication flow of the larger society. The corporate state bureaucracy, or bureaucracies of church, labor union, and voluntary organizations are basically oriented to their own survival and housekeeping needs. But they also carry adverse content of messages and symbols through the relevant populations, by-products irrelevant to the carrying organization, from jokes to propaganda. And, at the same time, communication becomes itself a specialized network of formal organizations, for it becomes a social product with exchange value at the market place. The mass-media industries arise, allowing a form of direct communication with a very large proportion of the total population that bypasses organizational structures."[116] Mass communication serves as a systemic linkage of interaction whereby one or more elements of at least two social systems, personal and social, are articulated in the urbanization process.

Boundary maintenance. Increased boundary maintenance may be achieved by assigning higher primacy or evaluation to the activities characteristic of the external pattern, such as the pursuit of a broadened economic goal, in which case the elements ends, power and rank may be expected to increase in primacy. "As ambiguities attached to ends are removed, as the identities and responsibilities of power figures are clarified, and as ranks consonant with the total operation are established, integration and solidarity are heightened."[117] Boundaries may be further sharpened for the social system by participation of members in ritual and sentimental activities which express the internal pattern. Boundary maintenance devices may be primarily physical, as in private property, political boundaries, zoning restrictions, and separate but not equal facilities. They may be social as in the case of endogamy, recruitment of leadership from within a bureaucracy, or membership in a professional association. The devices may also be symbolic in nature, as in the case of language, and they may be based on sex, age, ethnicity, or occupation which aside from physical or social proximity may limit interaction and segregate members according to the meaning and value attached to their respective status-roles within the socio-cultural system. The enforcement of Equal Employment Opportunity legislation in large scale organizations is made more difficult when symbolic boundaries separate members of the society.

The concept of "Three Worlds of Development" implies physical, social, and symbolic boundaries.[118] When the "First World," as the United States with the "more" developed societies; the "Second World," as the Soviet Union, and the "Third World," the "less" developed societies are viewed, each is characterized by physical and demographic, social and ideological features which function to give it a differentiated identity and solidarity. Revolution and militarism represent a coercive aspect of boundary maintenance.

Horowitz acknowledges the activity of an additional "world" in the "ideology of militarism."

The national independence of nearly every Third World nation — the old nations of Latin America and Asia, as well as the newer nations of Africa — has been ensured through revolution and secured through the armed might and organizational skills of revolutionists. The use of coercion, when it ceases to be a monopoly of the state, heralds the arrival of the revolutionary movement; for it is at that moment when the organized use of terror is neither confined to the ruling class nor accepted by wide masses that a revolutionary situation can be said to exist. The mass character of revolution in the Third World can hardly be ignored. And this requires an appreciation of the mass character of the

military apparatus that neither sustains or thwarts the revolutionists
in their struggles . . . The chief reason that the military potential of the
Third World remained unexplored in the pre-World War II period was
that the nation-state, which is an essential prerequisite for the existence of a national military complex, hardly existed in Asia and Africa.[119]

Systemic linkage.   Systemic linkage as previously noted may be
defined as the process whereby one or more of the elements of at least
two social systems is articulated in such a manner that the two
systems in some ways and on some occasions may be viewed as a
single unit. Whereas the process of boundary maintenance refers to
the limits set upon group contact, the process of systemic linkage
refers to the organizational arrangements for group interdependen-
cies.[120]

Empirical research conducted by the junior author of this chapter on linkages of Mexico and the United States tested hypotheses
including "Evaluation of Religious Activity" among others.[121] One
stated: *"Mexicans engage in more religious activity and evaluate religious organizations to which they belong more highly than do citizens
of the United States."* All the data available and related to this
hypothesis as gathered in the study support it. Mexicans report
attending church more frequently than do Americans. Answers to
specific questions support it.

"Taking all of these groups [in which respondents belonged and
participated] into consideration, which ONE is the most important to
you?" Almost 9 out of 10 Mexicans gave a religious group as an
answer; whereas only about one-third of the Anglo citizens claimed
such a group as most important.[122] Such findings indicate the extent
of normative integration and systemic linkage between the two countries and indicate how values of interacting persons influence Americans and Mexicans.

The subjective content of belief, knowledge and norms has linkage implications for inter-group integration. One of Max Weber's
important theses, often ignored, is that Protestants, especially the
Calvinists, Methodists, Baptists, and Pietists, internalized norms of
brotherhood and honesty which were supposed to be applicable to all
mankind, thus being effective far beyond family and religious sect,
and in this way are different from those of the Jews, Pharees, and
similar groups.[123] The belief in exogamous marriage, or marrying
outside the social system, is integrative for those societies which
tolerate and encourage this type of linkage. Exogamous marriage
would not take place except for the articulation of common norms and
sentiments within the linked relations.

The linkage of systems in the corporate world, and the development of the multi-national corporation has significant implications for both the "more" as well as the "less" developed societies. Warner observes that "the incorporation of smaller units into larger ones, marked in most enterprises, reduces local community autonomy and increases the strength of national enterprises with common centers of control. The lateral extension of vast enterprises throughout the country, associated with the elaboration of corporate and other hierarchies to manage such enterprises, increases . . . the circulation of the managerial elite from community to community and reduces the proportion of those of high status who live out their lives in one place."[124] The lateral extension of the multi-national corporation articulates the norms of a large-scale organization in two or more societies which operates with little concern for the needs of any single community or society. The "multi-national corporation" is actually "a cluster of companies of different nationalities under varying degrees of financial and managerial control by a parent company that is usually American . . . The U.S. has a vital interest, for example, in making sure that technology that would strengthen the Soviet Union military is not exported to Russia by foreign affiliates of U.S. firms.[125]

For the "less developed" societies the "multinational corporation" fills a vacuum. There is an increasing misfit between the fact of global economic life and the political organization of the world, in one hundred and forty local, so-called sovereign states. They aren't really sovereign because they are dependent upon the rest of the world for raw materials, and sometimes for food itself, in order to live. But they are as sovereign as they can continue to be. "Most of the economic troubles of the world are due to the misfit between the anticipated political setup of local states and the real, global economic setup . . . Multinational corporations precisely bridge the gap."[126]

The linkage of the multinational corporation, public and private, imposes independency relations upon communities as observed by Burgen.

Government and business have grown big and complex, and it becomes harder and harder to determine where one ends and the other begins. How much of a major defense contractor is in the private sector and how much in the public sector? New York State will help bail out financially distressed Consolidated Edison. Multinational companies are often bigger in terms of wealth than the country in which they operate. Where is the line between what is public and what is private to be drawn? The corporation could once be seen as simply the organizer of capital and labor to produce goods and services. That is still true today, of course, but that notion underplays the impact that the modern-day corporation has upon society. The corporation hires and fires and can bring about a sociological revolution if it begins hiring and promoting more blacks and more women. It can stay in a community and keep it prosperous or move out and leave it destitute. It can pollute the environment or it can help clean it up. The corporation is an integral part of society today — more so than ever before because it is bigger and richer than ever before.[127]

The linkage of systems by status-roles influences the development of the self. The linkage of large-scale organizations and bureaucracies in the multinational corporation imposes external controls upon communities in the "less" as well as the "more" developed societies of the world. The incongruities of status-roles and normative structures for sub-systems within society is not without consequences. In the case of programs of planned change, linkage must involve the norms of the change agents with the norms of the target systems that are to undergo development and change.

Socialization. The senior author of this chapter presents in his study of value patterns the normative aspect of the socialization process in the following proposition (No. 4)[128]: "The value profile(s) of the human organism, the self, represents an incorporation of 'self values' and 'self-other values' which are internalized in the process of value-role-taking in a given situation and ecological environment. This continuous incorporation and integration of 'self-values' and 'self-other values' constitutes the growth of personality."[129]

The personality system involves the adaptation of the human organism to the biological energy system, the beliefs and normative order of the culture, and the status-roles of the social system in which interaction takes place. The cognitive and personal developmental aspect of these linkages for the self, according to Mead, is accomplished in role-taking. "This role-taking enables (the self) to share the perspectives of others. Concurrent with role-taking, the self develops, i.e., the capacity to act toward one's self. Action toward oneself comes to take the form of viewing oneself from the standpoint, or perspective of the *generalized other* (the composite representative of others, of society, within the individual) which implies defining one's behavior in terms of the expectations of others.[130] The intrapersonal action and linkage within the individual as "I"; and the *generalized other* as "me" in role-taking, constitutes the social emergence of personality and the personality aspect of development.

McClelland[131] presents the view that early childhood socialization, and "the economic development of a country is, in part, a social-psychological process, since it is highly correlated with the cultural

pattern of early independence training and a high need for achievement."[132] In Bronfenbrenner's study of the differential socialization
in *Two Worlds of Childhood, U.S. and U.S.S.R.* — two highly industrialized societies —

> the major difference between the two cultures lies in the localization of
> primary responsibility for the upbringing of children. In the United
> States, we ordinarily think of this responsibility as centered in the
> family . . . in the Union of Soviet Socialist Republics . . . the duty of a
> father toward his children is a particular form of his duty toward
> society. . . . In handing over to you a certain measure of social authority,
> the Soviet state demands from you correct upbringing of future citizens
> . . . if you wish to give birth to a citizen and do without parental love,
> then be so kind as to warn society that you wish to play such an
> underhanded trick. People brought up without parental love are often
> deformed people; . . . nor is the family the sole or even the principal
> delegate of the society for the upbringing of children. Such primary
> responsibility is vested in still another social structure, the *children's
> collective*, defined as 'a group of children united in common goal-oriented
> activity and the communal organization of this activity.'[133]

An observation drawn by Bronfenbrenner in studying the major
environmental forces which can influence the behavior and development of children in each society is stated:

*"It follows that any appreciable, enduring improvement in the
child's development can be affected only through an appreciable, enduring change in the environment and behavior of the persons intimately associated with the child on a day-to-day basis."*[134]

The normative and status-role disparities which exists within
and between highly differentiated cultural, social and personality
systems have important consequences for members of communities
and societies in transition. The socialization and urbanization process represents the linkage of the human organism with environments both physical and social. The senior author of this chapter
presents the problem of adaptation to these environments within the
context of socialization. The following proposition supported by his
investigations illustrates this.

"The consistencies and inconsistencies of value profiles of cultural systems and persons, as well as the value-role-taking ability or
inability of members, have implications for human motivation,
[development], and health when viewed from the perspective of the
self-realization of the human organism."[135]

Socialization represents a behaviorial component of self and
society. Self-realization may be facilitated and, at the same time,

limited by the constraints of the physical and social environment in
the "less" as well as the "more" developed societies of the world.

Institutionalization. As noted earlier, institutionalization is
the process through which normative structures, including sanctions, become organized in the behavior of members of the community. Williams states that "in operation, institutional norms are also
likely to be persistent, enforced through definite social organs, and
reciprocally binding on the occupants of designated social positions.
In the fully developed case, institutional norms are: (1) widely
known, accepted, and applied; (2) widely enforced by strong sanctions
cautiously applied; (3) based on revered sources of authority; (4)
internalized in individual personalities; (5) inculcated and strongly
reinforced early in life; and (6) objects of consistent and prevalent
conformity. For example, there would be no doubt whatever that
judged by these criteria the prohibitions of murder, treason, can-
nibalism, and rape represent institutional norms in American Society."[136] And Parsons adds that "Although institutionalization is a
matter of degree, its opposite is *anomie* in which the structured
complementarity of the interaction process is absent and the normative order breaks down."[137]

The institutions which pattern work and production in subsistence societies center in the family as a work team; in highly
specialized societies they center in the integrative norms of the
large-scale organization — the corporation — with its emphasis upon
efficiency and predictable economic activity.

Social control. The elements and processes most closely related
to social control are norms, power, and sanctions.[138] Levy observes
that the scarcity of means, frustrations of expectations and imperfec-
tions of socialization makes this process a requisite in the function of
society.[139] Merton indicates that "a group cannot persist without
substantial measure of social control."[140] Other processes than
norms, power, and sanctions, such as status-role and facility, are
utilized in the professions and bureaucracies to institutionalize social
control so that "deviancy is permitted for a time. Such a status-role is
that of the sick person. Psychiatrists . . . and doctors through the
supportive action of friends and relatives employ many mechanisms
to restore the deviant to 'normalcy.' "[141]

The mechanisms of "sick leave" and "leave without pay" are an
institutionalization of behavior to allow for exceptions to work norms
without disrupting the social system. Institutional norms differ from
other cultural norms, "primarily in the intensity of social sanctions
and in the degree of consensus with which they are supported and
applied."[142] The sacred society is "facilitated by completely *primary*

contacts, articulated by expectations of *complete conformity* to *unchanging* and *well-defined situations* and *sanctioned* by general aversion, indignation, and traditional and spontaneous verbal or corporal chastisement" reinforced by gossip.[143] In rational bureaucratic organizations, the guides to behavior are preserved in *"principles,* where social relations are impersonal, . . . articulated by expectations of *varying degrees* of *conformity* to a fairly complex, *steadily* changing and not always defined situation, sanctioned by formally and legally codified punishment."[144] An "abuse of power" is condemned by "impeachment" proceedings as a measure of social control in the social system.

The threatened normative structures of sovereignty and independence within societies dominated by the multinational corporation has promoted the need for a social control mechanism embracing the "more" and the "less" developed societies. In June, 1974 after nearly a year of studying multinational corporations, a twenty member panel appointed by Secretary General Kurt Waldheim, called for establishment of a permanent United Nations commission on multinational corporations. One objective is "to promote a series of international agreements on such issues as taxation, antitrust, and jurisdictional disputes involving global companies, aiming eventually at a 'General Agreement on Multinational Corporations' that would provide for enforcement machinery and sanctions. The U.N. would also set up a special office to collect and analyze information on multinational companies and provide aid to governments of developing countries in dealing with multinational investors."[145]

CONDITIONS OF ACTION

Territoriality; size; time.   The social system in space is significantly affected by the adaptation of human populations to different physical environments. Changing population composition and planned change as well as change emerging "naturally" in the social system, and systemic linkages to other systems are affected by territorality. The organization of families and villages in space, how services of farmers are related in space,[146] and the relation of prices to markets, has been the concern of agricultural social scientists at least from Von Thuenen's time to the time of Galpin, Christaller, Loesch, Berry and others.[147]

The territoriality condition of action as determined by changes in population size, density, and heterogeneity in contemporary societies is identified by Philip Hauser in his 1969 presidential address to the American Sociological Association entitled "The Chaotic Society:

Product of the Social Morphological Revolution."[148] Four factors emerge in the social morphological revolution: namely, (1) the population explosion; (2) the population "implosion" — the increasing proportion of populations living in cities; (3) population diversification — differentation in the way of life and/or occupational specialization; and (4) the related technological and social changes following from the first three factors.

Hauser indicates a multiplier effect on Potential Human Interaction with Increased Population Density in a Fixed Land Area.[149] The United States in 1900 had an assumed density of 314 persons in a circle of a 10 mile radius; Manhattan in 1960 had a density of 23,550,000. The U.S. Population Density by State for 1970 is shown graphically in the three-dimensional map (Figure 6) illustrating the concentration in the Northeastern United States.

Durkheim observed in the late-nineteenth century: "Whereas lower societies are spread over immense areas according to population, with more advanced people population always tends to concentrate"[150] . . . A surplus-producing division of labor in an agricultural society undergoing development frees non-agricultural workers to work and live in cities. Table 2, Levels of Urban Concentration, illustrates the significantly higher percentage of the population living in localities of 20,000 and over in the more developed regions of the world in contrast to the less developed regions, with England and Wales in 1951 having 69 per cent as compared to Haiti in 1950 having 5 per cent.[151] Durkheim's observation regarding population concentration and community transformation is still valid at the mid-point in the twentieth century.

In the decade of the 1950's, however, Keyfitz[152] has observed the percentage of people living in urban places increased by 25 per cent for the more developed societies; and the less developed increased by 55 per cent according to Bourgeois-Pichat.[153] Keyfitz asks: "How could that 55 per cent increase occur?" The surplus food of the Asian peasantry did not increase by 55 per cent in the 1950's; it hardly increased at all. How can Djakarta be five times as populous as it was before World War II? . . . The answer, of course, is that it draws food from foreign territories, including the United States: some of it paid for with the export of raw materials; some of it borrowed; some as gifts . . . Once the local countryside can no longer produce enough food for its own inhabitants so that these must be supported by foreign food, they tend naturally to gather into such seaport cities as Djakarta, Calcutta, and Rio de Janiero, as close as possible to the spot where the boats will discharge their cargoes of American, or occasionally Burmese or Cambodian, grain. If people are to be fed from abroad it is

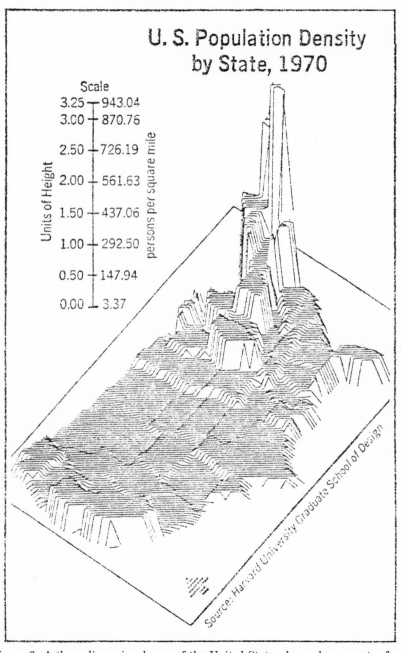

Figure 6. A three-dimensional map of the United States drawn by computer from census data.

cheaper to have them at the seaports than dispersed through the countryside; . . . if population continues to increase in the countryside and food does not, one can expect further flight to those cities.[154] The "population explosion" in the "less" developed societies (Table 1) is represented by a rapid decrease in the death rate, with the birth rate remaining high. This net population increase is advancing at an increasing rate in the developing societies and accentuates the numbers of people forced to the cities for food in these areas.

Keyfitz identifies "two sorts of dense agglomerations of people . . . The one is wealthy, modern, productive, highly differentiated by occupation, handling complex symbol systems, dominating the environment. The other is poor, traditional, non-productive except for services that are not badly wanted, less differentiated by occupation, illiterate or barely literate, highly dependent on the environment. Our rich American cities contain a minority which is taking refuge from rural poverty. Some Asian cities consist of a majority of such refugees."[155]

"Population explosion" dynamics in the developing societies; and, systemic linkages between the "more" and the "less" developed societies are producing major social changes in the traditional modes of adaptation of human populations to old communities and new territorial environments. Further adaptations are required to new and emerging urbanizing environments. A WHO (World Health Organization) study in Tunisia, emphasizes "the importance of modernization, both of health facilities and socio-cultural characteristics of the population as the major factor in promoting use of health services. Looked at another way . . . the *degree of coverage and utilization* of the health services is a good indicator of the level of modernization of a region or country."[156]

Malthus[157] did not anticipate the "voluntary" fertility control which has taken place in the "more" developed societies during the past century (Table 1).

Urbanization, the process of change in values, roles, and life styles, imposes the necessity to adapt to new physical and socio-cultural environments. This process whether imposed upon individuals and collectivities as a result of population "explosions," or as a result of population "implosions" pushing or pulling persons to urban centers, is occurring on a world-wide scale. One of Myrdal's considerations regarding the direction of change is that societies may be moving toward more common valuations.[158] Gesellschaft-like relations dominate the urbanized landscape including the agricultural village where persons are forced to migrate for physical survival, or where they choose to stay or move for greater alternative opportunity

TABLE 2. LEVELS OF URBAN CONCENTRATION

Region	Year	Percent of Population in Localities of	
		20,000 and over	2,500 and over
More Developed			
England and Wales	1951	69	
Japan	1955	66	
Australia	1958	64	
United States	1950	43	
United States	1960		69.9
United States	1970		73.5
USSR	1959	36	
Sweden	1950	35	
France	1954	33	
Less Developed			
United Arab Republic	1947	29	
Mexico	1950	24	
Brazil	1950	20	
India	1951	12	
Guatemala	1950	11	
Pakistan	1951	8	
Haiti	1950	5	

Sources: United Nations and U.S. Bureau of the Census.

and, since World War II, sprawling suburbs have been built all over the western world for the mobile who must move to new jobs in different places.[159] The very moving of people in the Gesellschaft-like urban society helps produce the interchangeable actor. The great suburban residential movement sweeping over the western world is a manifestation of the search for quiet and clean places to live which may also provide a degree of the internal interaction pattern for the residents of the Gesellschaft-like systems. The large cities, for all their urbanity, seem to contain an impressive degree of local community life within their metropolitan limits.[160] There is a persistence of ethnic and religious groupings in residential patterning reported by Glazer and Moynihan in "Beyond the Melting Pot," at least for those below the upper-middle class.[161] The interchangeability of actors in space seems to encourage a search for community and cultural identity in the urban setting. The survival of cultural pluralism and the continued emergence of "normative differentiation" in cities is suggested, but the urbanization process is complex. Populations in the process of urbanization and development tend to become relatively less dependent upon the immediate territorial environment for subsistence; and increasingly dependent upon large scale social systems and systemic linkages in urban locations on a regional and a world-wide territorial basis.

URBANIZATION AND THE PLANNED SOCIETY

The process of urbanization in Britain is represented by a transition from "town" differentiated settlements to a decline in propinquity. Throughout history, towns have been characterized by containment.

The wall has characterized endless towns from Jericho to the late nineteenth-century Paris, a symbol of separation and distinctiveness in style of living and in values . . . A distinction has arisen between town and country; . . . physically the division between town and country, particularly in a country like Britain, has become blurred . . . It was the desire to escape from the towns which at the peak of industrialization reached the nadir of human environment; a desire first indulged in by the middle classes, but later shared by a steadily increasing number of the less affluent as new means of transportation made possible that schism between workplace and home which is now the outstanding characteristic of all our towns and cities; . . . suburbs tried to create an illusion of country as near as possible to the city center for people still tied to it by work and services . . .

In fact containment was one of the main reactions to the increasing spread of cities which reached a peak in this country between the two world wars . . . In 1951, four out of five people in England and Wales lived in towns; . . . accretion has certainly been suburban, and already in a physical sense probably nine out of ten people live in towns. But in a social sense this country is rapidly becoming a hundred percent urban, for many aspects of urban life are no longer spatially differentiated. Taken literally . . . the concept of the central place need no longer apply. The towns can be replaced by a non-place urban realm.

Many of the desirable criteria of an adequate environment can be met within the limits of so-called high density. A more critical need is to realize that different groups in society, particularly age groups, have different requirements . . . Propinquity is loosening its grip.[162]

Town planning during the next 30 years in Britain, according to Jones, will need to be cognizant of continuing urbanization and social change.[163]

By the year 2,000 the population of the UK will probably be about 75 million and the number of houses that will have been built between now and then, at present rates, will be about 15 million. But the quality of living will have changed also . . . Even by 1985, great changes can be foreseen; . . . the working day will be considerably shorter than it is today, real income will be doubled, the amount of time spent on education more than doubled . . . Demands on the land are going to change . . .

... A massive increase in recreational demands on the countryside can be expected if present day trends continue. Affluence and increased mobility could turn the whole of Britain into a summer madness; ... nowhere in Britain is more than 70 miles from the sea ...

... If green belts and their probable extensions are added, it means that a considerable percentage of the land area — possibly a third — must be strictly controlled; ... no weekenders would be tolerated casually crossing a factory floor, and it may well be that much of farming in the future will demand the same protection ... There is much to be said for living in very compact settlements during a working week if we are allowed the use of a cottage or caravan on the Welsh uplands during the weekend. There is even some value in calculating density not so much by the amount of land on which a house stands, but by the areas accessible to and used by households. In this respect, perhaps we should lean less toward the American pattern but examine the Scandinavian in more detail.

Jean Gottman,[164] whose concept of "megalopolis" entails a network of interlocking associations based on new levels of transportation and communication in the Boston-New York-Philadelphia-Lancaster-Baltimore-Washington-Newport News corridor, suggests that programs of urban planning and development may be already obsolete. The nature and directions of "the urbanization process" may become more important for the contribution of social scientists to planning than earlier mechanistic approaches to renewal and development.

NOTES

1. For references to concepts and subject matter of this chapter see especially Charles P. Loomis and J. Allan Beegle, *A Strategy of Rural Change* (New York: Schenkman, Halsted and John Wiley, 1975). A work team may be defined as collectively composed of at least two members who accept a common objective in creating, transforming, moving and/or marketing goods and services, and cooperate to achieve it; the community is defined as a collectivity encompassing a territorial unit within which members pursue most of their everyday activities necessary in satisfying common needs.

2. Society is defined as the collectivity which furnishes the primary referents for cognitive, expressive, moral and purposeful activities of communities and their social systems.

3. Human ecology may be defined as the study of the form and development of the community in human population. Amos H. Hawley, *Human Ecology: A Theory of Community Structure* (New York: The Ronald Press Co., 1950), p. 68.

4. Urbanization is defined as a process of change in values, roles, and life styles, and the necessity to adapt to new physical and social environments as activities of the center when compared with those of the field become increasingly important.

5. Development is defined as a process of change: "A psychological unit built around a social value . . . a desire for accelerated industrialization and rapid modernization . . . the ideology of the (Developing) Third World is a response to the pervasive problem of how to gain worldly preeminence." Irving Louis Horowitz, *Three Worlds of Development: The Theory and Practice of International Stratification* (New York: Oxford University Press, 1972).

6. *The Point Four Program.* Publication 3347. Economic Cooperation Series 23, Division of Publications, Department of State (Washington, D.C.: Government Printing Office, 1949).

7. Robert F. Eshleman, "Value Profiles, Value-Role-Taking, and Health," *International Journal: Social Science and Medicine* (July 1970), pp. 113-130. Pergamon Press, Printed in Great Britain.

8. Pitirim A. Sorokin, in the foreword to Ferdinand Toennies, *Community and Society-Gemeinschaft and Gesellschaft:* translated and introduced by Charles P. Loomis, (East Lansing Michigan: Michigan State University Press, 1957), pp. lx-x. Also New York and London: Harper and Row.

9. Ferdinand Toennies, *Community and Society-Gemeinschaft and Gesellschaft*, op. cit.

10. Charles P. Loomis, *Social Systems: Essays on Their Persistence and Change* (Princeton, New Jersey: D. Van Nostrand Co., Inc., 1960), pp. 58-60.

11. Loomis, op. cit., pp. 58-60.

12. John C. McKinney, "Methodology, Procedures and Techniques in Sociology," in Howard Becker and Alvin Boskoff, eds., *Modern Sociological Theory* (New York: The Dryden Press, 1957), p. 225.

13. Robert K. Merton, *Social Theory and Social Structure*, rev. ed., (New York: The Free Press, 1957), pp. 3-16.

14. Karl Marx, *A Contribution to the Critique of Political Economy* (Chicago: Kerr Publishing Co., 1911).

15. Loomis, op. cit., p. 63.

16. Ibid., p. 62.

17. Curt Tausky, *Work Organizations: Major Theoretical Perspectives* (Itasca, Ill., Peacock Pub., 1970), pp. 8-9.

18. Loomis, op. cit., pp. 64-65.

19. Wilbert E. Moore, in a letter to the junior author. See also Godfrey and Monica Wilson, *The Analysis of Social Change Based on Observations in Central Africa* (Cambridge: Cambridge University Press, 1954), Ch. 2.

20. Loomis, op. cit., p. 120. Also Max Weber, *Essays in Sociology*, ed., and translated by H.H. Gerth and C. Wright Mills (New York: Oxford University Press, 1946).

21. Loomis, op. cit., p. 66.

22. Ibid., p. 67.

23. Kenneth A. Boulding, *A Primer on Social Dynamic History as Dialectives and Development* (New York: The Free Press, 1970).

24. Max Weber, *The Protestant Ethic and the Spirit of Capitalism* (New York: Charles Scribner's Sons, 1968).

25. Karl Marx, *A Contribution to the Critique of Political Economy* (Chicago: Kerr Publishing Co., 1911).

26. Loomis, op. cit., p. 68.

27. W.I. Thomas and Florian Znaniecki, *The Polish Peasant in Europe and America*, Vol. 1. (New York: Alfred Knopf, 1927), p. 319.

28. Weber, op. cit.

29. Loomis, op. cit., p. 69.

30. Emile Durkheim, *The Division of Labor in Society*. Translated by George Simpson, (New York: The Free Press, 1933), p. 277.

31. Robert Redfield, *The Little Community: Peasant Society and Culture* (Chicago: Phoenix Books, The University of Chicago Press, 1961), p. 64.

32. Loomis, op. cit., p. 13.

33. Charles P. Loomis, and Zona K. Loomis, *Modern Social Theories. Selected American Writers*, 2nd ed. (Huntington, N.Y.: Robert Krieger Publishing Co., 1975). p. 35.

34. Alvin W. Gouldner, *Patterns of Industrial Bureaucracy* (The Free Press, Glencoe, Illinois, 1954), p. 163.

35. Gouldner, op. cit., p. 175.

36. Loomis and Loomis, op. cit., p. 692.

37. Alvin W. Gouldner, ed., "The Problem of Succession in Bureaucracy," in *Studies in Leadership* (New York: Harper and Bros., 1950) pp. 644-662.

38. Robin M. Williams, Jr., *American Society: A Sociological Interpretation*. 3rd ed. (New York: Alfred A. Knopf, 1970) p. 70.

39. Williams, Jr., op. cit., pp. 174-175.

40. Act 195 (as signed into law, July 23, 1970). The General Assembly of Pennsylvania from Article VII, Section 701, known as the "Public Employee Relation Act."

41. Loomis, op. cit., p. 15.

42. See Arnold Van Gennep, *The Rites of Passage* (Chicago: University of Chicago Press, 1960).

43. Loomis, op. cit., p. 15.

44. Robert K. Merton, *Social Theory and Social Structure* (Glencoe: Ill.: The Free Press, 1957), Revised and enlarged ed., p. 204.

45. Ibid., p. 196.

46. Robin M. Williams, Jr., *American Society*. 2nd ed. (New York: Alfred Knopf, 1960), p. 288.

47. Loomis, and Zona K. Loomis, op. cit., p. 514.

48. Ibid., p. 515.

49. Williams, Jr., *American Society*, op. cit., p. 498-510.

50. Loomis, and Zona K. Loomis, op. cit., p. 516.

51. Robin M. Williams, Jr., *The Reduction of Intergroup Tensions: A Survey of Research of Ethnic, Racial and Religious Group Relations* (New York: Social Science Research Council, 1947), p. 57.

52. Misha Jezernik, "Changes in the Hierarchy of Motivational Factors and Social Values in Slovenian Industry," The *Journal of Social Issues: Social Psychological Research in Developing Countries*, 24, (April, 1969), pp. 103-111.

53. Loomis, op. cit., pp. 15, 73.

54. Mubeccel Kiray, "Values, Social Stratification, and Development," The *Journal of Social Issues: Social Psychological Research in Developing Countries*, 23, (April, 1968), pp. 87-100.

55. Kingsley Davis, *Human Society* (New York: The Macmillan Co., 1949), p. 526.

56. Merton, op. cit., p. 51.

57. Loomis, op. cit., p. 15.

58. Ibid., p. 76.

59. Alvin W. Gouldner, "Organizational Analysis," in Robert K. Merton, Leonard Broom, Leonard S. Cattrell, Jr., *Sociology Today: Problems and Prospects* (New York: Basic Books, Inc., Publishers), pp. 404-405.

60. F.J. Roethlisberger, W. J. Dickson, and W.A. Wright, *Management and The Worker* (Cambridge: Harvard University Press, 1939), p. 565.

61. E. Josephson and M. Josephson, eds., *Man Alone: Alienation in Modern Society* (New York: Dell Publishing Society, 1962), pp. 97-98.

62. Hans H. Gerth and C. Wright Mills, *From Max Weber: Essays in Sociology* (New York: Oxford University Press, 1946), p. 50.

63. Melvin Seeman, "On the Meaning of Alienation," *American Sociological Review*, 24, (December, 1950), pp. 783-791.

64. Emile Durkheim, *Suicide*. (Glencoe, Illinois: Free Press, 1951).

65. Merton, op. cit.

66. Loomis, op. cit., p. 17.

67. Robin M. Williams, Jr., *American Society: A Sociological Interpretation*. 3rd ed. (New York: Alfred A. Knopf, 1970), pp. 442-443.

68. Robert F. Eshleman, "A Study of Changes in Value Patterns (A Study of a Religious Ethnic Cultural System)," (Unpublished Ph.D. Dissertation, Cornell University, February, 1948).

69. Robert F. Eshleman, "Value-Profiles, Value-Role-Taking, and Health," in *Social Science and Medicine*, 4, (Printed in Great Britain: Pergamon Press, 1970), pp. 114-118.

70. H.H. Hyman, "The Psychology of Status," *Archives of Psychology*, 38, (1942), p. 15.

71. M. Sherif, "The Concept of Reference Groups in Human Relations," in M. Sherif, and M.D. Wilson, eds. *Group Relations at the Crossroads* (New York: Harper and Bro., 1953), pp. 203-231.

72. Robert K. Merton and A. Kitt, "Contributions to the Theory of Reference Group Behavior," in Robert K. Merton and P.F. Lazansfeld, eds., *Studies in the Scope and Method of The American Soldier* (Glencoe, Ill.: Free Press, 1950), pp. 49-50.

73. Tamatsu Shibutani, "Reference Groups as Perspectives," *American Journal of Sociology*, 60, (May, 1955), pp. 562-569.

74. Eshleman, op. cit., p. 114.

75. Ibid.

76. F.S.C. Northrop, *The Meeting of East and West* (New York: Macmillan Co., 1947), p. 549.

77. Loomis, op. cit., p. 81.

78. Ibid., p. 83.

79. Ronald M. Povalko, *Sociology of Occupations and Professions* (Itasca, Ill.: F.E. Peacock, Publ., 1971), pp. 17-27.

80. Ibid., p. 14.

81. Florian Znaniecki, *Social Actions* (New York: Holt, Rinehart and Winston, 1936), p. 615.

82. Florian Znaniecki, *The·Social Role of the Man of Knowledge* (New York: Columbia University Press, 1940), p. 33.

83. Povalko, op. cit., p. 189.

84. Loomis, op. cit., p. 24.

85. Pitirim Sorokin, *Social Mobility* (New York: Harper Bros., 1927), p. 12.

86. Thorstein Veblen, *The Theory of the Leisure Class*. Mentor edition, (New York: The New American Library, 1953), p. 66.

87. Loomis, op. cit., p. 25.

88. Gwyn E. Jones, *Rural Life Patterns and Processes* (New York: Longman, 1973), p. 31.

89. Ibid., p. 30.

90. Loomis, op. cit., p. 26.

91. William H. Sewell, Archibald O. Haller, and George W. Ohlendorf, "The Educational and Early Occupational Status Attainment Process: Replication and Revision," *American Sociological Review*, 35, (December, 1970), p. 1023.

92. Loomis, op. cit., p. 94.

93. Amitai Etzioni, *A Comparative Analysis of Complex Organizations* (Glencoe, Ill.: Free Press, 1961), pp. 3-67.

94. See also Curt Tausky, *Work Organizations: Major Theoretical Perspectives* (Itasca, Ill.: F.E. Peacock Publishers, 1970), pp. 1-23; Richard H. Hall, Eugene J. Haas, and Norman J. Johnson, "An Examination of the Blau, Scott and Etzioni Typologies," *Administrative Science Quarterly*, 12, (1967), pp. 126-134.

95. Loomis, op. cit., p. 22.

96. Ibid., p. 95.

97. Talcott Parsons, ed., *Max Weber: The Theory of Social and Economic Organization* (Glencoe, Ill.: The Free Press, 1947), pp. 324-406; H.W. Gerth, and C. Wright Mills, *From Max Weber: Essays in Sociology* (New York: Oxford University Press, 1958), pp. 245-264.

98. Loomis, op. cit., p. 99.

99. Ibid., p. 26.

100. Thomas and Znaniecki, op. cit., p. 1218.

101. Bayard Rustin, "The Watts' Manifesto and the McCone Report," *Commentary*, (March, 1966), pp. 29-35; in Max Birbaum and John Mogey, *Social Change in Urban America* (New York: Harper and Row, 1972), pp. 28-29.

102. Public Employee Relations Act 195, op. cit.

103. Loomis, op. cit., p. 100.

104. F.J. Roethlisberger and W. J. Dickson, *Management and the Worker* (Boston: Harvard University Press, 1939).

105. Robin M. Williams, Jr., *American Society* (New York: Alfred A. Knopf, 2nd ed., 1960), pp. 187-188.

106. Loomis and Loomis, op. cit., p. 555.

107. Horowitz, *Three Worlds of Development*, op. cit., p. 77.

108. Arthur R. Mosher, "Agricultural Development," in J. Paul Leagans and Charles P. Loomis, *Behavioral Change in Agriculture* (Ithaca and London: Cornell University Press, 1971), pp. 12-26.

109. Carolina Maria deJesus, *Child of the Dark* (New York: E.P. Dutton & Co., 1962); and Oscar Lewis, *The Children of Sanchez: Autobiography of a Mexican Family* (New York: Random House, 1961).

110. Horowitz, op. cit., p. 77.

111. Philip M. Mbithi, "Conquering The Economy Through Rural Development," *CERES FAO Review and Development* (Rome: May-June, 1974), pp. 26-29.

112. Horowitz, op. cit., pp. xvi.

113. Loomis, op. cit., pp. 30-31.

114. Frederick Frey, "Development Aspects of Administration," Leagans and Loomis, op. cit., p. 266.

115. George H. Mead, *Mind, Self and Society*, edited by Charles Morris. (Chicago: University of Chicago Press, 1934). Bernard Meltzer, "Mead's Social Psychology," in Jerome G. Manis, and Bernard M. Meltzer, *Symbolic Interaction: A Reader in Social Psychology*, 2nd ed., (Boston: Allyn Bacon, 1972), p. 12.

116. Gino Germani, *Modernization, Urbanization, and the Urban Crisis* (Boston: Little Brown and Co., 1973), p. 205.

117. Loomis, op. cit., p. 31.

118. Horowitz, op. cit.

119. Ibid., pp. 341-376.

120. Loomis, op. cit., p. 32.

121. Charles P. Loomis, Zona K. Loomis and Jeanne E. Gullahorn, "Linkages of Mexico and the United States," Research Bulletin 14, Agricultural Experiment Station, Michigan State University (1966), pp. 55-56.

122. Ibid., pp. 55-56.

123. Ibid., p. 402.

124. W. Lloyd Warner, "Big Corporations," in Philip Ehrensaft and Amitai Etzioni, *Anatomies of America: Sociological Perspectives* (London: The Macmillan Co., 1969), p. 175.

125. "Sovereignty vs. the Multinationals," *Business Week*, (April 20, 1974), p. 22.

126. Flanigan James, "Arnold Toynbee: Are Businessmen Creating a New Pax Romana," *Forbes*, (April 15, 1974), p. 68.

127. Carl G. Burgen, "Commentary/Chief Executive," *Business Week*, (May 4, 1974), p. 85.

128. In Eshleman, op. cit., 1948.

129. Ibid., p. 114.

130. Mead, op. cit., pp. 17-18.

131. David McClelland, *The Achieving Society* (New York: Van Nostrand Reinhold, 1961).

132. William W. Lambert and Wallace E. Lambert, *Social Psychology*, 2nd ed. (Englewood Cliffs, New Jersey: Prentice-Hall, Inc., 1973), p. 151.

133. Urie Bronfenbrenner, *Two Worlds of Childhood U.S. and U.S.S.R.* (New York: Simon Schuster, 1972), pp. 4-6.

134. Ibid., p. 142.

135. Eshleman, op. cit., p. 114.

136. Williams, Jr., *American Society*, op. cit., p. 37.

137. Talcott Parson, *The Social System* (Glencoe, Ill.: The Free Press, 1951), p. 39.

138. Ibid., p. 206.

139. Marion J. Levy, Jr., *The Structure of Society* (Princeton: Princeton University Press, 1952), p. 191.

140. Merton, op. cit., p. 341.

141. Loomis, op. cit., pp. 35-36.

142. Williams, Jr. *American Society*, op. cit., p. 37.

143. Howard Becker, *Man in Reciprocity: Introductory Lectures on Culture, Society and Personality* (New York: F.A. Praeger, 1956), p. 192.

144. Loomis and Loomis, op. cit., pp. 78-79.

145. "A U.N. Plan to Monitor the Multinationals," *Business Week*, (June 15, 1974), p. 85.

146. Charles P. Loomis, "Social Science," ch. 10, in Leagans and Loomis, op. cit., pp. 432-433.

147. Johann Heinrich von Thuenen, *Der isolierte Staat in Beziehung auf Landwirtschaft und Nationaloekonomie* (Jena: Fischer, 1930); Charles J. Galpin, *The*

Social Anatomy of an Agricultural Community, Wisconsin Agricultural Experiment Station Research Bulletin #34, (Madison, 1915); Walter Christaller, *Die Zentralen Orte in Sueddeutschland* (Jena: Fischer, 1933); August Loesch, *Die Raumliche Ordnung der Wirtschaft* (Jena: Fischer, 1941); and Brian J. L. Berry, *Geography of Market Centers and Retail Distribution* (Englewood Cliffs, N.J.: Prentice-Hall, 1967).

148. Philip M. Hauser, "The Chaotic Society: Product of the Social Morphological Revolution," *American Sociological Review*, 34, (February, 1960), pp. 1-19.

149. Ibid., p. 34.

150. Emile Durkheim, *The Division of Labor in Society*, translated from the French by George Simpson, (Glencoe, Ill.: The Free Press, 1952), p. 257.

151. The migration of populations from rural poverty to urban places contributes to "urban growth" — the absolute increase of the urban population. By contrast, "urbanization," demographically, is the proportionate increase in the urban population — a greater increase than that of the total population of a given country or region over a period of time.

152. Nathan Keyfitz, "Population Density and Style of Social Life." Reprinted with permission from *Bioscience*, 16, (December, 1966), pp. 868-73; in Rudolf H. Moos and Paul M. Insel, *Issues in Social Ecology: Human Milieus* (New York: National Press Books, 1974), pp. 126-127.

153. Jean Bourgeois-Pichat, *Population Growth and Development*, International Conciliation, No. 556, Carnegie Endowment for International Peace. (January, 1966).

154. Keyfitz, op. cit., pp. 868-73.

155. Keyfitz, op. cit., p. 134; in Moos and Insel, op. cit., pp. 126-127.

156. Amos Benyoussef and Albert F. Wessen, "Utilization of Health Services in Developing Countries — Tunisia," *Internal Journal: Social Science and Medicine*, 8, (May, 1974), p. 303. Pergamon Press. Printed in Great Britain.

157. Thomas Malthus, an English Clergyman, in 1798 published his: *First Essay on Population* in which he proposed that population is necessarily limited by the means of subsistence unless prevented from growing by (a) *positive* checks such as war, disease and famine; or (b) by *preventive* checks such as the prevention of births *by celibacy or delay of the time of marriage*. "Population, when unchecked, increases in geometric ratio, subsistence only in an arithmetic ratio." Thomas R. Malthus, *An Essay on the Principle of Population as it Affects the Future Improvement of Society, with Remarks on the Speculations of Mr. Godwin, M. Condorcet, and other Writers* (Macmillan Ltd. London, 1926), p. 14.

158. Gunnar Myrdal, *An American Dilemma*, Vol. 2, Appendix. (New York: Harper & Row, 1944). See also his *Asian Drama: an Inquiry into the Poverty of Nations*, (New York: Pantheon, 1968).

159. Loomis, op. cit., p. 119.

160. Ibid.

161. N. Glazer and D.P. Moynihan, *Beyond the Melting Pot* (Cambridge, Mass.: M.I.T. Press), 1963.

162. Emrys Jones, "Some Geographical Aspects of Urbanization," in W.D.C. Wright and D.H. Stewart, *The Exploding City* (Edinburg: The University Press, 1972), pp. 85-89.

163. Ibid., pp. 91-93.

164. Jean Gottman, *Megalopolis: The Urbanized Northeastern Seaboard of the United States* (New York: The Twentieth Century Fund, 1961).

Chapter 7

Educational
Social Systems*

INTRODUCTION

In a general sense, observed Wittlin,[1] every waking moment of life, from birth to death, is an educational experience. The saying goes: experience is the best teacher. The primitives gained experience as they lived and died. Such experience passed from one generation to the other through word of mouth, memory, folklore and legends. The moderns acquire their experiences carefully, note them down in written form, check, recheck and refine them on the basis of newer experiences. Since every society must face and solve the inescapable problems of collective life e.g., socialization, mastery of nature, and social control,[2] formalized education has emerged as the most effective medium to achieve these ends. "All societies organize — or institutionalize — education in order to socialize their human generations, and to secure their social and cultural survival."[3]

In a broad sense again, education secures the preservation and transmission of culture. In a pluralistic society where diverse values and norms are pursued, education becomes all the more meaningful and important if the cultural and the sub-cultural values are to be preserved. "Education is charged with the conservation of the most highly prized beliefs and intellectual skills in the cultural heritage."[4]

Education, especially liberal education, may in the thinking of Ehlers and Lee,[5] be deemed as that which stimulates in each person a compelling urge to explore the unknown and to exercise to a fuller degree the vast possibilities of his mind. In this interpretation of education truths are neither final nor absolute, nor values inflexible, but rather are always subject to modification, correction and refinement.

*By Proshanta K. Nandi, Charles P. Loomis, and Everett D. Dyer

The task of educating successive generations is one of the most important tasks found in all societies. The family and informal groups in every society assume part of the responsibility, but no modern society permits the entire task to be assumed by these groups. "All social systems, large or small contain occasions for learning and participate to some degree in transmitting culture and in socializing the individual. But the degree of educational involvement is often minor, since many systems of regular transactions leave instruction undifferentiated and incidental and are not characterized by their educational effort."[6] In all Western societies elaborate systems have been built for the explicit purpose of educating the young.

In this essay we are primarily concerned with those formalized systems, particularly the schools, which have been established for educational purposes. Since the schools are society's vehicles by which the prevailing culture is transmitted to the young, it follows that there can be no great enduring divergence and inconsistency between the elements and processes that articulate the society and those that articulate the educational system.

The character of an educational system reflects the value orientation of the society producing it.

By education, then, we mean the process by which the cultural heritage is transmitted. Included in cultural heritage are "skills, ideas, reaction patterns, moral values, social attitudes, and the beliefs which constitute citizenship and personality."[7]

IMPORTANCE OF EDUCATION AS A SOCIAL SYSTEM IN AMERICA

In America nearly everybody goes to school. The magnitude of the educational enterprise, as reflected by school enrollments, is impressive. In 1970, about 6 out of every 10 persons between 5 and 34 years of age in the United States were in school. More than 99 percent of all youth, white and nonwhite, in the age group from 7 to 14 were in school. And approximately 1/5 of whites and about 1/6 of blacks between 20 and 24 years old were in school.[8] Even a large proportion (37.5 percent) of preprimary children 3 to 5 years old were in school in 1970. This latter percentage is much larger than in 1965 when slightly more than 1/4 (27.1 percent) were enrolled.[9]

The school is also a training ground of another variety, for the school supplies a meeting ground for diverse racial, ethnic, cultural, and social class groups. The child's first contact with groups other than his/her own often occurs at school. The provision of an opportunity for youth to interact with various segments of the community appears to be an extremely important function of the school system.

ELEMENTS AND PROCESSES OF EDUCATIONAL SOCIAL SYSTEMS

KNOWING

Belief (knowledge) as an element.   The belief is strong in America that education is the answer to most problems. The degree to which education is sought and the amount of money spent for education support this contention. In the words of Wissler: "Our culture is characterized by an overruling belief in something we call education — a kind of mechanism to propitiate the intent of nature in the manifestation of culture. Our implicit faith that this formula, or method, will cause this purpose to be more happily fulfilled, is our real religion."[10]

Reduced to simplest terms the beliefs basic to the educational system of the United States can be summed up as follows:

> Democracy cannot flourish without an informed citizenry; the school is a training ground not only for the dissemination of information; it is also a laboratory in democratic principles.

Many American statesmen have expressed these basic beliefs as they have viewed their country's educational system. Thomas Jefferson in a letter to George Washington in 1786 emphasized the political importance of education. He wrote, "It is an axiom in my mind that our liberty can never be safe but in the hands of the people themselves, and that, too, of the people with a certain degree of instruction."[11]

Cognitive mapping and validation as process.   In the United States where the pragmatic approach is important, intellectual activity relies more on a theoretical framework to which cognitive systems such as applied mathematics and symbolic logic are germane[12] than on systems where more reliance is placed upon the intuitive, aesthetic component and where "music, drawing, and manual arts are enlisted for their expressive, artistic and coordinative values."[13] However, while the curriculum tends to emphasize rational and scientific ways of knowing, the matrix of school attendance, school support, or school control is certainly not totally devoid of expressive sentiment.

FEELING

Sentiment as an element; tension management and communication of sentiment as processes.[14]   In the United States adults have feelings about what education should be; they believe that the educative process passes knowledge on to the succeeding generations. They also have a deep and abiding faith, which transcends cognitive belief, that the next generation will be improved and that education itself will ultimately solve problems and dispel evil.

Coupled with this faith in the ameliorative process of "educatin 'em up to it" is an emotional naïveté which, like the belief system, is characteristic of the greater society and is transmitted, reproduced, and reenacted in miniature in the educational system. "Everyone will be nice to you if you're nice to them" is, in the eyes of some observers, a prevailing and valid sentiment that has been substituted for principle and self-discipline. One may or may not agree with Walter Lippmann's observations that a kind of unsophisticated emotionalism permeates our schools, is sustained by an organized philosophy, and has led to hideous blunders in the assessment of the international situation.[15] But even the unconvinced are likely to recognize an aspect of American education here:

> American education is friendly, relaxed, sentimental, humanitarian, imprecise, and amiable as a spaniel puppy. It assumes that kindliness and gentle curiosity will always be met by a neighborly smile. The pleasant thing about America for the three-quarters of a century following Reconstruction is that within our borders this has largely proved true . . . [The error of our misinformation about Russia], perhaps the most colossal error in all history on the part of a highly literate nation provided with hecatombs of libraries and printing presses, stemmed from this same relaxed, friendly, sentimental, and humanitarian education — not simply in the schools and universities but in most articulated American thought. The cost of that error has not yet been revealed to us.[16]

The pious, humanitarian sentiments of America, which may be unsuited to her comparatively new role of world power figure, may be necessary in a society in which disparate and varying national strains are being rapidly integrated into a whole. If the varying ethnic groupings did not progress toward integration into a solidarity, these currently existing sentiments would disappear. New and altered educational sentiments more appropriate to the role of a world power figure would then develop.

Data for the United States indicate teachers experience great stress from their ambiguous status-role definitions and their lack of complete professionalization. Some of the stress arises in interaction inside the system. Thus one investigation indicates that the teacher in high school is subjected to stress because of the conflict between "the requirements of . . . two sets of expectations which operated in the classroom, those presented by the teacher and those which the informal system defined."[17] The results of the study suggested that it was possible for a teacher to "articulate both sets of roles," but that the more the teacher became linked to the internal pattern of informal student groups or to the formal extracurricular organizations the more he was tempted to permit a student's rank in the community and other personal considerations to be substituted for high scholarly achievement standards.

Inherent in the status-role of the school administrator are ambiguities and consequent unresolved tension. Due to the prevailing emphasis on equalitarianism in the United States both teachers and administrators idealize equality and democratic action in decision-making. The administrator who is aggressive and effectively utilizes prestige and rank outside the school system to provide the facilities needed to the system often labors under stress in relations with his teachers. School administrators suffer from guilt feelings if the situation does not permit them to be equalitarian and democratic.[18]

Various rites of passage are utilized which are enacted as sacred religious involvements as in baccalaureate services in the United States. Various initiation ceremonies, so extreme at one time, are now being superseded by rationalized orientation programs. More study of these various rites as well as rites of intensification would no doubt lead to useful comparisons.

The Stouffer study[19] reveals that no factor analyzed in nationwide study was so important in producing tolerance toward Communists, atheists, and socialists as education — the more education the greater the tolerance. The people in those regions with lower educational attainment and standards, such as the South and farm and rural areas, were less tolerant than were those in the urban areas of the East and West with higher educational attainments.

"Democracy" taken to mean an ideal state of equality accompanied by a degree of almost unlimited personal liberty if not license, and the antithesis of all authority is certainly not the democracy that is a *form of government* with highly institutionalized democratic *controls* of equality and liberty — the Constitution, the Bill of Rights, the courts of law, trial by jury, and due process of law which means notice, hearing, and judgment. If Lippman and Chalmers are right in assigning to the schools a confusion which causes the replacement of the latter meaning of democracy by the former — and this confusion has been such a popular and prevalent error that the schools could hardly have escaped it — then indeed democracy has been sentimentally interpreted and not without repercussions.

ACHIEVEMENT

End, goal, or objective as element.   The specific objectives of the United States educational system can be examined most fruitfully against a general statement of educational objectives. Durkheim gives such a general statement:

> Education is the influence exercised by adult generations on those that are not yet ready for social life. Its object is to arouse and to develop in the child a certain number of physical, intellectual and moral states which are demanded of him by both the political society as a whole and the special milieu for which he is specifically destined.[20]

There is a dual objective — the demands of society and the demands of self-realization.[21]

The ends of education for the Americans are a composite of social skills, vocational training, and mastery of knowledge in fields dictated by the personal interests of the individual student. The net result in any society of the accomplishment of ends is in the transformation of a child into an incumbent of an adult status-role. Society, in effect, is training the child so that he may, upon becoming an adult, effectively participate in society's division of labor.

The laws in the USA protect the rights of the individual from infringements and attacks by the state. Good citizenship and democratic principles can be and often are a part of the state-sponsored education of United States youth, but it is incidental to the training considered necessary to give full expression to individual capabilities. The central objective or the fundamental purpose of the schools in every instance is the same: to provide an educational program that will stimulate and guide each individual in developing his abilities to their fullest extent for useful, satisfying living.[22]

While this is the present generalized goal of education, it has not always been this way nor is it true today in every kind of community.

Formerly the ends and objectives of the rural neighborhood school were understood to be the teaching of the three R's. With the growing complexity of modern society and the increasing contact between rural and urban areas, the rural school's objectives have been broadened and redefined. "As a society undergoes industrialization and modernization, its instruction of the young becomes extensively differentiated, internally complex, and elaborately connected with other features of society."[23]

Considering the broad aims of modern education in relation to achievement, the less satisfactory schools in the United States were found for the most part in rural areas in the south prior to 1960. In a period of rapid urbanization with consequent disruption in rural areas, it is not surprising that the ends and objectives of rural schools were not reoriented to the needs of a nonrural society. However, the situation has changed rapidly. Most midwestern states, for example, do not have rural or country schools exclusively any more but have developed consolidated school districts and new curricula offering more subjects and better teaching staffs. Perhaps the rural schools are still strong in the South but with greater share of the federal and state money, the emphases have changed, particularly in the recent years.

Goal attaining and concomitant "latent" activity as process. In the United States adolescents in school mix book learning, lecture, study, and laboratory training with courting and other activities involving both sexes. The amount of school and university activity which has its prime function in the mingling of the sexes is greatest in the United States.

Teaching methods in the United States have occasioned more and more discussion. One study describes the high school situation in the following way:

> The teachers' perspective of the classroom was one in which behavior was defined according to an ideally conceived classroom situation in which performance approximated the ability and knowledge of the students. According to this perspective, discussion operated in ping-pong fashion between teacher and pupils and among pupils, limited only by considerations of knowledge and limitations of personality.[24]

With the development of broadened and redefined objectives a concomitant alteration of methods has occurred. Gone are the days where the goals and methods of educational attainment could be summed up in the familiar lines: "School-days, school-days, dear old golden rule days, readin and 'riten' and 'rithmetic, taught to the tune of a hick'ry stick."

NORMING, STANDARDIZING, AND PATTERNING

Norm as an Element. It is hard to generalize about norms in the United States, because the kind of local control which prevails encourages a highly varied normative pattern. "Progressive" education and educational policies by other names designed to organize a school for pupil self-growth and self-expression as well as for group decision and activity and democratic living are subjects that are continually discussed and argued about. There is the educator who decries the fact that

> Our classrooms have been arranged in terms of an authoritarian conception of living. Seats and desks were screwed to the floor. The teacher's desk was sometimes on a raised platform so placed as to facilitate command of the class. The taskmaster stood before the class and issued orders. Perhaps he lectured to the students on the virtues of democracy.[25]

Other educators equally vigorously denounce the kind of educational latitude which equates democracy with casual self-discipline and with a kind of normless "growing." Here, for example, John Dewey whose educational philosophy is still having a sizeable impact on norms in the American schoolroom is taken to task.

> Professor Dewey used the metaphor of a growing organism without reference to standards of good or right, leaving grave uncertainty whether the growth stimulated by education would, for example, be partial, one-sided, bad, or good ... [His] account of man is clear: that he is naturally good, being liable to evil only if affected by bad social arrangements, that he is a child of nature, and that the child in his innocence should provide the central preoccupation of all *Paideia*. [Although the revisions brought about by application of such a philosophy were] executed in the direction of extreme democracy ... the net result of these social reforms has been good. [For the future, however,] those dated and limited ideas cannot possibly affirm the purpose of learning for the second half of the century ... Our liberties are not secured primarily by democracy. They are secured by constitutionalism.[26]

Most parents probably hope that their children will encounter teachers who are helpful and interested in each student but who inculcate self-discipline as well as self-expression.

The norms of a number of social systems influence teacher and teacher-student relationships. This is true, of course, of many important status-roles in rural and urban areas. A factory foreman, for instance, may be a member of a family, bowling team, a church, and possibly several other groups that impose different norms of behavior.[27] As will be indicated in the discussion of sanctions, the teacher may give the primacy to the norms of (1) the community, (2) the immediate social system of the school, or (3) the professional organizations and groupings of colleagues. The early neighborhood school was rooted in the neighborhood community and in many respects functioned as an extension of the family. The norms of the school system per se and the profession were generally less important than those of the neighborhood community. School discipline, like family discipline, tended to be strict and would now be considered authoritarian. But there is evidence that rigorous discipline as a part of a general expectancy pattern yields different results than does discipline applied in the impersonal atmosphere of a larger bureaucratic organization. In the neighborhood school motivation was based more largely upon the personal and often affectual appeal of the teacher than in the trade center community school. Norms and standards of achievement varied greatly from neighborhood to neighborhood. The instances of teachers being bullied by lower class ruffians in frontier communities attest to the fact that the neighborhood schools were not always controlled as exclusively by the norms of the middle class as they are today.

Another area which is rich in normative behavior of particular interest to students has to do with the "rules" which operate only within the student world and by which students are judged by their peers. Few if any nonstudents fully understand these rules. Among college students in the United States it is not generally considered "good form" to allow a professor to wield much influence on the basic attitudes of the student. The norms of the student group are generally important in governing what courses should be selected, how much studying should be done, and the degree to which it is socially acceptable to have one's views altered by subject matter in course work. A studied wall of imperviousness to mental excitement or curiosity is necessary for social success among the student peers.

The neighborhood school, like the church, tends to function as a conserver of values rather than an initiator of change. Many authorities attempted to prevent the teaching of evolution. However, educators see the reflection of enlightenment in the leadership of modern schools. Stouffer, for example, found that the presidents of school boards and of Parent-Teacher Associations (although in general less tolerant of communists, socialists, atheists, and persons accused of radicalism than were some other leaders, such as presidents of library boards, industrial leaders, and newspaper publishers) were much more tolerant than the average citizen.[28]

Evaluation as a process. One kind of evaluation of the educational system is a highly measurable and quantitative one. It amounts simply to how much people are willing to pay for education. This may be measured in a number of ways. "How many dollars per pupil" is one measurement, although this does not reveal the amount spent in relation to the ability to pay. Thus, within the United States, it is possible that some of the states spending a small amount per pupil are spending a relatively larger proportion of their total budget on education than some wealthier states whose dollar per pupil rate shows up advantageously. There is a wide range in the percentage of income in the various states in the United States spent on education. Some rural states such as the Dakotas, New Mexico and Utah allocate relatively the largest proportions and Delaware, Maryland and Michigan give relatively small proportions of their incomes for education. There is a persistent belief in America that the worthwhile in education is the immediately practical. Evaluation of what is indeed practical falters when such an unpromising and theoretical subject as nuclear physics suddenly becomes as practical as a coal mine or an oil gusher. The state legislatures cautiously and many times parsimoniously evaluate research in the great state-supported institutions of higher learning.

Americans are preoccupied with an evaluative comparison of their own and foreign educational systems. Reasons for this competitive kind of evaluation are many. Chief among them are the need to vindicate belief systems which are diametrically opposed and a fear of the physical and mental consequences of success of the adversary.

DIVIDING THE FUNCTIONS

Status-roles incorporating both element and process.   The core status-roles for all educational systems are those of pupil and teacher. However, the status-role of school administrator becomes increasingly important as educational systems become more complex. It is the teacher's job to transmit knowledge to the pupil; it is the pupil's job to learn it. The determination of *what* knowledge will be transmitted (curriculum) and *how* it will be transmitted (method) may be the responsibility of the teacher, the school administration, or both. In a highly centralized system of education the precise content of the curriculum is controlled by top level administrative decisions.

In the United States, teachers must impart information or knowledge, must perfect skills in some limited way (in vocational courses, for example) and must support the nation and its institutions. A 1954 survey revealed that an overwhelming number of citizens (91 percent) believed that a high school teacher found to be a communist should be fired. Only a slightly smaller percentage thought that such a teacher in a college setting should be fired.[29] The public school teacher in the United States is expected to be in the community, but not a full member of it. The activities in which teacher may openly and approvedly engage are frequently limited to school functions, church affairs, and the work of certain other acceptable organizations. Traditionally they are not expected to function in political life or to associate freely with the other citizens in such social affairs as dancing, visiting, or attending clubs.[30]

While the last two decades may have brought some changes in the role expectations of the school teacher, this traditional image is still likely to be true of teachers in parochial schools and certain religious communities.

The most important status-role in all school systems are those of the student and teacher. We shall center our discussion here on the teacher role and the relationship between teacher and student. Numerous classifications of teacher roles have been outlined but we will utilize that developed by Kinney to illustrate the multifaceted complexity of the teacher's status-roles.[31] The six roles specified by Kinney are described as follows: (1) director of learning; (2) guidance and counseling person; (3) mediator of culture; (4) member of the school community; (5) liaison between school and community; and (6) member of the profession.[32] While most teachers occupy the roles specified, there is great variation in the extent to which each is performed and the importance attached to each role.

As pointed out by Goslin, "the ultimate unit of the educational process is the two-person group made up of the teacher and the student."[33] While this teacher-student relationship may vary widely in regard to frequency of interaction and the degree to which the relationship is expressive or affectively neutral, certain stable characteristics can be cited. As Goslin observes, the teacher-student relationship is ordinarily one of status inequality in which the teacher is expected to make more demands on the behavior of the student than vice versa. In addition, only one of the participants (the student) in the relationship is expected to change behavior during the course of the relationship. Further, the teacher role requires that the student be induced to change behavior in some respect. "There can be little doubt," Goslin argues, "that many of the problems that teachers as well as students encounter in the establishment of an integrated and productive role relationship resulting from a lack of agreement on the amount of specificity in the system of mutual expectations about each other's behavior."[34]

The United States teacher model is a middle class female. Less than 1/3 of all public elementary and secondary school teachers in the United States are males. Historically, a large proportion of school teachers at this level have been women. Since 1920, the proportion of male elementary and secondary school teachers has risen gradually from 14.1 percent at that date to 31.5 percent in 1968.[35] Although the function of the woman teacher in American society is not completely understood, Parsons has hypothesized that it is the female teacher who may have "a significance connected with the process of emancipation from earlier attachments to the mother." This he believes to be of particular importance because "dependence on the mother is particularly intense in the American kinship system."[36]

The neighborhood teacher has frequently been characterized as a "baby-sitter" who, under the authority of the family and neighborhood community, has charge of the children for a few hours five days a week. In more recent times the larger systems have nurtured the growth of a certain amount of professionalism which permits affectually neutral relationships between student and teacher, at least in the more advanced grades. Under such conditions the teacher is held responsible for only specific functions at specific times, is judged by performance and is rewarded by more universalistic standards of achievement than in the neighborhood school.

Even in the larger, more bureaucratic school systems, however, teachers and school administrators find it necessary to involve the parents. Through participation in the Parent-Teachers Associations and other groups, ways have been developed to keep teachers in the social systems of the community. This is necessary if adequate financial support is to be made available and social linkage between community and school maintained.

RANKING

Rank as an element, evaluation as a process in ranking, and allocation of status-roles.[37]   Depending on one's point of view and what it is that he is trying to discover, one could choose from among the dozens of ways in which rank appears in connection with educational systems. How the student is ranked, for example, and the advantages and disadvantages of testing and marking systems are important pedagogical subjects. The methods of ranking teachers with other teachers as bases for good personnel practice and for pay increases is another important consideration. How the students of a particular kind of school rank with students of another kind of school would be useful information under some circumstances, as would the rank the teacher holds among other adults of different occupations. Here the discussion of rank will be confined to: (1) the rank of the teacher by the larger society; and (2) the relation between an individual's education and the rank accorded him by the larger society.

The rank of the teacher by the larger society. In the United States a rather definite ranking system of those engaged in education carries across the various educational levels and units. The range of rank for those engaged in teaching extends from the meager standing accorded a very low paid Negro teacher in the South to the high rank accorded the full professor of one of the prestigeful universities. In general it may be stated that, "school teachers, especially those in grammar and high schools, are the economic proletarians of the professions . . . Some 31 percent of all professional people are school teachers of one sort or another."[38] Of 90 occupations selected from a national cross-section study, there were 35 occupations having higher rank in 1947. However, only six status-roles included in the study ranked higher than college professor. They were U.S. Supreme Court Justice, physician, state governor, cabinet member, diplomat, and mayor of a large city in that order.[39] Actually, the rank accorded the teacher varies by the subject taught and the kind of educational institution with which the teacher is connected.

Although the rural teacher in the trade center community school may have higher social rank than the neighborhood school teacher, the status-role of public school teacher, in contrast to that of a college professor, does not have high social rank in American society. In fact, of the 90 occupations selected from the national cross section study, there were in 1963, 29 occupations having higher rank. The public school teacher (30th in rank) although slightly higher than in 1947, 16 years earlier, was only somewhat higher than the farm owner and operator (43rd in rank).[40] Nevertheless, the rural teacher's social rank is higher than the power attached to the rank. This is in part, no doubt, due to the relatively great respect in American society for those having learning.

Education is widely regarded throughout the United States as a mechanism through which the individual may improve his social standing. For many rural people, education is a requisite in the process of migration and eventual urban adjustment. Education also assists in the process of advancing middle class values. The interrelations of social rank and education are numerous, and thus far a complete study of the ramifications has not been made.

The relation between an individual's education and the rank accorded him by the larger society. Education bears a close relationship to the rank ordering of the individuals within a social system. The potential rank that his education is able to bestow upon an individual is probably the most important aspect of rank in relation to the educational system, at least in the United States, where by all odds the most important ranking hierarchy is that of occupation. Increasingly, a job applicant must have certain standards of education even to compete for a job.

What is true for the white collar jobs is also valid for thousands of jobs a cut below the white collar level; in the first instance a college education is required before one can compete for the job; in the second case a high school diploma is the sine qua non. No matter what the level, there is ample proof that income and prestige (both good indicators of rank) increase with level of education.[41]

One of the most direct and readily observable associations between social class and education is that all social classes do not have free access to education. Access to equal educational opportunity, as we have pointed out before, is a major problem for most children growing up in rural areas. An especially succinct statement of the dynamics of the "opportunity gap" is found in *Schools and Inequality*. The authors point out that both the family and society invest larger sums in the growth and development of the higher than the low socio-economic status (SES) child. Whether rural or urban, the low SES child is more likely to suffer prenatal malnutrition and to be exposed to inadequate medical and dental care. He is also more likely to live in a modest physical environment in which the family income precludes exposure to a whole host of enriching and stimulating experiences. Parental attention is likely to be less and the lower educational attainment of the parents severely restricts the knowledge that can be transmitted to the low SES child.[42]

It is generally accepted that teachers are usually recruited from the middle class and represent middle class values. Their social class background leads them to select these traits in students for praise and approval.

CONTROLLING

Power as an element.   There are very different aspects of power involved in educational situations. Who is eligible to attend the school? Does the student pursue the course he wishes? Does he get a passing grade or a failing one? What textbooks are adopted for use? What subjects are in the curriculum? Shall a new high school be built? How much financial support comes to the school system and from what sources? The answers to these and many other questions indicate that although the teacher is indeed a power figure from the point of view of the pupil, the teacher has little or no claim to much of the power involved in the total situation. Besides having a good deal of direct power over the student in the classroom (even in permissive settings), the teacher's behavior often serves as an adult model for the growing child, as is attested by many biographies.

One might expect that the more centralized the educational system, the more the power outside the teacher's scope would be concentrated in a few individuals.

The United States educational system is similar to the Mexican system in philosophy but entirely unlike either the Soviet or the Mexican systems in organization, structure, and locus of power. At the national level there is the United States Office of Education which has no power except as the professional leadership emanating from that office can motivate professional educators to take a stand, which in turn must be accepted and acted upon by the local school district. The educational offices at the state level have somewhat more power, although in most cases they too perform an advisory and leadership function rather than a control function.

While we speak of the American educational system as a state system, and while the Americans look to the state for leadership, belief in vigorous local units with large responsibility for education is deeply embedded in the American society. Seldom does one encounter an American who favors what he calls a highly centralized system of education.[43]

Americans avoid centralization because it may jeopardize "local control," but often do not realize that local control is frequently in the hands of a few local power figures. In the United States the insulating barriers which the state has set up to protect the agencies of popular education from the impact of social forces are relatively ineffective. In our great cities scarcely a day passes that fails to see some interest in the community seeking in one way or another to influence the program of the schools.[44] Moreover, "the politics with which the schools are beset at the present time are injected into the schools just as frequently by school boards as by representatives of the legislative or executive branches of political government."[45] The truth of these observations has been demonstrated over and over again as citizens have been blocked from passing increased tax levies, from changing the location of a school, or making other basic changes. Form and Miller report, for example, a case in which the PTA, Board of Education, organized labor, and teacher groups favored an increased levy but the newspapers and organized taxpayer groups defeated it.[46] Various pressures force the public school in many of its activities to conform to the wishes of those in power. This is not to say that the linkage of the educational system to the related governmental systems is weaker than are most subgovernmental organizations. It means only that the realities of democratic government obtain for the educational system as they do for other subsystems. To an American the chances for an educational system that is responsive to the will of the people seem greatest in a society in which authority is checked and balanced by counter authority and in which the influence of one power group can be challenged by the influence of other power groups.

Although the modern large school system is more often under the domination of the elite of the community than many other systems, the rights of the teacher and administrators have increased as the trade center community school has supplanted the neighborhood school. Both student and teacher are more subject to the impersonal nature of bureaucracy than ever before. Much has been written[47] about the relative merits of what has been called the authoritarian versus the democratic relationships within the classroom and within the authority structure of the staff of the school system. Brookover observes that "it may be suggested that at the lower grade levels. children respond to the authoritarian or dominating teacher with resistance and patterns of domination in relation to their peers. At the same level the children respond to the integrative, democratic teacher with initiative, spontaneous contributions, and cooperation. The secondary school youth express unfavorable reactions to the authoritarian teacher, but learn more from him. The opposite is true of their reactions to the friendly democratic teacher."[48]

Decision-making and its initiation into action as process. Decision-making as it goes into operation in the United States is as difficult to pinpoint as is the locus of power. Commercial and industrial groups within the community might be expected to marshal their forces about decisions concerning a large school building program, for example. Patriotic organizations, on the other hand, might be much more concerned about curriculum content or teacher slant which in their opinion gave too much favorable attention to untraditional or foreign forms of governments. Liberal forces have been known to rally around an issue which in their opinion represents freedom of thought and inquiry; parents' organizations frequently throw their weight behind decisions that affect the teacher-child relationship. The skillful administrator will somehow juggle and compromise the desires of all the would-be decision makers. Through the school board, which is composed of the elected or appointed representatives of the people, the administrator informs and is informed of the community climate of opinion. It is easy to understand, once the diffuse decision making process is known, why it has been claimed that although "no one can rightfully say that we have not a very great system for extending popular education in the

United States . . . surely it is a very unsystematic system."[49] Although the "unsystematic system" clearly lacks the ability to quickly respond to a new situation which a highly centralized system possesses, it certainly is in the end more responsive to the will of the people whose children are being educated than any system of similar magnitude in the world.

The greatest weakness in the current treatment of power in relation to its effect within social systems is the failure to analyze in a systematic manner the situations within which power is applied. The strict teacher in the neighborhood school of earlier times usually conformed to the expectancy patterns of the community, and teachers who behaved in ways that are now called democratic and friendly were often ridiculed. Their permissiveness usually caused frustration, because students were unaccustomed to or could not predict the teacher's behavior. In general, the authority of the typical neighborhood teacher was more Gemeinschaft-like. By this we mean that teacher-student relations were more affectual, more personal or particularistic, and responsibilities were more diffuse. In the larger, more bureaucratized trade center school system, the authority of the teacher in teacher-student relations is more affectively neutral, less personal, and responsibilities are more specific. Attainment of positions of authority is more dependent upon achievement in the profession. Thus power in the older neighborhood school is of a different order than power in the large school systems.

Most reports reveal that rural people are not as active as the town people in decision-making affecting school policy. Many factors are responsible for this, one of the most important being that other nonfarm economic and social agencies, such as banks, stores, and businesses, are usually owned and operated by townspeople. When no reorganization takes place, and high school attendance areas develop based on the size of the trade center school and ability of neighborhood districts to pay tuition, the middle class in the trade center rather than the rural people are in control. Under these conditions rural people are disenfranchised.

In most large centers the school teachers and administrative staff are not as important in decision-making for the school and community as are the businessmen and political leaders. In general, the teachers, often with superior knowledge and frequently with considerable experience, have relatively little power in the community. Their power is also not great in the final determination of school support and facilities.[50] School administrators, however, must have access to those with power in order to operate the schools. To be successful, they must establish working relationships with potentates in the communities.

Vidich and Bensman, in *Small Town in Mass Society*, recount the paternal dynamics of decision making between the principal and a country-dominated school board. The principal successfully attained the status of technical expert and administrator of board policies. In effect, the school board simply rubber-stamped the principal's prior decisions. His strategy, according to Vidich and Bensman, was as follows:

1. Become aware of all the facts in the case.
2. On the basis of these facts, paying special attention to the reactions of the significant people involved, reach a decision.
3. Formulate a definite plan of action based on the decision, implementing every step of action in detail.
4. Come to the board meeting fully prepared with the detailed solution of the problem and then present the problem as though you just realized the problem existed and "could the board help you with some advice since you are new and inexperienced in Springdale and they are familiar with the precedent."
5. Let the board knock it about for a while while you sit back and size up their individual stands on the issue.
6. Present the facts and the carefully worked-out solution, countering every argument with a better one, being, of course, very tactful.
7. Wait for Jones to make the motion that your plan be adopted.[51]

SANCTIONING

Sanctions as an element and application of sanctions as process. The rewards for teaching, particularly salaries, are low considering the training and intelligence required for the status-role. This is particularly true for rural teachers. In part due to unionization, the salaries of teachers have increased greatly. While the following salaries have not been adjusted for price changes, approximately 88 percent of public elementary and secondary teachers received under $6,500 in 1960; about 58 percent received this salary in 1966, and only 8.7 percent received this amount in 1971. About 41 percent of all teachers in public schools received salaries of $9,500 or more in 1971.[53]

In a study of involvement as related to teacher stress, Washburn[54] attempted to appraise the importance of: (1) economic gain and security; (2) status in the community; (3) authority or recognition and approval by varying agents of authority within the school system; and (4) professional status of orientation toward teaching as a profession. Obviously, achievement in any one of these areas might be regarded as rewarding; failure to achieve might be regarded as penalizing. The important fact is that attempting to achieve in all areas simultaneously might well bring stress. Washburne's study of a small group of men teachers in a city school concludes that a teacher "is caught in the center of a confused mixture of orders which place conflicting demands on him. Stated over-simply: He is caught between the structural demands of bureaucratic organization, the traditional demands of the community, and a series of 'ideal' demands associated with the profession."[55] It is our thesis that the pressures from the community are greater in the rural schools. Brookover supports this thesis when he says:

> The chances of stress are probably less in large school systems, where authority is more clearly defined in a bureaucratic structure and where the teacher's relations with the community are less personal. At the other extreme, the teachers of the small, one-room rural school can also probably identify with a predominant source of authority more easily. It is in the great number of town and village schools that role conflict seems most likely to occur.[56]

In the United States the sanctions applied to students include eligibility, based on grades, for participation in extracurricular activities and late hour privileges; being campused and expelled; and letter awards, scholarships and fellowships. The monetary rewards for professors are not so great in the United States as they are in some other foreign countries.

> Between 1940 and 1954, the real income of lawyers, physicians, and industrial workers rose from 10 to 80 percent, while that of faculty members dropped five percent. The people of the United States have a virtually unlimited faith in higher education. They know what it means for their own children, and what it means to the future of America. But they do not yet understand that this precious national resource is built squarely on the vitality of the teaching profession.[57]

FACILITATING

Facilities as an element and utilization of facilities as process.[58] Since school age youth generally comprise roughly 20 percent of the total population, the facilities needed for the mere physical housing of that number of people is tremendous. We face the never-ending challenge of providing enough schools in which to educate our young.

A 1959 New York Times survey reported that 300,000 new classrooms supported by a ten billion dollar construction budget would be essential by 1965.[59] As the birth rate in America declines as projected, the total number of required additional classrooms will decline. However, there is a continual need for reconstruction as school buildings deteriorate.

The school building, of course, is but one facility. Such rudimentary equipment as paper and pencils are prized facilities in some of the hinterlands, and everywhere there is the problem of maintaining a nice balance between supply and need of such equipment as textbooks, visual aids, scientific apparatus, shop equipment, and typewriters. In the United States the desired curriculum is sometimes compromised by the lack of shop and laboratory equipment.

> The high schools in the small rural districts cannot provide either the equipment or the teachers for effective vocational training programs . . . Small classes are among the most serious handicaps faced by small school districts that attempt to provide educational opportunities of this kind . . . The cost of providing equipment and teachers for such small numbers of pupils is likely to eliminate vocational subjects from the high school curriculum which then is confined to general academic courses that require little or no laboratory or shop equipment.[60]

Nor have the institutions of higher education been able to supply adequate space or equipment.

> Adequate financial support is not a matter to be viewed with alarm or with discouragement. The fact seems to be that we are today devoting a smaller fraction of our national income to the support of public and private higher education than was true in 1929 . . . One . . . problem is how to do a quality job with more prospective students on campuses already far too congested and in individual classes which in some state universities number hundreds, if not over a thousand, in size.[61]

Facilities in the United States schools, which only a few years ago were regarded by many as nice to have but somehow rather "extra" and certainly expensive, were suddenly seen in a new light after the advent of Sputnik. Certain it is that "the little red school house" is currently an inadequate symbol for an expression of educational facilities.

With respect to facilities of all kinds, rural schools tend to lag about a decade behind the urban schools. In the United States as a whole, even the reorganized, consolidated rural schools are inferior to those in urban areas. Teachers' salaries are lower, teachers' preparation inferior, school terms shorter, library services poorer, health services and remedial care more limited, and high school training more inadequate. Of course, urban schools have their share of problems, but those are of a different character.

COMPREHENSIVE OR MASTER PROCESSES

Communication.   One of the primary functions of the school, whether rural or urban, is to provide an arena for communication. It is clear that learning will not occur if the teacher fails to communicate with pupils. Of great importance in the learning process is the communication among students. Barriers to interaction and communication among peers include numerous hierarchical cleavages most often based upon social class, color, and ethnic origin. Cliques composed of like-minded peers are found in all school systems and are not only often serious barriers to interaction but may also effectively isolate certain students in and outside the classroom.

Many educators believe that the interaction which comes about by being thrown together in the schools has already affected and will continue to "provide a basis for the growth of mutual understanding between different cultural, religious, and occupational groups . . . Free schools where the future doctor, lawyer, and manual worker have studied and played together from the ages of 15 to 17 are a characteristic of large sections of the United States; they are an American invention."[62] The student mores that tend to erect a barrier between the students and the teaching staff affect the quantity and kind of communication as well as the impact it is permitted to make. Communication in large enough quantities and of the stuff which could change attitudes was found only in a few colleges such as Antioch, Bennington, and Sara Lawrence, and even here the attitudes were changed relatively little. The atmosphere created by "the community of liberal-minded scholars" apparently abounded less in the many other institutions relying on mass education such as the huge state universities and the large privately supported universities. The barriers to interaction and extensive communication were more severe here, and attitudes did not change perceptibly at these institutions.[63]

One may think of numerous other kinds of communication involving the school. There must be reciprocal communication between school administrators and teachers. When school systems become large, communication often becomes impersonal, through mimeographed announcements and directives. In such systems teachers may feel that they do not have adequate access to the principal. There is also the need for the school to communicate with the community of which it is a part. And of course, communication in the opposite direction is also necessary.

The media used in the schools vary greatly from system to system. Where the supply is ample and the variety great the experimental use of television-instructed classes has begun. What kind of educational television will ultimately be used in schools is not known. Its present supporters envision the truly great teacher reaching thousands of students all over the land, and its critics see in it a totalitarian potential. Whether or not it is used directly by the schools for course instruction, there is no question that it, along with radio and the expanded products of the printing press, has greatly enlarged the school child's world. Thanks to the media the modern school student knows something about a great many more things than did the last generation of students.

Coincident with school consolidation, school children from rural areas find themselves in classes with town and city children. Historically, pupils from rural areas are generally regarded as inferior by those living in the towns and cities. Such cleavages based upon residence may be severe, but most commonly today the initial bias tends to be transitory.[64] Ethnic cleavages and consequent lack of interaction and breakdown of communication remain important in rural and urban schools.

Boundary Maintenance. In the United States professional educators, political scientists, and thousands of private citizens who have studied the situation have agreed for almost half a century that there are too many independent school districts for the maintenance of effective school systems within each district. No better evidence that boundary maintenance is effective is needed than that there still are over 100,000 such school districts. The function of such boundary maintenance would seem to lie in the extremely high value attached to localism and local control. It is expressed by local groups rather than the schools themselves.[65] This particular form of boundary maintenance can be expected to diminish in importance as meaningful systemic linkages between the small locality and the larger centers become institutionalized.

The school as a system seems to be in a very difficult position. Since the professional and administrative personnel have relatively little power in the community, great emphasis must be placed upon gaining community support. This means that the professional status of the teacher and the school administrator in many instances is less important than being on good terms with persons influential in the community and with influential parents. Moreover, the public school and those who support it attempt to prevent the system establishing closure through boundary maintenance. Thus, community colleges often find it difficult to develop high standards for academic freedom because of community linkage with the educational system. An attempt is made to have parents participate in programs, visit classes, and insofar as possible determine policy. Since support for the school depends upon good public relations, and since the teacher and administrator have not established their own areas of competence as superior to those of the citizens, there is usually much greater interference with the teacher's performance of his role by those outside of the school system than would be permitted by such professional groups as doctors and lawyers.

A large complex of traditions and values are connected with the citizens' devotion to the maintenance of his small school district: his personal knowledge of his neighbors who are school board members; his traditional idea that the school which his child attends must be a part of an easily accessible central organization; his desire that the child not have to walk too far or ride a bus too long; his hope that taxes will not be too burdensome and that school finances remain simple enough that he can understand them; and his preferences for the present system with its known strengths and weaknesses over a proposed system with unknown qualities. Few of these cherished conditions which comprise the rationale of school district boundary maintenance would be violated by most school district rearrangements, but as was demonstrated above, the decision-making process is sufficiently laborious that it is safe to predict that the boundaries as they exist in the United States will be maintained, only to be realigned piecemeal and slowly.

Other boundaries of a more subtle nature are maintained throughout the educational systems. Clique groupings exert subtle social pressures and racial and ethnic groupings can be found in some schools. Competition among teachers for the sole devotion of the student's extracurricular time to particular activities can create boundaries, for example, between the band group and the basketball group or the yearbook group and the debate team. Schisms over subject matter, research grants, personalities, and administrative support develop in college and university faculties with student adherents to both factions constituting somewhat separate entities. The student sub-systems that erect effective barriers against anything but a minimum of faculty-academic influence is maintaining dysfunctional boundaries.

The "captive audience" which each school houses some six or seven hours a day, with a direct pipeline to most homes in the area, is a tempting target for many organizations which flourish within the community. Special education groups — such as those interested in health, safety, world government, the humane treatment of animals, community philanthropy, and many other subjects — eye the classrooms as likely vehicles for the reception of special literature and for the support of special projects. How much of this can be incorporated into a well-balanced school program and where the line should be drawn is a boundary maintenance question.

Systemic Linkage.   Few social systems are more used by change agents to reach out into the community than the schools. It is obvious that change agents in both developed and developing societies see the school population as an economical target to reach large numbers of parents and friends directly, or indirectly.

The most important link in the chain which binds the school system to other social systems is manifest in compulsory school attendance. While it is true that most people are inevitably linked to most of the important social systems of society there is, in the United States at least, a certain amount of choice inherent in the linkage. If a family has a child, however, it is inevitably linked to the school system for a period of eight to twelve years or longer. Furthermore, in the United States, by law and by tradition the school systems are legally linked to the community through the school board and to the state and to the nation by constitutional mandate.

The process of systemic linkage as it concerns the public school is not so much how to establish such linkage as how to maintain a desirable balance among all of the systems with which it is linked. Ideas like the community-school promote the close integration of every community activity into a school-linked activity.

The increasingly specialized, urban and Gesellschaft-like setting of American society has at least two characteristics with implications for the feasibility of a curriculum based on linkages to the community. The migration of people and technological change make problematic the advantages of extreme systemic linkage for the student.

Because schools are a function of society, a great many educators think it the duty of the schools . . . to "adapt" the young to the society in which they are to live. Needless to say, if each generation of young is merely fitted to the existing order of things, we will end up with a Byzantine, not a Western civilization.

Schools are a part of society but they should not be a complete mirror of society. They should offer not a repetition of experience, but a challenge of and an extension of experience . . . Yet at a time when schools are in a better position to emancipate themselves from community pressures than ever before, and whèn the necessity of challenge and experimentation is perhaps stronger than ever before, our schools seem to make a fetish of adaptation and conformity.[66]

Of the linkages beyond the community, the most important and universal in the United States is that to the state. The closeness of that link is shown by the following:

Because of the fundamental belief of our people in the right of local self-government, these units of local government often assume a degree of authority which they do not actually possess. With reference to the administration of a school system, local officials often assume that inherent within local government are the rights and powers essential to the control of that system. This is not the case, however. The only rights which local government has over the schools are those which are specifically delegated to it by the legislature, and those that are necessarily implied from those delegated.[67]

In the United States the linkages with higher levels of government are by and large kept as weak as possible by most local educational systems. States have, on the whole, shown tremendous restraint in changing school district organization to a more efficient pattern, despite the tremendous financial drain multitudinous school districts have made on state finances. Although the schools' financial dependence on the state has increased many times over and although the state has not exacted compliance as a price for financial aid, the local school district still tends to regard linkage with both the state and the federal governments as tantamount to forfeiture of its autonomy.

One final type of systemic linkage occurs with all public school systems whose graduates matriculate at a college or university. Such linkages often are cursory, beginning and ending in an exchange of reports concerning the student. Some preparatory schools are in close linkage with certain colleges at which a high proportion of their graduates matriculate. Certain steps in that direction have been taken to link the state-supported colleges and universities more effectively with the public school systems. For example, the high school counsellors may visit the nearby colleges or universities and talk with the recently graduated high school student in an attempt to find out the students' reaction to their high school preparation.

Socialization. For a large segment of the population school begins the initiation into the larger society. For many children, especially in rural areas, preschool social interaction has been restricted largely to family and kinship groupings and to the play group. In the environment of the school, the child learns to respond to a more impersonal type of authority than he had previously encountered. It is here also that he learns new status-roles — those of student, teacher, and schoolmate, for example. Furthermore, he is in a position to learn the bases of new social ranking systems, not only those within the school system but also those established by his peers. Even the least perceptive student will observe that a ranking system exists among the teachers themselves, and that the teachers use different criteria to ascertain rank or standing in school work. Therefore, the school must be regarded as a training ground, completely apart from substantive training, for the social order to which the child must eventually adapt.

Perhaps the greatest part the school plays in the total process of socialization is in furnishing the child an institutionalized framework within which to develop into adulthood with a consequent sloughing off of dependence upon the family. What is contributed toward a child's socialization in the school is not unique in the sense that much of the same socializing process would take place no matter where the child was. The school, then, merely provides the continuity by which he is immersed in friendship groups, gradually withdrawn from his family, and has before him selected adult models whose behavior in different kinds of interaction he can observe. Although Brookover admits a dearth of evidence on the subject, he attempts to examine the range of adult models provided to youth by the average school system in the United States.[68] Among his conclusions are:

1) the fact that opportunities for introducing youth to a wide variety of professional and occupational models are extremely limited;
2) that many more opportunities abound for exposure to middle and upper class models than for exposure to lower class models;
3) that there are few chances to see models from countries with markedly different cultures;
4) that there is a variously met need to have youth exposed to models who are flexible and adaptable in reacting to many different situations;
5) that the teacher as a model is scarcely representative of a cross section of adult status-role behavior.

The implications are, of course, that for the socializing for adult life, the school is necessarily very limited as a social laboratory where life models demonstrate the anticipated conduct of social living.

The practice in social interaction provided by the peer groups, by the opportunities for cooperation and for competition, as well as the socializing force of an intimate friendship group, is likely to be the most vital part of socialization provided within the setting of the school. "In typical middle class American life the importance of these later secondary-group contacts, with their relative abruptness and demands for adjustment, is very great."[69]

It is during the stressful high school period that in American culture the long "mate seeking" period, with its various institutionalized procedures for interacting with the opposite sex, begins. Kinsey found great differences in the sexual behavior of persons who finish only grammar school as compared with those who finish high school, and those who go to college.[70] Certainly the experiences in high school modify the basic patterns learned in the family through socialization. The claim of population experts is that industrialization and commercialization of a culture develops a rational or Gesellschaft-like set of sentiments which leads to birth control or family planning, and consequent reduction of the replacement rates.[71] When the social milieu of a large mass of adolescents tends to idealize early love and marriage, interaction in the school inevitably plays a part in socializing the youth in behavior acceptable to and expected by the opposite sex.

CONDITIONS OF SOCIAL ACTION

Territoriality. The geographical relation of the school to the home and community is a central consideration in educational policy. Many schools are located in centers of such heavy population that their enrollment tends to be bigger than educators believe wise. Also many schools are located in areas of such sparse population that their enrollment and supporting tax base does not begin to provide the facilities educators and parents alike think necessary. The neighborhood schools in the rural areas of the United States are gradually being replaced by the trade center community school which is much larger than the district school and, ideally, has all the elementary and secondary facilities and may have the beginning years of college. Although the lack of facilities of the typical, traditional rural school is generally deplored, its passing from the scene is nevertheless regretted by many.

Many professional educators recognize the necessity of retraining the Gemeinschaft-like characteristics of the old neighborhood school through planning attendance areas that correspond to the more dynamic locality groupings. This means that as the older neighborhoods decrease in population and lose their vigor, the attendance area must shift from the neighborhood to the trade center community. How to retain the advantages of the intimate neighborhood associations and at the same time to take advantage of the efficiencies of larger attendance areas is a crucial problem in rural life.

It was from the Gemeinschaft-like neighborhood school of the frontier period that the United States inherited the most locally and democratically controlled school system in the world. The larger, more bureaucratic school can without question yield more instructional materials and better trained personnel, but it has a difficult time matching the atmosphere in which the teacher was known intimately to all the parents and to all the students. In these schools the students' families knew each other well, the neighborhood was but an extension of the home, and but one step removed from the most primary of relations. The huge high schools, having 5,000 or more students and the huge colleges and universities having 10,000 or more students can scarcely avoid the kind of bureaucracy which has won for them the questionably distinctive title of "education factories." The use of many tempering techniques such as "home rooms," "personal advisors," "guidance staffs," and "house tutors" mitigate but do not completely remedy some of the machine-like characteristics of the large Gesellschaft-like school.

In many rural communities throughout the nation, the school is a primary integrative agency. In the light of this consideration it would seem obvious that school district reorganization should exercise care to preserve boundaries of communities which are true systems of social interaction. "The high school attendance area should, insofar as possible, be identified with the area in which people associate together in aspects of community life."[72]

Smith and Zopf argue cogently that rural schools be consolidated *within the community.* "School consolidation should accompany, but not anticipate, the expansion of the community area; and the first few grades might well be handled on a different basis from the upper grades. In the consolidation of schools, the ignoring of community interests and boundaries and of the fact that the community is the locality grouping that embraces virtually all aspects of the lives of its people, might well result in a form of educational absenteeism fully as vicious as absentee landownership."[73]

Size and Related Factors.   A source of stress in higher educational institutions is not unlike that resulting from rationalization and industrialization of underdeveloped areas. One of the most important studies of pressures upon social scientists in universities of the United States divides the organizations into those called "traditional" and those called "secular." In reality this division is not unlike the Gemeinschaft-Gesellschaft dichotomy used in the present monograph,

> Anthropologists and sociologists often . . . talk about the traditional ways of life that are found in rural communities or in societies not yet invaded by industrialization. They stress certain characteristics shared by these traditional social organisms: close social ties, belief in authority, distrust of change. In societies at the opposite extreme one finds more division of labor, greater emphasis on personal success and achievement, and on intellectual values.[74]

The investigators then, with some qualifications, type denominational and teachers colleges as "traditional" and "tax-supported and privately endowed colleges" as more "secular." Secular colleges have the most distinguished professors, the highest achievors, the most "liberal" and the highest paid staffs. However, it is the traditional and small colleges where the largest proportion of teachers report unusually good relations between faculty and administration and among faculty members. Here the traditional or Gemeinschaft-like systems provide such rewards which may compensate in part for lower salaries. The affectively neutral and functionally specific relationship of the large universities with their universalistic achievement standards place more stress upon individual achievement than do the smaller organizations.

NOTES

1. Alma S. Wittlin, "The Teacher" in Kenneth S. Lynn and editors of Daedalus, *The Professions in America* (Boston: Houghton Mifflin Company, 1965), p. 91.

2. Don Martindale, *Social Life and Cultural Change* (New York: D. Van Nostrand Company, Inc., 1962), pp. 31-59.

3. John Sirjamaki, "Education as a Social Institution" in D.A. Hansen and J.E. Gerstl, eds., *On Education — Sociological Perspectives* (New York: John Wiley & Sons, Inc., 1967), p. 40.

4. A.H. Halsey, "The Changing Functions of Universities" in A.H. Halsey, J. Floud, and C.A. Anderson, eds., *Education, Economy, and Society* (New York: The Free Press, 1961), p. 456.

5. Henry Ehlers and Gordon C. Lee, eds., *Crucial Issues in Education* (New York: Holt, Rinehart and Winston, 1964), p. 3.

6. Burton R. Clark, "The Study of Educational Systems" in *International Encyclopedia of the Social Sciences*, 4, p. 510.

7. Bronislaw Malinowski, "The Pan-African Problem of Culture Contact," *American Journal of Sociology*, 48, (1943), pp. 649-665; see also C.P. Loomis and J.A. Beegle, *Rural Social Systems* (New York: Prentice-Hall, Inc., 1960), p. 457.

8. Bureau of the Census, *Current Population Reports*, Series P-20, and unpublished data.

9. Department of Health, Education and Welfare, Office of Education, Annual Report, *Preprimary Enrollment Trends of Children Under 6*.

10. Clark Wissler, *Man and Culture* (New York: Thomas Y. Crowell Co., 1932), p. 8. Christopher Jencks and associates argue that quality education will not reduce socioeconomic inequality; Mary Jo Bane and Christopher Jencks. "The Schools and Equal Opportunity," *Saturday Review*, (October, 1972), pp. 37-42.

11. Roy J. Honeywell, *The Educational Work of Thomas Jefferson* (Cambridge, Mass.: Harvard University Press, 1931), p. 13.

12. F.S.C. Northrop, *The Meeting of East and West: An Inquiry Concerning World Understanding* (New York: The Macmillan Company, 1947), p. 454.

13. George Kneller, *The Education of the Mexican Nation* (New York: Columbia University Press, 1951), p. 104.

14. The separation of elements and processes for a given social action category serves the purpose of enabling the investigator to separate analysis of static and dynamic aspects of a system. Insufficient space is available in the present essay to specify and separate the categories "communication of sentiment" and "tension management," processes of great importance.

15. Walter Lippman, *Essays in the Public Philosophy* (Boston: Little Brown and Co., 1955), cited by Gordon Keith Chalmers, "The Purpose of Learning" in *Annals of American Academy of Political and Social Science*, 301, (September, 1955), 7ff.

16. Chalmers, op. cit., pp. 7-8.

17. C. Wayne Gordon, *The Social System of the High School* (Glencoe, Ill.: The Free Press, 1957), p. 42.

18. Melvin Seeman, "Role Conflict and Ambivalence in Leadership," *American Sociological Review*, 18, (Aug., 1953), pp. 373ff. See also Neal Gross, et. al., *Exploration in Role Analysis*, (New York: John Wiley and Sons, 1957). The lack of role consensus among school board members and superintendents is well documented by this study.

19. Samuel A. Stouffer, *Communism, Conformity, and Civil Liberties: A Cross-Section of the Nation Speaks Its Mind* (Garden City, New York: Doubleday and Co., 1955), p. 107.

20. Emile Durkheim, *Education and Sociology*, Sherwood D. Fox, ed., (Glencoe, Ill.: The Free Press, 1956), p. 71.

21. *Your School District*, The Report of the National Commission of School District Reorganization (Washington, D.C.: National Education Association, 1948), p. 61.

22. Ibid., p. 73.

23. Clark, op. cit., p. 510.

24. Gordon, op. cit., p. 45.

25. Harold Alberty, "How May the Schools Further Democracy" in *Annals of the American Academy of Political and Social Science*, 265, (September, 1949), p. 20.

26. Chalmers, op. cit., pp. 9-10.

27. Delbert Miller and William Form, *Industrial Sociology* (New York: Harper and Brothers, 1951), p. 208ff.

28. Stouffer, op. cit., p. 107.

29. Ibid., pp. 40 and 43.

30. Wilbur B. Brookover, *A Sociology of Education* (New York: American Book Co., 1955), pp. 238-239.

31. Havighurst and Neugarten, for example, provide a classification of "roles in relation to adults in school system" such as employee, colleague, leader, and of "roles in relation to pupils" such as mediator of learning, disciplinarian, parent substitute. R.J. Havighurst and B.L. Neugarten, *Society and Education* (Boston: Allyn & Bacon, Inc., 1957).

32. L.B. Kinney, *Measure of a Good Teacher* (San Francisco: California Teachers Association, 1952).

33. David A. Goslin, *The School in Contemporary Society* (Glenview: Scott, Foresman and Co., 1965), p. 20.

34. Ibid., p. 22.

35. U.S. Bureau of the Census, *Statistical Abstract of the United States* (Washington, 1971), p. 113.

36. Talcott Parsons, *The Social System* (Glencoe: The Free Press, 1951), p. 241.

37. Insufficient space was available for the author to specify and separate "rank as element" and "evaluation as process" in ranking and allocation of status-roles.

38. C. Wright Mills, *White Collar — The American Middle Classes* (New York: Oxford University Press, 1956), p. 129.

39. Cecil C. North and Paul K. Hatt, "Jobs and Occupations: A Popular Evaluation," *Opinion News*, (September 1, 1947), p. 129.

40. Robert W. Hodge, Paul M. Siegel, and Peter B. Rossi, "Occupational Prestige in the United States, 1952-1963," *American Journal of Sociology*, 70, (November, 1964), pp. 286-302. See also Melvin L. Defleur, William V. D'Antonio and Lois B. Defleur, *Sociology: Man in Society* (Glenview: Scott, Foresman and Co., 1971), p. 228.

41. Various United States Census Reports show the relation between education and income.

42. James W. Guthrie, George B. Kleindorfer, Henry M. Levin, and Robert T. Stout, *Schools and Inequality* (Cambridge: The MIT Press, 1971), pp. 141-142.

43. Theodore L. Reller, "Organization of the Educational System," *Annals of the American Academy of Political and Social Science*, 265, (September, 1949), pp. 38-39.

44. Ibid.

45. N.B. Henry and J.G. Kerwin, *Schools and City Government* (Chicago: University of Chicago Press, 1938), pp. 65-66.

46. William Form and Delbert Miller, *Industry and the Community* (New York: Harpers, 1960).

47. See N.L. Gage, ed., *Handbook of Research on Teaching* (Chicago: Rand McNally and Co., 1963), chapters 10 and 11. See also Ronald Lippitt, "An Experimental Study of Authoritarian and Democratic Group Atmospheres," University of Iowa Studies in Child Welfare, 3, (1940).

48. W.B. Brookover, *The Sociology of Education* (New York: American Book Co., 1955), p. 311.

49. Andrew S. Draper, *Journal of Proceedings and Addresses* (National Educational Association, 1896), p. 201 as cited by Edgar W. Knight, "The Evolving and Expanding Common School," *Annals of the American Academy of Political and Social Science* (September, 1949), 265, p. 92.

50. Floyd Hunter, *Community Power Structure — A Study of Decision-Makers* (Chapel Hill: University of North Carolina Press, 1953).

51. Arthur J. Vidich and Joseph Bensman, *Small Town in Mass Society* (Princeton: Princeton University Press, 1968), p. 193.

52. It seems unnecessary to specify and separate "sanction as an element" from "application of sanctions as process" for present purposes.

53. Statistical Abstract, 1971.

54. Chandler Washburne, *Involvement as a Basis for Stress Analysis: A Study of High School Teachers* (East Lansing: Michigan State College doctoral dissertation, 1953).

55. Ibid., p. 118.

56. Brookover, op. cit., p. 284.

57. Carnegie Foundation for the Advancement of Teaching, *Annual Report*, cited by Max Ascoli, "Our Cut-Rate Education," an editorial, *The Reporter*, (February 20, 1958), p. 9.

58. It seems unnecessary for present purposes to specify and separate "facility as an element" and "utilization of facilities as process."

59. Edgar W. Knight, "The Evolving and Expanding Common School," in *Annals of the American Academy of Political and Social Science*, 265, (September, 1949), p. 99.

60. *Your School District*, p. 18.

61. Ordway Tead, "New Frontiers in Higher Education," in *Annals of the American Academy of Political and Social Science*, Vol. 265, (September, 1949), pp. 118-119.

62. James Bryant Conant, *Education and Liberty — The Role of the Schools in a Modern Democracy* (Cambridge, Mass.: Harvard University Press, 1953), pp. 62 and 87.

63. Philip E. Jacob, *Changing Values in College* (New Haven, Connecticut: The Edward W. Hazen Foundation, 1956), p. 12.

64. See Charles P. Loomis, *Studies in Applied and Theoretical and Social Science* (East Lansing: Michigan State College Press, 1950), Chapter 12.

65. Arnold Anderson comments that our focus here should be the school since boundary maintenance is the other side of systemic linkage. The two are inseparable (from correspondence). His point is well taken but in the resistance to school reorganization and consolidation the local school and locality groups are so linked that they fuse. They maintain boundaries against larger systems, both school and locality group, which they feel will "gobble them up."

66. *The Story of Holtville*, Southern Association Study, Holtville (Ala.) Public Schools, 1944. As cited by Harold Alberty, "How May the Schools Further Democracy?", *Annals of the American Academy of Political and Social Science*, 265, (September, 1949), p. 23.

67. Henry Steel Commager, "Victims of Success," *Saturday Review*, (May 3, 1958), p. 13.

68. Brookover, op. cit., p. 340ff.

69. Conant, op. cit., p. 58.

70. Alfred C. Kinsey et. al., *Sexual Behavior in the Human Male* (Philadelphia: W. B. Saunders Co., 1948), p. 334.

71. Roderich von Ungern Sternberg, *The Causes of the Decline in Birth-Rate Within the European Sphere of Civilization* (Cold Spring Harbor, Long Island: Eugenics Research Association, Monograph Series No. IV, 1931), p. 202.

72. Shirley Cooper, "Characteristics of Satisfactory Attendance Units," in *Characteristics of Good School Districts*, School of Education, University of Wisconsin, (Madison: University of Wisconsin, 1948), p. 13.

73. T. Lynn Smith and Paul E. Zopf, *Principles of Inductive Rural Sociology* (Philadelphia: F.A. Davis Co., 1970), p. 332.

74. Paul F. Lazarsfeld and Wagner Thielens, Jr., *The Academic Mind* (Glencoe, Ill.: The Free Press, 1958), p. 27. See also Theodore Caplow and Reece J. McGee, *The Academic Marketplace* (New York: Basic Books, Inc., 1958).

Chapter 8

Small Informal
Social Systems*

INTRODUCTION

An earlier chapter showed the importance of the family and kinship system in the socialization of the child and the stabilization of adult personality. In most societies of the world the small clique, informal, friendship, or mutual-aid group rank next in importance in the performance of these functions.

In order to delineate different social organizations sociologists sometimes construct ideal types of opposite concepts. The German sociologist Ferdinand Toennies used the terms Gemeinschaft and Gesellschaft to describe the nature of interaction within two opposite types of social systems. A relatively small group held together by bonds of friendship and kinship, a common religion, a strong spirit of mutual helpfulness and a sense of commitment is Gemeinschaft-like. As an organic and harmonious whole it may be infused with a warm and loving aura, "unity of human wills," "mutual affirmation" and intimacy. Toennies not only mentioned the mother-child relation as a prototype of Gemeinschaft. He also noted that relations among friends and neighbors were Gemeinschaft-like.

An early American sociologist Charles Cooley used the term "primary group" to describe groups to which individuals are exposed first, where most intimate and cooperative relationships exist and which are fundamental and universal to all human societies. Cooley gives an acceptable definition of the term:

By primary groups I mean those characterized by intimate face-to-face association and cooperation. They are primary in several senses, but chiefly in that they are fundamental in forming the social nature and

*By Charles P. Loomis and M. Francis Abraham

ideals of the individual. The result of intimate association, psychologically, is a certain fusion of individualities in a common whole, so that
one's very self, for many purposes at least, is the common life and
purpose of the group. Perhaps the simplest way of describing this
wholeness is by saying that it is a 'we'; it involves the sort of sympathy
and mutual identification for which 'we' is the natural expression. One
lives in the feeling of the whole and finds the chief aims of his will in that
feeling.[1]

TABLE I*

Primary group (Cooley)	Gemeinschaft (Toennies)
Characteristics	
1. Face-to-face association	1. Unity of human will and an equilibrium of individual wills in mutual inter-dependence
2. The unspecialized character of that association	2. A division of labor based on mutual aid, helpfulness and the spirit of brotherhood
3. Relative permanence	3. Reciprocal and binding sentiments reinforced by diffuse obligations, common language, customs and beliefs
4. The small number of persons involved	4. Common habitat and common action directed toward common goals understood as given
5. The relative intimacy among the participants	5. Mutual possession and enjoyment
6. We-feeling, sense of belonging together and the common spirit	6. Authority based on age, wisdom, benevolent force and sacred tradition

*Adapted from John C. McKinney and Charles P. Loomis, "The Typological
Tradition" in Joseph S. Roucek, ed. *Contemporary Sociology* (New York: Philosophical
Library, 1958), pp. 557-83.

Table I provides an overview of the overlapping attributes of
primary groups and Gemeinschaft-like communities. It must, however, be pointed out that some of these characteristics are neither
essential nor sufficient to form informal social systems. A small
discussion group, the relationship between a prostitute and her client
and a small committee of the U.N. General Assembly may meet some
or even most of these criteria but they are, by no means, representative of primary groups. On the other hand, members of the family,
kinship and peer groups may be somewhat dispersed and yet they
might continue most intimate and personal relationships. Therefore,
a primary group may be defined as an informal group whose members
are related to one another in personal and affective ways as friends or
relatives rather than as mere categories. The primary relationship
consists in a mesh of total interaction, mutual aid and helpfulness
and a full range of human emotions.

Such groups, whether called friendship groups, congeniality
groups, cliques, informal groups, or autonomous groups, are all

Gemeinschaft-like in nature. In size they vary from two to thirty or so members. When they become larger they tend to break into subsystems. They are informal in the sense that they do not have explicit norms of entrance, membership or exit. Nor do they have written constitutions, by-laws or procedures. Members speak of nonmembers as outsiders, as "they" but of fellow members and themselves as "we." The small informal group, of course, has many forms; among hundreds of examples, the children's play group, the clique in the Chamber of Commerce, the neighborhood coffee klatch, the boy's gang on a street corner, or the clientele of Tony's Tavern are equally representative. The phenomena of the small intimate group and its importance in social interaction have received attention from sociological theorists and served as a favorite subject for empirical investigation. The observations of both the theorists and the re-, searchers will be used here to develop the essential elements and related processes of the small informal social system.

ELEMENTS AND PROCESSES OF THE SMALL, INFORMAL SOCIAL SYSTEM

KNOWING

Belief (knowledge) as an element.   Although members need not subscribe to a common set of beliefs as a prerequisite to membership in a small informal group, a selective factor probably tends to unite those of similar beliefs in the first place; once in the group, shared experiences and group interaction tend to breed common beliefs, or to maximize those commonly held and to minimize conflicting beliefs.

Studies in interpersonal influence[2] have shown that the opinions and beliefs of people are affected more by membership in face-to-face associations than impersonal forces of modern complex society like the mass media. They indicate a high degree of homogeneity of opinions and beliefs among members of the same family, among co-workers, friends, and companions. Joseph Precker's study[3] of students and faculty of Bard College showed that students were inclined to select associates, either as post-college friends, or as academic advisers, whose values and beliefs resemble their own and that the greatest homogeneity of beliefs occurred in those cases where friendship choices on the sociometric questionnaire were mutual rather than unilateral. Now, if you like, set up your own experiment and see to what extent you and your closest associates share the same beliefs and opinions.

Not only does frequent interaction among members of an informal social system tend to stereotype their values and beliefs, it also enhances the knowledge of self and others, facilitating a total involvement of personalities.

Simmel notes:

> . . . just as our apprehension of external nature, along with elusions and inadequacies, nevertheless attains the truth required for the life and progress of our species, so everybody knows, by and large correctly, the other person with whom he has to deal, so that interaction and relation become possible . . . One can never know another person *absolutely*, which would involve knowledge of every single thought and mood. Nevertheless, one forms some personal unity out of those of his fragments in which alone he is accessible to us. This unity, therefore, depends upon the portion of him which our standpoint permits us to see.[4]

The typology of *Gemeinschaft* and *Gesellschaft* is harmonious with the Simmel theory that a highly specialized relationship (i.e. a Gesellschaft-like relationship) is the first to eliminate from the interaction what Simmel calls "reciprocal knowledge" of the other person. At one end of the continuum there is extreme atomization of knowledge. What we know about the other person is restricted to a specific, narrowly defined area, of occasional interaction. Your knowledge about the bank clerk, the chauffeur of the university bus or the hairdresser is just that — a pure business acquaintance. But at the other end of the continuum we have the state of friendship which (even more than the state of marriage with its erotic preoccupations, according to Simmel) "may . . . connect a whole person with another person in its entirety; it may melt reserves more easily than love does — if not as stormily, yet on a larger scale and in a more enduring sequence."[5] True friendship knows no limit, we say. The stuff of which this kind of knowledge consists, "self-revelation and self-restraint, with their complements of tresspass and discretion" are the stuff of personality, too; the argument is compelling that the intimate friendship groups throughout life provide the training ground for the accumulation of this vital kind of knowledge and an absolutely necessary setting for its continued use.

These observations are supported by Suttles' study of *The Social Order of the Slum* which exemplifies the importance of personal knowledge as a cementing factor for street corner gangs in the slum.

> The function of the named street corner group in counteracting anonymity where personal acquaintance is out of reach points up the importance of personal knowledge whenever it is practicable. Addams area residents often know a wide arc of people personally and appeal to group

identities only as a last resort. This practice places great emphasis upon individual identities, intimate personal disclosures, and a close adherence to those personal precedents that have been laid down. The local street corner groups are private worlds in which personal precedents can become known and binding. The street corner groups not only make their members known to the remainder of the neighborhood, but create a network of personal acquaintances that augment those already in existence.[6]

Cognitive mapping and validation as process. In primary groups knowledge is validated by the emotional solidarity and normative integration of the group. The processes of questioning, criticizing, attacking, and substituting are accomplished through emotional encounters, revelations and self-sacrifices rather than the scientific processes of rational and impersonal verifications. In other words, beliefs and values are validated by personal testimony; mutual trust and personal attraction reinforce collectively held beliefs and opinions. Also primary groups sometimes develop ingenious devices to safeguard members' knowledge of self and others against inappropriate and dangerous exposures. Nicknames and inside jokes in friendship cliques and gangs and *ometra* of the Mafia are illustrations in point.

The relationship of the small informal group to the belief system of an individual member evinces itself on two planes: 1) subjectively, the individual's knowledge (and ignorance) of himself and of others; and 2) objectively, the individual's knowledge of and belief in the phenomena of the world he lives in, man-made, natural or supernatural. This latter kind of belief is fascinatingly revealed in small group context by a study which seeks to answer the question: what happens to the commonly held belief of a small group when incontestable evidence proves the belief to be wrong? The investigators conducting the study noted that in many movements a belief was not terminated by evidence of its falsity.[7] They were able to study the phenomena of group-belief endurance at close range when they located a cult whose members believed that their leaders had established contact with Outer Space. The messages from "divine" sources predicted that most of the earth would be flooded, but that the believers would be picked up by space ships and in time transported to a safe place on earth where mankind could begin anew. Unbeknown to the believing members who counted among their number a medical doctor and his wife, a chemical engineer, and a number of undergraduate students as well as people with rather average academic backgrounds, the investigators succeeded in infiltrating the small group. They participated, remembered and recorded through the quiet days of contemplation and study, the turbulent days of national publicity, "divine" commands and meticulous preparation, and finally through the tormenting hours of last-ditch waiting in sub-zero weather with eyes fixed on the sky out of which would come the space-saviors. In the great anti-climax of unfulfilled hope, an electrifying message came from Outer Space: the complete faith of the group had made it unnecessary for God to destroy the world by flood. The members quickly recovered their zeal and the investigators concluded that a large movement could have been started had the group been missionary-minded. A follow-up of the members and a check on their subsequent belief revealed that *those members who had easy access to other believers* persisted in their beliefs; those members who, through force of circumstance *were completely out of touch with other believers for a period lost their belief*. This was true, for example, of some of the undergraduate students for whom an extended Christmas vacation removed them from other believers for a three-week period.

The question is posed by this study as well as by others, as to whether many ordinary methods of demonstration and teaching are effective methods of leading groups to accept reality contrary to their beliefs. Studies indicate that such changes in belief systems might be accomplished more readily 1) if the adherents of the belief were not interacting or in contact with one another when the attempted change was made, and 2) if the adherents were not made to feel the "dissonance" of their beliefs in a manner which brings discomfort from devaluation of the self, in which case the individual tends to hold the belief and to be willing to proselyte for it. Research seems to demonstrate that people tend to give heed only to those opinions and attitudes which support their own pre-conceptions; that pre-conceptions not strengthened by similar opinions of others tend to be weakened; and that "reality" tends to become equated with the attitudes and opinions held and shared by those with whom the individual is in close communication.

FEELING

Sentiment as an element.   Everyone has experienced the sentiments of the small friendship group. Few can recall their most intimate clique groups without re-feeling the sentiments of fondness, security, perhaps competition and argument too, but with the comfortable feeling of belonging associated with these intimate groups. Cooley equates the sentiments engendered by the primary group particularly with "sympathy and the innumerable sentiments into which sympathy enters, such as love, resentment, ambition, vanity, hero-worship, and the feeling of right and wrong."[8] The same writer is quick to point out, however, that the purely individual nature of the sentiments evoked by the primary group soon are transmitted into an "ideal of moral unity" under which prevails the discipline of a common spirit, the allegiance to common standards, the sentiment of loyalty which includes truth, service and kindness to the intimate group. A deep sense of belonging, sentimental identification and "familistic" relations account for the cohesion and solidarity of primary groups. What is generally known as homesickness consists in the absence of the warmth and pleasures of close emotional ties associated with the primary groups from which we have temporarily removed ourselves.

In another chapter we referred to "in-groups" and "out-groups." Our attitude toward an out-group depends largely on how strongly we feel for 'our' group as well as the nature of sentiments — favorable or unfavorable — between "our" group and "their" group. Robert Bierstedt looks at this relationship in terms of two sociological principles:[9]

1. In-group members tend to stereotype those who are in the out-group. "Our" group is somehow "better" than "their" group, and we are inclined to react to members of our primary group as individuals and those in out-groups as members of a stereotyped category.

2. Any threat, imaginary or real, from an out-group tends to intensify the cohesion and solidarity of the in-group. An outsider will be foolish to interfere in an occasional quarrel between members of a healthy family. The members of a gang may not hesitate to mount a concerted attack on an outsider who "intruded" into their private business. A cohesive primary group rests on the solid foundation of a strong "collective consciousness."

These sentiments are well documented by William Foote Whyte who studied life in an Italian slum neighborhood in Boston. He observed the process of interaction among 13 young men aged twenty to twenty-nine who grew up in the neighborhood and regularly assembled on the Norton Street corner. These young men spent far more time on the corner with each other than at home with their families and also spent their little savings on each other. Doc, the leader of the Norton street group, explains the difference between his own gang and Chick's club:

Chick says that self-preservation is the first law of nature. Now that's right to a certain extent. You have to look out for yourself first. But Chick would step on the neck of his best friend if he could get a better by doing it . . . We were talking one night on the corner about that, and I was sucking him in. I got him to admit it — that he would turn against his best friend if he could profit by it . . . I would never do that, Bill. I would never step on Danny even if I could get myself a $50.00-a-week job by doing it. None of my boys would do that.[10]

Doc's feelings for his group are so strong that he admits:

I suppose my boys have kept me from getting ahead . . . But if I were to start over again — if God said to me, "Look, here, Doc, you're going to start over again, and you can pick out your friends in advance," still, I would make sure that my boys were among them — even if I could pick Rockefeller and Carnegie. . . . Many times people in the settlement (a social welfare agency in the area) and some of the Sunsets (a socially mobile girls' club), have said to me, "Why do you hang around those fellows?" I would tell them, "Why not? They're my friends."[11]

Tension management and communication of sentiments as process. Primary groups as well as large-scale organizations have mechanisms that protect the system from the disintegration potential in uncontrolled affective relations among its members. The informal, Gemeinschaft-like groups represent a fusion of sentiments; here the various passions of members are "socialized by sympathy" and brought "under the discipline of a common spirit." They serve as shock absorbers for the individuals, and to the extent to which individuals are integrated into the informal group they receive great strength and support from this emotional involvement. "To stick by my buddies" has always been the best way to avoid feelings of tension and psychological alienation.

A number of studies indicate that an *individual's sentiment pattern is influenced* by the type of interaction within small groups. The Rileys' study[12] is one example. Fifth and seventh grade children, some being well integrated into a peer group and others having little social life outside their families, were compared in regard to the kind of sentiments they experienced from certain mass-media programs. The children who were members of peer groups needed fantasy subjects less whereas those without a peer group turned to programs for fantasy and escape. While the former group used the program content for their own group activities, such as playing cowboy, the latter group liked action and violence programs and tended to live in a world of fantasy.

Another type of sentiment pattern in the small group relationship may be summed up in the word "morale." Cooley called it "moral unity" and characterized it thus:

... In its most general form it is that of a moral whole or community wherein individual minds are merged and the higher capacities of the members find total and adequate expression. And it grows up because familiar association fills our minds with imaginations of the thought and feeling of other members of the group, and of the group as a whole, so that, for many purposes, we really make them a part of ourselves and identify our self-feeling with them.[13]

Whatever its genesis, the powerful force of group spirit or morale has been incontrovertibly documented in widely different situations. A study[14] of the morale in Nazi Germany demonstrates that, contrary to the belief of many Americans, the Allies' propaganda had little effect in decreasing morale because German soldiers were fully integrated into their immediate primary group. The High Command used the Gemeinschaft idea and made every possible effort to maintain the primary nature of the fighting unit. Units were withdrawn from active service together, moved to another location together, when new members had to be added to the unit they were put in one or two at a time with sufficient time intervening to insure group absorption before more newcomers had to be dealt with. A "hard core" of a few men well indoctrinated in Nazi philosophy were the liaison between the unit and the High Command, but they too were part of the primary group. It was found that the men could endure defeat, physical deprivation, and unbelievable suffering as long as they were sustained by the primary group. Only under the most extreme circumstances, usually when the exigencies of battle forced physical separation of the members of a unit and when widespread disorganization prevented the unit from getting back together again, were the primary bonds dissolved. Dissolution of the primary group inevitably meant dissolution of individual morale as no other circumstance of war had done.

Similarly, a study[15] of the Korean front describes a tremendous amount of interest and energy exerted to prevent recruits and others from ideological or other motivations showing "heroism" which might endanger the group or upset the equilibrium. In the Korean and Chinese prison camps Communists "evolved a means of isolating every person emotionally from every other person" and since "there was practically no communication among the men, and most of them withdrew into a life of inactivity" many American troops created a most shameful image of American personality.[16] With the emotional insulation which had been produced, one third of the American prisoners entered into some sort of collaboration with the enemy; twenty-eight per cent died, a death rate which seems, comparatively, to be related to the breakdown of the primary social systems. By contrast, for example, the Turks who retained their group structure suffered no prison camp deaths, although half of them had been wounded in the same operation. "When a Turk got sick, the rest nursed him back to health."[17] These studies amplify the tension management role of primary groups and demonstrate the need for communication of sentiments and expressive behavior in times of great crisis. They are matched by investigations which show the importance of the primary group's sentiments in the daily grind of earning a living.

ACHIEVING

Ends, goals or objectives.   Friendship, companionship and affection suffuse the small intimate group. To the extent that these emotions prevail, to that extent it is difficult or impossible for most participants to specify the ends of the group. Whereas one may be able to state why he belongs to or holds stock in a credit union he may find it difficult to specify why he is part of a friendship group. In other words, primary groups are not goal-directed structures in the rigid sense of the term. The group may engage in a variety of activities — golfing, fishing, hunting, playing cards, mountaineering, skiing or smoking pot — but it is not these particular activities that determine the nature and function of the group. Rather, the group exists because of the members' concern, love and attraction for one another, and the activities are only the manifest expressions of their close, personal feelings. In a word, the importance of the group for its members consisted, not in any explicit goals it pursues, but in the intrinsic satisfaction the members derived from their shared activities and collective sentiments.

The distinguishing characteristic of the informal social system is its functional diffuseness. There is no sharp demarcation between different types of activities or different status-roles. Nor is there a time schedule to carry on the work of primary groups. Expressive goals as well as considerations of love and mutual obligations overshadow purely utilitarian goals. The individual's own needs and aspirations are conditioned by his orientation to the group. Cooley has put it succinctly: "The individual will be ambitious, but the chief object of his ambition will be some desired place in the thought of the others, and he will feel allegiance to common standards of service and fair play. So the boy will dispute with his fellows a place on the team, but above such disputes will place the common glory of his class and school."[18]

In the American society success is very highly evaluated and our culture places great emphasis upon the "getting ahead" theme. However, despite the cultural emphasis on social ascent or common success goals for all members of the society, levels of individual aspiration vary considerably. Several social scientists attribute the difference in motivation to childhood experiences and primary group ties. Russell Dynes and his colleagues[19] studied 350 university students enrolled in introductory and advanced sociology classes in terms of their aspirations and family experiences. Their conclusion: 42 per cent of the "high" aspirers had unsatisfactory interpersonal relationships in the family of orientation, or more specifically, had experienced feelings of not being wanted by their fathers; only 25 per cent of those in the 'low' group had reported experiencing strained parent-child relationships. While it is impossible to generalize from this limited sample, the study does point to the importance of primary groups in shaping one's achievement motivation.

Goal attaining and concomitant "latent" activity as process. The primary group is, as we have repeatedly noted, an expressive social system. Indeed, it is not even deliberately created by members; rather, informal groups just grow — in the neighborhood, in the school, or in the factory. Members identify themselves with these groups for various reasons — for companionship, for security, for emotional support, for "rep," or for just passing the time.

Friendship and companionship forms the integral part of such Gemeinschaft-like relationships making them ends in and of themselves and for that reason making their ends or functions more obvious to the objective outside observer than to the member who spontaneously plays his status-role in achieving them. Suttles' analysis of primary groups in the inner city illustrates this point:

Lacking anything like a daily agenda or a clearly defined set of group values, each group operates largely with a set of amoral assumptions and precedents that help define each situation. These assumptions and precedents, however, are equally well-known to the older residents. There is, for example, the general belief that each named group is up to something, acting tough, or in need of a strong hand. Specific group antagonisms are well-known, and group reputations are widespread. The location, movement, and age of each group can be interpreted by most of the residents. For instance, if a Mexican group is seen around Sheridan Park, people assume they are looking for trouble. When the boys enter a store, the management immediately takes precautions against shoplifting. If a group of boys are seen "hanging" in a dark alley, it "means" they are drinking. If the boys approach a girl, they are "on the make." When they "hang on the corner" they are just "wasting their time."[20]

Because of the high degree of normative integration within the small informal system any group activity, whether explicitly goal-oriented or not, is certainly functional in that it maintains group solidarity. Peter Blau's study of *Cooperation and Competition in a Bureaucracy*[21] illustrates how informal relations among the employees in a government office made them "good" and productive workers, whereas the absence of warmth and friendship made workers "inefficient" and less productive. The members of Section A, for example, were not very friendly with one another. They seldom shared lunch or coffee breaks. They never got together after working hours. Anxiety over meeting the official target of work output led to unhealthy competition and strained relations among workers. They all hoarded jobs while at the same time trying to prevent others from doing so, thus antagonizing their colleagues. Now they found it necessary to indulge in routine and insincere efforts to befriend and conciliate co-workers whom their competitive practices had alienated. Thus workers in Section A wasted a good deal of time and energy in unproductive behavior. But members of Section B were congenial, friendly and relaxed with another. They formed a well integrated informal group. Since their practices on the job did not antagonize colleagues, they were not forced to display false shows of friendship. This group was cohesive; it developed cooperation spontaneously and all members shared the common goals. Social cohesion of the group sustained employees' sense of security and reduced their status anxiety. Employees enjoyed their work. And the most important "latent" function of their informal social system was that the friendly relations which employees enjoyed with one another increased their levels of productivity and efficiency.

NORMING, STANDARDIZING, OR PATTERNING

Norm as an element.   Although there are no formalized or written rules, informal norms integrate primary groups and make patterns of interaction stable and predictable. The groups develop nicknames, inside jokes, special phrases and unique expressions which can be understood only by members of the same informal system. And institutionalized traditions developed through recurrent collective action exert pressures through relatively subtle influences exercised during the normal communication process.

The norms of a primary group are internalized by its members who form expectations of each other's behavior based on these norms. Members want to conform to them not only because they form an integral part of their social selves but also because they feel uncomfortable, or guilty, when they violate these norms. The great potency

of group norms is suggested by the following incident related by a
teen-age girl:

> The way they looked at me and the way they would be silent when I
> came into the tent, I could tell how upset they were, and not mad so
> much as sad for what I had done. I guess they kind of understand too,
> better than all the delegates who aren't in our gang, the reason I
> sneaked out and stayed off grounds after hours. All the rest of them have
> boy friends right in our church or at least right in our high school.
> Russell is my boy friend — or I like to think so anyway — and he lives
> thirty miles away. Well, here he is at the Institute. What do I do, spend
> all of the time with the gang and let some other girl snatch Russell? Or
> let my own very best friends do all our "last summer together" things
> without me, so that I can run when Russell beckons? This after hours
> arrangement wasn't anything very bad, really. But it was bad enough
> for our League to lose the attendance and service award, and for all the
> rest of the League to blame our gang for it. If my friends in the tent had
> only told that I wasn't there when I should have been, we would only
> have had a little demerit. But they didn't tell on me, and I got them into
> trouble. I surely messed up our "last vacation together." It feels right
> now as though I'll never get over it.[22]

This teen-age vignette shows that the strain attendant upon
breaking the norms was felt by the intimate group as well as by the
individual member; this is not uncommon among small intimate
groups whose integration is so related to sentiment.

Cooley observed that "human nature is not something existing
separately in the individual, but a group nature or primary phase of
society, a relatively simple and general condition of the social
mind."[23] The assumption will be made then, that small informal
groups exist because man is a gregarious creature and the small
group accomplishes the objective of providing him with an outlet for
his "group nature." Precisely as the family's ends could scarcely be
distinguished from its rules and norms, so do the ends and norms of
the small group merge. Friendly behavior, loyalty to members of the
group, helpfulness and service, self-sacrifice, are the rules or norms of
member behavior just as they are the *raison d'etre* for the group's
existence. These norms are not creations of definite purpose and writ
but unconsciously set in operation through personal involvement. In
other words, they are the "natural" and "right" ways of doing things
sustained by group cohesiveness and normative integration.

Evaluation as process.   In the Gemeinschaft-like social system
high evaluation is placed upon particularism, affectivity, functional

diffuseness and expressive processes. Norms are not simply means of rational, utilitarian ends; they are part and parcel of "collective consciousness" anchored in stable concensus, reflecting the solidarity, cohesion and likeness among members of small informal social systems. Norms are evaluated not in terms of rational instrumentality but in terms of friendship and kinship considerations and group cohesiveness. The pressures that induce conformity in the intimate groups relate to the following:

1. Attractiveness of the group. Individuals find it unpleasant to associate with groups whose ends and norms differ greatly from their own, and if they happen to join, they seek to change their own norms upon becoming a part of the group, or are induced to leave if they deviate too markedly from it. The attractiveness, or positive valence, of an informal social system depends on the number of intimate associates one has in it and on the extent of emotional ties between them.

2. Group identification. We may conform to the norms of an informal social group, not because we are afraid of sanctions, but because we recognize conformity as a means to express our identification with the group. Roethlisberger and Dickson's study[24] of the Bank Wiring Room demonstrated that individual production varied substantially around the established work norms of the group rather than the official norms set by the employers. Despite a group wage-incentive system set up by the management to boost production, workers established their own definition of a reasonable day's work and informal social pressures discouraged anyone from being a "rate-buster" — by working too hard, or a "chiseler" — by doing too little. In other words, workers conformed to the norms of the group with which they identified themselves.

3. Usefulness of the group. Individuals conform to the norms of the group insofar as it mediates certain goals which are highly evaluated by them. The group is considered functional by the individual in fulfilling some of his social, psychological or emotional needs — whether for power, prestige, social status or self-expression.

4. Group cohesiveness. We use the term group cohesiveness in the broadest sense, and include in it leadership, patterns of interpersonal influence, frequency of interaction, and the legitimacy of the group's traditions — whether authoritarian or democratic. If it is a well-knit group based on regular face-to-face communication and cooperative enterprise, such an informal social system will strengthen itself by enforcing conformity through subtle means of interpersonal influence.

DIVIDING THE FUNCTIONS

Status-role as both element and process. Status-roles of Gemeinschaft-like or primary groups by and large provide a more perfect fit in structuring personality attributes and needs than do those of Gesellschaft-like bureaucratic organizations. The loss of a key member due to death, migration, or other cause is much more likely to result in the disruption of informal Gemeinschaft-like groups than of the more formally organized groups such as armies, churches, industries or schools. This is because the informal group reflects the personality attributes and needs of members, in contrast to the opposite condition in which a group selects or moulds personalities to fit the social structure of the group, including its status-roles, pattern of power, and rank. Also the status-roles of informal, Gemeinschaft-like and primary groups, unlike the more formal, Gesellschaft-like and secondary groups commit a larger proportion of the personality and at less specified times and ways. Whereas the employee feels he owes his employer eight hours of labor of a specific kind, friendship is no eight-hours affair. True friendship systems function in "fair and bad weather" and they do not have "off and on" hours. They are thus functionally diffuse or "unlimited" in the demands they place upon the individual member. Because the personality attributes and needs of the members are so important to the relationship, the norms of particular importance to status-roles are personal and particularistic rather than universalistic. True friendships do not "blow hot and cold"; they are governed by affectivety, not affective neutrality.

Activities of small informal groups are not always planned according to some preexisting scheme of things; nor are the tasks assigned in any systematic manner. Rather, as tasks are identified, members just take charge of things. In this sense, it is probably more apt to say that leaders just grow; they are seldom chosen formally and deliberately. Referring to street corner groups in the slum, Suttles points out:

> Despite the absence of explicit rules and any impersonal division of labor, the boys seem to possess a vast and detailed set of preconceptions about what each member is apt to do. In the eyes of a boy, however, these are not "role expectations" but a mere knowledge of each other's "true," personal character. In this sense, their expectations are tailored to each individual by the precedents, promises, and commitments laid down in his known history.

> This importance attached to "remaining true" to one's established identity is readily apparent in most groups. If a member behaves inconsis-

tently in terms of what is expected of him he is not criticized or disturbed about doing something "wrong," but merely disbelieved or suspected of being "phony" or a "con artist." When street workers attempt to introduce explicit roles, like president or secretary, the boys tend to think them very funny. Apparently, the incongruity of someone "playing his part" is too much for them and "breaks them up." Thus, when elected to an office, most boys find it almost impossible to keep a "straight face."[25]

There appear to be two kinds of leaders in most groups: (a) the instrumental leader who is task-oriented and sees that the job is done, and (b) the popular or expressive leader who by bonhomie and good fellowship helps ease the tensions of the group. In the intimate friendship group no one person is delegated to a status role as in the case of a formal organization. Nevertheless, many friendship groups could designate those whom they consider "efficient" and perhaps somewhat dominating, and they could also indicate the jolly fellow or the peace-maker. Nicknames used in informal groups are clues to status-roles within them. One study revealed a "senator," a "judge" and a "public prosecutor."[26] The overzealous or industrious may be called names like "eager beaver" while "professor" or "preacher" may refer to wisdom or morality, or if used tauntingly, to their opposites.

The discussion group has been one of the most studied of groups. Some of the status-roles found to exist in the discussion group are: activity initiator, summarizer and feasibility tester. With no particular difficulty the duties and/or functions inherent in some of these status-roles could be seen to exist within the small friendship group too, where most likely the member who played one of the roles in a given situation would be playing another role in another situation (e.g., the information seeker at one point might be the information giver at another.)

RANKING

Rank as an element. In our society where equality and opportunity for equality are highly valued, differences in rank, particularly among friendship groups are likely to be a distasteful idea to some. Simmel suggests conditions under which ranking can take place (as it always will, he infers) among equals, or those engaged in "direct interaction of free, coordinate individuals."

> ... This coordination can perhaps be reached even if superordination and subordination continue to exist — provided they are reciprocal. We would then have an ideal organization, in which A is superordinate to B in one respect or time, but in which, in another respect or at another

time, B is superordinate to A. This arrangement would preserve the organizational value of super-subordination, while removing its oppressiveness, one-sidedness, and injustice. As a matter of fact, there are a great many phenomena of social life in which this form-type is realized, even though only in an embroyonic, mutilated, and covert way . . . Simultaneous superordination and subordination is one of the most powerful forms of interaction. In its correct distribution over numerous fields, it can constitute a very strong bond between individuals, merely by the close interaction entailed by it.[27]

The symbols of differentiation in low and high rank are blurred in the informal social system. Little difference in standing, for example, could be detected in the neighborhood play group of children, the street corner gang or a friendship clique. Unlike the boss in the office or the foreman in the factory who are assigned supervisory roles by higher authority, the boy who aspires to "lead" a gang or a play group has no higher authority to back him. He has to win leadership status by gaining the approval and administration of the group, often through the creation of situations which call for the display of characteristics highly valued by the group.

For a long time sociological literature as well as that of management, administration and psychology has sought to isolate the characteristics of a leader. Research would seem to indicate that much of the discourse about leadership has been misleading and fruitless. Findings seem to bear out the conclusion, not that there are "born" leaders with unfailing leadership traits, but rather than leadership is held now by one person and then by another within the same group and within a short span of time. Who will be the leader and what will be his characteristics will be determined by the situation in which the group finds itself rather than by any overall and general traits of leadership.

Research would tend to support some generalizations concerning rank. For example, the higher a man's social rank, the more he accepts the group's norms, ends, beliefs and sanctions, the more frequently he interacts with persons outside his own group, and the greater the number of persons for whom he originates interaction, either directly or through intermediaries. Research to date does not specify to what extent and under what conditions the individual brings his occupational rank, his community rank, his family rank with him to the small group. There is obviously no simple answer to this. The youth's gang, for example, for whom rank might be measured with skill and daring at illegal exploits, might not be unduly impressed with community standing or family rank accorded an individual member's family. The same youth's high or low rank in the fraternity or in the country club might not be entirely unrelated to his family's rank on the other hand.

Evaluation of actors and allocation of status-roles as process.   Be it a gang, a clique, or a work group, it is often difficult to appreciate the ramifications of individuals' status-roles and motivations without an understanding of their salient reference groups. As Merton and Kit have noted:

> An army private bucking for promotion may only in a narrow and theoretically superficial sense be regarded as engaging in behavior different from that of an immigrant assimilating the values of a native group, or of a lower-middle-class individual conforming to his conception of upper-middle-class pattern of behavior, or of a boy in a slum area orienting himself to the values of the street corner gang, or of a Bennington student abandoning the conservative beliefs of her parents to adopt the more liberal ideas of her college associates, or of a lower-class Catholic departing from the pattern of his in-group by casting a Republican vote, or of an eighteenth century French aristocrat aligning himself with a revolutionary group of the time.[28]

Individuals tend to orient their aspirations and actions to groups with which they identify themselves or which they aspire to join.

In the case of primary groups such orientations manifest themselves in expressive behavior. Evaluation of actors in the informal social systems is influenced by these expressive processes as evidenced by ties of kinship and friendship. A leader's prestige is bound up with the total network of interpersonal relationships. Indeed, 'leader' may not even be the best term, for none is too tall or too short in an intimate friendship group. However, some ranking systems develop within every informal social group although overwhelming personal relationships keep the distinction between the leaders and the led to the minimum. Even such an informal system as the Norton street gang had an hierarchical form with a leader, "Doc," and several lieutenants who exercised considerable influence on the rest of the members. The higher the individual's position in the hierarchy, the greater was the freedom he enjoyed in the initiation of action for those below him. Whyte was able to observe the ebb and tide of Doc's popularity among his street corner boys. Doc's unemployment and subsequent inability to buy favors with money for his boys, his failure in the political campaign and his inability to fulfill the obligations toward the gang affected his place in the group. As Whyte put it:

> Not all the corner boys live up to their obligations equally well, and this factor partly accounts for the differentiation in status among them. The man with a low status may violate his obligations without much change

in his position. His fellows know that he has failed to discharge the certain obligations in the past, and his position reflects his past performances. On the other hand, the leader is depended upon by all members to meet his personal obligations. He cannot fail to do so without causing confusion and endangering his position.[29]

Short and Strodtbeck who studied a dozen Chicago gangs for a period of three years also delineated conditions that favored the risk of, as well as sustained, leadership.[30] In conflict-oriented gangs in which violent action was admired, a good fighter with a reputation for playing it "cool" by being quick with fists rises to leadership. But the researchers found that not all street corner gangs respected toughness and violence. For example, in the drug-using gang of boys, the leader's status depended on his competence in enjoying a drug "kick" and "getting high" rather than on his physical strength or aggressiveness.

In summary, then, of status-roles and social rank as they occur in the small informal group, it may be said that the informality of the group does not negate these elements within itself, but that it does impart to them a less specific and more amorphous form than is true in more formal social systems. Even where status-role and rank are readily discernible in the small informal friendship group they are likely to be blurred by the expressions of common sentiment which dominate the small informal group.

CONTROLLING

Power as an element.   Ample evidence has already been given in this chapter to prove that the influence aspect of power is potent among members of the small group. The dynamics which built the powerful morale observable in the army units, the similarities of beliefs, sentiments and norms are all results of the reciprocal influences which intimate group members exert on each other. The greater the importance of the authority aspect of power, the more specificity the status roles will have. In intimate groups with a relatively high degree of structure, as in a boy's gang where there is an obvious and recognized leader, power and, of course, influence are easily traced. As was shown under status-role there are some groups where leadership is now in one place and again in another, depending upon the skills required for a particular situation. Influence could be assumed to be as mercurial as leadership in such groups. The elusive quality of influence, like leadership, will have to be related to the question of "influence for what?"

One significant aspect of influence of the small group is connected with the completely voluntary nature of the association and the pleasure that comes from being together. Since the members seem to be drawn together by common beliefs, sentiments, norms and objectives, the friendship group tends to participate together as sub-groups in other social systems. They may be together at the citizens' meeting when the school annexation is discussed, or at the Women's Club when the plea for aid to retarded children is made. Their poten-tial for disproportionate power because of their semi-organized state within these larger groups must be recognized in connection with their influence in community affairs. This matter will be explored further below in this chapter under *Systemic linkage*.

Authors of the Westgate study delineate two aspects of the power structure of informal social systems. The first is referred to as "inter-nal power" of the group. A group has the ability to induce changes in the direction of the forces which act on the members, its internal power being defined in terms of the magnitude of the change which it can induce on its members. Groups can induce members to work hard or to be lazy, to vote democratic or not to vote at all, to dress for dinner or to lead a "bohemian life."[31]

The second aspect is called the "power field" of the group. In order to appreciate the dynamics of power operating in a group we must understand not only how it induces conformity to establish ends and means but also the range of activities over which the group has power. The power of an informal friendship group may be confined to a specific recreational activity whereas a work group may be influen-tial in inducing conformity to a work norm as well as shaping political opinions and beliefs.

Decision-making and its initiation into action as process.   Most readers will have heard of the experiment in which a perfectly healthy person is told over and over again by a group of his associates that he looks sick. He very soon feels sick. The device used is essen-tially the same as that of a famous experiment conducted by Sherif.[32] Using the "autokinetic effect" which is the illusion of movement made when a stationary pinpoint of light is flashed on in a completely darkened room, he had students estimate the distance the light moved each time it was lit. First the students performed the experi-ment separately. Once the separate students had made their indi-vidual estimates they again performed the experiment in two's and three's. The first estimate played some part in the new estimate but the differences resulted in compromises until a group estimate was reached. Knowing the first individual estimates it was possible to judge who was most influential in the group norm. When the experi-ment was reversed by having students make the group estimate first and then make separate estimates later, the individuals like the healthy student mentioned above all accepted the group estimate.

Likewise, in another experiment which required students to match three lines with one which was equal in length to only one of the three, groups of seven were independently instructed to give the wrong evaluation. One student who had no instruction in each group made the evaluation last after observing the evaluation of the seven others. Although the intentional errors were large and very obvious, one third of the "uninstructed evaluators" went with the other seven. In another set of groups in which there were no intentional errors there were almost no errors. Among the "yielders" in the "propagandized" group were those whose perceptions changed, those whose judgments were distorted and those who knew that the majority was wrong but "went along."[33]

Studies in interpersonal influence have demonstrated the importance of opinion leaders in the flow of information and influence. Lazarsfeld and his colleagues showed that friends and coworkers influenced people's voting choice more than mass media did. In the Decatur study Katz and Lazarsfeld stressed the advantages of interpersonal aspects of face-to-face communication in affecting marketing, fashion and movie selections among women. Other studies point out that drug adoption by physicians, diffusion of innovations among farmers and the spread of information about events are invariably influenced by friends, relatives, neighbors, and co-workers far more than by various mass media. It is now generally conceded that individuals rooted in small informal groups are greatly influenced by the opinions, ideas and beliefs that prevail in the group.

It thus seems to be documented beyond any doubt that individual members of a group, particularly of primary groups, are affected by the group when evaluation and decision-making are involved, even in situations when the evaluation seems to the group member to be an individual decision. When evaluation and decision-making must be authenticated by subsequent action, thus making the decision more public and visible, investigators have been interested in knowing whether some methods of decision-making and evaluation are more action-prone than others. It seems to be established that more change comes about if the evaluation and decision-making has been done in the discussion group setting than if the same kind of information is given the group by the lecture method. Katz and Lazarsfeld, who consider this matter in the light of many investigations treated in their volume, suggest that the discussion method itself may not be so important as some of the interplay of small group attributes which the discussion method puts into motion: the recital of norms commonly held and respected by the group at hand as well as by other groups of which the participants are likely to be members; the perception of others' views of who supports what position; the therapeutic effect of talking out areas that might be emotion-laden. The suggestion is clearly established that the decision-reaching result is a function of the informal group rather than a function of a particular method of imparting information.[34] In short, most studies of decision-making attest to the importance of informal groups even when the decision represents a formal group like a legislature.

SANCTIONING

Sanction as element and application of sanctions as process. Common expressions attest to the general acceptance of pressures and sanctions of the in-group. "He is a good boy, but got mixed up in a wild gang", really signifies that the sanctions of the gang or intimate group can be more persuasive than a person's own original moral convictions or those of his family. The degree of punishment and its form meted out by the group varies with the group as well as with the kind of encroachment the individual has made on group norms, beliefs, or whatever. In keeping with the informal nature of the organization of the intimate group, nothing so structured as black-balling or trying a person usually occurs.

> ... Every group, in the measure of its organization, controls its members and exacts from them conformity to certain standards of conduct. If they do not conform to these standards the group inflicts failure upon them and casts them out. This control or casting out is accomplished in a great variety of ways — most of which do not imply deliberate purpose.[35]

Since the members of an intimate group know each other so well, subtleties of behavior that are not evident to the outsider can be a sanction against a wayward member. Since rational intention has little to do with expressive behavior which is the stock in trade of the small group, no amount of planned good intentions on the part of the deviant, and similarly, no amount of planned reward or punishment on the part of the group is likely to be ultimately successful in providing bulwarks to group integration. Unless full friendship is given spontaneously by members after the defection by one of its group, the recalcitrant individual is not and cannot be a "full member." No doubt, the need for spontaneity in the whole approval-disapproval pattern, if the interaction is to be meaningful, is what Cooley referred to when he talked of punishments which did not imply "deliberate purpose."

Sanctions in informal groups range all the way on the penalty side from practical jokes to lynchings; reward may range from permitting a leader to talk more than his share to giving a tip which will result in huge profits or stock dividends. Ridicule in a peer group, gossip in an old-fashioned neighborhood, and heckling and razzing in a street gang are examples of more or less effective sanctions. The fact that these sanctions are administered by no formal courts of law with elaborate procedures need not detract from their effectiveness in social control.

FACILITATING

Facility as element and utilization of facilities as process. As will be pointed out in the following section under territoriality, propinquity is a great factor in the maintenance of face-to-face relationships characteristic of the informal group. Facilities which conquer space take on added importance to the informal group as cities become large, as neighborhoods lose their primary character, and as suburbia drains into opposite directions people who are members of cliques in occupational systems or in old disintegrating neighborhoods. Chief among the "space conquerors" are the telephone, the automobile, and for the young, even the bicycle and motorcycle. The current rash of cartoons and stories about teen-agers and the use of the telephone and young adults who want a car more than any other possession can easily be related to the difficulty that the age-group experiences in maintaining primary contacts in an increasingly Gesellschaft-like community. Time must also be regarded as a facility. Probably one of the reasons that the intimate group which exists solely for the friendship it affords its members is out-numbered by the other clique groups such as those within the occupational organizations and special-purpose organizations is that the specialized and divergent schedules of group members in an increasingly specialized society do not provide a common meeting time to members.

But modern cities have developed new facilities which are designed to overcome these difficulties. Boskoff writes:

In the last few years, a relatively unique form of clique or quasi-clique has developed among young adults in the central city. This is the "swingle set" of single, employed, college educated, recent migrants (male and female) in New Orleans, Atlanta, Birmingham, Charlotte, Memphis, Jacksonville, etc., who participate in a personal, mass culture of partying, dating, swimming, and all the sex the market will bear. Two ingredients are indispensable: (1) a convenient apartment complex, designed for singles (but unofficial though temporary additions are quite common), with spacious swimming pools and indulgent neighbors, and (2) one or more "in" restaurants in the vicinity, which encourages singles to use the facilities (food, drink, and dance floor) as a focal meeting-place. It has been asserted, with some accuracy, that these otherwise favored migrants are isolated from the family life and the suburban residences of their co-workers and office mates. Consequently, the swingles form their own subculture, which, it has been suggested, is not unlike the pace and flavor of fraternity and sorority life in college.[36]

CONDITIONS OF SOCIAL ACTION

Kingsley Davis has provided three essential conditions of primary groups:[37] (1) close physical proximity, (2) smallness of the group, and (3) duration of the relationship.

They correspond closely to the Conditions of Social Action, namely Territoriality, Size and Time, in the PAS Model.

Territoriality. Territoriality or physical proximity is essential to clique group life in the following respects:

(1) A spatial setting provides opportunity for interaction out of which the intimate group can grow; (2) a well-located place or places for continued meetings must exist; (3) termination of the group is related to member mobility, greater distance tending to cause less interaction and the dissolution of the group.

Territoriality in terms of proximity of residence is especially important in new settlements, rural as well as urban. Both closeness of residence and likeness of backgrounds and interests are important factors in the establishment and maintenance of informal groups. Next-door neighbors or families living close by usually form clique groupings in early periods of settlement. The more homogeneous a new community, the larger the proportions of associates who live adjacent will be and the longer the propinquitous relationships will persist. In less homogeneous communities and in older communities, the members of informal groups tend to be more scattered.[38] Referring to the "ecological determinants of group structure," Festinger and his associates illustrate:

> The dependence of friendship formation on the mere physical arrangement of the houses (in the housing colony). People who live close to one another became friendly with each other, while people who lived far apart did not. Mere "accidents" of where a path went or whose doorway a staircase passed were major determinants of who became friends within this community. The small face-to-face social groups which formed, to a large extent, were determined by the fact that a number of people lived in the same apartment building or in the same court.[39]

In *The Social Order of the Slum*, Suttles delineates the process of slum formation in the inner city. Poor people of "low-status" minority groups who fail to conform to the vigorous standards of American society are relegated to "slums" and "skid rows" so that "respectable and essential citizens can carry on their corporate life undisturbed by their own apprehensions." This process of territorial aggregation segregates the poor, the unsuccessful and the disreputable into slum neighborhoods. Thus society forces the unfortunate members to compromise the ideals of public mortality or alienates them permanently. The new spatial arrangement necessitates closer communication and informal social relationships among the slum-dwellers. Suttles observes:

> The segregation of age, sex, and territorial groups, however, provides a structural starting point from which face-to-face relations can grow and reach beyond each small territorial aggregation. The development of personal relations furnished both a moral formula and a structural bridge between groups. Within each small, localized peer group, continuing face-to-face relations can eventually provide a personalistic order. Once these groups are established, a single personal relation between them can extend the range of such an order. With the acceptance of age grading and territorial usufruct, it becomes possible for slum neighborhoods to work out a moral order that includes most of their residents.[40]

Several studies on intimate groups in middle-sized and large cities indicate that the stereotype of the cold, unfriendly, impersonal and atomized social relationship of the urban region may be an overgeneralization, for intimate social relationships are prevalent in the city and are found both within local residential areas and are spread throughout the city. Local sub-areas also support intimate friendship groups. Boskoff delineates four major sources of close friendship in the urban region:[41]

1. In childhood and young manhood, school and college are frequent gardens of friendship.
2. Church affiliation, particularly among middle status urbanites and in the suburban ring, is a consistent factor in stimulating close personal ties for young people, and to some extent for adults. Indeed, most congregations encourage their young members to participate in a variety of social events — Sunday School, discussion groups, dances, bazaars, parties, musical activities, etc.
3. For the urban adult, office, shop, and factory are not only economic locations, but also excellent opportunities for informal contacts with fellow workers.

4. Several recent studies — mainly in the newer areas of the
    urban region and among medium status families — strongly
    suggest that urban friendships with close neighbors and with
    families within a limited radius of blocks are more numerous
    than had been expected.

However, it must be pointed out that urban sociology has not
extensively examined the networks of urban friendship and clique
formations. While the impersonality of the city and the anonymity of
its inhabitants have been generally exaggerated, anyone who is
familiar with a really small or rural place knows that unknown
identities and unexplained behavior seldom exist in an old peasant
community or other similar rural settings, whereas there are places
in the city where such anonymity is not only possible but even
inevitable.

Size and time.   Now let us briefly consider size and time, the two
other conditions of social action. A primary group must be limited in
size so that members may involve themselves fully and emotionally
in the mesh of social relationships and derive intrinsic satisfaction
from such personal interaction. "As the group becomes larger each
person counts less as a unique personality but more as a sheer cipher
or unit; the group tends to acquire a more complex and formal organization."[42] With very small groups the addition or withdrawal of even
one member might make a world of difference.

The importance of the concept of time for informal social systems
is exemplified by the enduring nature of primary ties. As Davis
remarked:

> Intimacy is largely a matter of the frequency and intensity of associa-
> tion. Other things equal, the longer the group remains together the
> more numerous and deeper are the contacts between its members.
> Social ties deepen in time through the gradual development of inter-
> locking habits. An oft-repeated association, like any other experience,
> becomes part of one's way of life.[43]

COMPREHENSIVE OR MASTER SOCIAL PROCESSES

Communication.   If intimate friendship groups can be said to
have one latent function which supersedes others, it surely would be
the provision of a communication network. Where friendship exists
active channels of communication exist too, and the more intimate
the friendship, the wider the range of subjects covered and the less
restraint upon communication. Even within formal organizations

like the factory, a large department of the government, or the army, individuals who are in frequent contact with one another tend to establish networks of personal relationships. To combat the "beast of monotony" or to escape impersonality, they band together into cliques and friendship groups. The term informal structure is often used to describe such networks of spontaneous interaction and communication. These groups develop informal norms, exchange confidential information, and stand united as a defense against any arbitrary action by management. However informal, such primary groups with their interlocking lines of communication and personal influence are often powerful enough to thwart the officially approved chain of command and formal channels of communication. Though much of what flows through communication channels in a friendship group is trivial except to the participants, that the channel is there, no matter what it carries most of the time, is the important sociological fact.

The importance of such communication channels when other forms of communication fail is discussed at greater length by the senior author in the essay dealing with "Systems Under Stress," where disaster and disruption are shown to make informal communication channels imperative.[44] The chapter dealing with governmental social systems will show the importance of such channels when, as in the Soviet Union, the official communication channels are inadequate. One study on the Soviet Union reveals something of the character of the informal groups which use the informal communication system, and of the saliency of the communication content.[45] In this setting where communication is rigidly controlled by the government, word-of-mouth communication composes 50 per cent of the regular sources of information and its "staying power" or saliency is rated higher than the information gleaned in any other way. The class pattern of informal communication follows what researchers have found it to be in the United States: the higher placed the individual is, the more he hears. Of the professional respondents 52 per cent report frequent exposure to informal communication while only 13 per cent of the peasants make that claim. The members of the upper class, however, attach less significance to the word-of-mouth communication that they hear than do the members of the lower classes.

One of the most enduring studies of communication in small groups is Robert Bales' *Interaction Process Analysis*.[46] Bales experimented with discussion groups varying in size from 3 to 8 men. He observed the process of interaction and systematically recorded each and every communicative act directed by and to any person in the group. He then constructed a hierarchy of rank in terms of the number of communicative acts directed toward every member of the group. Having repeated the experiment with several laboratory groups, Bales came to the striking conclusion that the man who ranked first in small discussion groups of up to 8 members received 45 per cent of all action in the group; the second received about 18 per cent; the remainder of all actions was systematically distributed among other members depending on the size of the group.

Very interesting experiments have been carried out with planted rumor. In one class known to the authors, at the next to the final meeting, the professor purposely told one student in an off-hand way that there would be no final examination. At the final session the members of the class revealed when and from whom they had heard the good news. The clique of the student in whom the professor had confided had been the first to hear, and one very bashful girl with few acquaintances in the class had been the last, having overheard talk about it as she came into the classroom. Sociometry, or a system of revealing social cliques by members' indications of whom they would choose for specific activities and in what order, is a useful device for many different kinds of information about groups. It is a diagram of the informal relations within a group, showing who are sought out by the majority of members or ignored by many. According to Katz and Lazarsfeld, "The sociometric method permits the study of communications flow in terms of an objectively delineable pattern of individual relationships. Thus, a rumor or a bit of news or an action-stimulant introduced into a social group whose sociometric connections are known, can be watched almost the way the doctor watches the flow of chalky liquid introduced into the human body during a fluoroscopic examination.[47] The spread of the news (concerning the cancellation of examination) among classmates clearly followed sociometric lines.

Boundary maintenance. There is probably no social system with less defined boundaries than the intimate friendship group. The reader will have noted in the preceding chapters that there is little or no doubt as to whether or not one is an Amishman, or whether or not one is a family member; in the succeeding chapters, the boundaries of such systems as occupational systems, governmental systems and others will be seen to have more or less well defined standards of membership. Although an individual *knows* when he is a member of a friendship group, and knows, sometimes by imperceptible degree when his membership in a friendship is waxing or waning, he by no means knows exact criteria for his own or others' membership. As was pointed out under the section above on *Beliefs*, it is impossible ever to know another person completely. Small intimate groups seem to thrive on the pooling of significant "self-revelations and intrusions" as Simmel expressed it. Everyone has experienced the social situation, (in reality, boundary maintenance) when some intrusion inappropriate to the group or to the occasion develops.

> The physical structure of an encounter itself is usually accorded certain symbolic implications, sometimes leading a participant against his will to project claims about himself that are false and embarrassing. Physical closeness easily implies social closeness, as anyone knows who has happened upon an intimate gathering not meant for him or who has found it necessary to carry on fraternal 'small talk' with someone too high or low or strange to ever be a brother.[48]

The awkward intrusion may, of course, come from one of the individual members as well as from an outsider. If a member of an intimate group too often for the group's comfort, well-being and integration, indulges in self-revelations inappropriate to the group or intrudes into what the others please to reveal about themselves in an indiscreet way, he will be rewarded with less and less intimate interaction until he no longer is an intimate member of the group.

What has been said so far should be true of the boundaries of any intimate group with respect to its most important function, its expressive sentiments, its comradeship, its ease of social interaction, its comfortable friendships. To the extent that any intimate group is likely to have a particular orientation, a few generally shared interests that supersede other interests, the form of boundary maintenance will not only have the general characteristics described above, but will be marked by barriers appropriate to the special interests. These latter may be unexpressed or may be quite openly subscribed to. For example, a group of adolescent girls bound together by ties of expressive friendship, may openly or secretly maintain the boundaries of their group to a prospective member by either acceptance or rejection on the basis of her success with boy friends. The girl who is markedly superior or inferior with respect to boy friends probably will not be a member of the group, although it may be equally true that the group does not exist as a friendship group merely to acquire boy friends.

> In the seventh and eighth grade there was this group of girls who shut themselves off from the rest . . . If some new girl came into school that had a new dress for every day in the week, seemed to attract the boys and was able to throw parties where they could sneak a little beer and smoke a bit, then they would all come together and vote on whether she could run around with them or not.[49]

The teen-age group of boys of whom the following was written, were oriented quite differently from the group just considered, but their boundary maintenance devices worked very similarly:

So strongly integrated a primary group curtailed its members with outsiders. Each member was involved in a most satisfying network of relationships and therefore did not seek more than marginal contact with others . . . Symptomatic of their ethnocentrism was the defensiveness of "the boys." They would argue that other groups and other people offered very little of interest; that others were interested in dances, football, parties and the like, to the exclusion of the important matters of the mind that occupied *their* group.[50]

The particular kinds of boundary maintenance could take countless forms; a certain freedom from adult-prescribed norms and intellectuality have been shown in the examples just given. Other common forms are exclusions by age, sex, education, kinds of abilities like athletic or musical training, occupation, and place of residence. No matter the form, the social function performed by the boundary of the small intimate group is the maintenance of the group in a condition in which it is able to minister most effectively to the emotional needs of its members.

Systemic linkage. In contrast to the primary group stands another kind of group; it exists for a specific purpose and sociologists know it by various names: associational, formal, or secondary. This kind of group — a work group or a civic club, or some other example of formal group — often provides the scene in which the small friendship group is operative. Even the small friendship group whose members live in the same neighborhood might not be sustained as a group solely from the interaction which takes place on the residence basis. Neighbors, for example, may belong to formal organizations such as civic clubs, or work at the same plant. Out of interaction at all such points of contact the friendship group — or informal structure as we termed it under *Communication* above — may develop, or if already developed, be sustained.

To argue that the formal association is not an important activity in the city is to fly in the face of the obvious evidence. However, in spite of the great number of formal associations . . . and their generally widespread membership, the question arises as to just how impersonal and anonymous are the relationships . . . It appears that attendance at a formal meeting serves in part to bring men together in relationships of a primary nature. For example, over 51 per cent of the members of formal associations in each of the neighborhoods report that they have nine or more close personal friends who also are members. Conversely, less than 17 per cent report that they have no close personal friends in their associations at all. Thus most individuals find the formal association by no means as impersonal as often assumed.[51]

Not only is the "formal" association not nearly so formal, investigation actually reveals that its efficiency in accomplishing its objectives often depends upon the utilization of the informal friendship groups in its midst. Often when the president of a formal organization appoints a committee, for example, there is much more likelihoɔd of the committee's fulfilling its obligations with the least amount of lost motion and intra-committee strife if he appoints a congenial friendship group to do the job, especially if the group is supportive of the formal organization. Outside of special committee assignments the friendship groups too, facilitate the regular day-by-day flow of work with their broader knowledge of the potentialities and limitations of their members and with their great ease of communication without the emotional barriers common to communication between relative strangers. "An organization would soon break down if everybody in it did only what his formal job description called for, and did it 'according to the book.' "[52]

The Russian Communists were aware of the importance of the informal friendship group and of the necessity of systemic linkage to it when, in the great industrial transformation it was thought necessary to create the status-role of the "agitator", the people most often chosen to fill this role were the informal group leaders. The agitator was relied on to know "not only how each person in his shop works, but also how he lives, what his family is like, what his living conditions are, and whether or not he needs advice on some personal problem; .. the successful agitator bases his success largely on . . . personal relationship with his audience."[53] The study does not reveal how long any agitator could maintain his "audience segregation" or what happened to his membership in the informal group once his agitator-self had been revealed to his friendship group audience!

Systemic linkage involving small friendship groups means simply that friendship group members belong to other groups too. Although it is technically correct to view two social systems as linked upon evidence that they share common members, how effectively they are linked is not revealed until the degree of involvement each system holds for the member is demonstrated. The Civic Group to which the medical social worker addresses her remarks on Monday is sure to contain a number of friends who will hear the appeal of the school superintendent at the PTA meeting. The network of friendship groups is obviously important, but the strength of their linkage to the Civic Group or to the PTA may also be a determinant of whose appeal is responded to most satisfactorily. Students of national economy have sometimes chosen a given number of business and industrial firms, and have listed all the members of the board of directors for each. It is considered significant very often if the vice-president of a huge industrial firm will be a vice-president of a large investment house with which the industrial firm does business; that the chairman of a center operation (the manufacture of automobiles, for example) will also be the chairman of a related field operation (the mining of iron, for example). Such a system of inter-locking director-ships as they are called, would likely be found on a miniature scale in every community for most social activities from the Ladies' Baked Food Sale to the Get Out to Vote campaign. It is of the highly unstandardized amalgam of the emotional ties of the friendship groups, the occupationally competitive ties of the working group, the demands and responses to the family group, and the semi-citizenship semi-professional ties of the civic group that the stuff of systemic linkage is composed.

Socialization. Cooley recognized the importance of primary groups in the socialization of individuals when he referred to them as "the nurseries of human nature." The first and most important primary group is the family where culture transmission begins. Parental influence, sibling rivalry and co-operation, sex education, rejection or over-acceptance by parents, eliminatory processes, and the arduous training intended to initiate the individual into the culture of the community are all part of the socialization process that goes on in the family. Next in importance are peer groups — spontaneous play groups of neighborhood children and associates in school. Acquisition of culture goes on through frequent interaction among them. Then, there is the transition to adolescence — the period characterized by a more positive evaluation of the information and guidance teen-agers receive from their contemporaries and a tacit rejection of parental influence.

The process of socialization does not, however, stop with family and school; it is a life-long process. Work groups in an industrial plant, pressure groups in local politics, sponsors of a community campaign, church groups and coffee clubs may at once be informal social systems and agents of socialization. The voting study by Lazarsfeld and others cited earlier in the chapter showed that even the influence of mass media on adult audience is far from direct. The study indicated that personal influence affected voting decisions more than the mass media did. In fact, the researchers found almost no direct influence of the mass media on voting patterns; instead, interpersonal influence from opinion leaders in informal social groups was recognized as an important intervening mechanism which operated between the mass media messages and their effects on human behavior.

Now let us look at the process of socialization from a theoretical perspective. We begin with two fundamental questions: How do we acquire our culture? How do we come to formulate a conception of ourselves? Several sociologists and psychologists have addressed themselves to these questions. Most of them tend to agree that an individual acquires self-consciousness as well as culture only because he first acquires a society. According to Cooley, "self and society are twin-born, we know one as immediately as we know the other, and the notion of a separate and independent ego is an illusion."[54] But it is George Herbert Mead who has given us the most elaborate exposition of what has come to be called the symbolic interaction theory. Mead insists that 'self' is neither a psychological organism nor a biological entity but essentially a social structure which arises in the process of social experience and activity. Social interaction, communication and group processes introduce the self into which the individual organizes all his experiences. Thus an individual comes to acquire the concept of self from the social group with which he has meaningful interaction. How does a girl, for instance, come to formulate her self-concept of being beautiful? Now, according to the symbolic interaction theory, she is beautiful not because she thinks she is beautiful, and she is not beautiful because others think she is beautiful, but she is beautiful because she thinks others think she is beautiful. It is the response of the boys and her experience with her peers that gave her the self-concept of being beautiful.

According to Mead, the "self" is made up of the "I" and the "me". "The 'I' is the response of the organism to the attitudes of others; the 'me' is the organized set of attitudes of others which one himself assumes. The attitudes of the others constitute the organized 'me', and then one reacts toward that as an 'I'."[55] In other words, the "I" represents the spontaneous behavior of the human infant — that behavior which is unconditioned and undisciplined. Over time, the process of continuous interaction with parents and others, gives rise to the concept of "me" which seeks to restrain and regulate the behavior of "I" in accordance with the established norms of the group or society. Mead delineates three stages in which the concept of "self" arises and develops. First, there is the spontaneous play children engage in. Play is only a set of responses and the child learns to mimic his parents, the mailman or the policemen but has not yet developed a whole self. Secondly, there is the game which has to be played in accordance with set rules and regulations and an individual has to assume the role of every other participant in the group. Consider the game of chess for a moment. Everything that a participant does is in response to what the other one does, or in accordance with one's perception of what the other will do. Social life is a game of chess that we continue to play all our lives. The third stage identified by Mead is the *generalized other*. It is the organized community or social group to which individuals belong. Very often it is the primary group with which the individual identifies himself that gives him his unity of self. The individual does not experience himself directly but only indirectly from the attitude of the generalized other. The individual's self-consciousness is, then, a product of social interaction or more specifically, of his perception of the responses of others toward him. In short, a primary group with which an individual identifies himself may make him a "coward", an "intelligent" person, a "handsome" guy, a "good mixer", or a "bashful introvert" depending on the self-concept the group has induced in him.

In predicting or understanding motivation and action it is important to know the salient reference group of the individual. Family, of course, orients the individual towards those values and beliefs which it considers important. The school, the community, and the society at large continue the process of socialization of the individual. However, it is the intimate friendship group which exerts the most influence. Peer groups in school, for example, have been found to have more influence upon the opinions of students than do the teachers;[56] and parents have less influence upon food likes and dislikes than peers.[57] Teen-age peer groups transmit norms concerning modes of dress, dance forms, hair styles, sexual conduct, drinking and other aspects of behavior. Referring to the emergent youth culture among urban adolescents, Boskoff writes:

> Its major values are the intrinsic importance of fun, amusement, recreation; withdrawal from "responsible" activities and concerns, as defined by adults; an emphasis on physical skills, such as complex dancing steps, sports, driving and dismantling automobiles; a love of constant minor novelties in dress, jargon, amusements; the acceptance of conformity to peer group standards; and the emphasis on gregariousness, on direct personal interaction with one's peers, accompanied by an apparent fear of isolation or extended privacy.[58]

"Kids" from "respectable" upper middle class families who opt for a hippie style of life or take to marijuana smoking illustrate the influence of peer groups.

What is often termed as the "generation gap" is not so much a radical difference in the ideology of the old and the new generations as it is a socialization gap. The older generations that grew up in a different social context acquired self-conceptions which were part of their upbringing but which could not be projected on to the modern youth whose social milieu is markedly different. When the older generation fails to perceive the emerging self-conceptions of contemporary youth against the backdrop of their social environment, there is a lag in the rate of socialization and "Never trust anyone over thirty-five" becomes the resounding slogan of the new radical movement (as was the case with Berkeley student movement). Recent trends in communal movements and counter-cultures only point to a fragment of the violent reaction of the youth to the pervasive malady of loneliness and alienation characteristic of modern mass society.

Alienation, that is, deterioration of primary relations. It is over sixty years since Cooley described the primary group based on "intimate association", "moral unity", and "common spirit" such as the family, the neighborhood and the community group of elders. The past decades have seen systematic erosion of primary ties in the wake of expanding urbanization and industrialization which brought forth the complex mass society based on cold, anonymous and formal relationships. Individuals living in today's mass society acquire what Simmel calls the "blasé attitude" which involves antipathy, repulsion, unmerciful matter-of-factness and utmost particularization. This attitude precludes them from interacting with other men as full, emotional and concerned human beings. As Durkheim observed: "A society composed of an infinite number of unorganized individuals that a hypertrophied state is forced to oppress and contain, constitutes a veritable sociological monstrosity."[59] A great volume of literature has come to be accumulated on the crisis of modern society which, in the words of Riesman, is a 'lonely crowd', or according to Homans, "a dust heap of individuals without links to one another."[60] And when the Beatles sang of "all the lonely people" they epitomized these sentiments.

American communities are sometimes called bedroom communities because of their transient nature. One out of every five Americans changes residence each year. Such frequent spatial mobility upsets primary ties and even causes disintegration of some intimate groups. Loss of primary ties develops anxiety and insecurity. "Rent-a-Gent" and "Rent-a-Bird" services furnished by big city travel bureaus to touring business executives, instant computer dating services, and singles' week-ends attest to willingness of lonely people to pay for even one evening of warmth and personal relationship. As

Time magazine reports: "Providing services for singles is obviously a growth industry, as attested to by the proliferation of singles bars, singles apartment projects, singles nights at resorts and computerized dating firms. The high divorce rate, particularly among the middle class, brings many new customers to the field yearly."[61]

The disintegration of primary ties and the waning influence of family and church on the individual are often cited as factors responsible for the alienation of the modern man "felt alone, cut off, unwanted, unloved, unvalued."[62] MacIver defines alienation as "the state of mind of one who has been pulled up by his moral roots, who has no longer any sense of continuity, of folk, of obligation."[63] Feelings of loneliness and lack of belonging are aggravated not only by frequent spatial mobility and the "rat race" but also by changes in the family structure. Home closes down during the day, so to speak, as spouses are at work and children left in the custody of teachers. The disintegration of primary groups manifests itself in a variety of ways.

Waldorf's recent book, *Careers in Dope*, demonstrates that "the experience of a family and particularly its dissolution or breakdown has a strong effect upon a person's subsequent life — the way that he views himself, the kind of adjustment that he makes, the way he raises his children and so forth. The experience of growing up in a broken family stays with most of those who suffer it."[64] Here is Waldorf's startling finding on the relationship between family disorganization and drug addiction.

> Only 1 in 3 (34%) of the women drug addicts reported that they had lived with both parents through their fifteenth year, while almost half of the men reported living with both mother and father until they were 15 years old. By far the majority of women (66%) grew up in homes that were broken by divorce, separation, or death, while considerably fewer (54%) of the males experienced such disorganization. Furthermore, 6% of the males and 13% of the females reported that they had not at any of these ages lived with both parents.

> It was more often the father who was absent from the home — 2 out of every 5 (40%) of the females reported that they had not lived either with a father or a stepfather when they were five, ten, fifteen, or twenty years of age. An additional 13% reported that they had not lived with their mothers at any of these ages, and a still larger number, 23%, reported that they had lived only with their mothers when they were five or ten.[65]

Retreatism of the drug addicts, political activism of the young radicals, escapism of the hippie communes and the deviant life styles of counter-cultures are only manifest expressions of the malady of "all the lonely people". Secondary relationships which demand only partial involvement fail to provide for the fullest expression of man's total self and produce feelings of rootlessness in individuals who then prefer a nostalgic return to things of the past, buy large tracts of land and grow their own staples. Theodore Razak, author of *The Making of Counter Culture*, shows how contemporary politics, technocratic totalitarianism, and the urban sprawl have sickened and disenchanted the young who want an "epochal transformation". And *The Greening of America* by Charles Reich predicts a non-violent revolution that will originate within the individual. Reich argues that many young people drop out because they have become skeptical that "technology makes possible a new life, a new permissiveness, a new freedom, and new expansion of human possibility."[66] On the other hand, prevailing technoculture has upset man's balance with nature, failed to respond to real human needs and to draw the best in the individual, but keeps us from interacting with each other as full, emotional human beings. The result is that many individuals seek to form communal living groups, set up counter cultures, experiment with new utopian communities or return to some fundamental religious expressions.

Many Americans are finding a measure of transcendence in the growing ranks of new religious movements like the Jesus movement or Krishna consciousness movement while others turn to an appreciation of mysticism, particularly Eastern mysticism. The popularity of transcendental meditation, integral Yoga weekend retreats, new live-in communities and the "current fascination of Buddhism in the United States" betray a growing under-current of disillusion about man's ability to transform either himself or his world.[67] Robert S. Ellwood Jr., author of *Religious and Spiritual Groups in Modern America*, believes that there are several million Americans who are either directly involved with Eastern religious practices or are fellow-travellers — students of transcendental meditation, practitioners of yoga or readers of books on mysticism. Some of these new religious movements form what Shils calls "ideological primary groups" characterized by "a very intense solidarity" and "an extreme 'we consciousness'."[68]

The preceding paragraphs show how the deterioration or breakdown of primary groups breeds alienation and insecurity and how men seek to compensate for this loss of personal relationships by returning to nature or new fundamental religious expressions, by forming utopian communities or through the new professional services of the "singles trade."

A CHRONICLE OF "ITCHY FEET": WHAT MADE THE SETTLERS MOVE?[69]

I. THE PROBLEM.

Each major depression brings with it a "back-to-the-land" movement in which jobless people everywhere attempt to find cheaper housing and some land on which they can produce some food-stuffs. During the last great depression the federal government established subsistence homestead projects, rehabilitation and relocation centers to reduce relief loads. Dyess Colony, Arkansas, was one such settlement. The project, conceived by the Congressmen from Arkansas, and publicized by local newspapers throughout the state, was described as a golden opportunity for inexpensive farm ownership, a prospect which naturally held great appeal to the impoverished share-croppers of the area who composed the bulk of the persons wishing to be relocated. The applications for farms in the colony far exceed the 484 families which the colony could accommodate. The chosen few, selected on the basis of financial need and personal dependability insofar as these factors could be determined by a brief questionnaire, were jubilant at being selected and apparently envisioned, on the basis of the newspaper stories, a rosy and prosperous future; the rejected applicants felt that the gates of paradise had been closed to them. And comparatively speaking, the resettled families *did* prosper. Previous to resettlement the families had each year consumed goods and services valued at $667. That figure rose to $895 shortly after resettlement.[70] Value of dwelling rose from $308 which represented the average share-cropper shack which had been "home" to $1500 for a house in the colony upon which payments would be made and which the colonist would eventually own. Most important, these property-less families who for so long had worked other people's land and who now literally faced starvation, had the opportunity to live from the products of land which in time they would own — land in the Mississippi delta, among the richest and most productive lands in the United States, twenty to forty acres of it. The cooperative grocery store, the cooperative hospital with the two-doctor clinic, the lending library with books for both children and adults were among the community services which similarly contributed to a new high in level of living for the new colonists. Nevertheless, in a two-year period 40 per cent of the families left the project. How can this exodus, equalled on none of the dozens of federal projects built during the period, be explained?[71] This is the problem posed for this case.

II. SEQUENCE OF EVENTS.

What confronted the colonists when they arrived at their new homes? They found 13,000 acres of rich but jungle-covered land, cleared only as much as was necessary for the erection of 484 homes and a few community buildings with rather primitive roads providing no more than access to the houses and the buildings. They found a project administrator whose orders concerning project policy came from Washington — an administrator prevented from giving much individual and personal attention to each family because of the simultaneous arrival of 484 families and the actual beginning of the resettlement. In due time they found that the clearing of the jungle and the preparation of the soil, the actual creating of farms out of wilderness, was a back-breaking process. They found that flood waters of the Mississippi sometimes threatened; that sometimes the co-op store did not carry the kind of food items they wanted; that contractual details concerning the purchase of the farm were changed in Washington, and that the new terms were not exactly clear. They found themselves in the midst of contradictory rumors about monthly payments and other matters concerning their very livelihood. They saw that the administrator and other federal personnel who were their only contacts with their "landlord" — the U.S. government — frequently changed, and that a promise or explanation from one would be empty since it in no way obligated his successor. All these and many more conditions prevailed and made up the day-by-day life of the colonists. These were the things that stuck in the memory and were reported to the investigating social scientists who tried to find out what had gone wrong with the project.

III. RELEVANT FACTORS.

It is true, of course, that unexpected and uncontrollable conditions like the change of personnel, or contract alterations, are frustrating and sometimes baffling; also, that hewing farms out of a wilderness, which is back-breaking work at its best, becomes worse when each stroke of it must be contrasted with the rosy, unrealistic preconception which had been held. But it is just as true that pre-colony life on a near-starvation share-cropping basis had its frustrations too, and that colony life offered many material benefits at the same time that it brought at least a normal share of disappointments. The administrator, whose reputation was tied up with the success of the colony, and the remaining colonists — the sixty per cent who had stayed, had done much speculating about the factors which had led to the exodus of almost half of the colony. Each reason given was no doubt a contributing factor and the social scientists examined them all.

Among the factors mentioned were: 1) The habit of moving, locally called "itchy feet." Some thought that life as share-croppers had ingrained into many of the people the expectation that after a short stay they would be moving on. Even when security lay within reach this habit of moving, some thought, was strong enough that some families felt compelled to move. 2) Differences in social ability and popularity. Some speculated that perhaps those who had moved were more likely to have been mal-contents, unable to socialize successfully with their fellow colonists, thus unhappy, and ready to seek new locations where they could try again. 3) Disappointments in the colony. These were frequently interjected as people tried to figure out what had gone wrong. "If it hadn't sounded so good in the newspaper," would say one. "If the government had not changed the time we have to pay," would say another. Without discounting any of these three classes of "reasons for moving" the social scientists examined each claim and established: 1) There was no appreciable difference in "habit of moving" among those who left and those who remained. 2) There was no great difference in the social abilities and the popularity of those who left and those who remained. (Those who stayed did have relatively more children of school age.) 3) All of the other similar resettlement colonies had frustrating circumstances similar to those at Dyess Colony, yet none of them lost such a large number of colonists in such a short time. The "gripes" must be regarded as "straws in the wind."

IV. WHAT THE INVESTIGATORS FOUND.

The clue to the real cause of settler exodus was unwittingly revealed by the administrator. He said, "It seems to me that a lot of folk have to lose a good thing before they learn how to appreciate it. The families who griped the loudest and tried the hardest to get out are the ones right now who are begging to come back. Here at the colony they were sort of cut off from the rest of the world; they kind of forgot that there are troubles elsewhere too. Of course it's against administrative policy to let any come back, but I have a notion that if some of the families who were the worst gripers when they were here, were to be allowed to move back they could teach a good lesson to some of the present colonists who think things are going bad for them." The investigators were immediately interested. Why should the same situation lead to one evaluation *in* the colony and to quite another outside? Why should so many people change their mind about a decision? On the hunch that informal groups within the colony had a great deal to do with the case, sociometric charts were drawn up. It is significant that the informal friendship groups thus revealed also compose predominantly the movers or the non-movers. With each frustrating circumstance such as a change in governmental regulations there was an increase in interaction among the settlers. The movers interacted less with the outside world than the non-movers. Those who kept in close touch with social systems outside the colony tended to have a much more relative and balanced view point concerning life at the colony. Those whose informal group in the colony had "talked things over" to the point of feverish rage and anger left the colony in that spirit. Outside the colony, their informal group was dispersed, group evaluation had nothing to sustain it, and individual evaluation of the situation proved to be quite different than the old group evaluation back at the colony. That there was this difference was substantiated by many letters received by the administration asking for reinstatement in the colony.

The sociologist sees in the Dyess Colony situation many currents and cross-currents which cannot be examined here. Dominant, however, are the two systems, the government and the colonists. The first had all the Gesellschaft-like formalism which bureaucracy — be it the public or private kind — brings in its wake. Few decisions could be made with personal and particularistic considerations in mind. Policy had to be broad enough and general enough to apply to the average situation, and each person affected had to do some of the adjusting to what that policy called for. The second, essentially an informal Gemeinschaft-like system, was composed of two subsystems of the most informal and intimate nature, the groupings of which were in great part fortuitous. Movers, non-movers; popular, less popular; industrious, less industrious; the younger, the older — all of these categories as bases for friendship patterns were superceded by a frontier situation. "Whom did you live near when you came to the colony?" "Was there a lake of mud between you and your neighbor across the road?" "A high dry path to the neighbor who lived back of you?" These were the factors which determined the friendship groups. "Did you visit with and write to the folks you knew outside the colony?" "Did your intimate neighbors have outside contacts too?" This circumstance determined to a large extent what people thought of the local situation. Such were the chance and near-chance factors which determined membership in Group A (the leavers) or Group B (the stayers). And if chance nudged the family into one group the chances were that it would move; if into the other group, chances were that it would stay.

V. THE OUTCOME.

People *did* stay; sixty per cent of the original settlers. And many others were anxious to take the place of those who had left. The coming of new colonists, the trading of farms, improved roads and transportation resulted in a re-arrangement of the informal groupings, so that small social systems with the closed geographical "pocket" disappeared. Intimate friendship groups might now contain settlers from all parts of the colony. Each part of the colony might have within it parts of a dozen or so of intimate friendship groups forming a complicated mosaic of relations throughout the whole colony with few "location" or "pocket" cores which had at first existed.

As the years passed and the federal government finally withdrew, selling its equity, arrangements which prevail in rural America generally replaced the original bureaucratic structure of the colony. The development of community facilities, the clearing of the land, the settlement to permanent families was finished. The process, compressed in time to a few short years, resembled in a way the decades in the history of the country in which settlers carved homes, farms and communities out of the wilderness. Should circumstances in the future require that re-location and re-settlement again be provided the details no doubt will differ, but it is fairly safe to predict that the evaluation and decision of the individual will bear the marks of the vitality and influence of his small primary friendship group.

NOTES

1. Charles H. Cooley, *Social Organization* (New York: Charles Scribner's Sons, 1909), p. 23.

2. Paul F. Lazarsfeld, Bernard Berelson, and Hazel Gaudet, *The People's Choice* (New York: Columbia University Press, 1948). See also Elihu Katz and Paul F. Lazarsfeld, *Personal Influence* (New York: Free Press, 1955).

3. Joseph A. Precker, "Similarity of Valuings as a Factor in Selection of Peers and Near-Authority Figures," *Journal of Abnormal and Social Psychology*, 47, (1952), pp. 406-414.

4. Georg Simmel, *Sociology*, translated and edited with introduction by Kurt H. Wolff, (Glencoe, Illinois: The Free Press, 1950), pp. 307-8.

5. Ibid., pp. 325-6.

6. Gerald D. Suttles, *The Social Order of the Slum* (Chicago: The University of Chicago Press, 1970), p. 173.

7. Leon Festinger, Henry W. Riecken and Stanley Schacter, *When Prophecy Fails* (Minneapolis: University of Minnesota Press), 1956.

8. Charles H. Cooley, *Two Major Works: Social Organization*, and *Human Nature and the Social Order* (Glencoe, Illinois: The Free Press, 1956), p. 28.

9. Robert Bierstedt, *The Social Order*, 3rd ed. (New York: McGraw-Hill, 1970), pp. 290-294.

10. William Foote Whyte, *Street Corner Society*, 2nd ed. (Chicago: The University of Chicago Press, 1955), p. 107.

11. Ibid., p. 108.

12. Matilda White Riley and John W. Riley, Jr. "A Sociological Approach to Communications Research", *Public Opinion Quarterly*, 15, (1951), pp. 445-460.

13. Cooley, op. cit., p. 33.

14. Edward H. Shils and Morris Jonowitz, "Cohesion and Disintegration in the Wehrmacht in World War II", *Public Opinion Quarterly*, 12, (Summer, 1947), pp. 280-315. Reprinted in Ronald Freedman et al., *Principles of Sociology* (New York: Henry Holt and Co. 1956), pp. 96-105.

15. Roger Little, "A Study of the relationship between collective solidarity and combat role performance," Ph.D. dissertation, Department of Sociology and Anthropology, East Lansing: Michigan State University, 1955).

16. Eugene Kinkenad, "A Study of Something New in History", *The New Yorker*, (October 26, 1957), pp. 114.

17. Ibid., p. 154.

18. Cooley, op. cit., pp. 23-24.

19. Russell R. Dynes, Alfred C. Clarke, and Simon Dinitz, "Levels of Occupational Aspiration: Some Aspects of Family Experience as a Variable," *American Sociological Review*, 21, (April, 1956), pp. 212-215.

20. Suttles, op. cit., p. 184.

21. Peter M. Blau. "Co-operation and Competition in a Bureaucracy," *American Journal of Sociology*, 59, (May 1954), pp. 530-535.

22. As recounted to the senior author by a respondent drawing from teen-age reminiscences.

23. Cooley, op. cit., p. 29.

24. F.J. Roethlisberger and W.J. Dickson, *Management and the Worker* (Cambridge, Mass.: Harvard University Press), 1939.

25. Suttles, op. cit., pp. 185-186.

26. Conrad M. Arensberg, *The Irish Countryman* (New York: The Macmillan Co., 1937), p. 125ff. See a systematic analysis of this in Charles P. Loomis and J. Allan Beegle, *Rural Sociology: The Strategy of Change* (Englewood Cliffs: Prentice-Hall, 1957), pp. 112. See also Charles Loomis and J.A. Beegle *A Strategy for Rural Change*, (New York: Schenkman, 1975), pp.110ff. (Distributed by Halsted.)

27. Simmel, op. cit., p. 285.

28. Robert K. Merton and Alice Kitt, "Contributions to the Theory of Reference Group Behavior," in Merton and Lazarsfeld, eds., *Continuities in Social Research* (Glencoe, Ill.: Free Press, 1950).

29. Whyte, op. cit., p. 257.

30. James F. Short, Jr. and Fred L. Strodtbeck, "The Response of Gang Leaders to Status Threats: An Observation on Group Process and Delinquent Behavior," *American Journal of Sociology*, 68, (March 1963), pp. 571-579.

31. Leon Festinger, Stanley Schater and Kurt Back, *Social Pressures in Informal Groups: A Study of Human Factors in Housing* (New York: Harper and Brothers, 1950), p. 165.

32. Muzafer Sherif, "A Study of Some Social Factors in Perception," *Archives of Psychology*, 27, (1935).

33. Solomon E. Asch, *Social Psychology* (New York: Prentice-Hall, 1952).

34. Katz and Lazarsfeld, op. cit., pp. 74-81.

35. Charles H. Cooley, "Competition and Social Placement," in Borgatta and Myer, eds., *Sociological Theory* (New York: Alfred Knopf, 1956), p. 172.

36. Alvin Boskoff, *The Sociology of Urban Regions*, 2nd. ed. (New York: Appleton-Century-Crofts. 1970), p. 165.

37. Kingsley Davis, *Human Society* (New York: The Macmillan Co., 1949), pp. 289-301.

38. Charles P. Loomis and J. Allan Beegle, op. cit., p. 110 and 111. Here studies by several authors which support the above generalizations are summarized.

39. Festinger, Schachter, and Back, op. cit., p. 10.

40. Ibid., p. 10.

41. Boskoff, op. cit., pp. 162-70.

42. Davis, op. cit., p. 293.

43. Ibid., p. 293.

44. Loomis, *Social Systems*, op. cit., Essay 3.

45. Raymond A. Bauer and David B. Gleicher, "Word-of-Mouth Communication in the Soviet Union," *Public Opinion Quarterly*, (Fall, 1953), pp. 299-301.

46. Robert F. Bales, *Interaction Process Analysis* (Cambridge: Addison-Wesley, 1951). See also his *Personality and Interpersonal Bahavior* (New York: Holt Rinehart and Winston, 1970).

47. Katz and Lazarsfeld, op. cit., p. 85.

48. Erving Goffman, "Embarrassment and Social Organization," *American Journal of Sociology*, 62, (Nov. 1956), p. 269.

49. Wayne Gordon, *The Social System of the High School*. (Glencoe, Ill: Free Press, 1957), p. 110.

50. Murray B. Seidler and M. Jerome Ravitz, "A Jewish Peer Group", *American Journal of Sociology*, 61, (July 1955), p. 13.

51. Wendell Bell and Marion D. Boot, "Urban Neighborhoods and Informal Social Relations," *American Journal of Sociology*, 62, (January 1957), p. 398.

52. Robert Dubin, *Human Relations in Administration* (New York: Prentice-Hall, 1951), p. 57.

53. Alex Inkeles, *Public Opinion in Soviet Russia* (Cambridge, Mass.: Harvard University Press, 1950), cited in Katz and Lazarsfeld, op. cit., p. 122.

54. Cooley, op. cit., p. 5.

55. George H. Mead, *Mind, Self and Society* (Chicago: The University of Chicago Press, 1934), pp. 173-75.

56. Ruth W. Beranda, *The Influence of the Group on the Judgments of Children* (New York: Columbia University Press, 1950).

57. Karl Duncker, "Experimental Modifications of Children's Food Preferences Through Social Suggestion", *Journal of Abnormal and Social Psychology*, 33, pp. 489-507.

58. Boskoff, op. cit., p. 166.

59. Emile Durkheim, *The Division of Labor in Society*, trans. by George Simpson, (New York: Free Press, 1947), Preface to 2nd ed., p. 28.

60. George C. Homans, *The Human Group* (New York: Harcourt, 1950), p. 133.

61. *Time*, (April 9, 1973), p. 67.

62. Harold Lasswell, "The Threat to Privacy", in Robert MacIver, ed., *Conflict of Loyalties* (New York: Macmillan, 1952).

63. Robert M. MacIver, *The Ramparts We Guard* (New York: Macmillan, 1950), pp. 84-92.

64. Dan Waldorf, *Careers in Dope* (Englewood Cliffs, N.J.: Prentice-Hall, 1973), p. 162.

65. Ibid., p. 163.

66. Charles A. Reich, *The Greening of America* (New York: Random House, 1970), p. 218.

67. *Time*, (April 9, 1973), pp. 90-93.

68. Edward Shils, "Primordial, Personal, Sacred and Civil Ties", *British Journal of Sociology*, 7, (June, 1957), p. 138.

69. For the original analyses upon which this case is based see Charles P. Loomis, *Studies of Rural Social Organization in the United States, Latin America, and Germany* (East Lansing, Michigan: State College Book Store, 1945), Chapter 2; and "Sociometrics and the Study of New Rural Communities", *Sociometry*, 2, (January, 1939).

70. Charles P. Loomis and Dwight M. Davidson, *Standards of Living of the Residents of Seven Rural Resettlement Communities* (Washington, D.C.: U.S.D.A. Social Research Report No. 11, 1938).

71. For descriptions and analyses of these colonies see Charles P. Loomis, op. cit., and Russell Lord, Paul H. Johnstone, et al., *A Place on Earth: A Critical Appraisal of Subsistence Homesteads* (Washington, D.C.: U.S.D.A., 1942).

Chapter **9**

The Mexican American Community*

INTRODUCTION

Whether or not there exists a Mexican American community in the United States depends to some extent on what is meant by the word "community." If the community is thought of as a social entity larger than the family but smaller than such units as the nation or its political subdivisions such as states to which people belong, certainly there is a Mexican American community and there is also a black community. Nevertheless, there is disagreement concerning the size and nature of the social unit made up of the people in the United States who are of Mexican descent. In fact some would maintain that there are several quite distinct Mexican American groupings or communities. Attention has been called to the fact that Spanish-speaking peoples and their descendents in Northern New Mexico and Southern Colorado, whose ancestors settled long before either the United States or Mexico existed as nations, are culturally and socially different from more recent arrivals of Mexican origin living in South Texas and other places. Although the scene is changing rapidly there are substantial differences in the manner in which people of Spanish-speaking background identify themselves. Thus some younger more activist persons want to be known as Chicanos, a word which was not much used until recently. Some others prefer not to be known as Chicanos. Some prefer to be known as Mexican Americans, some as Spanish Americans, etc. In fact the ethnic designations preferred by people of Mexican descent has varied through time and region.[1]

It is a theme of the present chapter that there is an emerging community at present centered in Southwestern United States

*By Charles P. Loomis and Anthony Gary Dworkin

composed of peoples who came there from Mexico or the area which is now Mexico and that eventually there will emerge consensus on the designation or title by which they prefer to be known. In a sense we are arguing that the Mexican American community is in the process of being born. In data collected by the junior author, it has been shown that for groups of Mexican Americans who are geographically more disparate, the present Chicano Movement has tended to sensitize members of the Mexican American communities to a common sense of identity, such that greater ideological and attitudinal similarities exist between them now than ever before.

Since it is claimed that in the United States various immigrant communities have died, we may ask, "Will the Mexican American community eventually die?" The other immigrant communities have "died" as a result of assimilation into the larger Anglo society. In a sense there have been considerable pressures upon Mexican Americans to do likewise. Community death involves the loss of a cultural heritage, usually through the loss of an ability to speak the language of the community, a loss of other culturally-bounded social institutions, including religion, belief system, and social structure, and the loss of the individual's identity as a member of the community. Thus when the symbols of the community and the consciousness of the community wane, the community approaches death.

The culture of the dominant society (Anglo society in this case) often overwhelms that of the minority community. Political, legal, and social institutions demand obedience to the language, norms, values, and orientations of the dominant society and frequently punished for participation in the minority culture. Historically the key to success in American society (and in most other numerically and politically dominant societies) has been for the minority group member to renounce his own culture and "assimilate" into the larger society. Public school teachers often punished minority children for speaking their native language on the school grounds. Those individuals who dressed differently, believed in different values, etc., were frequently the subjects of overt discrimination, and more recently more covert exclusion. It is not surprising then to learn that many middle class Mexican Americans cannot speak Spanish; their children cannot speak Spanish; and they have moved out of Mexican American neighborhoods into communities where Spanish is not understood. As one Mexican American lawyer, who had changed his name from Hernandez to Henderson, moved into an Anglo neighborhood, and changed his religion from Catholic to Episcopal once recounted, "To be Mexican is to be poor. I do not want to bequeath that kind of heritage to my children."[2] Thus, it was not uncommon in the two decades after World War II for middle class Mexican Americans to become middle class Anglo Americans — in name, culture, identity, and beliefs — the key elements which perpetuate the presence of a community.

Despite these signs of community "death" there are other indicators which suggest that there is a growing pride in being a Mexican American. Recently Dworkin and Eckberg[3] reported that although many Mexican Americans disavowed the term Chicano, the vast majority endorsed support for "brown power," pride in being of Mexican heritage, and admiration for Mexican American leaders, including activists.

Despite the pressures on Mexican Americans which have previously forced the assimilation and demise of immigrant communities such as those of the Germans, Irish, Poles, Italians, Japanese, etc., there are some significant differences present in the Mexican American community. Minority communities survive to the extent to which they provide rewards and support functional entities of their members. Discrimination on the part of the dominant society notwithstanding, minority or immigrant communities frequently survived as long as the members of the community defined their sojourn in the United States as transitory. Italians were less likely to assimilate than Germans in the earlier part of this century not only because of the relatively later arrival of the former, but because the Italians intended to live in the United States only as long as it was necessary in order to make their fortunes and then return to Italy, whereas the Germans had no such expectation.

American expatriots living abroad often gather together in "American" enclaves, resist adopting the dominant culture of the country in which they live, and treat the native population as "foreigners," mainly because they foresee a time in the future when they may return to the United States. This is certainly true of those expatriots living in Europe, Mexico, and Australia. As long as it is possible to return to one's native land, or as long as one shares a geographic propinquity with the land of one's heritage, then pressures for assimilation into the dominant Anglo society will be countered by pressures to maintain the minority culture. As long as Mexico and the United States exist as separate entities there will be forces which maintain the existence of a Mexican American community. In fact, we may also contend with support from data presented under *Territoriality* below that the closer the Mexican American community is to the U.S.-Mexican border, the greater the probability that the community will retain Mexican cultural elements. It is for that reason that in the border states (California, Texas, New Mexico,

Arizona, and Colorado) the influence of Mexico on Mexican American communities is the greatest and pressures to exert the Mexican heritage loom largest against the pressures for assimilation imposed by the Anglo community.

But Mexican American culture and the Mexican American community is not an isomorphism with Mexican culture and the Mexican community in Mexico. In his dynamic *Chicano Manifesto*, Armendo Rendon[4] noted that Chicano or Mexican American culture is a hybrid not just of Spanish and Indian heritages as in the case of Mexico, but of Anglo heritages as well. Thus the Anglo and his institutions are in fact part of the synthesis which makes up modern Mexican Americans. *Pachuchismo*, or the language of the barrios, is a merger of Spanish and English, and is often not unaerstood in Mexico. Thus the Mexican American community must be viewed as a hybrid, a marginal culture, providing for its members an identity, a value system, a manner of interpreting the exegencies of social life, which is at once part of the greater American society, part of the Mexican society South of the Border, and something of a uniqueness of its own. Gist and Dworkin[5] identified it as such and noted the relative isolation needed to convert the psychologically devastating aspects of marginality into the solidifying and nurturing aspects of a separate marginal culture. Marginal cultures, cultures which emerge when people who are hybrids of two or more cultures and integrated fully into neither, are always in transition. Whether the culture of the Mexican American community will tend to become more like that of the United States, more like that of Mexico or become distinctly different from both, we cannot know with any precision now. We hope in the discussion to follow to bring various possibilities under consideration. Obviously the relations of Mexico and the United States as these are played out in the arena of the border and world generally will have great importance for the future of the Mexican American community.

Identifying the Mexican American Community: A Demographic Problem. In attempting to determine how many Mexican Americans live in the United States we encounter a problem in that the U.S. Census does not distinguish between Mexican Americans and other Spanish-speaking groups. The Census indicates that there are approximately 9.25 million individuals of Spanish surname; this of course includes Puerto Ricans, Cubans, Latin Americans of countries other than Mexico, Spaniards, and of course Mexican Americans. It does not include, however, those middle class Mexican Americans who have chosen to pass and have changed their names, nor does it include Mexican American women who have married men without

Spanish surnames. Most Mexican Americans live in the five Border States of the Southwest, and a total of 4.7 million individuals in these states have Spanish surnames — 2.2 million in California, 1.7 million in Texas, and the balance divided among Arizona, New Mexico, and Colorado. We can reduce the error in estimating the number of Mexican Americans in the Southwest by deleting all non-Whites from the category, as the Census and many of the courts have not accorded non-white status to Mexican Americans despite petitions by many Chicanos. This gives us a total of 4.5 million persons of Spanish surname. Approximately 3.8 million of these individuals are native born (U.S. born), while only .7 million are foreign born. About 570,000 of the foreign born report births in Mexico, while 158,000 report other locations or fail to indicate a country of birth.

One additional difficulty in attempting to estimate the total number of Mexican Americans is that even if the Census had asked for ethnicity, with the multitude of terms used by Mexican Americas to describe themselves, we would be no better off in using some of the more common terms than in attempting to figure from Spanish surname, then controlling by white, and then by reported Mexican parentage or born in Mexico. We are still left with something of a large standard error of estimate. Presented below is a fair approximation of the numbers:

FIGURE 1

	Spanish surname	Mexican Parentage Born in Mexico
Foreign born (1st generation)	727,961 (16.0%)	570,040
Native born of foreign of mixed parentage (2nd generation)	1,303,258 (28.7%)	1,119,550
Native born of native born parentage (3rd or more generation)	2,514,478 (55.3%)	(?) Mexican ancestry
TOTAL	4,514,478	

Source: 1970 Census of Population, Subject Reports: Persons of Spanish-surname. PC(2)-10. (Washington, D.C.: U.S. Department of Commerce, Bureau of The Census, 1973).

The popular image held by Anglos of the Mexican Americans is that they are rural people who return to Mexico once the harvests are over. This is more of a stereotype than a reality today, as nearly 85 per cent of all Mexican Americans are native born U.S. citizens and 87 per cent live in urban areas as of 1970.

Despite the large influx of Anglos to the Southwest, the percentage of Mexican Americans in the Southwest has increased as a percentage of the total population. In 1950, 10.8 per cent of the persons in the five Border States were of Spanish surname. The figure climbed to 12.0 per cent in 1960, and to 12.9 per cent in 1970. Thus, Spanish surname persons are increasing in numbers more rapidly than non-Spanish surname individuals, even though there have been substantial migrations of Anglos to the newer cities of the region over the past twenty years. Since native born Mexican Americans represent the vast majority of all Spanish-surname people in the Southwest, restrictions have existed on the immigration of Mexicans to the United States, and most Mexican Americans live in the Southwest, we may conclude that the increase in the Spanish surname population is principally due to natural increases. Communities in Mexico, typically with very high population fertility and replacement rates are linked in many ways to the Mexican American Community of the United States. The latter contains counties which also have very high fertility and replacement rates. Comparable differences in fertility and replacement rates in the Southwestern United States would suggest that the size and importance of the Mexican American community will increase. It is not at all visionary to foresee a Southwestern United States dominated by what we are here identifying as the Mexican American community.

SOCIO-CULTURAL VALUES AND ATTITUDES OF MEXICAN AMERICANS

In the sections which follow attention will be focused on a comparative analysis of the socio-cultural activities, values and attitudes of Mexican Americans, with special attention given to those which may promote boundary maintenance and solidarity within as well as foster linkages outside the Mexican American community. For each separate theme and heading, findings from survey data for which the senior author is primarily responsible will be presented. Also comparable data from other studies will be brought in for comparative purposes.

Included in the other studies are three stratified random samples of Mexican Americans and Anglo Americans collected by the junior author in 1963, 1967-68, and 1971. The purpose of the three samplings was to monitor stereotype changes over time in the Mexican American and Anglo American communities. Fishman[6] and Dworkin and Eckberg[7] have demonstrated the functional linkage between changes in stereotype and changes in the relationship between stereotyper and the target (stereotyped) group. The 1963 sample reflects a time period prior to the rise of the most recent Chicano Movement; the 1967-68 sample was collected during the emergence of the movement; and the 1971 sample represents a time period after the full public awareness of the movement.

The 1963 sample consists of 174 Chicanos and 328 Anglos randomly drawn from college and junior college campuses and representative census tracts throughout Los Angeles County. The 1967-68 sample was drawn from Denver and Los Angeles County and represented a random sample stratified by sex, ethnicity, and education (college and non-college). A total of 131 Chicanos and 200 Anglos were in that sample. Finally, the 1971 sample was drawn from the *barrios* and neighborhoods as well as college campuses in Los Angeles, Kansas City, Kansas, and Kansas City, Missouri. The 1971 sample consisted of 227 Chicanos and 251 Anglos.

With each sample stereotypes were enumerated using an open-ended format which allows the Mexican Americans to articulate their own descriptions, rather than limiting them to pre-determined check-list items with their inherent methodological problems. In some of the 1963 samples and in all cases in the 1967-68 and 1971 samples, interviewers who administered the schedules were matched with the subjects not only by ethnicity, but by age and sex as well. The subjects involved in the open ended format reported here were all between the ages of 18 and 30 for the samplings.

In Figure 2 we present the most frequently mentioned stereotypes and self-images collected during the three sampling periods. The table is presented in four parts: Anglo self-images, Anglo images of Mexican Americans, Mexican American images of Anglos, and Mexican American self-images. Within each part are displayed the number and percentage of individuals endorsing a given image at each of the three sampling periods. We shall continually refer to these images in our ensuing discussion.

It should be noted that there was a strong tendency across the sampling periods for the percentage of respondents endorsing given stereotypes to change. Of the 106 different stereotypes free associated by the subjects, statistically significant changes in the percentage of endorsement were found for 67 of the images. At this point it may be useful to give a summary of the Figure. An inspection of the percentages indicates that there is no one curve of change in the data. Both rising and falling lines emerged, as did curvilinear lines of change. There was evidence, however, that the "old," prejudicial stereotypes regarding Chicanos, as held by Anglos, were dropping greatly. Examples abound. Such images as "clannish," "dirty,"

"greasy," "low intelligence," "lazy," and "dark skin" showed continual drops in percentage of endorsement while "emotional,"
"Catholics," "religious," and "broken homes" showed unsustained
drops. The stereotypes receiving the greatest percentage of endorsement in the first testing showed the greatest drop in percentage of
endorsement.[8]

While some stereotypes dropped sufficiently in endorsement to
fall from our list of stereotypes, new stereotypes emerged to replace
them. Thus, "fat," "immoral," and "artistic" and "greasy" appear to
no longer be closely associated with the group "Mexican-Americans."
At the same time, two terms which were mentioned by *no* Anglos in
the original study, "discriminated against" and "militant" have come
to be endorsed by 16.3 and 11.6 per cent of respondents respectively.

Chicano's autostereotypes have undergone less apparent change
than has the Anglo's view of him. Only four words fell significantly
from the original sample's percentage of endorsements. These were
"uneducated," "Catholics," "large families," and "pessimistic." Seven
words *rose* in endorsement, however, all of which can be seen as tying
into a theme of self-worth and *group* achievement. The specific terms
are: proud, ambitious, intelligent, militant, aggressive, brown and
superior. "Superior," especially, is interesting in that it was endorsed
by no one in the 1963 sample.

Along with the seeming upgrading in the image of the Chicano
comes a more disparaging view of the Anglo by both groups. Most
images of Anglos held by Chicanos changed significantly, and some
strong themes emerged. Anglo "personality-characteristics," for
example, especially those which might become important in intergroup relations, changed negatively. Thus, endorsements of bigoted,
greedy, prejudiced, and boastful increased, while endorsement of
friendly, well-mannered, and humanitarian dropped across time.

For Anglos, too, the view of the generalized "Anglo" has changed.
"Bigoted" and "prejudiced" have increased in endorsement, while
"friendly," and "civic-minded" have dropped. Several other of what
might be considered positive traits have dropped also: active,
hard-working, well-dressed, etc., have all dropped greatly in per cent
of endorsement.

Stereotypes are relational and comparative statements. They
tell us not only what the stereotyper thinks about the target group;
they tell us what the stereotyper thinks about himself. It is therefore
significant that we note a growing convergence between the Chicano
self-stereotype and stereotypes of Anglos, as well as the Anglo
self-stereotypes and stereotypes of Chicanos. With each sampling,
Chicanos, for example, are seen as continually more intelligent,

FIGURE 2

Itemization of Stereotypes Across Time and Targets

Anglo Subjects/Anglo Targets

Image	1963 1 = 328		1967-68 N = 200		1971-72 N = 251	
	n	%	n	%	n	%
Well educated	197	60.06	40	20.00	61	24.30
Intelligent	173	52.74	49	24.50	70	27.89
Fair skin	139	42.38	13	6.50	18	7.17
Ambitious	126	38.41	66	33.00	69	27.47
Good family life	103	31.40	11	5.50	33	13.15
High economic level	93	28.35	37	18.50	44	17.53
Religious	89	27.13	60	30.00	68	27.09
Education	82	25.00	20	10.00	42	16.73
Hard working	77	23.47	11	5.50	21	8.36
Well dressed	69	21.03	21	10.50	30	11.95
Neat	68	20.73	15	7.50	14	5.58
Active	67	20.42	13	6.50	20	7.97
Clean appearance	66	20.12	20	10.00	31	12.35
Civic minded	64	19.51	9	4.50	7	2.79
Social	59	17.99	17	8.50	34	13.54
Friendly	55	16.77	19	9.50	25	9.96
Athletic	51	15.55	16	8.00	24	9.56
Conservative	51	15.55	14	7.00	20	7.97
Reserved emotions	19	14.94	9	4.50	14	5.58
Tense and anxious	40	12.19	6	3.00	18	7.17
Not religious	35	10.67	15	7.50	26	10.36
Average	34	10.36	10	5.00	16	6.37
Snob	30	9.15	10	5.00	39	15.54
Society conscious	26	7.93	10	5.00	16	6.37
Tall	26	7.93	8	4.00	11	4.38
Clannish	25	7.62	13	6.50	27	10.75
Bigoted	23	7.01	28	14.00	45	17.93
Prejudiced	19	5.79	24	12.00	73	29.08
Mature	17	5.18	21	10.50	18	7.19
Poor family life	16	4.88	12	6.00	21	8.36

Chicano Subjects/Anglo Targets

Image	1963 N = 174		1967-68 N = 131		1971-72 N = 227	
	n	%	n	%	n	%
Friendly	106	60.92	12	9.16	21	9.25
Light complexioned	91	52.30	11	8.40	28	12.33
Intelligent	89	51.15	25	19.08	37	16.30
Well educated	84	48.28	33	25.20	51	22.46
Ambitious	65	37.35	13	9.92	16	11.45
Well dressed	51	29.31	13	9.92	22	9.70

High economic level	47	27.01	38	29.00	59	26.00
High social position	44	25.29	16	12.21	42	18.50
Well mannered	43	24.71	13	9.92	10	4.40
Religious	41	23.56	8	6.10	15	6.61
Athletic	34	19.54	14	10.68	23	10.13
Superiority	34	19.54	28	21.37	64	28.19
Snob	30	17.24	9	6.87	19	8.37
Humanitarian	29	16.66	10	8.40	4	1.76
Social	27	15.52	9	6.87	23	10.13
Average social position	18	10.34	11	8.40	26	11.45
Prejudiced	16	9.20	15	11.45	48	21.14
Average intelligence	15	8.62	9	6.87	13	5.73
Good family life	15	8.62	9	6.87	16	7.05
Greedy	14	8.05	16	12.21	41	18.06
Poor family life	12	6.90	8	6.10	20	8.81
Untrustworthy	12	6.90	7	5.34	22	9.70
Boastful	9	5.17	18	13.74	30	13.21
Sloppy	9	5.17	7	5.34	8	3.52
Bigoted	8	4.60	22	16.80	50	22.02

Anglo Subjects/Chicano Targets

Image	1963 N = 328		1967-68 N = 200		1971-72 N = 251	
	n	%	n	%	n	%
Dark skin	272	82.92	61	30.50	70	27.89
Uneducated	213	64.94	66	33.00	102	46.64
Catholics	206	62.80	46	23.00	65	65.89
Religious	184	56.10	45	22.50	79	31.47
Lazy	157	47.86	65	32.50	47	18.72
Poor	151	46.03	84	42.00	118	47.01
Greasy	131	39.94	11	5.50	12	4.78
Low intelligence	115	35.06	37	18.50	36	14.34
Dirty	108	32.93	16	8.00	13	5.18
Large families	101	30.80	50	25.00	60	23.90
Emotional	92	28.05	17	8.50	22	8.76
Dress loud	75	22.86	45	22.50	48	19.12
Friendly	74	22.56	12	6.00	54	21.51
Speak Spanish	69	21.03	20	10.00	49	19.52
Clannish	63	19.21	18	9.00	22	8.76
Broken homes	57	17.38	14	7.00	23	9.16
Dress sloppy	50	15.24	32	16.00	37	14.74
Dark hair	49	14.94	24	12.00	33	13.15
Happy people	47	14.33	10	5.00	30	11.95
Close family life	45	13.72	26	13.00	70	27.89
Accent	36	10.97	20	10.00	27	10.75
Artistic	21	6.40	7	3.50	10	3.98
Athletic	20	6.10	4	2.00	17	6.77
Immoral	18	5.49	3	4.00	9	3.58
Fat	17	5.18	2	1.00	4	1.59
Discriminated against	0	0	9	4.50	41	16.33
Militant	0	0	6	3.00	29	11.55

FIGURE 2 (Continued)

Itemization of Stereotypes Across Time and Targets

Chicano Subjects/Chicano Targets

Image	1963 N = 174		1967-68 N = 131		1971-72 N = 227	
	n	%	n	%	n	%
Religious	65	37.35	49	37.40	70	30.84
Friendly	61	35.05	40	30.53	74	32.60
Uneducated	53	30.46	24	18.32	41	18.06
Catholics	51	29.31	15	11.45	28	12.33
Lazy	49	28.16	29	22.14	42	18.50
Poor	48	27.58	27	20.61	53	23.35
Large families	47	27.01	13	13.74	30	13.21
Hardworking	36	20.69	26	19.85	59	25.99
Pessimistic	33	18.96	11	8.39	20	8.81
Proud	31	17.81	34	25.95	86	37.88
Shy	27	15.52	15	11.45	25	11.01
Intelligent	25	14.37	22	16.79	67	29.51
Emotional	23	13.22	20	15.27	39	17.18
Good family life	20	11.50	14	10.69	35	15.42
Close family life	19	10.92	15	11.45	33	14.54
Ambitious	14	8.05	12	9.16	42	18.50
Broken homes	14	8.05	11	8.39	18	7.93
Brown	13	7.47	11	8.39	80	35.24
Party goers	12	6.90	10	7.63	11	4.84
Humorous	10	5.75	8	6.10	14	6.17
Average intelligence	9	5.17	10	7.63	22	9.70
Aggressive	6	3.45	8	6.10	24	10.57
Militant	1	.57	5	3.81	28	12.33
Superior	0	0	5	3.81	17	7.49

Anglos as less so. Anglos are less clean, and Chicanos less "dirty." Anglo-directed "well-educated" drops as does Chicano-directed "uneducated."

Using the Mexican American sample as a focus, five universes of citizens in Mexico and the United States were sampled by the senior author. From these five universes, modified probability samples of informants 21 years of age and over were drawn. The respective universes were: a) the general public of the United States, b) rural persons in Michigan, c) rural Mexicans, d) urban Mexicans, and e) Mexican-Americans in the Southwest. Sampling details for all the universes are presented elsewhere.[9] It may be of interest to note that the data for what we are calling the Mexican American Community were drawn by the Gallup Organization for California, Arizona, Texas, New Mexico and Colorado. From these states 30 counties were selected by random sampling procedures with restrictions calculated to increase the probability of selection determined by the percentage of Spanish-surname people in the counties as enumerated in the 1960 census. In each of the 30 counties four informants were drawn in a manner calculated to make the proportion of rural and urban informants in the sample approximately the same as that determined by the number of Spanish-surname people designated in the 1960 census enumeration. From the study based upon the data from these samples those parts most pertinent for the analysis of the socio-cultural activities, values and attitudes of the Mexican American Community were used.

Processes of boundary maintenance and systemic linkage in system analysis. For a meaningful discussion of the sociological issues which attend the origin, development and death of pluralities whether these be communities, societies or a possible one world, we find the concepts *systemic linkage* and *boundary maintenance* useful. Systemic linkage is the process whereby the actors composing at least two organizations or systems function as a single unit in some respects and on some occasions. Marriage may be considered as a prototype of systemic linkage. Through it two families of orientation are united to form a family of procreation. Some of the sufficient and necessary conditions for successful marriages and families of procreation may be the same as those required if a community, society, a nation or humanity are to become integrated wholes composed of interlinked units or subsystems. As Arnold Toynbee in *One World and India* stated emphatically, "we are each other's keepers . . . we ought to live with each other like members of a single family."[10] In a world such as we now have in which a self-selected unit or group may destroy all others through exchange of nuclear or other devices such a statement takes on added meaning.

Through boundary maintenance, the other process employed throughout this chapter, actors of a system preserve the system's identity and power. For any social unit boundary maintenance of the system itself is important and necessary. Typically larger systems, such as a society or even a community are composed of subsystems, such as families, industrial organizations, government bureaus and schools, each of which manifests a certain amount of boundary maintenance. The extent and type of boundary maintenance of the subsystem and its relation to other subsystems and to the larger system is indeed important for the integration, existence, or disintegration of the whole.

As we view the Mexican American Community we shall want to note how the two processes of boundary maintenance and systemic linkage are kept in balance. On the one hand members may gain self-assurance and respect from a solidary community with which they identify. On the other hand tolerance, respect and understanding for representatives of the national communities of the countries to which the solidary community is linked may promote advantages for all.

FIGURE 3

Rejection Rates in Percentages

Social distance responses: A — relatives by marriage whom the informants would prefer not to have; B — neighbors whom the informants would prefer not to have; C — co-workers whom the informants would prefer not to have; and D — citizens by naturalization whom the informants would prefer not to have. (Based on the following numbers of interviews reading from the left column to the right: 158, 1357, 1528, 306, 105, 1126 and 288.)

Category	Negroes	Whites***	United States			Mexico	
			General Public	Rural Michigan	Spanish-Speaking	Urban	Rural
A. Relatives by Marriage							
Protestants	2.6	5.9	5.7	3.0	31.0	67.7	74.9
Catholics	7.9	19.3	17.4	10.9	3.6	1.8	2.1
Jews	25.8	31.7	30.7	31.0	34.7	70.6	81.5
Negroes	3.3	89.4	77.1	87.3	62.8	59.0	78.4
Whites*	25.8	1.4	4.2	.6	3.8	22.6	39.0
Mexicans*	25.2	59.7	55.1	58.9	1.0	—	—
North Americans**	—	—	—	—	—	36.0	56.1
Indians speaking Spanish**	—	—	—	—	—	27.1	31.4
Indians not speaking Spanish**	—	—	—	—	—	28.0	59.5
Japanese*	30.5	66.7	61.0	60.2	42.5	—	—
All are acceptable	61.6	8.4	14.1	6.5	27.8	18.2	11.5
B. Neighbors							
Protestants	—	.3	.3	—	3.1	59.6	77.8
Catholics	1.3	2.0	2.3	1.8	1.8	1.6	2.8
Jews	3.8	6.1	6.0	6.3	7.6	62.4	79.5
Negroes	1.3	50.7	43.7	45.4	21.4	43.2	71.5
Whites*	2.6	.03	.6	.2	1.2	17.9	33.3
Mexicans*	6.4	23.3	21.3	22.5	—	—	—
North Americans**	—	—	—	—	—	25.8	49.0

(356)

Indians speaking Spanish**	—	—	—	—	—	15.3	27.8
Indians not speaking Spanish**	—	—	—	—	—	35.5	53.5
Japanese*	8.9	20.2	18.6	17.1	14.9	—	—
All are acceptable	88.5	45.7	47.6	48.6	71.4	28.4	14.9
C. Co-workers							
Protestants	.6	.1	.1	—	—	56.0	72.1
Catholics	3.2	1.5	1.5	.5	1.2	1.3	1.4
Jews	3.2	4.2	4.1	4.5	10.5	59.3	75.6
Negroes	3.2	21.1	19.2	17.3	8.0	39.2	70.0
Whites	1.3	.1	.2	.2	.5	17.9	33.4
Mexicans*	3.2	11.7	11.5	9.8	—	—	—
North Americans**	—	—	—	—	—	25.6	48.1
Indians speaking Spanish**	—	—	—	—	—	15.2	24.2
Indians not speaking Spanish**	—	—	—	—	—	37.2	51.9
Japanese*	3.8	10.9	10.3	8.4	7.2	—	—
All are acceptable	92.4	74.4	73.5	73.4	79.4	31.6	17.4
D. Citizens by Naturalization							
Protestants	—	.01	.1	—	—	46.7	71.8
Catholics	1.3	.8	.8	.2	.8	1.3	2.4
Jews	—	2.0	1.9	3.6	1.8	60.6	79.1
Negroes	1.3	5.1	5.2	8.5	4.3	41.5	74.9
Whites	4.4	6.7	6.9	6.5	.8	18.2	35.5
Mexicans*	—	—	—	—	—	—	—
North Americans**	—	—	—	—	—	24.9	52.3
Indians speaking Spanish**	—	—	—	—	—	14.1	24.4
Indians not speaking Spanish**	—	—	—	—	—	28.2	46.7
Japanese*	5.7	8.3	8.2	9.0	9.3	—	—
All are acceptable	85.4	86.4	84.6	81.5	85.3	32.8	13.6

*Not analyzed for the Mexican samples.

**Not included in the United States samples.

***Approximately 1 percent are non-whites and non-Negroes.

Social distance; implying both systemic linkage and boundary maintenance. To appraise the boundary maintenance, that process which may prevent death by absorption of the Mexican American community, let us turn to a study of social distance. Forty years ago Park and Bogardus introduced into sociology the concept and measurement of social distance.[11] For our consideration of boundary maintenance four social distance categories or status-roles were employed for races, language and religious groups ranging from the close primary union specified as willingness or unwillingness to intermarry, to that of becoming a neighbor, work colleague or partner, and citizen.

As Figure 3 reveals, the Mexican American informants in the study report considerably less prejudice and/or boundary maintenance than white Anglo Americans but more than blacks as these are reflected in the social distance measures. Considering the high boundary maintenance generally reflected in the percentages of both urban and rural Mexicans who reject various categories for various status-roles, the relatively low rejection rates on the part of the Mexican Americans may be surprising. We take it as a good omen for the potential function of the Mexican American Community as a potential "broker" or linking agent between the United States and Mexico. One category in Figure 3, namely, "All are acceptable" in its way reflects potential for linkage. It is interesting to note that on this category blacks and Mexican Americans have comparable scores indicating low boundary maintenance, except that for inter-marriage the Mexican Americans report higher boundary maintenance, as measured by the social distance instrument.

Behavioral linkage. A theme of the present chapter is that the Mexican American Community of the United States is a great resource, not always used to its potential, but always available as a sort of "brokerage facility" and repository of a fund of good will which may be of great importance to both Mexico and the United States. We shall not explore this idea further here but merely ask the question: "Why does not the Community provide more ambassadors, consuls and other officials for countries both north and south?" Let us now turn to an analysis of what we shall call behavioral linkage, actual linkages of the members of the Mexican American Community, and, for comparative purposes, actual linkages of Mexicans and others across the Mexican-American border.

Ten items in the study, made by the senior author, brought forth information about actual contacts the informants had: visits to the other country, friends there, encounters in church, in other organizations, among relatives, among neighbors, among work associates, and second-hand contacts through a relative, close friend or spouse.

Figure 5 describes the manner in which these separate items of the behavioral linkage scales were combined in our effort to find out what factors were related to the actual linkages and contacts.

FIRST HAND LINKAGE AND CONTACT

Friendship linkages. Figure 4 summarizes responses to the question: "Do you, yourself, have any Mexican friends?" (or " . . . North American friends" in the case of the Mexicans). The linking function of the Mexican-American Community of the Southwest is demonstrated by the more than two-thirds who claim friendship with Mexican nationals. The interview schedule used for this sample was written in Spanish, and the designation for the nationality of the friends was "Mexicano", with the additional phrase, "that is to say, people who are natives of Mexico."

FIGURE 4

Citizens of Mexico and the United States Who Have Friends Among the Citizens of the Country Across the Border

Friends Across the Border	United States			Mexico	
	General Public	Rural Michigan	Mexican American	Urban	Rural
Yes, have friends across the border	18.7	19.5	68.4	15.8	4.2
No, do not have friends across the border	81.8	80.5	31.6	83.8	95.8
No response	.2	—	—	.4	—
TOTAL PERCENT	100.0	100.0	100.0	100.0	100.0

The slightly greater tendency of rural Michigan to claim Mexican friendships than is true of the general public may reflect the considerable number of Mexicans who through the years have come to Michigan as transient farm workers. Rural Mexicans are less mobile and claim fewer across the border friends than others in Figure 4.

Travel across the border. Besides Friendship, travel to the country across the border completes the items designated as "firsthand" across-the-border contacts. Of the Mexican American Community sample, 58 per cent indicated such contact. In contrast, over one-fifth of the general public of the United States and the urban population of Mexico had either visited or lived in the country across the border. Interestingly, rural Michigan as well as rural Mexico each reported slightly more than 13 per cent as having visited or lived on the other side of the border of their home countries.

FIGURE 5

Schematic Pyramiding of Indexes

a_1 What is a wetback?*
a_2 What states in the United States once belonged to Mexico?

Big A-Knowledge about Mexico/United States

b_1 What Mexican/United States radio-television programs do you hear?
b_2 What Mexican/United States magazines do you read?
b_3 What Mexican/United States newspapers do you read?

Big B-Mass media communication**

d_1 Have you any Mexican/American friends?
d_2 Have you ever been to Mexico/United States?

Big D-First-hand contact with Mexico/Mexicans, with United States-Americans

e_1 Have you contacts in church with Spanish-speaking/North Americans?
e_2 Have you contacts in other formal groups with Spanish-speaking/North Americans?
e_3 Have you any contacts among relatives with Spanish-speaking/North Americans?
e_4 Have you any contacts among neighbors with Spanish-speaking/North Americans?
e_5 Have you any contacts among work associates with Spanish-speaking/North Americans?

Big E-Contact with Spanish-speaking, Mexicans/North Americans in interaction arenas

HUGE A—Actual contacts with Mexico/United States
BEHAVIORAL LINKAGE

f_1 Have you any contacts with Spanish-speaking/North Americans via relatives?
f_2 Have you any contacts with Spanish-speaking/North Americans via close friends?
f_3 Have you any contacts with Spanish-speaking/North Americans via your spouse?

Big F-Second-hand contact with Mexico/United States

g_1 Our leaders should cooperate
g_2 We should have closer connections
g_3 Would consider moving to Mexico/United States
g_4 Ladder rating Mexico United States as a nation

Big G-Attitudes toward Mexico/United States and linkage with, as a nation

h_1 Desire to have more Mexican/American friends
h_2 Friendliness toward people of Mexico/United States

Big H-Attitudes toward and linkage with Mexicans/North Americans as people

HUGE B—Attitudes toward Mexico/United States
DESIRED LINKAGE

i_1 Prefer not to have as neighbors, Mexicans/North Americans
i_2 Prefer not to have as co-workers, Mexicans/North Americans
i_3 Prefer not to have as family members, Mexicans/North Americans
i_4 Prefer not to have as citizens, Mexicans/North Americans

Big I-Social distance from Mexico/United States

*For tabulation of answers to these questions and other separate items below, see: Charles P. Loomis, Zona K. Loomis and Jeanne E. Gullahorn, *op. cit.* For coefficients indicating the relationship of this particular item to those below, see *ibid.*

**Ibid.* Because mass media were infrequently used across the border, these items were not employed in the study below.

While visits of North Americans tend to be short, Mexicans who cross the border tend to stay longer. When informants who have visited the cross-the-border country are compared with those who have not, in terms of their scores on other items measuring behavioral and desired linkage, a consistent positive correlation for the general public of the United States and for the Mexican urban samples is noted. Having friends across the border is similarly related to all of the other linkage items. Although informants in the United States who have been to Mexico seemed not to differ in educational attainment from those who had not been there, those from urban Mexico who had visited the United States had lower educational attainment than those who had not. This no doubt reflects the fact that large numbers of unskilled laborers with low educational attainment work in the United States. The importance of this in the prejudice non-Mexican Americans in the United States have for Mexican Americans living there should not be discounted.

LINKAGES OF HOME BOUND INTERACTION

We move now to consideration of what has been called consciousness of kind and congeniality of interaction. Although they do not cross the border themselves, some individuals engage in home-bound interaction with nationals from the other side of the border or with fellow citizens of a different ethnic and/or language derivation, in encounters at work, at church, in other formal organizations, in their neighborhoods, or among relatives. Do people so situated have more behavioral linkage as a result of what often might be a more formal contact than do others without such contact? Does the interaction spread from the initial arena to other arenas of life? The present focus is on these questions, much of the data for which appears in Figure 6.

Church linkage. Figure 6 presents data on the percentages of respondents in the five samples who reported that *most* of their associates in church were from groups stemming from across the border as well as the percentages who reported that *some* stem from there.[12]

Two gradations of linkage, that is, "most," and "any" or "some", of the ethnic and/or language composition stemming from the other side of the border were used in the index. When these two are combined, between 6 and 9 percent in rural Michigan and the general public of the United States may be considered linked with Mexican Americans in church. Only 4 and 1 per cent, respectively of the urban and rural respondents in Mexico were so linked with Anglos. By far the greatest linkage, as would be expected, is the Mexican-American Community of the Southwest with the English-speaking associates in church.

FIGURE 6

Potential Basis for Systemic Linkage Through Home-Bound Interaction Arenas with People Who Stem from across the Border

Arenas of Interaction	United States									Mexico					
	General Public			Rural Michigan			Mexican Americans			Urban			Rural		
	Associates are Spanish-speaking to the following extent:**			Associates are Spanish-speaking to the following extent:**			Associates are Spanish-speaking to the following extent:**			Associates are Spanish-speaking to the following extent:**					
	Most	Some	Total	Most	Some	Total	Most	Some	Total	Most	Some	Total	Most	Some	Total
Friends, neighbors and co-workers off the job	1.4	7.0	8.4	—	3.9	3.9	70.9 (14.0)*	10.2 (37.0)	81.1 (51.0)	—	3.0	3.0	—	—	—
Relatives not living in informant's home	2.1	1.3	3.4	.3	1.1	1.4	86.8 (4.5)	2.7 (16.5)	89.5 (21.0)	—	4.0	4.0	—	—	—
Members of church known personally	1.4	7.2	8.6	.2	6.3	6.5	67.0 (22.7)	12.9 (16.5)	79.9 (38.2)	—	4.0	4.0	—	1.0	1.0
Members known personally in informant's most important formal organization (non-religious)	.3	5.7	6.0	.1	4.0	4.1	10.5 (8.8)	6.4 (5.5)	16.9 (14.3)	—	1.1	1.1	—	—	—
Co-workers on the job	.8	7.0	7.8	.5	4.4	4.9	27.2 (10.5)	10.7 (14.6)	37.9 (25.1)	—	1.2	1.2	—	—	—

*Percentages in parentheses are for English-speaking associates.

**Percentages for Mexico and the United States are not exactly comparable because the category, "Spanish-speaking background" appeared in the schedule as used in the United States, whereas the Spanish schedule as used in Mexico did not have the category "English speaking" on it but the percentages were derived from those listed by the interviewer under a category "other."

(362)

Persons who are linked in church tend to have behavioral linkages in other interaction arenas of the home-bound type discussed in the present section. Likewise those linked in church tend to desire more linkage in terms of the measures discussed in the sections below. Since many, perhaps most, Mexican Americans reporting church linkages are Catholics, the linkage factor may merely reflect the influence of an intervening variable, the Catholic religion. In none of the samples do respondents with church linkage appear significantly different in educational attainment from those without such linkages.

Linkage in non-church formal organizations. For information on this type of linkage, informants were asked about their membership organizations that meet more or less regularly such as civic societies, fraternal organizations, educational groups or recreational organizations, labor unions, farm organizations, or business or professional organizations. They then were asked, "Among these non-religious groups and organizations that you have mentioned in the last two questions, which ONE is the most important to you?"[13]

As will be noted in Figure 6, there are fewer linkages in non-religious formal organizations than in the church. Mexicans in particular reported few linkages in formal organizations of the non-religious type. Nevertheless, the linkage performance of the Mexican American Community is relatively great in all arenas. There was some tendency for informants in the United States general public sample who were linked in the formal organizations to have higher education status when there were "some" Spanish-speaking members and to have lower attainment when "most" were of this language and ethnic background.

Linkage with relatives stemming from across the border. As with linkages in church and other formal organizations just discussed, an effort was made to ascertain the extent of linkage of informants with relatives not living at home but who lived in or stemmed from the country across the border. Not only was each informant asked, "How often do you get together with any of your relatives, other than those living at home with you?" but also "To which of the following language or racial backgrounds do MOST of these relatives belong?" Here the same set of procedures and set of categories were used as in the last two items.

As will be noted in Figure 6, about 4 per cent of the United States general public and the urban sample of Mexico interact with relatives who stemmed from across the border. The extensive linkage of the Mexican Americans of Southwestern United States is well documented in Figure 6. Almost 9 out of 10 report that they interact with relatives stemming from Mexico, and 2 out of 10 interact with relatives stemming from white English-speaking associates of the United States. These proportions demonstrate the linkage potential of the Mexican American community of the United States. Only 1.4 per cent of the rural Michigan, and none of the rural Mexican informants, reported having relatives with whom they interact and who stemmed from across the border.

Comparisons of educational attainment revealed no differences in the three samples for which data are available between those linked with relatives and those without such linkage. So far as educational attainment measures social rank, interacting with relatives from the other side of the border appears not to be class or caste bound.

Linkages with neighbors stemming from across the border. Informants in all of the five samples were asked, "How often do you get together with any of your neighbors?" "How often do you get together, *outside of work*, with any of the people you (your husband) work(s) with?" and, "How often do you get together with any other friends?"[14]

Figure 7 indicates the extent and frequency of linkage in friendship, neighbor and co-worker off-the-job arenas of contact and social interaction. As with the other items already discussed, only members of the Mexican-American Community of Southwestern United States report extensive linkage. The 8.4 per cent of the informants in the United States general public sample who report linkages with neighbors, off-work and other acquaintances who stem from across the border (Figure 6), are much more frequently linked in other activities and generally more favorably disposed to more linkages than are those without this form of linkage. The 3.9 per cent of the informants in rural Michigan sample who are thus linked more frequently report linkages with fellow workers, relatives and friends who stem from across the border than those who do not report these linkages.

Informants in the United States general public sample who report the above linkages tend to have higher educational status than those who do not have such linkages. For the other samples studied in this regard, namely, rural Michigan and urban Mexico, differences were not statistically significant. But for rural Michigan there appeared a tendency for those reporting this type of linkage to have lower educational achievement than those without such linkage. There is again indication that linkages of Anglos and Mexican Americans in rural Michigan take place at lower educational and

FIGURE 7

Frequency of Interaction of Citizens of Mexico and of the United States with Neighbors, Co-workers, in Situations off the Job, and with Other Friends

Frequency of Interaction	United States									Mexico					
	General Public			Rural Michigan			Mexican Americans			Urban			Rural		
	Neighbors	Co-workers Off the Job	Other Friends	Neighbors	Co-workers Off the Job	Other Friends	Neighbors	Co-workers Off the Job	Other Friends	Neighbors	Co-workers Off the Job	Other Friends	Neighbors	Co-workers Off the Job	Other Friends
About everyday	18.6	4.3	5.5	17.4	2.0	2.3	23.0	23.9	7.8	29.6	18.9	18.0	43.5	30.0	23.7
At least once a week	25.7	15.2	30.8	26.4	16.6	29.2	30.6	13.4	44.7	15.7	12.4	17.3	20.6	13.6	14.6
A few times a month	11.3	12.0	19.7	14.2	8.1	18.4	3.4	1.0	5.2	3.5	3.0	4.0	4.2	2.4	5.2
About once a month	9.4	10.9	17.0	6.3	8.3	18.4	15.4	11.2	19.6	7.9	8.5	11.0	7.7	4.5	9.1
A few times a year	9.6	14.4	15.8	11.3	17.0	19.1	5.6	4.6	6.8	5.2	6.1	5.6	3.5	3.5	8.0
About once a year or less	4.0	7.5	2.6	4.7	12.4	5.1	1.8	9.1	5.0	7.4	5.3	6.7	3.8	2.4	3.1
Never	20.9	32.2	8.5	19.7	32.8	7.5	18.8	29.3	10.9	30.3	45.2	37.0	16.4	42.9	35.3
No response	.5	3.5	.1	—	2.8	—	1.4	7.5	—	.4	.6	.4	.3	.7	1.0
TOTAL PERCENT	100.0	100.0	100.0	100.0	100.0	100.0	100.0	100.0	100.0	100.0	100.0	100.0	100.0	100.0	100.0

class levels. Figure 7 indicates that members of the Mexican American Community generally interact with neighbors more frequently than do Anglo-Americans.

Linkages with work associates on the job. In addition to the data just discussed concerning co-worker off-the-job linkages, linkages on the job were also studied. On-the-job associations often differ from off-the-job associations. Figure 6 summarizes the percentages of informants in the five samples who report on-the-job linkage with co-workers stemming from across the border. Again by all odds the members of the Mexican American Community of the Southwestern United States surpass all others in linkages both with fellow members and with English speaking associates. Few Mexicans report working on the job with North Americans, but almost 8 per cent of the United States general public and almost 5 per cent of the rural Michigan informants report contacts with Spanish-speaking workers on the job. Furthermore, a larger proportion of these Mexican-Americans are farmers or farm laborers than is characteristic of the other samples, except rural Mexican. Often farm work is more or less family work, and hence does not involve people of other backgrounds. The much more frequent interaction of co-workers off the job among Mexicans than among Anglo-Americans indicates that life takes place in a less-differentiated society in Mexico than in the United States. (Figure 7). Workers, many of whom are kinfolk and old time friends, may return to neighborhoods within which they have lived for long periods. As we shall note below, the mobility of Mexicans is much more restricted than that of Anglo-Americans, with Mexican-Americans taking an in-between position in this regard.

SECOND HAND OR INDIRECT LINKAGE AND ITS CONTRIBUTION

What contributions do indirect linkages make toward producing favorable attitudes toward desire for linkage? Here will be considered the possible impact on the informant of relatives and close friends, who, although they may live in an actor's home country, have been across the border. In an attempt to provide answers to this question all informants were asked whether their own spouses, friends, and relatives with whom they were in contact had been to the country across the border. A considerably larger proportion of informants have close friends and relatives who have been to the country across the border than have been there themselves. Potential intimate sources of information about the across-the-border country are explored in the following discussion of items.

Second-hand linkage via relatives. As would be expected, Mexican-Americans of the Southwestern United States have much greater linkage (67 per cent) through relatives with the country across the border than any of the other groups in the study. Approximately one-third of informants in the general public of the United States, rural Michigan, and rural Mexico have this indirect form of linkage through such relatives. So that the second-hand or indirect linkage through relatives may reflect the influence of time spent across the border, informants were asked to think of the relative who had spent the most time across the border and to indicate how long he had been there. As in the case of the informants' own visits across the border, relatives of the United States nationals differ markedly from those of Mexicans in the length of their visits. In general, the status-role of temporary tourist best characterizes the relatives of the United States citizens visiting Mexico. Among relatives of Mexicans a large number have been in the United States for one year or more, indicating that they are, or were, there as workers or students, and some may have acquired United States citizenship.

Second-hand Linkages via Close Friends. Slightly less than one-fourth of the informants in urban Mexico and slightly less than one-third of the informants from the United States general public report that they have such indirect linkages as close friends who have visited the country across the border. The percentage of Mexican Americans of the Southwestern United States was 58.8 per cent indicating again the strong linkage potential of this gr up. Rural Mexicans and rural Michiganders less frequently reported close friends who had visited across the border, these proportions being respectively 16.0 and 18.7. In general, the informants who had this form of linkage had a higher educational status than those without such linkage. The United States general public sample manifests the greatest differences between those informants who claim second-hand linkages through close friends as compared with those who do not make this claim. For example, those having such friends are more prone to state that they would be willing to move to Mexico.

For the rural Michigan sample, the 19 per cent who claim close friends who have visited Mexico when compared with the remaining 81 per cent show the following differences: They more frequently claim to have Mexican friends, more frequently have been to Mexico, have more frequently been in contact with Spanish-speaking neighbors and fellow workers, and place Mexico higher on the "friendship ladder," discussed below.

The patterns of duration of stay or visit in the country across the border for those close friends follow the general pattern discussed earlier; Mexicans as workers, students, etc., seem to stay longer in the United States than United States citizens as tourists stay in Mexico.

The third item in the second-hand linkage index was linkage via the spouse. In general the proportion of informants who reported a spouse who had been to the across-the-border country was not greatly different from that of the respondents themselves. In fact many married couples crossed the border together. The significance of independent visits made by the spouse when the informant did not go remains to be appraised.

ELEMENTS AND PROCESSES OF THE MEXICAN AMERICAN COMMUNITY AS A SOCIAL SYSTEM

Having had a comparative look at the Mexican American Community as a boundary maintaining and linking system let us analyze it in respect to these processes and their potentials as a social system. In analyzing social pluralities of various types the so-called processually articulated structural model[15] (hereafter called the PAS Model) will be used. Table 1 gives the essence of the PAS Model. It will be noted that the model incorporates both social structure and process or change. Wilbert Moore metaphorized about the PAS model: It "made a notable advance by inviting in ... the strangers (process and change) to put the house on rollers and permit it to move, while furnishing the interior with flexible and movable partitions and occasionally discordant inhabitants."[16] The PAS Model will furnish the means of organization for a continuation of the analysis of the Mexican American Community.

KNOWING

We begin with the action category, Knowing, i.e., the element "belief," articulated by "cognitive mapping" as a process (see Table 1). Of course this cognitive component which we shall attempt to analyze is in the empirical world comingled with feelings and with moral components.

Belief as an element. A belief is any proposition about the universe which is thought to be true. Here we shall probe our informants' beliefs about beliefs. They were requested to indicate the extent of their agreement or disagreement with the statement: "I believe the world would be a better place if more people had the same beliefs which I have." Slightly over half (52 per cent) of the Mexican Americans interviewed agreed with the statement. A larger proportion of Mexicans agreed with it (93 per cent). Unfortunately data are not available on what specific beliefs the informant had in mind as he gave these responses. The Mexican Americans are closer to the gen-

TABLE 1. ELEMENTS, PROCESSES AND CONDITIONS
OF ACTION OF SOCIAL SYSTEMS
THE PROCESSUALLY ARTICULATED STRUCTURAL
MODEL (PASM)*

Processes (Elemental)	Social Action Categories	Elements
1) Cognitive mapping and validation	Knowing	Belief (knowledge)
2) a) Tension management and b) Communication of sentiment	Feeling	Sentiment
3) a) Goal attaining activity and b) Concomitant "latent" activity as process	Achieving	End, goal, or objective
4) Evaluation	Norming, Standard-izing, Patterning	Norm
5) Status-role performance	Dividing the functions	Status-role (position)
6) a) Evaluation of actors and b) Allocation of status-roles	Ranking	Rank
7) a) Decision making and b) Initiation of action	Controlling	Power
8) Application of sanctions	Sanctioning	Sanction
9) Utilization of facilities	Facilitating	Facility
Comprehensive or Master Processes 1) Communication 2) Boundary maintenance	3) Systemic linkage 4) Institutionalization	5) Socialization 6) Social control
Conditions of Social Action 1) Territoriality	2) Size	3) Time

*Charles P. Loomis, *Social Systems: Essays on Their Persistence and Change* (Princeton, N.J.; D. Van Nostrand Co., Inc., 1960), Fig. 1, p. 8.

FIGURE 8

Perceived Religiousity in Mexico and the United States:
Percent Placing Themselves on Various Ladder Steps

Ladder Step	United States			Mexico	
	General Public	Rural Michigan	Mexican Americans	Urban	Rural
TOP					
10	23.0	19.2	35.3	25.9	25.0
9	8.7	9.4	16.8	12.0	17.8
8	16.4	15.9	11.3	19.2	15.6
7	10.6	11.3	10.5	9.6	9.4
6	8.1	11.4	5.9	7.1	6.2
5	16.4	18.2	9.6	13.5	7.6
4	3.5	1.6	1.0	3.0	3.8
3	4.2	3.2	2.3	3.7	3.1
2	2.5	2.8	1.5	1.5	2.8
1	3.2	4.2	2.4	1.1	—
0	3.0	2.8	2.4	2.0	2.1
Don't know, refusals, etc.	.4	—	1.0	1.4	6.6
TOTAL PERCENT	100.0	100.0	100.0	100.0	100.0

eral public of the United States sample, among whom only 48.5 per cent agreed, than to the respondents in the Mexican samples.

This question leads to others posed to find how informants considered religion. As noted above in our analysis of social distance (Figure 3) Mexican Americans, most of whom are Catholic, are much more tolerant of Protestants than are Mexicans across the border. This should, however, not be taken to mean that Mexican Americans give religion low primacy in support and evaluation. To get some judgment of "how religious" informants thought themselves to be each was asked to place himself on a self-anchoring scale (a picture of a ladder which he held in his hand) with the top of the ladder representing those who regarded religion to be very important and the bottom of the ladder representing those who thought it was of little or no importance. As Figure 8 indicates, the Mexican Americans place themselves higher on the ladder than do other citizens of the United States and higher also than do Mexicans. Dworkin and Eckberg[17] noted that Mexican Americans considered themselves much more religious than Anglos, but also more tolerant of others of different religions than Anglos.

FIGURE 9

Informants from Mexico/United States Who Report Seeking God's Help in Decision Making, and Frequency with which Such Help Is Sought

| Seek God's Help and Frequency | United States | | | Mexico | |
	General Public	Rural Michigan	Mexican Americans	Urban	Rural
Yes	70.4	74.2	91.5	90.2	89.2
No	28.9	25.5	8.5	9.5	10.8
Refuse to answer, don't know, etc.	.7	.3	—	.3	—
TOTAL PERCENT	100.0	100.0	100.0	100.0	100.0
FREQUENCY					
Always	18.4	14.3	50.7	56.4	65.8
Most of the time	27.3	36.2	29.5	23.7	18.9
Sometimes	23.9	23.2	10.1	10.1	4.5
No response	29.5	25.9	8.5	9.8	10.8
Refuse to answer, don't know, etc.	.9	.4	1.2	—	—
TOTAL PERCENT	100.0	100.0	100.0	100.0	100.0

Cognitive mapping and validation as process. Cognitive mapping and validation may be defined as the activity by which knowledge, or what is considered true and what false, is developed. It is not unrelated to how people approach reality and how they think they perceive it. It may be illustrated by another question included in the study — a question previously used by Lenski[18] as one of his measures of *devotionalism*: "When you have a decision to make in your everyday life do you ask yourself what GOD would want you to do?" As Figure 9 indicates, almost all Mexican Americans and Mexicans answered this question with, "Yes." These same informants engaged in this prayerful activity much more frequently than did the United States general public and the rural Michiganders.

Dworkin[19] found that Mexican Americans born in the United States thought of themselves as "unscientific" while they characterized Anglo-Americans as "scientific." Interestingly, Dworkin reports that lower class Mexican Americans who were born in Mexico think of themselves as "practical". For this group the trait of being "scientific" or "unscientific" is not frequently referred to with respect to themselves or to Anglo-Americans. Dworkin hypothesizes that longer experience in the United States reduces the self-respect of Mexican Americans and also their general regard for Anglo-Americans. From this and other evidence not possible to explore here, there is plenty to support the idea that the Mexican American community is cognitively constituted to continue its function as a linking agency between the United States and Mexico, and for its importance to increase in this respect.

It should be noted that in a restudy of Mexican American stereotypes and self images conducted during the rise of the present Chicano Movement, Dworkin noted that (1) the time period required for foreign born Mexican Americans to change their beliefs and images such that they coincide with the images held by native born Mexican Americans was less than six months, and (2) that such image changes were accompanied by greater endorsements of militant ideologies. The creation of such value consensus, and shifts from Mexico to U.S.-barrio-based reference groups, noted by Dworkin[20] suggest further the presence of a sense of community among Mexican Americans.

DIVIDING THE FUNCTIONS

Status-role as a unit incorporating both element and process. Nothing is more important for self-identification than what one does and is expected to do in one's status-roles. As a part of the study all informants, after a brief introduction were told: "Ask this question of yourself, 'Who am I?' Think of as many answers as you can in answer to the question, 'Who am I?' . . . Now, please make what you consider to be the *most important* statement about yourself." Respondents were probed further in an effort to get ten responses or more to the question: "Who am I?"

It is interesting to note that twelve years ago in responding to the question "Who am I" not a single respondent in the Mexican American sample claimed identity with this minority group. This stands in contrast to Blacks (N = 158) 13.3 per cent of whom in one way or another mentioned their own race. The results from our interviews with Mexican Americans in 1963 stand in even greater contrast when compared with those from Mexican American family members (N = 335) who were interviewed in the Yakima Valley of Washington State in 1970 with practically the same questions and procedures.[21] In this latter study no less than one out of four among informants in any of the categories of respondents identified themselves ethnically. In the more politicized urban areas such as Los Angeles, Dworkin found one in ten Mexican Americans identified themselves ethnically in 1963 and three in four did so in 1971. It is our opinion from these and other indications that emphasis on ethnicity in self-identification for Mexican Americans has greatly increased in the last decade.

At this point we cannot take up the element of sentiment, and its many behavior manifestations such as patriotism. Because many of the findings related to that category impinge upon that of status-role, we shall just state here that Mexican-Americans value their family, community and occupational roles highly. If we can attach any prognostic importance to the high evaluation the Mexican-Americans in our study placed upon the political party and political party membership, then there is no doubt that Mexican-American political power will increase (see Figure 10).

Sex status-roles are important in every society but several studies have found that females in traditional cultures perform more boundary maintaining functions than do males.[22] For example, in such cultures males usually marry outside their ethnic, racial or national group more often than do females. When all the indexes measuring systematic linkage are combined after the model in Figure 5 for Anglo-Americans and Mexicans, women have lower behavioral as well as attitudinal linkages across the border than do men. For the Mexican Americans the opposite is the case. This may indicate that culturally, women in the Mexican American Community are slower to adopt Anglo norms and goals than men. It may also indicate that Mexican American women harbor close cultural "consciousness of kind" with the people of Mexico.

FIGURE 10

Respondents' Evaluations of Community, Family, Country, Occupation and Political Party in Relation to Himself

Ladder Step	United States — General Public					United States — Rural Michigan					United States — Mexican Americans					Mexico — Urban					Mexico — Rural				
	Community	Family	Country	Occupation	Political Party	Community	Family	Country	Occupation	Political Party	Community	Family	Country	Occupation	Political Party	Community	Family	Country	Occupation	Political Party	Community	Family	Country	Occupation	Political Party
TOP 10	10.6	52.4	46.2	21.9	10.0	15.2	49.1	52.1	24.2	11.7	23.7	50.0	53.4	29.6	23.2	23.4	32.8	69.3	22.3	20.7	13.5	19.1	56.2	18.0	—
9	7.7	15.7	14.0	9.3	4.9	6.7	19.1	12.4	9.3	3.5	6.1	14.0	9.4	14.4	10.2	15.2	16.0	12.8	12.8	12.4	14.9	13.2	16.0	9.0	—
8	18.5	12.9	15.3	14.2	9.4	18.5	11.1	11.6	13.1	9.4	16.6	11.9	14.4	12.9	4.2	17.9	16.1	8.5	13.4	11.2	16.3	19.2	10.8	11.1	—
7	18.3	5.8	6.9	10.7	10.4	17.8	5.6	8.8	11.1	9.2	12.1	6.7	5.4	9.0	9.5	16.9	11.9	4.3	12.0	11.4	14.9	16.3	4.2	14.2	—
6	17.5	4.9	7.9	11.4	11.7	20.9	6.9	8.2	11.6	11.6	14.7	5.2	4.5	9.7	10.5	16.0	12.5	2.1	16.9	13.9	19.9	11.1	3.5	20.3	—
5	6.6	4.5	2.6	7.3	8.3	6.5	4.4	3.3	6.3	10.2	6.8	5.8	10.3	10.9	10.7	2.5	4.0	.3	5.6	5.6	3.1	6.2	.3	7.3	—
4	11.6	1.7	3.8	11.4	19.1	8.4	1.8	1.5	10.2	17.3	9.8	2.1	—	7.0	16.2	3.0	3.2	—	9.7	9.3	4.2	2.8	.7	4.5	—
3	4.5	.5	.6	5.4	9.9	2.0	.2	.2	3.6	6.1	4.3	—	1.0	4.9	3.1	.9	.4	.3	2.0	3.5	2.1	1.4	1.0	3.1	—
2	1.0	.1	.5	2.5	5.0	.7	.2	.7	3.9	6.1	1.0	1.4	—	.6	2.7	1.2	.5	—	1.1	1.8	1.7	—	—	1.0	—
1	.9	.3	.7	1.4	3.7	1.4	—	—	.6	4.1	1.0	—	—	—	1.4	.4	.6	.1	.7	1.1	.7	.3	—	—	—
0	1.2	.2	.4	1.8	4.4	.3	.9	—	3.8	5.5	1.0	—	—	—	.8	.4	.4	.1	1.5	2.4	—	—	—	.7	—
Don't know, refuse, etc.	1.6	1.0	1.1	2.7	3.2	1.6	.7	1.2	2.3	5.3	2.9	2.4	1.6	1.0	7.5	2.2	1.6	1.7	2.0	6.7	8.7	8.7	7.3	10.1	—
TOTAL PERCENT	100.0	100.0	100.0	100.0	100.0	100.0	100.0	100.0	100.0	100.0	100.0	100.0	100.0	100.0	100.0	100.0	100.0	100.0	100.0	100.0	100.0	100.0	100.0	100.0	100.0

In the above discussions of linkages of the Mexican American Community with both the United States and Mexico, the importance of the status-roles of friend, relative, citizen, etc. has been discussed. Dworkin's studies of stereotypes contributes to what is being considered here as explicating status-role. He found for example, that Mexican-Americans who were born in Mexico thought of themselves as having "strong family ties", "being athletic", "being friendly", and "being field workers." Their self-descriptions project status-roles such as friend, father, mother, son, basket-ball player, farmer and rancher. The Mexican-American informants born in the United States were much more inclined to present stereotypes of themselves which were derogatory and which less easily connoted status-roles. This unfortunate disparaging attitude may be in part counter-balanced by the increasing identification with "la raza" and the Mexican-American Community.

In closing this section on identity and status-role in relation to boundary maintenance and to the linking potentials of Mexican Americans it may be observed that the linkage potential is in no small measure related to what is often in the sociological literature referred to as the status-role of the *marginal man*. Park referred to this identity as "a man on the margin of two cultures and two societies, which never completely interpenetrated and fused."[23] Gist and Dworkin[24] have noted that at various times Mexican Americans have been "marginal" culturally "in terms of language and religion," "marginal" socially in terms of prejudice and rejection by Anglos, and before World War II politically marginal as segregation legislation affected them.

While recognizing that among so-called marginal persons are to be found great creativity and many innovators, it is also true that the very forces which are responsible for these traits and which make them potential "cultural brokers," communicators, and linkers of the two countries can produce unhappiness, identity crises, and anomie. As is well known and as pointed out by Durkheim, if anomie is produced the lack of social certitude, lack of status crystalization, and lack of identity bring on that form of suicide known as anomic suicide along with various other pathologies.

It is only natural, therefore, that the quest for identity by the marginal person takes on special forms. It may be accompanied by withdrawal or drug addiction. It may also result in activism, revolt and formation of group identifications of various kinds. The development of "black power" for blacks or "Chicano power" for Mexican Americans may not be unrelated to this and other forms of relative deprivation.

In fact, it is just this conclusion that Dworkin and Eckberg[25] reach as they note the role of the Chicano Movement in (1) redefining the meanings Mexican Americans ascribe to images they have previously held, and (2) adopting stereotype patterns which demonstrate more positive self-imagery and more hostile imagery toward the dominant Anglo community. Utilizing a factor analytic technique Dworkin generated a summary score for stereotypes and self images which presented the "meanings" of the words used by the individuals. Words used in pre-Chicano Movement sampling which were found in later samplings no longer had the same connotations as defined by the Mexican American subjects; other words, also evaluated as positive traits for Mexican Americans and as negative for Anglos appeared in the images held by the subjects.

Referring back to the list of stereotypes presented in Figure 2, we observe that 57 per cent of the stereotypes Anglos held of themselves changed in meaning over the 1963 through 1971 time period. Images such as "ambitious," "religious," "tall," "active," "educated," and "athletic" shifted from favorable to neutral images, while "conservative" changed from a neutral to an unfavorable quality. Anglo images of Chicanos likewise underwent change. Fifty-two per cent of the stereotypes shifted. "Dark skin" and "dark hair," which in 1963 were unfavorable qualities, by 1971 became favorable ones. The images "emotional," "large families," "Catholics," "Speak Spanish," "accent," and "militant" moved from unfavorable to neutral, or from neutral to favorable traits.

Among Mexican Americans, 32 per cent of their images of Anglos shifted in meaning over the decade. No stereotype became more positive, as the general trend was for Mexican Americans to evaluate Anglos more negatively over time. Anglo traits of "athletic," "high social position," "light complexioned," and "social" moved from favorable to neutral or neutral to unfavorable evaluations. No Mexican American self image became less favorable, as Mexican Americans have tended to upgrade their self image as a result of the Chicano Movement, but 50 per cent of the images became more positive. Previously unfavorable or neutral self images (as of 1963) became neutral or favorable by 1971. These included the traits "shy," "Catholic," "emotional," "poor," "large families," and "brown."

RANKING

Rank as an element.   Rank or standing represents the value an actor has for the system in which the rank is accorded. Actors of similar rank may form a social class, common in industrial societies;

an estate, common in feudal societies; or a caste, common in highly traditional societies in which rank is determined by birth.

How and why various ethnic and other similar groupings come to form strata in terms of prestige, power and/or economic rewards they enjoy is a very much debated subject about which much has been written. Here we are interested in rank primarily as it relates to the emerging Mexican American community's role in boundary maintenance and systemic linkage. Several authors[26] have concluded that the ranking accorded to blacks and Mexican Americans results from ethnocentrism, differential social power (a subject to be discussed in the next section) and competition. Thus an ethnic group member who is regarded and/or regards himself as different, who has less power than the majority group member, and who competes with members of the majority society will be accorded lower rank.

Evaluation of actors and allocation of status-roles as process. What was stated about boundary maintenance and systemic linkage above is not unimportant in the ranking accorded the Mexican American community. Any informed person knows that the ranking of Mexican Americans, Negroes and American Indians results in discrimination in employment and in treatment at most levels for these minorities. This fact is documented with considerable precision.[27] It has been reported to the surprise of some that for all non-black minority groups except the Mexican Americans and American Indians that the so-called melting pot theory has actually worked; that is, those parents whose children have been educated more than they were might live to see these children climb the occupational ladder at about the same rate as white Anglo-Saxon Protestants. However, for Mexican Americans and blacks the situation has been different. According to these studies, if we assume that all attain an equal educational standing at a given starting point, and call this par, Mexican Americans are handicapped one point, and blacks by twelve points in job opportunities on the scale used in measuring occupational advancement. Of course, a Mexican American's education "depends to a considerable degree on the socioeconomic status of his father."[28]

The educational status of the informants who represent all ranks in our study is presented in Figure 11. Whereas 65 per cent of the United States general public reported completing at least 12 years of schooling only 36 per cent of the Mexican Americans reported having done this. As Figure 12 reveals a larger percentage of Mexican Americans when asked: "If you were asked to describe your social class, to which class would you say you belonged — working, lower, lower-middle, upper-middle and upper?" said they were in the middle

FIGURE 11

Formal Educational Attainment of Informants

Level of Education	United States			Mexico	
	General Public	Rural Michigan	Mexican Americans	Urban	Rural
None	—	—	—	19.0	38.9
1-4 years	5.0	4.4	29.3	40.0	53.9
5-8 years	30.1	36.2	33.1	30.0	6.9
9-12 years	42.5	42.0	23.5	8.0	—
13 years and over	22.3	17.4	12.7	2.0	—
Don't know, no response	.1	—	1.4	1.0	.3
TOTAL PERCENT	100.0	100.0	100.0	100.0	100.0

FIGURE 12

Self-Assigned Class Status or Rank: Citizens of Mexico and the United States

Class status or Rank*	United States			Mexico	
	General Public	Rural Michigan	Mexican Americans	Urban	Rural
In the United States					
Working	29.0	34.6	14.6	—	—
Lower	2.8	1.3	5.5	—	—
Lower middle	8.7	12.2	14.0	—	—
Middle	40.1	42.2	43.8	—	—
Upper middle	16.5	9.1	16.4	—	—
Upper	2.3	.6	4.3	—	—
Don't know, etc.	.6	—	1.4	—	—
TOTAL PERCENT	100.0	100.0	100.0	100.0	100.0
In Mexico					
Poor	—	—	—	53.3	83.7
Middle	—	—	—	45.8	16.0
Upper	—	—	—	.9	.3
TOTAL PERCENT	100.0	100.0	100.0	100.0	100.0

*These designations were used both because they had been found to be effective in getting informant response, and to make the data comparable with other studies.

classes than did the respondents in the United States general public. May we assume that this indicates that the Mexican American community is moored in the American social structure and value orientation? This is dubious for those who think of themselves as belonging in the lower ranks. Dworkin[29] found that lower class Mexican Americans in 1963 born in the United States stereotyped themselves as "Poor and of low social class," and "Uneducated or poorly-educated." As mentioned above under Status-Role, those Mexican Americans in this study who were born in Mexico mentioned that they are "Field workers." As indicated by Figure 13 Mexican Americans show equal respect for such "hand work," such as that in fields, as do Mexicans. As a matter of fact insofar as the data in Figure 13 accurately measure the evaluation of hand work Mexican Americans do not deprecate it; and contrary to much of the anthropological literature, hand work is not deprecated in Mexico.

CONTROLLING

Power as an element. Power as the term is used here is the capacity to control others. Authority is that component of power which is built into the status-role and is hence a right of the incumbent. Unlegitimized coercion and voluntary influence are non-authoritative, and will not be discussed below.

Two items with variation taken from the classical study *The Authoritarian Personality*[30] as presented in Figure 14 indicate that Mexican Americans in 1963 responded in a more "authoritarian" manner than Anglo Americans though slightly less so than the Mexicans. The extent of agreement with these statements, namely, "Whatever we do, it is necessary that our leaders outline carefully what it is to be done and exactly how to go about it," and "Children should be taught that there is only one right way to do things," is negatively related for the United States general public to educational attainment. For the urban Mexican sample no such relationship held. Unfortunately we do not have comparable data for Mexican Americans from this study by the senior author. Dworkin's data[31] leads to the belief that Mexican Americans now are less likely to stereotype themselves as authoritarian than before the Chicano movement began. Although he[32] found that before the movement began the various stereotypes lower class Mexican Americans born in the United States held of themselves, "Authoritarian" stood in third place with only "Emotional" and "Unscientific" standing higher in the proportions of the informants who agreed that the stereotypes characterized them, important changes have taken place since then. Thus, "Authoritarian" as a stereotype vanishes from the post-Chicano Move-

FIGURE 13

Evaluation of Hand Labor Versus Office Work: Responses to the Statement: "The Man Who Works With His Hands Has More Self Respect Than the Man Who Does Office Work"

| | United States | | | Mexico | |
Responses	General Public	Rural Michigan	Mexican Americans	Urban	Rural
Yes, strongly agree	14.4	18.0	40.6	31.7	39.7
Yes, slightly agree	10.5	19.0	16.0	25.6	31.9
Don't know	8.6	7.5	13.8	8.9	9.7
No, slightly disagree	26.7	21.5	7.7	17.2	9.7
No, strongly disagree	39.1	34.0	19.2	16.5	9.0
Refusal to answer, etc.	.7	—	2.7	.1	—
TOTAL PERCENT	100.0	100.0	100.0	100.0	100.0

FIGURE 14

Responses to Items Measuring Authoritarianism

| | United States | | | Mexico | |
Items Measuring Authoritarianism	General Public	Rural Michigan	Mexican Americans	Urban	Rural
Authoritarianism of leaders					
Yes, strongly agree	36.6	33.8	56.9	46.2	42.7
Yes, slightly agree	26.6	29.1	17.3	36.5	35.4
Don't know	7.0	5.0	4.2	6.3	15.3
No, slightly disagree	13.7	16.7	6.8	5.6	4.5
No, strongly disagree	15.1	15.1	12.1	5.4	2.1
Refused to answer, etc.	1.0	.3	2.7	—	—
TOTAL PERCENT	100.0	100.0	100.0	100.0	100.0
Authoritarianism in family					
Yes, strongly agree	40.8	43.9	72.0	78.2	71.6
Yes, slightly agree	18.9	20.3	15.1	16.0	25.3
Don't know	2.9	1.3	.8	1.6	1.7
No, slightly disagree	16.8	17.9	1.5	2.6	.7
No, strongly disagree	20.0	16.6	7.9	1.6	.7
Refused to answer, etc.	.6	—	2.7	—	—
TOTAL PERCENT	100.0	100.0	100.0	100.0	100.0
Need for definite rules					
Yes, strongly agree	23.5	20.0	47.3	39.1	34.7
Yes, slightly agree	25.7	36.7	23.2	32.4	35.8
Don't know	3.0	1.4	3.0	8.2	15.6
No, slightly disagree	26.7	29.5	5.9	11.8	9.4
No, strongly disagree	20.3	22.4	17.9	8.5	4.5
Refused to answer, etc.	.8	—	2.7	—	—
TOTAL PERCENT	100.0	100.0	100.0	100.0	100.0

ment samples of 1967-68 and 1971. We hypothesize that the Mexican American Community is changing the self-image of its members and that "Authoritarian" no longer applies.

Decision making and its initiation into action as process. In Figure 15 are responses indicating extent of agreement and disagreement with the following statements: "The only way to provide good medical care for all the people is through some program of governmental health insurance," "Rural youth who remain on the farm should be given more training to make them better farmers, even if we have to pay more taxes to provide that training," and "Health experts say adding certain chemicals to drinking water results in less decay in people's teeth. If you could add these chemicals to your water with little cost to you, would you be willing to have the chemicals added?" As Figure 15 indicates Mexican Americans take an in-between position on the last two statements with Mexicans in all cases agreeing more than Anglos.

NORMING

Norm as an element. The rules which prescribe what is acceptable or unacceptable are the norms of the social system. All informants in the study were asked to specify the extent of their agreement and disagreement with the statement, "I find it easier to follow rules than to do things on my own." Mexican Americans and Mexicans, who responded similarly to this statement, agree much more with it than do Anglo Americans as indicated in Figure 14. These results may explain why Dworkin found that Mexican Americans who were born in Mexico stereotyped Anglo Americans as "Individualistic." However, these lower class informants also stereotyped Anglo Americans as "Democratic," "Hard-working," and "Clean and neat." The Mexican American informants who were born in the United States were less complimentary and stereotyped Anglo Americans as "Conformists" and "Puritanical."

Mexican Americans in our probability survey displayed more alienation than others in their responses to the single item: "Peoples' ideas change so much that I wonder if we'll ever have anything to depend upon." (See Figure 16). On another item in Figure 16, namely, "I often wonder what the meaning of life really is," the Mexican Americans appear to manifest relatively less alienation. These normative reactions are, of course, manifestations of the process of evaluation.

Evaluation as a process. The process through which positive and negative priorities or values are assigned to concepts, objects, actors, or collectivities, or to events and activities, either past, present or future is identified as evaluation. Now that the world faces both serious pollution of the environment and shortages of energy some Catholics and most non-Catholics evaluate birth control positively. As may be noted from our earlier discussion, Mexican Americans and Mexicans have very high birth and population replacement rates — rates which stand among the highest in the world. These rates as may be noted in Figure 17 are coupled with the evaluation of birth control as wrong much more frequently than is the case with Anglo Americans. In the case of Anglo Americans the greater the tendency to approve birth control the higher the educational attainment. For Mexicans there was no demonstrable correlation between the two variables.

To elicit each informant's evaluation of the nation across the border on a scale ranging from good to bad, a self-anchoring scale was used.[33] This scale employs the device of a 10-step ladder with the

FIGURE 15

Responses to Items Concerning Government Assistance and Fluoridation of Water

| Items on Governmental Assistance and Fluoridation | United States | | | Mexico | |
	General Public	Rural Michigan	Mexican Americans	Urban	Rural
Governmental health insurance					
Yes, strongly agree	36.9	27.2	62.6	59.8	62.2
Yes, slightly agree	21.1	21.1	12.7	22.5	28.5
Don't know	5.9	7.1	6.2	4.0	6.9
No, sightly disagree	13.9	19.2	1.7	6.7	2.1
No, strongly disagree	21.7	25.4	14.1	7.0	.3
Refused to answer, etc.	.5	—	2.7	—	—
TOTAL PERCENT	100.0	100.0	100.0	100.0	100.0
Training of rural youth					
Yes, strongly agree	32.9	29.5	59.2	69.5	77.1
Yes, slightly agree	25.9	27.2	15.5	22.8	19.1
Don't know	8.1	3.5	10.5	2.5	3.8
No, slightly disagree	15.6	16.5	7.2	3.2	—
No, strongly disagree	17.4	22.5	7.6	2.0	—
Refused to answer, etc.	.1	1.0	—	—	—
TOTAL PERCENT	100.0	100.0	100.0	100.0	100.0
Fluoridation of water					
Yes	63.9	54.1	72.4	74.7	71.5
Maybe	9.3	6.9	7.9	7.3	6.9
Probably not	4.5	10.0	6.8	1.5	2.1
No	15.5	20.8	5.5	13.8	13.9
Don't know, refuse, etc.	6.8	8.2	7.4	2.7	5.6
TOTAL PERCENT	100.0	100.0	100.0	100.0	100.0

concept of the ideal or best being at the top and the least ideal or worst at the bottom. By the time in the interview when the items reported here were considered the informant had had considerable experience with this self-anchoring procedure. The interviewer described the informant's task as follows: "Now let's think of the top of the ladder as the place where things stand that are very good, and the bottom of the ladder as the place where things stand that are very bad. On which step would you place (name of your home country)? Where would you place (name of the country across the border)? Where would you place the Soviet Union?" Figure 18 presents the results of these evaluations. Mexicans place the United States higher on the ladder than the citizens of the United States placed Mexico. The Mexican Americans of the Southwestern United States make the highest evaluation of the United States recorded but their evaluation of Mexico is also higher than that given by fellow citizens of Anglo origin. Here again their marginality shows up and even this evaluation indicates their role as agents of linkages; loyal to their home country but favorably disposed to Mexico and Mexicans.

FIGURE 16

Responses to Items Concerning Normlessness

Items Concerning Normlessness	United States			Mexico	
	General Public	Rural Michigan	Mexican Americans	Urban	Rural
Normlessness in the midst of change					
Yes, strongly agree	18.1	21.3	56.9	49.8	35.1
Yes, slightly agree	25.7	25.7	24.5	32.0	29.2
Don't know	6.4	4.3	5.1	3.1	10.4
No, slightly disagree	26.4	26.7	5.9	8.8	11.5
No, strongly disagree	22.6	22.0	6.2	6.3	3.8
Refusal to answer, etc.	.8	—	1.4	—	—
TOTAL PERCENT	100.0	100.0	100.0	100.0	100.0
Normlessness and the meaning of life					
Yes, strongly agree	26.5	27.9	35.2	37.0	24.7
Yes, slightly agree	28.9	28.8	19.8	38.6	40.6
Don't know	8.3	5.1	15.7	8.1	22.2
No, slightly disagree	14.3	14.5	9.2	10.9	10.4
No, strongly disagree	21.4	23.7	18.7	5.4	2.1
Refusal to answer, etc.	.6	—	1.4	—	—
TOTAL PERCENT	100.0	100.0	100.0	100.0	100.0

In line with Max Weber's thought that Protestantism, the dominant religion of the United States, promotes confidence between people not bound together by kinship, the informants were requested to specify the extent of their agreement and disagreement with the statement: "People can be trusted." As indicated by Figure 19 a much larger proportion of Americans agree with this statement despite the Mexican tendency to answer in the affirmative tends to support our hunch as derived from Max Weber. The Mexican Americans did not differ much from the Anglo Americans in their responses to this item. Replying to another item on the authoritarian scale, namely, "Everyone should think the same about what is right and what is wrong," over 9 out of 10 Mexicans agreed as compared with 5 Anglo Americans. About 8 out of 10 Mexican Americans agreed to this, again placing them between Anglos and Mexicans.

To find how the informants evaluated their community, family, country, occupation and political party cooperatively a special procedure was used. In the interview in which the self-anchoring procedure was again employed, the informant was told, "Now, let's use the ladder in a different way. I would like you to think of yourself as compared to such things as . . . these organizations. On this card imagine that you are in the middle step of the ladder right now . . . at the top stand the things that are *most important* and at the bottom things that are *least important*. On what step would you put your family?" Figure 10 contains these placements. It will come as a surprise to some to note that Anglo Americans evaluate the family

FIGURE 17

Readiness to Accept Change — Birth Control: Responses to the Statement: "Family Planning or Birth Control Has Been Discussed by Many People. What is Your Feeling About a Married Couple Practicing Birth Control? If You Had to Decide, Which ONE of These Statements Best Expresses Your Point of View?

| | United States | | | Mexico | |
Response	General Public	Rural Michigan	Mexican Americans	Urban	Rural
It is always right	23.8	18.5	27.0	25.1	29.9
It is usually right	38.8	46.9	10.7	18.9	12.5
Don't know	13.0	11.8	25.9	6.9	13.9
It is usually wrong	11.6	11.9	20.8	26.4	17.4
It is always wrong	12.6	10.9	16.2	22.7	26.0
Other responses	.2	—	—	—	.3
TOTAL PERCENT	100.0	100.0	100.0	100.0	100.0

FIGURE 18

Mexico, United States and Russia, Evaluated as Nations at Various Steps on a Continuum from Good to Bad

| | United States | | | | | | Mexican Americans | | | Mexico | | | | | |
| | General Public | | | Rural Michigan | | | | | | Urban | | | Rural | | |
Ladder Step	Mexico	United States	Russia	Mexico	United States	Russia	Mexico	United States	Russia	Mexico	United States	Russia	Mexico	United States	Russia
Top 10	1.6	45.3	1.5	1.6	41.4	.6	11.9	80.9	2.1	44.5	37.3	9.7	49.4	25.1	5.9
9	2.3	15.5	3.0	1.5	15.5	2.1	25.4	11.3	4.1	17.3	27.4	11.6	15.3	27.2	8.0
8	3.6	18.8	6.7	2.5	16.8	3.7	10.8	5.2	5.8	18.1	15.8	14.4	14.6	18.0	18.7
7	5.3	8.2	10.5	5.2	13.0	7.8	12.2	1.8	7.6	7.1	6.7	10.0	4.5	7.6	8.7
6	8.8	3.3	10.0	5.5	6.6	10.6	12.5	—	6.1	4.9	3.8	8.5	5.2	5.6	9.7
5	19.9	4.2	17.5	23.0	3.7	12.7	13.0	—	4.9	4.6	2.5	9.3	2.8	2.4	4.9
4	16.1	1.0	8.5	8.8	1.1	13.4	8.6	—	8.1	.6	.9	5.9	.3	1.0	6.9
3	15.5	.8	10.1	14.9	—	12.7	1.8	—	12.5	.3	.8	4.6	.3	1.0	3.5
2	9.6	.2	8.4	12.4	.5	7.6	—	—	11.1	.1	.4	3.8	—	.3	2.8
1	5.9	.2	9.1	7.3	—	8.5	.8	—	6.5	.3	.1	2.3	—	.3	3.8
0	2.5	.2	9.7	4.6	.3	14.3	1.4	—	27.6	.1	1.1	14.4	.3	1.4	12.5
Don't know, refusal etc.	8.9	2.3	5.0	12.7	1.1	6.0	1.6	.8	3.6	2.1	3.2	5.5	7.3	10.1	14.6
TOTAL PERCENT	100.0	100.0	100.0	100.0	100.0	100.0	100.0	100.0	100.0	100.0	100.0	100.0	100.0	100.0	100.0

(384)

higher than do Mexicans following this procedure. Mexicans evaluate their country higher than do Anglo Americans. Mexican Americans give country, family, occupation, and community relatively high evaluations. They also give a higher evaluation to political party than do Anglos. Does this mean that they will use political activity to bring social justice?

Dworkin[34] found that lower class Mexican Americans born in the United States expressed stereotypes of themselves as being "Old fashioned," "Lazy, indifferent and unambitious." Those born in Mexico referred to themselves as "Religious" and "Well adjusted." There is implied a disparagement of self on the part of those born in and/or living a long time in the United States. Again, such images declined significantly in post-Chicano Movement samples regardless of nationality of the Mexican Americans. If any single statement can be made about the impact on stereotype of the movement or of changes in the social climate since the 1963 sampling, it is that it has significantly reduced what could once have been called minority group self-hatred.

FEELING

Sentiment as an element. Whereas beliefs, as discussed above under *KNOWING*, embody thoughts, sentiments embody feelings about the world. The sentiment of friendliness will receive our first consideration. After informants had used the self-anchoring ladder to evaluate the United States, Mexico, and Russia as reported in Figure 18, each was told, "Now, let's think of the top of the ladder as the place where those nations stand whose *people* you feel most friendly toward, and the bottom of the ladder as the place where the nations

FIGURE 19

Responses to the Statement: "People Can Be Trusted"

	United States			Mexico	
Responses	General Public	Rural Michigan	Mexican Americans	Urban	Rural
Yes, strongly agree	25.4	24.5	16.9	9.7	12.2
Yes, slightly agree	39.0	47.2	33.8	30.4	37.1
Don't know	2.8	2.2	4.4	3.4	4.5
No, slightly disagree	20.7	16.7	26.4	27.8	24.7
No, strongly disagree	11.5	8.8	15.8	28.7	21.5
Refused to answer, etc.	.6	.6	2.7	—	—
TOTAL PERCENT	100.0	100.0	100.0	100.0	100.0

FIGURE 20

Friendliness Felt Toward People of Mexico, United States, and Russia

| | United States | | | | | | | | | Mexico | | | | | |
| | General Public | | | Rural Michigan | | | Mexican Americans | | | Urban | | | Rural | | |
Ladder Step	Mexico	United States	Russia	Mexico	United States	Russia	Mexico	United States	Russia	Mexico	United States	Russia	Mexico	United States	Russia
Top 10	13.4	72.3	7.1	12.0	73.7	7.8	69.0	45.3	2.9	74.8	27.5	5.1	66.8	18.7	4.5
9	10.5	11.0	4.6	6.9	7.9	3.0	12.2	21.1	3.3	11.3	34.5	5.0	9.4	34.0	5.2
8	14.2	8.9	8.7	12.2	10.2	7.1	8.5	10.3	2.0	6.0	16.3	14.4	8.3	17.7	14.6
7	10.9	2.1	6.8	11.8	3.7	9.7	3.9	4.8	3.9	2.2	6.4	7.9	2.8	4.2	7.6
6	9.5	1.5	7.3	5.3	3.3	8.6	.8	9.0	7.1	1.9	4.0	10.0	2.8	3.8	6.9
5	16.7	2.2	17.0	16.9	.1	12.4	2.4	5.9	10.2	.8	3.5	10.5	1.7	4.9	9.0
4	5.0	.3	8.0	7.8	—	9.9	1.4	2.0	13.5	.8	1.4	6.2	.7	1.7	5.6
3	4.9	—	8.5	8.3	—	8.2	1.0	—	10.3	.3	.9	3.5	.3	2.1	3.5
2	4.5	—	5.1	3.0	—	7.2	—	—	9.1	.3	.6	6.3	.3	—	6.2
1	2.0	.1	9.6	2.6	.2	7.3	—	.8	5.5	—	.4	3.9	—	.7	3.8
0	2.2	—	12.1	4.6	.9	14.1	—	—	29.4	—	1.4	22.1	.3	2.8	20.3
Don't know, refusal etc.	6.2	1.6	5.2	8.6		4.7	.8	.8	2.8	2.3	3.1	5.1	6.6	9.4	12.8
TOTAL PERCENT	100.0	100.0	100.0	100.0	100.0	100.0	100.0	100.0	100.0	100.0	100.0	100.0	100.0	100.0	100.0

stand whose *people* you feel least friendly to? On which step would you place the *people* of (here the home country was named)? Where would you place (here the across the border country was named). Where would you place the Russian *people*?"

The results of this questioning are tabulated in Figure 20. The informants in the various samples with the exception of the Mexican Americans of the Southwestern United States placed the people of their home nation in such a manner as to produce much the same pattern. Almost three out of four placed the people of the home country on the top step, and a negligible number placed them on the bottom. How the Mexican Americans responded is highly informative. A comparison of their placement of the home country on the "friendship ladder" (Figure 20) and on the "evaluation of the nation ladder" (Figure 18) indicates that whereas they evaluate their home country, the United States as a nation, more highly than the informants of any of the other four samples, when it comes to the feeling of friendliness toward a country's people, they place Mexico slightly above their home country. Mexicans report that they feel more friendly toward the people of the United States than Anglo Americans of the United States say that they feel toward the Mexican people. Friendliness toward the people of Russia is not great for any of the samples.

For the general public of the United States, rural Michigan, and urban Mexico the samples for which data measuring the relationship between educational attainment and placement on the friendship ladder were available, the correlation was positive — the more educated the informant, the higher he was likely to place the people across the border. Product moment correlation coefficients for the three samples were respectively .14, .26, and .20.

As indicated above in Figure 4, 68.4 per cent of Mexican Americans interviewed said they had friends across the border. Of these, 60.4 per cent reported that they "would like to have some more friends across the border." The powerful linking potential of the Mexican American Community is indicated when these results are compared with those depicting the informants of the other samples. Only 4.8 per cent of those in the United States general public who already had friends in Mexico (18.7 per cent) said they would like to have more. Comparable figures for the urban and rural Mexicans are 4.1 and 1.4. None of the variables included in the study is more generally related to other "little" indexes of desired linkage and the various indexes of behavioral linkage (Figure 5) than that of desire to have across the border friends, or actually having such friends, as discussed above. For most of the samples those informants who

FIGURE 21

Worry About the Future: Citizens of Mexico/United States Assigning Themselves to Ladder Steps on the Basis of Their Conceived Worry About the Future — Responses to the Following: "Suppose at the Top of the Ladder Stands a Person Who Is Completely Free from Worry About the Future. At the Bottom of the Ladder is a Person with Many Worries About the Future. What Step of the Ladder Do You Stand on Right Now? . . . Stood on Five Years Ago? . . . Will Be on Five Years From Now?

| Ladder Step | United States | | | | | | | | | Mexico | | | | | |
| | General Public | | | Rural Michigan | | | Mexican Americans | | | Urban | | | Rural | | |
	Now	5 years ago	5 years hence	Now	5 years ago	5 years hence	Now	5 years ago	5 years hence	Now	5 years ago	5 years hence	Now	5 years ago	5 years hence
TOP 10	10.8	12.7	18.7	16.1	17.8	20.5	8.5	14.1	18.2	4.5	5.2	8.3	4.9	5.2	5.2
9	7.1	6.2	12.1	5.9	8.4	10.3	8.2	5.0	16.1	3.5	3.8	9.6	3.8	2.8	5.6
8	15.0	13.0	18.6	15.0	11.4	14.3	17.0	10.0	20.3	8.0	8.0	14.7	5.2	6.2	5.3
7	13.7	14.3	12.4	13.3	10.6	16.2	16.6	14.5	9.0	7.0	7.4	10.6	8.0	5.2	6.2
6	11.0	11.4	9.4	9.2	15.2	6.3	4.4	10.3	4.6	10.9	9.0	11.9	10.1	10.4	11.8
5	18.0	18.6	10.5	21.7	15.9	13.8	14.0	13.7	11.7	16.2	16.2	11.3	11.1	12.5	12.1
4	6.8	8.5	4.6	4.5	5.2	2.7	7.9	8.4	8.4	11.2	13.7	7.9	15.6	12.9	10.9
3	6.8	6.3	3.6	4.6	4.8	5.1	3.1	7.1	2.4	10.2	11.9	6.9	8.7	12.1	10.4
2	3.6	4.2	1.8	5.0	4.2	1.2	6.6	1.6	1.0	8.4	9.5	5.9	8.0	11.5	6.9
1	3.8	2.9	2.3	2.1	1.7	1.0	2.7	8.4	2.7	5.3	4.9	2.5	6.2	5.6	5.2
0	2.7	1.2	1.6	2.6	4.6	3.0	11.0	6.9	1.4	12.8	8.2	5.7	10.1	6.9	6.6
Don't know, refusal etc.	.7	.7	4.4	—	.2	5.6	—	—	4.2	2.0	2.2	4.7	8.3	8.7	13.2
TOTAL PERCENT	100.0	100.0	100.0	100.0	100.0	100.0	100.0	100.0	100.0	100.0	100.0	100.0	100.0	100.0	100.0

reported that they desired across the border friends are closer to the people across the border on the social distance scales; that is, they are less likely to reject them as neighbors, co-workers, citizens and as family members. Furthermore, in the United States general public as well as the rural Michigan samples, those desiring more friends than they now have across the border more frequently interact with across the border friends and neighbors, also they more frequently have second-hand contact *via* close friends, more frequently desire collaboration between the two nations, and feel more friendly toward the people across the border.[35]

Tension management as process.   This process may be defined as action by which elements of the social system are articulated in such a manner as to 1) prevent sentiments from obstructing goal-directed activity, and 2) avail the system of their motivating force in achieving goals. Prayer is among the many tension-managing activities. As indicated by Figure 9, the Mexican American and Mexican informants almost all pray and they pray frequently.

Some writers have pictured Mexico as the land of resignation, devoid of worry. Figure 21 reports results obtained from permitting informants to place themselves on a ladder in terms of how much they worry about the future. It argues against such worry-free claims. The level of worry now and five years from now is much higher in Mexico as ascertained from this "worry-ladder" than in the United States. Mexican Americans place themselves on this "worry ladder" much as do North Americans generally. In terms of worry as reflected by this procedure the hope for the future is very great for Mexican Americans and the other United States citizens; it is less so for the Mexicans.

Dworkin[36] found that lower class Mexican Americans included in his study who were born in the United States frequently stereotyped Anglo Americans as "Scientific" which might mean that they manage tensions. Also, they more frequently than those born in Mexico stereotyped Anglos as "Puritanical" and "Tense, anxious, and neurotic." These same informants stereotyped themselves as "Emotional" and "Unscientific." Those born in Mexico stereotyped Americans as "Friendly" although "Proper and respectable," and "Well-adjusted."

Communication of sentiment as process.   Through this process action is taken by the members of a social system which leads to motivation to achieve goals, conform to norms, and carry out systemic action through transfer of feeling by symbols. Dworkin in the study mentioned above found that Mexican Americans of lower class born in Mexico stereotyped themselves as "Happy," "Friendly," and "Proud" with "Strong family ties." Those born in the United States stereotyped themselves as "Emotional," "Mistrusted" but "Proud." Mexican Americans and Mexicans are noted for the sentiments they communicate in kinship and friendship relations.

The word "emotional," as the evaluation of the "Stereotype Ethnocentrism" indicators on Dworkin's 1963, 1967-68, and 1971 studies indicate, is a particularly interesting term. In 1963, the word was defined by Mexican Americans as the opposite of scientific, which typified Anglos. However, by the time of the Chicano Movement and afterwards, the term became a favorable trait implying that for Mexican Americans it was a property of having "soul." To be emotional suggested that one was not an automaton like the Anglo, but able to enjoy life fully.

ACHIEVING

End, goal, or objective as an element.   The end, goal, or objective is the change (or in some cases the retention of the status quo) that members of a social system expect to accomplish through appropriate action. Here we shall be interested in some obvious goals of informants and in addition our own goal of improving relations among the groups and nations studied.

In terms of hopes for a better future none of the informants in the study comparing Mexico, the United States and Mexican Americans of the Southwest of the United States were more optimistic than the Mexican Americans. This is revealed in Figure 22 and we may predict that pressures may be generated from unfulfilled expectations. Such unfulfilled expectations have no doubt resulted for all the population studied. In Dworkin's study[37] of lower class Mexican Americans those born in the United States frequently stereotyped Anglo Americans as "Materialistic" and "Education-minded" but they stereotyped themselves as having "Little care for education," and as being "Lazy, indifferent, and unambitious." In the later samplings "Materialistic" became a negative trait, depicting a grasping greedy individual. In reality the group seems to be voicing an unhappy concern for their own perceived low status educationally. This latter may be a "reverse stereotype" because many studies[38] reveal a great desire on the part of Mexican Americans for education. Thus, a "latent" goal may be here expressed.

Goal attaining and concomitant "latent" activity as process.   Dworkin observes that those born in the United States "perhaps developed their strongly negative stereotypes of the Anglo, which generally picture him as grasping and dishonest, in order to explain his relatively superior position . . . (and the negative stereotypes of themselves) as lazy and uneducated . . . to justify their own relatively inferior position within society."[39]

FIGURE 22

Self-Perceived Level of Living: Citizens of Mexico/United States Assigning Themselves to Ladder Steps on the Basis of the Following Instructions: "Now, Let's Change Things Which Stand at the Top and Bottom of the Ladder. Suppose We Say That at the Top of the Ladder Stands a Person Who Is Living the Best Possible Life and at the Bottom Stands a Person Who Is Living the Worst Possible Life. What Step of the Ladder Do You Feel You Personally Stand on Right Now? . . . Stood on Five Years Ago . . . Will Be on Five Years from Now?

| Ladder Step | United States | | | | | | | | | Mexico | | | | | |
| | General Public | | | Rural Michigan | | | Mexican Americans | | | Urban | | | Rural | | |
	Now	5 years ago	5 years hence	Now	5 years ago	5 years hence	Now	5 years ago	5 years hence	Now	5 years ago	5 years hence	Now	5 years ago	5 years hence
TOP 10	16.0	13.2	26.7	19.0	16.3	23.7	17.8	14.3	26.7	3.3	3.8	12.0	4.2	2.3	6.9
9	6.3	6.4	15.6	7.2	5.5	10.7	4.7	2.6	15.6	2.3	1.7	9.8	2.1	3.2	6.6
8	20.1	14.2	18.5	15.7	12.5	20.2	21.2	10.6	18.5	5.1	3.8	13.7	4.9	4.5	12.1
7	14.0	13.2	12.9	17.3	14.9	13.1	13.3	10.6	12.9	7.1	3.1	15.6	9.4	5.1	9.4
6	14.2	12.5	7.3	9.7	9.6	5.3	11.4	14.7	7.3	11.8	9.7	12.4	9.7	8.6	10.8
5	18.8	20.8	9.6	22.1	21.9	10.5	19.0	21.9	9.6	25.9	8.7	12.7	15.2	18.6	10.4
4	5.3	8.0	2.2	1.8	5.4	2.8	4.4	9.7	2.2	11.4	10.8	5.6	9.0	14.7	11.8
3	2.3	5.3	1.2	1.1	4.2	1.5	3.0	6.2	1.2	9.2	15.3	6.1	10.8	11.9	6.6
2	.7	2.5	.5	1.3	3.7	—	1.8	3.2	.5	9.6	11.1	3.9	12.5	14.5	5.2
1	.6	1.9	.6	.5	2.3	1.4	—	2.7	.6	5.3	9.4	2.0	8.3	6.6	3.8
0	1.0	1.1	.9	3.2	2.6	4.4	2.0	2.1	.9	7.4	14.3	2.5	5.6	8.2	3.8
Don't know, refusal etc.	.7	.9	4.0	1.1	1.1	6.4	1.4	1.4	4.0	1.6	8.3	3.7	8.3	1.8	12.6
TOTAL PERCENT	100.0	100.0	100.0	100.0	100.0	100.0	100.0	100.0	100.0	100.0	100.0	100.0	100.0	100.0	100.0

(391)

In our consideration of how to improve relations between Mexico and the United States, the following line of inquiry was developed. Informants were asked to express the extent of their agreement or disagreement with the following statements: "Our country should have closer connection and ties with Mexico (or the United States)" and "Our leaders should be working more with leaders of Mexico (or the United States)." The Mexican American informants as revealed in Figure 23 are overwhelmingly in favor of more cooperation. Here again their potential role as "brokers" and links between the two nations is manifest.

SANCTIONING

Sanction as an element and application of sanctions as process. Sanction may be defined as the rewards and penalties used to attain conformity to ends and norms. Many writers, including Whetten[40] consider the taking of bribes by government officials one of the greatest, if not the greatest, deterrent to progress in Mexico. Figure 24 indicates differences in responses from the various samples when

FIGURE 23

Desire for Greater Linkage Between the United States and Mexico: Desire for More Cooperation Between Leaders and Desire for Closer Ties

	United States			Mexico	
Responses	General Public	Rural Michigan	Mexican Americans	Urban	Rural
DESIRE MORE COOPERATION					
Yes, strongly agree	25.5	21.1	62.0	37.4	36.5
Yes, slightly agree	29.1	30.0	14.4	34.1	32.3
Don't know	26.1	26.6	9.3	7.4	14.9
No, slightly disagree	10.5	13.5	8.7	11.6	7.3
No, strongly disagree	8.0	8.4	2.9	9.2	9.0
Refusal, other	.8	.4	2.7	.3	—
TOTAL PERCENT	100.0	100.0	100.0	100.0	100.0
DESIRE CLOSER TIES					
Yes, strongly agree	29.4	24.0	68.2	42.6	39.1
Yes, slightly agree	30.6	33.6	12.6	36.0	35.8
Don't know	22.9	21.9	8.6	7.3	15.3
No, slightly disagree	10.3	12.9	4.4	7.5	5.6
No, strongly disagree	6.1	7.2	3.5	6.3	4.2
Refusal, other	.7	.4	2.7	.3	—
TOTAL PERCENT	100.0	100.0	100.0	100.0	100.0

informants were presented with the following proposition: "Some people in public office take bribes. What form of punishment do you think should be given to those public officials who do take bribes?" Perhaps the greatest difference in the response of the Mexican Americans as compared with others is the much larger proportion of informants that believe the culprits should be removed from office (98.3 per cent). Although other informants in the United States in general specify more severe punishments than Mexican informants the differences are not so great as the literature on the subject of bribery in public office would suggest.

FACILITATING

Facility as an element and facilitating as a process. A facility is a means used within the system to attain the members' ends. Scarce resources used as facilities is the subject of economics, but sociologists cannot avoid considering it. Many writers have noted that norms concerning private property and its unrestricted accumulation through free enterprise are highly evaluated and may approach sacredness. Thus Northrup[41] writes about the "Anglo-American Lockean doctrine of the primacy of property rights [maintaining that it] is this ... principle ... of property rights over human, social or economic needs . . . that Mexico and [other Latin American] countries are refusing to accept." The rural Mexican *ejido*, a voluntary cooperative type of ownership of rural lands, has no counterpart in North

FIGURE 24

Sanctions Against Particularism and Nepotism in Government:
Responses to the Question: "What Forms of Punishment, If Any, Do
You Think Should Be Given to Those Public Officials
Who . . . Take Bribes

| | United States | | | Mexico | |
Response	General Public	Rural Michigan	Mexican Americans	Urban	Rural
Punishment Recommended					
Death penalty	1.4	2.7	1.4	2.2	3.1
Imprisonment	44.1	37.3	37.6	29.8	33.4
Heavy fine	45.3	44.7	32.2	25.4	13.2
Light fine	3.9	5.0	1.8	16.0	16.4
Removal from office	75.9	79.1	98.3	56.8	41.1
No punishment	.7	.8	7.3	1.7	6.3
Other treatment	2.6	3.3	3.4	1.0	.7
Don't know or refusal	1.3	1.8	1.4	2.8	5.9

America. To get at attitudes concerning property as a facility and its use as process, respondents were asked their reactions to two statements: 1) "Some people have too much property and others don't have enough," and 2) "Property is something that should be shared." The results are presented in Figure 25. Mexicans agree with these statements more than do Anglo Americans. The Mexican Americans take a position in between. From these results may we ask: Are Mexicans nearer socialism than Americans?

THE MASTER PROCESSES

Of the six master processes of the PAS model, communication, boundary maintenance, systemic linkage, socialization, institutionalization, and social control, the two: boundary maintenance and systemic linkage, have been made focal to the whole inquiry. They were discussed above at the outset.

Communication. Communication is the process by which information, decisions, and directives pass through the system and by which knowledge is transmitted and sentiment is formed or modified. Figure 26 indicates the languages spoken by informants in the five samples. The Mexican Americans demonstrate their linking capacity with the largest proportion speaking the across-the-border language in their homes. With the high proportion of that group also speaking English, about 85 per cent appear to be bilingual. As the high fertility and other factors increase the proportion of Mexican Americans who inhabit the Southwest of the United States Spanish will become increasingly common.

Informants were also questioned about their use of mass media both at home and from across the border. Whereas 33.3 per cent of the Mexican Americans report listening to radio and viewing television programs, "only from across the border" the comparable figures for the United States general public and urban Mexico were respectively .7 and 17. Considerable linkage may be noted here on the part of Mexicans and Mexican Americans, and it may be expected to increase. Whereas 28.9 per cent of the urban Mexican informants reported reading magazines "only from across the border" few of the other informants seemed to be heavily influenced by newspapers and magazines from across the border.[42]

Institutionalization. This is the process through which organizations are given structure and social action and interaction are made predictable. As Durkheim noted institutionalization is a matter of degree, not of absolute presence or absence. Whereas in "over-institutionalization" actors may take their lives in the case of failure

FIGURE 25

Responses to Items Concerning Property

Items Concerning Property	United States General Public	United States Rural Michigan	United States Mexican Americans	Mexico Urban	Mexico Rural
Division of property unfair					
Yes, strongly agree	38.6	33.0	62.0	59.3	57.0
Yes, slightly agree	23.4	25.4	15.3	22.5	23.6
Don't know	7.5	3.3	5.9	3.5	7.6
No, slightly disagree	12.3	17.2	5.5	9.0	8.7
No, strongly disagree	17.7	20.7	8.6	5.7	3.1
Refusal to answer, etc.	.5	.4	2.7	—	—
TOTAL PERCENT	100.0	100.0	100.0	100.0	100.0
Property should be shared					
Yes, strongly agree	21.3	27.9	31.4	28.9	28.5
Yes, slightly agree	18.9	20.3	13.2	33.0	36.5
Don't know	10.0	6.3	7.3	5.1	8.7
No, slightly disagree	15.8	15.9	10.1	15.4	12.8
No, strongly disagree	33.5	29.4	33.6	17.6	13.5
Refusal to answer, etc.	.5	.2	2.4	—	—
TOTAL PERCENT	100.0	100.0	100.0	100.0	100.0

FIGURE 26

Citizens of Mexico and the United States Who Speak "Foreign" Languages, and Spanish and English in Their Homes

Language Spoken	United States General Public	United States Rural Michigan	United States Mexican Americans**	Mexico Urban	Mexico Rural
Language foreign to country	13.7	8.9	86.0	11.4	8.7
No foreign language	86.1	91.1	14.0	88.1	91.3
No response	.2	—	—	.5	—
TOTAL PERCENT	100.0	100.0	100.0	100.0	100.0
Percent speaking:					
Spanish	3.2	.2	86.0	96.0*	97.0*
English	92.5*	99.0*	85.4	8.0	—

*Interviewer's statement concerning language background.
**Originally.

to conform resulting in altruistic suicide, in periods of rapid change there may be "underinstitutionalization" resulting in egoistic and/or anomic suicide.

It is frequently assumed that Mexicans do not evaluate change as a general phenomenon as favorably as do North Americans. Although this generalization is a popular theme in the literature comparing the two countries, little in the present study supports this thesis. Two questions were designed to test it: "Some people are more set in their ways than others. How would you rate yourself — do you find it very easy to change your ways, somewhat easy to change your ways, slightly difficult to change, or very difficult to change?" and "I like the kind of work that lets me do things about the same way from one week to the next," with opportunity in the case of the latter to express degree of agreement or disagreement. As Figure 27 indicates, Mexicans rate themselves as more easily adjusting to change than do North Americans. In evaluating their preferences for stability in work expectancy patterns, however, Mexicans indicate they generally prefer work that involves the same routine from one week to the next. Interestingly, the greater the educational attainment the less the agreement with the statement. On no other single item do Mexican Americans differ from fellow United States citizens and also from Mexicans more than on this one. Eight out of 10 agree with the statement. On this they are closer to the Mexicans. Could this response be a desire for security resulting in part from insecurity and from a marginal position? Dworkin[43] in his 1963 study, found that those born in the United States thought of themselves as "Old-fashioned." May we assume that those who thus stereotype themselves, and are conservative or dislike change may be expressing a favorable self-image whereas those desiring to change are expressing just the opposite?

Socialization. This is the process whereby the social and cultural heritage is transmitted. Although socialization goes on in almost all pluralities in no modern society are the family and school unimportant in its conduct. Dworkin[44] found that Mexican Americans, both those born in Mexico and those born in the United States, stereotyped Anglos as "education-minded." However, those born in the United States stereotyped Anglos as having "Little family loyalty." However, persons of societies with different courtship, divorce and other norms relating to the family may, in their evaluations and also in their designation of weaknesses, be focusing on very different phenomena. In other words observers voicing honest condemnation and/or praise of one or the other family system may be talking past one another. The function of a nuclear family in an industrial society such as the United States may be different from the function of the more extended less mobile family in Mexico. In any case, as indicated above in Figures 10 and 28, in terms of both evaluation and interaction of members there is no basis for considering the Anglo American family weak. The very high rate of interaction of Mexican Americans with relatives not living in the same house and the higher rate of such interaction on the part of Anglo Americans than of Mexicans must be important for socialization. The senior author's field experience bears this out.[45] The family cannot be written off as unimportant in either country. Mexican Americans born in Mexico, reported above in Dworkin's study, stereotyped themselves as having "Strong family ties."

How does education contribute to boundary maintenance and systemic linkage of Mexicans and Americans? When scores for each item for either behavioral linkage are combined as indicated in Figure 5 (Huge A), the resulting score is significantly related to educational attainment. This holds also for desired linkage for all except the Mexican Americans as registered by the Pearsonian r. The C coefficient for this latter item is significant. (See Figure 29). We must conclude that education has potential for improving relations between the countries and groups here considered.

FIGURE 27

Responses to Items Concerning Readiness to Accept Change

| | United States | | | Mexico | |
Responses	General Public	Rural Michigan	Mexican Americans	Urban	Rural
Ease in accepting change					
Very easy	11.5	11.4	14.5	18.6	19.4
Somewhat easy	30.6	30.9	14.8	27.1	32.3
Don't know	2.6	.9	21.1	3.1	4.5
Slightly difficult	39.1	40.1	30.8	27.0	21.9
Very difficult	16.2	16.7	16.7	24.2	21.9
Other answers	—	—	2.1	—	—
TOTAL PERCENT	100.0	100.0	100.0	100.0	100.0
Stability in work patterns					
Yes, strongly agree	31.0	38.0	60.9	44.7	40.0
Yes, slightly agree	21.8	22.0	18.4	32.3	37.2
Don't know	3.1	1.1	.8	6.1	13.5
No, slightly disagree	21.1	20.0	7.1	11.7	6.9
No, strongly disagree	22.4	18.9	10.1	5.2	2.4
Refuse to answer, etc.	.6	—	2.7	—	—
TOTAL PERCENT	100.0	100.0	100.0	100.0	100.0

As indicated above under *Status-role*, Mexican Americans are marginal in the sense that Park and others used the term. To explore the nature of this marginality, a special study[46] was made in which the hypothesis that the greater the interaction within the Mexican American community the greater would be the desire for this linkage and linkage with Mexico, was tested. The hypothesis was supported only for Mexican Americans with the following combination of traits and experience: relatively high education, urbanity of residence and youth (21-40 years of age). Since the data for the study as used above were gathered in 1963-1964 we may speculate that then there was beginning among people with these characteristics, a movement which was to grow into a great effort on the part of Mexican Americans to improve their lot and deepen their identification as Mexican Americans. It is significant that education is playing an important part in this.

Social control.   Social control is the process by which deviancy is counteracted. Under the heading *SANCTIONING* social control was discussed above. Mexican Americans of lower class, born in the United States, are reported by Dworkin[47] to stereotype Anglo Americans as "Conformists" and "Puritanical." This seems a bit ironical in view of the great effort on the part of the sophisticated younger Anglos to "green" America. For them perhaps as they try to do their "own thing" the stereotype Mexican Americans born in Mexico apply to Anglos, namely, that of being "Individualistic" may be appropriate.

CONDITIONS OF SOCIAL ACTION

The elements and processes considered above constitute the working components; i.e., the parts and articulating processes, of the social system. Not all aspects of social action are encompassed in these concepts, but the remaining components are only partly systemic, that is, partly structured and partly under the control of the actors of the system. Territoriality or space, time and size are such components.

Territoriality.   The setting of the social system in space is called its territoriality, and it determines within limits how much space each person or group may have, the frequency and intensity of interaction within the group, and probabilities of systemic linkages between groups. Of course, both opportunities for and participation in across-the-border linkage is greater in border states than in non-border states. This holds for both Mexico and the United States. Following the United States Bureau of the Census practice in the publications on "Spanish-Name Persons," Arizona, California, Colorado, New Mexico and Texas are here designated as "border states." Baja California, (R.N.), Sonora, Coahuila, Chihuahua, Nuevo Leon and Tamulipas were designated as the border states of Mexico.

When separate indexes of linkage reported above and combined as indicated in Figure 5 are considered, the informants in the border states report the highest scores except that in rural Mexico the 20 informants failed to so respond. (See Figure 30). Since all of the Mexican Americans subjected to intensive analysis live in the border states they do not influence this comparison. No doubt the 49 informants in the United States general public who report themselves as bilingual Mexican and/or Indian influence the scores.

When traditional societies begin "placing a positive value on *mobility* ... a revolutionary change" is in the offing.[48] As indicated by Figure 31, Mexican Americans are certainly not immobile. In both Mexico and the United States, there is plenty of movement. Those who yearn for stability and the "good old days" may yearn for the world of the grandparents of the Mexicans, and the Mexican Ameri-

FIGURE 28

Frequency of Interaction With Kin and Relatives: Citizens of Mexico/United States Who Report on Frequency of Getting Together With Relatives Not Living in the Same House as Informant*

| Frequency of Interaction | United States | | | Mexico | |
	General Public	Rural Michigan	Mexican Americans	Urban	Rural
At least once a week	39.2	45.5	57.2	33.7	37.2
A few times a month	17.3	15.6	12.9	7.4	8.7
About once a month	10.9	8.9	9.5	12.8	18.1
A few times a year	18.1	17.9	6.9	16.1	6.6
Once a year	6.7	7.6	7.9	16.9	12.8
Less than once a year	4.0	2.7	2.1	2.8	2.4
Never	3.6	1.4	3.0	9.2	13.9
No response	.2	.4	.5	1.1	.3
TOTAL PERCENT	100.0	100.0	100.0	100.0	100.0

*It is possible that some family interaction for the Mexican samples is excluded from the responses by the specification that it must take place with relatives outside the home. The investigators do not know the degree to which the Mexican samples represent extended families in which most meaningful family interaction would take place inside the home. However, the high scoring of the Spanish-speaking Latinos of the southwestern United States, who also have extended families, would suggest that no great modification would have to be made if information on the Mexican extended family were available, especially for the urban Mexican sample.

FIGURE 29

Relation of Behavioral Linkage (Huge A) with Desired Linkage (Huge B), by Education, and Relation of Desired Linkage (Huge B) with Education, by Desired Linkage (Huge B)*

Behavioral Linkage (Huge A) with Desired Linkage (Huge B)

Control Variables	Sample**	C	x^2	d.f.	r
Whole sample	1	.40	300.4	130	.27
	2	.53	121.5	100	.33
	3	.68	90.9	65	.29
	4	.37	177.1	120	.22
	5	.53	113.5	90	.08
Education Low Grades	1	.42	146.5	120	.23
	2	.63	92.3	70	.34
United States 0-4	3	.69	67.8	60	.41
Mexico 0-2	4	.45	172.3	120	.16
	5	.55	115.5	90	.06
High	1	.45	211.2	130	.27
United States 5	2	.58	82.8	90	.29
and over	3	.78	46.0	44	.10
Mexico 3 and over	4	.43	95.8	120	.14
	5	.71	19.9	24	—

Desired Linkage (Huge B) with Education

Control Variables	Sample**	C	x^2	d.f.	r
Whole sample	1	.27	123.2	70	.17
	2	.49	94.9	70	.26
	3	.58	52.5	40	.03
	4	.39	198.9	80	.31
	5	.37	46.5	40	.20
Huge B Low scores	1	.41	83.0	63	.22
	2	.50	30.3	24	.19
	3***	—	—	—	—
	4	.47	64.2	56	.20
	5	.45	27.0	15	.31
High scores	1	.38	190.4	91	.24
	2	.55	94.0	70	.26
	3	.71	106.9	104	.31
	4	.45	224.8	96	.35
	5	.38	30.0	32	.15

*See Footnote 9 for references containing statistical indices similar to those above for other variables in Table 1.
**Sample numbers refer to the following populations: 1 = United States general public; 2 = Rural Michigan; 3= Mexican Americans of the Southwestern United States; 4 = Urban Mexico; 5 = Rural Mexico.
***Less than 1 percent.

(400)

cans. In answer to the question "Have you ever considered moving from this town?" 29 per cent of the Mexican Americans answered, "Yes" as compared with 48, 30 and 18, respectively for the U.S. general public, urban Mexico and rural Mexico.

Time.   The frequently asserted idea that *"Hora española* and *mañana*, not *hora englesa* and *today"* prevails in Mexico, while not without some support, as is true for many traditionally oriented societies, is not generally accurate. In support of it are the responses to the following statement: "Nowadays a person has to live pretty much for today and let tomorrow take care of itself," as tabulated in Figure 32. It is worthy of note that almost two-thirds of the Mexican Americans agree with the statement, and it seems to be more frequently affirmed in Mexico than in the United States. They and the Mexicans seem to conform to Max Weber's characterization of the traditional society as governed by the "authority of an eternal yesterday." Yet as Figure 21 indicates, there is no shortage of worry about the future in Mexico and among Mexican Americans, and they appear to think it will increase. Also one may judge from Figure 16 that these same informants wish that there were less change.

Size.   As Figure 33 indicates, the size of the place of residence is positively correlated to the component indexes of both behavioral and desired linkages for Mexican Americans. Although less consistently, so it is also related in the same way for the other samples. It appears then that both urbanization and education as discussed above, may foster linkage and desire for linkage.

CONCLUDING REMARKS

As other investigators have noted, life experiences that expose individuals to a broader range of human differences — whether ideological, racial, or cultural — also tend to liberalize attitudes. For those interested in the relations of Mexico and the United States, the Mexican American community has a great potential for articulating interaction and promoting favorable across-the-border attitudes.

FIGURE 30

Mean Scores and Standard Deviations of Behavioral Linkage (Huge A) and Desire for Linkage (Huge B) for Informants by Residence, Region, Ethnicity, Religion, Sex and Educational Level

Residence, Region, Ethnicity, Religion, Sex and Education	General Public No.	Mean A	Mean B	SD A	SD B	Rural Michigan No.	Mean A	Mean B	SD A	SD B	Mexican Americans No.	Mean A	Mean B	SD A	SD B	Urban No.	Mean A	Mean B	SD A	SD B	Rural No.	Mean A	Mean B	SD A	SD B
Place of residence																									
Rural farm less than 2,500	120	1.42	5.28	1.66	2.22	63	1.32	5.65	1.71	2.33	24	7.21	8.08	2.57	1.06	—	—	—	—	—	158	1.76	5.50	2.30	2.74
Open country non-farm	327	1.27	5.42	1.84	2.11	243	1.50	5.63	1.78	2.15	28	2.07	7.89	2.79	1.10	—	—	—	—	—	119	1.36	5.84	1.71	2.66
Places 2,500-49,999	230	2.21	5.76	2.42	2.40	—	—	—	—	—	16	8.00	8.56	2.13	.73	503	2.01	6.26	2.44	2.66	—	—	—	—	—
Places 50,000-499,999	376	1.94	5.76	2.24	2.19	—	—	—	—	—	24	9.25	8.46	3.55	1.18	265	2.47	6.77	2.66	2.41	—	—	—	—	—
Places 500,000 and over	475	2.62	6.22	2.87	1.99	—	—	—	—	—	13	7.69	8.77	3.64	.83	358	2.40	7.29	2.59	2.10	—	—	—	—	—
Total sample*	1528	2.01	5.79	2.42	2.17	306	1.46	5.63	1.77	2.19	105	7.55	8.28	3.13	1.06	1126	2.24	6.71	2.55	2.47	277	1.56	5.65	2.07	2.71
Region																									
Non-border states	1262	1.43	5.68	1.86	2.19	—	—	—	—	—	—	—	—	—	—	852	1.80	6.71	2.24	2.49	268	1.34	5.69	1.81	2.70
Border states	266	4.73	6.33	2.87	2.01	—	—	—	—	—	—	—	—	—	—	274	3.61	6.72	2.93	2.40	20	4.45	4.75	2.87	2.86
Ethnicity *(United States / Mexico)*																									
Anglo-white / Mexican only	1299	2.01	5.66	2.30	2.18	299	1.45	5.61	1.77	2.21	—	—	—	—	—	1048	2.29	6.72	2.54	2.47	2.46	1.69	5.57	2.72	2.70
Spanish-speaking / Mexican Spanish-speaking Bi-lingual Mexican and Indian	49	5.53	6.96	3.67	2.02	2	1.50	6.50	2.12	.71	105	7.55	8.28	3.13	1.06	47	1.51	6.87	2.07	2.09	32	.69	6.69	1.38	2.47
Negroes / Non-Spanish-speaking Indian	171	.96	6.44	1.88	1.98	5	1.80	6.40	1.92	1.14	—	—	—	—	—	10	—	3.70	—	1.83	—	—	—	—	—
Others / Negroes and others	9	1.78	5.89	1.72	1.45	—	—	—	—	—	—	—	—	—	—	29	2.38	6.97	3.31	2.61	10	1.29	3.80	1.69	2.90
Religion																									
None	42	2.81	6.45	2.57	2.00	11	1.45	5.00	1.92	2.53	1	11.00	7.00	—	—	6	1.67	5.00	2.88	3.90	4	.50	6.25	1.00	4.19
Protestant	1016	1.86	5.66	2.35	2.22	229	1.39	5.54	1.70	2.23	7	6.14	7.86	3.08	.90	37	3.14	7.78	2.51	1.72	10	2.60	7.50	2.84	2.27
Catholic	398	2.25	6.02	2.57	2.06	62	1.65	6.18	1.78	1.79	96	7.60	8.31	3.13	1.07	1063	2.18	6.68	2.52	2.47	265	1.50	5.51	2.03	2.70
Jewish	48	1.83	5.78	2.05	1.93	—	—	—	—	—	—	—	—	—	—	1	7.00	9.00	—	—	—	—	—	—	—
Agnostic/Atheist	7	4.29	7.14	3.09	1.77	2	5.00	7.00	5.66	—	—	—	—	—	—	16	3.63	6.88	3.48	2.06	2	2.00	6.50	2.86	3.54
Other	14	3.00	6.79	2.45	1.67	2	—	1.00	—	—	1	9.00	9.00	—	—	1	4.00	1.00	—	—	7	2.71	6.71	1.75	2.43
Sex																									
Male	734	2.15	6.02	2.47	2.17	146	1.71	5.86	2.03	2.32	52	5.28	5.56	3.22	.78	414	2.71	7.16	2.70	2.26	138	1.94	5.96	2.29	2.53
Female	794	1.87	5.59	2.37	2.16	160	1.23	5.42	1.46	2.05	53	6.89	8.00	2.91	1.22	698	1.99	6.46	2.43	2.53	142	1.20	5.37	1.76	2.87
Education *(United States / Mexico)*																									
0-4 years / 0-2 years	672	1.56	5.44	2.25	2.24	138	1.14	5.27	1.58	2.31	75	6.93	8.28	2.89	1.02	693	1.62	6.18	2.15	2.62	267	1.49	5.50	2.03	2.74
5-over / 3-over	847	2.36	6.07	2.49	2.08	168	1.73	5.93	1.87	2.05	30	9.10	8.27	3.21	1.17	424	3.18	7.58	2.82	1.93	20	2.45	7.30	2.31	1.89

*Totals may differ slightly due to no response, don't know etc.

FIGURE 31

**Mobility: Present Address Related to Place of Birth
for Citizens of Mexico/United States**

Place of Birth	United States			Mexico	
	General Public	Rural Michigan	Mexican Americans	Urban	Rural
Data for informants:					
Born in same city, (town) as present residence	30.5	36.7	31.7	39.3	36.5
Born in different city, but same state as present residence	26.7	31.0	34.5	23.1	48.3
Born in different state, but same nation as present residence	35.3	28.4	10.2	35.0	13.5
Born in different nation from present residence	6.5	3.7	23.6	1.4	.3
Don't know, refusal, etc.	1.0	.2	—	1.2	1.4
TOTAL PERCENT	100.0	100.0	100.0	100.0	100.0
Data for informants' parents or grandparents:					
All born in respondent's country	40.4	52.0	59.5	94.4	98.3
Not all born in respondent's country	58.7	44.8	38.7	4.0	.3
Don't know, refusal, other	.9	3.2	1.8	1.6	1.4
TOTAL PERCENT	100.0	100.0	100.0	100.0	100.0

FIGURE 32

**Responses to the Statement: "Nowadays a Person Has to Live Pretty
Much for Today and Let Tomorrow Take Care of Itself"**

Responses	United States			Mexico	
	General Public	Rural Michigan	Mexican Americans	Urban	Rural
Yes, strongly agree	28.6	26.9	60.6	42.0	33.7
Yes, slightly agree	18.4	18.8	8.3	33.4	34.3
Don't know	2.2	1.1	4.1	6.6	18.1
No, slightly disagree	22.0	19.8	8.7	11.3	7.6
No, strongly disagree	28.4	32.7	14.2	6.7	6.3
Refusal to answer, etc.	.4	.7	4.1	—	—
TOTAL PERCENT	100.0	100.0	100.0	100.0	100.0

FIGURE 33

Measures of Relationship of Behavioral, Desired Linkage Indexes and Educational Level to Other Sociological Variables

Indexes S(a)	Educational Attainment C	x²	df	r	Regions: Non-Border Border C	x²	df	r	Size of Place of Residence (b) C	x²	df	r	Language and/or Ethnic or Racial Background (c) C	x²	df	r	Social Class, Self-Determined (d) C	x²	df	r	Religion (e) C	x²	df	r	Sex C	x²	df	r	Age C	x²	df	r
Big A 1	.39	265.9	14	.39	.27	116.6	2	.27	.16	40.1	8	.13	.28	133.7	6	-.23	.26	107.2	10	.22	.11	19.4	10	.01	.16	38.3	2	-.16	.11	19.6	10	-.04
2	.36	45.1	14	.33	—	—	—	—	.06	1.2	2	.06	.08	1.7	4	.02	.24	18.5	10	.19	.18	10.2	8	.04	.27	23.0	2	-.26	.22	14.8	10	-.01
3	.47	29.4	16	.44	.20	45.6	2	.18	.51	36.0	8	.13	—	—	—	—	.28	8.7	10	.02	.20	4.5	6	—	.10	1.1	2	-.09	.31	10.7	10	-.10
4	.47	320.9	16	.49	.22	15.2	2	.18	.21	50.1	8	.19	.14	22.0	6	-.04	.35	153.0	10	.37	.15	26.1	10	-.04	.33	139.4	2	-.35	.15	25.4	10	-.08
5	.36	41.7	8	.34	.10	15.1	1	.10	.06	.9	2	.03	.14	5.7	4	-.07	.18	10.1	4	.11	.19	10.4	8	-.02	.33	35.2	2	-.34	.16	7.7	10	.03
Big B 1	.13	25.0	7	—	.10	15.1	1	.10	.06	4.6	4	.03	.19	57.4	3	.05	.05	3.6	5	-.04	.07	7.0	5	.03	.03	1.1	1	.03	.07	8.4	5	.04
2	.12	4.1	7	—	—	—	—	—	.03	.3	1	.03	.01	.3	2	—	.08	2.0	5	-.08	.03	.3	4	-.02	.06	.9	1	.06	.13	5.4	5	.03
3	.33	12.7	24	-.01	—	—	—	—	.29	9.8	12	.07	—	—	—	—	.31	11.1	15	-.13	.13	1.7	9	—	.13	1.9	3	-.19	.28	8.4	15	-.12
4	.52	419.9	24	.42	.12	16.5	3	.10	.12	15.5	6	.08	.13	20.6	9	-.01	.31	118.5	6	.32	.12	16.9	15	-.02	.19	43.5	3	-.19	.15	24.6	15	-.10
5	.35	40.2	8	.32	.21	13.8	3	.19	.09	2.4	2	-.08	.09	2.5	4	.03	.13	4.7	4	.11	.29	27.2	8	.16	.19	10.5	3	-.19	.19	10.4	10	-.09
Big D 1	.24	91.6	21	.19	.45	382.5	3	.49	.19	54.5	12	.16	.23	81.3	9	-.05	.14	30.8	15	.10	.14	29.0	15	-.01	.12	21.1	3	-.11	.10	15.7	15	-.03
2	.33	38.5	21	.20	—	—	—	—	.08	2.1	3	-.01	.10	3.0	6	.03	.21	13.6	15	.06	.39	55.5	12	.09	.13	5.6	3	-.10	.26	22.8	15	-.05
3	.46	27.4	24	.23	—	—	—	—	.46	27.4	12	.29	—	—	—	—	.39	18.8	15	.03	.22	5.3	9	-.08	.17	3.1	3	-.10	.17	18.6	15	-.01
4	.37	172.3	24	.31	.31	115.8	3	.30	.14	23.8	6	.07	.10	11.2	9	-.04	.31	117.5	6	.28	.17	31.6	15	.02	.21	53.2	3	-.21	.17	32.0	15	.02
5	.17	9.0	12	.09	.43	64.3	3	.36	.16	7.5	3	-.15	.11	3.6	4	-.05	.06	.9	6	.01	.19	10.7	12	-.03	.27	22.8	3	-.27	.23	16.3	15	.14
Big E 1	.21	66.7	35	.06	.36	221.9	5	.35	.22	76.8	20	.19	.49	484.4	15	-.08	.14	32.1	25	-.05	.13	92.2	25	.10	.13	25.8	5	-.09	.14	28.2	25	-.08
2	.24	20.6	21	.02	—	—	—	—	.09	2.5	3	-.04	.05	.8	6	-.01	.25	20.5	25	-.01	.26	21.4	12	-.01	.22	15.2	5	-.22	.14	14.6	15	-.12
3	.59	56.2	40	.27	—	—	—	—	.47	30.0	20	.03	—	—	—	—	.48	31.2	25	-.22	.32	11.8	15	.08	.36	15.5	5	-.33	.40	19.0	25	-.12
4	.31	115.2	32	.22	.20	47.3	4	.20	.09	8.8	8	.01	.17	31.7	12	.07	.27	89.3	8	.23	.21	49.9	20	-.03	.06	3.6	4	-.05	.12	16.4	20	-.10
5	.20	12.0	8	.13	.36	42.8	2	.36	.12	3.8	2	-.10	.06	.9	4	-.04	.14	6.0	4	.08	.14	5.8	8	-.04	.09	2.1	4	.09	.14	5.3	10	.01
Big F 1	.35	218.3	42	.28	.38	263.5	6	.40	.21	68.4	24	.12	.26	107.0	18	-.15	.23	82.7	30	.17	.17	45.0	30	.04	.06	4.6	6	.01	.17	46.0	30	-.04
2	.41	62.4	42	.29	—	—	—	—	.17	8.7	6	.08	.17	9.2	12	.03	.26	22.2	30	.12	.48	89.9	24	.05	.10	2.8	6	-.06	.30	29.3	30	-.04
3	.51	36.9	48	.21	—	—	—	—	.46	28.9	24	.20	—	—	—	—	.47	29.5	30	.03	.41	21.3	18	.08	.12	1.5	6	-.09	.50	34.2	30	-.06
4	.37	179.0	48	.32	.28	94.3	6	.24	.11	13.8	12	.06	.14	21.1	18	-.06	.33	134.5	12	.32	.14	21.6	30	.04	.11	13.2	6	-.08	.17	31.2	30	-.06
5	.20	40.2	20	.21	.30	27.9	5	.29	.12	3.8	5	-.06	.14	11.2	4	-.11	.23	14.0	4	.12	.23	16.5	20	.09	.13	4.8	5	-.10	.26	20.0	25	—
Big G 1	.23	87.0	28	.17	.12	23.3	4	.12	.13	26.8	16	.04	.12	23.7	12	-.03	.13	25.5	20	.09	.12	22.2	20	-.01	.13	25.4	4	.14	.14	31.1	20	-.10
2	.33	38.3	28	.19	—	—	—	—	.14	6.2	4	.01	.11	3.4	8	—	.35	42.0	20	.08	.36	38.8	16	.01	.16	8.3	4	-.15	.27	24.5	20	-.14
3	.50	34.5	32	-.03	—	—	—	—	.42	21.8	16	.24	—	—	—	—	.33	12.5	20	-.11	.30	10.2	12	.17	.32	11.8	4	-.31	.43	23.5	20	—
4	.27	84.5	32	.13	.09	8.2	4	—	.13	20.4	8	.06	.17	34.2	12	-.02	.12	16.8	8	.08	.19	43.4	20	-.03	.13	19.8	4	-.12	.16	30.1	20	-.06
5	.29	26.0	16	.18	.13	5.0	4	—	.11	3.3	4	.09	.24	18.2	8	.13	.21	13.7	8	.13	.32	33.8	16	.06	.20	12.1	4	-.18	.16	7.7	20	-.02

	r	M	N	r	r	M	N	r	r	M	N	r	r	M	N	r	r	M	N	r	r	M	N	r	r	M	N	r	r	M	N	r
Big H 1	.19	58.3	14	.16	.11	18.8	2	.11	.14	31.4	8	.12	.13	26.0	6	.08	.08	10.9	10	.04	.09	11.6	10	.04	.07	7.1	2	.06	.20	62.3	10	-.17
2	.27	23.5	14	.24	—	—	2	—	.02	.1	2	-.01	.12	4.3	4	.01	.17	8.6	10	.07	.18	10.6	8	.08	.08	2.1	2	-.06	.17	8.9	10	-.11
3	.23	18.5	16	-.04	.05	2.9	2	.05	.22	5.4	8	.10	—	—	—	—	.24	6.5	10	.07	.17	3.0	6	.07	.07	.5	2	.06	.25	6.6	10	.08
4	.28	95.9	16	.25	.10	2.9	2	-.10	.08	7.4	4	.07	.22	59.6	6	-.06	.19	40.0	4	.18	.12	17.6	10	-.03	.15	24.9	2	-.13	.17	33.0	10	-.12
5	.20	12.2	8	.15	—	—	4	.02	.07	1.5	2	.07	.15	6.2	4	-.04	.16	7.4	4	.13	.17	8.7	8	.02	.10	2.8	2	-.09	.14	5.8	10	-.07
Big I 1	.19	58.9	28	.05	.06	5.3	4	.02	.23	82.0	16	.16	.29	139.9	12	.23	.19	54.5	20	-.12	.20	60.1	20	.10	.07	7.8	4	-.02	.19	58.7	20	-.13
2	.30	30.2	28	.16	—	—	4	—	.10	2.8	4	-.02	.18	10.5	8	.11	.33	37.2	20	-.01	.32	35.7	16	-.01	.11	3.6	4	—	.22	15.2	20	-.04
3	.15	2.3	8	.10	—	—	4	—	.18	3.4	4	.13	.09	—	—	—	.24	6.5	5	.04	.03	.1	3	-.02	.09	1.0	4	.10	.13	12.0	5	-.16
4	.34	141.4	32	.30	-.02	5.6	4	-.02	.23	63.3	8	.21	.09	10.1	12	.01	.18	50.0	8	.20	.18	36.8	20	-.01	.09	9.7	4	-.08	.17	17.6	20	-.10
5	.30	27.7	16	.14	-.10	3.8	4	-.10	.12	3.9	4	.02	.17	8.3	8	.03	.16	7.8	8	.09	.23	15.8	16	-.07	.18	9.4	4	-.03	.24	17.3	20	.06
Huge A 1	.36	230.1	91	.25	.52	438.3	13	.52	.28	127.0	52	.19	.43	337.1	39	-.08	.27	115.0	65	.12	.26	107.5	65	.06	.13	18.7	13	-.06	.21	69.2	65	-.06
2	.54	122.8	70	.28	—	—	13	—	.26	21.8	10	.04	.20	12.4	20	.02	.38	50.6	40	.10	.59	167.1	40	.21	.21	14.2	10	-.14	.40	51.5	50	-.08
3	.71	106.9	104	.31	—	—	—	—	.61	62.3	52	.23	—	—	—	—	.55	45.9	60	-.05	.47	29.9	39	.05	.13	16.1	13	-.22	.64	72.6	65	-.08
4	.45	289.2	96	.37	.30	113.1	12	.31	.16	29.0	24	.07	.21	51.8	36	-.04	.38	185.9	24	.36	.30	111.0	60	.03	.12	34.5	12	-.14	.21	50.6	60	-.05
5	.36	41.6	36	.20	.45	72.2	9	.39	.21	13.0	9	-.11	.26	20.4	18	-.11	.22	14.8	18	.10	.37	44.7	36	.06	.23	15.1	9	-.18	.36	41.8	45	.05
Huge B 1	.27	123.2	70	.17	.11	33.2	10	.11	.20	63.7	40	.14	.20	62.8	30	.13	.18	51.9	50	—	.20	61.8	50	.06	.10	23.6	10	-.10	.25	98.2	50	-.18
2	.49	94.9	70	.26	—	—	10	—	.17	8.7	10	-.01	.15	7.3	20	.05	.48	90.5	50	.07	.54	124.3	40	.03	.10	16.1	10	-.10	.39	54.9	50	-.13
3	.58	52.5	40	-.03	—	—	—	—	.47	29.3	20	.25	—	—	—	—	.33	12.8	25	-.08	.29	9.4	15	.17	.42	9.5	10	-.26	.64	21.9	25	.03
4	.39	198.9	80	.31	.07	5.4	10	-.08	.21	51.7	20	.18	.20	45.5	30	-.02	.23	60.5	20	.21	.28	93.0	50	-.03	.10	22.9	10	-.14	.25	70.9	50	-.12
5	.37	46.5	40	.20	.19	10.4	10	-.08	.20	11.5	10	.06	.28	25.0	20	-.04	.28	24.6	20	.14	.31	31.3	40	-.02	.10	10.7	10	-.11	.34	36.6	50	.01
Education 1	—	—	—	—	.08	17.9	3	.08	—	—	—	—	.15	55.2	12	.15	.10	18.9	15	.10	—	—	—	—	.12	27.8	3	.05	.15	400.1	177	-.30
2	—	—	—	—	—	—	—	—	.04	.5	3	.04	.06	15.9	9	.06	—	—	—	—	.33	12.5	12	.06	.03	13.3	3	.05	.26	206.0	171	-.26
4	—	—	—	—	.03	2.5	4	.03	.25	81.3	8	.25	-.18	62.8	20	-.18	—	—	—	—	.49	103.5	20	.05	.05	36.5	4	-.17	.27	304.3	228	-.27

*Big A-Knowledge about Mexico/United States; Big B-Mass media communication; Big D-First-hand contact with Mexico-Mexicans with United States-Americans; Big E-Contact with Spanish Americans in interaction arenas; Big F-Second-hand contact with Mexico-United States; Big G-Attitudes toward Mexico/United States; and linkage with, as a nation; Big H-Attitude toward and linkage with Mexicans/North Americans as people; Big I-Social distance from Mexico/United States; HUGE A-Actual contacts with Mexico/United States Behavioral Linkage; HUGE B-Attitudes toward Mexico/United States Desired Linkage.

(a) Sample numbers throughout refer to the following populations: 1=United States general public; 2=rural Michigan; 3=Mexican-Americans of Southwestern United States; 4=urban Mexico; 5=rural Mexico.

(b) Rural farm; open country non-farm; 2,500-49,999; 50,000-499,999; over 500,000.

(c) United States: Anglo; Spanish-speaking; Negro; Other. Mexico: Mexican only Spanish-speaking; Bi-lingual Mexican and Indian; Non-Spanish-speaking Indians; Negroes and Others.

(d) Codes used in statistical analysis for social class were the following: United States: working; lower; lower-middle; middle; upper-middle; and upper. Mexico: pobre (poor); media (middle); and alta (high).

(e) Religion: None; Protestant; Catholic; Jewish; Agnostic/Atheist; Other.

NOTES

1. John Burma has attempted to categorize by region the various terms used by Mexican Americans. See John H. Burma, ed., *Mexican Americans in the United States* (Cambridge, Mass: Shenkman, 1970), pp. 7-8.

2. A.G. Dworkin, "No Siesta Mañana," In Raymond W. Mack, ed., *Our Children's Burden* (New York: Random House, 1968).

3. A.G. Dworkin and D.L. Eckberg, "Stereotypes: The Language of Prejudices" American Sociological Assn. (New York, 1973). See also Dworkin and Eckberg. "Consciousness and Reality: The Impact of the Chicano Movement in Natural Stereotyping," in John H. Burma and Miquel Tirado, eds., *Mexican Americans in the United States*, 2nd ed., (New York: Canfield Press, 1975).

4. Armando Rendon, *Chicano Manifesto* (New York: Macmillan, 1971).

5. Noel P. Gist and Anthony Gary Dworkin, *The Blending of Races: Identity and Marginality in World Perspective* (New York: Wiley, 1972).

6. J. Fishman, "An Examination of the Process and Function of Social Stereotyping," *Journal of Social Psychology*, 43, (February, 1956): 27-64.

7. Dworkin and Eckberg, 1973, 1975, op. cit.

8. While part of the drop can be explained via the regression phenomenon, it should be noted that (1) the stereotypes with originally high endorsement percentages were basically those which had *traditionally* been strongly endorsed, (See Richards, 1950; Tuck, 1946; Simmons, 1961; Katz and Braly, 1933; Meenes, 1943; Gilbert, 1951) and (2) some of the most highly endorsed stereotypes, notably "poor" and "uneducated," either did not drop significantly or showed a rebounding effect. For details of the works cited here the reader may consult the references in footnote 7, above.

9. Charles P. Loomis, Zona K. Loomis, and Jeanne E. Gullahorn, *Linkages of Mexico and the United States* (East Lansing, Michigan; Michigan State University Agricultural Experiment Station, Research Bulletin, 19, 1966).

10. New Delhi, 1960, p. 36.

11. Emory S. Bogardus, "Measuring Social Distance," *Journal of Applied Sociology*; and also see his *Immigration and Race Attitudes* (Boston: Heath, 1928). See also Robert E. Park, "The Concept of Social Distance," *Journal of Applied Sociology*, (July-August, 1924), pp. 339-344. See also Emory S. Bogardus, *Social Distance* (Yellow Springs, Ohio: The Antioch Press, 1959).

12. To obtain the data presented in Figure 6 informants were asked: "Consider only the members of your church whom you know personally. Which of the following language or racial backgrounds do MOST OF THESE PEOPLE belong to?" For the United States samples these were as follows: "1) White, English-speaking, 2) Spanish-speaking background, 3) Negro, English-speaking, 4) Other, specify: _____." Schedules used in Mexico had the following categories: "Now, do ANY of them come from any other background: If 'yes' ask 'Which background?'" 1) Mexicanos qué no hablan ninguna lengua indigena, 2) Indigenas qué no hablan Español, 3) Mexicanos or indigenas que hablan Español e indimos indigenas, 4) Negroes qué hablan Español, 5) Otro. (The interviewer had the above categories on the schedule.)

13. After ascertaining the attendance at this organization and its nature, the following question was asked: "Now, consider only those members of these organizations *whom you know personally* . . . consider the language or racial backgrounds of those members *whom you know personally*. To which one of the following language or racial backgrounds do MOST of them belong?" Categories listed above on church linkage were used here also. "Now do ANY of the members *whom you know personally* come from any other language or racial background?"

14. For the purposes of the present section they were then asked, "Now, consider the language or racial backgrounds of these friends, neighbors and co-workers. To which of the following groups do MOST of them belong?" "Now, are ANY of your friends, neighbors, and co-workers of different language or racial background?" The language and racial categories used are the same as those in the preceding items.

15. Charles P. Loomis, *Social Systems: Essays on Their Persistence and Change* (Princeton, New Jersey: D. Van Nostrand, 1960) p. 8.

16. Wilbert E. Moore, "Editorial Introduction," to Charles P. Loomis and Zona K. Loomis, *Modern Social Theories* (Huntington, N.Y.: Krieger, 1975).

17. Dworkin and Eckberg, op. cit.

18. Gerhard Lenski, *The Religious Factor* (Garden City, New York: Doubleday & Co., 1961), p. 53.

19. Anthony Gary Dworkin, "Stereotypes and Self-Images Held by Native-Born Mexican Americans," *Sociology and Social Research*, 49, (Jan. 1965), pp. 214-224.

20. See Dworkin, 1965, op. cit; Dworkin, "Epilogue to Stereotypes and Self-Images Held by Native-Born and Foreign-Born Mexican Americans," in John H. Burma, ed., op. cit., (1970); Dworkin, "National Origin and Ghetto Experience as variables in Mexican American Stereotype," in N. Wagner and M.J. Haug, *Chicanos: Social and Psychological Perspectives* (St. Louis: Mosby, 1971).

21. Victor Gecas, "Self-Conceptions of Migrant and Settled Mexican Americans," *Social Science Quarterly*, 54, (Dec. 1973). For a summary of data concerning self-identification for the informants in the senior author's 1963 study see Charles P. Loomis, "A Backward Glance at Self-Identification of Blacks and Chicanos," *Rural Sociology*, 36, (Spring, 1974).

22. For references to such studies see Jeanne E. Gullahorn and Charles P. Loomis, "A Comparison of Social Distance Attitudes in the United States and Mexico," *Studies in Comparative International Development*, 11, Social Science Institute, (St. Louis, Mo.: Washington University, 1966).

23. Robert E. Park, "Human Migration and the Marginal Man," *American Journal of Sociology*, 33, (May, 1928), p. 892.

24. Noel P. Gist and Anthony Gary Dworkin, op. cit., pp. 14-22. See also Dworkin, "The Peoples of *La Raza:* The Mexican-Americans of Los Angeles," Ibid., Ch. 9.

25. See Dworkin and Eckberg 1973, 1975, op. cit.

26. See S. Dale McLemore, "The Origins of Mexican Americans Subordination in Texas," *Social Science Quarterly*, 53, (March, 1973); Donald L. Noel, "A Theory of the Origin of Ethnic Stratification," *Social Problems*, 15, (Fall, 1968), pp. 157-172.

27. Beverly Duncan and Otis Dudley Duncan, "Minorities and the Process of Stratification," *American Sociological Review*, 33, (1968); and Peter M. Blau and Otis Dudley Duncan, *The American Occupational Structure* (New York: Wiley, 1967).

28. Peter M. Blau and Otis D. Duncan, "Occupational Mobility in the United States," in Celia Heller, *Structured Social Inequality: A Reader in Social Stratification* (New York: The Macmillan Co., 1969), pp. 340-352.

29. Anthony Gary Dworkin, "Stereotypes and Self-Images Held by Native-Born Mexican Americans," op. cit.

30. T.W. Adorno, et. al., (New York: Harpers, 1950).

31. Dworkin, "Stereotypes and Self Images Held by Native-Born Mexican Americans," op. cit.

32. Ibid.

33. F.F. Kirkpatrick and Hadley Cantril, "Self-Anchoring Scaling: A Measure of Individual's Unique Reality Worlds," (Washington, D.C., The Brookings Institution, 1960).

34. Dworkin, "Stereotypes and Self-Images Held by Native-Born Mexican Americans," op. cit.

35. For these and other correlations see the reference in Note 9. In this reference see the appendix and other tables.

36. Dworkin, "Stereotypes and Self-Images Held by Native-Born Mexican Americans," op. cit.

37. Ibid.

38. Dworkin and Eckberg, op. cit.

39. See for example Armando Morales in Wagner and Haury, op. cit., p. xci.

40. Nathan L. Whetten, *Rural Mexico* (Chicago: University of Chicago Press, 1948).

41. E.S.C. Northrup, *The Meeting of East and West* (New York: Macmillan Co., 1947), p. 45.

42. See references in Note 9 above for details.

43. Dworkin, "Stereotypes and Self-Images Held by Native-Born Mexican Americans," op. cit.

44. Ibid.

45. Olen Leonard and Charles P. Loomis, *El Cerrito, New Mexico* (Washington, D.C.: U.S.D.A., November, 1941).

46. Jacqueline D. Bass, *The Southwest Spanish-speaking Minority: A Study of Assimilation and Boundary Maintenance* (Michigan State University, M.S. Thesis, 1970).

47. Dworkin, "Stereotypes and Self-Images Held by Native-Born Mexican Americans," op. cit.

48. Wilbert E. Moore, "Creation of a Common Culture," *Confluence*, 4, p. 235.

Chapter 10

Behavioral Change: Strategies and Concepts

INTRODUCTION

In the previous chapters we have concentrated upon the more important social systems composing society. Where feasible we have attempted to point out major changes and the direction of change for these systems. Especially for directed social action, the change agent-change target model is basic for the analysis of social organization and processes of change.[1] The change agent is the person or organization attempting to introduce or effect a change; the target is the group or individual at which the change is aimed. For example, if an agricultural extension service in a given community or village is attempting to organize the rice growers there into a one-variety rice production community, the extension service is the change agent system and the community involved is the target system. The supervised loan illustrates a simple example of the change agent — change target system.

Change Agent-Change Target Systems and the PAS Model. Figure 1 in Chapter 1 presents the essence of the PAS Model that incorporates the elements and processes used in previous chapters and includes elements and processes mentioned in the paragraphs above, but it includes more. The model systematically incorporates both statics and dynamics, social structure and process or change. Wilbert Moore notes that the above-mentioned characteristics make the PAS Model a highly flexible analytical tool, and that it made possible a notable advance in social systems analysis.[2] As was the case for the previous chapters, the PAS model will furnish the means of organization for most of this chapter. It will be relied

By Charles P. Loomis

upon to perform the same function as it has elsewhere: to furnish a basis for possible comparison among activities involving socioeconomic change in general.[3] Also it will be used to organize certain findings that are relevant for agricultural development from the MSU Five-Nation Study.[4] In order that the chapter may be assigned separately some concepts even though previously defined are again defined in this chapter.

Because an example seems the best means to convey the abstractions of social change, we propose to deviate from the non-focused use of the term "system" and to treat social change involved in change and institution building by treating the social relationships studied in two farming villages near Turrialba, Costa Rica, not far from the Inter-American Institute of Agricultural Sciences, one of the eight Organizations of American States. (See Figures 1 and 2).

AN EFFORT TO MODERNIZE VILLAGES: A CASE OF NEAR FAILURE

That Costa Rica's educational system is one of the most effective and advanced in Latin America is the frequent claim of both the Costa Ricans and others who write about this country. "We have more teachers than soldiers" is a slogan not outmoded by war.[5] Less than 20 percent of the general population and less than 30 percent of the rural population are illiterate. In Latin America, only Argentina, Uruguay, and Chile have such small percentages of illiterates. In 1965, 20 percent of tax funds in Costa Rica went for education.[6]

The rural teacher as out-of-school change agent. The goal of the proposed program was the improvement of agriculture and health in the area. Although fairly broad in its aims, the ends and activities were reasonably specific, two of which were to provide chlordane for the elimination of field ants that cause great damage to crops, and to build privies to cut down on the incidence of hookworms. The Inter-American Institute of Agricultural Sciences at Turrialba enlisted the help of the national ministry of education and the teachers of the thirty-two villages surrounding Turrialba to carry out the program. At about the same time that this program was launched, early in the 1950's, an all-out effort was being made to vitalize the national agricultural service. In order to avoid interference with that effort and to try another approach, the decision was made to use change agents other than the extension workers. The presence of a school in every village of any size and the services of one or more teachers in each of the schools made the rural school teacher a natural choice. During the school vacation period special workshops and courses in simple agricultural and health procedures that would improve life in the area were conducted for the elementary teachers. The program was begun with considerable enthusiasm and it was reasonably well financed.

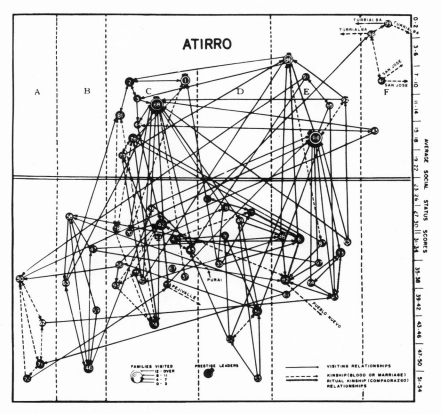

Figure 1. Social relationships in Atirro. The circles represent families. The size of a circle is determined by the number of visits to the family. Arrows on the lines which connect circles indicate the direction of the visiting. Broken lines indicate visiting between kin; crosshatching, ritual kinship, e.g., godfather. The families depicted by the larger circles hold key positions in the network of visiting and are popular leaders. Those depicted by circles with blocks above are prestige leaders. The family-friendship groups are separated by vertical broken lines and identified by letters. Social status is indicated by the position of the circles on the vertical axis — high status families are at the top, as indicated by the scale of average status scores at the right margin of the chart.

At the onset it seemed that the teachers as change agents had some valuable advantages. Most of the teachers were men, their knowledgeability over that of the ordinary village dweller was recognized, and they were held in high esteem.[7] Careful studies based on probability samples of specific areas as well as the whole country demonstrated that few professionals, if known personally to the informant, were considered to be as reliable in the advice or information imparted as the teachers.[8] However, when teachers were not known personally, they were accorded relatively low reliability and credibility as compared with priests and medical doctors who were not known personally to the informant. Sociologists who specialize in the study of the professions have noted this phenomenon with respect to groups other than teachers. When incumbents of status-roles are evaluated as inferior in reliability and accorded low confidence because of not being known personally, we may assume that the professionalization of the status-role leaves something to be desired.

Let us turn to a discussion of this and other aspects of status-role

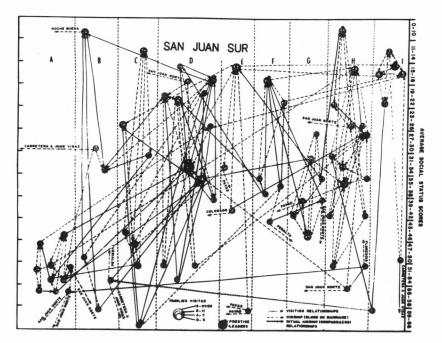

Figure 2. Social relationships in San Juan Sur (see Figure 1 for explanation).

as used in the PAS model. We shall be watching for evidence that might throw light on reasons for the failure of the rural teachers as change agents.

ELEMENTS AND PROCESSES OF SOCIAL SYSTEMS

DIVIDING THE FUNCTIONS

Status-role as a unit incorporating both element and process. The two-term entity, status-role, contains the concept of a status, a cultural element implying position, and the concept of role or functional process. Both are important determinants of what is to be expected from an incumbent. Although in both industrialized and traditional societies the size of communities is correlated positively with the number and variety of status-roles available to members, it is well to remember that a high level of living has never been attained in a society without a considerable division of labor, i.e., differentiation of status-roles. "A nation can be wealthy only if few of its resources are required to produce food for subsistence,"[9] and if there are many status-roles for its citizens. As traditional societies are modernized and the proliferation of status-roles occurs, "economic development of various primitive and agrarian economies will produce greater similarity among world cultures."[10]

In modern cultures, societies are dynamic because high evaluation is placed upon the quest for knowledge. The scientists and philosophers, like Max Weber's ethical prophets, see to it that change is omnipresent. No successful scientist can differ much from his fellow scientist in the fulfillment of his status-role. This holds true whether he is in the "hard" sciences or in the social sciences, irrespective of other attributes such as his nationality. In peasant cultures there is considerably more room for an individualized interpretation of the status-role from society to society. In non-traditional societies the range of status-roles available to an individual is wide, but there is not much variation in playing a given role. A Norwegian physicist will do pretty much the same thing as an Italian or Japanese physicist. Whether we consider the scientist who is responsive to the world of science or the peasant of traditional society, culture through the status-role largely determines what is expected locally. The following oversimplified description may serve to illustrate how culture in a traditional society is important in the status-role of the farmer or herdsman.

> To draw an analogy . . . assume that a social scientist, upon returning from summer vacation, finds on his desk invitations to lecture before various women's clubs, to join an administrative committee of his

university, and to run for political office in his community. These invitations draw him away from what he had been before — a research worker. In this situation the Yaqui Indian would accept every invitation but would also continue his research; each activity (or what a Yaqui farmer or herdsman actually does) would be well organized . . . The Pueblo would probably refuse all invitations so as to remain a pure scientist (i.e., farmer), but even if he did accept just one he would never lose his research perspective . . . The Navaho would not understand the invitations and would leave at the first opportunity for another vacation.[11]

Presumably the Yaquis, Pueblos, and Navahos manifest consensus on expectancy patterns within their own societies. If a given Pueblo farmer would start behaving as a Navaho farmer in the above mentioned aspects, he would appear as a deviant and sanctions would be applied. In a sense this is what happened with the effort to use school teachers as change agents in the Turrialba area. Popular expectations of what could and should be done within the status-role of teacher were violated. This is what happened from the villagers' point of view.

The teachers had to be concerned with the installation of privies. The villagers who respected the teacher's knowledge in the classroom and who were willing to be influenced by the teacher's opinions about non-school matters, nevertheless found themselves uneasy when they talked about privies with the teacher. They felt it was not an easy subject to talk about with someone to whom one normally shows a certain amount of deference. Privies were not properly a concern of teachers. The school inspectors felt very uncomfortable about the new work of the teachers. Ordinarily it was their task to supervise the teachers and to rate them on their classroom activity. They had no standards for rating them on this new task, and so there was ambiguity in both status-roles, that of the supervisors and that of the supervised. Pressure was exerted within the village toward the end of pushing the teacher out of this new agricultural extension status-role and back into the familiar teaching status-role. Even though the teachers could ordinarily muster considerable influence, they could not resist this solidary and sustained pressure.

In sociological terms, the filling of the new status-roles by incumbents having had different roles had never been legitimized. Although the process of legitimation is not elaborated here since it is more clearly a part of norming which is treated later, suffice it to say that by this process change is made rightful in the eyes of the members of the change agent-change target systems. Even after legitimation has been achieved the change agents must "deliver the goods;" that is, they must act to achieve their objectives. This will be discussed later under *ACHIEVING*. Any concept — status-role, for example — represents a distillation of a number of interrelated thoughts. It says something to another scientist only if it stands for the same interrelated thoughts to both. It often happens that terms are used that convey somewhat different meanings to different readers.

In this discussion it is maintained that the field of psychology specializes in personality systems, that the fields of sociology and political science specialize in the phenomena studied through the use of the concept of the social system, and that the cultural anthropologist specializes in that field conceptualized in the cultural system. Each field has its own conceptual scheme, and not all of the concepts used in explanation and prediction in one specialty are applicable in another. This, of course, may seem obvious, but the frequency with which psychologists, for instance, describe social systems using psychological concepts often surprises sociologists. A number of social psychologists think they have overcome this difficulty. They believe that in articulating the relationships between the social system, the personality system, and the cultural system the one common term used by all is that of status-role.

In Figure 3, an attempt is made to indicate how the three systems may be interrelated with the status-role forming the interlinking triangle using the terms Toennies developed. "T" on the chart indicates a tentative location of the status role of the traditional man of knowledge in a peasant village. As will be noted, he is heavily influenced by social and cultural factors that place him in the status of Gemeinschaft-like value orientation. The empirical scientist, of course, falls in the rational or Gesellschaft-like orientation and would, in Toennies' thinking be governed by the societal components of rationality derived from Gesellschaft.

The personality system is influenced of course by "energy" from the biological system. Beliefs, values, and expressive symbols contribute to the "actor" in role and these come from the cultural system. The status-role of the social system influences this "actor" in various ways, determining in part what is expected from him.

RANKING

Rank as an element. Rank as used here is equivalent to "standing" and always has reference to a specific act, system, or subsystem. Rank, then, represents the value an actor has for a system in which the rank is accorded. The position of the spheres ranging from bottom to top of Figures 1 and 2 is determined by the ranking a family received when knowledgeable judges who were living in the villages evaluated the family in terms of its "importance for the community." It is not difficult to perceive that in the large estate community, Atirro (Figure 1), a type of "proletariat" or work group holds the positions at the bottom. Above this "proletariat" are the intermediary supervisors and professionals who form a sort of "middle class;" above them are the owners of the hacienda, the commissary, and the coffee mill noted in the upper right side of Figure 1. The location of the horizontal line shows at what point interaction decreases up and down the social class structure. If the figure represented a social system in which a very few members formed an "upper crust" who interacted almost exclusively with each other, and everyone else in the social system formed the hoi polloi among whom there was no significant difference in rank, the horizontal line would be very close to the top of the figure. The ranking system of Atirro (Figure 1) is a modified version of such a

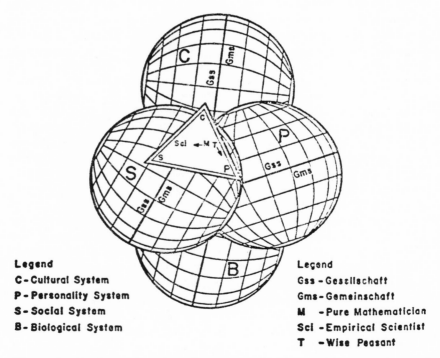

Legend
C - Cultural System
P - Personality System
S - Social System
B - Biological System

Legend
Gss - Gesellschaft
Gms - Gemeinschaft
M   - Pure Mathematician
Sci - Empirical Scientist
T   - Wise Peasant

Figure 3.   Linkage of systems by status-roles in cognitive mapping and validation — a tentative model.

pattern. Statistical procedures determine the location of the line that figuratively separates the lower from the upper classes. By such a device one can "see" three classes in Figure 1.

The stratification structure in the family-sized farming community of San Juan Sur (Figure 2) is far less obvious. In fact, there is no point at which interaction from the bottom to the top is significantly less than that which prevails among the members at the top and among the members at the bottom. Although differential ranking is assigned to the members of this social system, the rate and frequency of interaction is apparently not a function of ranking. Figure 2 portrays a much more unitary social system than does Figure 1. It is not possible from charts such as Figure 2 to find points at which interaction was class or caste structured as was possible in Figure 1. In this respect description of the stratification structure in the relationships of the family-sized farming community presented in Figure 2 is not as simple as that in Figure 1.

It should be obvious that such ranking patterns in target systems are of great importance in plans for directed change and institutional building made by change agents. They should be taken into account in both tactics and strategy as developed by change agents interested in modernizing agriculture. In the large estate community of Atirro for instance it would be quite easy for the administrator to change the facilities and processes of some agricultural operations such as pruning the coffee trees. All he would have to do would be to provide the facilities and order the *jornaleros* through their supervisor to carry out the required instruction and to initiate the change. At most, simple demonstrations would be needed. It would be quite a different matter to accomplish this objective in the family-sized farming community, the relationships of which are depicted in Figure 2. This will be discussed further in the treatment of the concepts, *CONTROLLING* and *boundary maintenance*.

Evaluation of actors and allocation of status-roles as process. In the communities depicted in Figures 1 and 2, rank is accorded as is usual in Costa Rica. Rank comes from various qualities such as (1) authority and power, the legitimized and nonlegitimized ability to influence others; (2) kinship relations; (3) personal attributes and achievements such as age, sex, beauty, skill, and ability; and (4) property holdings and wealth. The latter may function as symbols of social status or means of initiating action by which authority or power over others is established. However, rank does not necessarily derive alone from wealth and power. Each of the judges here who ranked the families gave reasons for their placements. Often they said the man they had placed high was *muy honrado*, very honorable.

In a way this could be thought of as comparable to the Brahmin in India who might be without wealth and power and yet have high prestige. The owner of the hacienda, Atirro, derives his social rank mostly from the first and last criterion mentioned above. The principal leader in San Juan Sur (number 66, Figure 2) derives his social rank mostly from the third criterion. He is a very clever and effective speaker and although possessing only two years of education has many human relations skills.

In a conference on agricultural development Harry Triandis,[12] a social psychologist, in an effort to explain the presence of chaperones among family groups of mixed sex condones the practice and condemns societies which do not have this need to protect brothers and sisters from engaging in sex. Thus, he writes, "In cultures . . . in Western societies the needs of the parents 'have introduced internal controls [guilt] into the child's personality'." He writes further, "The custom of chaperoning [practiced in various cultures] with strong taboos prohibiting brothers and sisters to find themselves together unchaperoned . . . seems to an American silly, wasteful, time-consuming, old-fashioned . . . but he does not realize that he may be paying a price in excessive sexual maladjustment for not having this custom." The sociologist might not be so prone to condemn guilt for violating the incest and other taboos. We would argue that the existence of a transcendental god in a given culture provides a built-in support for father figures who may help inculcate the superego. Probably the actors in such cultures have more inter-nalized guilt than others. Max Weber might have observed that the honesty of the Puritan Boston and Quaker Philadelphia bankers was based upon the guilt they might feel if they filched funds. We believe it is important that this "social psychological consideration" be given attention in developing status-roles for change agents in developing societies. Business and trading might not be very profitable if it were necessary in every business transaction to have the equivalent of a chaperone stand by. One of Max Weber's important theses, often ignored, is that the Protestants, especially the Calvinists, Methodists, Baptists, and Pietists, internalized norms of brotherhood and honesty which were supposed to be applicable to all mankind. Thus they were effective far beyond the family and religious sect, and in this way different from those of the Jews, Parsees, Jains, and similar groups that have also amassed capital, but under less universalistic norms.

CONTROLLING

Powers as an element.   Power as defined here is the capacity to control others. It has many components that may be classified as authoritative and nonauthoritative control. Authority is the right to control, determined and legitimized by the members of the social system and built into status-roles as discussed previously. Unlegitimized coercion and voluntary influence are nonauthoritative. Two somewhat different manifestations of the power structure in the villages (Figures 1 and 2) may be noted. On the one hand there are so-called "grass-roots" or popular leaders with many visiting relationships; on the other, there are leaders called "prestige leaders," who are those individuals who would be chosen to make representations for the village to the governor of the state. Power as derived from social relationships described on the charts comes largely from clique groups or what some call congeniality groupings. These groupings are delineated by the vertical lines on the charts and are determined by the answers of all informants to the question, "In case of a death in the family, whom would you notify first?" The rank of the cliques descends from right to left on the charts. In each of the communities these systems of relationships are important for change agents who may wish to reach all members of a given clique through one or more leaders. As will be noted on the charts, most of the so-called prestige leaders are in the upper classes in the large estate communities and occupy higher positions of rank in both communities than most other members. It is obvious that grass-roots or congeniality leaders as well as the prestige leaders have power. Of course, the large estate community is so organized that the most powerful individual is the owner and usually he has made the administrator the second most important person. The owners of haciendas in the area do not all live on the haciendas. Some spend considerable time abroad or in San Jose. It is of interest to those change agents advancing improved agricultural practices and stocks that very often the ordinary worker manifests more antagonism toward the manager than toward the owner, who is generally called the patron. Not infrequently the patron and the administrator play a sort of game by which the patron retains both his power, prestige, and even esteem. Generally the manager cannot be both loved and in control. When he takes his position as administrator he muy well know or even be informed that he will be hated. Workers frequently told the interviewers that some of the things about which they were most bitter and complained most would be corrected if only the patron knew about them. Often a large fiesta takes place when the patron, who has been away, visits the hacienda. At this time the patron plays the game of over-riding the administrator and granting certain small favors in order to retain prestige and esteem, and even quite often appears to be affectionate.

Decision-making and its initiation into action as process. Since charts such as Figures 1 and 2 were available for all thirty villages in the municipality of Turrialba, (all in the sphere of influence of the Inter-American Institute of Agricultural Sciences), some interesting consequences developed. As a sort of experiment the Director of the Institute invited all of the prestige and popular leaders to a demonstration at which chlordane was used to eliminate ants that infested the area and greatly reduced crop production. The day after the demonstration hundreds of villagers appeared at the Institute requesting the chlordane. Another example of the power of influence and informal leadership occurred when interviewing began in the village represented in Figure 2. Villagers were hesitant to provide the data that the interviewers requested. Some refused to be interviewed. We noted that Maximino Torres, (number 66, at the top of the clique H) left in a hurry on foot to walk five miles to the trade center in Turrialba. We learned later that he went directly to the Jefe Politico, the most powerful representative of the government in the municipality, to find out what we were doing. Fortunately, we had previously visited the Jefe Politico and explained the purpose of the study and its connection with the Institute. After Maximino Torres returned to the village, in a matter of hours young and old, men and women, from all parts of the village began coming to the interviewers inviting them to come and interview them. Often refreshments were served. Two years after the interviewing the senior author had occasion to walk into the village again, the only way to get there during the rainy season. He was surprised to find a substantial new concrete bridge across the small river in place of the usual narrow wooden bridge. Upon inquiry he found another manifestation of how decisions are made and initiated into action in the village. On her way home from school during the rainy season a small girl fell in this river and was drowned. This created a crisis in the village. All who could walk gathered and marched behind Maximino Torres the five miles to the office of the Jefe Politico where they demanded a bridge. It was installed as soon as the dry season came and materials could be hauled in.

Those familiar with the village culture of Latin America will recognize that in the family-sized farming villages this type of action is very common. The informal leaders usually rise to prominence both because of personal characteristics and other qualities such as wealth and education. Maximino Torres does not own the largest farm in the community and his education is little more than two years. However, no one could talk with him long without noting that he has qualities of leadership, including some measure of charisma, that quality mentioned by Max Weber in connection with ethical prophets. When Maximino delivers an oration, his command of the language is superb. He is influential and nonauthoritarian. His power does not derive from formal office. Such informal leadership crops up in most social systems, and no doubt it exists on the large estate as well as in the community of small, family-owned farms. But its manifestations in the hacienda community are quite different. In a power-centered situation such as that on the hacienda, where the power is concentrated in the hands of the owner, the manager, and the various supervisors, it would be unthinkable that nonformal power such as that held by Maximino Torres could be articulated for community endeavors such as bridge-building. In neither type of community was the teacher mentioned as a prestige leader unless he or she was a member of a village farm family. Although the local priest has high prestige and, of course, considerable power, he likewise is not mentioned as a prestige leader. In the networks of relations designated in Figures 1 and 2, neither the teacher nor the priest appears as prominent in either the visiting patterns among the villagers or among those who would be chosen to represent the village before the governor, namely the prestige leaders.

Of course, the effort of the Institute to use the teacher as a change agent met with very different results in villages with family-sized farming units and in hacienda villages. In point of fact the project was designed more for the family-sized villages. On the large estates many changes such as disposal of refuse, for which privies were built on family-sized farms, could be handled as an expenditure of the hacienda. On large estates how ants are to be killed and waste disposed of can be determined by the patron, the administrator, and other similar power figures. Likewise if these actors were to oppose the changes advocated by the teacher as change agent, the teacher's position would be in jeopardy.

NORMING, STANDARDIZING, PATTERNING

Norm as an element. The rules that prescribe what is acceptable or unacceptable are the norms of the social system. Among the most important norms for the change agent to understand are those by which the three most generalized values of society are allocated: power, wealth, and prestige and esteem. Force is often used to obtain wealth and power but prestige and esteem or general ranking accorded by an actor's fellows and peers is less often so achieved. Max Weber noted that the ethical prophet might, because of his charisma, be highly evaluated by immediate followers but if he were to establish an organization meant to bridge generations and fit himself and followers into status-roles, the charisma must be routinized. The high evaluation formerly accorded the personal qualities of the individual must be transferred to qualifications attached to position, the elemental component of the status-role.

Norms for change agents.   Karl Deutsch dramatized the restraints peasants in traditional societies place on innovative behavior. He noted that "in traditional cultures that have moved up to the very limit of subsistence, further innovations promise very modest and marginal rewards, but swift and terrible risks that are intensely salient. To this degree, a traditional agriculture that fills up its Malthusian process to the limits of subsistence becomes an engine for teaching its people to fear and distrust innovations. It becomes a Pavlovian conditioning mechanism against innovation." Thus, from experience, members of traditional society learn to fear innovators who, unless they have charisma, will be negatively sanctioned as deviants. As Durkheim observed, the traditional society is anchored in stable consensus which he called "mechanical solidarity" supported by repressive norms.

George Foster, an anthropologist, presents a somewhat different explanation for the conservative nature of traditional society.[13] He maintains that the members of traditional society explain achieving in economic activities in accordance with "pure conflict" conditions of the zero-sum type. This form of explanation is more generally used for political activities by conflict theorists (Marx, Weber, and others). According to Foster, norms for activity in peasant and traditional societies restrict individuals from achievement because, as in the zero-sum type game, the total that all actors considered together can achieve is given. Under these circumstances any achiever who adds to his original portion has done so in the view of himself and others only at the expense of taking it away from others. (This basic way of viewing the world would be more correctly treated later under *"KNOWING,"* but here we are interested in the norms that result from this type of cognitive mapping.) In societies in which it is believed that all may gain from individual attainment of wealth, the norms or rules of the game do not prohibit competitive striving as much as in traditional societies.

In the case of the effort to make teachers into change agents in the Turrialba area the inspectors' norms did not lead them to approve the extra income the teachers might earn by engaging in the project. Likewise villagers were opposed if not indignant when teachers advised them on agricultural and sanitation matters. It was as if they might say: "Let them stick to doing what they know something about. Let them teach our children as best they can, but don't let them try to teach me what to do."

Evaluation as a process.   The process through which positive and negative priorities or values are assigned to concepts, objects, actors, or collectivities, or to events and activities, either past, present, or future is identified as evaluation in the PAS model. If the values of individuals and pluralities result from the process of evaluation defined in this manner, all of the nine elements in Figure 1 Chapter 1 can under certain conditions, be values; likewise the social action categories can also be thought of as values. Activities such as birth control or family planning can be evaluated.

In the Michigan State University Five-Nation Study, informants from probability samples drawn from among those twenty-one-years of age and older in Costa Rica, Mexico, Japan, Finland, and the United States were questioned to ascertain their evaluations of birth control as an activity.[14] It was considered wrong for married couples in Costa Rica, rural Mexico, urban Mexico, Japan, Finland, and the United States respectively by the following percentages of informants: 55.2, 49.1, 43.4, 24.5, 11.7, and 23.9. In few nations is population increasing so rapidly as in Costa Rica and Mexico, but obviously these figures indicate that birth control is evaluated much more negatively there than in the United States, Japan, and Finland. Obvious also is the importance of this evaluation for change agents who are attempting to reduce the birth rate. If the teachers who were attempting to change health and agricultural practices in the Turrialba area of Costa Rica had attempted to advance birth control (which they did not), disapproval of their activities would have been greater than it was.

Evaluation and legitimation of change and change agents. Elsewhere we have attempted to specify the processes that are crucial for the change agent as he attempts to bring about directed change through institution building. Here only the crucial part evaluation plays will be mentioned. The processes of initiation, legitimation, and execution are important for institution building but it is the process of legitimation that is most akin to evaluation. Legitimation is the process whereby the proposed change is made "rightful" to the target system. Prestigeful sponsors, rituals, prayers, and other legitimizing procedures are used in this aspect of the strategy of change. Of course, those actors with legitimizing authority vary from culture to culture. In cultures such as that of the United States they may be prestigeful personalities from the scientific, literary, sports, entertainment, military, judiciary, and religious worlds. For some programs in India, Brahmins or other priests may be helpful. In Russia, outstanding Communist party members may be important.

In this connection it is pertinent to report a case of belated legitimation which the senior author had occasion to observe as he attended a workshop held at the Inter-American Institute of Agricultural Sciences in Costa Rica for agricultural workers. Monsignor L.G.

Ligutti, the executive director of the National Catholic Rural Life
Conference, in his formal address to the extension agents and other
administrative personnel from all parts of Latin America, advised
them to call upon local Catholic priests to help with important
agricultural and health programs. His words came too late to save the
efforts of the teachers in the Turrialba experiment, but having seen
how this effective Catholic leader works, the senior author believes
that if Monsignor Ligutti had advised the village teachers of the area
to have the local priests support the program and if he had himself
helped with the legitimation in the local Catholic system, the
program would not have failed. He told the extension agents from the
Latin American countries to let him know if a priest refused to help,
and he would see that the reluctant priest changed his mind. He
implied that the priest would hear from him or Rome.

ACHIEVING

End, goal, or objective as an element.   The end, goal, or objective
is the change (or in some cases the retention of the status quo) that
members of a social system expect to accomplish through appropriate
interaction. In Marxist thought, interests or what we call ends, are of
central .importance, but norms and evaluation, and beliefs and
sentiments (and the relevant articulating processes) are considered
to be epiphenomena. It is, of course, true that in acts actually
executed or experienced, there is a merging of ends, norms, beliefs,
and sentiments. Students of change and change agents, however, can
achieve a precision of thought not otherwise possible if the various
elements are separated for analytical purposes. There is a degree of
actual separation in real life too, as societies become increasingly
differentiated. For example, those agencies responsible for cognitive,
cathectic and moral activities such as schools, cultural and recreational centers, law courts, and churches are differentiated.

One of the problems common to areas in the process of development is that of rising but unfulfillable expectations. In a probability
sample drawn from Costa Rica, 1,500 informants twenty years of age
or older were asked: "How many years of school would you like your
son(s) to complete?" (or: "If you had sons of school age . . . .?"). The
percentages who wanted university, high school, and elementary
schooling for their sons were as follows: 43.6, 23.3, and 20.2.
Informants were then asked, "Do you consider this to be possible?"
Percentages of those answering yes, no, don't know, or giving no
information were respectively as follows: 65.1, 23.6, 10.1, and 1.1.[15]
Of course, in Costa Rica and elsewhere outside of the Communist

world, educational achievement of children is highly related to the income of parents. About the same proportion of informants want university training for their children as have family incomes of less than $1,000 per year. With only about 3 per cent of the population having family incomes of $4,000 and above there seems to be plenty of evidence here of rising unfulfillable aspirations.

In an effort to discover how people regard their conditions of life in relation to where they want to be, the so-called "self-anchoring" scale was used.[16] Informants in the Five-Nation Study were told: "Now here is a picture of a ladder. Suppose we say that at the top of the ladder stands a person who is living under the best possible conditions of life, and at the bottom stands a person who is living under the worst possible conditions of life. On what step would you say you are at present?" The percentages of informants who placed themselves on the bottom three steps of the ten-step ladder for the general public of Costa Rica, urban Mexico, rural Mexico, Japan, Finland, and the United States were respectively as follows: 20.2, 22.7, 26.4, 9.0, 6.1, and 2.6. Looked at another way, the average step placement on the ladder for Costa Rica, Mexico, Japan, Finland, and the United States was respectively as follows: 4.6, 4.4, 4.7, 5.5, and 6.8.

The pressures of rising expectations in Mexico, Japan, and Costa Rica may be noted from the manner in which the same informants responded when asked to place themselves on this hypothetical ladder as they thought they would stand in five years. The average step placement on the ladder respectively as above was: 6.0, 6.1, 6.0, 6.3, and 7.8. Only about half as many of the Costa Ricans, Mexicans, and Japanese placed themselves on the bottom three rungs as five years in the future. For the Americans and for the Finns those on the three bottom steps, although in the same direction, indicated an anticipated change which in absolute numbers was negligible. Obviously, relatively large proportions of Costa Ricans, and Mexicans are not satisfied with life as it is. The belief that people in traditional societies are "happily poor" is nonsense. The programs the change agents initiate, legitimize, and execute must be those that offer improved conditions of life for the members of the change target system. Apparently the rural people in the thirty-two villages in the Turrialba area were not convinced that the agricultural and health programs advanced by the village teachers would make a better life for them.

Goal attaining and concomitant "latent" activity as process. There is frequent reference in discussions such as this to what is called rational action. Usually rational action is manifest and not latent. It is manifest because its relation to the goal is both recognized and intended by the actor. Of a different order is latent action; that is, action that produces results that either are not intended by the actor or that come about without his knowing it. As an example of manifest activity, the Inter-American Institute of Agricultural Sciences gave a demonstration on the use of chlordane in the control of ants to the leaders of the thirty-two villages in their immediate sphere of influence. The calculated objective was to induce the villagers to wish to adopt the use of chlordane for ant control. The objective was realized very much as anticipated. If the villagers had, as the result of the demonstration, pronounced the director of the Institute a God or even a prophet, it would have been latent activity because the result would not have been intended. Very often the unintended results strengthen the target system by providing it integration. An example is the rain dance of the Hopi Indians, which unifies the society even though it does not rain. A latent result in the thinking of many change agents of various types of directed change in developing as well as developed countries is the flight of rural people to the ghettos of the cities as modernization and development shuffle and relocate them.

KNOWING

Belief (knowledge) as an element.   A belief is any proposition about the universe that is thought to be true. The present section deals with the cognitive aspect of an actor's behavior.

In the Five-Nation Study, beliefs were probed using a Lickert-type question to find the extent of belief in the following proposition: "I believe the world would really be a better place if more people had the same religious beliefs I have." The percentages of informants for the general public of Costa Rica, urban Mexico, rural Mexico, Japan, Finland, and the United States who agreed with the statement are as follows: 73.4, 82.6, 93.4, 27.3, 52.4, and 48.5. Obviously the responses reported here did not come from scientists, who subscribe to the following norms as identified by Merton: universalism, communism (in the sense that the substantive findings of science are a product of social collaboration and are assigned to the community, constituting a common heritage from which the discoverer's equity is limited or removed), disinterestedness, and organized skepticism.[17] Skepticism, criticism, and disinterestedness, of course, cannot exist in the minds of those who know that only they are always right. Even for those who are not scientists the application of scientific norms to what one will and will not believe would appreciably change the task of the change agent and the nature of the change target. This brings us to the process of cognitive mapping and validation.

Cognitive mapping and validation as process. Cognitive mapping and validation may be defined as the activity by which knowledge, or what is considered true and what false, is developed. In the national probability samples from the Five-Nation Study, another difference in cognitive mapping emerges. Informants were asked to indicate whether they agreed or disagreed, and to what extent, with the following statement: "Everyone should think the same about what is right and what is wrong." The percentages agreeing for Costa Rica, Mexico, Japan, Finland, and the United States were respectively 90.0, 94.9, 65.5, 86.9, and 49.0.

When the proportions agreeing to this proposition for different levels of education are studied, the part the teacher may play in developing the scientific attitude may be contemplated. In the United States, the higher the level of education the less likely the informant was to agree with the above dogmatic statement. However, the informants in urban Mexico who disagreed with the above statement were not better educated than those who agreed. We hypothesize that teachers and education in Costa Rica and in Mexico do not reduce dogmatism to the same extent that they appear to in the United States. We have no proof of a connection, but we speculate that this may be another reason for the failure of the effort of the teachers in the Turrialba area as change agents in health and agriculture. We are led further to speculate that open-mindedness, tolerance, and flexibility are not only functions of the number of years of exposure to the educational process, but are also functions of the content of the educational program. An understanding of the many guises with which "truth" has been viewed through the ages by the people of the world is of special importance in this regard.

FEELING

Sentiment as an element. Whereas beliefs embody thoughts, sentiments embody feelings about the world. Some change agents appeal to the patriotism of decision makers in the change target. In general, as traditional and new nations begin to modernize, nationalism and patriotism increase. In the Five-Nation Study, we obtained answers to the following "self-anchoring" question: "Imagine that you are on the middle step of a 10-step ladder. On the top steps of the ladder are things which, in your judgment, are more important than you as an individual. And on the bottom steps are things less important than you are as an individual. On what steps would you put your country?" The respective average step placement for Costa Rica, Mexico, Japan, Finland, and the United States was as follows: 9.00, 9.35, 5.84, 7.92, and 8.47. It is obvious that if this approach measures the loyalty people might have for their countries, both Costa Ricans and Mexicans are highly imbued with this sentiment.

In an effort to ascertain some measure of the attachment respondents have for their countries these same persons were asked, "Can you imagine that conditions could get to the point that you would consider moving to another country?" The percentage of informants answering this question in the negative for Costa Rica was 82.4, and for whites and blacks respectively in the United States, 85.4, and 77.5[18] For Mexicans, Japanese, and Finns the percentages were 83.6, 88.3, and 74.4. These differences are not great and our hypothesis that the percentage for Costa Rica would be higher than for the United States was not validated.

In the study from which these data come, another hypothesis was not validated, namely, that "the family (as evaluated) in terms of the amount of interaction taking place among its members and in terms of its members' evaluation (of it in comparison with other organizations) is more important in both Costa Rica and Mexico than in the United States."[19] The directors of the study were surprised that these data indicate that appeals to family sentiments would be no stronger in Costa Rica and Mexico than in the United States.

To what extent could one use loyalty to his community for motivational purposes? To ascertain to what extent the community of residence was a true home base and not just a way station the respondents of the Five-Nation Study were asked, "Have you ever considered moving from this town or community?" The proportions answering, "No," were 69.0, 72.7, 67.7, 51.4, and 51.7. From this we may judge that if Turrialba is typical of Costa Rica, the sentiment of community loyalty may be used for motivation purposes by change agents.

Tension management as process. This process may be defined as action by which elements of the social system are articulated in such a manner as to (1) prevent sentiments from obstructing goal-directed activity, and (2) avail the system of their motivating force in achieving goals. Prayer is among the many tension-managing activities, and the only one to be discussed here. For the probability samples mentioned above drawn in the United States and Mexico informants were asked, "When you have a decision to make in your everyday life do you ask yourself what GOD would want you to do?"[20] For urban Mexico, rural Mexico, and the United States the proportions answering in the affirmative were respectively 90.2, 89.2, and 70.4. The frequency with which this prayerful activity was engaged in is indicated by the percentages of informants who answered "Always" when questioned. For these samples the percentages were respectively 56.4, 65.8, and 18.4. Assuming that the same proportions as reported for Mexico would hold for Costa Rica, for which we do not have comparable data, we could assume a high level of religiousity in Costa Rica. This impression is reinforced by the religiousity manifested in the Costa Rican villages in which the senior author worked. It reinforces the impression that had the church legitimized and supported the efforts of the teachers in the Turrialba area, the attempts to effect change might have been more successful.

Communication of sentiment as process. Through this process action is taken by the members of a social system which leads to motivation to achieve goals, conform to norms, and carry out systemic action through transfer of feeling by symbols. Elsewhere an attempt was made to demonstrate how the two processes, tension management and communication of sentiment, are utilized in the promotion of change by communists after social systems are torn by disruption, and how they may be used as communities are disabled by disasters.[21] There is no doubt that within the realm of sentiment communication, much dynamic force exists which, if understood more clearly, could be harnessed.

FACILITATING

Facility as an element. A facility is a means that, except for slaves, is nonhuman and is used within the system to attain the members' ends or goals. Mass media is one such facility that often is used effectively to help change agents attain goals. In the effort of the teachers in the Turrialba area to advance agricultural and health practices little use was made of mass media, and radio and television were not used at all. Radios, purchased by the Institute, and placed in each village, might have increased the chances for success, if pertinent radio programs and forums on the subject had been planned.

Another facility prominent in this particular attempt at change was the use of chlordane. Village leaders saw it and were enthusiastic. They communicated their enthusiasm to the villagers who came in unprecedented numbers to stock up. The quantity held by the Institute was insufficient, and many went away empty handed.

Utilization of facilities as process. From the point of view of the change target, how members use their facilities presupposes some surplus over subsistence and some choice among facilities. Concerning the first supposition of surplus, the informants in the Five-Nation

Study provide some information. "Property is something that should be shared" was the statement to which informants in Costa Rica, Mexico, Japan, Finland, and the United States agreed by the following percentages: 62.5, 63.5, 52.6, 18.0, and 40.2. It is tempting to speculate that the remarkably lower number agreeing with the statement in Finland is connected with Finland's proximity to Russia and its unhappy experiences with that country. A related statement: "Some people have too much property and others don't have enough" elicited the following percentages respectively: 84.3, 82.3, 56.8, 80.8, and 61.2. From these figures can we argue that countries in Latin America could easily go the route of Cuba insofar as the relation of facilities and private property is concerned?

We ask the informants in our Five-Nation Study, "Do you own stock or any other shares in any private enterprise?" The percentages responding "Yes," were as follows: 3.3, 12.4, 18.1, 15.9, and 24.1. The same informants were also asked: "Have you ever thought about buying stock or other shares in any private enterprise?" The percentages responding "Yes," were as follows: 13.9, 42.4, 26.1, 35.4, and 59.7. It is interesting to compare the Costa Rican and Mexican responses with those of the Finns on these questions in relation to the matter of "sharing property" and giving consideration to leaving the home land. One is tempted to speculate that Finland's proximity and experience with Russia conditions these answers. Will Cuba produce the same results for our neighbors?

An important question for the change agent is "How does the change target use its surplus?" In the Turrialba area, for example, would a farmer be more likely to buy a votice candle or a bag of chlordane? If the farmer is already attempting to exterminate ants by some means, the change agent's job (to switch him to a more effective ant control) is far different than if the farmer protects ants because they are the friends of the monkey-god as in India. Many times the utilization of facilities is not done as effectively as it might be simply because the members of the change target do not know what is available. They use the facilities with which they are familiar because they have not seen and do not know about improved means. It can be something as simple as substituting a fly swatter for a piece of paper, or something as complicated as installing electricity to replace candles. Media devoted to description and sale of facilities are of invaluable aid in extending the horizons of the change target. Mail-order catalogs and county fairs are examples of media that fill this function. Of course the availability of a facility does not insure that it will be extensively used. Credit offices offering loans at low rates of interest and easily understood methods of saving such as postal savings accounts are examples of facilities that require considerably more than availability to insure use.

COMPREHENSIVE OR MASTER PROCESSES

Of the six master processes of the PAS model, communication, boundary maintenance, systemic linkage, socialization, institutionalization, and social control, there is only space to discuss briefly the first four, which are, we believe, the most important in the analysis and discussion of institution building and the strategy of change.

Communication.   Communication is the process by which information, decisions, and directives pass through the system and by which knowledge is transmitted and sentiment is formed or modified. In addition to the numberless ramifications of communication through personal means, other means such as mass media, mail service, telephone lines, highways, and advertising devices should be included.

In the efforts of the officials of the Inter-American Institute of Agricultural Sciences to reach the target population, sociograms depicting interrelationships were of assistance. How the complete network of personal communications was achieved by one demonstration to a few leaders substantiated to the Institute administrators the value of the sociogram. Likewise the teachers studied such charts in the courses they took on the strategy of change at the Institute. Since these teachers who were to become change agents lived in the villages the charts were of great interest to them.

As revealed by the Five-Nation Study, communication through the various mass media reaches the largest percentage of people in Finland and the United States and the least in Costa Rica and Mexico.[22] It has been hypothesized that certain adoptions (such as the plow, for example) are brought about, not so much by a man's change in receptiveness or by an increase in his psychological motivation, as by his seeing that the tool exists, is available and is used by others with whom he has a chance to interact. According to this hypothesis travel to a city might make people adopters of many things seen there. This observation recalls Ralph Beals who observes that in potential for producing change "one road is worth about three schools and about 50 administrators."[23] Various diffusion studies have found urban contact, urban pull, mass media contact, etc., very important in the adoption of agricultural and health practices. The available evidence indicates that any society which becomes isolated from the activities that take place in the world's major routes of transport, cities, and knowledge centers will be disadvantaged by a lower level of living than would otherwise be the case. Iron curtains, bamboo curtains, and high tariffs exact their penalty in terms of an opportunity to develop.

Boundary maintenance. Through boundary maintenance the solidarity, identity, and interaction patterns within social systems are maintained. If a change agent is working on the problems of a small village, the boundaries that might prove difficult between him and the change target could be the resistance to change by a hacienda owner who sees no advantage to himself in improvements for his laborers as long as labor is cheap. It could also be the resistance to a poultry program if the change agent is a man and poultry is viewed as women's work.[24] Another type of boundary would be encountered if the proposed change espoused by the change agent were to be directly in conflict with cherished beliefs and sentiments of those who comprise the change target as might well be the case for ant extermination in parts of India or birth control in a traditional Catholic country.

On a larger front it might be fear of institutional innovation that provides the change target with a boundary that might be formidable for a change agent. While the local power structure might not be opposed ipso facto to more goods and services, only a little projection might reveal that such institutions as company stores or company credit would be drastically altered by modernization; that people could move about more freely and that the local reservoir of cheap labor might dry up; that extensive small land-holdings might change the relation of the big estate to the government. Many of the feared consequences are often vaguely visualized but are no less threatening because of it.

On a still larger front is the barrier posed by free or restricted trade, depending upon which side of the argument one finds himself. Of course, boundary maintenance affects the extent of international collaboration which is possible. Informants in the Five-Nation Study responded to the following statement indicating whether and to what extent they agreed with it: "It is a good thing for companies and business firms from other countries to do business and have factories in our country." For Costa Rica, Mexico, Japan, Finland, and the United States the percentages respectively agreeing were: 68.7, 68.1, 35.6, 41.0, and 57.2. It is interesting to speculate whether the Cubans before Castro would not have responded as did Costa Ricans, and Mexicans. Although we tend to think of underdeveloped economies as exercising high boundary maintenance, here is an instance where the more modernized societies express a greater desire for boundaries than do the less developed ones.[25]

Systemic linkage.   This is the process whereby the elements of at least two social systems come to be articulated so that in some ways and on some occasions they may be viewed as a single system. Whereas the processes previously discussed deal chiefly with interaction within a system, systemic linkage relates members of at least two systems.

Several linking processes were involved in the Inter-American Institute of Agricultural Sciences' institution building activities, that used the local village teachers as agricultural and health change agents. First the Institute involved and obtained agreement on the part of the National Ministry of Education for the experiment, and in effect the two agencies became the change agent system. The change target systems to which the change agent system was to be linked, of course, were each of the thirty-two villages. This linkage, for reasons discussed above, was never finalized to a significant extent. The linkage that proved most productive and of greatest duration was that between teacher and such groups as athletic clubs, especially soccer clubs.

Depending upon the objective, a few people may comprise the change target for the attempt to be successful or a very high percentage may have to be involved. A community's drinking water, for example, may be chlorinated with a relatively few people linking with the change agent before the decision. Karl Deutsch mentions an example of the opposite situation, where a great number have to be involved. Literacy and the birth rate are negatively correlated. It is, however, not enough that a few people become literate for the birth rate to show a change. Even when literacy is extended from 10 percent to 60 percent of the population, there is no correlation. But by the time literacy reaches 80 percent of the population the birth rate begins to drop. His idea of the "threshold" at which point changes can be observed because of a wider and wider linkage should be of interest to change agents involved in system building.

The so-called "package program" of Indian agriculture is an illustration of a systemic linkage designed to insure an input from all relevant facilities and services in such a way that there will be an optimal or "highest profit combination" output. Nations that are unabashedly planners, such as India and Russia, seem to encounter considerable difficulty in effectively linking many systems. Nonetheless, nations that are only occasionally planners and that then go about planning a bit furtively, as the United States, link a good many sub-systems not ordinarily thought of as compatible bedfellows (such as the private and public sector) when an otherwise unobtainable goal is important. Molders of public opinion who ordinarily denounce socialistic tendencies if there is any deviation from private enterprise were peculiarly silent about criticism and noticeably jubilant about results when the race for leadership in the space program led to the moon landings. If it is just as imperative in the eyes of the people of Guatemala and Pakistan to increase food supply and to modernize as it seems to be in the eyes of Americans to maintain space leadership, perhaps their motives in systemically linking the government with the private and industrial sectors should appear no more threatening than our own motives in the space adventure. That we still view any such alliance with deep suspicion is shown by the Five-Nation Study. Informants were asked whether and to what extent they agreed with the following statement: "The only way to provide good medical care for all of the people is through some program of governmental health insurance." The percentages respectively agreeing for Costa Rica, Mexico, Japan, Finland, and the United States were as follows: 84.9, 84.1, 90.3, 83.9, and 57.2.

Socialization. Socialization is the process whereby the social and cultural heritage is transmitted. In primitive and developing societies the family is of crucial importance for socialization. In industrialized societies specialized institutions of various types carry on socialization in addition to that which the child receives in the family and from friends and neighbors. The high evaluation which Costa Ricans place on schools and education has been mentioned. In an effort to ascertain how people generally feel about socialization for agricultural development, informants included in the Five-Nation Study were asked the following question: "Some people believe that the government should play a bigger part in training rural youth in agricultural practices. What is your feeling on this statement: 'Rural youth who remain on the farm should be given more training to make them better farmers, even if we have to pay more taxes.'?" Proportions of informants from the various countries who agreed with this statement are respectively as follows: 82.6, 93.3, 42.7, 78.1, and 59.4. If these figures are a valid indication there seems to be no question about the readiness of Costa Ricans and Mexicans for agricultural development. Such answers might indicate that the Costa Rican Ministry of Education and the Inter-American Institute of Agricultural Sciences might well have trained vocational agricultural teachers to give this type of training directly to Costa Rican rural youth.

Other findings from the Five-Nation Study indicate that both in Costa Rica and in Mexico the people have been socialized to accept thoroughly the society in which they were reared. The informants were asked to indicate whether and to what extent they agreed with

the following statement from the well-known F-Scale used by Leo
Srole to measure authoritarianism: "Children should be taught that
there is only one correct way to do things." The percentages respectively agreeing are as follows: 78.3, 94.8, 58.8, 63.9, and 60.2. These
data substantiate the contention that industrialization, urbanization, and other processes involved in modernization change people;
such a milieu seems to exert a socializing process of its own.

CONDITIONS OF SOCIAL INTERACTION

The elements and processes constitute the working components,
i.e., the parts and articulating processes, of the social system. Not all
aspects of social action are encompassed in these concepts, but the
remaining components are partly systemic, that is, partly structured
and partly under the control of the actors of the system. Space, time,
and size are such components.

Territoriality. The setting of the social system in space is called
its territoriality, and it determines within limits how much space
each person or group may have, the frequency and intensity of interaction within the group, and probabilities of systemic linkages
between groups and between change agent and change target systems. In the Turrialba area a rather simple consideration involving
the change agent-change target relation was studied. A study was
made in one of the communities to ascertain a location where most
people could see a poster display. On the large estate of Aquiares it
was found that the greatest number of contacts are made at the
butcher shop. Since no local refrigeration exists, a steer or hog is
butchered almost every day and the people come to buy fresh meat as
it is needed. It was recommended that certain posters developed by
change agents be displayed in the butcher shop.

How services of farmers are related in space and the relation of
prices to markets has been the concern of agricultural social scientists at least from von Thuenen's time to the time of Galpin, Christaller, Loesch, Berry and others.[26] Effective directed change and institution building require considerable knowledge of interrelations and
linkages of locality groups. Unfortunately time and space will not
permit further elaboration but the importance of understanding such
linkages may be illustrated by the statement of the economist, Kenneth Boulding, to the effect that central place theory, the discipline
and science devoted to these matters, may be the "queen of the
sciences."

Time. Time as a condition is inexorable and cannot be completely controlled by man. Even though man is the only animal that

bridges the generations through the transmission of culture, he is nonetheless time-bound and this is reflected in all studies of the strategy of change. In the effort to use teachers as change agents in the Turrialba area, time often came into consideration. Training for the change agent role was carried on when school was not in session. In this area people are not as time conscious as they are in industrialized societies. *Hora española* and *mañana,* not *hora englesa* and today, describe timing of events to which change agents must become accustomed.

In institution building and directed social change, when to act or start programs and when not to act is as important to change agents as it is to military strategists. Just as the successful military strategists are often said to have a superb sense of timing, so also must effective change agents have the ability to correctly time their actions.

Size.   Insofar as size of social systems is not controlled by the actors, it may be discussed as a condition of social action. Although inventions that improve man's efficiency in the use of energy tend to increase the size of certain systems, various systems in different organizations, societies, and epochs are remarkably similar. It is interesting to note how frequently eight and twelve persons comprise the supervisory unit in various organizations. The original squad in armies is an example. Another aspect of size as a condition is the number of persons per unit of space. Some think this is a condition and uncontrolled because of man's inability to manage reproduction; others, such as many Catholics, consider it a moral issue. The extent to which beliefs in countries such as Costa Rica and Mexico affect the evaluation of birth control was discussed above. Ralph Cummings[27] of the Rockefeller Foundation thinks the present runaway growth of population will continue so that if famine is to be avoided food production per year must be doubled or tripled. At the present time, concern about famine and the rapid pollution of man's environment has made the problem of population size most important.

SUMMARY

Institution building and development are not simple processes to be achieved by the separate contributions of a society's economy, polity, or its research and educational establishments. Nor can one academic discipline alone claim success in predicting or explaining the course of social and economic development. In reality it depends on favorable conditions not only in rural institutions but in the sectors of "agri-climate," which supply transport, market, finance, purchase, and provide the technical advantages and inventions as well as a stable governmental administration for agricultural production. The complexity and magnitude of the processes involved in effective institution building are so great that many scientific disciplines must be brought to bear on them if they are to be predicted, understood, and furthered. This being true, it is necessary to assist specialists in the various scientific disciplines involved in institution building to understand each others' frames of reference and concepts.

Often in the past, disproportionate efforts have been made to educate the agricultural producer. The enlightenment of the peasant is important, but too little attention has been given to institution building aimed at improving his incentives, technology, and facilities, which would encourage and enable him to respond as desired. Policy and strategy must deal with all sectors of the total system and its sub-systems that affect the producer. Most sectors of the whole society must change. The approach must be macroeconomic in order to permit and encourage microeconomic change.

As agriculture in developing societies becomes increasingly dependent upon the development of other sectors, the coordinating and service roles of government become increasingly complex and important. Moreover, the traditional agriculturist, exploited and neglected by representatives of the larger society for many generations, distrusts governmental and educational officials. Also governmental and other administrative officials may lack the required administrative capabilities for either institution building or operation. Their traditional origins may foster corruption and nepotism. Changes in incentives of government and organizational structure may be required to get results. Often a government's use of political power to attain development objectives involves political costs exceeding immediate political gains. Nevertheless, societies must develop governmental strategies for the economical and effective use of their power. Professionally trained, socially minded, and adequately supported and organized administrative personnel are the indispensible condition of system building and development.

If traditional agricultural societies are to modernize, hindrances must be removed that prevent freedom of effective human action and prevent use of resources for human betterment. Land tenure systems, marketing arrangements, and human relations generally must not only permit but facilitate efficient action and economical use of both human and nonhuman resources. The concepts and tools developed in fields such as agricultural economics and rural sociology are applicable for system building and its evaluation. However, the optimum combinations of labor, capital, land, entrepreneurship, and other "inputs" will be different in developing countries than in industrialized societies. Developing societies are universally burdened with underemployment of labor and heavy farm-family food requirements. The prescriptions carried over to developing societies by agricultural economists from industrial societies may be more pertinent to the commercial pockets of agriculture generally found in developing countries than to subsistence farming. Nevertheless, the potential rationality and desire for an improved life on the part of the traditional agriculturists should not be underestimated.

Science applied to the control of disease has resulted in such decreasing death rates and consequent rapid population growth rates that the world faces critical food and other shortages on a scale never before known. Unless agricultural science produces disease-resistant and otherwise regionally suitable plants and animal stocks and improves cultural practices and agricultural knowledge generally, famine appears to be inevitable. If famine is to be avoided through worldwide institution building and agricultural development, all scientific disciplines must team up on the problem. Control of environmental pollution requires a similar approach. This holds whether the sciences focus on nature in general, scarce resources in particular, the personality, human power, or politics, culture, health. and education.

There is not sufficient stored knowledge available to save us, but much knowledge now available is ineffectively used. It is in the behavioral sciences that knowledge necessary for agricultural development is most lacking. While effective and economically feasible birth control measures are now available to slow the rate of population growth, the behavioral sciences do not possess sufficient knowledge concerning the organization and motivation of people to greatly increase the use of them. The potential contribution of the behavioral sciences should make it possible to speed up institution building for agricultural and societal development generally without undue application of force, violence, or cruelty.

NOTES

1. See a presentation of the change agent-change target model in Charles P. Loomis "Toward a Theory of Systemic Social Change," in Irwin T. Sanders, ed., *Interprofessional Training Goals for Technical Assistance Personnel Abroad, Council on Social Work Education* (New York, New York, 1950). For an earlier presentation of the PAS model see Charles P. Loomis, *Social Systems: Essays on Their Persistence and Change* (D. Van Nostrand, Princeton, N.J., 1960).

2. "Editorial Introduction" in Charles P. and Zona K. Loomis, *Modern Social Theories* (Huntington, N.Y.: Robert E. Krieger Publishing Co., 1975), p. xxiii.

3. This was first published as a chapter in a government bulletin in Spanish under the title "Variables Culturales en el Desarrollo Institucional," by Charles P. Loomis in *Desarrollo Institucional — Seminario Sobre Desarrollo Institucional* (Patrocinadores: Ministerio de Agricultura y Ganaderia de El Salvador y A.I.D., Washington, D.C., San Salvador, 1971). For an effort to relate the change agent-change target to the PAS model in the analysis of social change see, J. Paul Leagans and Charles P. Loomis, eds., *Behavioral Change in Agriculture — Concepts and Strategies for Influencing Transition*, (Ithaca, New York: Cornell University Press, 1971). See especially Chapter 10 by Loomis and Editors' introductions throughout. Also see Charles P. Loomis and Zona K. Loomis, *Socioeconomic Change and the Religious Factor in India* (New Delhi: Affiliated East West Press, 1969), Charles P. Loomis and Joan Huber, *Marxist Theory and Indian Communism*. (East Lansing: Michigan State University Press, 1970); and *Modern Social Theories* by Charles P. Loomis and Zona K. Loomis, op. cit., is also organized on the PAS model.

4. The study was planned and/or carried through by Hideya Kumata, Charles P. Loomis, Robert Stewart, Fredrick Waisanen and associates. The study is based upon modified probability samples drawn from among persons aged 21 and over in Costa Rica, Mexico, Japan, Finland, and the United States. (All figures as given in the text refer to the countries in this order.) It was financed by the Carnegie Corporation, the Ford Foundation, the National Institutes of Health and the Mich. Agri. Exp. Sta. The useable interviews were: 1,040 from Costa Rica, 1,414 from Mexico (1,126 from places 2,500 and over and 288 from rural areas), 990 from Japan, 893 from Finland and 1,528 from the United States.

Writings based upon data from this study authored and/or coauthored by the present writer include the following: Charles P. Loomis, Zona K. Loomis, and Jeanne E. Gullahorn, *Linkages of Mexico and the United States*, Bul. 14, Mich. Agri. Exp. Sta. Res. (East Lansing: 1966). In this residents of rural and urban Mexico, the Spanish-speaking Chicanos of the U.S. Southwest, and the general public of U.S. are compared on various dimensions. Jeanne E. Gullahorn and Charles P. Loomis, "A Comparison of Social Distance Attitudes in the United States and Mexico," *Studies in Comparative International Development*, 11, (1966). Charles P. Loomis, "In Praise of Conflict and Its Resolution," *American Sociological Review*, 32, (Dec., 1967). Charles P. Loomis, "In Defense of Integration," *Centennial Review*, 14, (Spring, 1970). In this publication U.S. blacks at varying levels of education are compared with categories mentioned in Loomis, Loomis, and Gullahorn.

5. John and Mavis Biesanz, *Costa Rican Life* (New York: Columbia University Press, 1946), p. 10. Also see Eduardo Arze Louriera and Roy A. Clifford, "Educational Systems," in Charles P. Loomis, et al., eds., *Turrialba: Social Systems and the Introduction of Change* (Glencoe, Ill.: The Free Press, 1953), p. 172.

6. F.B. Waisanen and J.T. Durlak, *The Impact of Communication on Rural Development: An Investigation in Costa Rica*, A Final Report submitted to UNESCO/NS/2516/65, Article 1.4, (Paris, France: December 1967), p. 13.

7. Ibid., p. 17. One report implies that in Costa Rica teachers are "natural" change agents who in an area comparable to that in Turrialba "by their high credibility, expertise, developmental concern and continued presence in the village . . . are the principal change agents of this (San Isidro del General) and other rural areas of Costa Rica."

8. Waisanen and Durlak used the "self-anchoring" scale to study the reputed reliability and credibility of various professionals and mass media especially for change agents. After introducing the notion of the ten-step ladder the informant was told "Let's suppose at the top of the ladder stand all those things in which you have *complete confidence* and which you are *ready to believe* with little doubt. At the *bottom* of the ladder are those things which are unreliable, unbelievable, and

in which you have no *confidence*. On which step would you place (the following; each presented with a separate discussion) 'School teachers whom you know personally,' 'School teachers whom you do not know personally,' 'Medical doctors whom you know personally'? (etc.). Teachers "known personally" were more highly evaluated in reliability and credibility than medical doctors, priests, nurses, and midwives who were likewise "known personally." How important the condition "known personally" turns out to be is given in the text, above. F.B. Waisanen and J.T. Durlak, *A Survey of Attitudes Related to Costa Rican Population Dynamics* (San Jose, Costa Rica: American International Association for Economic and Social Development, 1966), pp. 132-139.

9. E.O. Heady and J. Ackerman, "Farm Adjustment Problems and Their Importance to Sociologists," *Rural Sociology*, 24, (December, 1959), pp. 315.

10. Wilbert E. Moore, "Creation of a Common Culture," *Confluence*, 4, (1958), pp. 232-233.

11. Edward M. Bruner, "Differential Cultural Changes: Report on the Inter-University Summer Research Seminar, 1956," *Social Science Research Council Items*, 11, (March, 1957).

12. Leagans and Loomis, *Behavioral Change*, op. cit., pp. 401-402.

13. George M. Foster, "Peasant Society and Image of Limited Good," *American Anthropologist*, 67, (April, 1965), 293-315; and 68, (Fall, 1966), 210-214. See also *Human Organization* (Winter, 1970) 303-323.

14. See Footnote 4. The manner in which questions are stated is, of course, important in such research. Our birth control question was stated as follows: "Family planning or birth control has been discussed by many people. What is your feeling about a married couple practicing birth control? If you had to decide which one of these statements best expresses your point of view: It is always right; It is usually right; It is usually wrong; It is always wrong." Of course, provision was made for, No answer, Don't know, etc.

15. Waisanen and Durlak, *A Survey of Attitudes*, op. cit., pp. 166-167.

16. For a discussion of the scale see F. P. Kilpatrick and Hadley Cantrill, *Self-Anchoring Scaling: A Measure of Individuals' Unique Reality Worlds* (Washington, D.C.: The Brookings Institution, 1960).

17. Robert K. Merton, *Social Theory and Social Structure* (Glencoe, Ill.: The Free Press, 1957), p. 553.

18. Loomis, "In Praise of Conflict," op. cit., pp. 890.

19. Loomis, Loomis, and Gullahorn, *Linkages of Mexico*, op. cit. For the following frequency categories of relatives getting together outside the home; namely: never; 1-few times a year; 2-once a month; 3-few times a month; 4-once a week for Costa Rica were: 13.9, 22.0, 12.6, 19.9 and 31.6; for Mexico 10.8, 18.7, 13.8, 14.4 and 42.2; for Japan 3.8, 37.1, 23.7, 17.7 and 17.7; for Finland .6, 24.6, 33.8, 14.8 and 26.2; for the United States 3.7, 10.2, 17.1, 11.7 and 57.4.

20. Ibid., p. 57.

21. Loomis, "In Praise of Conflict," op. cit.

22. The percentages of informants respectively reporting not viewing television were as follows: 90.9, 63.9, 14.1, 43.3, and 11.5. The percentages not listening to radio as reported were: 36.3, 23.3, 53.5, 7.8, and 20.5; those reporting not reading newspapers were: 45.1, 64.7, 9.7, .7, and 18.2; and those reporting not reading magazines were: 76.3, 42.9, 48.2, 7.4, and 5.6.

23. "Notes on Acculturation," in Sol Tax, et al., *Heritage of Conquest* (Glencoe, Ill.: The Free Press, 1952), p. 232.

24. Thomas L. Norris, "Economic Systems: Large and Small Land Holdings," in Loomis, et al., *Turrialba*, op. cit., pp. 102-103.

25. Henri Mendras, *Les Paysans et la modernisation de l'agriculture* (Paris: Centre National de la Recherche Scientifique, 1958).

26. Johann Heinrich von Thuenen, *Der isolierte Staat in Beziehung auf Landwirt-schaft und Nationaloekonomie* (Jena: Fischer, 1930); Charles J. Galpin, *The Social Anatomy of an Agricultural Community*, Wisconsin Agricultural Experiment Station Research Bulletin No. 34, (Madison, Wisc., 1915); Walter Christaller, *Die zentralen Orte in Sueddeutschland* (Jena: Fischer, 1933); August Loesch, *Die raeumliche Ordnung der Wirtschaft* (Jena: Fischer, 1941); and Brian J.L. Berry, *Geography of Market Centers and Retail Distribution* (Englewood Cliffs, N.J.: Prentice-Hall, 1967).

27. Leagans and Loomis, *Behavioral Change*, op. cit., p. 79.

Index of Names

Subject Index

DATE DUE

RETURNED	RETURNED
RETURNED	
JUN 2 8 1982 UWL	
RETURNED UWL	
OCT 2 1982 UWL	
RETURNED UWL	
RETURNED UWL	
NOV 8 1982	